INDIA

INDIA

5,000 Years of History on the Subcontinent

Audrey Truschke

Princeton University Press
Princeton & Oxford

Published by Princeton University Press
41 William Street, Princeton, New Jersey 08540
99 Banbury Road, Oxford OX2 6JX

press.princeton.edu

GPSR Authorized Representative: Easy Access System Europe - Mustamäe tee 50, 10621 Tallinn, Estonia, gpsr.requests@easproject.com

Library of Congress Cataloging-in-Publication Data is available

ISBN 9780691221229
ISBN (e-book) 9780691221236

British Library Cataloging-in-Publication Data is available

Editorial: Priya Nelson, Emma Wagh
Production Editorial: Elizabeth Byrd
Jacket: Katie Osborne
Production: Danielle Amatucci
Publicity: Maria Whelan (US), Carmen Jimenez (UK)
Interior Design: Wanda España

Jacket Credit: *Soldiers at the hookah stall and commotion in the bazaar*, c. 1775–1800, paper, natural color, 25 × 35 cm.

This book has been composed in Minion Pro

Printed in the United States of America

10 9 8 7 6 5 4 3 2 1

Contents

Scholarly Conventions

I aim for accuracy and legibility throughout this book, and those twin goals have guided my choices of scholarly conventions.

Specialist Terms. I shy away from specialist terminology when I can, eschewing terms beloved by experts but unintelligible to others (e.g., "Persianate" and "Islamicate"). I also decline to use acronyms, which are somewhere between off-putting and maddening to nonspecialists. And so, I spell out the Indus Valley Civilization (rather than resorting to IVC) and use the titles of Sanskrit texts such as the Mahabharata (not MBh); I make small exceptions when the acronym is more common than the full name (e.g., RSS). Readers who want a more in-depth take on my vocabulary choices should see the Historiography essay.

Diacritics. Many words in this book are transliterated from a rich plethora of South Asian languages, including Sanskrit, Tamil, Pali, Persian, Urdu, Hindi, Telugu, and Bengali. To be easy on the eyes, I forgo diacritics (including for European languages). For earlier periods, I follow standard transliteration schemes, although with some variations to use familiar English spellings (e.g., Ashoka, not Asoka, and Mahmud Gawan, not Gavan) or for clarity (e.g., Brahmin for the social class, not Brahman).

Names and Spellings. For proper names of people in the colonial period and later, I tend to employ the transliteration adopted by the person in question. Accordingly, I write about Duleep Singh (not Dalip Singh), Sikhdhar (not Sikdar), and Anandibai Joshee (not Joshi).

For places, I use names and spellings in vogue at the time, and so I recount events in Bombay, Calcutta, and Madras in British India (in the twenty-first century, Mumbai, Kolkata, and Chennai, respectively); similarly, I detail how Malik Ambar built up the central Indian city of Khirki (i.e., Aurangabad, after the Mughal renaming). This practice results in multiple spellings of some places depending on the timeframe in question (e.g., Sind in premodernity and Sindh today). In some cases, spellings were not standardized, and I let small variations stand (e.g., I use Baluchistan and Balochistan, Kandahar and Qandahar). I make an exception to the practice of adopting time-appropriate names for the Indus (Valley) Civilization, since we do not know what they called their cities or themselves and so must resort to modern terms. For English words, I generally follow American spelling conventions.

Honorifics. I avoid honorifics for historical figures, writing of Alexander of Macedon rather than Alexander the Great, William Jones sans his knighted title of Sir, Jinnah rather than Quaid-i-Azam (Great Leader), Ambedkar rather than Baba Saheb (Respected Father), and Jyotirao Phule and Mohandas Gandhi by their respective given names rather than their shared appellation of Mahatma (Great Souled). Some may find this practice jarring or even disrespectful, although it is meant only to signal an appropriate critical distance. My goal is to understand the historical roles of flawed women and men in their times and places, and I find positioning those people on pedestals ill-suited for such an endeavor. My non-honorific preference also applies to religious figures, such that I tend to write of Nanak and Jesus (rather than Guru Nanak and Jesus Christ, respectively). Notably, when I write about such figures here, I do so pursuant to excavating the histories of specific religions in South Asia, especially through the ideas and actions of practitioners. As a historian, I do not and cannot give credence to theological claims. Accordingly, I speak of deities as part of Indian intellectual history and without veneration, writing of Ram, Allah, and Krishna sans further qualification. I make small exceptions to these guidelines and include honorifics when not doing so would likely cause confusion. For instance, I refer to the Maratha warrior-king Shivaji (rather than Shiva, which is more commonly the name of a Hindu god) and the Prophet Muhammad (since there are many Muhammads in Indian history).

Dates. I give all dates in the Gregorian calendar since it is, by far, the most common calendar used worldwide today. I always use the acronym BCE (Before Common Era). I only include CE (Common Era) upon first usage or where there is a likelihood of confusion. I strive to give dates, instead of or alongside referents meaningfully only to certain groups of scholars. For instance, South Asia–focused archaeologists may all know when the Neolithic period began on the subcontinent, but most scholars who work on later periods do not. Likewise, I can recite Mughal regnal dates in my sleep, but I would not expect "Akbar's rule" to immediately anchor a Vedic specialist much less a more casual reader of South Asian history.

Quotes. In quotes from primary and secondary sources, I often adjust spellings, grammar, and italics and omit diacritics for the sake of consistency and readability. I also sometimes introduce parenthetical glosses for clarity. For English-medium primary sources, I retain older spellings when doing so does not compromise intelligibility. I often cite to translations of primary sources for wider accessibility.

Citations. Some premodern Indian names lend themselves to the modern Western convention of citation by surname, and others do not. I use and alphabetize as appropriate to the specific name and do not awkwardly force South Asian names into Western conventions (e.g., I cite Abul Fazl and not Fazl, Abul, but I cite Vivekananda, Swami). Most sources are listed in the bibliography, with one big exception and one small exception. In the last few chapters, I cite to many contemporary news sources and often include full citations in the notes. This avoids the awkward question of whether such sources are best categorized as primary or secondary. It also signals my more limited use of contemporary news sources, which I do not endorse as equivalent with scholarship. On a smaller scale, I cite some modern poetry and novels in the introduction and elsewhere, including full citations in the notes.

Translations. Unless noted, all translations are my own. Readers should know that I agree with many scholars of South Asia—both historians and literary scholars—that a little flexibility produces more accurate translations than rigid adherence to the original text, especially regarding grammar. As the historian A. L. Basham—one of my predecessors in writing an overarching history of South Asia—put it, "I have, however, allowed myself in places great liberties with the original, mainly in order to make the point of the verse more clear to English listeners" (India Office Records manuscript Eur f147/94, British Library, p. 11). Indeed, I translate as I judge can best communicate a primary source's original sense and thereby, hopefully, allow Indians from the past to speak to readers in the twenty-first century.

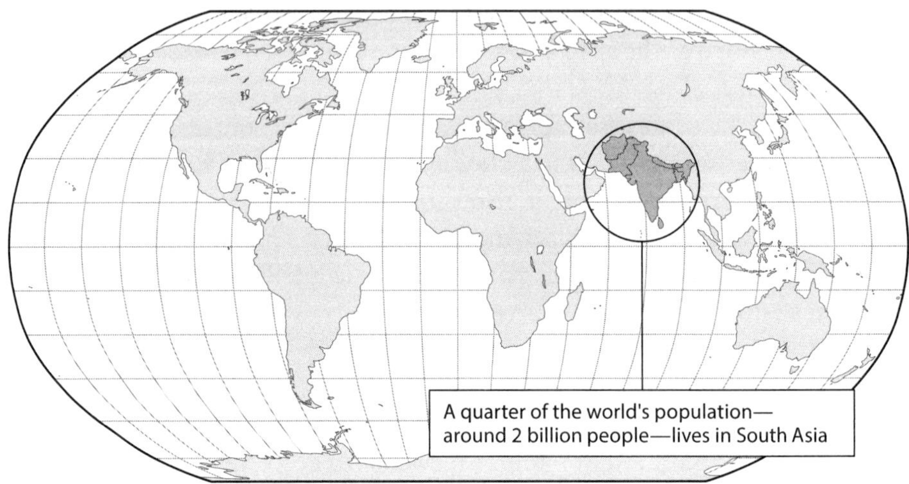

Modern South Asia's population density.

Starting Points

Twenty centuries of ancient baggage
heaped together, slung across
our backs,
we began our long journey.

—R. Murugaiyan (d. 2009), Sri Lankan Tamil poet[1]

Indian stories are continually retold, and I follow that grand tradition by narrating afresh nearly 5,000 years of human experiences on and near the subcontinent. This history matters. In modern times, a quarter of humanity lives in South Asia. For the rest of us, our lives are shaped by South Asian cultures—from the films we watch, to the spices that flavor our foods, to the clothes we wear, to how we exercise, to (for many) the religions we practice. In brief, South Asia and its myriad traditions are critical to the human experience, and so we all ought to know a bit—maybe more than a bit—about the region's history. This book offers an overview of South Asian history with a focus on the Indian subcontinent, aimed at avid and casual readers alike, including those taking their first dive into this fascinating subject. For the non-initiated, maybe you are already confused, wondering what, exactly, constitutes "South Asia" and "India." I explain that and more in this brief chapter as I introduce Indian and South Asian history as an under-told set of stories brimming with an astonishing diversity of people and experiences.

This book narrates the wondrously dense and complex history of life on the Indian subcontinent (i.e., largely what is now Pakistan, India, and

Bangladesh), with periodic appearances from Sri Lanka and other surrounding areas (i.e., modern-day Afghanistan, Nepal, Bhutan, and the Maldive Islands). Collectively, we call the region inhabited by these eight modern nations "South Asia." I also use "India" throughout this book, referring predominantly to the subcontinent, not the more modest contemporary nation-state (a historian's privilege, as elaborated below). Still, this book is not a history of land, of either South Asia or India, but rather of the many communities who have made these places home over millennia. My focus on people—on South Asians—stands at the core of this book, and I strive to tell the stories of many different South Asian groups, from rich to poor, from high class to low class, from the builders of the Indus Civilization about 4,600 years ago (chapter 1) to everyday people in Bangladesh, Pakistan, and other countries in the twenty-first century (chapter 24). Primary sources anchor every chapter—including box quotes drawn from many Indian sources and languages—so that, to the extent possible, you can hear for yourself the voices of prior generations of South Asians.

South Asian history is lengthy and diverse, but that diversity itself provides a kind of glue that holds together a wide-ranging set of narratives. Across time and regions, South Asians engaged in robust cross-cultural exchanges between groups on the subcontinent and with migrants. They forged connections via trade and travel with people living in other parts of Asia and, in more recent centuries, the rest of the world. Partly owing to their ever-changing contexts and contacts, South Asians repeatedly innovated in the religious and political spheres, making adaptation and change recurrent, even consistent, parts of their lived experiences. Throughout this book, I return to these persistent threads of diversity, cross-cultural exchanges, and innovation, since they offer anchors to ground us within South Asia's mosaic of history.

India and South Asia

This book is a history of India—in its historical sense of the subcontinent (i.e., the area covered by modern-day Pakistan, India, and Bangladesh)—with some journeys into other areas of South Asia (especially Afghanistan and Sri Lanka), and I use both terms aware of their virtues and drawbacks. "South Asia" is a modern, social science term, imposed from outside the region, and defined geographically as the land area bounded on the north by the Hindu Kush, Himalayan, and Karakoram mountains and on the south by the Indian Ocean. "South Asia" is useful for shaking scholars out of nationalist boundaries, themselves rather new.[2] But the phrase lacks history and is commonly confused with Southeast Asia.[3] "India" is a far older term and has been used for millennia to refer to the subcontinent. There are two additional reasons, beyond its historical weight, that I use "India" throughout this book. It is a widely understood term, far more so than "South Asia." Also, I do not cover all of South Asia equally, devoting more time to the subcontinent than, say, Sri Lanka, and using "India" honestly reflects that choice.

Despite these reasons, using "India" to refer to the entire subcontinent will jar readers who are accustomed to India denoting only the post-1947 nation-state. For them, I hope the different sense of "India"—as a broader, not politically demarcated, geography—proves a useful disruption. It can remind us that, in this book, we peruse the halls of history where societies and states were quite different than they are today. In this sense, my insistence on using "India" is also a corrective against gross presentism. The Indian nation-state is quite new in human history, and its recent advent does not require us to abandon the deeper, more historically grounded sense of "India" as the broader subcontinent.

Many Indian Histories

The celebrated scholar A. K. Ramanujan once asked, "Is there an Indian way of thinking?" He answered yes, there are many Indian ways of thinking, depending on the inquirer's tone and intentions.[4] Similarly, answers abound to the deceptively simple question—What is Indian (or South Asian) history? It depends on what you want to know, whom you consider to be important, and which historical changes you deem essential to understand. This book includes a little of everything, including cultural, religious, social, literary, economic, and intellectual histories. I trace larger trends, such as India's first urbanization (third millennium BCE), second urbanization (first millennium BCE), the advent of temple-based Hindu practices (first millennium CE), and the spread of

Indo-Persian culture (second millennium CE). I also take significant forays into biographical history, detailing the lives of individuals from Ashoka (third century BCE) to Pandita Ramabai (nineteenth century CE). Readers will find a fair amount of political history in these pages, although I have at times chosen to accommodate a broader array of stories rather than narrowly focusing on state affairs (I elaborate on this choice in the Historiography essay). Overall, I aim to make significant strides forward in terms of breadth and inclusion in how we narrate South Asian history, according to a few distinct choices.

This book presents a greater diversity of voices than we often hear in South Asian history in terms of gender, caste, class, region, language, and religion. In concrete terms, that means that readers will encounter more women, Dalits, lower castes, poor and disadvantaged communities, south Indians, non-Indian South Asians, non-Sanskrit speakers, and non-Hindus. Diversity helps us better understand Indian history, both its underappreciated aspects and, also, its dominant groups. To again become concrete, I detail the oppression of Dalits and lower castes, in theory and practice, in the first millennium CE (chapters 7 and 8). This helps readers gain important knowledge about life for a sizeable chunk of the ancient Indian population who are often neglected in traditional historical accounts. It also grants a richer, contextual perspective on more well-researched elite topics, such as Brahminical Sanskrit literature by the law theorist Manu and the famed poet Kalidasa.

Parts of the Indian subcontinent developed according to distinct rhythms, as did discrete communities. India was often more a cluster of regions than a unified whole and its people, as a geneticist has observed, "a large number of small populations."[5] Even when we can hazard larger categories, such as north and south India, they often diverged for centuries, even millennia, in their historical development. To address this reality, I do a certain amount of tacking back and forth, and I devote some chapters to covering discrete regions (especially chapters 12, 14, and 16). Throughout, I strive to incorporate south Indian history especially, as a corrective to our standard narrative of Indian history being unapologetically north Indian-centric. For instance, I highlight material evidence of early social practices in Karnataka (chapter 3), detail Chola rule and culture (chapter 9), cover Nayaka and Maratha ruling lineages (chapter 15), and incorporate colonial-era activities from Madras (chapter 19). I also bring in Sri Lanka (known at earlier points in history as Taprobane or Ceylon). I freely admit that I fall short of adequate geographic diversity in these pages, and some regions still receive less airtime than others (e.g., Assam). Still, I hope to have taken a sizable step toward correcting enduring geographic biases in the discipline of South Asian history.

I do not entirely confine myself to the region of South Asia in these pages, and this calls for explanation. As the sociologist Janet Abu-Lughod noted, India was "on the way to everywhere."[6] As a result, South Asian history sometimes spills into other world areas, through migration, trade, travel, pilgrimage, and other human movements. I look beyond the confines of South Asia at numerous points, including to explain ancient migrations (chapters 1 and 2), the diffusion of Sanskrit-based knowledge and stories (chapter 8), Chola conquests in Southeast Asia (chapter 9), Indian participation in the Persian literary sphere (chapter 10), the Bahmani kingdom's connections with Iran (chapter 11), and European colonialism (chapters 12 and 16–22). I use maps as a visual aid to highlight specific points and moments of connection. Still, I have sought to keep the focus on the relevance of these transregional links for those living in South Asia.

I mention select migrations out of the subcontinent, although I am not thorough on this point. There is much to say about the impact of South Asians on other world areas, but that is a different history than I recount here. Accordingly, I mention major outward movements of groups, such as indentured laborers in the mid-nineteenth to the early twentieth centuries CE (chapter 20), late twentieth to early twenty-first-century migrant workers (chapter 24), and the contemporary diaspora (afterword). But, with a few brief exceptions, I stop short of following these groups to their new homes, at which point they become part of histories set in those regions.

Premodernity forms the core of South Asian history. So often, we forget this truism, because it is easiest to focus on events close to our own time. I am not immune from the pull of the present, and I cover shorter time periods in each chapter as the book moves forward through the centuries. Still, most of this book centers on premodern South Asia (pre-1750 CE), as it should since that is the bulk of known human history in the region. This emphasis should help readers better contextualize contemporary trends, such as Hindu-Muslim conflict that largely dates in its current form to the nineteenth century and was preceded by centuries in which religious identities were more fluid (chapters 10–16). Focusing on the deeper past might also help us provincialize ourselves and our own moment in time.[7] After all, we are not the endpoint of history, and soon enough we too will be part of a far longer past.

Indian History before Us

There is a certain amount of unavoidable disconnect in Indian history, which is a collection of chronological stories that overlap but do not fully cohere. In this sense, an overview history of South Asia is a little like the *Panchatantra*, a famous collection of animal fables from India that became a premodern bestseller across Asia and Europe (chapter 8). In the *Panchatantra*, Karataka tells story after story to exemplify ethics to Damanaka, who sometimes takes the moral to heart and other times ignores the lesson. The *Panchatantra* contains dozens of discrete tales, connected by the thin thread of this meta conversation between two friends. Indian and South Asian history, too, is a series of discrete stories that do not feed into a grand, singular narrative. And so I make no attempt to offer an overarching storyline here, opting instead for the more modest and intellectually honest approach of repeated themes.

Amid this book's complex, slightly unwieldly narrative of subcontinental history—with its multipronged focus, diverse voices, and ambitious geographical and temporal breadth—I use a set of recurrent themes to give readers a navigable path beyond chronology. As mentioned above, diversity has long been a shared feature across Indian communities and so may serve as a connecting thread in history too. Additionally, migration is a repeated phenomenon as waves of people came to the subcontinent over the millennia. New groups brought their own ideas and interacted with indigenous and earlier migrant populations, resulting in a kaleidoscope of syncretic South Asian traditions. Another strand worth mentioning at the outset is that South Asians evinced an ongoing interest in history, telling stories about times past, which I include as part of Indian intellectual, social, and religious trends. Also, the mundane persists, such as what people wore and ate, how they worked, and their family and community ties. Such things are part of all human experiences, and they are often knowable even without written records, which makes them especially helpful as connecting topics across close to 5,000 years of history. Last, more difficult subjects recur in numerous time periods as well, such as social stratification and climate change.

We face limits in accessing the past imposed by archival sources, which I strive to overcome where possible. Archives are "rags of realities," as a French scholar has put it, always incomplete and insufficient.[8] A compounding issue is that, to quote an Africanist, "the documents we read were not written for us."[9] As a result, historical documents—primary sources such as political texts, travelogues, edicts, and inscriptions—often do not convey the kinds of information that we seek, especially about historically oppressed communities. More prosaically, South Asia's hot, wet climate is anathema to paper preservation, and multiple South Asian nations do not provide easy archival access.[10] Still, difficulty ought not to be mistaken for impossibility, and I decline to continue the uninspiring pattern of using only the most accessible sources in the most straightforward ways. Instead, I strive to listen to the "whisperings" of history—to read against the grain of well-used sources and seek out hitherto neglected ones—to reconstruct more vibrant, accurate South Asian historical narratives.[11]

Sometimes archival challenges are compounded by modern biases, and two prejudices recur with numbing frequency in modern South Asian histories: sexism and casteism. Many historians write out women entirely, filling chapters upon chapters with only men. Most mention the caste-oppressed but too often only through an upper-caste lens that dehumanizes and disempowers. In contrast, the experiences and writings of nuns are central to my narrative of early Buddhism (chapter 3), and, millennia later, I include female voices amid India's nineteenth-century reformers (chapters 19 and 20). Oppressed castes do not speak to us directly in ancient Indian texts, but I found works about them that rendered insights when read through a lens that inverts the works' Brahminical gaze (chapter 7). For modernity, I elaborate lower-caste, Dalit, and Adivasi movements at some length, underscoring their internal diversity and attempts to improve South Asian lives (chapters 20–24).

My goal is to diversify the standard cast of South Asian history. More boldly, I aim to challenge what we take to be standard and offer a more comprehensive, representational, and compelling approach to the South Asian past.

History is full of sad stories, with and without silver linings. To quote the Ghanaian American novelist Yaa Gyasi, "Some people make it out of their stories unscathed, thriving. Some people don't."[12] I narrate moments of loss, pain, and difficulty—for South Asian individuals and communities—without sugarcoating and thereby honor them and their lives. I know that some prefer a more celebratory tone to historical narratives, but fulfilling that modern desire requires that we elide many premodern peoples' harsh realities. Over time, it means that we collectively forget huge parts of history, which is antithetical to the historian's charge to remember. In these pages, I seek to evoke the breadth and depth of South Asian lived experiences.

Embedded in my embrace of historical breadth is a broad-ranging empathy. I consider not only the feelings of the living but also of the dead, honoring past generations of South Asians by being accurate about their experiences. I invite readers to do likewise, working through their modern emotions—surprise, uncertainty, discomfort, distaste, and anger—at the pain and travails of the past (and that I recount them in an unvarnished fashion). Thereby, readers might encounter the treasures of history, including the perspectives and realities of earlier generations. I cannot promise a tale of beautiful things, for that is the prerogative of fiction. But I offer true stories in these pages and so contribute to what the American poet Amanda Gorman has described as "the preservation of a light so terrible."[13]

The intended result of my efforts is an innovative history of India with notable appearances from the rest South Asia. Narrative renewal is good since, as the Jain scholar Merutunga wrote in Sanskrit about 700 years ago, "Because they have been heard ad nauseum, / old stories no longer gratify the minds of the wise."[14] I offer here a new history, crafted to be relevant in the twenty-first century while avoiding a perspective warped by contemporary ideas. It can be hard not to make the past, implausibly, about us moderns since, as the Sri Lankan novelist Anuk Arudpragasam has put it, "The present, we assume is eternally before us, one of the few things in life from which we cannot be parted."[15]

But this is a misperception since the present is always becoming the past. In truth, the past is eternally before us, an ever-expanding catalog of human experiences. I turn next to the earliest points of human habitation on the Indian subcontinent to begin our exciting, circuitous journey through South Asian history.

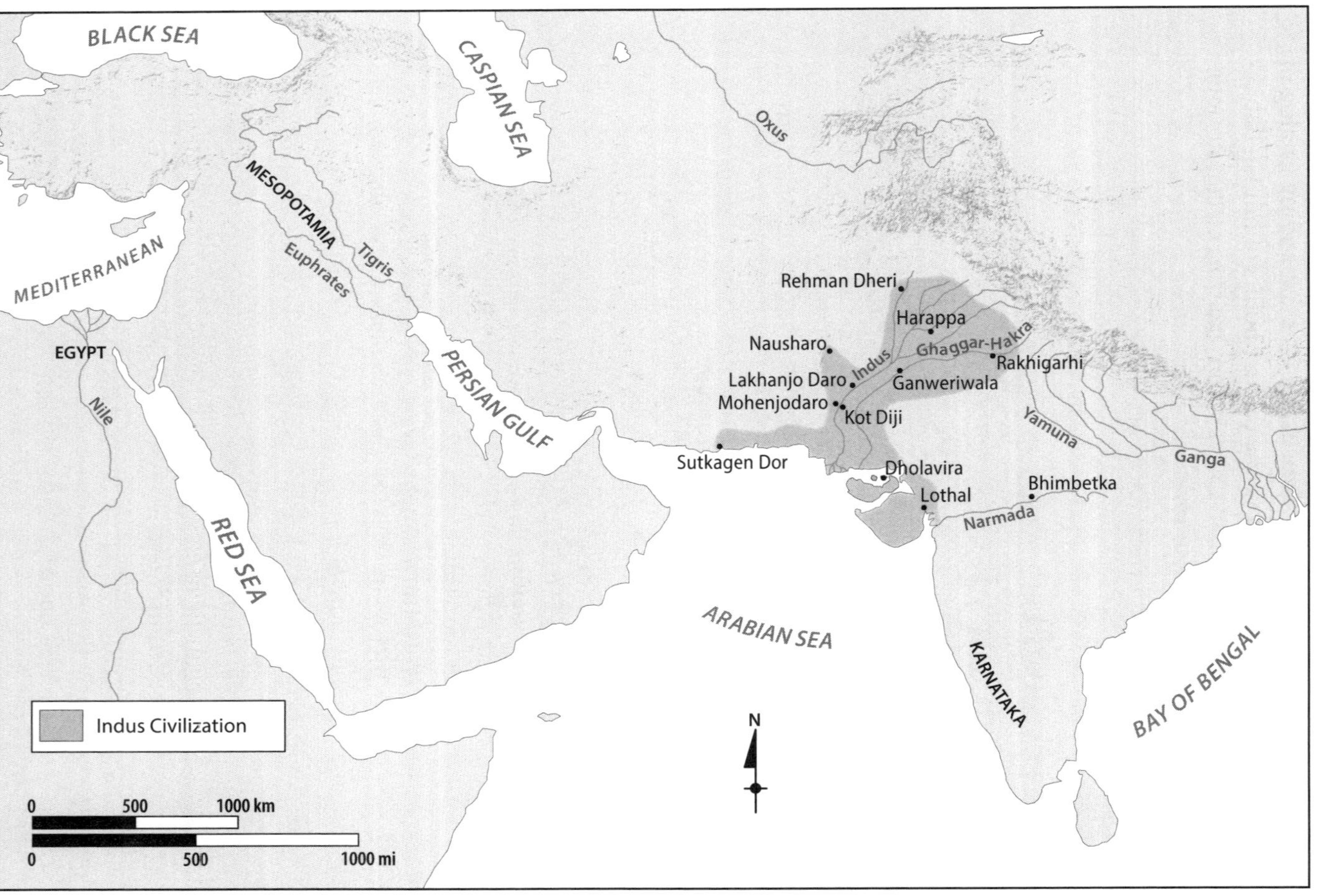

Ancient India, ca. 2500 BCE.

1

Indus Valley Civilization, 2600–1900 BCE

May the land of Meluhha load precious desirable carnelian, mes wood of Magan, and the best abba wood into large ships for you.

—"Enki and Ninhursag," Mesopotamia (Sumerian), ca. 2000 BCE[1]

In 2000 BCE, the most populous cities on earth thrived in northwestern India within a society called Meluhha by ancient Mesopotamians.[2] Today, most prefer the name "Indus Valley Civilization" for this ancient South Asian culture that flourished from 2600 to 1900 BCE and was centered partly around the Himalayan-fed Indus River.[3] We do not know what the Indus Civilization inhabitants called themselves, because we cannot decipher their writing. But, through archaeology, we have recovered much about how the Indus people—ancient India's first city builders—lived, including their trade relations with ancient Mesopotamia. I cover highlights of India's first urbanization here, preceded by an account of how people came to populate the subcontinent in the first place and began to farm and domesticate animals. I close with the collapse of the Indus Valley Civilization by 1700 BCE, after which Indus cities were soon covered by dust. The ancient Indus Civilization constitutes an early flourishing of Indian urbanization and mercantile prosperity, which built upon thousands of years of human ingenuity and lifestyle changes.

First Indians

Humans initially populated the Indian subcontinent through waves of migrations. They hailed from Africa, as we all did originally, with the first homo sapiens setting foot on subcontinental soil as early as 120,000 years ago.[4] These initial migrants left no surviving lineage, however.[5] The first people from whom modern Indians are partially descended (i.e., the first Indians) arrived in South Asia maybe 65,000 years ago.[6] They were succeeded by numerous other eastward-moving groups in subsequent millennia (e.g., the first farmers ca. 7000 BCE, Indo-European speakers ca. 1500 BCE that are discussed in chapter 2, and so forth). As migrants, the first Indians anchored South Asia, even in its prehistory era, as connected with other parts of the world.

The first Indians experienced a subcontinent rather different than it appears to modern people today. Many food items we take for granted as important to South Asian cuisines and cultures were unknown in prehistoric India, including dominant varieties of wheat, barley, and sugarcane; all new world crops (e.g., potatoes, tomatoes, and chilis); and maybe even sandalwood.[7] When ancient migrants first arrived in the northwestern subcontinent, there were neither cities nor farming, and they survived as hunter-gatherers.[8]

Still, the first Indians encountered one thing that remains familiar in our time: the annual monsoon. Every spring and summer, water evaporates from South Asia's surrounding oceans, aided by rising temperatures. The moisture is moved north by winds and trapped by the high mountain peaks of the Himalayas, a towering range created by the geological collision of two tectonic plates fifty million years ago and still rising every year. The water cools and condenses as it is pushed upward, forming clouds that roll back across South Asia, dumping torrential summer rains in an annual pattern.[9] South Asian monsoons have fluctuated in volume through the eras, but the basic phenomenon has been experienced by all humans who have made the subcontinent their home.

Archaeological evidence is meagre for the first 110,000 years of human habitation in India, until about 7000 BCE. That dearth of material explains why so many scholars, me included, talk around prehistory, about weather and the like. Still, even the scant archaeological record furnishes evidence of two trends: people continued moving around, populating various corners of South Asia, and they made art. For example, people inhabited Bhimbetka, a site near Bhopal in central India, probably 100,000 years ago and lived there frequently thereafter, if not necessarily continuously.[10] As early as 10,000 BCE, Bhimbetka inhabitants carved impressions on cave walls and rock shelters, and they painted red images of humans and wild animals, including hunting.[11] Humans arrived in Sri Lanka maybe 35,000 years ago as per skeletal evidence found in caves on the island, and they made adornments such as shell beads as early as 25,000 years ago.[12]

Between 7000 and 2500 BCE, numerous Indian communities began to farm and domesticate animals. These shifts toward sedentary life came on the heels of worldwide climate change as the last ice age ended about 12,000 years ago and the earth began to warm.[13] Pollen trapped within lake sediment records the intertwined stories of climate change and farming, proffering clear evidence that the two converged temporally.[14] Among India's first farmers were people who probably imported agricultural technology developed in Western Asia's fertile crescent. They, perhaps alongside groups who had lived on the subcontinent for longer, cultivated cereals such as barley and wheat at Mehrgarh in Balochistan (modern-day Pakistan) before 6000 BCE.[15] Over the next several millennia, numerous discrete communities across the subcontinent—including in southern India, eastern India, Gujarat, and the Gangetic Basin—cultivated crops on their own, especially indigenous millets and rice.[16] Material evidence indicates a roughly parallel pattern of multiple origins for domesticated animals in South Asia, with the earliest being goats, sheep, and cattle.

The move toward sedentary life—radical in the history of human experiences up until that point—enabled denser living conditions for some Indians and gave rise to early trade networks beyond South Asia. At Mehrgarh, people built multiroom houses in 5000 BCE or even earlier, painting the external walls red or with red, white, and black geometric patterns.[17] Early inhabitants of Mehrgarh crafted human and animal clay figurines, threw pottery on wheels, and performed dental work, such as molar crowns.[18] Some Indian communities figured out that they had natural resources for which others would pay handsomely, such as the brilliant blue gemstone lapis lazuli mined in Badakhshan (northeastern Afghanistan). We are not clear who exactly exported it, but Badakhshan-sourced lapis lazuli had reached Tepe Gawra on the Tigris River as early as 4100 BCE and was relatively common in Mesopotamia by 3550 BCE.[19]

By 3300 BCE, proto-cities began to emerge in South Asia, generally tied to the Indus River. These served as important predecessors to the large-scale urban centers of the Indus Valley Civilization 700 years later. For instance, Rehman Dheri was established around 3300 BCE, with a fortification wall, town planning, and perhaps a population of several thousand.[20] Founded roughly contemporaneously, Kot Diji in Sindh also lay along a branch of the Indus River and has become synonymous for a pre-Indus or early Indus Civilization.[21] At many sites, even before 2600 BCE, northwestern Indians developed early versions of things that later became central to Indus culture, including seals, pottery techniques, and a standard ratio for bricks.[22] It is critical to cognize that the Indus Civilization built on earlier foundations, stretching back millennia in the case of domesticated agriculture and centuries regarding definitional design elements and cultural features. Still, the scale of the Indus Valley Civilization—in both its largest cities and its broader cultural complex—were new as of around 2600 BCE and are worth setting apart.

India's First City Builders

The Indus Valley Civilization flourished in the northwestern subcontinent for 700 years (2600–1900 BCE). I focus in the next section on the Indus Civilization's economic position amid other river-based, urban Asian cultures of its day and in the section thereafter on its decline, dating to roughly 1900–1700 BCE. Here I outline the breadth of the Indus Civilization and key features of life, especially for its city dwellers who enjoyed an urban lifestyle without precedent in South Asian history. These early urbanites depended on a far larger rural population for their food, and so—as is still true today—sustained agriculture enabled cities. Still, urban dwellings set the Indus people apart, as a civilization (a word cognate with city), and so I focus here on life for South Asia's first city dwellers.

The Indus Valley Civilization stretched across roughly one million square kilometers, with urban sites clustered along three bodies of water: the Indus River, the (now largely dried-up) Ghaggar-Hakra River that ran roughly parallel a bit east, and the Arabian Sea along the Gujarat coastline.[23] All three areas were different than they appear today. The Indus River ran a different course in parts, the Ghaggar-Hakra was a robust river, and the Gujarat coast was more extensive than at present.[24]

The Indus Civilization's biggest cities lay along the Indus River, including its three largest known urban centers: Mohenjo Daro, Harappa, and Lakhanjo Daro, which, at their heights, each housed tens of thousands of people.[25] Other cities were a fraction of the size, such as Dholavira in Gujarat (less than half of Mohenjo Daro's extent) as well as Rakhigarhi and Ganweriwala (both along the Ghaggar-Hakra River).[26] The Indus Civilization also included numerous smaller urban centers and towns, including trade outposts such as Lothal in Gujarat and Sutkagen Dor in Balochistan (near modern-day Pakistan's border with Iran).[27] Dozens of Indus sites have been excavated, although some remain nearly untouched (e.g., Lakhanjo Daro, which is largely located beneath the modern Pakistani city of Sukkur). All Indus sites shared certain features that mark them as part of a civilizational complex.

The Indus Civilization people erected cities, big and small, with well laid out streets and remarkable construction. They used consistently sized bricks and generally aligned their roads along the cardinal directions. Some major thoroughfares were quite broad, whereas streets in residential areas were so narrow you could touch the homes on either side as you walked. Houses were sometimes organized around courtyards, had multiple rooms, and stood up to two stories tall. Whether by design or organic usage, Indus cities often had discrete areas for specific crafts. Big cities also maintained some larger buildings, although their purposes remain uncertain with theories ranging from storage units to town halls.[28] People sometimes moved hundreds of kilometers from home to live in bustling metropolises like Harappa (figure 1.1).[29]

Indus city builders were highly skilled at managing water, an important aspect of all urban planning and a cultural focus for this civilization. Each city developed its own method of ensuring drinking water for its populace, with Dholavira's residents using cisterns and reservoirs to collect rainwater while Mohenjo Daro residents dug wells every few houses. Today, some of Mohenjo Daro's wells are deceptive to view, standing high like towers due to excavation to levels further down. An unusual feature of Mohenjo Daro is the Great Bath, a tank measuring 12 meters by 7 meters that was watertight and filled by either rainwater or buckets. We do not know its purpose. But whether it served a practical function as a reservoir or a religious one as a ritual bathing site, it was surely of civic importance and underscores the centrality of water in Indus society.[30]

Figure 1.1. Mound "F" excavation at Harappa, ca. 2450 BCE, Punjab, Pakistan.

Some city residents enjoyed private indoor bathrooms, including at Mohenjo Daro and Harappa, and the facilities were remarkable for the time, even while they had their downsides. The Indus peoples constructed their bathroom floors to be watertight, and some gently sloped downward for drainage to city streets. Also, some Indus Civilization bathrooms featured pots sunk into the ground that required regular cleaning, what we call "manual scavenging" in South Asia today. Certainly, such facilities were convenient for the elites, although less so for those (whether workers, servants, or slaves) who cleaned these latrines. And Indus cities likely stank of raw sewage, especially in hot summers.[31]

Signs of social hierarchy abound in the Indus Valley Civilization, including in city planning. Many Indus Civilization cities were walled, and while some walls served defensive purposes, others enforced social segregation. Large cities like Mohenjo Daro, Harappa, and Dholavira each comprised several discrete walled areas inhabited by distinct populations.[32] The gate to each area was often narrow, which signals a high degree of civil control regarding the movement of people.[33] Some groups lived just outside of Indus city walls, and they often had a poorer quality of life in comparison to their better-off brethren within the city proper. For instance, one archaeologist conducted an in-depth study of discarded animal bones at Gola Dhoro, a small Indus Civilization site in Gujarat. He found diet differences between residents within and beyond the walls for significant stretches of time, with the city dwellers enjoying a richer diet consisting of more fish and mutton (both ate beef).[34]

We remain in the dark regarding the bases of social stratification in the Indus Valley Civilization. Did they discriminate based on ancestry, wealth, gender, skin color, language, religion, sexual orientation, age, or some combination thereof? Maybe they disregarded all of these, which are preoccupations of our times, and cared about other factors instead. At present, there is no way to know. Even without recovering the terms of their social organization, a hierarchy is evident in the material record and worth emphasizing here for two reasons. One, many features of life in the Indus Valley Civilization—such as wearing nice jewelry and having personal seals (both discussed next)—were not enjoyed equally by all inhabitants. We ought to be precise when we speak about elites and see how their lifestyle was enabled by unequal access to resources. Two, some have tended to idealize the Indus Civilization as egalitarian in ways that, to my eyes, project modern fantasies onto the past.[35] I seek to avoid rose-tinted glasses in my attempt to recover the Indus Valley Civilization and indeed the rest of South Asian history.

Indus Civilization people excelled in numerous crafts, which are notable for their artistry and as indicative of economic flourishing. They made distinctive jewelry, including orange and red carnelian beads etched with white designs and shell bangles crafted with a specialized bronze saw.[36] Some artists crafted animal and human figurines, with the two most famous being from Mohenjo Daro. A white steatite rock sculpture depicts a bearded man with adornments on his forehead and right arm and a decorated cloth slung over his left shoulder, measuring at around 7 inches tall (it may have been bigger originally).[37] Standing even shorter, at about 5 inches, a bronze statue shows a naked girl wearing a necklace and dozens of bangles, one hand poised on her hip in what some see as dancing.[38] Other celebrated Indus Civilization sculptures include terracotta carts and boats that were perhaps children's toys.[39] Animals, too, appear on Indus art items, especially seals that merit further discussion.

Figure 1.2. Indus Civilization unicorn seal and modern impression, 2600–1900 BCE, Punjab, Pakistan, steatite stone and clay, 3.8×3.8×1 cm.

Several thousand Indus Civilization seals—fired stones measuring 1 to 5 centimeters square or rectangular—are known today. The seals typically feature an animal, design, or a few characters of writing, and make a positive imprint when pressed on clay or another soft surface.[40] There are also a handful of cylindrical seals that work similarly. We cannot read the Indus script, and we are also unclear about the meaning of the most common animal on seals: a mythical unicorn (figure 1.2).[41] Unicorns appear on seals throughout the entire time span of the Indus Civilization and in terracotta figurines.[42] They are among the features that mark this civilization as distinct from later Indian cultures, in which unicorns are rare.

Even while we remain uncertain what, exactly, Indus seal iconography like the unicorn meant, we have a decent sense of how the seals were likely used. People carried Indus seals around, as evidenced by a semicircular boss on the back of many for threading a cord. Indus seals have been found as far away as Mesopotamia. At Indus Civilization sites, seals are often discovered clustered in certain areas, such as in markets and around gateways, and they have also been found in some houses and not others.[43] A small concentration of seal impressions was found in Lothal, a trading outpost.[44] Collectively, these patterns suggests that seals may have enabled access to specific urban areas, for some people, and facilitated trade. They were produced by specialist workshops in Indus cities (especially at Mohenjo Daro and Harappa, where the vast majority have been found) and seem to have been regulated by Indus elites. In brief, Indus seals set their users apart from others within their society.

Indus Civilization people also distinguished themselves internally through death rituals, even if we have a poor understanding of this. For instance, some groups were buried with shell bangles, whereas other were not.[45] Archaeologists have unearthed burial sites from across the Indus Civilization, although they have not found the number of burials one would expect within the world's most populous ancient civilization. The most likely explanation is the simplest one: many Indus people probably cremated their dead. Still, the relatively few burials we have found demonstrate inequality in death, likely reflecting inequality in life.

There are many things we do not know regarding the Indus Valley Civilization, including their governments, religions, languages, and warfare tactics. Many archaeologists have speculated on these Indus Civilization unknowns, but I decline to recount their various theories here because all are necessarily premised on perilously thin evidence.[46] Still, two things are important to note regarding Indus Civilization unknowns and theories thereof. First, a lack of excavated surviving stone structures does not constitute evidence for a historical absence. For instance, we have found no huge tombs for rulers at Indus sites, on the scale of the gigantic pyramids made for roughly contemporary Egyptian pharaohs. One might see it as prudent to not divert massive resources to constructing royal tombs, no doubt at the expense of everyday people, but, critically, we do not know whether the Indus peoples did this or not. We only know that we cannot identify any funerary structures at present, for which there are many possible explanations other than that they never existed (e.g., they did not survive, are unexcavated, or are presently misidentified). Two, we should not assume a static or singular nature for Indus Civilization unknowns. For example, the Indus peoples may well have had multiple successive governments, since few states survive for 700 years, or there may have been coexisting rulers in different areas. Indus society was likely religiously and linguistically diverse, given that pluralism in these areas is a persistent trend in South Asian history.

Undeciphered Script of the Indus Valley Civilization

A corpus of several thousand Indus Civilization objects bear writing, demonstrating hundreds of discrete script symbols. Still, Indus script examples are all brief and undeciphered. The vast majority of examples of the Indus script are a symbol or two in length, and the longest piece of surviving Indus writing is only seventeen symbols long.[47] Most known specimens of the Indus script are on seals, which are a few centimeters. The physically largest example of Indus writing is a 3-meter signboard of ten symbols (one of them repeats four times) found at Dholavira. We have no bilingual or bi-scriptal writing that includes the Indus script (e.g., like the Rosetta Stone that repeats the same edict in Greek, Demotic, and ancient Egyptian Hieroglyphics and thereby enabled archaeologists to decode Hieroglyphics). There have been dozens of claims to have cracked the Indus script in print over the last 150 years (and at least one forgery to get the job done[48]), but none are widely accepted or convincing.

Deciphering the Indus script is an alluring prize given what access to writing has enabled us to learn about other ancient cultures. But we have a severe handicap when it comes to decoding the Indus script, since we do not know what language or languages the Indus Civilization people spoke or wrote. We do not even know what family tree (or trees) their language (or languages) belonged to nor whether their languages have known descendants today. Some have speculated about the Indus Civilization language tree(s), with Dravidian and Munda being the best guesses, but there is no conclusive historical evidence at present.[49] Many scholars believe the Indus script to be multilingual, similar to Cuneiform script that was used to write Sumerian and Akkadian, which further complicates decoding efforts.[50] Frustrated by a meagre archive, some propose that the full script has not survived.[51]

A minority of scholars propose that the Indus script does not represent language at all but rather consists of non-linguistic signs.[52] This theory sees the "script" as likely a mixture of personal and professional identifications and talismanic symbols, akin (to resort to modern examples) to a swirl of logos, coats of arms, and emojis. The idea has gained little traction beyond its original proposers. We know certain things about the Indus script, such as that it was usually written from right to left. Some seals contain smushed characters on the left as the scribe ran out of room.[53] That might offer a beginning for decrypting, but there remains no decisive evidence or scholarly consensus regarding whether the Indus script represents a language, languages, or non-linguistic communication.

Many historians hold out hope that the Indus script will be decoded someday, despite the obstacles that currently seem insurmountable. But, even if we can one day read what the Indus peoples wrote, we have only short bursts of writing from them and no texts beyond seventeen characters. As a result, even if we do decipher the Indus script, material evidence will likely remain our bedrock for analyzing the Indus Valley Civilization. We are fortunate to have good chances of further archaeological discoveries given that many Indus Valley sites are only partially excavated, such as Mohenjo Daro, and the vast majority remain unexcavated entirely.

Indus Civilization in a Global Context

The Indus Valley Civilization was one of the four centers of the ancient world, alongside Egypt, Mesopotamia, and China. The Indus Civilization was geographically larger than Mesopotamia and Egypt combined and probably significantly more populated.[54] It also coexisted with other slightly smaller civilizational structures on or near the subcontinent. For instance, the Bactria-Margiana Archaeological Complex flourished between 2300 and 1900 BCE (and perhaps a few centuries later too) around the Oxus River in northern Afghanistan.[55] Indus peoples connected through commercial and travel networks with these cultures and others, especially Mesopotamia.

Indus peoples cultivated a bustling trade of imports, exports, and goods that they re-exported. For instance, Indus traders imported lapis lazuli from Afghanistan, often exporting it to Mesopotamia and (perhaps through other intermediaries) to Egypt, where it was used for jewelry and pharaonic funeral masks. Indus peoples imported turquoise from Central Asia and probably copper from Oman.[56] Indus beads were widely sought after and may have inspired similar styles in China.[57] To measure these items—and perhaps goods harder to glimpse in the archaeological record such as spices and grains—Indus traders used standardized cubical weights. These weights were often fashioned from stone mined in Upper Sindh's Rohri Hills.[58] They have been found across the Indus Civilization and as far afield as Mesopotamia.[59]

The Indus Civilization's largest transregional trading partner was Mesopotamia. A ca. 2300 BCE inscription of Sargon, founder of the Akkadian Empire, lists ships traveling to his realm from far away, with the furthest land named as Meluhha (i.e., the Indus Valley Civilization).[60] Despite the distance, the scale of Indus-Mesopotamian trade was likely quite large, including both sea and land routes.[61] Indus peoples exported sesame oil, timber, beads, animals, lapis lazuli, and more to their Mesopotamian contemporaries. Indus Civilization carnelian beads have been found at the royal cemetery at Ur (ca. 2600–2550 BCE, in modern-day Iraq), material proof for ancient Sumerian texts that speak of "precious desirable carnelian" coming from Meluhha (see the chapter epigraph).[62] A few centuries later, Sumerian texts speak of "slabs of lapis lazuli" coming from the east (lapis was mined in Afghanistan).[63] We are uncertain what the Indus Civilization imported from Mesopotamia in exchange for such riches, perhaps raw materials or other things that would not leave a clear archaeological record.[64]

People, too, traveled west from the Indus Valley Civilization to Mesopotamia. Some Indus Civilization people perhaps worked as interpreters in Mesopotamia, with a cylindrical seal bearing the identification "Shu-ilishu, Meluhha interpreter."[65] The existence of an interpreter implies there were Indians working in other capacities in Mesopotamia, perhaps as traders. Indeed, an Akkadian text from ca. 2300 BCE mentions Lu-Sunzida, a "man of Meluhha" who paid in silver to fix a broken tooth.[66] Several dozen Indus seals have been found in Mesopotamian cities, presumably carried there by their ancient Indian users.[67] Ancient Mesopotamians also used seals, although in different ways than their Indian counterparts.[68]

Tracing cultural influences is a dicey proposition, especially for ancient history, but there are limited indications that aspects of the Indus Civilization were informed by cultures further west. Specifically, the Indus Civilization bears marks of Elamite culture, which flourished in west and southwest Persia in the third millennium BCE. Proto-Elamite script remains the best candidate for any known connection with the undeciphered Indus script.[69] More convincing is that Indus peoples adapted certain mythical ideas from Elamite traditions, whether they learned about them firsthand or through intermediaries. For instance, a famous seal from the Indus Valley Civilization depicts a known Eurasian deity, "lord of the animals," who sits cross-legged with a "bulging loincloth knot" and a horned headdress.[70] The depiction is similar to proto-Elamite seals, including the seated position.[71] Such borrowings also involved local adaptations, and in this case Indus peoples substituted what is typically a bull or bison headdress on proto-Elamite seals with a headdress from a water buffalo, an important animal in Indus culture.

In being open to outside influences and cultivating robust trade connections, the Indus Civilization people foreshadowed many subsequent Indian communities. Put another way, trends of Indians seeking transregional contact far outlived the Indus Valley Civilization. But this specific large-scale culture fell apart in the second millennium BCE, and I turn next to the evidence of its foundering and debates about possible causes.

Indus Civilization Collapse

The Indus Valley Civilization declined—meaning its cities lost population, saw a decrease in the quality of urban life, and were ultimately largely abandoned—between 1900 and 1700 BCE. For some Indus Civilization centers, the decline began even earlier. At Mohenjo Daro, the Great Bath fell into disuse around 2200 BCE as the city faced difficulties maintaining earlier construction.[72] From 1900 BCE onward, things worsened in many Indus cities. In Harappa and Mohenjo Daro, residents suffered drain maintenance failures.[73] Dholavira was abandoned twice between 1900 and 1750 BCE.[74] Across the civilization's expanse, the Indus script and cubic weights became rare, with the former ultimately ceasing altogether. Transregional trade reduced in this period. Like many other sites, the once bustling trade outpost of Lothal shrank to a "squatter's settlement," as people moved out and probably east.[75]

Scholars have proposed an array of possible triggers for the fall of the Indus Civilization, with many current theories centering around climate change. Monsoon shifts about 4,000 years ago led to drier weather, which was perhaps unfriendly to urban life in northwestern India.[76] Droughts also likely brought on periodic flooding (although there is no evidence for a single catastrophic flooding event). Some key rivers dried up in parts, especially the Ghaggar-Hakra, and other rivers changed course, especially the Indus.[77] Some have expressed skepticism that climate change could have caused the Indus cities to fall, arguing that "even while some [environmental] factors were pertinent to certain regions, none can account for the decline of the entire civilization."[78] I fail to see why not. Although I do wonder about the possible biases of our own time, in which we are facing potentially civilization-ending climate change (chapter 24) and so are perhaps primed to see it elsewhere. Climate change is a popular explanation at present for major shifts in ancient cultures from the Hittites to Neolithic China.[79]

A distinct issue is whether the end of Indus Civilization urbanity constituted a decline or improvement in human living standards in northwestern India. Certainly, for urban elites, much was lost. Still, even they escaped the smelly streets of Indus cities where backed-up gutters and litter were common by the end. But, for everybody else, returning to a mixture of rural and hunter-gatherer life had upsides. Indus cities had spread disease, with both tuberculosis and leprosy being attested in the skeletal record.[80] Also, cholera—an endemic Indian disease—perhaps spread amid decaying city infrastructure. In brief, as James Scott has recently argued for societies west of India, "The early states were fragile and liable to collapse, but the ensuing 'dark ages' may often have marked an actual improvement in human welfare."[81]

Elsewhere in South Asia, people probably did not even notice the decline of the Indus Civilization, since other Indian cultural formations developed on distinct timetables. Worth mentioning here are the large ashmounds of central and southern India, created between 2700 and 1200 BCE by people who burned cow dung and other material at high temperatures.[82] We do not know why south Indians—who herded livestock, farmed, and exploited wild plants—created over 100 such mounds by burning dung, again and again at the same spot, over centuries.[83] Perhaps, at first, they were just cleaning up. But it soon became a deliberate act, and one of the largest ashmounds at Kudatini (in modern Karnataka) is 130 meters wide by 10 meters high.[84] The ashmounds are often situated within habitation areas and so were perhaps central to daily life for their creators.[85] It would have been quite the experience to witness one of the burnings, gazing up at an awesome fire show and feeling the radiating heat that sometimes exceeded 1,200 degrees Celsius.[86] Through repeated burnings, people deliberately created these monumental structures that are still easily visible millennia later as part of the human-altered landscape in the southern Deccan, northeast Karnataka, and western Andhra Pradesh.

Conclusion: Vanishing and Continuing

While Indus Civilization cities were largely abandoned by around 1700 BCE, Indus people and their descendants continued to live in the region or nearby, albeit with different lifestyles. There are surely points of continuity between the Indus Civilization and later South Asian cultures, although scholars have trouble sorting out precise links due to limited evidence. Perhaps the most easily identifiable point of continuity from the Indus Civilization were orange and red carnelian beads etched in white, which spread across South Asia and remained popular for centuries (chapter 3). Dice, too, are first attested in India in the Indus Civilization and recur in other premodern periods (notably, in the Mahabharata, chapter 5). Other civilizations of the period, too, had lasting cultural legacies. For example, the namaste gesture—common in South Asia today—has antecedents in the Bactria-Margiana Archaeological Complex around Afghanistan's Oxus River ca. 2000 BCE.[87] On the other hand, many things died out with South Asia's first cities, ranging from the Indus script to the Indus Civilization's interest in unicorns (who rarely feature in later Indian cultures).[88] Also, Indians forgot about the Indus Civilization, and it was not rediscovered and properly identified until the nineteenth and twentieth centuries CE (chapter 19). Accordingly, this chapter of South Asian history stands apart, more than most others, from later Indian developments.

Further Reading

This is, by far, the most temporally expansive chapter of this book, and I drew accordingly on multiple discrete scholarly fields and subfields. On Indian prehistory, I relied on the work of David Reich on genetics, Dilip Chakrabarti on archaeology, and Yasodhar Mathpal on Bhimbetka. I found Tony Joseph's book a solid overview, sans jargon, of some key points of Indian prehistory. I looked beyond South Asianists for certain ideas, finding work compelling by James Scott, Peter Bellwood, and others for thinking about the human turn to agriculture. For the Indus Civilization, Jonathan Mark Kenoyer's scholarship is without parallel, and I also drew on Gregory Possehl, Nayanjot Lahiri, Rita Wright, and others, in addition to the online resource (maintained by scholars) harappa.com.

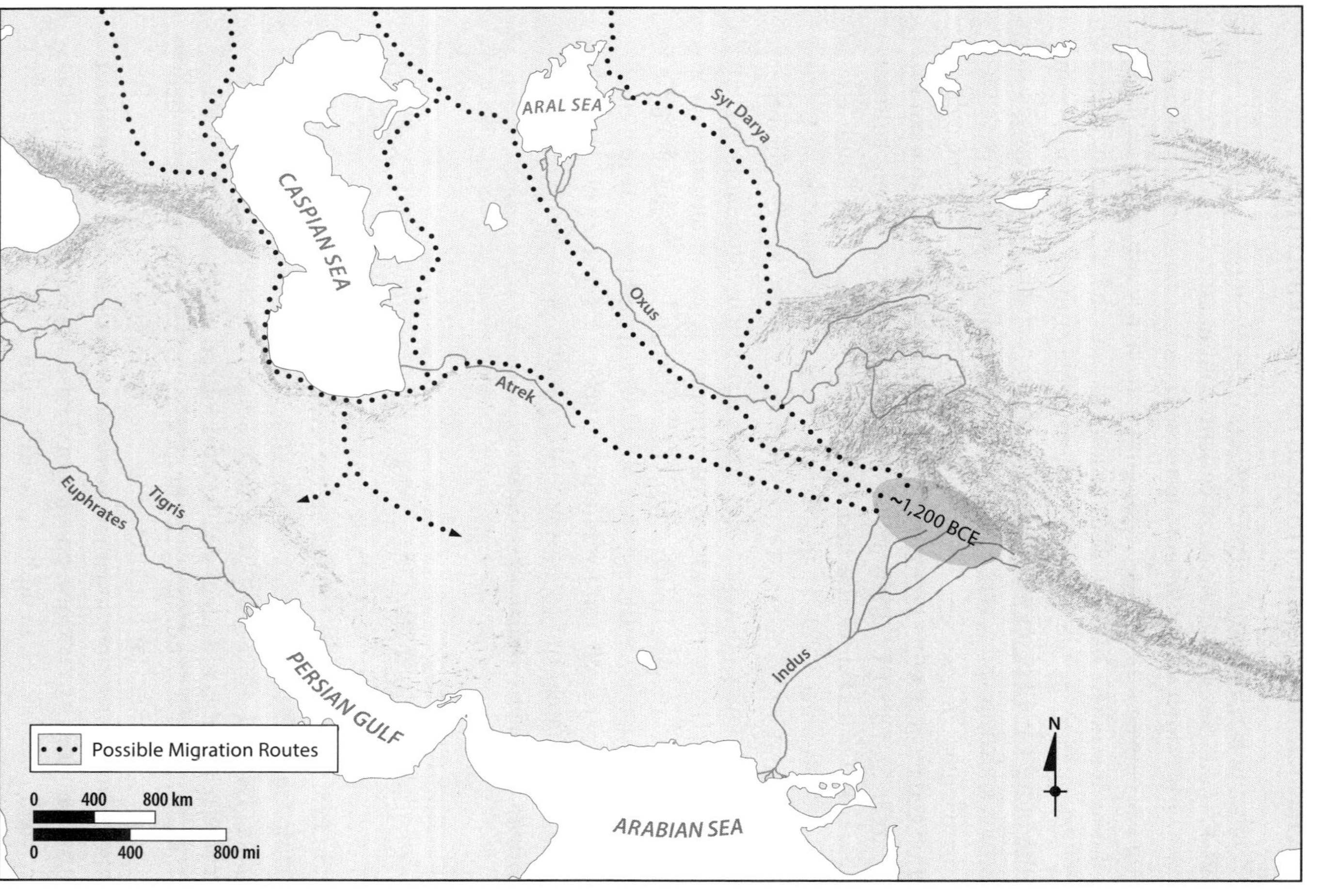

Indo-European-speaking migrations, ca. 1700–1200 BCE.

2

Ancient Migrants and Vedic Practices

He who studies understands, not the one who sleeps.

—Rig Veda, ca. 1200 BCE (Vedic Sanskrit)[1]

Around 1500 BCE, the Indian subcontinent was peopled by groups of diverse ethnic and linguistic backgrounds. Some communities had ancestors who had participated in the Indus Valley Civilization (chapter 1), but most did not.[2] We know few details about most residents of the subcontinent around 3,500 years ago, aside from what kind of pottery they favored. But one group, who migrated to parts of northwestern India around this time, left behind texts that offer substantial insight into their communities' values and culture: Indo-European speakers who authored and transmitted the Vedas. As per their modern designation, Indo-European speakers had roots outside of the subcontinent, migrating into the northwest. After hundreds of years of mixing culturally and through marriage with others already present in northwestern India (largely what is Afghanistan and Pakistan today), they developed Vedic Sanskrit and composed the hymns, chants, and formulas later grouped together as the four Vedas. The Vedas—our earliest surviving Indian texts—offer a peek into the lifestyles and ideas of their ancient authors. Also, while the influence of Vedic practices remained limited in these early centuries, that slowly changed. Over the next few thousand years, Brahmins and others who revered the Vedas shaped key aspects of South Asian languages, cultures, and religions.

Migrations of Indo-European Speakers

Over several hundred years, between 1700 and 1200 BCE, small groups of people who spoke an Indo-European language or languages migrated into northwestern India in search of land for farming and grazing. They perhaps came from the Caucasus and Persia, through the Hindu Kush Mountains (which they called Uparishyena, "Beyond where Falcons Go"), and settled in the dry Punjab region.[3] These small groups were pastoralists and nomadic cattle herders, sometimes clearing forests and other times cattle rustling or migrating further east. After a few hundred more years, perhaps around 1000 BCE, some had settled in villages along the comparatively wet and lush Gangetic plain.[4]

These ancient migrants called themselves "aryan" or "arya" (noble). And so, some scholars refer to them as such or, in a nod to their integration with people already in northern India, Indo-Aryans.[5] I prefer the more neutral descriptor "Vedic" or the linguistically accurate, "Indo-European speakers." Whatever we dub this linguistically defined migrant group, they trickled into the subcontinent in relatively small numbers, were themselves a series of fractured clans, and did not disrupt life for most Indians. So, why are we talking about them? In short, the long-term influence of Vedic culture far outsized its modest beginning and serves as one major strand that informs South Asian cultures throughout history and into today.

Specifically, Vedic rituals, social organization, relationships with certain animals, and languages developed and spread over later centuries, ultimately numbering among the many sources for what we now call Hinduism. That said, a lot has changed over the last 3,000 years. Most, possibly all, modern-day Hindus would find Vedic culture ca. 1000 BCE to be utterly foreign. Because of this disconnect, many scholars prefer to not use the anachronistic term "Hinduism" to describe the religion of these early clans, instead speaking of Vedic religion or Brahminism.[6] That disruption in common vocabulary is useful because it forces us to look more closely at what we know about these early Indo-European speaking migrants and, as they settled in parts of northern India, their evolving ideas and lifestyles.

Linguistic analysis provides the cornerstone evidence for migrations of Indo-European speakers into northern India in the second millennium BCE. Vedic Sanskrit and its slightly later descendent, classical Sanskrit, are cognate with a host of other Indo-European languages, including Greek, Latin, Persian (Old Persian and modern Farsi), and even modern English. We can still hear these ancient links in common words today, such as *mother* in English and *matr* in Sanskrit. Working backward, scholars have reconstructed proto-Indo-European, a language spoken perhaps around 4000–2500 BCE west of the subcontinent and of which Vedic Sanskrit is a linguistic descendent. Indo-European speaking migrants brought this language family to the subcontinent, and, over time, Sanskrit flourished as an elite tongue.[7] Today, most north Indian languages—including Urdu, Hindi, Bengali, Gujarati, Punjabi, and Marathi—are Indo-European in origin (although Sanskrit itself was never a spoken vernacular).

Modern people generally attribute the critical discovery that Sanskrit belongs to the Indo-European language family tree to William Jones, a late eighteenth-century British Indologist based in Calcutta (chapter 17). However, several decades before Jones, in the 1750s, the Delhi-based (and, at the end of his life, Lucknow-based) Indian thinker Khan-i Arzu unearthed the same connection in his Persian text *Musmir* (Fruitful).[8] That most remember the British Jones and few have even heard of the Indian Khan-i Arzu is a testament to the persistent privileging of Western traditions and the ongoing devaluation of premodern Indian knowledge, both of which this book seeks to help remedy.

The linguistic evidence is strong enough to stand alone as proof of ancient migrations by Indo-European speakers into northwestern India between 1700 and 1200 BCE, but it is supplemented by conceptual links. Vedic gods have parallels in cultures outside of India—including among Zoroastrians in Persia, Hittites in Anatolia, Mitanni in Syria and northern Mesopotamia, and Kassites in Babylon—which further suggests a common, non-subcontinental source.[9] Parallels are especially rich between the Vedas and the oldest Avestan texts, used by Zoroastrian communities in Persia (modern-day Iran).[10] Additionally, the Vedas mention places in Persia and Central Asia as well as how groups "crossed many rivers" and went "through narrow passages" in what are possible memories of historical migrations.[11]

In recent years, many people have been captivated by the possibility of genetic evidence for the ca. 1700–1200 BCE movements of Indo-European speakers into northwestern India. Indeed, recent genetic analysis shows significant differences between ancestral north Indians and ancestral south Indians, with the former group sharing genetic similarities with populations in Central Asia, the Middle East, and Europe.[12] Analyses of ancient skeletal remains indicate the introduction of Steppe ancestry in northwestern India (a marker of migrants to the region) after the Indus Civilization's decline and before the composition of the Vedas.[13] Both finds are consistent with ancient Indo-European speaking migrations.[14]

Material evidence furnishes little for further understanding these ancient migrations. Archaeologists have unearthed remains of various settlements in northern India around the times and places that Indo-European speakers lived in the second millennium BCE, but we have no means of linking the two. In any case, people who herded cows, planted crops, and held their religious rituals outdoors or in temporary structures may have left behind scant archaeological remains. Early Vedic communities did not even make bricks. Their light material footprint stands in stark contrast to the robust archaeological remains of the Indus Civilization (chapter 1). We find more robust resources for reconstructing Vedic worldviews and ritual practices in the earliest extant Indian texts that they composed and cherished: the Vedas.

Vedas as Oral Texts

The four Vedas—the Rig Veda, Sama Veda, Yajur Veda, and Atharva Veda—were composed in an archaic form of Sanskrit over a thousand-year period, roughly 1400–500 BCE, in northern parts of the subcontinent. Of the four Vedas, the Rig Veda is the oldest. In its current state, the Rig Veda comprises 1,028 hymns (*suktas*) organized in ten sections, but this compilation occurred sometime later. Initially, the earliest Rig Vedic hymns were composed over probably five or six generations by 1200 BCE and transmitted by individual lineages.[15] Many hymns have named authors, such as Vishvamitra, Bharadvaja, and Atri.[16] Their compositions and others were subsequently collected into the so-called family books (sections 2–7 of the Rig Veda).[17] Some later layers of the Rig Veda are ascribed to female authors, such as Apala Atreyi and Ghosha Kakshivati, although scholars have questioned the veracity of these attributions.[18]

The Vedic hymns were composed, anthologized, and transmitted orally. The Vedas themselves stress the power of *vach* (speech), especially for ritual purposes. Brahmins, the class of trained priests who preserved the Vedas, developed sophisticated recitation techniques—memorizing the text backwards and forwards and various other ways—that ensured accurate transmission over millennia. The Vedas were eventually written down, probably in the early second millennium CE, but, even then, oral transmission was preferred. An undated text on how to pronounce Vedic hymns warns that a pandit who reads (*likhita-pathaka*) ranks among the worst kinds of Vedic reciters.[19] A verse from the epic Mahabharata (ca. 100 CE) predicts that those who write the Vedas (*vedanam lekhaka*) will go to hell (*nirayagamina*).[20] Even today, select groups of Brahmins uphold traditional techniques of reciting the Vedas, and their methods have been documented by UNESCO as part of the "Intangible Cultural Heritage of Humanity."[21]

While we know what the four Vedas sound like, making sense of their contents is challenging. These ancient works, especially the Rig Veda's earliest layers, were composed thousands of years ago in a society radically different from any in modernity (and, frankly, from most in premodernity). In trying to bridge this formidable gap, we lack evidence external to the Rig Veda to infer how communities in this early period used these hymns. We must rely on Vedic literature alone to make sense of this society. And Vedic texts were not composed as historical records but rather as invocations to gods, curses, blessings, and so forth. Even reconstructing Vedic mythology is challenging, since many hymns refer to stories involving gods and other figures without elaborating the full tales, assuming that these would be familiar to all listeners. These difficulties are compounded by the language of the Vedas, which is not only ancient but, by design, abstruse. As modern scholars have explained, Vedic poets opted for difficult, recondite language as part of their aesthetics of appealing to various deities. What was crafted to delight the gods has confounded generations of interpreters.[22] As early as the mid-first millennium BCE, the lexicographer Yaska struggled to ascertain the meaning of many Vedic words.[23]

The Vedas promise to deliver wisdom. The very word *veda* means knowledge (*veda* has the same Indo-European root as the English *witness* and the German *wissen*). Despite the plethora of challenges, when read carefully, the enigmatic Vedas transmit a wealth of information about the people who authored and preserved these texts, both information that they meant to communicate and insights that were unintentionally preserved.

Vedic Social and Religious Life

The Rig Veda outlines two distinct communities that intermixed: the migrants who revered Vedic hymns and rituals and those they name as *dasa* or *dasyu*, autochthonous residents of northern India. Some hymns express a desire to conquer dasa groups, for instance appealing to the god Indra to deliver the dasas to (the rhetoric goes) the superior Vedic community.[24] But the Rig Veda also documents how the two broad groups intermingled. Some Vedic clans forged alliances with dasas.[25] Hymns authored by two separate families record rituals being performed for the dasa chiefs Bribu and Balbutha Taruksha, respectively.[26] The groups intermarried, likely unevenly with men more likely to take local wives. Later Vedic texts speak highly of Brahmin men born of dasa mothers, and genetic evidence bolsters claims of intermarriage.[27]

Language provides the most visceral evidence of cross-cultural exchanges. Many, possibly all, dasa groups spoke Dravidian and Munda languages, two linguistic families that preceded Indo-European tongues on the subcontinent.[28] Both Dravidian and Munda words appear in the Vedas, including the Rig Veda (the earliest of the four), which indicates communication between Indo-European speaking migrants and autochthonous communities. More fundamentally, Sanskrit's retroflex sounds—where your tongue curls back so that its underside touches the roof of your mouth—were borrowed from Dravidian languages.[29] In other words, the very language of the Vedas was produced through social and cultural mixing.

While Vedic groups adopted much from those already living in northwestern India, they also introduced new practices and technologies, such as domesticated horses. Before Indo-European speakers migrated, domesticated horses were not a major feature of any known subcontinental culture (including the Indus Valley Civilization), perhaps because the best areas for breeding horses were in Central Asia.[30] The Vedic peoples prized horses for practical, cultural, and religious reasons. Horses assured speedy travel and offered a military advantage. They were also a major sacrificial animal, especially in the *ashvamedha* (horse sacrifice) that became notably elaborate in the first millennium BCE. In later

Sanskrit-based traditions, kings and emperors used the ashvamedha to express real and imagined political power (chapter 7). Cattle were another important animal in Vedic culture, serving as sources of food and status markers. Vedic peoples were far from the first beefeaters in South Asia, and the animal was widely consumed within the Indus Civilization as well.[31] In Vedic culture, cattle held specific symbolic value. They were also used as currency, including to pay Brahmin priests to perform rituals.[32]

Vedic religious life was well suited to the clans' peripatetic lifestyle. As Stephanie Jamison has put it, the Vedic peoples constructed the "ideally portable religion," which had no fixed place of worship, no written texts, and no icons.[33] But one thing they had in abundance were gods. The conceptual world of the Rig Veda teems with divine figures, including deified natural phenomena such as the sun, earth, sky, and dawn. Other gods are referred to with fleeting references to their larger mythologies that we cannot fully reconstruct, such as Varuna, Mitra, and Indra. Some Vedic hymns are almost personal. One example is Vasishtha's poem to Varuna (god of the ocean), which is found in the oldest layer of the Rig Veda. Vasishtha addresses Varuna directly and, speaking in the first person, imagines the two of them sailing across an ocean toward the sun.[34] Other Vedic hymns are more esoteric, animated by an embrace of plurality and questioning, rather than appealing to a specific deity. One example that speaks remarkably well across time is Rig Veda hymn 10.129 that poses many unanswered questions in a meditation on the profundity of creation.

Rig Veda Hymn 10.129, ca. 1000 BCE

There was neither non-existence nor existence then; there was neither the realm of space nor the sky which is beyond. What stirred? Where? In whose protection? Was there water, bottomlessly deep?

There was neither death nor immortality then. There was no distinguishing sign of night nor of day. That one breathed, windless, by its own impulse. Other than that there was nothing beyond.

Darkness was hidden by darkness in the beginning; with no distinguishing sign, all this was water. The life force that was covered with emptiness, that one arose through the power of heat.

Desire came upon that one in the beginning; that was the first seed of mind. Poets seeking in their heart with wisdom found the bond of existence in non-existence.

Their cord was extended across. Was there below? Was there above? There were seed-placers; there were powers. There was impulse beneath; there was giving-forth above.

Who really knows? Who will here proclaim it? Whence was it produced? Whence is this creation? The gods came afterwards, with the creation of this universe. Who then knows whence it has arisen?

Whence this creation has arisen—perhaps it formed itself, or perhaps it did not—the one who looks down on it, in the highest heaven, only he knows—or perhaps he does not know.[35]

Among the Rig Veda's many deities, two stand out who served as ritual links between the human and divine worlds: Agni and Soma. Agni, fire, was central to Vedic sacrifices as a consumer of offered items. One could present items to many Vedic gods, but Agni alone could devour the offering via burning before the sacrificer's eyes. Soma has prompted much debate but was some kind of edible plant pressed into a beverage, probably with mind-altering qualities. In the eighth section of the Rig Veda, one hymn dwells on the euphoric effects of ingesting Soma once the substance has "settled down in every limb" and "enflamed me like a churned fire." Once verse reads:

> We have drunk the soma;
> we have become immortal;
> we have gone to the light;
> we have found the gods.[36]

Vedic communities performed sacrifices to their gods, and these rituals constituted a central part of their conceptual and social worlds. The Rig Veda is shot through with mention of sacrifice (*yajna*, *homa*), and many rites were further elaborated in later centuries. Public *shrauta* sacrifices were done outdoors or in temporary constructions. Shrauta rituals involved elements that would strike most modern people as esoteric and aspects that raise eyebrows today. The horse sacrifice (ashvamedha) is a prime example. A host of specialized Brahmin priests—each with his own title such as *udgatar* and *hotar*—were required to conduct the horse sacrifice, with each priest having his own tasks and price tag. The sacrifice could take up to a year to complete, most of which was spent allowing the horse to wander.

The ashvamedha's finale featured a ritualized enactment of aberrant sexuality. Specifically, the sacrificer's wife pantomimed having sex with the just strangled and, thus, erect horse while his other wives engaged in lurid banter with priests.[37] The bestiality aspect of this ritual finds rough parallels in other cultures, such as urban legends about Russia's Catherine II.[38] It caused colonial-era scholars' cheeks to redden, and some declined to translate the more graphic bits of Vedic texts.[39] But prudishness was a Victorian preoccupation, not a Vedic one. The themes of public intercourse and sexual jousting recur in other public gatherings of Vedic society, which also included forms of entertainment more comfortable to many today, such as singing, dancing, and riddles.[40] Vedic practitioners understood such sexual behavior as breaching ordinary conduct and so pursued it within a ritual context to allow for an unleashing of chaos within a controlled environment.[41] While many details of Vedic sacrifices have changed over time, the general emphasis on ritual has thrived within various Hindu communities. Even today, many practitioners and scholars define Hinduism by its rituals, by what people do, rather than by what individual Hindus may or may not believe.[42]

The Vedic emphasis on sacrifice prompted numerous additional social and intellectual developments between 1200 and 400 BCE. Many sacrifices required knowledge of mathematics, astrology, and astronomy to run properly.[43] Especially as sacrifices became more elaborate, they served to redistribute wealth and to concentrate it within two major groups: the sacrifice sponsors and the priests who performed the rituals. Eventually these two groups came to have names: Kshatriyas and Brahmins, respectively. A late addition to the Rig Veda describes the sacrifice of the cosmic man that created, among other things, a hierarchy of four social classes:

> When they divided up the man, how many parts did they make?
> What did they call his mouth, arms, thighs, and feet?
> The Brahmin was his mouth. His arms the ruler.
> His thighs were the Vaishya. From his feet came the Shudra.[44]

This fourfold theory of social organization no doubt contrasted with the messy reality of intermixed groups in ancient north India. But ideas hold

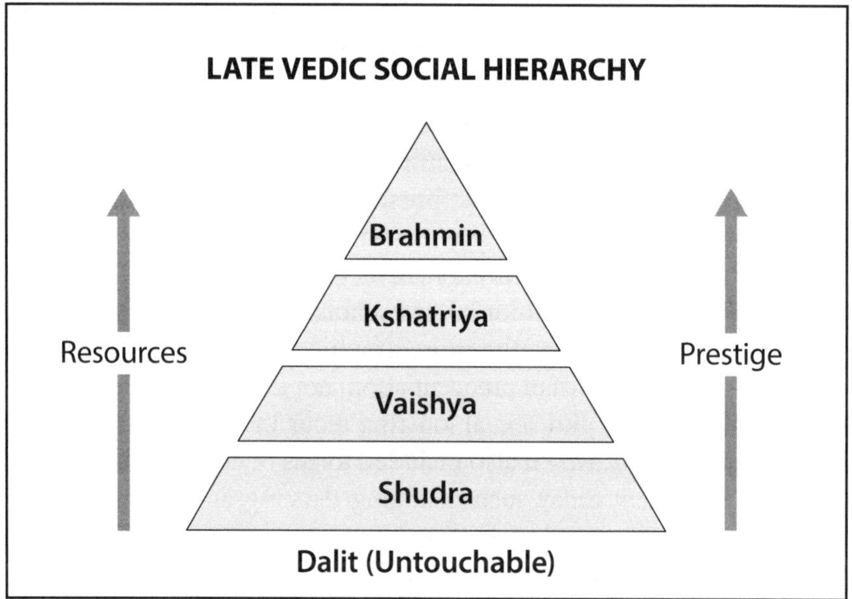

Figure 2.1. Social hierarchy as imagined in the Rig Veda, ca. 1000 BCE.

power, and this one became entrenched in later millennia along with ideas about Brahminical identity and superiority first expressed within Vedic culture (figure 2.1).

Notably, this first articulation of a new idea—the fourfold varna system—came couched within one of the most repeated, familiar aspects of Vedic society: ritual sacrifice. While both sacrificers and Brahmins were required for Vedic rituals, as funders and priests, respectively, the early Vedic texts are products of Brahminical thought. In fact, Brahmins claimed authority and special status in early Vedic society precisely because of their textual and ritual expertise. Brahmins alone, they proclaimed, had the *adhikara* (right) to knowledge contained within the Vedas and to perform Vedic rituals, the centerpiece of this social community.[45]

By looking at how rituals developed over the centuries, we can trace a Vedic historical consciousness across multiple texts. After the Rig Veda, three other Vedas were composed a bit later and elaborated on ritual practices. The Sama Veda largely overlaps in content with the Rig Veda. The Yajur Veda offers *mantras* (ritual formulas). Standing a bit apart from these first three, the Atharva Veda includes magical poems, life cycle rites, and far more. Composed perhaps around 800–600 BCE, Brahmana and Aranyaka works interpret Vedic rituals by providing further details of specific sacrifices and rituals. All these works, along with the Upanishads (discussed in the next section), are part of the broader Vedic tradition (and, somewhat confusingly, "Veda" can refer to the four Vedas or to this larger set of works). Many later Vedic texts flesh out stories and philosophies that highlight the sacrificial inclinations of this society. For instance, one story from the *Shatapatha Brahmana*, composed in the seventh to sixth centuries BCE, explains why animals are tied to a pole (*yupa*) at sacrificial grounds. The tale goes that animals used to walk upright on two legs, like humans, and opposed being immolated in the sacrificial fire. They were cowed into submission by the gods' thunderbolt, which is the sacrificial post.[46]

The voices we hear in the broad corpus of Vedic texts (1500 BCE–400 BCE) are overwhelmingly male and, to modern eyes, young (which we should keep in mind when discussing, say, creative sexual elements of the horse sacrifice), but women were also part of this world. Women recited mantras and were required to participate as wives in sacrifices.[47] Women still wielded limited power in Vedic society, and there are indications that their introduction to public sacrifices met with resistance.[48] Perhaps, then, it is unsurprising that we glimpse women in the Vedas most clearly in domestic concerns and regarding their relations with men. Some Rig Veda hymns promise to protect against miscarriage, and others assure a safe birth.[49] The text describes an incestuous rape in graphic terms.[50] Polygamy was practiced in Vedic society, and one hymn offers a woman the ability to "triumph over her rival wife," attracting all their shared husband's attention and ensuring that he "takes no pleasure in this person [his other wife]."[51] The Rig Veda also provides incantations for more prosaic concerns, such as a sleep charm that bids various household members to "Go to sleep!"[52]

A lullaby contrasts with how most people today imagine the four Vedas, and that is because few people read the Vedas and many interpretations of the Vedas are products of later centuries. As mentioned, sometime post-composition, people collated slightly more than a thousand hymns into the Rig Veda, thus making what had been the intellectual property of discrete clans into an anthology. Even after the Vedic tradition was codified, new ideas about it surfaced. For instance, one later idea is that the Vedas are *shruti* (heard) and thus especially authoritative, in contrast to other kinds of Hindu texts that are dubbed *smriti* (remembered). One influential philosophy known as Purva Mimamsa understood the Vedas to be *apaurusheya*, authorless, whereas many of the hymns' original authors put down their names.[53] Even in ancient India, the Vedas were reinterpreted, sometimes quite radically.

Thinking ahead, one big question that arises is: How important were the Vedas to later Hindu communities? No doubt the answer has varied, and even today their importance is debated, with some arguing that revering the Vedas is definitional to Hinduism and others describing them as irrelevant for the vast majority of lived Hindu experience. Either way, the Vedas are a set of texts that survived and were repeatedly analyzed and imbued with new meanings. In ancient India, the authors of the Upanishads constituted a key group of Vedic interpreters, who took the texts and thus the Hindu tradition in new directions.

New Ideas in the Upanishads

By 600 to 500 BCE, groups who honored the Vedas and used Sanskrit had spread across much of the northern subcontinent. They were far from culturally dominant and had not yet moved south of the Vindhya Mountains in central India.[54] But Vedic culture was known in and around the Gangetic plain, where fertile agriculture created ripe conditions for the rise of cities and accompanying lifestyle changes. Kingdoms that we will hear about again, such as Magadha (chapter 3), date to this period. As new urban centers emerged, people began to author texts called Upanishads that purported to explain the philosophy of the Vedas while, in actuality, introducing innovative ideas. The Upanishads number at fifty-two in some later northern traditions, and 108 in some later southern traditions. If we count all Sanskrit texts that bill themselves as "upanishad" (literally meaning "sitting near" and referring to a pupil sitting near a teacher), then there are hundreds, some composed as late as the sixteenth century CE.[55] Here I focus on the earliest Upanishads, the *Brihadaranyaka* and *Chandogya*, which, like the Vedas they claim to gloss, were initially composed and transmitted orally and were anthologized slightly later. These early Upanishads echo some of the prosaic concerns of the Vedas, offering rites to ensure safe childbirth and charms to render your wife's lover impotent.[56] The

Brihadaranyaka and *Chandogya Upanishad*s also offer substantial innovations that reinterpreted key Vedic ideas for a new audience enmeshed in shifting social realities.

The Upanishads are sometimes called *vedanta*, the end of the Vedas, and, appropriately given this description, they offer two major narratives for how Vedic sacrifice had developed over the prior centuries. The early Upanishads attest that Vedic rituals had become more elaborate and monied as compared to the evidence glimpsed in the Rig Veda. For instance, the *Brihadaranyaka Upanishad* records that Janaka, ruler of Videha, performed a sacrifice with "lavish renumeration" to the Brahmins who flocked from nearby regions, and so "corralled a thousand cows, tying ten pieces of gold to the horns of each one."[57] Even if this inflates the amount of cash thrown around at sacrifices in the sixth century BCE, it indicates that, in the years since the composition of the Rig Veda, Vedic rituals had become economic powerhouses whose financial offerings attracted priests from far and wide.

Alongside elaborate physical sacrifices, the Upanishads posited that *yajna* (sacrifice) could be internalized, a radically new idea within Vedic culture. As the *Chandogya Upanishad* puts it: "Now, what people call 'sacrifice' (*yajna*) is really being a celibate student (*brahmacharya*). Being a celibate student is how one finds the knower. What people call 'offering' (*ishta*) is really being a celibate student. Striving precisely by being a celibate student, one discovers the self."[58] In other words, the pursuit of knowledge, especially by being a celibate student (*brahmacharin*), could produce comparable results to physical Vedic sacrifice. This startling proposition would likely have met with opposition or perhaps just blank stares of non-comprehension by Vasishtha, Vishvamitra, and other Rig Veda poets. Here we glimpse astonishing innovation of the core Rig Vedic concept of the centrality of sacrifices, even while still using the basic language and grammar of ritual.

The *Brihadaranyaka* and *Chandogya Upanishad*s attest that asceticism—depriving oneself of pleasures, often including society and food—was emerging as a legitimate spiritual path by the middle of the first millennium BCE. Asceticism makes the most sense in an era of urbanization, when there were sufficient concentrations of wealth and people to renounce. Notably, in the early Upanishads, asceticism appears to be a lifestyle choice (not a stage of life, which was a later development).[59] Ascetic practices were designed to promote spiritual growth, and they also proved a useful set of tools for those who articulated religious paths that eschewed the Vedas, such as Buddhism and Jainism, in the coming centuries (chapter 3).

Karma is another idea that was seriously overhauled in the early Upanishads. Karma literally means "action." In the Vedas, karma denoted ritual action specifically and the ability of this highly regulated human activity to produce certain results (e.g., money, power, pleasing a god). In contrast, in the Upanishads, all human actions result in negative or positive implications for one's next life.[60] This expanded notion of karma and its consequences went along with the idea of *samsara*—the cycle of death and rebirth that characterizes all human existence—that became elaborated at this time.

In the Upanishads, just as in the Vedas, sacrifices could produce good karma, but so, too, could knowledge. At one point in the *Brihadaranyaka Upanishad*, Yajnavalkya explicitly argues to his wife Gargi that knowledge supersedes sacrifice: "Gargi! If a person gives offerings, performs sacrifices, and does austerities in this world for many thousands of years, but does not know that imperishable, then it comes to nothing. Wretched is the person who leaves this world without knowing that imperishable, Gargi!"[61] Some scholars have theorized that Kshatriyas introduced some of these new ideas in the early Upanishads, enriching a tradition that, until that point, had been dominated by Brahminical thought.[62] The theory finds limited support in some Upanishadic stories, but it remains uncertain. I am not even clear that it is historically accurate to talk about a cohesive Kshatriya identity or community in the sixth century BCE. We make far more headway on the important agenda to search for non-Brahmin voices in ancient India in the next chapter, by looking to communities that went beyond reinterpreting Brahminical practices, instead ignoring or rejecting them.

Some women speak up in the male-dominated philosophical debates within the early Upanishads. For instance, Gargi Vachaknavi and Maitreyi both talk philosophy with men. Some of Gargi's contributions echo the Rig Veda questioning hymn by dealing with similar queries about the origins of things in the world and wondering on what the universe is woven. Still, Gargi and Maitreyi are, perhaps, exceptions that prove the rule that Brahminical social conventions around the sixth century BCE usually excluded women from philosophical and ritual exegesis.[63] Nonetheless, there was some space for women in this world. The *Brihadaranyaka Upanishad* mentions a ritual one can perform to obtain an "educated daughter" (*duhita pandita*).[64]

A mother-son conversation between Jabala and Satyakama stands out for its display of female sexuality. In the exchange, Satyakama asks his mother, Jabala, for his gotra, meaning his line of patrilineal descent. Gotras are exogamous Brahmin lineages that became elaborated in later centuries and are, critically, patrilineal (in contrast to caste, which is generally understood to depend on the status of both parents).[65] Jabala states, rather nonplussed, that she slept around and does not know her son's father. She offers her own name as a substitute, and Satyakama is ultimately identified by his caste (see excerpt). In addition to the seeming easy acceptance of a woman's sexual promiscuity as Jabala "got around a lot as a working girl," the passage also offers an early example of the importance of caste identity, specifically being Brahmin.

Jabala and Satyakama on Being a Brahmin, Excerpt from the *Brihadaranyaka Upanishad*, ca. 500 BCE

Satyakama Jabala said to his mother Jabala: "I want to live as a Vedic student (*brahmacharya*). What is my lineage through my father (*gotra*)?" She answered: "My dear, I don't know your paternal lineage. In my youth, I got around a lot as a working girl, and you came along. So, I don't know your paternal lineage. But my name is Jabala. Your name is Satyakama. So, say that you are Satyakama Jabala."

Satyakama approached Haridrumata Gautama and said, "I want to live as a Vedic student. Please let me study under you."

Haridrumata asked him: "Son, what is your lineage through your father?" He replied: "Sir, I don't know my paternal lineage. When I asked my mother, she said: 'In my youth, I got around a lot as a working girl, and you came along. So, I don't know your paternal lineage. But my name is Jabala. Your name is Satyakama.' So, I am Satyakama Jabala, Sir."

Haridrumata said to him: "Nobody who was not a Brahmin could say that. Get some firewood, son. I will initiate you since you have not strayed from the truth."[66]

For many today, the most inspirational aspect of the early Upanishads is the repeated showcasing of philosophical inquiry. For instance, in one chapter of the *Brihadaranyaka Upanishad*, Vidagdha Shakalya asks Yajnavalkya seven times: "How many gods are there?"[67] Each time, Yajnavalkya gives a different answer, starting from several thousand and dwindling to one. His penultimate answer is cheeky: There are "one and a half" gods. This idea of a flexible number of deities, depending on one's perspective, connects with parts of the Vedas that identify specific gods with one another. Arguably, it also offers an early precedent for later strands of Hindu traditions—each with its own specific genealogy—that emphasize the unity of God (chapters 8 and 19).

Another example of the Upanishadic emphasis on philosophy is the recurrent subject of how the *atman* (self) relates to the *brahman* (ultimate reality). Speakers in the early Upanishads struggled to describe either concept clearly, sometimes resorting to negation.[68] For instance, Yajnavalkya says: "Describing this self (*atman*), we can only say 'not, not.' He is ungraspable since he cannot be grasped. He is undecaying since he is not subject to decay. He has nothing stuck to him since he cannot stick to anything. He is boundless, without being agitated or harmed."[69] Perhaps the most famous expression in the *Chandogya Upanishad* concerns the self: *tat tvam asi* (That's how you are).[70] This expresses some sort of relationship between atman and brahman, although its contours remain vague, to put it mildly. Perhaps that vagueness is what, in part, has allowed many modern people to feel that the Upanishads speak to core human concerns, in addition to being products of a specific time and place and thus of historical interest.

Conclusion: Sanskrit and Its Discontents

Speech was a powerful concept in the early Upanishads, like in the Vedas, although the language of the two bodies of materials differed substantially. The Sanskrit of the early Upanishads had lost many linguistic features of Vedic Sanskrit and approaches classical Sanskrit, a register more or less codified by the grammarian Panini who lived around the fourth century BCE in what is now Pakistan. Even as Sanskrit developed, Brahminical culture overall met with a decidedly mixed response. To put it bluntly, not everybody was charmed by the late stages of Vedic society. From the turn of the fifth century BCE onward, numerous philosophical and religious positions articulated ideas that had nothing to do with Vedic practices, and they all steered clear of Sanskrit, seen as a language closely associated with Brahminical practices. In the following chapter, I turn our attention to non-Vedic trends as well as accompanying political, economic, and social changes.

Further Reading

The Rig Veda has been published numerous times, and the Sanskrit text is available and searchable online. I consulted English translations by Stephanie Jamison and Joel Brereton (full translation) and by Wendy Doniger (select hymns). Those scholars, along with Laurie Patton, Frits Staal, and Michael Witzel, have produced significant scholarship interpreting the Vedas. For a grounded historical perspective on the Vedic period, Romila Thapar's work offers much to specialists and general readers alike. Patrick Olivelle's work on the Upanishads is detailed and careful; I also consulted Olivelle's Sanskrit edition of the early Upanishads.

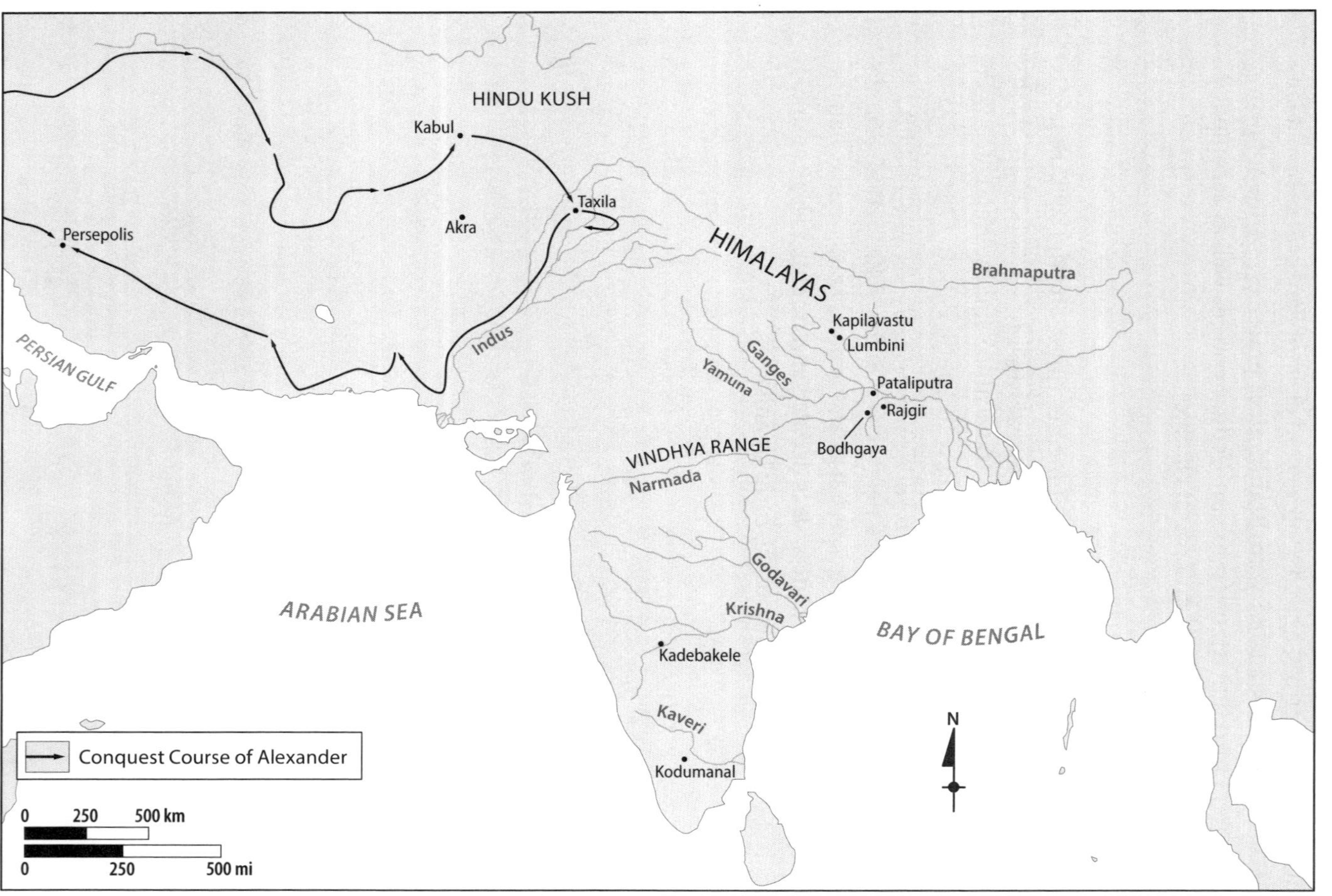

India's second urbanization, 550–325 BCE.

3

Building and Renouncing Cities, 550–325 BCE

You are called Freed, Mutta,
so be freed!
Be like the moon emerging from the darkness of an eclipse.

—Mutta, *Therigatha*, fourth-third century BCE (Pali)[1]

Between 550 and 325 BCE, Indian communities underwent a near explosion of interlinked cultural, political, religious, and economic innovations. A wave of urbanization constitutes the first South Asian experiences of city life since the fall of the Indus Civilization more than a millennium earlier (chapter 1). Building upon greater population density, rulers forged larger political formations, including empires, monarchies, and oligarchies. Others innovated in the religious realm, preaching new philosophies and lifestyles. This included the founders of Buddhism and Jainism, two traditions that remain part of the human experience today. Economic activity increased as trade expanded within and beyond the subcontinent and Indians minted their first coins. By focusing on these myriad shifts, we can glimpse human life in different parts of the subcontinent during the mid-first millennium BCE. South India, for instance, gets left out when we fixate on political dynasties but comes into focus when we explore trade routes and even fashion around 2,500 years ago. By surveying a mix of topics, we glimpse a layered picture of Indian experiences in different areas of the subcontinent during the dynamic sixth–fourth centuries BCE.

Urbanization and People's History

In the mid-first millennium BCE, Indians began to construct and inhabit cities. This trend toward urban life was witnessed in the northwest, eastern, and southern subcontinent, where it unfolded at slightly different paces and dates. Scholars sometimes dub this period India's "second urbanization," since the first occurred during the heyday of the Indus Valley Civilization (2600–1900 BCE). But, so far as we know, nobody in the first millennium BCE remembered that ancient history. From the perspective of those inhabiting Taxila, Kadebakele, Kodumanal, Rajgir, and other cities ca. 500 BCE, urban life was a new subcontinental phenomenon. Urbanization was helped by and, in turn, fostered technological advances. Many Indian communities had begun producing and using iron tools between 2000 and 1000 BCE, and by 500 BCE, iron tools helped people to clear forests and increase agricultural output, both of which created ripe conditions for cities.[2]

Urban life concentrated wealth and thus enabled inequality to blossom. For example, the *Anguttara Nikaya*, a Buddhist text composed several centuries later, mentions poor men being jailed for failing to pay their debts, whereas wealthy debtors walked free.[3] Class differences likely increased apace with urban growth, but further detail remains elusive. Perhaps society in, say, Taxila was partly organized according to the fourfold class system described in the Rig Veda (chapter 2). Perhaps people formulated an early version of the caste system that today includes thousands of *jatis* (endogamous social groups). We do not know, a situation unlikely to change since our major textual sources for this period date to the third century BCE and later. Instead, archaeological evidence constitutes our major contemporary sources for economic and social features of urban life in and around the Indus valley, the Gangetic plain, and south of the Vindhya Mountains around 500 BCE, best exemplified by focusing on a handful of cities.

Taxila flourished in the northwest from the sixth century BCE onward. Modern scholars first read in ancient texts about the city known as Takshashila (Taksha's Rock) in Sanskrit and Taxila in Greek. They identified its location in the nineteenth century (about thirty kilometers from Islamabad in modern-day Pakistan) and began excavations in the early 1900s.[4] Today, Taxila is among the most well-excavated premodern cities on the subcontinent, with the area dubbed Bhir mound housing the oldest layers of human occupation at the site, ca. sixth–fifth century BCE. The city probably grew organically, without centralizing planning, and possesses no identifiable granaries or warehouses, which perhaps indicates decentralized political power.[5]

Ancient Taxila's economy thrived, with shops that opened onto thoroughfares and streets that could accommodate wheeled, human, and animal traffic. Some street-facing houses even had wheel guards to prevent damage from passing chariots and carts.[6] You could probably procure some desirable goods in ancient Taxila—such as silver, gold, and deep-blue lapis lazuli—since the city was located on trade routes to Kashmir, Afghan regions, and Persia.[7] Taxila is often associated with the Persian Achaemenid Empire (discussed later in this chapter), although not all ancient Indian cities were tied to the rise of large polities, even in the northwest. A good example is Akra, located about 250 kilometers southwest of Taxila. Akra only began to be excavated in the 1990s, but it appears to have been an urban center with robust trade that predated the Achaemenid Empire's incursions into northwestern India.[8]

In southern India, too, urban centers grew during the mid-first millennium BCE with one striking example being Kadebakele, near modern-day Hampi in eastern Karnataka. During or before the mid-first millennium BCE, residents of Kadebakele managed water, including by erecting damns and building reservoirs. Others devoted their efforts to the arts, and at least two rock art sites date from this period, featuring red etched hourglass human figures with tousled hair.[9] In one panel, two people clutch an upside-down bovine, its legs tied together, while other people in the image hold hands, forming a human chain. The second panel includes more than twenty figures, plus animals, a crowd that calls to mind the population density of urban life (figure 3.1). Residents of ancient Kadebakele maintained separate areas for domestic and ritual activities. We even know a little bit about their taste in jewelry, a subject that merits further discussion.

Fashion, specifically of beads and other ornaments, offers one entry point into people's history that centers everyday life. This emphasis allows us to bring in southern India, even without knowing about its politics and elite life, for this ancient period. For instance, material evidence at Kadebakele attests that people wore carnelian beads that shone vibrant orange to dark red, strung one or a few together.[10] In a sign of being fashion conscious, designs on beads were often repeated,

Figure 3.1. Rock art showing a crowd of hourglass figures and animals at Kadebakele, 1200–400 BCE, Karnataka, India, red ochre on stone.

including at sites far away and over hundreds of years. For instance, 600 kilometers south at Kodumanal, some carnelian beads bear motifs that repeat those found in Kadebakele, while others feature fresh designs that had hit the market.[11] There is no carnelian in the Tamil Nadu region in which Kodumanal is located, and so this material must have been imported from further north along trade routes.[12]

Artisan skills, too, may have traveled long distances and been preserved through significant political upheaval. Strikingly, south Indians fashioned shell bangles, especially after 400 BCE, using a technique identical to that practiced in the Indus Valley Civilization. This raises the intriguing possibility that itinerant craftsman may have kept this specialized knowledge alive over centuries and transmitted it to communities far south of where the Indus Civilization flourished.[13]

Not all sites offer the rich archaeological materials found at Kadebakele and Kodumanal, but even with more limited evidence we can often glean something of ancient life. For example, Rajgir (Rajagriha) was

Figure 3.2. Punch-marked coin with images of an elephant, sun, six-armed symbol, and bull as well as an obverse-side small punch, sixth–second centuries BCE, northern India, silver.

a city in the Gangetic plain associated with the kingdom of Magadha and nestled between five hills.[14] No buildings survive from 2,500 years ago, but there are remains of a stone wall that ran across parts of the five hills surrounding Rajgir to mark the settlement's boundaries and were fortified around the entrances.[15] The stone wall stood up to eleven or twelve feet high and enhanced the natural defense of the hills, presumably against rival polities. Around the core of the city are remains of an earthen inner wall whose purpose was likely to protect Rajgir from water runoff down the hills during the annual monsoon rains.[16] While Rajgir's residents guarded their city from political and natural threats, they welcomed the movements of peoples and goods. The ancient city was said to be visited by religious teachers, most notably the Gautama Buddha (ca. 400s BCE).[17] Rajgir was located along trade routes extending south and west. For further information on Rajgir's economic life, the best material evidence is some of the smallest in physical size: punch-marked coins.

Beginning in perhaps the fifth century BCE, Indians in the northwest and the Gangetic plain began to mint silver punch-marked coins, which afford us several insights about their society. The coins were struck first by small states, and, later, larger kingdoms such as Magadha ran mints (in Magadha's case, probably first at Rajgir).[18] The coins contain no dates or names, leaving their exact origins unclear, but each was punched with five or six geometric or symbolic designs (figure 3.2). These designs surely communicated information to users, including, modern scholars have theorized, who minted the coin. For example, a six-armed symbol and a sun likely indicated Magadhan authority.[19] Hundreds of other images feature among the initial punch-marked designs, including elephants, horses, lions, plants, weapons, wheels, humped bulls, and more. To fit on the coins, such images were shrunk to only a few millimeters, a feat that attests to both technology and artistic talent. In addition to their original minting marks, many punch-marked coins bear later small punches that were added while the coins were in circulation. In many cases, merchants likely etched these later markings to mark coins of a specific weight, or even to create a tracking system as counterfeits emerged.[20] So much has changed about Indian society since the early days of punch-marked currency, but forgeries are still a problem in the twenty-first century. The antiquities market is awash in modern fakes of these ancient coins made by people seeking to profit from inventing a piece of Indian history.

Monarchies—Oligarchies—Empires

As subcontinental cities and economies expanded, the stage was set for the dawn of more complex political formations. Three major types of polities emerged in the mid-first millennium BCE in India that differed from one another in governance style and location within the subcontinent. Monarchies centered power in a single royal family, with the most well-known example being Magadha in the Gangetic plain. In oligarchies, a small group of families shared political power. Oligarchies were often dotted around Magadha's periphery, with the most prominent being the Shakyas in the Himalayan foothills and the Vajjis (Vrijjis) in Bihar. Transregional empires extended from western Asia into the northwestern subcontinent, including the Persian Achaemenid Empire and Alexander's Macedonian Empire. Between specific instantiations of these three types of kingdoms were large swaths of the subcontinent that were presumably under more local forms of control. For their many differences, the monarchies, oligarchies, and transregional empires from this period concurred on one point: none embraced Vedic culture.

It remains a judgment call how many kingdoms we ought to identify by name on the subcontinent between 550 and 325 BCE. Numerous lists survive that catalog specific monarchies and oligarchies. The most well known is the list of sixteen kingdoms (*mahajanapadas* in Sanskrit), found in Jain, Buddhist, and (later) Brahminical texts.[21] These lists post-date this period and are inconsistent, points that call their accuracy into question.[22] I am even less convinced of the validity of specific claims about most of these kingdoms, such as precise borders and lineages of rulers. In addition to lacking strong evidence for detailed information, there are other reasons to de-emphasize political history in this period. Listing dynasties is a dull approach. Also, a strong political focus distracts our attention from cultural, social, and religious developments that provide a more wholistic picture of ancient Indian communities. Accordingly, I limit my comments on political power to a handful of kingdoms, especially the Persian Achaemenid Empire and the kingdom of Magadha. For both, their historical existence stands on solid evidence, and they offer insights into cultural and social developments with repercussions far beyond their political boundaries.

Around 530 BCE, the Persian Emperor Cyrus crossed the Hindu Kush Mountains and incorporated parts of northwestern India into the Achaemenid Empire. Gandhara and two other provinces, named as Thatagus and Hindush in Achaemenid sources, formed the easternmost edges of this vast and culturally influential Persia-based empire for nearly 200 years.[23] We remain uncertain today about how much imperial control the Achaemenids exercised over their Indian territory, but residents sent impressive payments west to Persia. Writing around 425 BCE, Herodotus attests that northwestern Indians contributed the most robust tribute out of the Persian Empire's twenty provinces.[24] Herodotus recorded other things too, such as identifying the Indus River as a habitat for crocodiles.[25] He communicated less about the people who inhabited northwestern India and their role in the Achaemenid Empire beyond serving as financiers. In this line of inquiry, material evidence offers more.

A ca. fifth-century-BCE panel at Persepolis (figure 3.3) depicts a visiting Indian delegation to the city, evidence that some Indians were well integrated within the Achaemenid Empire. The Indian diplomats wore loincloths and sandals while exposing their upper bodies, sartorial choices that distinguished them from other groups depicted on the panels. Likely this was not a one-time visit since Indians also appear in reliefs on the tombs of Darius (r. 522–486 BCE) and subsequent Achaemenid kings.[26] Still, they likely did not travel quite as far from the

Figure 3.3. Indian delegation in a tribute procession on the eastern stairway at the Apadana, fifth century BCE, Persepolis, Iran.

subcontinent as their Indus Civilization counterparts 1,500 years earlier who journeyed as far as Mesopotamia (chapter 1).

For their part, the Achaemenids may have introduced the seeds of certain ideas—about writing and kingship—to the subcontinent. They wrote Aramaic on both papyrus and leather, which likely served as an inspiration and model for Kharoshthi, the oldest deciphered Indian script that was developed in the fourth to third century BCE.[27] Also, Darius sponsored numerous inscriptions where he speaks in the first person, a decision also made by Ashoka in the third century BCE to great political and cultural effect (chapter 4).[28]

More than 1,500 kilometers southeast of the Achaemenid's eastern border, in the Gangetic plain, the kingdom of Magadha flourished from the sixth century BCE onward. Magadha's kings practiced familial and state violence. Bimbisara, based in Rajgir and the earliest known historic ruler, is said to have been killed by his son Ajatashatru in the fifth century BCE. Sources diverge on the details of subsequent transfers of power, but fratricide is a recurrent theme.[29] An appetite for political violence was also evident in the thirst of Magadha's rulers for annexing further territory. Bimbisara is often dubbed *seniya*, "head of an army." Ajatashatru is credited with several conquests, including dominating the Vajji confederacy to the north.[30] At some point, Magadhan rulers shifted their capital city to Pataliputra (Patna), about eighty-five kilometers north of Rajgir and advantageously located along the Ganges River.

Culturally, Magadha was not dominated by Vedic practices. In fact, both Magadha and Vajji witnessed a burgeoning of new religious ideas and practices in the mid-first millennium BCE. Mahavira and Siddhartha Gautama, the historical founders of Jainism and Buddhism, respectively, were both born and lived in these regions in the fifth century BCE along with other religious leaders less well known today.

Founding Buddhism and Jainism

In the span of a few generations in the 400s BCE, numerous new religious communities—including Buddhists, Jains, Ajivikas, and Charvakas—emerged into historical view. Several founding leaders of these groups were contemporaries who operated in the same general region: the Gangetic plain and Himalayan foothills. Such aligned timing and geography are extraordinary. We can best explain this convergence by identifying the contexts, practices, and ideas common to these groups. Their new religious ideas embraced a shared vocabulary of karma and samsara that point to the purported centrality of human actions (karma) in determining one's fate over multiple lifetimes (samsara). This vocabulary is also found in the slightly earlier Upanishads (chapter 2). Each group tweaked their definitions of these shared ideas to outline distinct religious paths. None of these new traditions involved Vedic rites, animal sacrifice, or ritual purity. Although it remains uncertain whether such Brahminical ideas were widespread enough at this point in South Asian history to be consciously rejected, or, alternatively, if they were socially restricted enough to be ignored.

Jains, Ajivikas, Charvakas, and Buddhists all emerged against the backdrop of urban life. The most robust and, ultimately, long-lived of the new religious ideas—Buddhism, Jainism, and the Ajivikas—were part of the *shramana* tradition of renunciation where individuals declined to participate in material life and instead pursued higher truth.

Booming urbanity offered something tangible to reject and renounce (Charvakas, instead, embraced materiality). Typically, shramana renunciants of this period lived outside of populated areas and relied on deprivation, meditation, and philosophy to achieve insights into the true nature of existence. The shramana tradition also existed within the umbrella of Hindu practices, as evidenced by the embrace of asceticism within the early Upanishads at roughly this same time (chapter 2).

While converging with Upanishadic thought on asceticism, early Buddhists, Jains, and Ajivikas declined to use Sanskrit, which distinguished them from both Vedic and Upanishadic worldviews. The historical founders of all three traditions taught in vernaculars, sometimes named as Magadhi for Gautama, the founder of Buddhism.[31] Gautama's ideas were recorded, along with those of his contemporaries Mahavira (Jain) and Makkhali Gosala (Ajivika), in texts composed a few centuries later in various Prakrit languages (Pali for Buddhists and Ardha-Magadhi for Jains). We presume that the Ajivikas also composed their texts in a Prakrit language, but none of their own literature survives, a historiographical difficulty to which I return below. Prakrits are a set of languages that are etymologically related to Sanskrit but sounded, to many ancient Indian ears, closer to everyday speech. As such, they offered Buddhists, Jains, and Ajivikas a more seemingly accessible way to communicate religious ideas, quite different than the language of Vedic ritual and its restriction to upper-class men. Indeed, the newly coined Buddhists, Jains, and Ajivikas offered their insights to all people, in sharp contrast to the hierarchical and stratified nature of Vedic society.

Mahavira and Gautama, the founders of Jainism and Buddhism, respectively, were dynamic renunciants who lived at the same time in the fifth century BCE. Although they never met, their life stories share a broadly similar outline. Both men were born in oligarchies, in towns about 300 kilometers from each other. Mahavira was born at Kundagrama, quite close to the Vajji capital of Vaishali.[32] Siddhartha Gautama (or Siddhattha Gotama, as his name is given in Buddhist Prakrit sources) was born at Lumbini, in modern-day Nepal, and raised in Kapilavastu, a town associated with the Shakya oligarchy. Both left home as young men, shunning urban life. Each wandered in the forest for years, ultimately claiming to gain enlightenment through meditation. The two men then taught their respective insights for the rest of their lives so that others might follow their paths to *moksha* or *nirvana*, liberation from the cycle of death and rebirth (samsara). Mahavira was the elder of the two, dying around 420 BCE, and Gautama died around 400 BCE.[33]

This bare-bones outline of the lives of Gautama and Mahavira strips away much later embellishment, which is extensive for both figures. In so doing, I stick to history and avoid religious hagiography. But this approach also risks missing what their followers found inspirational about these teachers' life stories, whether real or imagined. I agree with other scholars who have argued that these men must have been charismatic leaders.[34] That said, most specific details of their lives are intellectual products of followers in subsequent centuries. I now turn to those hagiographies to capture the memories of these men, narrating them separately along with some additional early developments in each tradition, beginning with Buddhism.

After 400 BCE, narratives of the Gautama Buddha's life circulated and expanded. Our earliest source for Gautama's traditional hagiography is the Pali canon, a three-part collection (*tipitaka*) of Buddhist ideas and teachings compiled, perhaps, a few hundred years after his death. In that canon, we find many details appended to Gautama's life story that, regardless of their historical truth, tell us what most Buddhists have believed about their founder.

Siddhartha Gautama was born into an important family, even as a prince according to some later texts. His father sheltered him from life's harsh realities. And so, Siddhartha grew up, got married, and had his own child without ever learning the fundamental truths of human existence, including that we all grow old, are prone to illness, and will die. On a pleasure tour around Kapilavastu one day, he saw these ills in human flesh: an old man, a sick man, and a corpse. He realized that pain and sorrow are universal human experiences that would visit him, too, one day. Alarmed at this discovery, Siddhartha fled from his palace and family in the middle of the night, so that he might be free to discover a way out of the suffering endemic to human existence.

In the forest, Siddhartha Gautama deprived himself, very nearly starving to death at one point, in a bid to gain knowledge. This approach made him hungry but not enlightened. Finally, he sat under a bodhi tree and meditated, gaining nirvana (enlightenment) that would free him from samsara. Rather than leave this world immediately, Gautama chose to remain in his human form so that he could teach others his insights, his *dhamma* (Prakrit for Sanskrit *dharma*). He delivered his first sermon at Sarnath (in modern-day Uttar Pradesh) and spent the remainder of his life teaching the Buddhist dhamma, including a moderated approach to physical deprivation (a "middle way"). He attracted followers who were mendicants, like him, and followers who maintained their households. When Gautama died, Buddhists believe, he achieved his final nirvana (*parinibbana*), escaping from the ruthless cycle of constant rebirth fueled by karma.

Gautama's followers cremated his body and followed his teachings, ultimately forming a Buddhist community of monks and laity. The renunciants, male *bhikkhus* and female *bhikkhunis* who are collectively called the *sangha*, lived the dhamma, studied, and taught others. Buddhist monks and nuns were supported, in part, by lay Buddhists who followed Gautama's teachings within the confines of normal and, often, urban life. Some early Buddhists penned their own texts, preserved in the Pali canon. Among them, one group of voices stands out: the nuns whose poems comprise the *Therigatha*.

The *Therigatha* (Songs of enlightened women) is a groundbreaking work on several levels. It is an early set of Indian poems, composed between Gautama's death through perhaps the third century BCE.[35] Its authors—Chala, Tissa, Mitta, Isidasi, and so forth—offer a set of female voices that are often sorely lacking in ancient literature. In fact, the *Therigatha* is the first anthology of women's literature worldwide.[36] As its modern translator, Charles Hallisey, has put it, "As salt just seems to go with food, the adjective 'first' and the *Therigatha* seem to go together."[37]

Overall, women occupied a contested place in early Buddhism. It is unclear whether some skepticism about female followers dated back to Siddhartha himself. Certainly, parts of Pali canon offer a debasing view of women, such as one passage that reduces us to emotional temptresses of men:

> Womenfolk are uncontrolled, Ananda.
> Womenfolk are envious, Ananda.
> Womenfolk are greedy, Ananda.[38]

Against this dismissive backdrop, it is all the more important to recover the voices of the theris, enlightened Buddhist women who tell us why and how they followed the dhamma.

In the Therigatha poems, some of the earliest Buddhist nuns offer insight into their experiences, as both adopters of the Buddhist path and as women. Some theris dwelled on the freedom from domestic obligations that becoming a bhikkhuni offered, such as Mutta who said:

> The name I am called by means freed
> and I am quite free, well-free from three crooked things,
> mortar, pestle, and husband with his own crooked thing.[39]

Others talked about difficult pasts, such as Vasetthi who attests that following Gautama saved her from insensate grief over her dead son.[40] Addhakasi narrates how she gave up work as a prostitute to follow Buddhist teachings.[41] Female friendship is a recurrent theme as the women turn to each other for guidance. Several authors, including Chanda and Sona, credit other bhikkhunis, like Patachara, with setting them on the path toward enlightenment.[42] We lack further resources, beyond the poems themselves, to help us reconstruct these women's lives. But we are not the first to wish we had more information. Dhammapala wrote a commentary on the *Therigatha* in the sixth century CE in southern India, in which he imagines the theris' life stories to place them in larger social contexts.[43]

The *Therigatha* authors also help map the intellectual contours of the early Buddhist tradition more broadly. For instance, while there are plenty of indications of earthly sisterhood in their writings, the theris' end goal was, generally, freedom from rebirth. Several poems end with the phrase "I became cool, free," with the Pali word for "free" having the same root as *nirvana*. Many women claim to repeat wisdom imparted by Gautama (referred to as Gotama or Sugata, the well-gone one, in the text), such as warning against the (for Buddhists) false assumption that people have permanent souls.[44] Chanda offers a small indication of distinguishing the Buddhist dhamma from Vedic practices. Toward the end of her poem (see excerpt), Chanda mentions that she knows "three things," which a contemporary reader or listener would recognize as one's past lives, where and why others are reborn, and the elimination of one's own moral corruptions. The Pali term for this triad, *tevijja* echoes the Sanskrit *trayividya*, meaning the three Vedas (exempting the slightly later Atharva Veda), which women were forbidden from learning. In affirming her access to the Buddhist *tevijja*, Chanda declares both the place of women in Buddhism and issues a slight to exclusive Vedic claims of knowledge.[45]

Chanda, Becoming a Buddhist Nun, from the Pali *Therigatha*, ca. Fifth–Third Centuries BCE

In the past, I was poor, a widow, without children,
without friends or relatives, I did not get food or
clothing.

Taking a bowl and stick, I went begging from family to family,
I wandered for seven years, tormented by cold and heat.

Then I saw a nun as she was receiving food and drink.
Approaching her, I said, "Make me go forth to homelessness,"

And she was sympathetic to me and Patachara made me go forth,
she gave me advice and pointed me toward the highest goal.

I listened to her words and I put into action her advice.
That excellent woman's advice was not empty,
I know the three things that most don't know,
nothing fouls my heart.[46]

Vasetthi, Becoming a Buddhist Nun, from the Pali *Therigatha*, ca. Fifth–Third Centuries BCE

I was wounded by grief for my son,
mind unhinged, mad,
without clothes, hair unkempt,
I walked from place to place.

Resting on heaps of garbage in the streets,
in cemeteries, on highways
I wandered for three years,
always hungry and thirsty.

Then I saw the Sugata going toward Mithila,
tamer of the untamed, fully awake, afraid of no one and nothing.

Back in my right mind, I worshiped him and came close.
Gotama taught me the dhamma out of kindness toward me.

I listened to what he taught, I went forth to homelessness,
forming myself with what the Teacher said.
I knew at first hand the blissful state.

All sorrows are cut off, left behind,
this is their end,
now I understand things,
how could sorrow start again?[47]

Jain communities, too, expanded their teachings and religious hagiographies in the centuries after Mahavira's death or, as Jains saw it, his liberation. Jain texts from the second or first century BCE—the second book of the *Acharangasutra* and the *Kalpasutra*—offer some of our earliest glimpses of embellishments to Mahavira's life story.[48] Aspects of Mahavira's hagiography are beyond the historical realm, such as the transfer of an embryo from a Brahmin woman to a princess, Trishala, who then gestated and gave birth to Mahavira.

Other parts of Mahavira's tale are grounded in historical reality, especially his emphasis on *ahimsa* (nonviolence). Most notably, Mahavira had robust practices to avoid harming any living beings, such as refusing to wear clothing out of concern for insects that might hide in the folds of cloth. He was a strict vegetarian and spurned even root vegetables that must be dug up, thereby harming creatures living in the dirt. The *Acharangasutra*, one of the oldest Jain texts, likewise prescribes: "All breathing, existing, living, sentient creatures should not be slain, nor treated with violence, nor abused, nor tormented, nor driven away. This is the pure, unchangeable, eternal law which the clever ones, who understand the world, have proclaimed."[49] In Mahavira's teachings, avoiding harm to living creatures helps one to prevent the accumulation of bad karma, which Jains understand as a black substance that sticks to and weighs down one's soul. Only after a person is lightened of karma can he (or, for some Jains, she) achieve the ultimate goal of moksha, escape from repeated rebirth.

According to Jain tradition, Mahavira was the final in a line of twenty-four Jain teachers known as *tirthankaras* (ford-makers) since they offered teachings that promise to help people cross the ocean of rebirth. The prior twenty-three Tirthankaras (also called Jinas) are historically unverifiable, but their stories tell us about the beliefs and ideas of later Jains, including internal divisions.[50] For instance, Malli, the nineteenth ford-maker is believed to have been a woman by Shvetambaras but not by Digambaras.[51] These two branches of Jainism diverged in the early centuries CE and disagree on the status of women more generally. Shvetambaras believe that women can attain enlightenment, whereas Digambaras stipulate that women must be reborn as men to achieve moksha.[52]

Like Buddhists, Jain communities comprise renunciants and laity, with the latter providing financial support to the former. As per their names, Shvetambara (white-clad) monks wear white robes, whereas Digambara (sky-clad) monks go nude in imitation of Mahavira (nuns in both traditions wear clothing). Jain monks and nuns sometimes practice rather fulsome renunciation and deprivation, which stood, especially in early centuries, in contrast to the Buddhist middle way. For instance, Jain monks and nuns pull out their hair by the root, whereas Buddhist renunciants typically shave their heads. Even today, occasionally a Jain renunciant will take *sallekhana*, a voluntary fast to the death thought to hasten one's pursuit of liberation from samsara.[53] Still, such practices are limited to renunciants. Like most Buddhists, most Jains throughout history and today have practiced their religion as lay followers.

Ajivikas, Charvakas, and Other Religious Innovators

The Ajivikas were a third major religious group to emerge in the fifth century BCE in eastern India, but reconstructing their ideas and practices poses significant historiographical challenges. Makkhali Gosala, the historical founder or at least a major articulator of Ajivika views, was a contemporary of Gautama and Mahavira. Like Buddhists and Jains, Ajivikas probably wrote down their ideas and memories about Makkhali Gosala a few centuries after his death. But the Ajivika tradition went extinct in the early to mid-second millennium CE, and no Ajivika writings survive today. As a result, this once formidable religious community has the cruel fate of being known only through the criticisms of their competitors. Reconstructing from Jain and Buddhist sources, the Ajivikas were also shramana ascetics who attracted many followers. Some

Buddhist texts even suggest that Makkhali Gosala, not Mahavira, was the foremost rival of Siddhartha Gautama.[54] Buddhist and Jain sources appear to muddle Ajivika theology, however.

Today, we have inherited two major alleged characteristics of Ajivika thinking that seem to be at odds: a view of fate (*niyati*) as the organizing feature of the universe and severe ascetic practices, including sometimes starving themselves to death. Many scholars have tried to square the circle of why fatalists would bother with extreme deprivation (instead of reveling in life's sensual pleasures).[55] Ultimately it seems, to me, best to conclude that the Ajivikas' rivals probably bungled parts of their tradition. If we only knew which parts. Some Indians found Ajivika teachings and practices, whatever they were, compelling. The group flourished for centuries, surviving in southern India as late as the fourteenth century CE before dying out.[56] Buddhism, too, evaporated from most of the subcontinent before or during the early to mid-second millennium CE, although, unlike the Ajivika tradition, it survived in many places outside of India (including elsewhere in South Asia, such as Sri Lanka).

Other religious groups and leaders interacted with Gautama, Mahavira, and Makkhali Gosala, but recovering anything of their ideas and social realities is difficult. For instance, the Charvakas were materialists who, we think, rejected ideas of divinity and argued that the world as we experience it is all there is. To the Charvakas, the soul was no more permanent than "water bubbles" and only "those destitute of knowledge and manliness" would bother with sacrifices.[57] Like with the Ajivikas, no Charvaka writings survive, and we access their views through reports by their critics, who were merciless in ridiculing the materialists.[58] Nearly two millennia later, other Indians were still beating up on the Charvakas, although it is unclear whether any were around by that point or if their memory was just a convenient punching bag. Abul Fazl, an intellectual at the Mughal court in the late sixteenth century CE, described the Charvakas as having "written extensive books in contempt of others that serve as memorials of their own idiocy."[59] If the Charvakas, indeed, wrote books, none survive today.

In addition to the Charvakas, skeptic or agnostic leaders also feature in early Buddhist texts as conversation partners, although their views are presented as comically prevaricating. For instance, one passage depicts Sanjaya Belatthiputta, a skeptic, as answering a question with the gobbledygook: "I do not say it is not so, and I do not say that it is not not so."[60] In the sources we have, such people seem to serve as a foil for Buddhist ideas, rather than reflecting a historical reality of substantive intellectual debate.

Even with such fragmentary and imperfect records, it is clear that northern India in the fifth and fourth centuries BCE witnessed an efflorescence of religious thinkers and ideas. Moreover, the religious communities they founded shaped South Asian cultures and society for millennia. In subsequent chapters, I cover the end of certain traditions, such as premodern Indian Buddhism (chapter 10). Other groups, such as Jains, constitute a continuous religious tradition that still flourishes in contemporary times. For now, I turn briefly back to political events in the 300s BCE to round out this period of ancient Indian history.

Conclusion: Political Coda of Western Asian Empires

Alexander of Macedon crossed the Indus River in the mid-320s BCE, seeking to enlarge his already considerable kingdom that replaced the Achaemenid Empire and stretched west as far as Greece. Greek authors, like Strabo, wrote a few centuries later about Alexander's skirmishes in India and introduced fantastical elements, making it hard to say much for certain.[61] Alexander is said to have fought King Porus (maybe Puru in Sanskrit), but there is little further information available on this ruler or his alleged battle with the Macedonians. Certainly, the Macedonians noticed the Indian use of elephants in war, a broader trend of the period.[62] That military strategy and health challenges, such as dysentery and malaria, proved formidable obstacles to Alexander's army remaining in northwestern India very long.[63] During his brief time near Taxila, Alexander met a naked ascetic named Kalanos who subsequently traveled back to Persia with the Macedonian army. We cannot say what religious tradition Kalanos belonged to or if his tradition is one known today, but he constitutes an early example of an Indian religious figure traveling beyond the subcontinent.[64] Indian sources mention nothing of Alexander, who left behind a small group of Macedonians that initiated a line of Greek rulers in northwestern India who introduced Hellenistic art forms and religious ideas (chapter 6). Those cultural influences endured for centuries, but, politically, the Macedonians were soon dominated by the conquering Mauryans, a political dynasty that changed much about politics, society, and culture on the subcontinent.

Further Reading

Upinder Singh, Romila Thapar, and Johannes Bronkhorst offer extensive accounts of political and religious trends during this period. For the development of religious traditions, see Rupert Gethin on Buddhism, Paul Dundas on Jainism, and A. L. Basham on the Ajivikas. I consulted Charles Hallisey's edition and translation of the *Therigatha*. P. L. Gupta remains a strong authority for punch-marked coins. I relied on the work of Gwendolyn Kelly and K. Rajan on southern India. Dilip Chakrabarti offers an overview of archaeological evidence for this period.

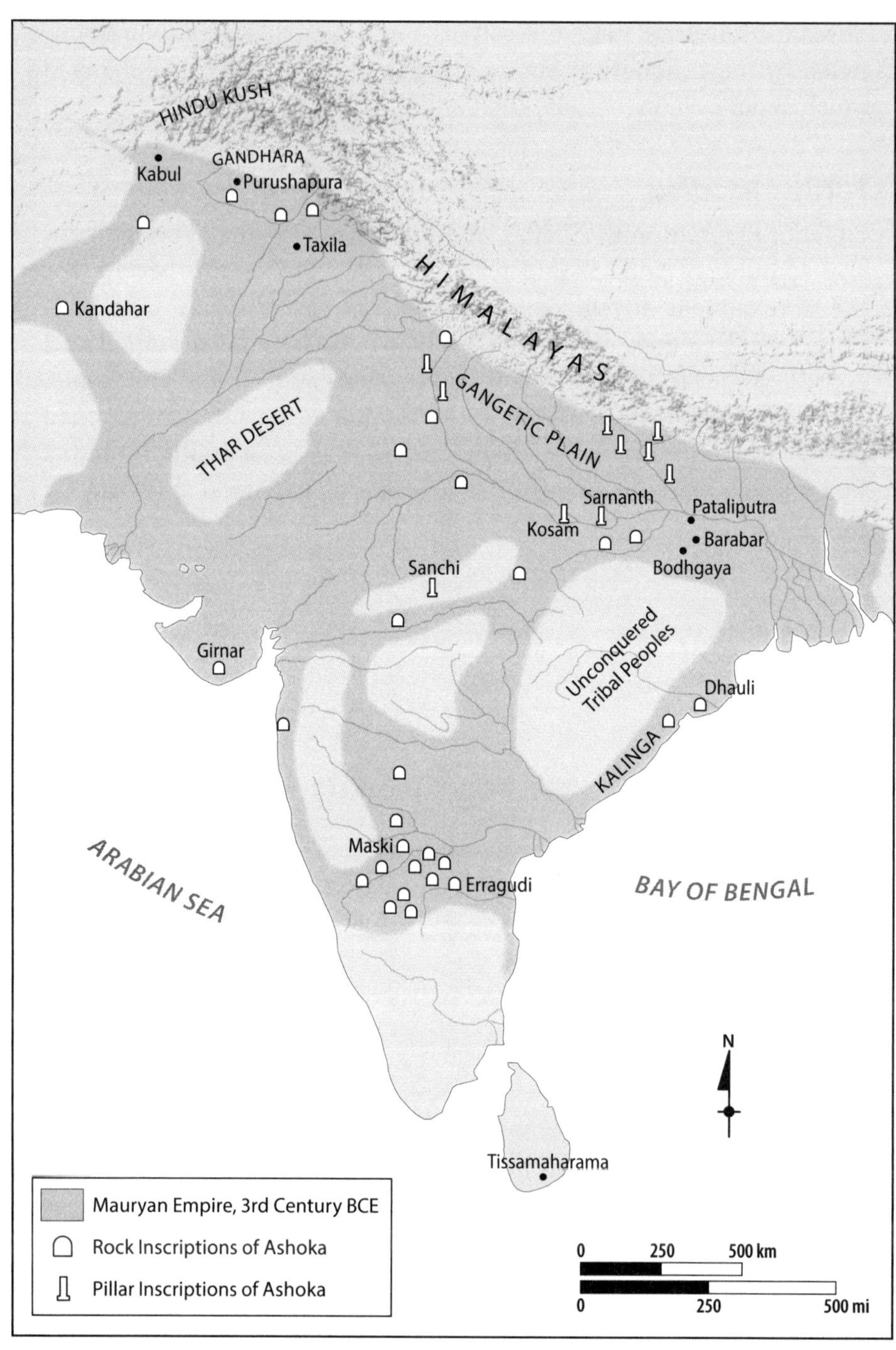

Mauryan Empire, third century BCE.

4

Ashoka's Mauryan Empire

Doing good is difficult.
It is hard to even start doing good.

—Ashoka, third century BCE (Prakrit)[1]

Ashoka is one of the most remembered kings in South Asian history, and he embodied many firsts. He ruled the Mauryan Empire, the first polity to stretch across much of northwestern and eastern India that flourished between 321 and 185 BCE. He numbers among the earliest Indian historical figures about whom we possess concrete, detailed information. He authored South Asia's first political inscriptions in a first-person voice, chiseling a striking set of ethical precepts on dozens of rocks and polished stone pillars. Through his life and words, Ashoka has enlivened imaginations for over 2,000 years. His story was adapted and retold by premodern Buddhists on the subcontinent and beyond. In the twentieth century, some of Ashoka's symbols of Mauryan sovereignty were repurposed as symbols for the Indian nation-state and still appear today on Indian rupees, the Indian flag, and more. Even historians who rail—for good reasons—against a "great man" approach to the past have found ourselves entranced by Ashoka.[2] There is scholarly consensus that Ashoka's voice—his "candid confessional style" as Upinder Singh has put it—is unique in South Asian history.[3] To contextualize this "singular" king,[4] I first narrate the founding of the Mauryan Empire by Ashoka's grandfather, Chandragupta, and then turn to Ashoka himself and the stunning epigraphy he left for posterity.

First Gangetic Plain Empire

Chandragupta (r. 321–297 BCE) established the Mauryan Empire by seizing the capital of Pataliputra (Patna) along the Ganges River and overthrowing the Nandas, possibly a Shudra lineage who had taken control of Magadha in the Gangetic plain around 350 BCE. From this base in eastern India, Chandragupta expanded Mauryan territory west toward the Indus River. This spatial orientation was unprecedented. Before the Mauryas, a series of smaller kingdoms ruled Magadha from Rajgir and, later, from Pataliputra, but emperors who sought large-scale territorial expansion had always pressed from the Indus River in the northwest further east into the subcontinent (chapter 3). Chandragupta reversed this. He led an army of archers, cavalry, elephants, and foot soldiers around 2,000 kilometers northwest of Pataliputra, through and beyond the thick forests and large stretches of grasslands that covered much of the Gangetic plain at the time.

Around the Indus River, Chandragupta met the army of the Seleucid Empire, which had filled part of the power vacuum left by Alexander of Macedon's death in 323 BCE. It is not clear if Seleucid and Mauryan forces fought or not initially, but they soon opted for a diplomatic solution. The Seleucids ceded some of their eastern territories, mainly in modern-day Afghanistan and Pakistan (including Gandhara), to the Mauryans in exchange for 500 elephants, an animal unknown in Asia outside of the subcontinent.[5] Seleucid representatives soon set out for Pataliputra in what constitutes the earliest clearly documented diplomatic envoy to the subcontinent.

The Seleucid convoy's journey to Pataliputra must have taken months. We can tentatively identify at least two members of the group: a female Seleucid relative who wed Chandragupta as part of the peace treaty and Megasthenes, the official ambassador of Seleucus I Nicator (ca. 358–281 BCE). These two and their entourage traveled along a road built, or at least maintained, by Chandragupta. Centuries later, parts of this road were integrated into northern sections of the Grand Trunk Road.[6] We know nothing about the daily rhythms of the Seleucid journey to the Mauryan capital or its security. After all, the Mauryan Empire likely exercised limited control beyond urban and core areas, something frequently misrepresented by modern maps.[7] On the other hand, Mauryan officials called *agoranomoi* by Megasthenes maintained the roads, including building wells every nine miles and erecting periodic signposts.[8]

We can reasonably speculate that the Seleucid travelers were stunned upon arriving at Pataliputra, one of the largest cities in the world in the late fourth century BCE. Megasthenes later wrote *Indica*, an ethnography about his experiences in Mauryan territory that survives through the reports of later Greek authors. He described Palimbothra, the Greek name for Pataliputra, as "a city eighty stadia [roughly 14 kilometers] in length and fifteen [2.5 kilometers] in breadth. It is of the shape of a parallelogram and is girded by a wooden wall, pierced with loopholes for the discharge of arrows. It has a ditch in front for defence and for receiving the sewage of the city."[9] Archaeologists have unearthed parts of ancient Pataliputra's wooden defense walls. They stand in two parallel rows fifteen feet high apiece, several feet higher than the stone wall at the former Magadhan capital of Rajgir (chapter 3).[10] Pataliputra's walls were made of Sal trees, which are uncommonly hard. They are estimated to have enclosed 25.5 square kilometers, making fortified Pataliputra nearly twice as large as Rome in the third century BCE and eleven times the size of Athens.[11] The walls were long ago buried under subsequent layers of habitation at Pataliputra, today known as Patna (population of more than two million). In modern times, villagers have sometimes hit Chandragupta's impenetrable defenses while digging wells and so been compelled to relocate their efforts.[12] Even millennia later, Mauryan fortifications still influence people's lives in eastern India.

Megasthenes furnished further details of Mauryan urban society, even as we must read carefully between the layers of this source. At times, Megasthenes participated in a tradition of Greek fantastic accounts of India in order, ironically, to make his ethnography believable to premodern Greek readers who expected India to bear mythical features.[13] For instance, he wrote that women of Pandaea (south of Mauryan territory) gave birth at the age of six and described Indian men with gaping holes where nostrils should be and legs twisted like snakes.[14] Additionally, as Paul Kosmin has deftly analyzed, Megasthenes wrote his *Indica* to explain away the loss of eastern parts of the Seleucid empire, as a sort of imperial apology.[15] As a result, the *Indica* tells us more about the Seleucids at times than the Mauryans. For instance, Megasthenes says that Indian society is divided into seven social classes, which seems to mirror the structure of Egyptian society rather than any Indian reality.[16] That said, Megasthenes identifies philosophers as the premier Indian social class and notes that they alone can intermarry with other classes. This may plausibly be taken to document an early iteration of the endogamy—marriage within a restricted social class—that is essential to the caste system and the privileges afforded to Brahmins (Megasthenes's philosophers) as per later Brahminical texts (chapter 7).[17]

Under Chandragupta and his son, Bindusara (r. 297–273 BCE), the Mauryans and Seleucids enjoyed ongoing diplomatic relations and trade. For decades, the Mauryans supplied the Seleucids with war elephants, which were important enough to appear as a sovereign symbol on coins, city walls, seals, and more.[18] More occasionally, the Mauryans likely sent tigers to their western neighbors.[19] In exchange, the Seleucids provided the Mauryans with aphrodisiacs, dried fruit, and wine. The Mauryans may have also been intrigued by Greek philosophy. One historian recorded that Bindusara asked Antiochus I, the second Seleucid ruler, to send, along with sweet wine and dried figs, a sophist. Antiochus I replied: "The figs and sweet wine we will send you, but it is not lawful among the Greeks for a sophist to be sold."[20] This exchange suggests that Mauryan-Seleucid relations involved a thirst for knowledge as well as trade.

Ashoka's Empire of Land and Words

After Bindusara died, Ashoka (r. 268–232 BCE) inherited the bustling, thriving Mauryan state. Our knowledge of Ashoka as a historical Mauryan ruler is interspliced with legends, many of which date back to premodernity. Even with this challenge, we know more about Ashoka than any prior figure in Indian history, and that alone makes him worthy of historical attention. Still, we are in the dark regarding Ashoka's princely years, including why there was a roughly four-year gap between Bindusara's death in 273 BCE and Ashoka's coronation in 269 or 268 BCE. There are premodern reports of a fratricidal struggle between Ashoka and his brothers during this period, and the idea is certainly plausible. Earlier Magadhan dynasties fought internally for the throne (chapter 3). More generally, bloody royal struggles recur throughout South Asian history. Such contests also feature in literature, and a family fight for political power constitutes the core narrative of the Mahabharata epic that was likely written down in the few centuries after Ashoka's death (chapter 5). That said, premodern narratives of Ashoka killing his brothers are inconsistent with one another, and all post-date Mauryan decline.[21] Whether true in their gist, their details, or not at all, the memory of Ashoka having come to power through personal and political violence heightens how many have interpreted his later public regrets about the Mauryan state inflicting human suffering.

During his thirty-six-year rule, Ashoka ordered dozens of inscriptions carved on rock faces and stone pillars that communicate information about his life and reign, including how he impacted other Indians of his day. He had his inscriptions placed across much of the subcontinent, including what is now modern-day India, Pakistan, Afghanistan, and Nepal. Many have called these writings "edicts," but I prefer "inscriptions" because it more accurately covers the wide range of subjects—including state policies, ethics, recent history, and even diet—on which Ashoka spoke through his stone-inscribed words. Modern scholars divide the inscriptions into three categories: numerous minor rock inscriptions, fourteen major rock inscriptions that together constitute an anthology, and seven pillar inscriptions.[22] The latter two groups were inscribed in multiple places, sometimes with small variations. For instance, the fourteen major rock inscriptions were copied thousands of kilometers apart at the furthest reaches (or, perhaps, ambitions) of Mauryan control, such as at Girnar in Gujarat, Erragudi in Andhra Pradesh, and Dhauli in Orissa. The pillar inscriptions tend to be clustered around the Gangetic plain, perhaps because these massive stone objects were difficult to move except via boat.

Before reading what Ashoka ordered inscribed on stones and pillars, their materiality confronts us, as it must have confronted premodern audiences. The pillars are colossal, weighing in between 8.6 and 51 tons apiece, plus a 2-ton carved capital on top.[23] For comparison, Asian male elephants weigh around 5 tons each. The pillars were also highly polished, as befits something intended to be monumental and to withstand the test of time. We do not know, of course, what percentage of Ashokan inscriptions survive. A 2016 computer model predicted more than one hundred additional sites where Ashokan inscriptions might have been placed and still might be (re)discovered.[24] More concretely, the premodern travelers Faxian (fifth century CE) and Xuanzang (seventh century CE) described pillars that have not (yet) been located.[25] The archive is never complete, but Ashoka's inscriptions constitute a rarity among

Figure 4.1. Four scripts of Ashokan inscriptions: Brahmi (Sarnath, India), Kharoshthi (Shahbazgarhi, Pakistan), and Greek and Aramaic (Kandahar, Afghanistan, now in Kabul Museum), third century BCE, stone.

premodern Indian texts: namely, they come down to us today in precisely the form in which they were inscribed, not in later copies.[26]

Most Ashokan inscriptions were written in a Prakrit language and in the Brahmi script. Prakrits were in use for centuries before Ashoka, preferred by many non-Brahmin communities in lieu of Sanskrit (chapter 3). Brahmi's origins are less clear, although writing at all was innovative within the strong oral culture of northern India shared by Vedic followers, early Buddhists, and early Jains.[27] In a display of regional sensitivity, Ashoka sponsored a handful of inscriptions in the northwest in other languages (Aramaic and Greek) and scripts (Kharoshthi) (figure 4.1). But the bulk of Ashokan inscriptions are in Brahmi script, which became the parent of nearly all later South Asian scripts, from Grantha in Tamil Nadu to Sharada in Kashmir. Some of Ashoka's inscribers were fluent in multiple scripts, such as Chapada who carved a Brahmi inscription in Karnataka and then added his name in Kharoshthi script.

In devising royal inscriptions at all, Ashoka acted without precedent in the history of South Asian rulers. He may have been familiar with

Darius, whose sixth century BCE Aramaic inscriptions further west laid out his vision of Achaemenid kingship. But comparing the voices of Ashoka and Darius in their respective inscriptions is comparing apples and oranges.[28] In terms of content, Ashoka stands alone.

Ashoka's earliest known rock inscription opens by sketching out the timeline of his turn to the Buddhist path. The inscription, located at Rupnath in Bihar, starts with "The Beloved of the gods (e.g., Ashoka) speaks thus" (*devanampiye hevam aha*) and continues: "I have been a Buddhist layman for more than two and a half years, but for a year I did not make much progress. Now for more than a year I have drawn close to the Buddhist community (*sagha upete*) and have become more ardent."[29] Here Ashoka tells of his personal religious convictions, a striking tone for a head of state. He does not communicate—in this inscription or anywhere else—what religion he converted from. Legends do not associate the Mauryans with Brahminical traditions, instead projecting Chandragupta as Jain and Bindusara as partial to the Ajivikas. Indeed, there is scant evidence of Vedic practices within Magadha, including among the Mauryans. That said, Ashoka was familiar with some Brahminical rituals since he condemns the ritual slaughter of animals—described using Vedic terms—in a later rock inscription.[30] While Ashoka positions himself as against some Brahminical practices, that does not tell us whether they were ever his own.

Ashoka declines to narrate why he became Buddhist (as opposed to following another religion), instead focusing on his activities as a convert. He calls himself a follower (*upasaka*) of an ancient tradition (*porana pakiti*).[31] He commemorates visiting Lumbini, where the Gautama Buddha had been born about two centuries earlier, in a pillar inscription still there today.[32] Later Sri Lankan materials remember Ashoka's wife, Devi, as playing a pivotal role in the king's turn toward Buddhism, and the idea is intriguing.[33] That said, Ashoka was no champion of women's religious activities in other contexts. In the ninth rock inscription, he condemned female-run life-cycle rites concerning marriage, birth, and travel. Many of these rituals (*mangala*s) are praised in roughly contemporary Brahminical texts known as the *Grihyasutras*.[34] I wish we knew more about Devi's life and influence, but here we confront a lack of contemporary evidence.

We are clearer on the limits of Buddhism within the Mauryan state. Certainly, Ashoka did not require his subjects to convert. Moreover, he continued the default policy for Indian rulers of supporting multiple religious traditions. For example, Ashoka sponsored the construction of caves with polished walls at Barabar in Bihar for Ajivikas.[35] When Ashoka exerted energy trying to persuade his subjects to follow a specific tradition, it was his own brand of dhamma, as discussed in the next section.

Ashoka's most significant territorial conquest in his thirty-six years on the Mauryan throne was the acquisition of Kalinga in 260 BCE. Kalinga is a band of land in eastern India around the border between Orissa and Andhra, south of Pataliputra, with access to growing sea trade routes (chapter 6). Ashoka himself recorded what we know about this conquest in the thirteenth rock inscription, claiming that Mauryan forces captured 150,000 people and killed more than 100,000 more (see rock inscription 13). Ashoka's round numbers have justly raised many skeptical eyebrows among historians. Even while seeing them as suggestive rather than documentary, the basic point remains that the Mauryans killed and enslaved many people at Kalinga.

Ashoka took no pride in this state-sponsored violence, which was unusual for Indian kings who—across regions, time periods, and religions—bragged about violent victories. Instead, Ashoka depicted himself as a reformed, or at least reforming, ruler who aspired to nonviolence. In so doing, he proclaimed a different kind of victory at Kalinga since, as per his own testimony, the battle prompted him to turn to dhamma or ethics. In the fourth rock inscription, too, Ashoka presents dhamma as supplanting military conquest, declaring, "The drums of war (*bheri-ghosha*) have been replaced by the sound of ethics (*dhamma-ghosha*)."[36] Ashoka wanted his fame and glory (*yasa* and *kiti*) to arise—not from military conquest—but from people following his ethical guidelines.[37] He was not shy about projecting himself as a moral leader, describing himself as "good looking" (*piyadassi*) and thereby reflecting inner virtue as well as "beloved of the gods."

Ashoka's Rock Inscription 13, ca. 260–258 BCE, Inscribed at Multiple Locations

In the eighth year of his reign, King Piyadassi, Beloved of the gods, conquered the area of Kalinga. 150,000 people were deported as captives, 100,000 were killed, and many more died.

Immediately after he conquered Kalinga, King Piyadassi began to devote himself to studying dhamma, yearning for dhamma, and teaching dhamma.

Upon conquering Kalinga, the Beloved of the gods felt regret. He experienced deep remorse and sorrow because conquering an independent people required killing, death, and deportation. It weighed heavy on his mind. But there is a graver reason for the king's regret. The Brahmins, ascetics (shramanas), followers of other traditions, and householders—who are obedient to their superiors, parents, and teachers as well as devoted and courteous to friends, acquaintances, companions, relatives, slaves, and servants—suffer from the assault, slaughter, and deportation of their loved ones. Even those lucky enough to escape calamity themselves are distressed by the misfortunes suffered by their beloved friends, acquaintances, companions, and relatives. Thus, everyone suffers, and this weighs heavily on King Piyadassi's mind.

There is no place where Brahmins and shramanas are not found, except among the Greeks, and everywhere people are attached to one religious tradition or another. Accordingly, even if fewer people—one-hundredth or one-thousandth the number—were killed, died, or were captured in Kalinga, it would still weigh heavily on the king's mind.

The Beloved of the gods now thinks that a person who does wrong ought to be forgiven, insofar as forgiveness is possible. He seeks to prompt even forest dwellers under his administration to adopt these ideas and actions, while still reminding them of his power to punish with lethal force, despite his remorse. King Piyadassi desires that all beings possess security, self-control, equanimity, and gentleness.

King Piyadassi considers the most important conquest to be victory by dhamma. And he has achieved this repeatedly, here and on every frontier, even thousands of miles away where the Greek king Antiyoka (Antiochus) rules, and even beyond Antiyoka's territory, at the realms of [other western] kings named Turamaya, Antikini, Maka, and Alikasudara,[38] to the south among the Cholas and Pandyas as far as Sri Lanka (*tambapanniya*). Similarly, here in royal domains among the Greeks, Kambojas, Nabhakas, Nabhitinis, Bhojas, Pitinikas, Andhras, and Palidas, everywhere people follow his instructions in dhamma. Even in places where King Piyadassi's messengers have not reached, people have heard about his conduct according to dhamma and his rules and teachings about dhamma, and so themselves follow dhamma and will continue to do so.

> This conquest is everywhere and repeatedly produces satisfaction. The king is pleased by this victory. This pleasure at victory by dhamma is, still, only a slight pleasure. Let them consider victory by dhamma the only true conquest.
>
> This inscription on dhamma has been engraved so that my sons and great grandsons after me do not think of pursuing new conquests. If they do conquer, they ought to exercise mercy and mild punishments. Let them consider victory by dhamma to be true conquest. This is good, in this world and the next. They should delight in abandoning other aims and delight only in dhamma. This is good, in this world and the next.[39]

Ashoka contrasts the ethical dimensions of war and dhamma, but in reality they were sequential. Military conquest paved the way for the third Maurya king to articulate an ethical vision through stone inscriptions. Ashoka relied on some measure of state power to place stones and pillars in various locations around the subcontinent, including some in regions beyond the day-to-day control of the Mauryas. A network of state scribes chiseled Ashoka's words into rock, and state officers were ordered to read out the inscriptions at regular intervals for the benefit of Mauryan subjects (most of whom were illiterate). Ashoka even commissioned imperial officers to preach the dhamma on tour every five years. For Ashoka, his empire and his dhamma were inextricably linked, especially through the state apparatus on which he relied to advocate his ideas.

Victory by Ethics

Ashoka outlines a set of ethical precepts, his dhamma, throughout his numerous rock inscriptions. Here I offer an overview of some key features, and two things are critical to note off the bat. One, Ashoka's dhamma was not coterminous with Buddhist dhamma. Ashoka articulates ideas that are broader than Buddhist teachings (e.g., obeying one's parents) and more specifically political (e.g., a class of Mauryan officials should promote dhamma among their subjects).[40] Two, Ashoka intended his dhamma for everyone. He wanted to guide all human beings in moral behavior, a sharp contrast with the Brahminical idea of *svadharma* that stipulated different ethics according to social class (or caste) and gender (chapters 2, 5, and 7). Ashoka spoke to Brahmins, Ajivikas, Jains, Buddhists, tribal peoples, and more, encouraging all to adopt his ideals.

The most consistent theme throughout Ashoka's dhamma is nonviolence against people and animals, two groups about which he often spoke similarly. For instance, Ashoka used the suggestive number of 100,000 for people killed in the Kalinga war and, pluralized to "hundreds of thousands," for animals slaughtered daily in his kitchen. He writes of his attempt to be vegetarian: "Formerly, in the kitchen of the Beloved of the gods . . . hundreds of thousands of animals were killed every day to make curry. But now with the writing of the *Inscriptions on Ethics*, only three creatures, two peacocks and a deer are killed—and the deer not always."[41] Ashoka exhorts his subjects to follow him in moving away from slaughtering animals, for food or any other purpose. He opens his major rock inscriptions as carved at Erragudi in Andhra Pradesh with the proclamation: "Here no living being should be slaughtered for sacrifice."[42] Ashoka sometimes placed inscriptions at places known for festivals that featured animal sacrifice with the goal of dissuading shedding animal blood.[43] Like other aspects of Ashoka's dhamma discussed earlier, his vegetarianism stands in sharp contrast to Brahminical traditions of the time, such as Yajnavalkya's pleasure at eating "tender beef" as per the *Shatapatha Brahmana*.[44]

Ashoka advocated mercy and nonviolence toward people, especially those unable to help themselves in Mauryan society such as prisoners. In one inscription, Ashoka attested that he ordered prisoners released repeatedly.[45] In another, he encouraged Mauryan officials to show empathy for the incarcerated and consider mitigating circumstance for their release, such as having a family to support.[46] Prisoners are among the most overlooked people in many cultures. Even today, in modern North America and South Asia, many of us easily accept dehumanization and brutality against incarcerated persons. In his suggested treatment of this community, Ashoka's dhamma challenges this common callousness.

Ashoka's dhamma had limits, and his relationship with the forest people (*atavika*) offers one case where the king deemed nonviolence an unaffordable luxury. In rock inscription thirteen, Ashoka addresses the forest people separately from the rest of his populace, reminding them: "[Ashoka has] power to punish with lethal force, despite his remorse." Such a thinly veiled threat of violence suggests that the forest people were beyond Ashoka's dhamma, or at least had the potential to push his ideals to a breaking point. Here, we see no accommodations for people who had a different lifestyle than those residing in the growing metropolis of Pataliputra. Rather, Ashoka's dictate to the forest people was to conform, or else risk Mauryan wrath. Practically, it does not appear that Ashoka had much success subduing forest-dwelling communities. Post-Mauryan authors, such as Kautilya who wrote his *Arthashastra* treatise on politics around 50–125 CE, depicted forest people (*atavika*, *atavi*) as reclusive, threatening, and requiring coercion.[47] Later kings, such as the Guptas (ca. fourth century CE) who imitated the Mauryans in various ways, still struggled with forest people as per an inscription of Samudragupta that mentions reducing forest chiefs to servants and was added, appropriately, to an Ashokan pillar.[48]

Arguably, Ashoka offered more empathy to forest animals and fauna than to forest-dwelling people. His fifth pillar inscription lists out numerous species of wild animals that ought not be killed.[49] The Mauryans also did not engage in large-scale forest clearing or burning. The Mahabharata mentions the cleansing of the Khandava Forest for Indraprastha being sanctioned by the Hindu god Agni (chapter 5), and so the idea is attested around this period that urbanization might require the sacrifice of forests along with their inhabitants.[50] It is tempting to depict Ashoka as ecologically conscious or interested in environmental sustainability, and maybe he was. Then again, maybe Ashoka just lacked the technology, power, or both to clear the forests of the Gangetic plain, which remained largely intact into the second millennium CE.[51] Regardless, Ashoka's comments on forest-dwellers clarify that his dhamma did not include a desire to preserve their way of life.

Many people in Ashoka's India seem to have ignored the king's ethical ideas, which comes into focus when we bring in archaeological evidence. For instance, remains in the Hindu Kush foothills indicate a robust carnivorous diet—of hunted wild sheep, goats, tortoises, foxes, jackals, deer, horses, and cattle—going back to the middle and upper paleolithic period (ca. 35,000–15,000 years ago).[52] Remains at the urban center of Mundigak, near Kandahar, as late as the second millennium BCE similarly suggest that people consumed an array of domestic and wild animals.[53] In brief, premodern inhabitants of what is now Afghanistan ate a lot of meat. One wonders, then, how this populace responded to an inscription that Ashoka placed at Kandahar around 248 BCE proclaiming (sans evidence) that the Mauryan king's virtue had inspired fisherman and hunters to give up their trades. Ashoka even had this inscription written in Aramaic and Greek so that it could be understood by local residents or, perhaps, to connect with memories of Achaemenid and Greek rule, respectively.[54] I agree with historian Nayanjot Lahiri's speculation that: "In this kind of context, might there have been hoots of laughter at the efforts on behalf of vegetarianism from distant Pataliputra?"[55]

Around 2,500 kilometers south of Kandahar, residents of Maski in Karnataka probably had little in common with those in Mundigak, except that they also disregarded Ashoka's dhamma. Maski was a center for gold mining in Ashoka's time, which was traded to bring in lapis lazuli and other desired materials from as far afield as Afghan regions. Despite Ashoka placing an inscription at Maski, material evidence suggests that residents continued to practice their own religious traditions and honor local deities.[56]

Despite some opposition, Ashoka personally attempted to spread his dhamma throughout his imperial territory. His first rock inscription ends by noting that the emperor had been on tour for 256 days (about eight months). Rock inscription eight offers further details about Ashoka's touring activities, describing an itinerary with features of a lecture circuit and a pilgrimage. Notably, he explicitly contrasted this dhamma journey with the pleasure tours of other kings, especially hunting (see rock inscription 8). It seems that Ashoka sought, in addition to military victories, a moral victory as a mark of royalty.

Ashoka's Rock Inscription 8, Third Century BCE, Inscribed at Multiple Locations

In the past, kings used to go on pleasure tours. On these tours, they hunted and indulged in other pastimes. King Piyadassi, however, became enlightened in wisdom ten years after his coronation. Since then his tours have been moral tours. He visits priests and ascetics and makes gifts to them; he visits the aged and gives them money; he visits the people of rural areas, instructing them in dhamma and discussing it with them. King Piyadassi takes great pleasure in these tours, far more than could result from other tours.[57]

Ashoka intended his inscriptions to guide successive Mauryan rulers. He closed the seventh pillar inscription, one of his last inscriptions, with these lines: "I have done all this so that among my sons and great grandsons and as long as the sun and moon endure, men may follow dhamma. For by following it one gains this world and the next. When I had been consecrated twenty-seven years, I had this inscription of dhamma engraved. The Beloved of the gods speaks thus: This inscription of dhamma is to be engraved wherever there are stone pillars or stone slabs, that it may last long."[58] Suffice it to say that Ashoka's sons and grandsons did not make him proud. After Ashoka's death in 232 BCE, the Mauryans cycled through a rapid succession of kings so tumultuous that we are not even sure of all their names. Fifty years later, in the mid-180s BCE, the last Mauryan ruler, Brihadratha, was assassinated by his Brahmin commander-in-chief who then founded the Shunga dynasty.[59] Even absent long-term dynastic success, however, Ashoka made lasting impacts on later South Asian history, rulers, and religions.

Ashoka's Legacies and Limits

Ashoka left behind material improvements and monumental objects on the subcontinent. He financed wells, rest houses, highways, and other public works. One large-scale example is a dam at Girnar in Gujarat. In Mauryan times, the dam wall stood 7.5 meters high and covered more than 40 meters; a visible rise of the land can still be seen today.[60] Ashoka also sponsored numerous pillars, not all of them inscribed, as well as caves. A less well-known example of the latter is the garage-sized Sitamarhi cave, cut into a solitary boulder in Bihar.[61] Perhaps the most famous piece of art from the Mauryan period is the four-lion pillar topper complete with a dharmachakra (wheel of dharma) at Sarnath (both symbols were adopted by the modern Indian nation-state; chapter 23). In some cases, the Mauryans employed local artisans, such as to carve a large elephant at Dhauli in Orissa, near a rock inscription.[62] Mauryan art also featured the royal family, and one of the gates at Sanchi—a growing Buddhist pilgrimage site—features a carving of Ashoka with two of his queens (figure 4.2). The family was also depicted on a smaller scale, and a punch-marked coin from Mauryan rule likely shows Ashoka with two of his wives.[63]

Figure 4.2. Ashoka with his queens on the southern gate at Sanchi, first century CE, Madhya Pradesh, India.

Many later Buddhist practitioners and some scholars have credited Ashoka with clarifying and spreading Buddhist teachings. Certainly, Ashoka projected himself into this role. In an inscription found at Sarnath, Sanchi, and Kosam (near Allahabad), Ashoka projected authority over Buddhist monks and nuns, criticizing internal divisions and expelling disruptive mendicants.[64] Ashoka also claimed to have sent Buddhist missionaries far beyond the subcontinent to seek converts (quoted earlier). Even if all of this is true, popular memory attributes Ashoka a far greater role in spreading Buddhism than is supported by available evidence. For instance, Ashoka is often believed to have hosted the Third Buddhist Council at Pataliputra.[65] Many associate the spread of stupas, rounded mounds that house relics of the Gautama Buddha, with Ashoka's patronage.[66] Sometimes Ashoka is thought to have sponsored mass building projects at Buddhist pilgrimage destinations like Lumbini and Sanchi.[67] Historical evidence dates many of these activities to post-Ashokan periods. For example, one of the earliest post-Ashokan Indian inscriptions records a relic of the Gautama Buddha being interred at Shinkot (in modern-day Afghanistan) during the second-century-BCE reign of an Indo-Greek king.[68] In part, some scholars have embellished Ashoka's impact because they have privileged written Buddhist materials, even those dated later, over material evidence that offers a more historically grounded picture for much of early Buddhist history.[69]

Tissamaharama along Sri Lanka's southern coast offers a case study in how material evidence allows us to displace Ashoka and instead see the formational roles played by other early Buddhist communities and individuals. The Brahmi script—favored by Ashoka—was known in parts of Sri Lanka around this time as per pottery fragments unearthed in Tissamaharama. Those pottery shards contain numerous inscriptions, include the names of laywomen—such as Tisya, Gupta, Sude, and Anuradha—who supported a community of predominantly Buddhist nuns.[70] Here, we glimpse few men, royal or otherwise. To the extent that the Mauryans played any role in forming the Buddhist community at Tissamaharama, the loss of Mauryan power in the mid-180s BCE to the Brahmin Shunga dynasty might have incentivized Buddhist leaders to travel south.[71] But this remains speculative, in contrast to the concrete material evidence available along Sri Lanka's southern coast for a female-centered Buddhist community. I imagine that the Theris, whom we encountered in chapter 3, would have approved.

Ashoka inspired kings far and wide, both during his life and long after his death. His later contemporary, Devanampiya Tissa of Lanka (r. ca. 247–207 BCE), took Ashoka's preferred name "Beloved of the gods" as his own.[72] Almost 800 years later, Emperor Wu of China (502–549 CE) imitated Ashoka (or who he imagined Ashoka to have been) by patronizing stupas and banning alcohol and meat.[73] Within India, Chandragupta and Ashoka both featured in later Sanskrit texts, including *Ashokavadana*, second century CE (Ashoka as a Buddhist figure) and *Mudrarakshasa*, sixth century CE (Chandragupta as an emperor). In the mid fourth century CE, a Gupta king named himself Chandragupta after the Mauryan founder. But Ashoka arguably never had worthy imitators in his inscriptional voice. As Richard Salomon has put it: "In terms of format, content, and tone, there is practically nothing in the later inscriptional corpus of the Indian world that even resembles Asoka's inscriptions."[74]

On the Indian subcontinent, one lasting impact of Ashoka's inscriptions was that they centered dhamma (dharma in Sanskrit) as a key concept for Indian rulers and religious traditions. Dharma was a somewhat marginal idea in the Vedas, and it is used infrequently in later Vedic texts too. Some scholars have suggested that it became a focal point in subsequent incarnations of Hindu traditions precisely because Brahmins were playing catch-up with Buddhists and political figures who made the concept of dhamma/dharma "impossible to ignore."[75] Ashoka—and his powerful voice—is part of that story. Even if nobody ever spoke quite like Ashoka again, many later kings, too, used the language of dharma, which Ashoka helped to develop into a broader political and social framework.[76]

Conclusion: Long Echoes of Ashoka

Long after Ashoka and his successors were gone, Mauryan material culture remained part of the Indian landscape. Carvings from a few hundred years after Ashoka's death show people venerating Ashokan pillars (figure 4.3).[77] In more recent times, some pillars have been repurposed as Shiva lingas.[78] More on point to Mauryan intentions, later rulers added inscriptions to Ashokan rocks and pillars, including Rudradaman (second century CE), the Guptas (fourth–fifth centuries CE), the Chauhans (twelfth century CE), and the Mughals (seventeenth century CE). Some ambitious kings even moved Ashokan pillars to centers of their own kingdoms. For instance, Firuz Shah Tughluq (r. 1351–1388) relied on thousands of laborers to package and transport two Ashokan pillars to Delhi, where they still stand today.[79] In a more prosaic reuse, nineteenth-century British colonialists used pieces of Ashokan pillars to roll out roads.[80] The British were not complete iconoclasts regarding Ashoka. In 1837, James Prinsep decoded the Brahmi script, which everybody had long ago forgotten how to read, and thus made Ashoka's words, once again, an active part of the Indian world. Ashokan inscriptions are still being recovered, with one of the more recent discoveries being at Ratanpurwa in Bihar in 2009.[81] One wonders if we have yet to hear all that this ancient Mauryan ruler has to say?

Figure 4.3. Indians venerating an Ashokan pillar on the southern gate at Sanchi, first century CE, Madhya Pradesh, India.

Further Reading

Nayanjot Lahiri is the foremost biographer of Ashoka in our day. I also consulted work by Sonam Kachru, Patrick Olivelle, Upinder Singh, and Romila Thapar on the Mauryans. For the Ashokan inscriptions, I relied on D. C. Sircar and E. Hultzsch. Harry Falk is strong on the archaeology of Mauryan India, and Gregory Schopen makes a compelling case for the importance of material evidence in reconstructing early Buddhism. Paul Kosmin's work on the Seleucids is strong, especially his discussion of spatiality in Megasthenes *Indica*.

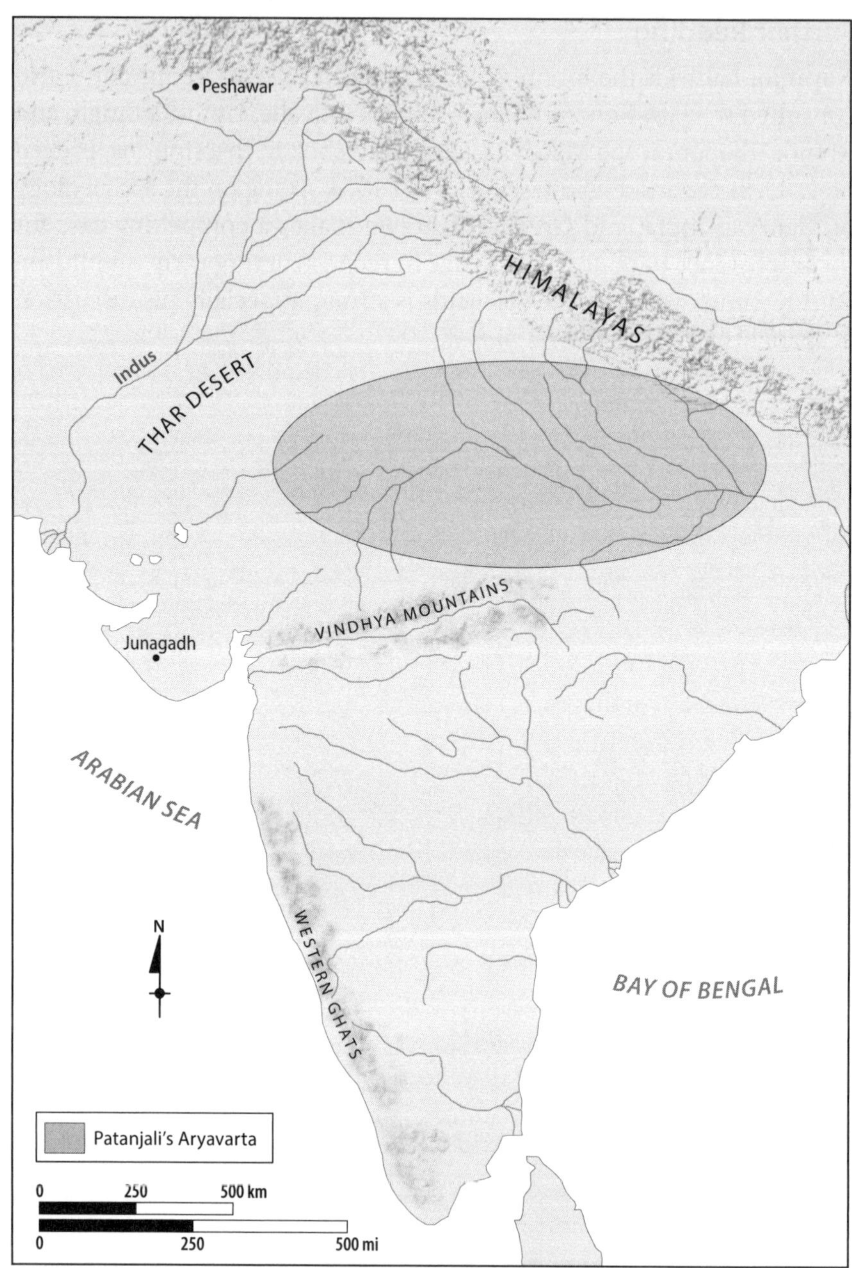

Projection of where Brahmins lived, second century BCE.

5

Mahabharata

A Tale of Ancient India

So long as mountains and rivers exist, Krishna,
there will always be celebrations of this fame.
Brahmins will narrate the great Mahabharata battle.

– Mahabharata, ca. 100–500 CE (Sanskrit)[1]

In an old Indian myth, a group of blind men stumble upon an elephant. Each feels a different part of the animal and concludes, based on his experience alone, that the elephant is like a rope (tail), a snake (trunk), a wall (side), and so forth. None of them comprehends the true nature of the enormous beast. We are all those blind men in seeking to grasp the Mahabharata, an epic story of a fratricidal war first written in Sanskrit close to 2,000 years ago and since retold in countless mediums and languages. The Mahabharata is a tale for all times. It explores enduring questions of the human condition, such as why good people do bad things and how we live with the human ability to commit atrocities. This tumultuous epic—specifically its Sanskrit version ascribed to Vyasa—is also a cultural product of ancient north India, furnishing upper-caste views on the vicious state violence unleashed in the transition from clans to kingdoms as well as evidence of changes in the tradition we now call Hinduism. Here I explore Vyasa's Mahabharata, a fantastical story that has gripped imaginations through two millennia, focusing on its insights regarding ancient social and religious developments.

Sanskrit beyond the Vedas

We have scarcely heard of Sanskrit—the language in which the Mahabharata attributed to Vyasa was first composed—in the prior two chapters, covering the sixth to third centuries BCE. That is because, during these centuries, Brahmins alone used Sanskrit, primarily to conduct specialized rituals. For everybody else—Buddhists, Jains, Ajivikas, and rulers of Magadha including the Mauryans—Prakrits were the major political and religious mediums of the day. How and why, then, did Brahmins (possibly with Kshatriya input) pen the Sanskrit Mahabharata, one of the most culturally influential texts ever composed, in the early centuries CE and subsequently disseminate it widely through storytelling bards? Three interrelated developments—dated between about 300 BCE and 150 CE—help to explain how Vyasa's Mahabharata burst onto the scene in northern India sometime around 100 or 200 CE: the geographical and political expansion of Sanskrit, a more robust hereditary caste system, and Brahminical integration of non-Vedic ideas. These trends are foundational for understanding why one of the most captivating stories ever told, anywhere on earth, was written in Sanskrit.

Over 500 years, between around 350 BCE and 150 CE, upper-caste north Indians began to use Sanskrit—hitherto an exclusive language of Vedic ritual and theology—to express wider cultural and, critically, political ideas. It started with grammar. Between 350 and 100 BCE, several Brahmins codified Sanskrit grammar: Panini near Peshawar, Katyayana in the Gangetic plain, and Patanjali north of the Gangetic plain. Of the three, Panini is the most extraordinary for linguistic history. Panini's *Ashtadhyayi* is a generative Sanskrit grammar that uses a maximally concise set of rules to express an immensely complicated grammatical system. Panini's brief aphorisms have struck many modern thinkers as remarkably elegant and complex, rivaling computer coding.[2]

Culturally, Panini and his two successors, Patanjali and Katyayana, projected themselves as living within a Sanskrit-dominated world. Patanjali is the most verbose, delimiting the "land of the pure" (*aryavarta*) as a geographical area of northern India inhabited by the *shishta*, Sanskrit-speaking Brahmin men.[3] It would be imprudent to take the grammarians at their word, assuming they accurately described a north Indian paradise sonorous with high-caste men conversing in Sanskrit. Most likely, Panini—who may have lived through Alexander of Macedon's incursion—was surrounded by chattering in Old Persian, Aramaic, and

Greek, whereas Katyayana and Patanjali probably heard Prakrits (or vernacular derivations thereof) most often (chapters 3–4). These men projected a Sanskrit Brahminical milieu that they considered ideal and, in their lifetimes, unachievable. Their imagined Vedic-centered world never became a reality. Rather, Sanskrit use became far more widespread in later centuries because of another key development: Sanskrit became desacralized and went political.

Up until the early centuries CE, Prakrits had been the major languages of north Indian politics, demonstrated most obviously by Ashoka's inscriptions. Then, in 150 CE, a king named Rudradaman sponsored a Sanskrit political inscription at Junagadh in Gujarat. The inscription praises Rudradaman (an otherwise forgettable ruler in the western Kshatrapa dynasty) for repairing a reservoir called Sudarshana (Lake Beautiful). This was entirely ordinary. Extraordinary is that the inscription was in Sanskrit and used a literary style that soon became definitional to texts and inscriptions grouped together as *kavya* (poetry and literary prose).[4] In fact, fluency in Sanskrit kavya quickly became a defining characteristic of Indian kings, and Rudradaman is lauded in the inscription as "skilled in the composition of kavyas in prose and verse, which are exquisitely ornamented by the confluence of clear, swift, sweet, wonderful, and pleasing language."[5] How we speak matters, and, after this, Indian kings increasingly spoke through inscriptions in poetic Sanskrit. Soon others too—including Buddhists and Jains who had abjured Sanskrit for centuries—began to use this language, and so Sanskrit ceased to be associated with elite Hindu religious practices alone (on this process, see chapter 6).[6] In the case of Rudradaman, he ordered his praise (*prashasti*) inscribed on the Ashokan rock inscriptions at Junagadh, seeming to proclaim by proximity that Sanskrit was supplanting Prakrit as the language of *rajaniti* (politics). Among many other things, Vyasa's Mahabharata is a poem (kavya) about politics.

Around the same century that Sanskrit began to be used for political purposes, caste groups began to practice more extreme forms of social segregation through endogamy, marrying within one's own caste community. Here, genetic evidence is critical. Most Indians today descend from a mix of discrete historical groups whose members commonly intermarried between about 4,000 and 2,000 years ago. But things shifted toward the end of that time range when Indians began to restrict marriage to caste groups.[7] As scientists have noted, these marriage restrictions were often severe, resulting in genetic markers today that would not have occurred if even one in one hundred community members had engaged in intercaste marriages from ca. 100 CE onward.[8] Separate hereditary communities organized in a social hierarchy, an idea articulated as early as the Rig Veda, now became a lived reality for many Indians.

Around 100 CE is also our best scholarly guess on the rough composition date of Vyasa's Mahabharata, which advocates caste-based ideals and distinct social roles for caste groups (*varnashramadharma*). The epic especially extols the two highest classes: Brahmins and Kshatriyas.[9] Caste continued to evolve—especially through spreading to new communities and the addition of new castes—throughout Indian history, as discussed in subsequent chapters. Consistently throughout premodernity, the caste system combined community, identity, and hierarchy in a way that many found attractive for wielding power and many more experienced as oppressive.

In the early centuries CE, Brahmins engaged in an additional activity that they do not write about explicitly, namely they adapted non-Vedic practices, ideas, and gods into their own tradition. This process is hidden from the historical record, except for the outcome. Brahminical culture includes the conceit that its core ideas never change. This theological commitment leads, from a historian's viewpoint, to patently contradictory notions, such as that the Vedas—which name individual authors—are eternal and of nonhuman origin (*apaurusheya*).[10] In reality, while vouching that their tradition was immutable, Brahmins enacted dynamic changes in certain arenas. The Mahabharata attests to several key shifts, such as the introduction of non-Vedic deities like Shiva and Krishna, who remain popular in Hinduism today. Indeed, the Mahabharata was the first Brahminical text not directly connected to the Vedas and thus itself embodies a significant expansion of this tradition.[11] I turn now to analyzing what was both a product of and a catalyst for religious and cultural changes: the Mahabharata, a Sanskrit myth about politics.

Truth of a Myth

The Mahabharata's core story concerns a clash for the north Indian throne of Hastinapura between two sets of cousins—the Kauravas and the Pandavas—which spirals into a devastating world war. The epic narrates this saga in a three-part structure (stretched over eighteen books, or twenty-four books in some southern versions). First, the hundred Kaurava brothers and five Pandava brothers attempt to settle their competing political claims without war. The two groups try splitting the kingdom, gambling for the throne, engaging in illicit murder (of the Pandavas, by the Kauravas), and more. When these strategies all fail, the cousins fight, propelling nearly all their relatives and the entire known world into battle. The last part of the epic follows the five Pandavas, survivors more than victors, as they struggle to rule within a postapocalyptic landscape. Eventually, they also die.

The Mahabharata is a myth, but it expresses truths about our world and, more specific to my purposes here, truths about ancient north Indian society. The text calls itself *itihasa* (lore).[12] For a modern historian, there is no possibility of the epic recording the literal past given that it features gods acting on earth, supernatural weapons, and a rash of other fantastical elements. But, as Anne Monius has argued, narrative had a unique power to communicate truth—in a higher sense—in premodern India.[13] The kingdoms mentioned in the Mahabharata may never have existed, but the epic explores the implications of the all-too-real political violence unleashed, again and again, by large-scale governments.

Even before the Mahabharata was written, Ashoka responded to large-scale warfare by decrying the human suffering he wrought in Kalinga, although he still threatened violence against forest dwellers (chapter 4). So many political figures since Ashoka have caused human anguish, in India and elsewhere, and yet have been unwilling to renounce political violence. Even in the twenty-first century, probably everyone reading these lines lives within states that exercise incredible violence. In a broad sense, we are still living in the brutal world of large-scale political formations that the Mahabharata describes. Perhaps our needs to continually explore this aspect of our lived experience explains why, as the editors of a recent collection of essays on the Mahabharata put it, "the most common response to the *Mahabharata* has been to recreate it."[14]

Notwithstanding my synopsis attempts throughout this chapter, the Mahabharata can never be definitively summed up for two reasons. One, the Sanskrit epic is gigantic. In the Western context, the term "epic" often calls to mind the Greek poems Iliad and Odyssey, but both are closer to short stories compared to the mammoth Mahabharata. Vyasa's Mahabharata is about seven times the length of the Iliad and the Odyssey combined or roughly fifteen times the length of the Christian Bible. Much of the verbose text is constituted by frame stories, side stories, and didactic sections that supplement the nucleus battle narrative.[15] These include tales of gender bending, pilgrimages, sexual assault, honeymoons, being a good king, and even a robust precis of the Ramayana, the other great Sanskrit epic (discussed in chapter 6). The Mahabharata celebrates its encyclopedic nature in a verse repeated in its opening and closing books:

> Whatever is found in this story
> regarding life's aims of righteousness, profit, pleasure, and
> liberation,
> you might find elsewhere.
> But what is missing here is found nowhere else.[16]

In addition to including everything and the kitchen sink, Vyasa's Mahabharata was also a fluid poem to which narrators added, verbally and in writing. Today, thousands of premodern handwritten copies of the Sanskrit Mahabharata survive, and no two are identical. With few exceptions, we do not know the names of the epic's countless premodern authors (Vyasa himself was a legendary poet and a character in the story). But Mahabharata texts, often grouped into regional versions, are the result of crowdsourcing over close to 2,000 years. For bards and poets alike, the Mahabharata's fluidity was a delightful invitation to rework the epic saga.

For a historian, the Mahabharata's mutability marks it as a special source. Temporally, we must analyze the epic as a cultural product refined from 100 CE onward, undergoing especially robust changes between 300 and 450 CE under a north Indian dynasty known as the Guptas.[17] An older generation of scholars mistakenly worked out the epic's temporality in the other direction. They projected the Mahabharata as representing a world that existed generations or even centuries before the myth was committed to writing. I think this approach blindly repeats the Mahabharata's self-conscious archaism. However appealing it might be to casually push the Mahabharata back in time, the evidence does not support it. Moreover, if we focus on Vyasa's Mahabharata as the result of layered additions from 100 CE forward, we can best highlight its polyphonic value. There is not a single voice that speaks through Vyasa's epic but rather a diverse cacophony, including less dominant Indian voices that we can hear if we listen closely to this gloriously complicated story.

Cataclysmic Political Violence

The Mahabharata devotes more attention to the intertwined issues of violence and political power than to any other subject, especially in its core battle saga. From the start, the Great War is presaged, even fated. For instance, in the first third of the epic, the eldest of the five Pandavas, Yudhishthira, lost an ill-advised dice game to the Kauravas and was forced into exile for thirteen years along with his four brothers and their joint wife, Draupadi. As the Pandavas exited the Kaurava capital of Hastinapura, the middle brother and ferocious archer, Arjuna, dropped handfuls of sand, each grain representing an enemy he would kill in the future war.[18] When the war happened, it was so abominable that it ushered in a new era of depravity, the Kali Yuga, the final and most corrupt of four eras.[19] Here, I explore three moments—before, during, and after the conflict, respectively—to draw out the epic's commentary on the thirst for political power and its ever-present companion of bloodshed.

On the morning of the first day of the Great War, the two sides amassed on the battlefield, and the blind king Dhritarashtra, father of the Kauravas and uncle of the Pandavas, asked:

dharmakshetre kurukshetre samaveta yuyutsavah
mamakah pandavashcaiva kimakurvata sanjaya

Tell me what happened, Sanjaya,
when mine and the Pandavas gathered, eager to fight
at Kurukshetra, the Kuru's field, the field of righteousness.[20]

This line opens the Bhagavadgita (Song of the Lord, or Gita, for short), a succinct eighteen-chapter section that serves as the epic's ethical crux. As asked, Sanjaya, advisor to Dhirtarashtra, next narrates the battlefield scene, which was an assault on the senses. Conches blew, cymbals banged, drums resounded, and troops roared, combining into a dreadful clamor. Men lined up ready to die on both sides, Sanjay tells Dhritarashtra, including Dhritarashtra's sons, trusted advisors, and dear friends.[21]

The Pandava warrior Arjuna, the third of five brothers and the most skilled archer, was among those ready to fight, but he hesitated. What Dhritarashtra heard from Sanjaya, Arjuna experienced with his own eyes and ears, and it overwhelmed the hero. Arjuna commanded his charioteer Krishna (also an incarnation of Vishnu) to drive into no man's land between the assembled armies and objected:

Krishna! I see my own family gathered here, eager to fight.

My limbs sink, and my mouth goes dry.
My body trembles, and my hairs bristle.

The Gandiva bow slips from my hand, and my skin burns.

> I cannot stand my ground, and my mind seems caught in a
> tailspin.
>
> I see bad omens, Krishna,
> and I see nothing good in killing my own family.[22]

Arjuna listed his reasons for wishing to avoid killing his kin, dubbing the kingdom such a slaughter would secure a "sorrow that desiccates my senses."[23] He slumped down, dropped his weapon, and protested "I will not fight!" (*no yotsya*).[24] If we wanted to put Arjuna's objection in philosophical language (and many premodern readers understood the Gita as a philosophical work), we would say that Arjuna perceived a clash between his duty to protect his family (*kuladharma*) and his caste duty to fight as a Kshatriya (*varnadharma*). Prioritizing the former, he suggested that he sit out the battle.[25] We can also put the dilemma in more universal and emotive terms. Arjuna recoiled at the idea of killing his family in exchange for political power, no matter what duty decreed.

In the remainder of the Bhagavadgita, Krishna used two strategies—logic and divine revelation—to convince Arjuna to fight. Krishna's most basic argument was that caste obligations outweigh all else and that Arjuna, as a Kshatriya, must participate in the battle. This idea of caste-based duty was oft repeated in subsequent Hindu texts. As the Gita puts it, "Better one's own dharma done poorly than another's done well."[26] Krishna also attempted to assuage Arjuna's conscience by claiming that the warrior lacks causality and merely appears to slaughter his enemies. Krishna claimed to be the true cause of the warriors' demise, and their souls are eternal in any case, he assured. Still, Arjuna must act for his own sake, performing *karmayoga* (practice of action) within caste-based prescriptions. "Focus on action, never its fruits," Krishna advised.[27]

Krishna's arguments go into considerably further depth than what I have sketched out here, and they have enthralled many thinkers over the centuries. Later Indian interpreters, including in premodernity, often read the Gita as a stand-alone text apart from the larger Mahabharata. In Krishna's words, readers have found arguments for violence and restraint, for renouncing the world and reveling in it.[28] As the medieval poet Jnandev saw it, the Gita is a wish-granting gem that satisfies all desires.[29] Maybe so, and even in the nineteenth and twentieth centuries, Indian independence leaders disagreed about whether the Gita recommended violence or nonviolence in the Indian independence struggle (chapter 21). Here, my interests remain more narrowly Krishna's argument in its epic context, namely that Arjuna ought to kill in accordance with his caste duties.

Krishna backed up his arguments and superseded logic by showing his true cosmic self. Krishna's divinity was truly news to Arjuna, who had encountered Krishna as a brother-in-law, advisor, and friend earlier in the epic. For readers or listeners in ancient India, Krishna was a relatively new deity in the Hindu pantheon, and so he perhaps meaningfully revealed his divinity to them as well. In fact, most of Krishna's backstory is absent from Vyasa's text, with some beloved Krishna myths being found in the Harivamsha, an appendix later affixed to the Mahabharata (of course, the world's longest poem has a lengthy appendix).[30] In the Gita, Krishna's cosmic form is beautiful and terrible, inspiring and horrifying (see excerpt). Above all, it is divine and so ended the debate. How can one argue with God? Arjuna picked up his bow, returned to the Pandava frontline, and rushed into battle.

Excerpts of the Divine Revelation of Krishna, Bhagavadgita, ca. 100 CE

Lord Krishna said: "Look at me, Arjuna! See my hundreds
of thousands of forms,
that are diverse, divine, a kaleidoscope of shapes and colors.
See the Vedic gods—Adityas, Vasus, Rudras, Ashvins, and Maruts—
and the many marvels never seen before, Arjuna!
Here and now see the universe with all its living creatures in one
place
in my body, Arjuna, along with whatever else you wish to see.
But you cannot look at me with your own eye.
I give you a divine eye. Look at my divine yoga!"

Sanjaya said, "Having said this, O King, then Krishna, the great lord
of yoga,
revealed his true divine form to Arjuna.
That amazing, multiform vision showed endless mouths and eyes,
countless celestial ornaments, and innumerable divine and drawn
weapons.

Wearing godly garlands and garments, glistening with divine perfume,
that infinite divinity filled all space and contained all marvelous things.
If the light of a thousand suns dawned all at once in the sky,
it would be like the brilliance of that great-souled one."

Arjuna said, "I see the gods in your body, God, throngs of all kinds of creatures,
Lord Brahma on his lotus throne, the seers, and all celestial serpents.
I see your unbounded form everywhere, with countless arms, stomachs, mouths, and eyes.
There is no beginning, no middle, and no end.
I see you are the Lord of All, Form of All!
Holding a crown, mace, and discus, you blaze with fierce rays
I see you, hard to glimpse in the enveloping light of sun and fire.
You should be known as the ultimate deity.
You are greatest treasure of the world.
You are the perpetual guardian of the eternal dharma.
You seem to me to be the eternal man . . .
Greedy to devour, you lick at the worlds around you
with your flaming mouths.
Your fires are filling the universe,
scorching it, Vishnu!
Tell me—Who are you in this horrible form, Lord?
Honor to you, Best of Gods! Have mercy.
I want to know who you truly are,
but I do not understand your actions."

Lord Krishna said, "I am time grown old, destroyer of worlds,
manifested here to obliterate the worlds.
Even without you, all these warriors prepared to fight will die.
Therefore, Get up! Seize fame!
Conquer your enemies! Enjoy the kingdom!
They are already killed by me. You are merely my instrument as archer.
I have killed Drona, Bhishma, Jayadratha, Karna, and the other heroic warriors.
Kill! Don't falter! Fight! You will defeat your enemies in battle."[31]

The carnage of the eighteen-day Mahabharata war is inconceivable, and the epic tries to evoke the horror, in part, through mind-numbing numbers. Vyasa's Mahabharata boasts that 1.6 billion people died on the battlefield of Kurukshetra in northern India, an unimaginable death toll in premodernity designed to highlight the clash's catastrophic nature.[32] The globe did not support this population until maybe 1900 CE, and humanity's bloodiest historical war to date, World War II, resulted in the deaths of about one-third that grotesque number. Sometimes, the epic and later texts explain the massacre as a sacrifice requiring the blood of an entire generation of Kshatriyas. If we follow this interpretation, the war is a notably messy sacrifice that contrasted sharply with the rigid rules of Vedic rites where even a mispronounced *akshara* (syllable) required correction.[33]

Moreover, Mahabharata characters often sought base revenge rather than virtuous ends in the war. For instance, Bhima, the second Pandava brother, fulfilled an earlier vow by breaking the thigh of the eldest Kaurava Duryodhana, literally hitting him below the belt. Bhima also hacked to death the second Kaurava brother, Duhshasana, by ripping off his arm and then clawing open his chest to drink his blood. Things were even worse on the Kaurava side. After eighteen days, the battle appeared over because nearly all the Kauravas and their allies lay dead. But after dark, one of the few survivors, Ashvatthaman, snuck into the Pandava camp and killed every man, woman, and child slumbering there, including all Draupadi's children by her five husbands. Some of these battle moments featured in later Sanskrit dramas from various corners of India.[34] But as much as people like hearing sad stories as literature, who would want to live through such devastation?

Not Yudhishthira, who no longer desired earthly power after the conflict ended. The war's victor—"out of his mind with grief"—leveled some of the fiercest criticisms of Kshatriya dharma and kingship known in Sanskrit literature.[35] He lamented that his "triumph" appeared more like defeat (*ajayakaro*),[36] proclaiming:

> Our enemies' plans have succeeded since the Kuru family has lost
> all direction.
> Having killed ourselves by ourselves, what possible virtuous result
> can we achieve?
>
> Damn Kshatriya customs! Damn might makes right!
> Damn rage, which has brought us to this calamity!

> Those who dwell in the forest always have patience, self-restraint, and honesty.
> They lack aggression and envy while embracing non-violence (*ahimsa*) and truthfulness.
>
> But we were greedy and deluded, clinging to arrogance and pride.
> We have fallen to this state because we coveted a mere kingdom.
>
> Having seen our relatives slain, over hungering for this morsel,
> nobody will make me happy to be king, even over the three worlds.[37]

Yudhishthira then envisioned the grief of parents who had lost children in the conflict, but we do not need Yudhishthira's imagination on that score. The Mahabharata devotes an entire book, the *Striparvan* (Book of Women) to the laments of mothers, wives, and daughters of those whose corpses rotted on the battlefield. One woman, Gandhari (mother of the hundred dead Kaurava brothers), described many fallen warriors and the women who grieved for them. She cursed Krishna—who had egged on the Pandavas and encouraged breaking the rules of war—to see his entire clan annihilated and to himself die, to be mourned by his wives.[38]

Whereas women can lament in the Mahabharata epic, Yudhishthira must rule. His four brothers and their wife Draupadi argued this point, expressing shock and anger at Yudhishthira's incapacitating empathy.[39] For instance, Arjuna (his earlier doubts forgotten) pontificated that there is virtuous violence (*sadhuhimsa*) and, for Kshatriyas specifically, "there is no fame without killing." "Even the gods are killers," Arjuna exclaimed.[40] They all scoffed at Yudhishthira's proposal to renounce the world and live in a forest as appropriate for a Brahmin sage but anathema for a Kshatriya fighter. Ultimately, the big gun was called in to assuage the reluctant king and, perhaps, disturbed readers and listeners as well: Bhishma, the family patriarch of both the Kauravas and the Pandavas.

Bhishma lay on a bed of arrows, mortally injured while leading the Kaurava army but able to choose the time of his death. From that prone position, he instructed Yudhishthira in how to rule. Some of Bhishma's advice is blunt, such as his opening maxim to Krishna who fixed the meeting with Yudhishthira:

> Just as the dharma of Brahmins is generosity, study, and asceticism,
> the dharma of Kshatriyas is striking down bodies in battle, Krishna![41]

Bhishma's instruction to Yudhishthira is lengthy, constituting nearly 25 percent of the entire Mahabharata.[42] He covered a lot of ground, including extensive discussion of duties specific to each caste and life stage (*varnashramadharma*) and how exceptional times call for exceptions to the rules (*apaddharma*). It is as if Bhishma's weighty wordage tries to fill the depopulated earth that is soaked in blood.

Eventually, Bhishma convinced Yudhishthira to ascend the Hastinapura throne, and the new ruler even completed the horse sacrifice, a late Vedic ritual of Kshatriya kingship. But sinister events continued to plague the Pandavas and their allies. As per Gandhari's curse, Krishna and his entire clan, the Vrishnis, perished in a drunken brawl. Eventually the Pandavas died and, to their surprise, went to hell. Soon enough the Pandavas wound up in heaven, but, in so doing, they left behind the kingdom that they had won by killing almost everyone they loved.

Analyzing the Mahabharata close to a millennium later, the ninth-century philosopher Anandavardhana proposed that the epic induces grief and aversion (*vairagya*). He argued that learning the dismal end of the Vrishnis and Pandavas might inspire us to shun the world and instead seek a feeling of peace (*shantarasa*) through liberation (*moksha*).[43] I find this a compelling reading. But before we turn away, there are further historical insights to be gained from this extraordinary epic.

New Hindu Gods and a Tightening Social Order

Vyasa's Mahabharata—including some of its later additions—records significant religious changes, such as the Brahminical incorporation of non-Vedic deities. The epic includes both Shiva and Krishna, Hindu gods to whom we find increasing references around this time. For instance, Indo-Greek dynasties and other northwest rulers of this age minted coins with imagery consistent with Shiva. Some have even suggested that the god Oesho on second-century-CE Kushan coins is Shiva.[44] Shiva and his wife Parvati appear in Hala's *Sattasai* (Seven Centuries), a collection of

Prakrit poetry compiled in the Deccan between the first and third centuries CE, such as in these suggestive lines:

> Long live Shiva's third eye
> which Parvati covered with kisses
> while covering his other two eyes with her hands
> when her skirt slipped off in the heat of love play.[45]

Still, Shiva's mythology became elaborated only later in the first millennium CE, largely through later Sanskrit texts known as *purana*s and popular practices (chapter 7). Krishna's stories were likewise fleshed out in the Harivamsha appendix to the Mahabharata (early to mid-first millennium CE) and the Bhagavata Purana (tenth century CE).

Not all Hindu gods that are part of the religion today appear in Vyasa's Mahabharata, and here the epic's later layers are helpful in tracking newcomers. For instance, Ganesha is an elephant-headed god known to modern Hindus as Shiva's son, the god of beginnings, and for his sweet tooth. But Ganesha is absent from the epic's core narrative and is never added to old Sanskrit versions common in Kashmir, Kerala, and Bengal. Ganesha appears only in a frame story—first found in a Tamil retelling of the epic and inserted maybe around the tenth century CE into Sanskrit versions across the Hindi belt—in which he wrote down Vyasa's narration, switching to his tusk when his pen broke.[46]

The Mahabharata elaborates on caste norms, presenting the varna system as a hierarchy in which human worth lessens as one moves down the pyramid. As mentioned, Vyasa's text projects an unabashedly upper-caste outlook. At one point, the epic explains the origins of the caste system as follows, playing on the literal meaning of "varna" as color:

> Brahmins who were partial to sensual pleasures, quick to anger, and rash in love
> abandoned their own dharma and became red-bodied Kshatriyas.
>
> Brahmins who herded cattle and farmed failed to act according to their own dharma and so became yellow Vaishyas.
>
> Brahmins who were fond of violence and deceit, greedy, and would do anything to make a living, fell from purity and became black Shudras.[47]

This ranking of human beings comes into play throughout the epic narrative in which Brahmin and Kshatriya men receive by far the most airtime and privileges. In the epic, caste is inborn, as demonstrated through the tale of Karna. Karna's mother Kunti had him out of wedlock and so abandoned the infant to hide her sexual impropriety, sending him down a river in a basket. Karna was found and raised by low-caste parents, but he always displayed the virility of a Kshatriya and, indeed, was eventually recognized as such and fought for the Kauravas in the war. The Mahabharata is less kind, and less individualistic, to lower castes and those outside of the four-fold varna system, such as forest-dwellers.

The Mahabharata offers several stories featuring Nishadas, tribal people who live in the forest, typically treating them as foils for upper-caste values. For instance, early in the epic, the Kauravas tried to burn the Pandavas alive in a wax house. The Pandavas escaped and, in their place, left a family of Nishadas to be incinerated. Vyasa's text shows a "cold-blooded disregard" for the fate of this tribal family that, perhaps inadvertently, captures something of what the premodern caste system may have looked like from the bottom.[48]

The saga of Ekalavya and Drona is another Mahabharata tale that features callous treatment of a Nishada. Drona was a Brahmin weapons teacher, and Ekalavya was an aspiring warrior and Nishada prince. Drona flatly refused to teach the young man of low birth. But after Ekalavya learned the arts of war on his own, with only a clay statue of Drona as his guide, real-life Drona demanded his teacher's fee (*guru-dakshina*). In the Mahabharata, gurus name their price, and Drona asked for Ekalavya's right thumb. Ekalavya complied, thus destroying his own archery superiority in deference to a Brahmin. Drona's justification for his unusual fee was steeped in caste norms, namely he wanted to uphold his promise that Arjuna, a Kshatriya, would be the best archer of the age. Through caste-based violence, Drona kept his word.

As narrated in Vyasa's text, the story of Ekalavya offers an upper-caste viewpoint. Ekalavya is depicted as having internalized caste prejudices, happily occupying the bottom of the social hierarchy and submitting to a Brahmin's cruelty. But this erasure of a Nishada perspective has, in modern times, had an unintended effect. Many from caste-oppressed communities have spoken about or on behalf of Ekalavya, using his name and story as a rallying cry for demanding civil rights and equality.[49] Whereas Ekalavya was not permitted to speak in an ancient Indian text, others have done so in our time, further developing an epic tradition that is never quite finished.

The Mahabharata also mentions large-scale acts of violence against forest dwellers, most prominently the burning of the Khandava Forest and all its inhabitants. The episode opens with the Vedic god Agni (Fire) enlisting Krishna and Arjuna to set the Khandava alight to sate Agni's merciless appetite.[50] The pair agreed and prevented all living things from escaping the flames:

> Krishna and Arjuna, tiger-like on their chariots, stood on both sides of the forest.
> They massacred living creatures in all directions.
>
> Wherever the two heroes saw living beings escaping from the Khandava,
> they captured them.
>
> Creatures found no escape from the two chariots
> that moved so fast the chariots and the charioteers blurred together.
>
> As the Khandava burned, living being by the thousands
> scrambling in every direction, screeching blood-curdling screams.
>
> Countless were burned in a single spot, and scores were incinerated elsewhere,
> shattered, scattered, confused, and their eyes cracking.
>
> Some hugged their sons, and others their moms and dads.
> Unable to let go of their loved ones, they met their end together.[51]

The genocidal scene goes on at length, at one point featuring Arjuna hacking up living beings and laughing as he throws mutilated pieces of flesh into the blazing forest.[52] Indra and other gods tried to halt the massacre, but they failed, and nearly everyone in the Khandava Forest died. The epic offers philosophical explanations for this extermination, but I am more interested in the possibility that it reflected real practices, admittedly with distortions.[53] Cities were expanding as Vyasa's Mahabharata was penned around 100 CE, and this urbanization required some forest clearing. The process was surely less sensational than depicted here and proceeded slowly, but deforestation entailed displacing forest-dwellers at times. In this story, such displacement is glorified as part of Kshatriya dharma.

Amid stories of men, Vyasa's Mahabharata features some unforgettable heroines. Most striking to most readers is Draupadi whose internal power is so fierce that she could not be disrobed in the public audience hall at Hastinapura. This scene of her sexual assault is one of the epic's most well-known episodes. Yudhishthira had lost everything to the Kauravas during a gambling match, including the Pandavas' shared wife Draupadi. The Kauravas dragged Draupadi into the hall of men, bleeding during her period, to humiliate her. Duhshasana rushed to tear off Draupadi's single garment but found that there was always more cloth to cover her body.[54] Most modern Hindus know this story with the variation that Krishna supplied Draupadi's extra clothing. Indeed, this version is common within epic retellings that emphasize devotion to Krishna, in Sanskrit and, later, in vernacular languages.[55] But in Vyasa's text as known across Bengal, Kashmir, and southern India, Krishna was nowhere to be seen.[56] Instead, Draupadi—a highly respected woman in Vyasa's narration—protected herself while a room of tight-lipped men watched her brutal assault.

Some later texts dub the Mahabharata as a "Veda for women and Shudras" (*strishudraveda*), both of whom Brahmin men prohibited from knowing the four proper Vedas. But the epic offers no single message, either to or about women. Rather, as Stephanie Jamison has put it, so many ancient Indian texts, the Mahabharata included, contain reams of "misogynist maxims" alongside "resourceful, energetic, and verbally and dharmically accomplished women."[57] Building upon the latter, some modern authors have retold the Mahabharata as Draupadi's story, upholding this fierce heroine as a proto-feminist icon.[58]

Speaking Historically by Omission

The Mahabharata says nothing about Buddhists, Jains, or Ajivikas in what is best read as a pointed omission rather than mere insouciance. Two thousand years ago, these three non-Vedic traditions thrived in parts of northern India that feature in the geography of Vyasa's story. For instance, images of Jain ascetics and laity—dating as early as the second century BCE with more from the first century CE—were carved into relief panels at Mathura.[59] The Buddhist pilgrimage site of Sanchi, in modern-day Madhya Pradesh, was built-up significantly in the late centuries BCE into the early centuries CE. The four gateways to Sanchi's

Great Stupa, erected during this time, still stand today and are iconic of the site.[60] Buddhism also flourished further north in Gandhara—whose Mahabharata namesake is Gandhari, mother of the Kaurava brothers—as evidenced by stupas and some of our oldest surviving manuscripts from South Asia (chapter 6). A set of first-century-CE Kharoshthi scrolls found in Gandhara narrate, among other things, conversations between the Gautama Buddha and a Brahmin.[61] But descriptions of interreligious dialogue do not appear in the Mahabharata.

Some scholars surmise covert references to Buddhist, Jain, and Ajivika traditions in Vyasa's text. For instance, in a conversation with the Pandavas, the sage Markandeya offers a dystopian vision of the world as it deteriorates through the four *yugas* (ages). Markandeya's signs of decline constitute a grab bag of male Brahminical anxieties of the time, including intercaste marriages, neglect of Vedic rituals, women talking back to their husbands, Shudras refusing to serve, and students ignoring their teachers.[62] A few of Markandeya's signs could plausibly be read as references to Buddhist structures, including people venerating mounds housing human remains (stupas?) and towers dotting the countryside (Ashokan pillars?).[63] Jains also venerated stupas during this period, and so could be indicated here.[64] Additionally, one could read the Gita's endorsement of violence as a response to Jain and Buddhist ethics of ahimsa, but the evidence is only circumstantial.

Whether we accept any of these as covert references or not, it is striking that the Mahabharata does not overtly name any religious tradition that rejects Brahminical authority. Vyasa's text claims to cover everything under the sun, and yet it conspicuously fails to mention major religious trends of the time and place of its composition. Some scholars see this pointed silence as a "projected antiquity," an attempt to bolster the epic's claim to represent an older world.[65] I think it may also be forward looking. One of the epic's idealistic visions—from an upper-caste viewpoint—is a world characterized by widespread, largely unchallenged acceptance of Brahminical authority. That this has never come to pass is yet another reason to understand the Mahabharata as a myth.

Conclusion: Only Facts

After so much fiction, let me conclude this chapter squarely within the confines of historical fact. People narrated the Mahabharata widely in ancient India, carrying manuscripts of Vyasa's epic far beyond the tale's internal geography of the northern subcontinent. Our oldest surviving manuscript fragments that mention the Mahabharata date to the third century CE and were found interred in the Qizil caves of the Uyghur region, currently in China and historically part of the northern Silk Roads trade routes. In a twist darkly appropriate to the epic's ruminations on political violence, parts of this manuscript (known as the Spitzer manuscript) were destroyed in Allied bombing of Nazi Germany during World War II.[66]

The Mahabharata also traveled north and south in the first millennium CE, carried by groups of migrating Brahmins. During the first millennium CE, Brahmins migrated north to Kashmir, and the version of the Mahabharata preserved in that region is thought to be among the oldest extant today.[67] Separately, the Purvashikha Brahmins—named for their front-tufted hair—moved to Tamil regions in the early centuries CE, and some later shifted to Kerala. A second group of Brahmins migrated to Tamil lands in the fifth to eighth centuries CE, remaining there into modern times.[68] Both south-bound groups of Brahmins carried Vyasa's epic with them, although in slightly different versions as people across India—and later Southeast Asia—adapted the Mahabharata and its enduring truths for their own communities.

Further Reading

Many scholars have written on the Mahabharata; I prioritize more recent scholarship and diverse voices, especially in terms of gender. For translations of the Mahabharata, John Smith offers a readable, single-volume rendering that follows the critical edition Sanskrit text. For poetry in modern English, I am partial to Carole Satyamurti's rendering. For a verse-by-verse translation, Chicago University Press volumes (by J.A.B. van Buitenen and James Fitzgerald, to date) follow the critical edition; volumes by multiple authors in the Clay Sanskrit Library follow Nilakantha's seventeenth-century vulgate. For independent volumes, Johnson's *Massacre at Night* translates the night attack in Book 10, Wendy Doniger's *After the War* renders books 15–18, and Simon Brodbeck's *Krishna's Lineage* translates the Harivamsha appendix.

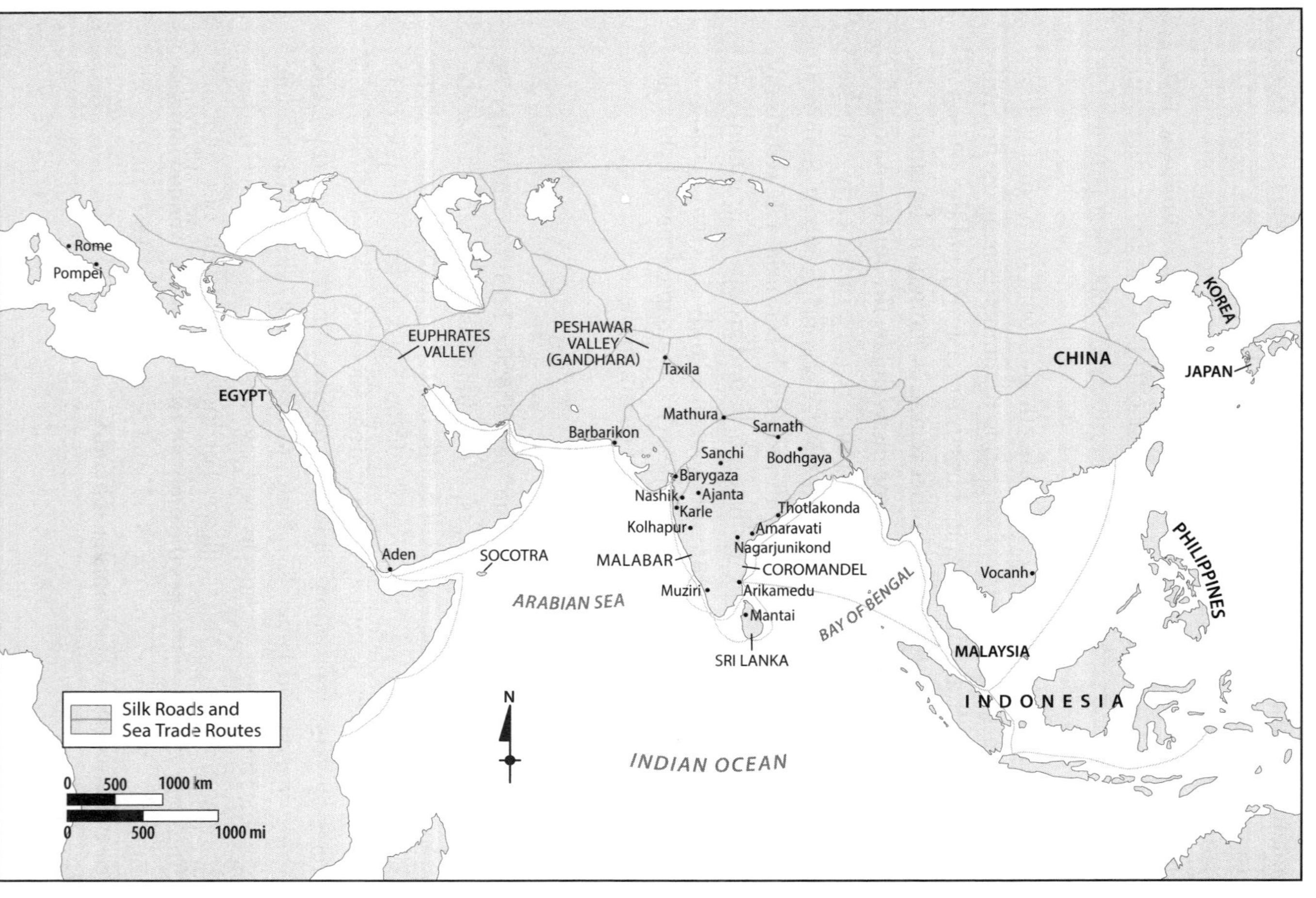

Silk roads and sea trade routes, ca. 100 CE.

6

South Asians Traveling, 200 BCE–300 CE

We will instead go away from here as rapidly
as the water of a river
rushing into the many waves of the ocean.

—Peruncittiranar, *Purananuru*, third century CE (Tamil)[1]

One autumn in the third century CE, Vishnudhara set sail from Bharuch in Gujarat and began a multi-month journey west. He captained a boat laden with spices, gems, pearls—and maybe peacocks and human slaves—cargo that would fetch a good price in Egypt or be transported further inland within the Roman Empire. Around February, Vishnudhara pulled into port at Socotra, an island about 185 miles south of the Arabian Peninsula and a frequent stopover point for sailors. There, Vishnudhara did what many of us have done at one point or another: he left a piece of graffiti. Using the Brahmi script native to South Asia, he etched his name on a cave wall amid dozens of others, such that we know that Isharadasa, Siha, Ravahaka, Thulaka, Devila, and "captain Vishnudhara from Bharukaccha" were there.[2] Vishnudhara was one of many ancient South Asians to brave the high seas in pursuit of wealth, religious evangelism, political gain, and more. In addition, some traveled over mountains during this period using the newly founded Silk Roads that connected China, Central Asia, northern India, and Mesopotamia. Even those who stayed home spun poems about rushing into the ocean, as per this chapter's epigraph, or told itinerant stories. Valmiki's Ramayana—a Sanskrit epic likely penned in the early centuries CE—imagines journeys to faraway lands peopled by sentient monkeys and talking bears as well as a demon-filled island. Travel was a material reality and literary interest that shaped South Asian life between 200 BCE and 300 CE.

Trade via Sea Routes and the Silk Roads

Communities in the northern, central, and southern subcontinent and Sri Lanka helped to create and traveled along the vast network of land and sea trade routes that traversed much of ancient Asia. These extensive trade links connected discrete South Asian communities, both with each other and far beyond the region. Trade east of the subcontinent likely came first, with shipping routes established from the fifth century BCE onward.[3] Numerous South Asian communities—from Sri Lanka to the Coromandel coast (southeastern Indian coast) to Bengal—traded with counterparts in Malaysia, Indonesia, the Philippines, Taiwan, and, likely through intermediaries, as far north as Korea.[4]

Trade west of the subcontinent—with Greeks, Egyptians, and others within the Roman Mediterranean—exploded between the first and third centuries CE due to two developments. First, Rome annexed Egypt in 30 BCE, which combined imperial resources with access to Indian Ocean trade. Second, sailors figured out how to use the annual monsoon winds such that they could complete a round trip between India and the Arabian or East African coast in under a year (typically, setting sail west from India in autumn and returning east to India in summer).[5] Indians and Sri Lankans used knowledge of the monsoon winds to sail across the south, southeast, and east Asian littoral zones, sometimes collectively dubbed "monsoon Asia."[6] Romans also traversed the Indian Ocean. In addition to sea trade, the Silk Roads were founded in the second century BCE as a series of land-based routes that linked northern India with Central Asia and China to the north and the Mediterranean to the west.

Using these various routes, Indian and Sri Lankan peoples, items, and ideas moved across ancient Asia, influencing many corners of the known world. Groups within Tamil Nadu and Kerala were especially active in sea trade. Pottery shards with Tamil-Brahmi script and cooking pots used to make Indian dishes attest that ancient Tamilians resided as far away as Egypt in this period.[7] Recent DNA evidence suggests that ancient south Indians were buried in the Euphrates valley.[8] Traveling east, Sanskrit and, quite possibly, south Indians made it as far as Vocanh on Vietnam's eastern coast by the second or third century CE, as evi-

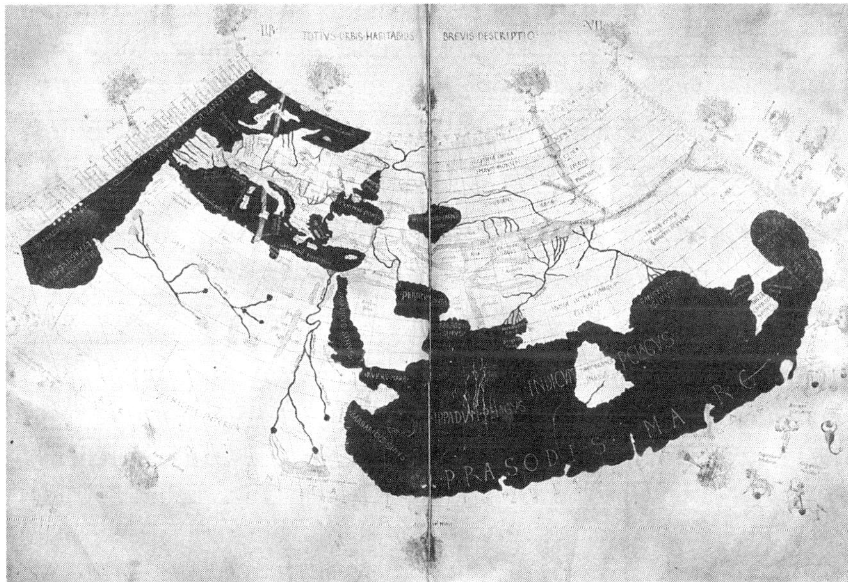

Figure 6.1. World map including India and Taprobane (Sri Lanka) based on Ptolemy's second-century *Geography*, 1450–1475 CE.

denced by a Sanskrit inscription there.[9] Sri Lankans, too, played important roles in burgeoning pan-Asian trade. In an imaginative reflection of this reality, one Roman author projected Taprobane (as they called Sri Lanka) as having continental proportions, nearly rivaling the subcontinent in size (figure 6.1).[10] Historians of South Asia overall still suffer from a general bias toward the north, which explains—but does not justify—the neglect of south India and Sri Lanka in overview histories.[11]

Many South Asians—from the subcontinent and Sri Lanka—worked in ancient port towns and cities at crossroads, such as Arikamedu (Pondicherry, Tamil Nadu), Barygaza (Bharuch, Gujarat), Barbarikon (near Karachi, Sindh), Muziri (Pattanam, Kerala), and Mantai (Sri Lanka). Port cities were bustling, as a mid-third century Chinese author described a north Indian port city: "There are always more than a hundred ships (in the harbor). The crowds gathering in the market are more than 10,000. Day and night they do business. Drums and horns are sounded on the ships. The clothes of these peoples resemble the clothes of the Chinese."[12] Some Indians captained boats that sailed from these ports, as mentioned. Many boats were large to weather monsoon storms (a downside of using monsoon winds to sail), and this likely centralized sea trade, at least to some degree, in the hands of those able to finance larger ventures.[13] Smaller-scale operators used more modest boats to transport goods inland and, conversely, to ports through a labyrinth of rivers on the subcontinent and Sri Lanka. Ports also served as clearing houses, re-exporting desired items west and east. For example, south Indian ports moved Southeast Asian spices further west, and north Indian cities did likewise for Chinese silks while sending Central Asian horses south to Sri Lanka.[14]

Tracing what we now call supply chains even further back to the source of goods, more groups come into focus as enmeshed in this burgeoning global trade. A north Indian pepper farmer might never have set foot on a ship or even seen the ocean, but he grew a spice that enlivened tastebuds in Italy. A Tamil bead-maker may never have left her village, but she crafted jewelry that adorned necks across the Indo-Pacific.[15] Such examples abound given the astonishing array of South Asian exports in this period. These included spices (such as pepper, ginger, cardamom, cloves, and saffron), animal products (such as ivory, tortoise shells, and various skins), gems and jewels (such as diamonds, emeralds, sardonyx, turquoise, sapphire, lapis lazuli, and onyx), pearls, pottery, wood (teak and sandal), textiles (cotton and silk), live animals (such as peacocks, parrots, rhinoceroses, and leopards), beads, raw glass, crafted statues, manuscripts, and—in an export that should always be set apart—slaves.[16] This list of goods and people gives some sense of why "India" was synonymous with wealth for much of premodernity. By focusing on details within this abundance, we can glimpse how South Asian exports shaped lived experiences around the ancient world.

Indian animals appear across the Roman Empire in the early centuries CE, prized for sport, beauty, and food. In Roman amphitheaters, one-horned rhinos, and perhaps panthers among other large wild animals, were torn apart by each other and by gladiators in front of cheering crowds.[17] Subjects of the Roman Empire also had less bloody ways of amusing themselves, such as inebriating green Indian parakeets. As Pliny put it, writing about a Roman party game in the late first century CE: "[The parrot] salutes emperors and repeats the words it hears, being especially outrageous in its speech when drunk with wine."[18] Recent scholarship confirms that birds—including parrots—will consume alcohol and suffer vocalization impairment.[19] Roman subjects also appreciated peacocks, for their beautiful feathers and as tasty fowl on the dinner table.

Other Indian exports were eye-catching in different ways. For instance, ivory and tortoise shells were used in jewelry and furniture.[20] Statues carved on the subcontinent were sometimes brought long distances. An intricate sculpture of a *yakshi* (tree spirit) was carved in central India, within the Satavahana kingdom, in the first century CE and exported to Pompeii (figure 6.2).[21] It was probably used as the leg of a small piece of furniture prior to being among the many items buried in Mount Vesuvius's volcanic ash in 79 CE.[22] In the same century, a statue of Poseidon, the Greek god of the sea, was brought to central India; it was uncovered in a dig at Kolhapur in Maharashtra (figure 6.3).[23] When viewed side by side, these two items stand as a visible testament to how Indian Ocean trade connected ancient Eurasia.

Amid luxury items for flashy consumption, more mundane Indian goods likely touched more peoples' lives. For instance, many Indian spices and rice featured in Roman medicines. As per Pliny, a Roman subject might spend his disposable income on Indian cinnamon to use as a diuretic, sleep aid, or solution to bad breath.[24] In the case of cinnamon, the Roman author Pliny identified it as sourced from India, but people commonly lost track of where specific items originated on the vast sea trade and Silk Roads networks.[25] One wonders, for example, if the glass beads we now call Indo-Pacific—made by a process of drawing glass perhaps developed by Tamil artisans in Arikamedu—were known as Indian or Tamilan among the communities that wore them, stretching from Ghana to Bali to South Korea.[26] Even today, we remain unclear if certain spices were exported west from ancient South Asia, Southeast Asia, or both. But there was one item uniquely associated with India across ancient trade routes: pepper.

In the ancient world, most pepper was grown in India, with long pepper being native to the north and black pepper native to the south. Bronze Age shipwrecks indicate that Indian communities exported pepper to the Mediterranean, probably to the Phoenicians, as early as the second millennium BCE.[27] Pepper exporting flourished as Indian Ocean trade accelerated in the early centuries CE to the point where, as per one historian, any Roman subject "except the most destitute" could afford a bit of this taste of India.[28] Romans used pepper, as we do today, to flavor food. The spice appears in over 80 percent of recipes in Apicius's fifth-century-CE cookbook, *De Re Coquinaria*, and peppercorns have surfaced during archaeological digs of the sewers that serviced private residences in Italy.[29] Pepper was also used across the Roman Mediterranean in

Figure 6.2. Yakshi, first century CE (before 79 CE), central India, ivory, excavated at Pompeii in October 1938.

medicines.[30] The spice was in such demand that Tamil sources often mention it being shipped in huge quantities, seemingly emblematic of the region's wealth (see the quoted poem by Paranar).

Ships returned across the Indian Ocean carrying cargo desired by South Asians, most notably gold. The Tamil poet Paranar (ca. third century CE) recorded, through a lyrical meditation on an unattainable woman, that immense wealth poured into southern India by trading pepper for gold (see the poem by Paranar). Another Tamil poet put it more bluntly: "Let the gold pile up in heaps!"[31] South Indians probably melted down most imported gold to cast jewelry, pitchers, and more.[32]

Figure 6.3. Poseidon, first century CE, Roman, copper alloy, found in Kolhapur, India.

But they saved some coins, and, in a small indication of the avalanche of imported gold during this period, thousands of Roman gold coins have been found in over 100 caches in southern India since the late eighteenth century, plus additional coins in Sri Lanka.[33] Some coins have loops and apertures, suggesting use as jewelry, and others are in near mint condition.[34] Roman sources of the period record the insatiable Indian appetite for gold, claiming a massive trade deficit, and Indian sources add that they also sought gold from other trading partners, referring for centuries to the alluring "land of gold" (*suvarnabhumi*) that lay to the east.[35]

There are exceptions to every rule, and Kushan gold coins (made ca. first to third century CE to match Roman coins in weight) have been found as far away as Ethiopia.[36] Still, overall, Indians imported gold. While little else has stayed the same over the millennia, the Indian thirst for gold still drives global markets today.[37]

Poem by Paranar, from the Tamil *Purananuru* (Four hundred songs), Third Century CE

"In Muciri with its drums, where the ocean roars,
where the paddy traded for fish and stacked high
on the boats makes boats and houses look the same
and the sacks of pepper raised up beside them
make the houses look the same as the tumultuous
shore and the golden wares brought by the ships
are carried to land in the servicing boats,
Kuttavan its king to whom toddy is no more
valuable than water, who wears a shining garland, gives out gifts
of goods from the mountains along with goods from the sea
to those who have come to him. Even if you humbly bring
and bestow as much fine and copious wealth as that city possesses,
she will not marry someone who is unworthy of her." So says
her father and will not grant her hand. Think! Will the tall city
suffer where sighing kites sleep on the middle wall of the fort,
the roads hard to conquer are filled with weapons,
but ladders have been thrown up by men who have come to force
their way in![38]

Horses were another item that premodern South Asians imported—and continued to import—for centuries. Horses had been important for some north Indian communities since the Indo-European migrations of the second millennium BCE had given rise to a Brahminical culture of valuing horses for practical and ritual reasons (chapter 2). But premodern Indians never raised horses as successfully as their Western and Central Asian counterparts.[39] As a result, Indians imported horses for millennia, using them for religious ceremonies, transportation, and warfare. Even the Mahabharata associated horses—an important animal within the epic story—with *yavana*s, namely people from the north (in that case, perhaps Indo-Greeks).[40]

A less discussed import is wine. Few think of ancient India as having a robust drinking culture, but pottery shards of wine containers—made in the Roman Empire and Mesopotamia—have been unearthed in cities across the subcontinent and Sri Lanka. This material evidence leaves little doubt that ancient South Asians drank imported wine, probably lots of it. Archaeological finds at Arikamedu in Tamil Nadu even indicate that importers were sensitive to local tastes, with a possible preference for the salty wine associated with the Greek island of Kos.[41] More lyrically, the Tamil poet Karikkannanar, wrote this about the ancient Indian love of wine:

> May you live on, with a sweet life,
> giving away precious ornaments to all those who come to you in need
> and never running out of them, while every day you take your pleasure as women
> wearing their shining bangles bring you the cool and fragrant wine
> carried here in their excellent ships by the Greeks and the women pour it
> for you out of pitchers made of gold that have been fashioned with high artistry.[42]

Even after South Asian trade with the Roman Empire declined later in the first millennium CE, Indians found other sources for wine, such as Sasanian Persia.[43] Later Indian stories indicate that some elites reveled in consuming alcohol.[44]

We have a dearth of information regarding the role of South Asian states in trade during this period. A first- or second-century-CE inscription at Godawaya in southern Sri Lanka records that customs were collective by King Gamani Abaya and given to a local *vihara* (Buddhist monastery). This suggests that both the state and religious institutions regulated trade. But on the subcontinent, evidence is scant on direct involvement by the Kushans in the northwest, the Satavahanas in central India, and the Cheras and Pandyas in the south. One thing that is clear is that ancient trade networks far outlived all these Indian dynasties, just as the Silk Roads in China and Central Asia persisted throughout political changes.[45]

In lieu of further excavating elite Indian political interests in trade, I instead end this survey of ancient mercantile exchanges by highlighting the experiences of the most non-elite involved: slaves.

Some South Asians were trafficked along sea routes and the Silk Roads, sold as property across the ancient Mediterranean. Conversely, slaves were also imported from the Roman Empire to serve Indian masters. Greco-Roman and Indian sources concur about the existence of a bidirectional slave trade in this ancient period, with people being sold in and out of the subcontinent as household help, entertainers, and more.[46] In the Roman world, the second-century-CE Alexandrian Tariff mentions a duty on Indian eunuchs, and Indian slaves may have contributed to Greek plays that depict Indians speaking incomprehensible languages (these may well have been south Indian languages).[47] Regarding India, a first-century-CE practical trade guide, titled *Periplus Maris Erythraei*, describes the ruler of Barygaza (Bharuch, Gujarat) as having a taste for importing "slave musicians" and "beautiful girls for concubinage."[48] The Indian interest in slaves also arises in literature, such as the legend of the Christian apostle Thomas being sold into slavery and taken to India in the first century CE (in reality, Christian communities arrived in southern India, via sea routes, in later centuries; see chapter 7).[49] We have few further details about the lives of the enslaved of this period, but it is worth underscoring that slavery was not limited to global trade networks. Many South Asian communities practiced forms of enslavement before, during, and after this period in what remains an understudied feature of the South Asian past.[50]

Indian Buddhism Goes Global

Buddhist monks and nuns used trade routes within and beyond South Asia to spread their religious tradition ca. 200 BCE–300 CE, traveling as far as China via the Silk Roads. Also, during this period, Buddhist ideas and practices changed substantially. Buddhists crafted corporeal images of the Gautama Buddha for the first time and initiated relic veneration centered around stupas (rounded cylindrical mounds). The Pali canon—a collection of Buddhist texts—came into clear view by the close of the first century BCE. Works within this three-part collection articulate what are today considered basic Buddhist principles, such as the four noble truths (or truths for nobles):[51]

1. Life is suffering.
2. Desire is the root of suffering.
3. Eliminating desire leads to liberation (nirvana).
4. Such liberation can be achieved via the eight-fold path.[52]

Another Buddhist idea that emerged during this time was the bodhisatta, a Buddhist monk or nun who defers nirvana to help others along the Buddhist path. Somewhat confusingly, "boddhisatta" can also describe the Gautama Buddha in one of his past lives, a set of stories collectively known as the *jataka* tales that began to be elaborated during these centuries (chapter 8). A split in Buddhism emerged in this period between the Theravada and Mahayana traditions, which subsequently developed distinct theologies and flourished in discrete areas. In brief, during this 500-year stretch, Indian Buddhism changed to include practices, ideas, and contours that, today, are commonly considered definitive of the tradition, and the Buddhist dhamma took root far beyond the subcontinent.

Money undergirded many of the changes within Indian Buddhism between 200 BCE and 300 CE. The Buddhist community—lay Buddhists, monks (bhikkhus), and nuns (bhikkhunis)—grew wealthier throughout this period from royal patronage, trade, and (for the sangha, i.e., monastic community) lay donations. Some financial support was recorded in stone inscriptions, allowing us to piece together ancient financial networks. In some cases, individuals underwrote the construction of monasteries, with a perfumer donating a door and a lay woman financing a pillar at the first-century-CE Karle caves in Maharashtra.[53] Less than 100 miles away, the similarly dated Kanheri caves were carved on an island off India's western coast and relied on support from visiting traders for centuries.[54] In terms of political powers, the Satavahanas in central India and the Kushans in the north both financed Buddhist communities, among other religious groups.

These diverse revenue streams enabled Buddhist monks and nuns to build an astonishing number of pilgrimage sites, monasteries, and educational institutions. Some Buddhist sites have come up earlier in our tour through South Asian history, such as Sanchi in central India and Taxila in the northwest (chapter 3). Other Buddhists sites come into view during this period, including Kanheri, Karle, Nashik, and Ajanta in Maharashtra; Amaravati, Nagarjunikond, and Thotlakonda in Andhra Pradesh;

and Bodhgaya in Bihar. I elaborate on some of these sites below as hosts for and examples of key trends in the development of Indian Buddhism.

Gandhara—an area in and around the Peshawar valley (in modern-day Pakistan and Afghanistan)—was a hotspot of ancient Buddhist activity, notable for written texts and arts. Milinda (Menander), a second-century-BCE Indo-Greek ruler in the region, is said to have converted to the Buddhist path. The Indo-Greeks were relatively short-lived in their political power, but their religious and cultural influences lingered. The story of Milinda as a prominent Buddhist convert reverberated for generations, known to many through an early first millennium CE Pali text that was also translated into Chinese: *Milindapanha* (Milinda's Questions).[55] Hellenistic influences were apparent in Gandharan art from the first century CE onward, such as in the folds of cloth that appear draped on smooth-skinned stone figures.[56] One striking sculpture is the starving Siddhartha (Gautama Buddha before his enlightenment), crafted in the Gandhara region between the second and third centuries CE and now in Lahore. Siddhartha's concave stomach and hollow cheeks speak to his failed attempt to gain enlightenment via severe asceticism (chapter 3), while his visible ribs and bulging forehead veins artistically mirror the cloth bunched in his lap (figure 6.4).

Gandharans also composed Buddhist texts, including a series of scrolls—written in a form of Prakrit we call Gandhari and in the Kharoshthi script—that someone stuffed into pots in the early first to the mid-second century CE, probably to discard them. The Gandharan scrolls contain fragments of poetry, narratives, Buddhist religious works, and even a (non-Buddhist) political treatise. These scrolls would not have survived almost anywhere else on the subcontinent, but Gandhara's dry climate and high altitude preserved some of them.[57] Today, they number among the oldest surviving South Asian manuscripts.

Buddhists created images of the Gautama Buddha from the first century CE onward, starting in Mathura in Uttar Pradesh. For the first several hundred years after Gautama's death, he was not represented in corporeal form and instead was invoked, most commonly, via depictions of footprints. At Bodhgaya in Bihar, where Gautama is said to have been enlightened, veneration of a bodhi tree is attested from the third century BCE onward, with statues appearing several hundred years later.[58] Bala's Buddha is one of our earliest statues of Gautama, which stands at a monumental ten foot tall and three feet across. While made in Mathura in the second century CE, it was erected 400 miles away in

Figure 6.4. Starving Siddhartha, second-third century CE, Gandhara, grey schist stone, Lahore, Pakistan.

Sarnath, a major Buddhist pilgrimage site. Once there, it inspired at least one local copy, and comparable images are also known from shortly thereafter.[59] That we call the statue "Bala's Buddha," after its male patron, Bala, is a sign of sexism in modern times. In fact, the statue had two premodern patrons, one of which was Buddhamitra (a woman), described in one inscription as one who "knows the three pitakas (the tripartite Pali canon)."[60] Women were frequent Buddhist donors during the tradition's early centuries.

Stupa veneration was a central Indian Buddhist practice by 300 CE. Stupas are rounded mounds that house human relics—bones or ash, usually—of the Gautama Buddha or other enlightened people. Early Buddhists understood these relics to be alive in a sense. For instance, in *The Lotus Sutra* (*Saddharmapundarikasutra*, a Mahayana work completed in the third century CE), there is a scene where a living buddha emerged from a stupa and revealed that he resides there with Gautama himself.[61] Some scholars date stupas to Ashoka's reign (268–232 BCE), but more substantial material evidence points to them being built during the second and first centuries BCE. Monastic and lay Buddhists venerated stupas, small and large, from northwestern India to Sri Lanka, in open-air contexts (such as at Sanchi) and within caves (such as at Karle, Maharashtra).[62] These two contexts may have had different audiences. In Karle, sixteen rock-cut caves date to the first century CE, including a *chaitya* hall defined by the stupa at its center (figure 6.5). Inscriptions shows a variety of individuals financed the chaitya cave, including Simhadata (a perfumer), Bhayila (a woman), and Sihadhaya (a yavana, probably meaning from the northwest).[63] Still, cave complexes like those at Karle were primarily made for monks and nuns, and entrance to chaitya halls may have been restricted.[64] In contrast, the huge open-air stupa at Sanchi drew both monastic and lay pilgrims during this period and long after. In both cases, Buddhists venerated stupas using items obtained via sea and land trade, such as gems, pearls, and silk.[65]

In addition to obtaining wealth, support, and goods through trade networks, Buddhist monks also used the Silk Roads and sea routes for religious evangelism. Texts within the Pali canon, such as the *Mahavagga*, placed the call to spread the Buddhist dhamma in the mouth of Gautama, instructing his followers:

> Go now, O Bhikkhus, and wander for the gain of the many, out of compassion for the world, for the good, for the gain, and for the welfare of gods and men. Let not two of you go the same way. Preach, O Bhikkhus, the doctrine which is glorious in the beginning, glorious in the middle, glorious in the end, in the spirit and in the letter; proclaim a consummate, perfect, and pure life of holiness. There are beings whose mental eyes are covered by scarcely any dust, but if the doctrine is not preached to them, they cannot attain salvation. They will understand the doctrine.[66]

Figure 6.5. Chaitya hall with stupa at the Karle caves, first century CE, Maharashtra, India.

Not everybody in premodern Asia wanted to hear the Buddhist teaching. For example, the *Mahavamsa* (a fifth-century-CE Sri Lankan chronicle) records opposition in Kashmir, where even mountains were said to have been thrown down to stop Buddhist monks (in vain, the text says).[67] But in the first century CE, Buddhist monks succeeded in one mission that changed the history of Buddhism forever: they spread the dhamma to China.

The adaption and spread of Buddhism within China falls outside of my purview here, but I mention the initial moment of its expansion beyond South Asia for two reasons. One, Buddhism and its material culture were among ancient India's chief exports. Alongside a dynamic set of religious practices, Indian Buddhists also shared manuscript technologies and texts. For instance, the Bamiyan tradition of pothi manuscripts—palm leaves held together by a string between wooden covers—spread via sea to Southeast Asia and via the Silk Roads to Tibet and Central Asia.[68] Regarding texts, *The Lotus Sutra* (mentioned earlier) was one of the most popular Buddhist texts ever written, especially in translations that circulated in Nepal, China, and Japan.[69] The second reason to mention the spread of Buddhism to China is because it serves as crucial background for explaining a later development, namely Chinese Buddhist monks who journeyed to premodern India as religious pilgrims in the mid- to late first millennium CE. These Chinese travelers visited Sanchi, worshipped at Bodhgaya, and searched for Sanskrit and Pali texts. A few pilgrims, such as Faxian and Xuanzang, also left travel accounts that offer substantial details about India in the fifth and seventh century CE, respectively (chapters 7 and 8).

Ramayana and Sanskrit Poetry

South Asians—whether they traveled or not—told stories about journeying far from home in this period, most famously Valmiki's Ramayana, a tale about a prince who traveled south to lands populated by talking monkeys, bears, and demons. Valmiki's Ramayana is the second Sanskrit epic, often paired with Vyasa's Mahabharata (including in premodernity), although the two myths are strikingly different. For one thing, unlike its unwieldly counterpart, the Ramayana can be briefly summarized. In the Treta Yuga, the second of four ages when dharma still stood firm, a nearly perfect man called Rama was born to King Dasharatha in Ayodhya. Rama's wicked stepmother, Kaikeyi, had him exiled to the forest for fourteen years, accompanied by Rama's beautiful wife Sita and his ever-faithful brother Lakshmana. While in the forest, Sita was stolen by the demon king Ravana, who lived on the southern island of Lanka. Rama traveled south, rustling up an army of monkeys and bears along the way, and engaged the demon army, killing Ravana and rescuing Sita. At this point, the fourteen years of exile had elapsed, and so Rama returned to Ayodhya and ascended the throne.

The Ramayana is easily the most famous Indian story ever told and the most generative. The tale was written down in Sanskrit, in a version we now call Valmiki's Ramayana, perhaps in the early centuries CE and thereafter became a bestseller, retold in more mediums and languages than anyone can count.[70] From the beginning, Rama's story was adapted by multiple religious groups, and among our earliest Ramayanas are the Buddhist *Dasaratha Jataka* and the Jain *Paumachariyam*.[71] Hindus, too, wrote (and still write) many new Ramayanas, and two premodern Hindu versions are worth mentioning here because they inform contemporary knowledge of the Ramayana myth: Kampan's twelfth-century Tamil rendering and Tulsidas's sixteenth-century Hindi version.[72] Many modern Indians know the Ramayana as reworked by one of these later authors, even if they have never heard of them by name, and, if that is you, dear reader, be forewarned. There are sharp edges to Valmiki's text, such as Rama's "cruelty" to Sita and Sita's periodic biting criticisms of the men in her life, that often get flattened in later retellings.[73] There are also narrative aspects underdeveloped in Valmiki, like Rama being an incarnation of Vishnu, that became robust in later versions.[74] These days, all Indians have heard the Ramayana, and that familiarity can make it difficult to see what were, when it was first written down, innovations in Valmiki's text as well as later versions, including projecting a geography from eastern and into southern India and claiming to invent poetry.

Rama, prince of Ayodhya, spends most of Valmiki's story far beyond his own northern kingdom, first in the Dandaka Forest and later further south as far as the island called Lanka. It is not clear that Valmiki—or whoever composed the Ramayana and was assigned that nom de plume—imagined his tale as occurring across the entire subcontinent. Many places mentioned in the Ramayana myth—including Ayodhya and Lanka—were likely identified with physical parts of South Asia in later centuries, and the Ramayana's original imagined geography was perhaps more circumscribed. Still, Valmiki was the first Sanskrit author to write in any detail about traveling to lands south of aryavarta, the area of north India defined (in theory) by Vedic practices. Valmiki does not offer a historical account in any sense but, rather, a fantastic fiction of encountering communities he viewed as utterly different and so characterized as monkeys, bears, and demons (*rakshasa*s).[75]

Parts of the story involve Rama foisting his Kshatriya traditions on those who live differently. For example, he slays the monkey Vali in accordance with, as Rama puts it, "my ancestral traditions."[76] As other scholars have noted, the Ramayana tale has in-built tools for othering one's enemies, including a "fully demonized Other" that later Indian kings found useful.[77] Such a perspective should remind us that cross-cultural contact sometimes prompted premodern people to condemn those they perceived to be different, a trend we have seen before in Brahminical texts and will encounter even more strongly in the next chapter.

The Ramayana claims to be the first Sanskrit poem (*adikavya*) in a story early in the text. In brief, the sage Valmiki saw a tribal Nishada shoot one of a pair of mating love birds (*krauncha* birds) and, out of grief, cursed the hunter in what has been said, ever since, to be the first lines of Sanskrit poetry (see excerpt). This story, like tales in the Mahabharata, uses a tribal person as a foil for elaborating upper-caste values (chapter 5). Indeed, the Ramayana is unapologetic about its commitment to upper-caste privilege throughout its narrative that showcases Rama as the ideal Kshatriya king. However, in the realm of poetry, Valmiki's Ramayana opened a Pandora's box that upper-caste Hindus never exclusively controlled going forward: classical Sanskrit literature.

Creation of Poetry: Excerpt from Valmiki's Sanskrit Ramayana, ca. 200 CE

Nearby, the sage Valmiki saw a tight-knit pair
of sweetly singing love birds flitting about.
But, as he watched, an evil, hateful Nishada
killed the male of that pair.
Having seen him fallen, covered with blood and writhing on the ground,
his wife cried out in sorrow.
The righteous sage also saw the bird struck down thus by the Nishada,
and he was filled with sorrow.
Knowing such sorrow, the Brahmin Valmiki thought, "this is wrong."
Hearing the cry of the female love bird, he said:
    Nishada! Since you have killed one of this pair of love birds,
    while they were making love, may you also not live for long!
As he was speaking and watching, the thought rose in his heart:
"Overcome with grief for this bird, what have I said?"
That learned, wise bull among sages thought about it,
and he decided. He said to his student:
"Metered, with even syllables, and appropriate for being sung,
let what I said overcome by pain (*shoka*) be called poetry (*shloka*) and nothing else."
Even as the sage spoke, the student was delighted to memorize his brilliant speech.
His teacher was pleased.[78]

Conclusion: Sanskrit Goes Viral

From the second century CE onward, people began to use Sanskrit—previously confined to the Vedas, epics, and grammar—to write a huge range of materials, including philosophy, scientific treatises, stories, poetry, satire, political propaganda, and far more. As Anne Monius put it, the two epics Mahabharata and Ramayana are "the tip of a very large iceberg" of Sanskrit narrative texts that were written between the second and eighteenth centuries CE.[79] In the end, more texts were written in Sanskrit than possibly any other premodern language on earth, and millions of handwritten manuscripts of premodern Sanskrit texts survive today.[80]

Critically, Hindus, Jains, and Buddhists all jumped on the Sanskrit literary bandwagon. Jains and Buddhists still wrote in Prakrits, but they also used Sanskrit going forward, liberating this language from its earlier exclusive relationship with Vedic traditions and making it one of the most robust mediums of written expression in the premodern world.[81] In fact, the author of the first major surviving Sanskrit poems (*mahakavyas*) after Valmiki was Ashvaghosa, a Buddhist at the Kushan court in the second century CE. Ashvaghosa wrote two lengthy poems in beautifully crafted Sanskrit, both about Buddhist figures.[82] Political leaders, too, shifted over to Sanskrit. The Satavahanas, who ruled over parts of central and southern India between the first century BCE and the early third century CE, were perhaps the last large-scale kingdom to predominantly use Prakrit, inaugurated by the Mauryan emperor Ashoka as a political medium.[83] Sanskrit remained a contested language in some circles, and, in the next chapter, we encounter Brahmin men who tried to circumscribe its use. But, just like ancient trade routes, the Sanskrit tradition could not be contained. Sanskrit was used widely and robustly by many South Asian communities in the coming centuries.

Further Reading

Indian Ocean trade is more thoroughly studied from a Western versus an Indian perspective, and I drew on scholars such as Matthew Cobb and Grant Parker even while unapologetically inverting their gaze to center India. I relied on Ingo Strauch on Socotra and Peter Francis on beads. Robert and Sally Goldman are the leading translators of the Valmiki Ramayana, and I found historical insights regarding this myth in scholarship by Richard Davis and Sheldon Pollock (who is also excellent on Sanskrit going viral). On material evidence and Buddhism, works by Frederick Asher and Gregory Schopen were informative.

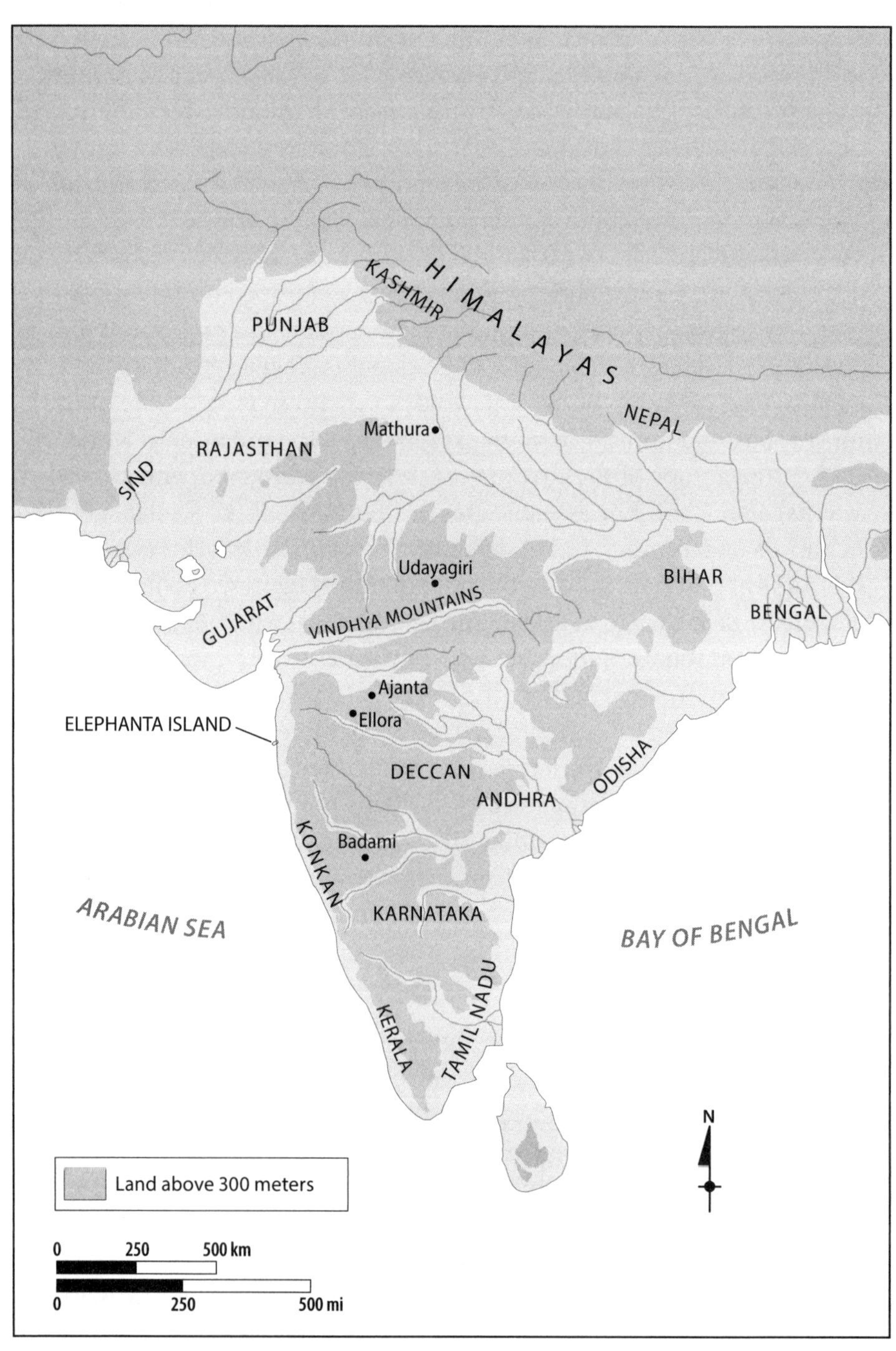

Regional areas in early India, ca. fifth century CE.

7

Inequality, Pleasure, and Power in Early India

The same fire that burns in an outcaste's home
also blazes on sacrificial grounds.
Do not spurn a man
just because of his low circumstances.

–*Sattasai*, second–fifth century CE (Prakrit)[1]

During the early to mid-first millennium CE, life got worse for many Indians—especially women and lower classes—as inequality became further systematized and entrenched. For a small sliver of high society, fortunes skyrocketed as poetry and the arts flourished. The two trends are connected. The extraction of wealth from the many financed the pleasure activities of the few. Elites, in turn, sometimes wrote about kinds of subjugation, such as patriarchy and the caste system. Most modern people readily accept that premodernity involved horrible things, but harder to grasp is the inversion of values as compared to the present day. Specifically, some premodern upper-caste men championed as virtues what most today see as vices: radical inequality and oppression. Here I present these ideas unvarnished as I trace the growth of larger trends in the early to mid-first millennium CE, including sectarian Hindu practices, Brahminical identity, multiple literary traditions, and the always intertwined phenomena of power and oppression.

Sectarian Hinduism and Temples

Many non-Vedic aspects of Hindu traditions began or were solidified during the first millennium CE,[2] including big shifts in the most emphasized gods and stories. Some of the most important Vedic deities—such as Indra, Varuna, and Soma—migrated to the periphery of Hindu practices. Meanwhile, the Goddess (often as Durga), Vishnu, and Shiva gained popularity during the first millennium. Some scholars describe this shift—along with the related developments of icon-based worship and temples—as "sectarian Hinduism." Indeed, followers of these ascendent deities often competed with one another, formulating identities not as Hindus (a word not yet used in India) but rather as, respectively, Shaktas (worshippers of the Goddess), Vaishnavas (worshippers of Vishnu), and Shaivas (worshippers of Shiva).

Durga, Vishnu, and Shiva appear in the epics (Mahabharata and Ramayana) and are each the subject of discrete *purana*s, a new genre of Sanskrit texts in the first millennium CE that reoriented Hindu worship around specific deities. The *Vishnupurana* focuses on myths of Vishnu, the *Devimahatmya* on the Goddess, and so forth.[3] The mythology of these gods blossomed as we find, for the first time, the story told of the goddess Durga slaying Mahisha, the buffalo demon.[4] Shiva's sexual prowess became legendary.[5] Vishnu became known for reincarnating himself in animal and human forms to save the world, including as Krishna and Rama in the respective epics. Notably, the number and lineup of Vishnu's incarnations fluctuated for centuries (early on, the god was said to have six avatars), and even today one sees variations on the standard number of ten.[6] Fluidity and plurality proved enduring features of premodern Hindu stories.

Sectarian Hinduism included the rise of icon-based worship within temples, a development that further entrenched Brahminical authority. This constituted a dramatic shift as compared to Vedic rituals, which were conducted outdoors and involved no icons. We remain in the dark about what, exactly, inspired Brahmins to begin venerating icons in permanent structures. As discussed, Buddhism and Jainism also emphasized reverence of physical sites and images from the last centuries BCE onward (chapter 6), and so one might see first-millennium Brahmins as participating in a wider set of Indian religious innovations. In fact, many early temple sites feature Hindu and Jain spaces side by side, such as the caves at Badami (sixth century CE) and Ellora, which also includes

Figure 7.1. Varaha (Vishnu's boar incarnation) panel at the Udayagiri Caves associated with the Gupta Dynasty, fourth–fifth century CE, Vidisha, India.

Buddhist sites (seventh–eighth century CE). Hindu temples also stood apart at times. For instance, Elephanta Island, off the coast near modern-day Bombay/Mumbai, boasts a series of rock-cut temples from the mid- to late first millennium CE with images of Shiva marrying, playing dice with Parvati, and letting the heavenly Ganges River flow through his hair to dilute its power so that it did not destroy the earth.[7]

Amid such lovely imagery were power dynamics. Brahmin priests mediated the access of worshippers to the divine, deriving power from controlling temples and positioning themselves as critical caretakers of icons. As Michael Willis has put it: "The complex theology of early Hinduism and its formal architecture did not emerge in a subconscious or organic fashion from some kind of socioreligious plasma. It was rather created and made possible by the priesthood."[8]

Inside temples, two major kinds of images represented—and continue today to represent—Hindu deities: iconic and aniconic. A stunning iconic image from the mid-first millennium CE is Udayagiri's large tableau of Vishnu as the boar-headed Varaha, an incarnation who rescued the earth from being submerged in the ocean by a demon (figure 7.1). In its heyday, water covered the ground beneath this carving, giving the

Figure 7.2. Shiva linga with one face, ca. 500 CE, northern or central India, pink sandstone.

impression of Varaha emerging from the sea's depths.[9] The Gupta kingdom (ca. 305–550 CE), discussed in more detail below, patronized Udayagiri, and so the caves doubled as religious sites and political propaganda, a common overlap in Hindu temples during later periods as well.

Aniconic Hindu images also thrived during the first millennium, and the Shiva linga deserves special attention owing to its popularity. A Shiva linga is a cylindrical mound, typically in a rounded base, that, in its form, parallels an erect phallus (the literal meaning of "linga") in honor of Shiva's creative power. Some Shiva lingas show the god's face (figure 7.2), although more are smooth.[10] To understand why Shiva is represented by a phallic cylindrical mound—as opposed to a ball, cube, triangle, or any other shape—we must invoke the god's sexual prowess, which is widely celebrated in Hindu mythology of this period. This has already arisen in this chapter (also, chapter 5), and here is another story, found in purana texts—Once time, Shiva's lovemaking with his wife Parvati was so protracted and intense that it threatened the cosmos. The gods wanted to intervene but feared the repercussions of seeing Parvati naked and compromising Shiva's enjoyment. Finally, they compelled Agni to interrupt the coupling pair, which saved the world but resulted in Shiva cursing Agni.[11]

Shiva is also a great ascetic, and the pairing of his virility and restraint, seeming contradictions, undergirds Hindu conceptions of Shiva's awesome power. Similarly, Shiva is also sometimes represented, combined with his consort Parvati, in an *ardhanarishvara* form, as half man and half woman (figure 7.3). Some modern people are a bit priggish about sex. But Shiva's sexuality was idealized, not shunned, in premodern Hindu thought. Accordingly, texts like the *Kurmapurana* (sixth–eighth century CE) contain stories that openly explain Shiva's sexual behavior that led to his representation via the linga.[12] The Gudimallam Lingam—one of our earliest lingas (maybe first century BCE)—has a notably phallic form.[13] Shiva lingas are often set in a yoni (literally, "vagina") base, a combination that invokes procreative energy.

Temple-based Hindu worship practices were and are diverse—depending on the region, god, and temple—and, for the first millennium CE, we often know more about the priests than the laity. As mentioned, much temple-based worship was mediated by Brahmins whose position enabled them to collect wealth from lay practitioners and royal patrons. In this, Brahmins followed in the footsteps of their Buddhist counterparts, whose monasteries sometimes experienced significant cashflow (chapter 6). Accordingly, Hindu temples were economic—in addition to religious and political—institutions in premodern India.[14] In terms of religious practices, new methods of Hindu worship (*puja*) emerged that focused on making offerings to a specific god believed to inhabit a physical icon.[15] But who were the worshippers? We are unclear about who, exactly, constituted the Hindu laity in the first millennium CE. But we do know that Brahmins simultaneously emphasized the need to ostracize (rather than include) lower castes and those without caste, while spreading their social hierarchy through migration, especially south.

Figure 7.3. Androgynous form of Shiva and Parvati (*ardhanarishvara*), eleventh century CE, Rajasthan, India, black schist stone.

By 300 CE, Brahmins imagined aryavarta—the land where Brahmins lived—to stretch west to east, from the Arabian Sea to the Bay of Bengal, but conceded that it did not permeate south of the Vindhya Mountains.[16] At the time, south Indian communities worshipped a panoply of their own deities. Old Tamil poetry records the names of some of these non-Vedic gods, the most well known of which is Murugan (Murukan), a handsome young warrior and lover.[17] During the first millennium CE, Brahmin communities migrated to southern India, such as the Purvashikha Brahmins who came to Tamil Nadu (some later moved to Kerala).[18] As Brahmins interacted with local communities (including some southern Indians newly identifying as Brahmin), north Indian and Dravidian deities became fused. Murugan, for instance, became associated with Karttikeya (also known as Skanda and Kumara), the god of war, and, in another ca. first millennium CE innovation, Shiva's son.[19] Still, regional differences remained robust. Karttikeya was a minor god in northern India and declined in prominence further, becoming "little more than a footnote" by 600 CE within the booming worship of Shiva.[20] In contrast, Murugan remains popular today as a Hindu god in the southern subcontinent.

Inequality as Dharma

Brahmins further demarcated their community in this period, in part by defining dharma. "Dharma" is a complicated term that first appeared in the Rig Veda but became a central Hindu concept later.[21] Some of its more common translations are law, virtue, duty, correct conduct, morality, and religion. Patrick Olivelle put it well when he defined dharma as "doing good and being good."[22] But how do we know what is good? Premodern Brahmins answered that question, in large part, through *dharmashastra* texts (ideal-based legal treatises) from the third century BCE onward. By far the most famous, quoted, and commented on dharmashastra text—both in premodernity and in our times—is Manu's second-century-CE *Manusmriti* (also known as *Manavadharmashastra*).[23] In recovering Manu's influential vision of dharma, it is wise to remember that one man's virtue is another man's vice (we will get into Manu's dismal view of women shortly). Indeed, texts like the *Manusmriti* have been described as "propaganda for the Brahmanical cosmopolitan world order."[24] I present, without soft-pedaling, the irreparable inequality that Manu and many Brahmin patriarchs following him upheld as the basis for their desired social system.

Manu argued that people were created unequal with specific obligations (dharma) as per their caste, gender, and—for upper-caste men specifically—life stage. He presents this as an ideal wherein an individual's *svadharma* (caste duty), *svakarman* (caste-determined occupation), and *svabhava* (inborn nature) are harmonious.[25] Critically, nothing was universal for Manu. Caste and gender determined distinct and uneven rules for social groups.[26] Manu even prescribed different punishments for transgressions depending on the caste of the offender and offended. For example, regarding verbal assault (*vakparushya*), he said: "For assailing a Brahmin, a Kshatriya ought to be fined 100, and a Vaishya 150 or 200; but a Shudra ought to suffer corporal punishment."[27]

As is often the case in systems of inequality, Manu displayed coarse disdain for those at the pyramid's bottom. He elaborates on the possible punishments for a Shudra who maligns a Brahmin by alluding to the Rig Vedic poem on the origins of the varna system (quoted in chapter 2): "If a Shudra hurls grossly abusive words at high-caste men, his tongue shall be cut off, for he originated from the lowest part. If he invokes their names and castes with disdain, a red-hot iron nail ten fingers long should be driven into his mouth. If he arrogantly gives instruction on the Law to Brahmins, the king should pour hot oil into his mouth and ears."[28] If the roles are reversed and a Brahmin abuses a Shudra, Manu says that a small fine suffices as a penalty.[29]

Manu's treatise and other dharmashastra works circulated throughout the first millennium CE among upper-caste communities who increasingly adhered to endogamy (marrying within one's social class), a foundational feature of the caste system. In this, controlling female sexuality was critical to maintaining caste purity, and here I advise the reader to steel herself for some severe views. The *Vasishtha Dharmasutra* (first century BCE) calls for public castigation of adulterous women. The woman is to be "shaved, smeared with ghee, and led naked along the highway on a donkey, whose color is determined by the varna of her lover, e.g., a black one when he is a shudra."[30] "Varna" also means "color," and the colorism of the caste system dates back two millennia, at least. Writing in the second century BCE, Patanjali listed being "fair-complexioned" among the qualities of a Brahmin.[31] Writing about 500 years later, Yajnavalkya (fourth–fifth century CE; different than the

Upanishadic Yajnavalkya) recommended keeping a woman who is unfaithful to her husband on a near starvation diet, "compelled to dwell deprived of any rights, wearing dirty clothes, living on just morsels of food, scorned, and sleeping on the ground."[32] This penalty may appear even darker to modern eyes once one realizes that Yajnavalkya does not specify if the woman's unfaithfulness was by choice or force.

For his part, Manu is the best spokesperson for his views on controlling women. He wrote: "Even in their own homes, a female—whether she is a child, a young woman, or an old lady—should never carry out any task independently. As a child, she must remain under her father's control; as a young woman, under her husband's; and when her husband is dead, under her sons'. She must never seek to live independently. She must never want to separate herself from her father, husband, or sons; for by separating herself from them, a woman brings disgrace on both families."[33] Manu and other like-minded Brahmin men invoked a theory of karma to justify policing caste and gender boundaries as well as the variable levels of human worth they assigned to members of this hierarchy.

As early as the Upanishads, karma (literally, "action") was expanded from its Vedic meaning of ritual activity to cover all human acts along with their associated positive or negative consequences. Karmic consequences were typically thought to manifest in one's circumstances in future rebirths, including by possibly spending time in heaven or hell (both are which were well-established Hindu concepts by this point in history).[34] Hindu thinkers of the first millennium CE posited that karmic debt could be transferred at times but never vacated in the cycle of rebirth (samsara). For example, a story in the *Markandeya Purana* (ca. sixth century CE) explains:

> Once, when his wife named Fatso had been in her fertile season, King Vipashchit did not sleep with her, as it was his duty to do, but slept instead with his other, beautiful wife, Kaikeyi. He went to hell briefly to expiate this one sin, but when he was about to leave for heaven, the people in hell begged him to stay, since the wind that touched his body dispelled their pain. "People cannot obtain in heaven or in the world of Brahma," said Vipashchit, "such happiness as arises from giving release (nirvana) to suffering creatures." And he refused to leave until Indra agreed

> to let the king's good deeds (karma) be used to release those people of evil karma from their torments in hell—though they all went from there immediately to another womb that was determined by the fruits of their own karma.[35]

Dharmashastra works posit a causal connection between karma and caste, arguing that everyone deserves their caste status as the "fruits of actions" (*karmanam phalonirvritti*).[36] Manu, for example, offers an extensive account of different rebirth scenarios ranked according to the caste pyramid.[37]

The Brahminical investment in caste also involved new social practices designed to set apart the Brahminical community and exclude others. Many Brahmins embraced dietary restrictions, such as forgoing alcohol and meat (in contrast, recall that Vedic-era Brahmins consumed beef ritually; see chapter 2). The idea of four life stages (*ashramas*) emerged as an ideal, positing that a Brahmin man should be, in order, a celibate student, householder, partially renouncing forest-dweller, and full renunciant (respectively, *brahmacharin*, *grihastha*, *vanaprastha*, and *sannyasi* or *sanyasi*).[38] The oft-repeated Sanskrit phrase *varnashrama-dharma* clubs together "behavior according to one's caste and life stage" as a Brahminical ideal. Brahmins admitted that reality often diverged from theory, and so dharmashastra works covered *varnasamskara* (mixing across caste lines) by elaborating the caste implications for the resulting progeny.[39] Still, Brahmins and other upper castes often enforced purity boundaries, which gave birth to a harsh practice first attested in the mid-first millennium CE and that persists in some South Asian communities today: untouchability.

One of premodern India's social taboos was human contact between upper castes and those deemed as having lesser worth. Untouchability as a premodern Hindu practice had two major forms: temporary (e.g., menstruating women) and permanent (e.g., those born lower caste or outside the caste system, such as Chandalas). Both kinds were oppressive, and the latter resulted in segregated living. Faxian, a Chinese Buddhist who traveled to India in the early 400s CE, wrote based on his observations around Mathura:

> Throughout the whole country, the people do not kill any living creature, nor drink intoxicating liquor, nor eat onions or garlic.

> The only exception is that of the Chandalas. The meaning of Chandala is "evil people," and they live apart from others. When they enter the gate of a city or a marketplace, they strike a piece of wood to make themselves known, so that men know and avoid them, and do not come into contact with them. In that country, they do not keep pigs or fowl and do not sell live cattle. In the markets there are no butchers' shops and no dealers in intoxicating drink. In buying and selling commodities they use cowries. Only the Chandalas are fishermen and hunters and sell flesh meat.[40]

Xuanzhang, another Chinese Buddhist, visited India in the seventh century CE and confirmed similar practices of segregation and untouchability.[41] We have no records on the matter from marginalized communities in ancient India, as much as I long to hear their perspectives on this oppression.

Life's Finer Things

Premodern Indian elites also wrote about pleasant things, such as *kama* (sensual pleasure), which emerged as an ideal in high society and literatures in multiple South Asian languages during the early to mid-first millennium CE. Kama included sex, as well as eating well, dressing nicely, ornamenting one's body, spending time in nice buildings, sporting high-end perfumes, reading beautiful poetry, and enjoying classy entertainment (see excerpt).[42] The most famous Sanskrit text on pleasure is Vatsyayana's *Kamasutra* (ca. late third century CE). Vatsyayana's treatise includes a chapter on sexual positions for which it enjoys popular infamy today, on display, for example, in the Indian-made Kamasutra brand of condoms.[43] The *Kamasutra*'s seven books also feature advice on wooing another man's wife, handling courtesans, and winning over a virgin. The work is written from a male perspective, although Vatsyayana says that knowledge of the art of love will help a wife "keep her husband in her power even if he has a thousand women in his harem."[44] Some of the sections on courtesans—such as how to bleed a smitten man dry of money—can be read either as warnings to men or tips for women.

Ideal Day for the Man-about-Town, Excerpt from Vatsyayana's *Kamasutra* (Sanskrit), ca. Late Third Century CE

He gets up in the morning, relieves himself, cleans his teeth, applies fragrant oils in small quantities, as well as incense, garlands, beeswax and red lac, looks at his face in a mirror, takes some mouthwash and betel, and attends to the things that need to be done. He bathes every day, has his limbs rubbed with oil every second day, a foam bath every third day, his face shaved every fourth day, and his body hair removed every fifth or tenth day. All of this is done without fail. And he continually cleans the sweat from his armpits. In the morning and afternoon he eats; "In the evening, too," says Charayana. After eating, he passes the time teaching his parrots and mynah birds to speak; goes to quail-fights, cock-fights, and ram-fights; engages in various arts and games; and passes the time with his libertine, pander, and clown. And he takes a nap. In the late afternoon, he gets dressed up and goes to salons to amuse himself.

And in the evening, there is music and singing. After that, on the bed in a bedroom carefully decorated and perfumed by sweet-smelling incense, he and his friends await the women who are slipping out for a rendezvous with them. He sends female messengers for them or goes to get them himself. And when the women arrive, he and his friends greet them with gentle conversation and courtesies that charm the mind and heart. If rain has soaked the clothing of women who have slipped out for a rendezvous in bad weather, he changes their clothes himself, or gets some of his friends to serve them. That is what he does by day and night.[45]

While its topic may be eye-catching, Vatsyayana's *Kamasutra* is emblematic of Sanskrit technical treatises more broadly in using cataloging as a means of expounding knowledge. Vatsyayana gives numerous sets of lists, including types of kisses, ways of scratching, varieties of erotic biting, and more. Sanskrit works on both *artha* (power and wealth) and dharma—which combined with kama make for the Brahminical *purushartha* (aims of life)—often similarly privilege enumeration as a means of knowledge.[46] In the case of kama, not all premoderns agreed that this methodology produced mastery of life's finer things. As a Prakrit poet argued:

Shame on those who cannot appreciate
this ambrosial Prakrit poetry
but pore instead
over treatises on love.[47]

Sanskrit thinkers did not admit defeat, however. Yashodhara's thirteenth-century commentary on the *Kamasutra* retorted to such sentiments by arguing that it is important to know things, correctly and thoroughly: "You can, of course, learn about pleasure from other teachings, just as you can read meaning into a hole shaped like a letter of the alphabet that a bookworm has eaten out of a page, but you do not understand what you should do and what you should not do."[48] Then again, doing what is forbidden is often alluring, an aspect of eroticism explored throughout the first millennium CE in Prakrit poetry.

The Prakrit *Sattasai* (Seven Centuries) offers a compelling case study in how poetry can play on transgressing social and sexual taboos. The work was attributed to Hala (a Satavahana king) and collected in the Deccan between the second and fifth centuries CE. Some *Sattasai* verses feature men calling their wives by their lovers' names, thus provoking domestic wrath. Other verses celebrate having sex with a woman on her period, which is sexy precisely because it is verboten:

Though people condemn it,
though it is highly inauspicious
and considered most improper,
the sight of a woman during her period
fills the heart with heavenly bliss.[49]

Like authors across languages in premodern South Asia, the *Sattasai* poets celebrated the female form, with lines such as:

Who is not captivated by a woman's breasts,
that, like a good poem,
are a pleasure to grasp,
are weighty, compact, and nicely ornamented?[50]

Prakrits and Sanskrit were often treated as complementary languages in premodern South Asian literature, appearing in plays to code the speech of different characters, for example. The most famous Prakrit work today is one that did not survive (if it was ever real): the *Brihatkatha* (Vast

Story) allegedly written in the lost language of Paishachi.[51] Indeed, Prakrits lost ground over time in premodern India to Sanskrit, a language whose very name means "refined" and came to embody an alluring cultural style.[52]

Sanskrit poetry flourished from the second century into the eighteenth century CE with Kalidasa (fourth–fifth century) being among the most celebrated Sanskrit poets and playwrights. Kalidasa retold mythological stories about Shakuntala, Urvashi (a celestial apsara), and Rama and his family.[53] Other works by Kalidasa unfold against historical backgrounds, such as *Malavikagnimitra* (Malavika and Agnimitra) set during the Shunga dynasty in the second century BCE.[54] Kalidasa also invented tales, such as *Meghaduta* (Cloud Messenger) about a yaksha (semi-divine tree spirit who often serves the god Kubera) who, slightly mad with longing for his faraway wife, instructed a cloud to deliver a message to her and in so doing lushly described parts of the subcontinent.[55] All three of Kalidasa's approaches—retelling old stories, using historical settings, and inventing new tales—recurred in Sanskrit literature for more than a millennium. One drama worth mentioning here given its historical backdrop is Vishakhadatta's *Mudrarakshasa* (Rakshasa's Ring, ca. sixth century CE) that narrates events set around 800 years earlier during Chandragupta Maurya's life (third century BCE).[56]

Much about Sanskrit literature is extraordinary, including the immense amount of beautiful poetry and its robust dramaturgical tradition. Sanskrit authors used carefully crafted language to elicit *rasa*s (aesthetic emotions), such as erotic love (*shringara*), tragedy (*karuna*), and heroism (*vira*).[57] Some of this poetry reads well across time, such as Amaru (first millennium CE) on pining for one's lover:

> She is in the house, she is everywhere.
> She is behind me, she is in front.
> She is inside in bed, she is outside on every road,
> when I am tortured by her absence.
> I am going out of my mind!
> The whole world is nothing to me,
> but she, she, she, she, she, she—
> what chatter of nondualism is this?[58]

Sanskrit poetry also reflected life's harshness for many in early India. Consider, for example, these lines by Bhartrhari (fourth–fifth century CE) on how life kicks you when you're down:

> A bald man, his forehead scorched by the sun's rays,
> hurries to a shady spot under a tree.
> But there a large piece of fruit falls and loudly cracks his head.
> Wherever those cursed by fate go, misfortunes follow.[59]

Other times, Sanskrit poets attested to their specific social norms. For example, an interlude in Kalidasa's *Shakuntala* features a king who held a deceased merchant's wealth in trust for the man's unborn son since the merchant's wives—as women—could not inherit property.[60] Kalidasa declined to elaborate on how the merchant's wives felt about this or how they fared as impoverished widows.

Parallel to Prakrit and Sanskrit, Tamil was the third great premodern literary tradition of South Asia. Our oldest Tamil texts are a corpus of ten poetic narratives and eight anthologies known collectively as Sangam literature.[61] Tamil Sangam literature is broadly devoted to love, politics, and warrior culture, which comes out in these lines by the female poet Kakkaipatiniyar Naccellaiyar:

> Many said,
> "That old woman, the one whose veins show
> on her weak, dry arms where the flesh is hanging,
> whose stomach is flat as a lotus leaf,
> has a son who lost his nerve in battle and fled."
> At that, she grew enraged and she said,
> "If he has run away in the thick of battle,
> I will cut off these breasts from which he sucked,"
> and, sword in hand, she turned over fallen corpses,
> groping her way on the red field.
> Then she saw her son lying there in pieces,
> and she rejoiced more than the day she bore him.[62]

Tamil Sangam poetry was designed to appear timeless, which makes for great literature and, simultaneously, a historian's nightmare regarding dating. Current academic opinion considers Sangam literature to have been composed between the second and eighth centuries CE, with widespread agreement that it was anthologized toward the end of this date range.[63] Maybe 10 percent of Sangam poets are Brahmins, postdating the migrations mentioned earlier.[64] But much Sangam literature evinces no awareness of Brahminical culture and may predate the arrival (or at least the extensive influence) of Brahmins in southern India. Consider, for example, the *Cilappatikaram* (Tale of an anklet), attributed to Prince Ilankovatikal who appears in the story as a Jain.[65] This tale concerns a woman who channels her rage as a wrongful widow into becoming a ferocious goddess. At the end of the story, she is memorialized as Orraimulaicci (Goddess with one breast), still worshipped today at Kodungallur along Kerala's Malabar coast (southwestern coast).[66] While premodern Indian poetry—in Sanskrit, Prakrit, and Tamil—sometimes transcends time and space, each was produced in specific political and social contexts to which I now turn.

Power and Propaganda

Statecraft in premodern India existed in practice and theory, and we should not confuse the two. In reality, a smorgasbord of kingdoms ruled parts of the Indian subcontinent during the early to mid-first millennium CE, of which the Pallavas are most well known in the south, the Vakatakas in the Deccan, and the Guptas in the north. In propaganda, specific rulers often projected their territory across impossibly vast areas and as divinely ordained. In accessing political realities and circulating propaganda of the period, the Gupta kings and their self-projections, respectively, offer useful case studies.

Between around 305 and 550 CE, Gupta kings held fragmented, limited power within a landlocked kingdom centered in the Gangetic heartland. We lack even a clear demarcation of Gupta regnal years, but the kingdom reached its height during the reigns of Samudragupta (r. ca. 335–375) and Chandragupta II (r. ca. 375–415).[67] The Guptas engaged in standard violent activities for premodern Indian sovereigns, such as fighting internally for succession and against neighboring kingdoms for territory, including the Kshatrapas to the west, Shakas to the north, and Vakatakas to the south.[68] Gupta rulers practiced polygamy, amassing substantial harems since they used marriages to solidify political alliances.[69] Most notably, Chandragupta I (r. ca. 320–335 or 350) elevated his lineage's social prestige by marrying a Licchavi princess from one of the old oligarchies in Nepal. The Guptas lost power throughout the fifth century due to Hun incursions from the north. Historians have often taken liberties with Gupta history, extrapolating from meagre inscriptional evidence to make sweeping generalizations.[70] I think we stand on firmer ground in focusing on how the Guptas projected themselves as Vishnu-worshipping kings and incredible conquerors.

The Guptas left behind significant material evidence of their agenda to present themselves as Vaishnava rulers. As mentioned, the Guptas patronized the Udayagiri caves, where they advertised themselves as Vishnu devotees. Gupta gold coins sometimes featured Lakshmi, Vishnu's wife and the goddess of wealth. Each Hindu god has an animal that they ride, and Garuda—Vishnu's eagle mount—was the Gupta lineage emblem.[71] In part, the Guptas partook of this period's burgeoning sectarian Hinduism, but simultaneously they also, as one scholar has put it, made a "conservative, conscious effort to restore the customs of the Vedic past."[72] For example, the Guptas (along with many other premodern Indian rulers) claimed to have performed the horse sacrifice, known as ashvamedha. We lack evidence to adjudicate if the Guptas conducted the ashvamedha rite or merely said they did. The Guptas were nearly as far removed in time from the Vedic period as we are from Gupta rule, and their claims of participating in a Vedic past were a project of imaginative recovery, not continuity.

The Guptas also tried to connect themselves to a specific political past, proposing links with the Maurya Empire (third century BCE) that had ruled across a far larger area. Two Gupta kings adopted the name of the Mauryan founder Chandragupta (a point that has confused history students ever since).[73] Sanskrit texts produced under Gupta patronage often cited Kautilya's *Arthashastra*, a treatise on statecraft often compared to Machiavelli's *The Prince*.[74] The *Arthashastra* was first composed in the first–second century CE and was substantially redacted in maybe the third century CE.[75] Likely the Guptas invented, or at least promoted, the (historically false) idea that its author was a Mauryan state advisor named Chanakya.[76] While the *Arthashastra* was popular in the Gupta kingdom, it was subsequently forgotten, being little read or commented on after the ninth century CE. The work barely survived into modernity in a handful of manuscripts.[77] Its rediscovery in modern times helps us better understand ancient India, although ongoing repetition of Gupta-era political ideas—such as misattributing the *Arthashastra* to a Mauryan court author—cuts against accurate recovery of the Indian past.

The Ashokan pillar inscription of Samudragupta (r. ca. 335–375) is an astonishing piece of premodern propaganda concerning territorial Hindu kingship. In the inscription, stretching over more than thirty lines, the poet Harishena praises Samudragupta for his Sanskrit learning and military dominance over other kings, while using Hindu religious imagery.[78] Much of this is fiction, such as the long list of kings that Samudragupta allegedly conquered, stretching from Nepal to Sri Lanka (as noted, the Gupta kingdom was territorially much more restricted). But, as Sheldon Pollock has argued, Samudragupta's claim to a "conquest of all the earth" (*sarvaprithivivijaya*) "exhausts the domain where the extension of a particular kind of political power has meaning."[79] Notably, however, the Guptas did not project political dominance beyond the subcontinent. Frederick Asher has described this as a "more insular world view" in contrast to what "might be expected from a south Indian contemporary."[80] Still, the idea of universal kingship—even if the universe was South Asia—had legs and recurred throughout premodernity in political inscriptions and poetry, including in Kalidasa's *Raghuvamsha* (Raghu's lineage).[81] Also popular was using Hindu religious imagery to proclaim political power, such as in these lines that invoke the materiality of the column on which they are engraved:

> This column is like an upraised arm of the earth pointing out the way for Samudragupta's fame. For having pervaded the whole world by the great success obtained from his conquest of all the earth, it now has acquired a graceful, easy step for going hence to the abode of the Lord of the Thirty Gods.

> By his generosity, military prowess, tranquility, and command of the shastras
> his glory mounts on high, up and up, by this path and that,
> and purifies the three worlds like the white water of the Ganga rushing down
> when released from the matted locks of Shiva, Lord of Beasts, that hold it in check.[82]

In a similar vein, Samudragupta's successor, Chandragupta II, built up the Vikramaditya legend about India's mythical first sovereign, and even adopted his name as a title.[83]

Turning back to reality, ancient Indian kings, including the Guptas, continued to patronize ecumenically. The Guptas supported Nalanda, a Buddhist monastery (vihara) in Bihar that became famous as far away as China as a center for studying philosophy and other subjects.[84] Close to Udayagiri, a Gupta official financed three statues of Jain teachers (Tirthankaras).[85] More spectacularly, the Vakatakas in the Deccan sponsored rock-cut Buddhist caves at Ajanta with stunning carvings and wall paintings. Today, the Ajanta caves attract substantial tourist traffic as a UNESCO world heritage site. In one cave, visitors encounter a large statue of the Gautama Buddha lying down and surrounded by the faithful at his parinibbana (the final enlightenment at death). The paintings, too, depict Buddhist imagery as well as political figures, including a Sasanian emissary from Persia.

Beautiful art notwithstanding, some sources capture life's grimness for many premodern Indians. For example, a Jain-authored Prakrit text offers a dystopian view of the Gupta kingdom, wherein Jains and other non-Hindu communities were taxed, imprisoned, exiled, and destroyed by a Hindu goddess incarnated as a stone cow.[86] As Paul Dundas has noted, this Jain work borrows from apocalyptic tropes in the Mahabharata and *Vishnupurana*.[87] More concrete evidence attests that forced labor was part of the landscape of northern, central, and southern India in this period. Notably, many kings gifted land to Brahmin communities, which sometimes came with lower-caste farmers who were compelled to work the soil.[88] Scholarship abounds on these tax-free land grants (the granted villages are often called *brahmadeya*s or *agrahara*s), but far more infrequent are mentions of the accompanying bonded labor. It is a shameful testament to modern biases that so many have focused on the few elites that benefited from these land grants, often without bothering to acknowledge the coercion of laborers that increased their value.

Many women underwent a decline in social status during the mid-first millennium CE. There was no formal education for women who, like Shudras, were forbidden from hearing the Vedas. Marriage appears to have been often decided by men without input from women.[89] Even royal women were traded in political bargains, such as the Gupta princess Prabhavatigupta who was married into the Vakataka family.[90] One of our earliest material records of *sati* (widow burning) is a 510 CE memorial stone in Eran in modern-day Madhya Pradesh. An inscription on the stone attests that a local chief named Goparaja died and was cremated along with his, until she entered the fire, still-living wife.[91] Sati is sometimes depicted as a woman's choice in premodern Indian texts, but historically we have little way of determining such agency.[92] A *Sattasai* verse reminds us that public emotions were sometimes disingenuous:

> The false woman bewailed her dead husband
> with such choking sobs
> that even her lover was afraid
> she might join him on the pyre.[93]

Additionally, there is the uncomfortable reality that sati economically benefited surviving sons, who were then left without an elderly dependent to support.[94] Other Hindu religious practices emerged or solidified during this period that reduced the social standing of widows, including prohibiting remarriage, expectations of severe fasts and asceticism, and treating widows as bad omens. As some scholars have pointed out, this may have left many widowed women with few good options.[95]

Conclusion: Old and New Indian Communities

Many non-Hindu communities—both old and new—thrived in early India, and it seems appropriate to close this chapter with two brief examples that, in different ways, invoke the trading routes that occupied our attention last chapter. Merchant communities prospered, and one such group in western Gujarat sponsored a list of customary rules (*acharas*) in 592 CE that gives us rare insight into first millennium CE legal codes.[96] This merchant community operated under the Maitraka dynasty, which had earlier been Gupta vassals.[97] Their legal code, known as the Charter of Vishnushena, contains more than seventy prescriptions, including barring forced entry into homes and banning a wife's arrest for her husband's crimes (see excerpt). It specifies that a court summons may not interrupt a wedding nor, in a nod to the presence of Brahminical groups, a Vedic sacrifice. It includes numerous directions regarding taxes and custom duties as well as provisions designed to curb frivolous lawsuits. Some of these rules were likely common across many Indian communities, and scattered inscriptions in Bengal, the Deccan, and elsewhere refer to "customary rules" governing property rights, marriages, and other subjects.[98] Still, the Charter of Vishnushena stands out as a unique collated set of legal codes from this early period that attests to community governance.

Excerpt from the Charter of Vishnushena (Sanskrit), 592 CE, from Western India

1. The property of a man with no son may not be seized [by escheat].
2. The king's officer should not violate the threshold [i.e., forcibly enter a home].
3. A contrived lawsuit should not be entertained.
4. Arrest on suspicion is not to be made.
5. A woman should not be arrested for the crime of her husband.
6. In the event that a safely laid fire spreads, no frivolous complaint shall be entertained.
7. In the event of a "self-shortened ear" (most likely, a self-inflicted injury designed to deceive), no frivolous complaint shall be entertained.
8. No suit is to be entertained where a plaintiff or a defendant is absent.
9. A frivolous complaint shall not be entertained from someone who is seated in the market.
10. An oxcart may not be seized.[99]

New groups entered the subcontinent in this period, such as Christians who alighted on India's southern shores via the same trade routes that had been in use since the second century BCE. In recovering the early establishment of Indian Christian communities, legend diverges from historical evidence. The apocryphal *Acts of Saint Thomas*, a Syriac text composed ca. the early third century CE, says that Thomas, one of Jesus's twelve apostles, traveled to India in the first century CE as a carpenter enslaved by an agent of an Indian king.[100] A parallel story of

Figure 7.4. Stone cross with Pahlavi inscription at St. George's Church in Kadamattom, late first millennium CE, Kerala, India.

Thomas (although the details vary considerably) is found in the early seventeenth-century *Thomma Parvam* in Malayalam.[101] In reality, the earliest evidence for Christians in southern India dates to the mid-first millennium CE when crosses with Pahlavi inscriptions (figure 7.4) began to appear along the southern coasts and in Sri Lanka.[102] A small Christian community—sometimes called Thomas Christians as per the legend—was continuous in southern India from this point forward.

Further Reading

Dharmashastra literature has been extensively explored and translated by Patrick Olivelle and Donald Davis, and Timothy Lubin's work is useful on real-world law. Wendy Doniger has translated and commented on the *Kamasutra*. Sheldon Pollock's analysis of Sanskrit literary culture is unparalleled, and I relied on Andrew Ollett regarding Prakrit. On Tamil literature, George Hart and Davis Shulman both offer insights. For translations of Sanskrit literary works, the Clay Sanskrit Library and Murty Classical Library of India volumes are a treasure trove.

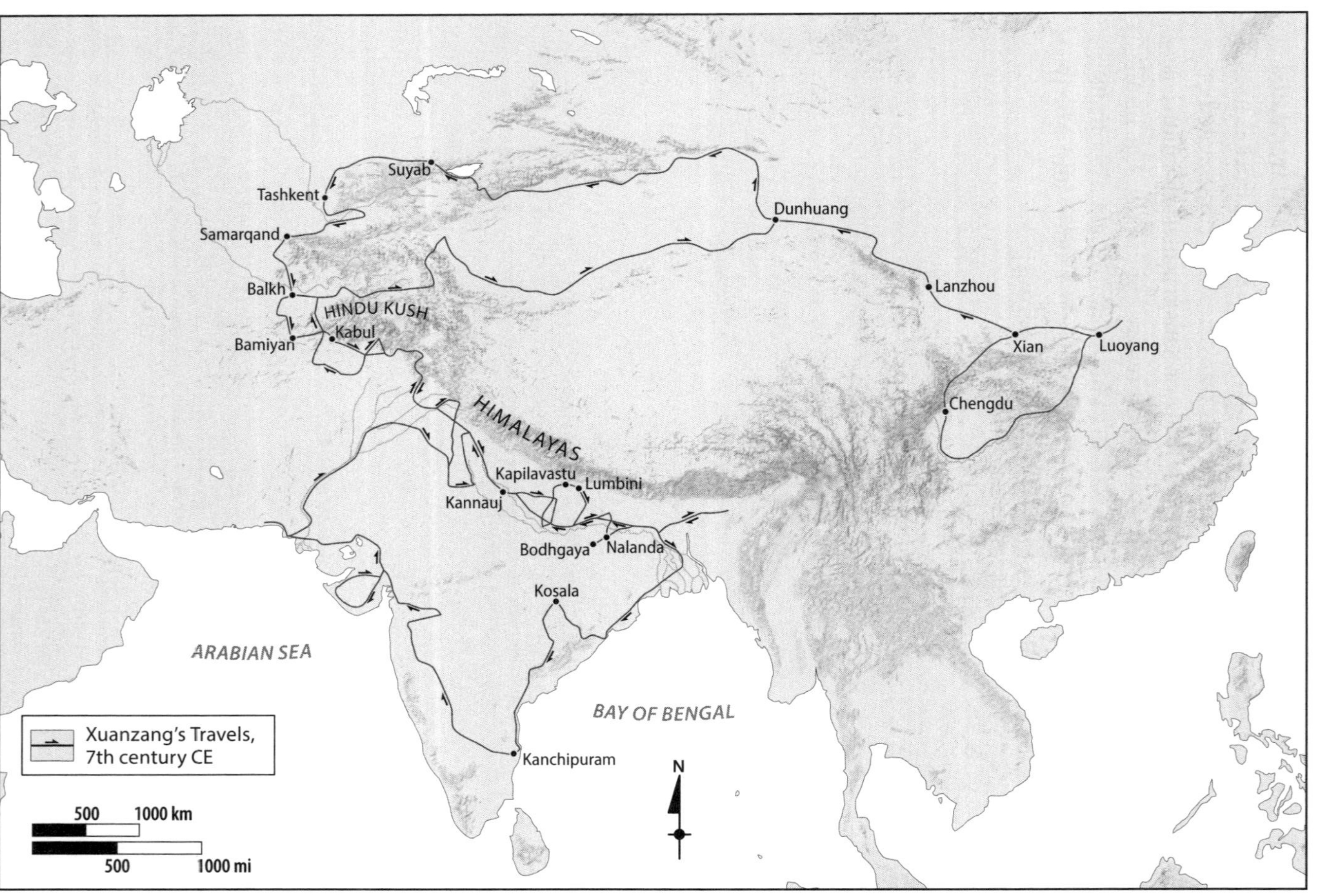

Xuanzang's travels, seventh century CE.

8

India in the World, ca. 700 CE

When a person becomes controlled by anger,
while ignorant of the facts,
he will soon be separated from his friend,
like the Brahmin from the mongoose.

—*Panchatantra*, first millennium CE (Sanskrit)[1]

> There was a poor Brahmin who had raised a mongoose from birth and, one day, left his infant son in the care of the tamed animal. A cobra tried to bite the child, and the mongoose valiantly tore apart the snake. When the Brahmin returned, he saw the mongoose guarding the door with his mouth covered in blood. Fearing that the animal had attacked his son, the Brahmin beat the mongoose to death with a stick. He then entered his home to find the baby sleeping soundly next to the shredded cobra's carcass. Realizing his error, the Brahmin was filled with remorse and so learned the hard way that one should not act hastily without being in full possession of the facts.[2]

This tale—demonstrating the risks of rash action—was in wide circulation within South Asia and beyond by 700 CE within a story collection known as *Panchatantra* (Five topics).[3] The anecdote's moral that ignorance and impulsiveness invite grief might be applied to the study of premodern India, warning us against impetuous assumptions. Perhaps the most basic presupposition about the Indian past is precisely that South Asia has a geographically confined history. In this chapter, I push past the limits of this bounded approach and instead position India in a global context that received travelers and exported cultural products (including the *Panchatantra*). Many of these exchanges utilized established Asian networks, including the Silk Roads, sea trade routes east and west, and Buddhist pilgrimage networks. A few—such as the transfer of scientific knowledge to Abbasid-controlled Baghdad in the eighth century—involved new communities that soon entered South Asia themselves. At the end of this chapter, I refocus attention within the subcontinent, including on some of its frontier regions where we can glimpse religious innovations that ultimately changed South Asian cultures more broadly.

Xuanzang and Indian Buddhism

Xuanzang—a Chinese Buddhist monk in the seventh century CE—was among the most well-traveled premodern visitors to India. He left China in 629 and began a multi-year journey to the Gautama Buddha's homeland. Xuanzang sought access to Buddhist texts and teachings that he felt had been fragmentarily transmitted in Chinese but would be available in full in India. Xuanzang was right. He found the texts he sought along with Indian teachers who instructed him in Sanskrit and helped him interpret Buddhist sources. Xuanzang left behind an account of his travels (called *The Record of Western Regions*), and his students also authored a biography.[4] Writings by and about Xuanzang—like every other premodern text—pursued agendas other than historical documentation. Xuanzang, for example, crafted his *Record* for pedagogical purposes, selecting episodes accordingly and even fictionalizing at times.[5] Still, if we read critically, Xuanzang and his students offer invaluable information about Indian social life, interactions between religious groups, and how South Asian communities participated in global trends and networks in the 630s and 640s.

Xuanzang followed the land-based Silk Roads—in use for close to a millennium by the seventh century CE—across China and through parts of Central Asia until reaching northwestern India. Along the way, he experienced the polyglot culture enabled by Silk Road trade. For example, in Suyab (in modern-day Kyrgyzstan), he feasted on a pilaf made with rice from China, sugarcane from India, and local grapes.[6] His Suyab hosts were Zoroastrians, and Xuanzang also encountered followers of Hellenistic religions, practitioners of local traditions, Shaivas, and, of course, Buddhists while traversing the Silk Roads. Xuanzang's journey was perilous at times, including facing state opposition to leaving China and more than one run-in with bandits.[7] It is a judgment call where we consider Xuanzang to have crossed into "South Asia," a modern descriptor of the region, but perhaps somewhere between Samarqand and Balkh.

Xuanzang found a thriving Buddhist community in Balkh and there began his study of Sanskrit Buddhist texts under a young teacher named Prajnakara. After a while, the pair headed southeast together, crossing the Hindu Kush Mountains (a later name; Xuanzang calls them "Snow Mountains") and visiting Bamiyan. At Bamiyan, Xuanzang saw two monumental Buddhist statues—towering 180 feet and 125 feet tall, respectively, that had been carved in the sixth century CE and seemingly stood guard for numerous Buddhist caves and rock paintings (figure 8.1).[8] For almost 1,400 more years, many travelers repeated Xuanzang's experience of gazing up at the towering Bamiyan Buddhas, until they were blown up by the Taliban in 2001. The historical archive is never complete, including due to modern destruction.

Xuanzang, too, recorded loss in his time. He notes multiple abandoned Buddhist sites in the several years during which he traveled from the northwest through Kashmir and into the Gangetic plain.[9] Historians are uncertain whether to take Xuanzang at his word on abandoned Buddhist sites or, more prudently, to see his comments as reflecting the contemporary prevalence of the narrative trope of decline.[10] Possibly both are true, and we find similarly conflicting accounts by later historians. For example, the ca. 1150 CE Sanskrit historian Kalhana reports Hindu-Buddhist conflict in sixth-century Kashmir, such as his (admittedly dubious) account of Mihirakula, a Shaivite ruler remembered for iconoclastic violence against Buddhists while granting land to Brahmins.[11] Still, Buddhism survived in the region since, after a 1123 fire burned Srinagar to the ground, the sole structure left standing was a "single great Buddha, homeless and blackened by smoke, like a burnt tree."[12] Traveling in the seventh century, between these two moments, Xuanzang participated in a vibrant Buddhist intellectual culture in numerous parts of the subcontinent.

Xuanzang spent five years studying Sanskrit texts at Nalanda, which hosted a large Buddhist monastic community by this point. He reports that Buddhist intellectuals far and wide sought entry into the famed

Figure 8.1. Bamiyan Buddha, sixth century CE, Bamiyan, Afghanistan, carved into rock face, destroyed by the Taliban in 2001.

Bihar monastery (vihara), seeing it as a premier intellectual institution: "Scholars from different places who want to enhance their reputation come here to resolve their doubts and establish their fame."[13] Nalanda's reputation was so robust that, as per Xuanzang, there was social cache to be gained by lying about an affiliation: "Those who travel about falsely claiming to have studied here are treated with the utmost respect."[14] Xuanzang was no charlatan, however, and was admitted to Nalanda after passing an oral exam.[15] He studied under Shilabhadra and attested to a vigorous scholarly community:

> With regard to the highly capable and broadly learned teachers here, they have all mastered the many types of knowledge and are wise men of supreme virtue. It is due to their collective brilliance that the path endures. As for Dharmapala and Chandragupta, they earned their fame by upholding the Buddha's teachings. Gunamati and Saramati made their name in the present day. Prabhamitra is known for clear arguments, Visheshamitra for lofty discussions. Jnanachandra is brilliant and quick; Shilabhadra is profound and virtuous. The people know that the virtue of these eminent men surpasses that of previous worthies. They are well versed in the old texts, and they have each produced more than ten commentaries, all of which are in broad circulation and viewed as treasures of our age.[16]

After passing five years in such stimulating company, Xuanzang resumed traveling, eventually reaching southern India and circling back to Nalanda. Along the way he continued to study, for example, spending a month in Kosala reading Dignaga, a well-regarded sixth-century Buddhist logician.[17]

Xuanzang traveled through many Indian kingdoms, and he offers a particularly intriguing snapshot of north Indian rulership norms in his description of King Harsha of Kannauj (r. 606–647) in eastern India. Specifically, Xuanzang reported witnessing a meeting with vassal rulers and described Harsha (whom he calls Shiladitya[18]) as appearing dressed as the Hindu god Indra along with an armored division of elephants, a known feature of Indian warfare since before the Mauryas. Harsha then venerated a Buddhist icon, offering precious jewels and silk in honor of the "three treasures" of Buddhism, namely the Gautama Buddha, the monastic community (sangha), and the dhamma (see the excerpt following).

Other sources confirm that Harsha was eclectic in his use of religious imagery for royal representation. For example, Bana's *Harshacharita*—a Sanskrit hagiography of the king written in his lifetime—describes one of Harsha's ancestors as participating in Shaiva rituals and characterizes Harsha as "calm in mind like Buddha himself, one who carries out all the rules for the castes and orders like Manu, and bears the rod of punishment as visibly as Yama."[19] This line clubs together upholding the Brahminical ideal of *varnashramadharma* and being like the Buddha in a single breath, views that many would see as theologically opposed. Critical is that both had wide cache across India by the seventh century CE, and so Harsha could benefit politically from drawing on numerous religious traditions.[20]

Harsha and Vassal Rulers at Kannauj, Excerpt from Xuanzang's *Record* (Chinese), Seventh Century

The kings emerged from the temporary palace and raised a concealed golden statue into the air. The statue, which was more than three feet tall, was kept behind a jeweled curtain on the back of a great elephant. King Shiladitya (Harsha), dressed as Indra and holding a jeweled canopy, attended on the left, while King Kumara (of Assam), appearing as Brahma holding a white-hair whisk, attended on the right. Each had an army of five hundred elephants completely encased in armor. Behind the Buddha image lumbered another hundred large elephants ridden by musicians beating a rhythm and making music. King Shiladitya scattered natural pearls, various jewels, gold, silver, and a variety of flowers in all directions as offerings to the Three Treasures [Gautama Buddha, sangha, and dhamma].

Arriving at the jeweled altar first, the king bathed the image with fragrant water and then carried it on his back up to the western terrace. He then made offerings of various precious jewels and hundreds of thousands of silken garments. At that time, just over twenty monks followed behind and various other kings served as guards. After everyone had eaten, groups gathered to engage in various studies, establishing the truth of the profound teachings and proclaiming the ultimate principle. When the sun began to sink, the kings returned to the temporary palace. In this way, the golden statue was delivered each day from the beginning to the end of the assembly.[21]

Another way to interpret Xuanzang's travels is through the lens of pilgrimage as he traveled across a landscape sacred to multiple religious communities. In this same period, Hindu pilgrims also imagined a sacred geography across the premodern subcontinent's natural and built landscapes, and sometimes Hindu pilgrimage networks overlapped with Buddhist ones.[22] For example, in the seventh century CE, Vaishnavas traveled to Bodhgaya to perform *shraddhas* (ancestral rites), and some attempted to repurpose key Buddhist sites therein.[23] Xuanzang mentions that a Hindu king had chopped down the Bodhi tree, under which Buddhists claimed Gautama had gained enlightenment. The same king also placed a Shiva statue in the main temple's central shrine, displacing a Buddhist icon.[24]

More broadly, Vaishnavas and Buddhists tried to appropriate each other's religious figures at times. Some Buddhist texts criticize Vishnu (and Shiva) as weak, and they are also incorporated into Buddhist cosmology as minor deities.[25] Premodern Vaishnavas identified the Gautama Buddha as one of Vishnu's avatars (incarnations) in a similar attempt to domesticate a rival. Still, Hindu and Buddhist communities shared sacred spaces for centuries. For instance, Hyecho, a Korean Buddhist pilgrim who traveled to India for several years in the 720s CE, noted both Buddhists and ash-smeared Shaivas around Varanasi.[26]

Xuanzang returned to China in 645, bringing with him more than 650 Sanskrit texts and dozens of relics and statues. He spent the better part of the next two decades overseeing a robust translation workshop that produced new Chinese editions of Buddhist Sanskrit texts.[27] In the assessment of one modern scholar, Xuanzang thus became the "second great translator in the Chinese Buddhist tradition," following the fifth-century Central Asian Buddhist Kumarajiva.[28] Xuanzang's trip sparked a flurry of India-China embassies over the next century as well as other itinerant scholars, although some took different routes. For example, in the 670s–690s, the Chinese monk Yijing traveled via sea through Southeast Asia and even stopped in Sumatra to study Sanskrit before continuing to Nalanda and other Buddhist pilgrimage sites in India.[29] Few premoderns journeyed as far and wide as Xuanzang and Yijing. But many Indian ideas, stories, and even languages traveled even further in the seventh and eighth centuries CE.

Indian Cultural Exports

Premodern India was a mass exporter of cultural and intellectual goods. Sometimes, we have a decent sense of how ideas traveled, such as when Buddhists spread the dhamma north into Central Asia and China via the Silk Roads and to Southeast Asia via sea trade routes (chapter 6). In other cases, we lack knowledge of how information spread and have only the results. For example, a story first recorded in Sanskrit in the early first millennium CE appeared centuries later as a Welsh folktale in the British Isles.[30] Ideas from the subcontinent spread north, west, and east, although not always the same ideas in all directions. Stories, games, and scientific knowledge traveled west from India, reaching communities in western Asia and, eventually, Europe. In Southeast Asia, many elites developed a taste for Sanskrit and the notions of rulership expressed in that medium. These two broad trends overlapped in some cases—especially regarding Sanskrit stories—but they were largely distinct in timing and outcome.

A set of Sanskrit animal fables known as *Panchatantra* proved wildly popular in premodernity. The Panchatantra tales were an "open canon," with various compilations made within India between 300 and 1200 CE.[31] Our oldest versions feature five books (the *tantra*s of the title), and later collations sometimes circulated under alternative names, including *Hitopadesha* (Good counsel) and, combined with other narratives, *Kathasaritsagara* (Ocean of the river of stories).[32] These animal fables were not bounded by religion, and one popular version was the Jain-collated *Panchakhyanaka* of Purnabhadra (twelfth century CE).[33] Trying to capture its immense circulation, some scholars have surmised that the *Panchatantra* is the most circulated book, except the Bible, ever.[34] If this is hyperbole, it is not by much, even as the meanings of Panchatantra tales shifted considerably with new audiences.

In premodern Indian contexts, Panchatantra stories generally traded on the idea of inborn nature and thus lend further insight into the development of the caste system. Most stories feature interactions between animals, who represent their species collectively.[35] Always, birth determines nature and is immutable. Many stories feature animals who perish by foolishly failing to realize this, such as the frogs who were tricked into helping a snake who ultimately, as any snake will do, gobbled up the helpful frogs.[36] McComas Taylor has described the social "discourse of division" in the *Panchatantra* that divides animals into jatis (caste groups).[37] Taylor further sees animal jatis as parallel to human varnas, arguing in his study of the *Panchatantra*: "We have observed a parallel between the jati, as the natural division of the forest realm, and the varna, its analogue in the idealized human society depicted in the hegemonic texts of the brahmanical archive. These are two complementary manifestations of a single discursive force: one in the metasocieties of the Panchatantra narrative, the other in human society. The discourse that divides the animals of the forest into jatis is the same discourse that classifies humankind by varnas."[38] Jatis also became critical to the human caste system, which generally became more complex, entrenched, and widespread over time in premodern India.[39]

The Panchatantra stories spread west from the 500s CE onward. First, they were translated from Sanskrit into Syriac and Pahlavi (Middle Persian) in the sixth century CE. The ca. 977–1010 CE Persian *Shahnama* (Book of kings) of Firdawsi contains a legendary narrative of this transmission. In brief, a learned man named Borzoi traveled to India in pursuit of a plant that could make the dead speak, which he failed to locate but instead found the *Panchatantra* and covertly copied it into Pahlavi.[40] The *Shahnama* is an epic, not history, but this narrative suggests that premodern India enjoyed a deserved reputation as a rich source of stories. From Pahlavi, the *Panchatantra* was translated into Arabic in the eighth century. In these early renderings, the story collection was called *Kalila wa Dimna*, after the two jackals (Karataka and Damanaka in Sanskrit) whose conversation constitutes a frame narrative. From Arabic, the Panchatantra tales spread like wildfire, appearing in Greek, New Persian, Hebrew, Latin, and Old Spanish (Castilian). By the nineteenth century, Panchatantra stories were known across much of the world in more than 250 languages, and many still circulate today.[41]

Some Panchatantra stories communicated ideas and values that transferred well between cultures and over time. For example, interfering in the affairs of others can go south fast, such as for the jackal who got between two fighting rams to lick up their blood and was pulverized. Brains can triumph over brawn, as per the hare who tricked a lion into attacking his own reflection in a well and thus drowning.[42]

In some cases, we find stories in different times and places that seem similar, even while communicating different values. For example, a Panchatantra tale features a Brahmin who builds castles in the sky, so to speak. He sees a pot filled with barley and visualizes selling it to buy some goats, and so his imagined transactions improve his lot until he envisions himself with a wife and young son. Still in his imaginary world, he hits his wife, but his arm lashes out in reality and knocks over his pot, thus spilling his barley on the ground and his dreams along with it.[43] An Aesop's fable about a milkmaid and her pail unfolds similarly. Like the

Brahmin, the milkmaid dreams of a brighter future that stems, for her, from selling the milk that she carries in a pail on her head. She eventually imagines herself pursued by many suitors and haughtily throws back her head at them all, thus spilling the milk. Both stories communicate the danger of getting ahead of oneself, but the Brahmin saga involves marital relations and a son, whereas the milkmaid tale concerns controlling female sexuality.[44] Scholars have rightly cautioned against mistaking familiarity for clear genealogy in the case of individual tales.[45] But the general point stands that many in premodern Asia and, eventually, Europe loved Indian fables sourced from the *Panchatantra*.

Other Indian stories also proved popular across wide areas, such as the *jataka* tales that spread west and east. The jatakas are a loose collection of narratives about the prior lives (bodhisattas) of enlightened beings (buddhas), especially the Gautama Buddha. The earliest written jataka collections are in Pali, a Prakrit language commonly used by premodern Buddhists, and stories circulated orally as well. Some date back to the last centuries BCE, whereas others were formulated (or reformulated) later. In Buddhist circles, the tales constituted teaching moments, offering good and bad examples that could help Buddhist monks and laity on the path to liberation.[46] In South Asia, jataka tales also appear in art, such as the story of the monkey king who sacrificed himself to save others that is illustrated in panels at Bharhut and Sarnath (both in modern-day Madhya Pradesh).[47] Jataka tales spread east, along with Buddhism, appearing in Java, Thailand, Laos, and elsewhere. A stunning example is the Borobudur Stupa (ca. 800 CE) in Java, whose outer walls bear stone carvings of jataka stories.[48] Jataka tales also moved west, becoming popular among Muslim communities and, later, giving rise to folklore themes in Chaucer and the *Arabian Nights*.[49]

Indian games, too, proved attractive beyond the subcontinent, such as *chaturanga* (an antecedent of modern chess) that was introduced to premodern Persia. We are not entirely clear on the original rules, but Firdawsi presents chaturanga as a game of war in the *Shahnama*. In Firdawsi's story, a north Indian raja sends the game to Persia as part of political negotiations in the sixth century CE, and the Sasanian minister Bozorjmehr cleverly figures out how to play.[50] Even without knowing whether this precise tale has roots in reality, there is little doubt that chess—a game played at some point by most readers of this book—originated in India.[51]

Among India's many premodern knowledge systems, astronomy—including mathematical components—garnered particular interest in the Perso-Arabic world, including among Muslims. Muslims were a new addition to Asia's religious diversity as of the early seventh century CE and, like premodern Buddhists, Muslims often sought converts. Islam thus constituted a multicultural and multiethnic tradition from nearly its beginning. Buddhists were among the earliest South Asian converts to Islam, including a Bactrian family who relocated from Balkh to Baghdad, capital of the Muslim-led Abbasid Empire, in the eighth century and became known as the Barmakids.

The Barmakids oversaw a knowledge transfer of Indian sources in eighth-century Baghdad, sponsoring some the earliest known translations of Sanskrit astronomical, ayurveda (pseudoscientific medicine), and scientific texts into Arabic.[52] The interest in astronomy possibly followed similar inclinations at the Tang court in contemporary China, which suggests awareness of ruling cultures across Asia.[53] Many Indian Sanskrit treatises contained considerable scientific knowledge. For example, Aryabhata (sixth century CE) and other Indian mathematicians had accurately postulated the causes of solar and lunar eclipses and had calculated pi.[54] One notable aspect of the Barmakids' eighth-century translation project is that it involved South Asians traveling to Baghdad and spending time within the Abbasid Empire while they assisted with textual translations. They were joined by Persian, Syriac, and Aramaic speakers and others, some of whom assisted with a parallel (and, ultimately, longer-lived) translation movement in Baghdad that centered on rendering Greek texts into Arabic.[55] The Baghdad-bound Indian travelers, along with their contemporaries who visited the Tang court, constitute early cases of South Asians who traveled abroad, not for trade or political negotiation, but for sharing knowledge.

The final premodern Indian cultural export that occupies my attention here is Sanskrit literature and conventions, which were embraced by political elites across Southeast Asia in premodernity. Most often in history, languages spread through migration, conquest, trade, or conversion, but literary Sanskrit was different. Across much of Southeast Asia—from Burma to Indonesia—elite communities adopted Sanskrit (as a literary language, not an everyday vernacular) seemingly because it offered them rhetorical resources and an aesthetic style otherwise unavailable.[56] This process began in the fourth century CE and lasted through the fifteenth century in some places, such as Java and Cambodia. The details differ, but relatively consistent was the use of Sanskrit as a technology of elite self-expression. Even today the study of political history in Southeast Asia involves, and sometimes heavily relies on, Sanskrit inscriptions. In terms of South Asian history, this process featured southern India quite strongly, especially the Coromandel coast during Pallava rule where Sanskrit intellectuals flourished around 700 CE (including Dandin, whose works were also popular in Sri Lanka).[57] It remains unclear what precise role Brahmins and members of other religions played in the spread of Sanskrit to Southeast Asia.[58] Clearer, if complex, was the religious scene at home on the subcontinent.

Premodern Religious Diversity

South Asia's religious scene was crowded, dynamic, and sometimes antagonistic in the seventh to eighth centuries CE. Brahmins fought intellectually with both Buddhists and Jains like snakes and mongooses (cats and dogs, in modern English idiom).[59] Jain, Buddhist, and Brahmin communities were each internally divided by sectarian differences. Jains had split into two branches: Shvetambara (white-clad) and Digambara (sky-clad) that differed, most visibly, in that Shvetambara monks wore white robes while Digambara monks walked around naked (chapter 3). Buddhists, too, had divided into the Theravada and Mahayana traditions. Brahminical thinkers boasted six philosophical systems (*shaddarshana*) that offered conflicting views on the nature of the Vedas and epistemology (i.e., how we know things). All these traditions were challenged by and ultimately adapted to include a new set of ritualistic practices that thrived during this period: tantra.[60] Here I outline some core features of tantra, along with the accompanying rise of Shaiva worship and the discrete innovations of yoga and Vaishnava non-dualism.

In the mid-first millennium CE, yoga constituted a set of meditative practices (*samadhi*) designed to achieve union (the literal meaning of *yoga*) with a higher being. Physical poses—today considered by many practitioners to be the entirety of the tradition—were only one component of an array of life choices, including celibacy. Yoga seems to come a bit out of left field in the early first millennium CE, with scant connections to earlier Brahminical ascetic practices, such as those described in the Mahabharata (chapter 5).[61] Some scholars have even suggested that Patanjali's foundational fourth-century *Yogasutra* was decidedly non-Hindu and was subsequently domesticated into a Brahminical treatise by Vyasa (a fourth–seventh-century-CE commentator; distinct from the Mahabharata's purported author).[62] Others cite more of a "patchwork" of Brahminical and other sources for early yoga, with "om" serving as a good example of how multiple sources may have converged.[63] Patanjali's *Yogasutra* prescribes the chanting of "om," a word that may have a Dravidian etymology but had been upheld as the essence of the Vedas since the first millennium BCE.[64] While disagreeing on the details, scholars generally agree that premodern yoga was multiform and malleable.[65]

The sacred syllable "om" also arose in the writings of Shankara (also known as Shankaracharya and Adi Shankara), a Brahmin thinker who lived in the eighth or ninth century CE and crafted a theory of non-duality. Shankara lived in Kerala and was Vaishnava, although later thinkers such as Ramanujan smeared him as a "crypto-Buddhist" (*pracchannabauddha*).[66] Shankara's ideas were innovative within Brahminical thought in proposing a non-dualistic interpretation of reality in which the atman (self) and brahman (ultimate reality) are one and any perceived distinction is illusion (*maya*).[67] In other ways, Shankara was decidedly standard for a Brahmin man of his time, accepting the four-fold varna system and endorsing sources that prescribe torturous punishments for anybody who studied the Vedas beyond upper-caste men.[68] Shankara's philosophy was known as Advaita Vedanta (non-dualistic Vedanta), and it is influential today among many Hindus.[69] But this is owing to later developments, especially the embrace of monotheism within the Hindu reform movements during the nineteenth–twentieth centuries (chapters 17 and 20). In his time, Shankara was less popular as compared to the connected religious developments of Shaiva worship and tantra.

Worship of Shiva (a non-Vedic god) and tantra (a wide-ranging set of ritual practices) grew exponentially between the fifth and thirteenth centuries CE, flourishing from the deep south up to Kashmir and the Kathmandu valley. Shaiva worship and tantra often overlapped as tantric rites became robust among Shaiva devotees and later fanned out, being adapted within Buddhist, Vaishnava, Shakti, and Jain traditions.[70] Tantric rituals vary widely by community but overall center around two types of practices: (1) chanting mantras and sacred sounds and (2) antinomian behaviors that promise liberation through being transgressive.[71] We know about premodern tantric practices today from texts called *tantra*s, composed in the eighth century CE and later, and through literary depictions of specific tantric communities, such as the Kapalikas.[72]

Premodern tantra must be understood within social contexts, especially Brahminical purity protocols that tantra was designed to prompt its followers to challenge. Tantra practitioners might consume impure items (including meat, semen, and blood), do impure things (like sleep with a woman on her period or sit on top of a corpse), or spend time in impure places (like cremation grounds).[73] These antinomian practices caused many people to bristle, and that was the point. In early India, Brahminical purity norms—largely centered around the caste system—spread and grew more potent, and some tantric practitioners positioned themselves in opposition pursuant to understanding true reality beyond social conventions.[74]

Premodern practices at the Kamakhya Temple in Assam's Brahmaputra valley allow us to see the tantric tradition among worshippers of the Goddess and enable us, even if briefly, to focus on the underexplored northeastern region in South Asian history. Numerous puranas record the legend of how the Kamakhya Temple was founded. In brief, Shiva was slighted by his father-in-law Daksha, who failed to invite the sometimes-unkempt god to a sacrifice. Sati—Shiva's wife and Daksha's daughter—immolated herself in protest at her husband's mistreatment, and Shiva was beside himself with grief at losing her. Shiva carried Sati's charred body across the subcontinent and parts of her fell in different areas that became known as the Goddess's power seats (*shakta pitha*s).[75] Sati's yoni (vagina + womb) fell in Assam, and the Kamakhya Temple served as a hub for tantric practice by the eighth century or earlier.[76]

Rituals at the Kamakhya Temple center around the annual menstrual cycle of the Goddess (called Kamakhya), who accepts blood sacrifices. As the *Kalikapurana* puts it: "One should satisfy Ganesha with sweet-meat, Surya with burnt-offering, Shiva with song, dance, and instrumental music, and Vishnu with observances," but the goddess is best propitiated with blood from birds, boars, buffalo, even "one's own body."[77] Animal sacrifice is one of the oldest Hindu practices, well attested in the

Vedas (chapter 2). However, following antinomian tendencies, tantric practitioners often intentionally inverted features of Vedic sacrifice, such as by using wild instead of domesticated animals.[78]

In premodernity, tantric practices were not everybody's cup of tea, although they proved hugely influential. Sometimes tantric practitioners were the butt of jokes, such as in Bana's *Kadambari*, a seventh-century Sanskrit prose work. Bana poked fun at the appearance, clumsiness, and exaggeration tendencies of an "old Dravidian holy man" who read Shaiva tantra texts and hung out at a Chandika temple in Malwa.[79] Xuanzang's biographers dismiss as worthless tantric practices that Xuanzang witnessed in India, noting: "Kapalikas make garlands of skulls to adorn their heads and hang around their necks. Shriveled and withered like piles of stone, they resemble yakshas beside tombs."[80] But tantra became widespread, even as it changed and was cleaned up for polite, high-caste society at times, such as in Abhinavagupta's eleventh-century *Tantraloka* (Elucidation of tantra).[81] Tantra also spread far beyond Shaiva communities. Buddhist tantric traditions became quite robust, leading to things like some Buddhists wearing a sacred thread, typically associated with Brahmin men, but "made of the twisted hair of corpses or human sinew."[82] Jains, too, developed tantric practices, even while they shied away from certain aspects, such as eating meat, and instead focused on mantras.[83] Jain and Shaiva ideas also overlapped in other ways, especially in southern India where some Shaivas shared the otherwise unique Jain interpretation of karma as a physical substance (as opposed to a causal sequence).[84]

While influencing one another, religious traditions in South Asia also competed for followers at times, such as Jains and Shaivas in seventh-century southern India. Some later sources and folk stories narrate that Shaiva ascetics impoverished Jainism's footprint in Tamil Nadu by impaling 8,000 Jains at Madurai in the seventh century CE.[85] This tale lacks historical evidence, but the two communities were rivals. For instance, the Tamil poet Sambandar (figure 8.2) had a litany of complaints about Jains, including that they were filthy, evil, destructive, wicked, indecent, ignorant, and criminals.[86] Sambandar, counted among the *nayanar*s (sixty-three Shaiva poet saints of Tamil Nadu), exhorted people to worship Shiva, proclaiming, "He can't be found in the false doctrines of the heretic Jain and Buddhist monks."[87] Sambandar's contemporary, Appar,

Figure 8.2. Tamil Shaiva poet-saint Sambandar, fourteenth century CE, Tamil Nadu, India, copper alloy.

converted from Jainism to Shaiva worship and tended to write in a calmer, but still polemical, tone, such as these lines:

O god who pierced the delusion
that afflicted me
when I joined the Jains
and became a wicked monk!
O bright flame, celestial being

who stands as the pure path,
bull among the immortals,
honey who dwells in Tiruvaiyaru [a town in Tamil Nadu]
I wander as your servant,
worshipping and singing at your feet.[88]

Others, too, abandoned their traditions to become Shaivas, such as the seventh-century Pallava king, Mahendravarman.[89] Mahendravarman steered clear of tantra's antinomian features, however, and he penned a drama, titled *Mattavilasa* (Drunkards' play), that mocks Kapalika ascetics as lascivious drunks.[90]

At the start of the seventh century CE, the South Asian religious scene was complicated and diverse. It included Jains, Buddhists, Shaivas, Vaishnavas, Shaktas, Brahmin pandits of numerous philosophical traditions, Christians, and those practicing a wide range of tribal religions. By around 700 CE, followers of two additional religions, namely Parsis and Muslims, had entered the subcontinent. Parsis follow the ancient religion of Zoroastrianism, which is about as old as Vedic traditions. In fact, the oldest Zoroastrian religious text, the *Avesta*, is composed in a language closely related to Vedic Sanskrit (this historical and linguistic link was not known in premodern India). Parsis traveled to India to escape the upheaval and pressure associated with the fall of Persia's Sasanian Empire and the advent of Muslim-led rule from the seventh century onward.[91] Around the same time that Parsis first arrived in India, a second new religious community, Muslims, also alighted on the subcontinent. I address this latter group separately, if briefly, since South Asian Muslims ultimately became both numerous and influential.

Muslims Enter South Asian History

In the late seventh and early eighth centuries, Muslims began to travel to southern coastal and northwestern parts of the subcontinent. Islam was founded in the early seventh century in Arabia by the Prophet Muhammad. From Arabia, Islam spread rapidly, especially east toward India. Within a century of there being Muslims on earth, members of this broad-based religious community had reached the subcontinent.[92] Like many before them, early Muslims came to India primarily as traders and merchants. Using overland routes, some Muslims entered northwestern regions, and via sea routes, other Muslims visited the Malabar and Coromandel coasts. Some were itinerant, and others stayed, with Muslims living in Kerala, for instance, from the ninth century onward.[93] These early Muslim communities brought a new religion and new languages (especially Arabic). Still, for centuries, Muslims had limited impact on wider Indian society, to the extent that it can be difficult to find concrete evidence about them.

In a single case in the first millennium CE, a Muslim leader pursued political power in South Asia. In 711, while still a teenager, Muhammad bin Qasim conquered Sind (now known as Sindh and in Pakistan). Sind remained under Arab-led rule for centuries, but Muslims—whether Muhammad bin Qasim's successors or anybody else—sought no further political expansion within the subcontinent for nearly 300 years.[94] That changed around the turn into the second millennium CE when Muslims of Turkish and other ethnic backgrounds traveled to northern India to raid and when, closer to 1200, some started to exercise political authority in northern India. But those are later developments (chapters 9 and 10). The initial entry of Muslims into the Indian subcontinent around 700 was, to be blunt, lackluster. Early Muslims did little to nothing to alter the lives of most South Asian communities, and they were often deeply acculturated into their new environment.

Conclusion: Global Perspectives

As of the late first millennium CE, many experienced and viewed India as connected with other parts of the world. This growing global perspective invited borrowing and comparison that sharpens our view of premodern India. For instance, the Buddhist traveler Xuanzang described Indian urban centers as follows, noting similarities to Chinese construction but also distinctive features of social segregation and adornment:

> As for cities and villages, they have a square [layout enclosed] by a tall, thick wall. Streets and alleys wind throughout, with shops lining the main roads and taverns set along the narrow lanes. The homes of butchers, fishmongers, entertainers, actors, executioners, and night soil collectors are marked with flags and relegated to outside the city. When these people come and go from the village, they must stay far to the left of the road. As for

> the construction of houses and city walls, since the terrain is low and damp, city walls are built of brick. The walls of buildings are constructed of woven bamboo or wood. Dwellings and viewing platforms are usually made of boards, plastered with lime, and covered with fired or sun-dried bricks. Various tall buildings are made in the same way as in China, using thatch, grass, bricks, and boards. They differ in the way that the walls are covered with lime and the ground is purified with cow dung and a scattering of seasonal flowers.[95]

Xuanzang was unusual in his day for engaging in extensive travels, even as ideas and languages seemed to move more freely. But India only became more integrated into a wider Asian context moving forward. This theme also arises in the next chapter, albeit from a different vantage point of focusing on southern India, especially dynastic innovations and robust cultural developments between the ninth and thirteenth centuries.

Further Reading

For Xuanzang, I utilized translations of primary sources and the scholarship of Benjamin Brose, Max Deeg, Stewart Gordon, and others. Patrick Olivelle has translated the *Panchatantra*, and I found McComas Taylor's analysis insightful. James Mallinson and Mark Singleton offer solid ideas regarding yoga, and I used Finnian M. M. Gerety's work on "om." Alexis Sanderson is the leading authority of premodern Shaiva traditions, and I drew on a variety of scholars regarding tantra.

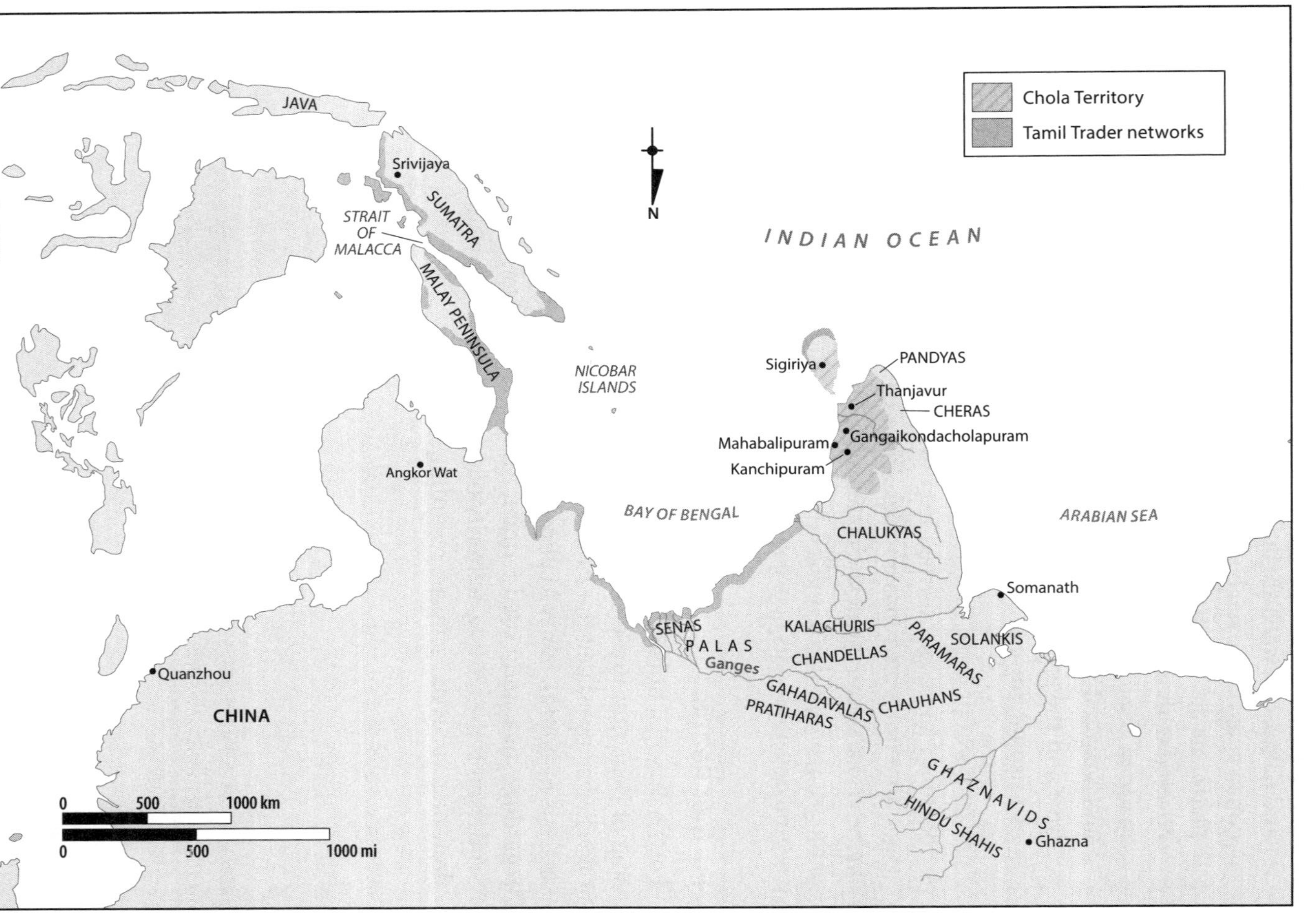

India and Southeast Asia, ca. 1050 CE.

9

Medieval South India

Though there is a flower in your hand and
  a gentle smile on your face,
in what manner can I sustain my heart
when you do not speak anything felicitous with me?

—Anonymous, ninth century, Sigiriya in Sri Lanka (Sinhalese)[1]

In the 1230s CE, two unscrupulous Brahmins abused their positions at a Shiva temple in Tamil Nadu in southern India. The priests-cum-thieves cooked the books, skimming money off the temple's income until they amassed a small fortune.[2] One even swiped a jewel that adorned an icon of the goddess and gave it to his concubine. The pair treated lower classes harshly, locking up in solitary confinement a servant who requested his daily food. They alternatively beat and drowned royal messengers and refused to pay state taxes. Ultimately, a combination of temple trustees, Shaiva devotees, and local residents convicted the two delinquents of crimes against Shiva (*shivadroha*) and the Chola king (*rajadroha*).[3] As punishment, the pair were expelled from the temple, and their property (including slaves) was confiscated. This roguish episode was repeated in different variations by many sticky-fingered individuals in medieval south India as the accumulation of wealth in temples created opportunities for affluence's ever-present companion of corruption.[4] This chapter surveys the developments that enabled such events—including the advent of large-scale Hindu temples and the Chola dynasty—focusing on southern India between the seventh and thirteenth centuries. I also comment on north Indian events around 1000 CE, but, by and large, I center a southern geography transformed by Chola rule.

Chola Raids and Campaigns

South India was home to many medieval dynasties, among which the Cholas (ca. 848–1279) stand out as the most territorially robust. The Chola dynasty was established around 850 CE when a man named Vijayalaya wrested control of Thanjavur, probably from the local Muttaraiyar family. Vijayalaya's origins are obscure, but he brazenly borrowed the name "Chola" from an ancient kingdom in Tamil Sangam literature.[5] The heartland of Vijayalaya's kingdom was the fertile Kaveri delta, sometimes called the rice bowl of Tamil Nadu.

The new Cholas fought with their neighboring dynasties to gain land, fame, and wealth. They experienced some early setbacks, such as the 948–949 battle at Takkolam, around twenty-five kilometers north of Kanchipuram, where they were soundly beat by the Rashtrakutas, a dynasty to the north. To make matters worse, the Chola crowned prince Rajaditya was pierced by an arrow while seated atop an elephant at Takkolam and died instantly.[6] They were also probably negatively impacted by a tenth-century tsunami that wrought considerable damage along the entire southern Indian coastline.[7] The Cholas recovered, however, and their empire reached its heyday in the eleventh century during the overlapping reigns of Rajaraja I (r. 985–1014) and his son, Rajendra I (r. 1012–1044). We know about Chola raids and campaigns predominantly from inscriptions, of which many thousands concerning the Cholas survive in Sanskrit or Tamil (13,000 on temple walls alone).[8] Less than half of Chola inscriptions are printed, and only a fraction of them are translated into English. But even a sliver of the archive offers rich access to Chola ambitions and activities.

The Cholas, unsurprisingly, gave glowing descriptions of their military prowess. They often described kings performing a *digvijaya* (conquest of the four directions) and other kinds of ritualized violence as per the conventions of premodern Sanskrit and Tamil literatures.[9] But the targets of real-world Chola aggression held alternative perspectives. For example, a 1007/1008 inscription criticizes Rajaraja I for leading a campaign into northern Karnataka in which the Chola army "ravaged the land; murdered women, children, and Brahmins; seized women; and destroyed the order of caste (jati)."[10] Sri Lankan chroniclers were similarly unflattering, referring to the Cholas as "blood-sucking vampires."[11] Many rejoiced when they routed the Cholas, such as Bilhana, a twelfth-century Sanskrit poet who celebrated when his Chalukya patron Vikramaditya VI filled the ocean "with swirls of rivers of blood streaming forth from destroying the Chola army."[12] The Cholas were quite standard among premodern Indian dynasties in pursuing political power through violence, but they were unusual in their success, which gave them influence across southern India and beyond.

The Cholas conducted military campaigns in Sri Lanka and Southeast Asia. Rajaraja I conquered northern parts of Sri Lanka and the Maldive Islands, and his successor, Rajendra I, raided parts of Sumatra (specifically the Srivijaya Kingdom) and the Malay Peninsula around 1025. I circle back below to Chola assaults in Southeast Asia, which concerned trade more than political control, whereas their interest in Sri Lanka was commercial and political. Sri Lanka offered a lucrative income of import taxes, given its location at the oceanic crossroads of Asian trade networks. The island also possessed pearl fisheries and copper deposits, whose goods were in demand within Chola India.[13] The Cholas boasted acquiring northern areas of Sri Lanka—land they held for roughly seventy-five years between the 990s and 1070—proudly naming the island first in lists of Chola conquests.[14] Military victory paved the way for cultural exchanges. Eleventh-century Sri Lankans built Shiva temples and imitated the widely famed Chola bronzes (discussed later in this chapter).

The northern part of Sri Lanka broke away from Chola control around 1070, an event that involved forging a Lankan-Burmese alliance. King Vijayabahu I (r. 1055–1110) of Sri Lanka's Polonnaruwa kingdom solicited help from King Anawrahta (r. 1044–1077) of Burma's Pagan kingdom. While it is unclear if the Burmese, in fact, sent material assistance, this is the earliest known case of Sri Lankan political overture aimed at a Southeast Asian polity.[15] Going forward, Burma and Sri Lanka—who both hosted substantial Buddhist populations—participated in periodic cultural exchanges of monks, relics, and manuscripts into the seventeenth century (chapter 14).

Chola imperial ambitions included much of southern and central India, where they engaged in an activity with significant precedent among South Asian (especially Hindu) kings: sacking temples and stealing religious icons. In the seventh century, the Pallavas looted an icon of Ganesha from the Chalukyas who, later that century, pilfered icons of Hindu goddesses in northern India.[16] In the ninth century, the Pandyan king

Shrimara Shrivallabha (r. 815–862) raided Sri Lanka and seized wealth, including a solid gold Buddha.[17] Some decades later, a Sinhala ruler sent an army to southern India and stole back the Buddha image. Rulers in north India, too, engaged in the political act of icon seizing. In the tenth century, the Pratiharas stole a solid gold Vishnu from the king of Kangra in the Himalayan foothills. Subsequently, the Chandellas took the same golden Vishnu icon from the Pratiharas and installed it at Khajuraho's Lakshmana Temple.[18]

South Asian temple plundering was undergirded by a widely shared idea that Hindu temples and icons were expressions of political authority. For example, the sixth-century-CE *Brihatsamhita* notes:

> If a temple or icon, like a Shiva linga, is broken, moves, sweats, cries, falls down, speaks or evinces some other foreboding action,
> it indicates the destruction of a king and his kingdom.[19]

Following this logic and earlier rulers, the Cholas raided their enemies' temples and plundered divine icons as war trophies. For example, in the early eleventh century, Rajendra I pillaged consecrated images of Durga, Shiva, Nandi (Shiva's bull), Ganesha, and Kali from the Chalukyas, Kalingas, and Palas and installed them in Chola temples.[20] He and other Chola kings often advertised the origins of the stolen icons and the violence required to seize them. For example, Rajadhiraja (r. 1044–1052) had inscribed on a Chalukyan image looted by his father, Rajendra I: "This is the door guardian brought by Lord Vijayarajendradeva after burning (the Chalukya capital) Kalyanapuram."[21] The Cholas displayed the icon in their capital city Gangaikondacholapuram. The capital's name translates as "city of the Chola who took the Ganges" and refers to a more unusual looting of a divine object, namely the Ganges River.[22]

In 1022, Rajendra I sent his army north to procure Ganges water and carry it in pots south to Chola territory. The Chola army traveled 1,600 kilometers from Thanjavur to fulfill their king's command.[23] The journey involved cutting across numerous kingdoms, and Chola inscriptions celebrated the ensuing military encounters and defeated kings.[24] The Ganges is both a Hindu goddess and a river, and so stealing Ganges water was akin to looting icons. Also, before the Cholas, both the Chalukyas and Rashtrakutas claimed to have raided north and brought back the Ganges and Yamuna (another Hindu goddess-cum-river). Scholars are unsure whether these two dynasties carried off stone images of the two goddesses, often situated at temple entrances, or pots of water from the respective rivers.[25] Either way, there was precedent for capturing the Ganges to claim a certain mantle of Indian kingship.

For centuries after the Cholas, Indian kings of various religious backgrounds treated Hindu temples and their icons as legitimate political targets. The Cholas, as enthusiastic and fairly early icon seizers, demonstrated two defining features of the premodern Indian imperial tradition of temple looting. First, this was typically political, not religious, targeting. The Cholas were Hindus in modern terms, as were nearly all the dynasties from which they seized icons (the Palas were Buddhist). But Indian kings competed for political power. Accordingly, when the Cholas stole a Ganesha icon, they did not intend to insult the elephant-headed god but rather the icon's patrons and prior caretakers: the Chalukyas.[26] Second, religious and political realms were not separate in premodern India, and one place they were tightly interwoven was at large, often royally sponsored temples. These two interrelated features of the imperial treatment of temples and icons persisted for centuries among Indian rulers, including Hindus, Buddhists, and, starting around 1000 CE, Muslims as well.[27]

North Indian Interlude of Ghaznavid Incursions

In 1025–1026, a few short years after Rajendra I's army captured the Ganges, Mahmud of Ghazna led troops south from Central Asia to raid the Somnath Temple in Gujarat. As Richard Eaton has noted, there were acute similarities and differences between the two expeditions. Mahmud's army, too, traveled around 1,600 kilometers and seized a representation of a Hindu deity. Like the Cholas, Ghaznavid iconoclasm was not religiously limited. Mahmud sacked Jain and Hindu temples as well as cities with Muslim populations, such as Ray (in modern-day Iran).[28] He mistreated religious objects at times, reportedly torching Islamic texts he deemed heretical in Ray and having Somnath's Shiva icon set in a floor in Ghazni to be trampled on.[29] Mahmud sought wealth, more than anything else, from his raids, which largely explains why he targeted numerous north Indian cities in the first quarter of the eleventh century. India was a rich land in many premodern eyes, with concentrations of wealth in royal treasuries and temples. Consider that Mahmud's 1029 raid of Ray brought in less than one million dinars' worth of spoils as compared to his 1025–1026 raid on Somnath that gained loot worth twenty million dinars.[30] Mahmud used his pillaged wealth to pay his professional army and advance his political interests, which stretched into northwestern parts of the subcontinent largely through vassal rulers.

Within India, Mahmud's raids had little effect we can discern. No contemporary surviving Brahminical (or other Hindu) source mentions any of Mahmud's attacks. A single Jain poet, Dhanapala, noted Mahmud's assaults, primarily to dwell on his alleged inability to harm a Mahavira icon in Rajasthan (a way of saying that the Jain community was strong).[31] In brief, Mahmud's raids were seemingly a non-event in Indian history at the time. Nonetheless, they constitute a major moment when Muslim political figures entered the subcontinent outside of Sind. Additionally, some of Mahmud's own poets and chroniclers wrote about his raids, and this marks one major introduction of Persian and Arabic historical sources into South Asian history.

Mahmud of Ghazna was a Persianized, Muslim, Turkish-descent son of an ex-slave. Scholars have struggled with how to succinctly describe the broad culture in which the Ghaznavids and subsequent Indo-Muslim political dynasties participated, with two favorite descriptors being "Islamicate" and "Persianate," meaning culturally Muslim and culturally Persian, respectively. I elect for the more succinct descriptors "Islamic" and "Muslim," as well as the less succinct but more accurate, especially for later figures, "Indo-Muslim" and "Indo-Persian." Whatever vocabulary we use to describe Muslim and, later, Indo-Muslim political figures, these groups brought new languages, cultural mores, and historical sources—in addition to a new religion—to the already diverse Indian subcontinent.

Like many comers to India before them, the Ghaznavids deployed assimilation strategies. For example, Mahmud had bilingual Sanskrit-Arabic coins struck in Lahore in 1027–1028 CE. One side bore the *kalima* (also known as the *shahada*), the Islamic statement of faith in Arabic that "there is no god but God, and Muhammad is God's messenger," and the reverse had the loose translation in Sanskrit, written in Sharada script (usually associated with Kashmir): "He who is invisible is One, Muhammad is his manifestation (avatar), Mahmud is king."[32]

Blending Hindu and Muslim religious vocabularies on coins had precedent. In the ninth century CE, Multan's Arab rulers minted coins inscribed on one side to God (*lillah*) or Muhammad and on the other to Hindu deities such as Lakshmi, Surya, and Varaha (Vishnu's boar incarnation).[33] Arguably the Ghaznavids went further by proposing loose approximations, such as that the Prophet Muhammad could be described as an avatar. Additionally, by combining the shahada and mention of Mahmud, the Ghaznavids linked Islamic expressions and political power. Both features were critical to later Indo-Muslim political culture, a topic that recurs throughout the next several chapters of this book. Here, I showcase two other new things introduced by the Ghaznavids to South Asian history: Perso-Arabic historical sources and theorizing a Hindu religious tradition.

Mahmud's court hosted intellectuals who wrote in Arabic and Persian about history and mythology. We have encountered Firdawsi's *Shahnama* already (chapter 8), a product of the Ghaznavid court and a foundational work of modern Persian. Ghaznavid intellectuals also wrote about contemporary events, and the raid at Somnath offers a case study for pointing up the promises and perils of this archive. The promise is that Persian- and Arabic-medium authors documented events that others did not. Without them, we would not even know of the 1025–1026 raid on Somnath, for example. But the peril is that they did not always tell the truth. For example, the poet Farrukhi (d. ca. 1040) wrote Persian panegyric poems (*qasida*s) for Mahmud in which he extols that Mahmud set the Somnath Temple aflame and "emptied the lands of India of fighting men and horrendous elephants."[34] We know that emptying India is an exaggeration that would have gone over well at the Ghaznavid court, which calls into question claims of arson as well. Likewise, historians like Gardizi, who wrote in a Persian genre known as *tarikh* (history), also exaggerated, flattered their patrons, and relied on older reports. For instance, Gardizi repeated Megasthenes's assertion, made more than 1,000 years earlier, that Indian society was divided into seven classes (chapter 4).[35] It is a truism in the study of history that we must be critical of premodern sources and not blithely assume they are always accurate, but I repeat the stipulation here because of the deceptive similarity that some perceive between premodern Persian-medium tarikh and modern history. Both weave together episodes from the past to narrate a coherent story.

But many tarikh authors played fast and loose with the facts, whereas any modern historian worth her salt does not.[36]

The polymath Biruni (or al-Biruni) was among the intellectuals at Mahmud of Ghazna's court and an early theorizer of a Hindu religious tradition. In his Arabic treatise known as *India*, Biruni began with a contrast, proclaiming that "the people [of *al-hind*] entirely differ from us in every respect."[37] He then elaborated three major points of difference, namely language, religion, and customs. The rest of his *India* discusses Hindu deities, cosmogony, dharmashastra, festivals, and more. Biruni was a learned man, and he appears to have studied Sanskrit while writing his detailed treatise that collates a broad array of ideas and practices under the umbrella of what, today, many would call Hinduism (Biruni used the Arabic term al-hind, i.e., "India"). But Biruni also saw Hindu traditions as fundamentally different from his own. He catalogs them but does not try to incorporate them into his worldview. In this sense, his project stood apart from the Arabic interest in Sanskrit sciences around the eighth century CE and the broad sharing of Panchatantra stories that began even earlier (chapter 8).

In any case, while Biruni's *India* is an important moment in Perso-Arabic intellectual history, it had little impact for centuries. Other Arabic- and Persian-medium authors largely forgot his work on Hinduism, and it moldered in obscurity until European colonial-era scholars rediscovered it.[38] Among Hindus of Biruni's day, there was no parallel interest in articulating a broad-based religious identity. Instead, both north and south Indians continued to forefront their differences, identifying most commonly by their region, caste, or favored god.

Royal Temples and Social Divisions

South Indian dynasties patronized the construction of large-scale temples and other religious sites that also had economic, social, and political dimensions. The Pallavas were early builders, sponsoring the Kailasanathar Temple (to Shiva) at Kanchipuram, rock-cut temples, and the stunning open-air relief at Mahabalipuram ca. 650–700 CE. The Mahabalipuram relief tells multiple stories through its iconography, and scholars are still teasing out its nuances.[39] Pallava temples such as Kailasanathar appear monochromatic today, but their sandstone used to shimmer with colorful paint. Temple-building reached its peak height-wise under the Cholas who devoted their major temples to Shiva. Thanjavur's Rajarajeshvaram Temple, completed under Rajaraja I in 1010 CE, stretched to 216 feet tall, making it "*the* skyscraper of its time, taller than anything built before it anywhere in India."[40] A thousand years later, it is still awe-inspiring to stand outside and gaze up at the soaring Rajarajeshvaram Temple, although that is all most medieval Indians probably ever did at these elite sites.

Chola royal temples were strongly associated with the state. For example, when Thanjavur's towering Rajarajeshvaram Temple was finished in 1010, it was gifted sixty bronze icons, with roughly one-third given, respectively, by the king, royal family, and Chola officials.[41] Chola temples were named after their royal sponsors (they are sometimes known by alternative names today).[42] They were often heavily inscribed, with Lord Rajaraja's Temple at Thanjavur alone containing hundreds of inscriptions that record donations, financial support, and other aspects of Chola state history.[43] In brief, Chola temples were dedicated to Hindu gods, usually Shiva, but they expressed Chola imperial identity and ambitions. Pursuing this intertwining of royalty and religion, Chola bronzes sometimes blurred the lines between deity and sovereign, such as an image of a woman who might be the tenth-century Chola queen Sembiyan Mahadevi, the goddess Parvati, or both.[44]

Chola temples hosted worship, although that too was elite-focused. Vidya Dehejia, an art historian who has spent decades working on the Cholas, has argued: "Temples built by chieftains, court officials, wealthy ladies, or Brahmins were built to be admired and applauded by their own circle of aristocratic peers. They were intended to portray the realm of the gods and the world of royalty, not that of the ordinary citizen."[45] Within temples, Brahmin priests held the exclusive ability to conduct rituals, which gave them power, wealth, and status. Larger temples also led to new Brahmin-led rituals and specialists, outlined in *agama* texts, composed between the eighth and twelfth centuries and associated with the Shaiva Siddhanta tradition.[46] Temple inscriptions attest to substantial elite support, even for smaller ongoing expenses such as providing fuel for lamps.[47] In contrast, villagers in medieval southern India worshipped at small local shrines and probably never set foot inside a Chola imperial temple.[48] Tribal communities continued their own traditions and engaged with other groups in nonreligious contexts, such as at coastal markets where some sold venison.[49]

Chola temples were expensive, even with imperial support, and were partly financed by taxes on a broad population. The Cholas directed entire villages—as far afield as Karnataka and Sri Lanka—to pay some or all their taxes directly to specific temples.[50] These villages were sometimes known by the euphemism *devadana* (literally, "giving to god"), although the wealth was directed to temple elites. Temples sometimes redistributed their income—such as sharing rice and vegetables on feast days—although largely with the temple's employees and devotees. Even centuries later, observers noted that grand south Indian temples were built at the financial expense of common people. For example, writing in the seventeenth century CE, Bhimsen noted that agricultural wealth was directed to erecting temples in southern India while the people ate coarse rice.[51]

In Chola times, people sometimes lost more than a good meal to royal temples. Some villagers were compelled to sell their land to temples to pay off fines imposed by the Chola state.[52] Other times, lower-class people sold themselves to temples, such as Nambanambi Kadugal Nangai who sold herself, her daughter, her grandson, his children, and others to a temple in Malapperumballam.[53] In 1201 CE, a man was watching his children starve to death and so sold himself and his two daughters to a temple in Tiruppamburam.[54] In such cases, reality and theory aligned. A dharmashastra text from the same century, written in south India, proclaims that famine or debt legitimizes slavery for everyone but Brahmins, who can properly only be slave owners and never slaves.[55] Numerous additional thirteenth-century inscriptions feature people in dire financial straits who sold themselves to Tamil Nadu temples.[56]

Slavery was practiced throughout medieval southern India. The eminent twentieth-century historian of the Cholas, Nilakanta Sastri, drew attention to "the most odious form of private property in human beings" in several inscriptions.[57] Sastri noted that slaves (*adimai*) often worked the fields, which makes sense since the Cholas supported rice, a labor intensive crop.[58] Slaves also provided domestic labor in private homes and in Hindu temples.[59] These bonded laborers were owned by a mix of Brahmins, military chiefs, political dynasties, merchants, and Hindu temples.[60] Like nonhuman forms of property within Chola domains, slaves could be confiscated as punishment to their owners and sold at auction.[61] Today, far more people associate sky-scrapping temples with Chola cultural achievements than slavery, and yet the two went together.

Outside of temples, Brahminical privilege and social segregation placed pressure on medieval south Indian society. As mentioned, Brahmin communities began to migrate from the north into Tamil Nadu during the first millennium CE. They soon started to receive royal land grants, a key means through which Brahmins across the subcontinent expanded their wealth and social standing. Some land grants to Brahmins had environmental implications in that they required forest clearing, a point explicitly mentioned in inscriptions in Goa (sixth century) and Tamil Nadu (eighth century).[62] By the tenth century, Brahmins were "influential landholders" in southern India.[63] There is limited evidence from the ninth–tenth centuries of less social stratification in non-Brahmin, as compared to Brahmin, villages.[64] Perhaps greater social inclusion—a vice for premodern Brahminical communities—was one reason that the Cholas directed that non-Brahmins sell their lands within Brahmin (*brahmadeya*) villages in the early eleventh century.[65] Overall caste distinctions became more pronounced over the subsequent few centuries in south India.[66]

Gender inequality was also a feature of medieval temples and associated religious activities. Elite women had the most options, but even they were circumscribed. For instance, a Chalukya queen patronized Rani ki Vav (Queen's step well) in Gujarat around 1085, and, as mentioned, Chola royal women sponsored icons. Beyond royalty, elite women served as donors to Hindu temples and other religious institutions in Tamil Nadu between the eighth and thirteenth centuries but far less frequently than men. Elite Hindu women also appear in the inscriptional record as patrons less often than their female Jain counterparts in the region.[67]

We have far more information about male religious activities, such as the establishment of mathas (monasteries) affiliated with Shaiva temples. The dawn of mathas heralded a larger shift of Hindu renunciant activity from individual ascetics who often lived outside of society to an organized structure that controlled entry and could amass resources.[68] Mathas also served other functions going forward, including as feeding houses and male educational institutions. At times, they even drew cross-religious patronage, such as a 926 Rashtrakuta grant in Maharashtra that records donations to a matha made by Madhumati (the Sanskrit version of Muhammad), a Muslim administrator who worked for the Rashtrakutas.[69]

Culture, Religion, and Pleasure

Perhaps the most emblematic objects associated with Chola rule are stunning bronze statues, most often of Hindu gods. South Indians began to cast bronze images in the eighth century, and the art form became refined under the Cholas between the ninth and thirteenth centuries.[70] Chola bronzes are typically 90–95 percent copper, which makes these exquisite objects extraordinarily heavy.[71] Artisans cast them using the lost wax technique, so called because it involves breaking the wax mold, and so each piece is unique.[72] Chola bronzes feature many subjects, with the most famous being dancing Shiva. This form was popularized by Queen Sembiyan (tenth century) and shows Shiva dancing on a dwarf who symbolizes ignorance while the god's dreadlocks spin out and he is surrounded by a ring of fire (figure 9.1).[73] The same artists who fashioned dancing Shivas also made images of Vishnu, the Gautama Buddha, and other figures.[74] Some striking statues feature the aged and emaciated Mother of Karaikkal (figure 9.2), one of sixty-three Shaiva saints who asked Shiva to take away her body's weight so she could watch him dance forever.[75] Chola artisanal skills were valued widely in their times, and the bronzes remain prized objects on the art market today.

Chola bronzes are usually displayed unadorned in modern museums, but this is not how they appeared and still appear to worshippers in religious contexts. Chola bronzes were covered with jewels, flowers, and silk clothing to honor the deity that these adornments invite to inhabit the icon. As mentioned, Chola temples probably drew an elite crowd, but bronze icons were slightly more accessible during periodic processions. On certain days, temple priests—along with dancers, elephants, and others—would chaperon bronze icons around a particular area.[76] Some Chola bronzes were cast with hoops precisely to enable them to be carried or tied to palanquins. During processions, whether in the Chola dynasty or today, the bronze image is not particularly visible since it is heavily adorned and is also typically shaded by a parasol. But the point is not to see the icon so much as to glimpse the divinity believed to inhabit it. This glimpse or *darshan* (from Sanskrit *darshana*) goes two ways in that the devotee and deity see one another.[77] Such processions inspired displays of personal religious devotion (*bhakti*) among devotees, which were sometimes recorded by south Indian poet saints, with Vaishnavas known as *alvar*s and Shaivas as *nayanar*s.

Figure 9.1. Shiva as lord of the dance (*nataraja*), Chola dynasty, eleventh century CE, Tamil Nadu, India, copper alloy.

Subcontinental dynasties beyond the Cholas also engaged in large-scale temple construction during this period, and the Chandellas (ca. 831–1308) are noteworthy for sponsoring sexual imagery in their temples at Khajuraho in central India. The Khajuraho temples date between the tenth and eleventh centuries and include a Jain temple, a Surya temple, and three large royal temples, one for Vishnu and two for Shiva.[78] The Chandellas adorned the outer walls of Khajuraho's royal temples with auspicious images of the gods, women, and erotic depictions. The first two were standard, but the third—which includes couples making love in

Figure 9.2. Shaiva saint Mother of Karaikkal, thirteenth century CE, Tamil Nadu, India, copper alloy.

different positions, oral sex, orgies, and bestiality—calls for further contextualization.[79] As discussed (chapter 7), premodern Hindu traditions embraced a broad range of human sexuality through the ideal of kama (sensual pleasure). The early eleventh-century *Shilpaprakasha*, an architectural treatise written in Orissa from a tantric perspective, proclaims: "A place devoid of erotic imagery is a place to be shunned."[80] In other words, the Chandellas placed erotic images on Vishnu and Shiva temple walls to mark them as religious spaces. Some modern scholars have offered additional interpretations, including that the erotic images encode secret *yantras* (diagrams), represent a higher union, or alleviate the need to perform sexual rituals.[81] Even these polyphonic readings rely on erotic depictions being considered a virtuous part of Hindu temple imagery.

Many premodern Indians found sexuality an interesting, pleasurable subject to include in various discussions. For example, the mid-twelfth century Brahmin Bhaskara was a renowned mathematician whose *Lilavati* includes verses such as:

> Whilst making love a necklace broke
> A row of pearls mislaid.
> One-sixth fell on the floor
> One-fifth fell on the bed
> The woman saved a third
> One-tenth were caught by her lover
> If six pearls remained on the string
> How many pearls were there altogether?[82]

The math problem is real (the answer is thirty), but more memorable than a basic equation to most people is the image of a pearl necklace snapping in the heat of passion. Medieval kings, too, drew on sexual imagery, such as in rhetoric celebrating political conquests. For example, a verse from the Tirukalangadu copper plates of Rajendra I (1018) describes how Vijayalaya, founder of the Chola dynasty, "took possession of Tanchapuri (Thanjavur)" like "he would seize his own wife" for love sport.[83]

One further Hindu religious development merits discussion here because it took an unusual approach to caste and gender: Virashaivas, also known as Lingayats. "Virashaiva" literally means "militant devotee of Shiva," and this group stood apart from their contemporaries in largely shunning temple-based worship and welcoming those from various caste backgrounds and women.[84] The Virashaivas still boasted elite, upper-caste, male leadership. Perhaps the most famous early Virashaiva was Basavanna, who also headed the Kalachuri treasury in the twelfth century.[85] Still, Virashaiva followers were more mixed, and women and lower-caste people are well represented among the more than 200 authors of the Kannada poems known as *vachanas* (utterances) in the twelfth and thirteenth centuries.[86] For example, Akka Mahadevi (twelfth century) is remembered to have sought only Shiva as her husband, rejecting traditional domestic life, while Sule Sankavva reflected on her former life as a prostitute.[87]

Virashaiva Vachana Poetry, by Two Women (Kannada), Twelfth-Thirteenth Centuries

Akka Mahadevi:

Husband inside,
lover outside.
I can't manage them both.

This world
and that other,
cannot manage them both.

O lord white as jasmine,

I cannot hold in one hand
both the round nut
and the long bow.[88]

I love the Handsome One:
he has no death
decay nor form
no place or side
no end nor birthmarks.
I love him O mother. Listen.

I love the Beautiful One
with no bond nor fear
no clan no land
no landmarks
for his beauty.

So my lord, white as jasmine, is my husband.

Take these husbands who die,
decay, and feed them
to your kitchen fires.[89]

Sule Sankavva:

In my harlot's trade
having taken one man's money.

I daren't accept a second man's, sir.
And if I do,
they'll stand me naked and kill me, sir.
And if I cohabit with the polluted,
my hands, nose, and ears
they'll cut off with a red-hot knife, sir.
Ah, never, no,
knowing you I will not.
My word on it, libertine Shiva.[90]

The vachanas were also part of the larger development of south Indian vernacular literature during this period. Poets had written in Kannada since the late first millennium CE, heavily borrowing from Sanskrit aesthetic theory.[91] The poet Nannaya—known as the first Telugu poet—wrote a Telugu Mahabharata in the eleventh century.[92] In this regard, south India far preceded the north, where vernacular literatures did not arise until the second millennium CE.[93]

Transregional Trade and Cultural Exchanges

Local and interregional trade flourished in medieval south India, with powerful merchant guilds taking leading roles. Most notably, a Tamil-origin guild known as Ainnurruvar (or Ayyavole) operated across southern India and as far away as Sumatra by the eleventh century.[94] Guilds described themselves using the standard language of praise poetry (*prashasti*) of their day, also common among dynasties. For example, an 1135 Kannada record invokes a plethora of mythological figures from the epics and other Hindu stories to compare the Ainnurruvar guild to "Rama in energy, Arjuna in prowess, Bhishma in purity, Bhima in boldness, Yudhishthira in righteousness, Sahadeva in knowledge, Indra in enjoyment, Kama in generosity, and Surya in brilliance."[95] The inscription follows this flattery—which depends on detailed knowledge of Hindu stories to grasp—with a list of names and jobs, including Vesapayya (a trader), Rava (a recorder), and Khapparayya (a sheriff).[96] The Ainnurruvar encompassed Hindus of different caste backgrounds and Jains, with some local concentrations of particular castes.[97] Like kings, medieval south Indian trade guilds patronized widely, including supporting

Vaishnava, Shaiva, Jain, Buddhist, and Muslim groups.[98] Guilds also took care of their own, such as giving breaks on taxes and customs to Revana around 1000 CE, after he avenged a merchant's murder.[99]

Tamil trade guilds benefited from and materially supported Chola power, which is visible in an early eleventh-century military altercation in Southeast Asia. A Sumatran dynasty known as the Srivijayas and the Cholas traded with one another. But the Srivijayas misrepresented the Cholas as their vassal in Chinese contexts, and they might have tried to issue levies on Tamil merchants sailing through the Strait of Malacca en route to China.[100] In 1023, the Chinese Song dynasty directed Arab traders to shift overland routes to sea trade, which probably placed additional pressure.[101] In 1025, in protection of trade interests, the Chola king Rajendra I sent ships to the Strait of Malacca and sacked Srivijayan cities on the Malay Peninsula, Nicobar Islands, and Sumatra.[102] In this action, the Cholas relied on an armada marshalled from trade vessels.[103]

Over the next several centuries, Tamil guild trade with China flourished, and Chola decline in the thirteenth century seemed to be irrelevant to this bustling commerce. Marco Polo visited the Chinese port city of Quanzhou in the late 1200s and attested that Indian ships alighted often, bearing spices, precious stones, pearls, and more.[104] The Tamil community in Quanzhou even built a Shiva temple in 1281 that bore a bilingual Tamil and Chinese inscription complete with a reference to Kublai Khan, the Mongol ruler at time.[105] The Shiva temple was one of many non-Chinese structures in medieval Quanzhou, which also housed six Arab-constructed mosques.[106] Chinese leaders also sought trade relations, including through force, with Sri Lanka. A trilingual stele—in Chinese, Persian, and Tamil—was erected in Galle, Sri Lanka, in 1409 to honor a trade-cum-military visit of the Chinese Ming commander Zheng He (1371–1433).[107]

Alongside trade, aspects of Indian culture and religions continued to circulate in Southeast Asia. Hindu artefacts have been found in southern Vietnam, including hundreds of small golden plaques of deities made throughout much of the first millennium CE.[108] More spectacularly, the twelfth-century Cambodian ruler Suryavarman II, who maintained diplomatic relations with the Cholas, built the large temple complex of Angkor Wat that still draws many visitors today.[109] The oldest Javanese Ramayana was penned in the tenth century based largely on a ca. 600 retelling of Rama's tale in Sanskrit.[110] Javanese translators adapted

Figure 9.3. Fresco of two ladies at Sigiriya, fifth century CE, Sri Lanka, painted on rock face.

the story to speak to local contexts such that their Ramayana can be read as narrating the victory of a local Javanese king over his rival or even the triumph of Shaiva traditions over Buddhism.[111]

In Sri Lanka, a public literary culture flourished at Sigiriya between the eighth and ninth centuries. Sigiriya is a large palace complex that includes frescoes of beautiful women painted in the fifth century (figure 9.3). It became a tourist hotspot in the late first millennium, and nearly 700 visitors, ranging from kings to merchants, inscribed verses of premodern Sinhalese poetry at the site.[112] Numerous verses refer to large crowds gathering at Sigiriya, with one proclaiming, "That rock, Sihigiri, captivates the minds of many people who have ascended it."[113] Many of the verses at Sigiriya analyze the fresco images of women in a multi-century art critique.[114] Some speak wistfully of the paintings, such as this chapter's epigraph in which a man wonders why one of these beautiful painted women remains silent. Several verses respond to one another, such as by borrowing another's words or trying to improve on an earlier bit of poetry.[115] At least one verse echoes Kalidasa's fifth-century *Meghaduta*, which attests to a broader literary exchange with the subcontinent.[116] A few authors even came from India to carve a verse at Sigiriya.[117]

Kerala's coast in southwestern India, too, was part of trade and cultural exchange networks. By the ninth century, the Malabar coast hosted Arab Muslim, Jewish, Persian, and Indian communities.[118] Sometimes, one group dominated over trade of a particular item, such as Arabs who controlled the horse trade.[119] Other times, there were partnerships, and one such example comes to us from the Geniza documents. The Geniza documents are a trash heap of writings discarded in twelfth-century Egypt that, among other things, contain information on a handful of Jewish traders who spent time in India.

One intriguing India-related Geniza story featured Abraham Ben Yiju who liberated a female slave named Ashu in Mangalore on the Malabar coast in the fall of 1132. Abraham gave Ashu the Jewish name Berakha and married her.[120] This marriage was enabled by the robust trade connections that had flourished for more than a millennium across the Arabian Sea, but it was still unusual. We do not know how the couple was received in India, where they resided for years while Abraham Ben Yiju ran a bronze factory that made custom orders for clients in Aden.[121] But, when the pair journeyed to Aden years later, they received the cold shoulder, because some within the Jewish community perceived the cross-cultural marriage involving a former master and slave as illegitimate.[122] Other aspects of the couple's lives were more standard for their times. For instance, Ashu bore three children, one of whom died in infancy or as a toddler.[123]

Conclusion: Cholas no More

The thirteenth century witnessed significant unrest in Tamil Nadu. A rash of temples instituted stricter rules on their administrators in the 1200s, signaling a rise in corruption (which had long cropped up in temple inscriptions).[124] Many Chola bronzes were buried in this period, and some still resurface today, tinted green from exposure to wet soil for centuries.[125] Chola territory shank to around Thanjavur, and the dynasty formally ended in 1279 when it was absorbed by the Pandyas. Dynastic fighting and falling was hardly unusual, but burying statues suggests additional uncertainty among southern Indians at the time. Then again, perhaps we just happen to glimpse at this moment the insecurity that probably characterized life for many in medieval India.

Further Reading

For the Cholas, I found the work of Vidya Dehejia, Noboru Karishma, and Y. Subbarayalu to be especially insightful. For trans-regional relations, the edited volume by Hermann Kulke, K. Kesavapany, and Vijay Sakhuja deserves special mention for focusing on connections east of India. I used S. D. Goitein and Mordechai Friedman's scholarship on the Geniza documents. On temple desecration, Richard Davis and Richard Eaton are the leading authorities. Finbarr Flood's work on the Ghaznavids is excellent, and the best analysis of Mahmud of Ghazna's raid of Somnath and accounts thereof is Romila Thapar's 2004 book.

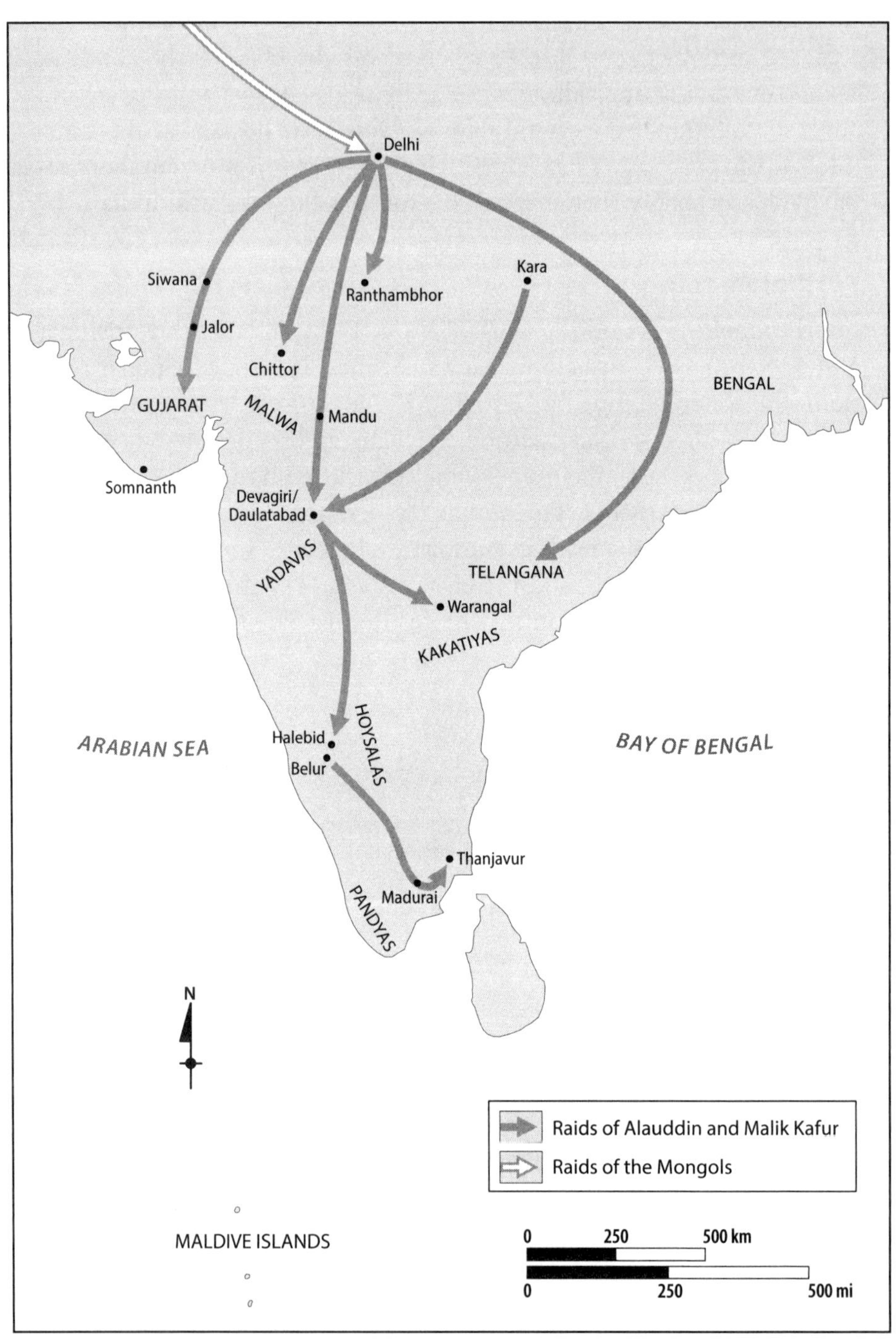

Khalji raids, 1299–1311.

10

Indo-Persian Rule and Culture, 1190–1350

I ask but this: that occasionally
you should come and cast a glance upon me.

—Nizamuddin Awliya, ca. 1300 CE (Persian)[1]

Around 1030 CE, a Buddhist author argued that upper-caste Hindus were on the fast track to becoming Muslims since both, in contrast to Buddhists, embraced violence: "In both Islam (*mlecchadharme*) and Vedic traditions (*vedadharme*), killing is required for the sake of the gods and one's ancestors. It is the same for Kshatriyas (*kshatradharme*). The Brahmin sages said, 'Having pleased your forefathers and gods, it is not an error to eat meat' and 'I see no error in a person who would injure an evil man.' Therefore, those who consider Vedic traditions authoritative will embrace Islam."[2] This Buddhist prediction—citing dharmashastra and religious treatises—proved incorrect. Over the course of the second millennium CE, many communities were incorporated into Hindu traditions through the spread of rituals and caste hierarchy, but most Indians did not become Muslim. Even as Islam remained (and remains today) a minority religion on the subcontinent, followers of this broad-based tradition—*musalmans* in north Indian vernacular—became embedded within the rich tapestry of South Asian life from the late twelfth century onward. This chapter traces some early threads in this integration, focusing on Indo-Muslim culture in Delhi and Daulatabad during the thirteenth and fourteenth centuries. Parts of this history feature political violence, a fact of premodern life shared by Indian rulers of all religious, cultural, and regional backgrounds.[3] The political success of Indo-Muslim dynasties paved the way for other changes, including large-scale building projects, the flourishing of Persian literature in India, and creative cultural achievements.

Indo-Muslim Rule from Delhi

In the 1180s–1190s, the Ghurids, a small dynasty from a mountainous region of Afghanistan, began to move into northern India, cannibalizing Ghaznavid holdings in the northwest and Punjab. They took Lahore in 1186 and conquered Delhi in 1192. The Ghurids brought with them myriad cultural innovations—including a rulership style, architectural agenda, languages (especially Persian), and religion—still unknown across most of India. Critically, the Ghurids were not a one-off. Rather, they were followed by five dynasties of Persian-speaking Muslims that sequentially ruled from Delhi (and, occasionally, from other Indian cities), collectively known as the Delhi Sultanate (1192–1526). Two Delhi Sultanate dynasties—the Khaljis (1290–1320) and the Tughluqs (1320–1414)—briefly conquered parts of central and southern India, a disruption that created the conditions for new kingdoms to rise (both Muslim-led and Hindu-led). These political activities also paved the way for rich cultural exchanges between subcontinental communities. Altogether, Indo-Persian, or Indo-Muslim, rule lasted into the nineteenth century in parts of South Asia, including in Delhi, and initiated a cascade of cultural, linguistic, political, social, and religious shifts.

Ghurid conquest proceeded rapidly in northern India, although little changed on the ground at first. The Ghurids benefited from upswings in military technology in the eleventh–twelfth centuries. Specifically, wider use of nailed shoes and stirrups made horses nimbler in warfare.[4] Indian rulers sometimes treated those they conquered harshly. For example, the *Manasollasa* (Mind's delight), a ca. 1130 Sanskrit encyclopedia penned in Karnataka by a Chalukya king, recommends: "The enemy's capital city should be burned—the palace of the king, beautiful buildings, palaces of princes, ministers and high-ranking officers, temples, streets with shops, horse and elephant stables."[5] But the Ghurids, relative newcomers to the subcontinent, followed a different custom of reinstating as vassal rulers those they decimated in battle. For instance, after dominating at the Battle of Tarain in 1192, the victorious

Ghurids reinstalled the defeated Prithviraj Chauhan as ruler of Ajmer.[6] After similar victories, the Ghurids restored thrones to the Gahadavalas in Benares, the Chalukyas in Patan, and the Pratiharas in Gwalior.[7] Such continuity meant that most Indians likely experienced minimal changes in their daily lives as their local rulers were demoted from independent to subsidiary kings.

The Ghurids also drew on preexisting north Indian religious and political idioms. In 1199, they converted from the Karramiya sect of Islam—which had distinct burial, prayer, and ablution practices—to mainstream Sunni Islam.[8] This decision gave them access to Islamic and Persian-based expressions of kingship, and, around the same time, Ghurid rulers also began calling themselves "sultans."[9] The Ghurids similarly adopted long-standing Indian approaches to sovereignty, such as invoking Sanskrit to boast territorial gain. After Muhammad bin Bakhtiyar Khalji sacked and reinstated the Senas of Bengal in 1204, he had a coin struck in Muhammad Ghuri's name proclaiming, in Sanskrit written in Devanagari script: *gauda vijaya* (on the conquest of Bengal). The coin also featured a horseman—a shared symbol of sovereignty across numerous Asian royal traditions—which was repeated on slightly later Delhi Sultanate coins.[10]

While maintaining local rulers, the Ghurids brought new customs to northern India, including a system of elite slavery (*bandagan-i khass*). Boys were captured or bought, preferably young, and separated from their families to break natal ties. They were raised to ensure undying loyalty to their master alone, a bond that persisted beyond manumission and that only expired with their master's death.[11] The slaves were highly educated and valued, with the most skillful earning high status in society and even becoming kings.[12] Ghurid elite slavery—also called military slavery and practiced by numerous Delhi Sultanate dynasties—was rather different than the unskilled, indigent enslavement we have encountered elsewhere in premodern India (chapters 6–9). As mentioned, Brahminical thinkers justified slavery as related to caste and gender within a broader social hierarchy of oppression. This slavery persisted during and after Delhi Sultanate rule.[13] Military slavery was distinct, including in its robust consequences for royal succession.

Again and again, former slaves ascended the Delhi Sultanate throne, including Aybek (r. 1206–1210), Iltutmish (r. 1210–1236), and Balban (r. 1266–1287). Some scholars refer to these rulers (and those in between them) as the Mamluk (Slave) dynasty. Delhi Sultanate kings (including former slaves) also had sons, and so an early tension was whether the throne should pass to a king's favorite slave or son.[14] Shihabuddin Ghuri preferred his slaves to rule, reportedly saying: "While other rulers may have one or two sons, I have many thousand sons, in other words my Turkish slaves, and my dominions will be their inheritance."[15] Indeed, after Shihabuddin's death in 1206, his favored slave Aybek ruled from Lahore for four years. Simultaneously, another slave, Iltutmish, consolidated his power in Delhi. Iltutmish formally ruled as sultan from 1210 onward, after Aybek's fatal fall from a horse while playing a fierce variety of polo known as *chaugan*.[16]

Aside from former slaves, one additional early Delhi Sultanate ruler stands out: Queen Raziyya (r. 1236–1240). Raziyya's father, Iltutmish, named her as the heir apparent in 1233, several years after her brother's death, and she was placed on the throne by her father's elite slaves.[17] There was precedent for thinking of women as kingmakers in Indian politics. For example, the *Chachnama*, a 1226 Persian transcreation of an Arabic text about Sind, features several Hindu women who swayed political events in the eighth century.[18] But female rulers were rare in premodern India. To survive in a man's world, Raziyya gender-bended, abandoning the seclusion (*purdah*) expected of Muslim women of her status and instead donning male dress. Amir Khusraw (1253–1325), a famous Persian poet of the era, described her emergence from purdah thus:

> For several months, her face was veiled—
> her sword's ray flashed, lightning-like, from behind the screen.
> Since the sword remained in the sheath,
> many rebellions were left unchecked.
> With a royal blow, she tore away the veil;
> she showed her face's sun from behind the screen.
> The lioness showed so much force that brave men bent low
> before her.[19]

Poetry aside, Raziyya's decision to abandon purdah yielded practical advantages, enabling her to mix freely at court and lead troops into battle from atop an elephant.[20]

Ultimately, however, Raziyya's independence sat ill with many powerful men. Raziyya had asked to be judged based on her ability to rule, saying:

If I am better than men,
then place me on the throne.
And if you see my qualities in another,
then throw the royal crown from my head.[21]

But the lone Delhi Sultanate queen did not get her wish, instead being deposed by elite male slaves of Turkish descent who were motivated, in part, by their displeasure at her close relationship with Jamaluddin Yaqut, a military slave of Ethiopian descent. In general, Turkish slaves were most highly valued and guarded their privilege, especially against those of Ethiopian and Indian origin.[22] Later historians, too, failed to judge Raziyya on her own merits, instead falling back on standard misogyny of their time. For example, writing about Raziyya in the Deccan around 1350, Isami maligned women as unfaithful and sexually uncontrollable to the point, he says, that even a pious woman (*zan-i parsa*) will sleep with a dog.[23] After Raziyya's rule, the Delhi Sultanates returned to their customary lineup of male sovereigns.

The Ghurids and subsequent Delhi Sultanate rulers were builders, especially of mosques, which enhanced the Indian landscape's religious diversity. Mosques had dotted parts of the subcontinent for close to half a millennium already, appearing in Sind in the eighth century and along southern coasts by the tenth century.[24] But Ghurid architecture was distinctive and their building agenda ambitious. For example, the Ghurids constructed Ajmer's Adhai ka Jhompra Mosque in the 1190s, reusing pillars from Jain and Hindu temples. Such reuse was common, and its precise form at sites in central and eastern Rajasthan suggests Hindu-Muslim collaboration.[25] Not all Ghurid structures survive in their original form, however. In the 1190s, the Ghurids built a mosque in Sadadi, Rajasthan that was later converted into a Shiva temple.[26]

Indians treated mosques like other places of worship in many respects. Sometimes, premodern South Asians called mosques *dharmashala*s (places of dharma), a term also used for Hindu temples (chapter 11). Mosques were incorporated into India's existing ecumenical patronage practices. For example, the thirteenth-century Jain merchant Jagadu sponsored mosques, Hindu temples, and Jain temples in Gujarat.[27] Muslim-sponsored mosques, too, often showed local accommodations, such as a mosque built in Veraval, Gujarat, in 1264 that was accompanied by a bilingual Arabic and Sanskrit inscription.[28] One difference worth noting is that, whereas Hindu temples were widely perceived to embody the authority of individual rulers (chapters 8–9), royally sponsored mosques were not. Accordingly, mosques in premodern India were more rarely targeted for political desecrations or destructions, in contrast to temples. But there were exceptions, such as the Rajput destruction of mosques in seventeenth-century Jodhpur during a political conflict.[29]

Delhi Sultanate building agendas left a strong mark in and around Delhi, a city of minor consequence previously but that henceforth served as the seat of power in northern India. Most visibly, the Ghurids and Delhi Sultanate dynasties built the Qutb complex, which today is a well-visited tourist site consisting of a large minar, congregational mosque, major gateway, numerous tombs, and other structures. The Ghurids began the large minar, which was added onto by many later Delhi Sultanate rulers and stands at 238 feet tall at present, slightly higher than Thanjavur's Rajarajeshvaram Temple built by the Cholas (chapter 9).[30] The Qutb Minar bears inscriptions in Persian, Arabic, and either corrupt Sanskrit or an early Hindavi vernacular, including Quranic verses and identification as a "victory tower" (*kiratirambha*, from Sanskrit *kirtistambha*).[31] The Qutb Minar complex also features an iron pillar of the Guptas (figure 10.1), which was possibly moved to Delhi by the Tomars, a minor dynasty that ruled from the early eleventh to mid-twelfth centuries.[32] Just as the Tomars had appropriated the iron pillar, so too did the Delhi Sultanate, incorporating it into the congregational mosque near the Qutb Minar in a case of "cultural continuity."[33]

Not all attempts to proclaim political strength at the Qutb complex succeeded, however. Within the site lays the ruined base of a minar begun by Alauddin Khalji (r. 1296–1316), who is notable for his extensive conquests in central and southern India (described later in this chapter).[34] The minar was intended to be twice the size of the Qutb Minar, but it was never completed, and its stunted, ruinous condition stands as a testament to human folly. As the famous fourteenth-century Persian poet Sadi wrote of the fleeting nature of earthly power: "Realize now, while you hold these good things in your hand, that fortune and kingship move from hand to hand."[35]

Delhi Sultanate rulers also altered the landscape around Delhi through forest clearing, thus making the city more accessible. Their actions displaced some forest communities. For example, the Meos people

Figure 10.1. Qutb Minar with Gupta iron pillar in foreground, twelfth-thirteenth centuries CE in Mehrauli (Qutb Minar), fourth-fifth centuries CE and maybe Madhya Pradesh (iron pillar), Qutb Complex, Delhi, India.

who lived in the hills in Mewat were forcibly resettled or enslaved in the late thirteenth century.[36] Presumably, forest dwellers resented losing their homes and freedom, a contrast to the many north Indian Hindu elites who welcomed Delhi's urbanization. The merchant Uddhara, for example, moved his family of twelve (including three wives) from Uch,

Sind to Delhi in the mid-thirteenth century.[37] In 1276, he sponsored a stepwell near Delhi for travelers, and a Sanskrit inscription marking the occasion celebrates the "great city called Delhi," likening it to a "treasure mine of amazing jewels."[38] The inscription also places the Delhi Sultanate in line with earlier rulers, including the Tomars and Chauhans.[39]

Uddhara's contemporaries offered similar positive assessments of Delhi under Sultanate rule, such as Amir Khusraw who imagined it as challenging Mecca, the holiest Islamic city:

> Excellent Delhi, the protection of religion and justice,
> it is the garden of Eden; may it flourish forever.
> It is like an earthly paradise in its qualities—
> May God guard it from all calamities! . . .
> If Mecca but heard of this garden
> it would circumambulate Hindustan.
> The city of the Prophet takes oaths by it;
> the city of God became deafened from its fame.[40]

Khusrau also described Delhi's inhabitants, especially its young men as was common in Indo-Persian poetry (see the ghazal in the following section). More broadly, Delhi Sultanate domains proved attractive to many migrants in the thirteenth century, including those seeking refuge from Mongol incursions further north.[41]

Delhi grew throughout the fourteenth century, with stone structures rising due to Khalji and Tughluq patronage. These dynasties built new forts—including Siri, Tughluqabad, and Firoz Shah Kotla—which can all be visited as ruins today. Firuz Shah Tughluq (r. 1351–1388) erected numerous pillars, including an Ashokan pillar that still stands at the center of Firoz Shah Kotla in southern Delhi and speaks to how Indian kings remembered and appropriated their predecessors. The pillar bears a third-century-BCE Mauryan Prakrit inscription in Brahmi script, which nobody could read by Firoz Shah's time 1,600 years later. But the pillar also has a Chauhan inscription dated to 1164 CE, written in Sanskrit in Devanagari script, which some people in Firoz Shah's Delhi could read. It celebrates Chauhan conquests, exaggerated as ranging from the Himalayas up north to the Vindhyas down south. Some premoderns even slotted Ashokan pillars into later myths or remembered history, imagining that they were walking sticks of Bhima from the Mahabharata or had been erected by Alexander of Macedon (who got nowhere near Delhi; chapter 3).[42] Even if in a very different way than us today, premodern Indians thought about their multi-sourced past.

Economically, Delhi Sultanate rulers introduced notable innovations. Iltutmish established the silver tanka, a coin to which the currencies of modern-day Bangladesh, Pakistan, India, and Sri Lanka can be traced.[43] In general, the establishment of the Delhi Sultanate meant that silver stayed within the subcontinent, rather than leaving as plunder.[44] Still, silver shortages arose at times, such as after the Delhi Sultanate lost control of Bengal to an independent Muslim dynasty in 1342.[45] This inspired Muhammad bin Tughluq (r. 1325–1351) to introduce token currency, where the value of coins exceeds their metallic components. Muhammad bin Tughluq knew of a similar scheme's success in China, but it failed spectacularly in India due to counterfeiting.[46] As Barani, a curmudgeonly fourteenth-century historian, put it, "every Hindu's house became a mint."[47]

Sufism, Persian, and Vernaculars

Military conquest paved the way for cultural exchanges, including the advent of Indian Sufism. As a mystical orientation within Islam, Sufism is not a distinct denomination but rather an approach that emphasizes a direct experience of God. People were often Sufis while holding other Islamic identities, such as being a jurist, ulama, Sunni, or Shia. Sufism appealed to both men and women as well as, in certain practices, to non-Muslims. There are numerous Sufi lineages (*silsilas*), of which the Chishtis are the most famous in premodern South Asia.[48] The Chishti founder in India, Muinuddin Chishti (d. 1236), migrated to Ajmer in the wake of the Ghurid conquest, possibly motivated by a desire to flee Mongol destruction. He lived in Ajmer the remainder of his life and was known as *gharib navaz* (comfort to the poor).[49] Shortly after his death, Muinuddin's shrine (*dargah*) became a pilgrimage destination where pilgrims sought—and still seek today—a blessing (*barakat*) by propitiating his grave.[50] Kings and princesses numbered among the premodern visitors to this dargah, and subsequent Chishti saints established their own centers in Delhi, the Deccan, and elsewhere.

Nizamuddin Awliya (d. 1325) is a slightly later Chishti who attracted the era's literary talent to his dargah in Delhi. His disciples included the Persian poets Amir Khusraw and Amir Hasan, along with the historian Barani. Amir Khusraw put Nizamuddin's relationship with kings thus:

> An emperor in a faqir's cell,
> a "Refuge of the World" for the heart of the world,
> a King of Kings without throne or crown,
> with kings in need of the dust of his feet.[51]

Indeed, Delhi Sultanate rulers sought out Nizamuddin, trying to access the legitimacy that this charismatic saint could bestow. That said, part of the mystique of Sufi saints derived precisely from them standing aloof from political power, and there are numerous stories that remember Nizamuddin avoiding meeting kings.[52] Amir Hasan recorded his master's teachings and poetry (e.g., this chapter's epigraph) in a *malfuzat* (recorded oral discourses), a popular Persian genre going forward.[53]

Persian literature gained popularity throughout the thirteenth and fourteenth centuries in South Asia and had both translocal and regional cache. On the one hand, Indo-Persian poets participated in a network of Persian literati that stretched across much of Asia. Their shared literary tongue facilitated connections and appreciation across great distances, such as when the Shirazi poet Hafiz (d. 1390) wrote: "All the Indian parrots will turn to crunching sugar with this Persian candy which is going to Bengal."[54] One such parrot—the so-called parrot of India—was Delhi-born Amir Khusraw, whose father was Turkish and mother Indian. Sitting in Shiraz, 2,400 kilometers west of Delhi, Hafiz read Khusraw, and a 1355 copy of Amir Khusraw's *khamsah* (collection of five poems) survives today in Hafiz's handwriting.[55]

Even while finding an audience abroad, authors like Amir Khusraw made Persian an Indian language from the late twelfth century onward and used Persian poetics to express identifiably Indian themes. For example, Amir Khusraw described the practice of sati (widow burning) thus: "In love there is none as mad as a Hindu woman. / Where else is the moth which burns in a dead flame?"[56] His descriptions of Delhi are arresting, drawing on literary tropes (such as an irresistible non-Muslim beloved) to express the allure of north India's growing metropolis (see ghazal).

Amir Khusraw's "Fine Lads of Delhi," Persian Ghazal, ca. 1290

Delhi and its fine lads
with their turbans and twisted beards
openly drinking lovers' blood
while secretly sipping wine.

Willful and full of airs
they pay no heed to anyone.

So close to the heart, they rob
your soul and tuck it safely away.

When they are out for a stroll
rose bushes bloom in the street.

When the breeze strikes them from behind,
see how the turbans topple from their heads.

When they walk, the lovers follow,
blood gushing from their eyes.

Their heads puffed up with beauty's pride,
their admirers' hearts are gone with the wind.

These cheeky, simple Indian lads have made
Muslims into worshippers of the sun.

Those fair Hindu boys
have led me to drunken ruin.
Trapped in the coils of their curly locks
Khusrau is a dog on a leash.[57]

The advent of Persian as an Indian vernacular and literary tongue was welcomed by most. A minority objected, specifically upper-caste Sanskrit intellectuals like Jayanaka (ca. 1200) who lamented the "pallid phonemes" of Persian speakers.[58] Gangadevi (ca. 1380), a female poet and Vijayanagara queen, likened Persian to the "screeching of owls."[59] But, overall, Indians of many different backgrounds adopted Persian as a language of literary expression, government employment, and even religion. Numerous Sanskrit Hindu texts were translated into Persian

Figure 10.2. Shvetambara Jain monk instructing a king, ca. 1300 CE, Gujarat, India, opaque watercolor on palm leaf.

during Delhi Sultanate rule, such as Varahamihira's sixth-century *Brihatsamhita* (Great Compendium) and the *Amritakunda* (Pool of Nectar) on yoga.[60] Some scholars, such as Shihabuddin Nagauri (ca. fourteenth century) studied both Greco-Arabic medicine (*tibb*) and ayurveda with yogis in and around Rajasthan.[61] The Jain monk Jinaprabhasuri (1261–1333)—who spent time at the Tughluq court and, following earlier and contemporary precedents (figure 10.2), interacted with the king—penned three works in Persian.[62] In one poem, he compared the Jina Rishabha, one of the legendary founders of Jainism, to the Islamic Allah.[63]

Just as religion proved no bar to writing in Persian, Muslims also engaged with existing Indian literatures. Amir Khusraw, for one, wrote laudatorily about numerous Indian languages, saying of Sanskrit: "If I knew it well, I would praise my sultan in it also."[64] He is credited with many Hindi verses that are popular today in *qawwali*, a form of Sufi devotional music.[65] Whereas claims about Amir Khusraw being multilingual are unclear historically, many Muslims of his time indeed learned Indian literary languages. A notable case is Abdur Rahman, who authored a Prakrit messenger poem called *Sandesarasaka* in Multan, which had been under Muslim-led rule for centuries. Abdur Rahman (Addahamana in Prakrit) boasted of being "the lotus of his family in Prakrit poetry" and imitated Kalidasa, a famous Sanskrit poet who had lived about 700 years earlier.[66] He even wrote about Hindu religious festivals, such as Diwali:

> Lamps for the festival Dipavali were offered at night,
> held in the hand like a streak of the new moon.
> The houses were ornamented with soft lights.
> Women apply sticks (carrying lamp-black as eyeshadow)
> to their eyes.[67]

Overall, Sanskrit and Prakrit literatures continued to flourish during the thirteenth and fourteenth centuries. In terms of philosophy, the *Mokshopaya* and its abbreviated version, the *Yogavasishtha*, were produced, likely, between the tenth and fourteenth centuries and impart esoteric ideas about liberation within a Vaishnava framework.[68] Other poets chose to write in vernacular tongues and sometimes expressed rather innovative ideas.

In 1290, a Brahmin named Jnandev wrote a commentary on the Bhagavadgita in Marathi, a vernacular language spoken in central India, that radically reinterpreted the text as for Hindus of all castes. Up until this point, readers had generally understood the Gita as articulating caste-based duties for a male, upper-caste audience.[69] But Jnandev argued that the Bhagavadgita was written in relatively simple Sanskrit so that it could reach "women, low castes (Shudras), and others."[70] Jnandev's Marathi translation made the work further accessible and stated that everyone possesses the right (*sarvadhikara*) to access Krishna's teachings.[71] Jnandev did not explicitly include Muslims in his capacious audience, although a roughly contemporary Marathi author, Chakradhar, (his *Lilacharitra* is dated 1278) professes that his teachings were, indeed, for Muslims (*mleccha*) as much as everyone else.[72]

Despite notable sentiments of inclusion, Jnandev's text proffers plenty of evidence for the quotidian reality of caste and gender distinctions in thirteenth-century Maharashtrian society. Moreover, Jnandev proved unable to transcend some biases of his time, advising—as Brahmin men had been advising for centuries—that Shudras should honor Brahmins.[73] Arguably, Jnandev's more lasting innovation was not his limited pushback on caste barriers but rather his emphasis on Krishna worship, a prospering part of Hindu religiosity in this period. For instance, Jayadeva wrote the Sanskrit *Gitagovinda*, which narrates Radha and Krishna's romance, in the twelfth century, and it soon spread from Bengal to Nepal, Gujarat, and elsewhere.[74]

Medieval Indian Buddhism

Buddhism continued as a living tradition in northern India in the twelfth and thirteenth centuries, including in Magadha that was home to key Buddhist sites such as Bodhgaya, Nalanda, and Vikramashila. Some monasteries were sacked by Muhammad bin Bakhtiyar Khalji in 1193, such as Odantapuri and Vikramashila, whereas the status of others remains uncertain. Similar to the targeting of Jain and Hindu temples, a mix of political associations and wealth seems to have informed Muhammad bin Bakhtiyar's selection of targets.[75] Also like earlier assaults on temples, stories about hitting Buddhist monasteries are full of rhetoric and exaggeration such that we cannot take them as straightforwardly true.[76] Material evidence attests that many Magadhan Buddhist sites thrived into the twelfth century and beyond.[77] For example, in the 1230s, a Tibetan monk named Dharmasvamin (ca. 1197–1264) traveled to Nalanda (which may have been hit by the Khaljis in the 1190s, but this remains unconfirmed) and Bodhgaya, where he saw lingering unrest but also ongoing Buddhist practices.[78] Dhyanabhadra was born in Kapilavastu in 1289 and later studied at Nalanda. He participated in a tradition that, by his time, was more than 1,500 years old of Indian Buddhists spreading the dhamma widely, traveling first to Sri Lanka and then spending the 1320s–1360s in Tibet, China, and possibly Korea.[79]

Buddhist practices continued elsewhere on the subcontinent, too, as late as the fifteenth century. For example, at Bodhgaya, the Mahabodhi Temple was maintained and hosted a monastic community into the thirteenth century.[80] Shariputra (d. 1426) was its last known abbot, a post he abdicated to spread the dhamma to China. He left behind an architectural legacy in Beijing.[81] Outside of monastic centers, Buddhist practices, too, flourished in medieval South Asia as lay Buddhist women in eastern India sponsored the production of many manuscripts between the eleventh and thirteenth centuries along with foreign Buddhist men visiting from Nepal or Tibet.[82] One manuscript, of thc *Kalachakratantra*, was dated 1446 and discusses the advent of Muslim-led rule in parts of South Asia.[83] In Kashmir, mentions of a Buddhist community and buildings, including viharas, persist into the fifteenth century.[84] In Assam's Brahmaputra valley, Buddhist monks and tantric practices, perhaps from Nepal, are attested into the seventeenth century.[85]

Even with such qualifiers and pockets on the subcontinent's outskirts, however, Buddhism—the most widely adopted religious tradition that India ever birthed—went extinct (or nearly so) in its homeland between 1250 and 1500 CE, with the exact timing varying by region and community. The pressure to explain Buddhism's disappearance in India stems from its ongoing appeal elsewhere in Asia. After all, Buddhism originated in the fifth century BCE in northern India with two other traditions: the Ajivikas and Jainism. Apart from the historian A. L. Basham, nobody has ever seemed much bothered with explaining the demise of the Ajivikas, who were last heard of in India in the thirteenth century.[86] Jainism never grew beyond the subcontinent (excepting modern immigration) and survives today as a minority South Asian tradition. But many premodern Asians adopted Buddhism, which raises the stakes of the question: Why did Indians give up the dhamma? The best answer probably features a mix of social, religious, and political changes, although more research is needed.[87] In any case, Indian Buddhism was not dead forever. It reemerged, in a radically different form, in twentieth-century conversions by Ambedkar and other Dalits (chapter 21).

Delhi Sultanate Expansion South and Court Culture

The early fourteenth century was a time of unrest and change throughout much of India owing to Delhi Sultanate raids. Alauddin Khalji (r. 1296–1316) and Muhammad bin Tughluq (r. 1325–1351) raided central and southern areas of the subcontinent in pursuit of wealth, land, and fame. They found all three, and their exploits—which reshaped South Asia—were highly discussed at the time. For example, in 1336, the Jain Sanskrit author Kakka described Alauddin's military feats, accurately and poetically, at Devagiri (1296), Ranthambhor (1301), Chittor (1303), Gujarat (1304), and Malwa (1305) (see excerpt). He did not mention Malik Kafur, a Maratha-descent eunuch slave who carried out some of the Delhi Sultanate's most spectacular military feats in southern India in 1310–1311. Aided by new weapons, such as crude grenades and catapults powerful enough to bring down fortification walls, Malik Kafur sacked all three western Chalukya successor states in the Deccan: the Yadavas, the Kakatiyas, and the Hoysalas.[88] He brought back to northern India nearly unimaginable riches, including gold, animals, and jewels. Tying together the violence of conquest with the acquisition of wealth, Amir Khusraw remarked, "For generations the mines will have to drink blood in the stream of the sun before rubies such as these are produced."[89]

Description of Alauddin Khalji's Conquests, Excerpt from Kakka's Jain Sanskrit Text, 1336

Then Sultan Alauddin, who pounds land with galloping horses,
like the ocean does with churning waves, became king.

He went to Devagiri and, having captured its ruler,
reinstalled him there like a victory tower to himself.

Having slain King Hammira, a proud hero and Chauhan ruler,
[Alauddin] gained all his territory.

Having captured the lord of Chittor Fort and having looted his wealth,
he sent him wandering about from city to city like a monkey chained by the neck.

Karna, ruler of Gujarat, was destroyed quickly by his might.
Karna went wandering to foreign lands and then died like a beggar.

Likewise, the fort-based ruler of Malwa was led out like a slave
over many days and died, sapped of all strength.

[Alauddin], shining with Indra's strength, conquered many kings,
including the rulers of Karnataka, Pandya territories, and Telangana.

He grasped towns such as Siwana and Jalor.
Who can count the many difficult places that he dominated?

He reacted to armies of the Mongol ruler that wandered into his land
such that those armies did not come again.[90]

The remarkable military successes of Alauddin Khalji and Malik Kafur allow us to glimpse the cultural fluidity of fourteenth-century South Asia. For example, before Alauddin's 1301 assault on Ranthambhor, three of that fort's four Hindu commanders betrayed their master, the Chauhan sovereign Hammira.[91] Meanwhile, Hammira's four Muslim commanders, all Mongol converts to Islam who had defected from the Khaljis, stood by the last Chauhan king to the bitter end. This episode illustrates a consistent trend in Indian premodernity: namely, people fought on all sides regardless of religious identity. Further details of Khalji raids illustrate the high degree to which, by the early fourteenth century, cultures and peoples were intermixed in India. For example, Hammira, the last Chauhan king, bore a name that was a loose Sanskrit adaptation of the Perso-Arabic "amir," like numerous Hindu kings before and after him.[92] For his part, Malik Kafur was a Maratha from Gujarat.[93] And so, some of the most ferocious raids in Indo-Muslim history were undertaken, not by Turkish-born rulers, but by an Indian whose grit and skills were forged through an imported system of elite slavery.

In the 1320s, the Tughluqs took over the Delhi Sultanate from the Khaljis and initiated further raids into southern India, even shifting their capital south for a time. Muhammad bin Tughluq chose the Deccani city of Devagiri (renamed Daulatabad) for his new capital and brought with him one-tenth of Delhi's population. Many perceived northern and southern India as distinct places at this point in Indian history, and many Delhiites moved south reluctantly. Some soon sank roots in their Deccan home, while others did not. Outsiders, however, seemed to have minded the shift less, such as the Moroccan traveler Ibn Battuta, who was impressed by the quality of the road between Delhi and Daulatabad.[94]

In Delhi and Daulatabad, the mid-fourteenth century Tughluq court brimmed with diverse peoples and practices, both of which were general features of Indo-Muslim dynasties. Those present included Turks, Ethiopians, Persians, north and south Indians, Arabs, and people born of intermarriage between these groups. The ulama, the learned men of Islam, attended court to vie for power, engage in commerce and warfare, and interpret Islamic law (even as they were often ignored on this point by rulers more interested in power and security than theology).[95] Jains participated in Tughluq court life as government employees, such as Thakkura Pheru who worked in the treasury, and as visitors, like the monk Jinaprabhasuri.[96] Hindu ascetics were also present, such as yogis who enjoyed private audiences with Muhammad bin Tughluq.[97]

Tughluq court ritual mixed symbols of royalty from numerous traditions. The king sat cross-legged, in the Indian fashion, surrounded by silks and cushions made of materials gathered from across Asia via ongoing sea and land trade. Some attending court chanted the Arabic phrase *bismillah* (in God's name), while the sovereign was kept free of flies by a whisk, a traditional symbol of Hindu kings (chapter 8). Both horses and elephants were visible at court, animals associated with political power by Asian rulers of many cultural backgrounds.[98] In brief, Indo-Muslim political court culture was syncretic and multi-sourced.

The Moroccan traveler Ibn Battuta (1304–1368/69) seemed to have felt at home in India, especially in Delhi where he served as a judge (*qazi*) between 1334 and 1342. Ibn Battuta's Arabic travelogue largely focuses on Indian Islamic practices but also contains some interesting nuggets about other cultural developments in South Asia.[99] For example, in Karnataka he witnessed a "Muslim yogi" who lived on a public platform during a multi-week fast.[100] Even after nearly a millennium of Brahminical incorporation, yoga traditions retained a certain flexibility that enabled them to be adapted across religious and cultural lines (chapter 8). Ibn Battuta also encountered Buddhists when a group of Chinese emissaries visited the Tughluq court in the early 1340s to request permission to rebuild a Himalayan Buddhist temple. Ibn Battuta was on rocky ground with Muhammad bin Tughluq by this point, and so left Delhi with the Chinese Buddhist delegation. They departed together from Gujarat, but their ship wrecked near Calicut, leaving Ibn Battuta one of the only survivors.[101]

After leaving India, Ibn Battuta had a dramatic eight-month sojourn in the Maldives that points up diversity within South Asian Muslim practices. The Moroccan initially received a warm welcome on the islands and was even appointed chief qazi, probably by misrepresenting his decidedly iffy relations with the Tughluq king of Delhi as warm. Ibn Battuta married four Maldive women rather quickly. But he was unsettled that Muslim women in the Maldives wore no head coverings nor, apparently, much clothing at all. During his time as judge, Ibn Battuta tried to change this but failed. As he put it, "I endeavoured to compel the women to wear clothes, but I was not able to get this done."[102] He had other clashes as well, such as when he ordered a harsh beating of a slave who had slept with a sultan's concubine. The punishment did not sit well with local elites, who soon compelled the Moroccan traveler to divorce his Maldivian wives and decamp from the islands.

Ibn Battuta next visited Sri Lanka, where he journeyed to Adam's Peak to see a nearly 6-foot-long footprint in rock believed to be that of Gautama Buddha, Shiva, and Adam by premodern Buddhists, Hindus, and Muslims, respectively. Ibn Battuta expressed no qualms about the cross-religious nature of this pilgrimage site, but his Maldive troubles were not yet over. Upon receiving word that one of his former Maldive wives had given birth to a son, he returned to claim the boy. Ibn Battuta lasted only five days on the islands before, again, being driven off while his son remained in the Maldives with his mother.[103] Perhaps, by this point, the Moroccan traveler had learned that sharing a religion was not always enough to overcome substantial cultural differences.

Conclusion: Losing Daulatabad

By the mid-1340s, about 150 years after the Ghurid conquest of Delhi, Indo-Persian rule had spurred myriad changes in premodern Indian cultures. And India, too, had changed its most recent newcomers, who had become integrated amid the subcontinent's diverse religious communities. Further cultural and political changes were on the horizon. While the Black Death, a bubonic plague, raged across much of Afro-Eurasia killing tens of millions between 1346 and 1352, in India it was a political crisis that spurred change.[104] During the 1340s, a contingent of north Indians (confusingly, later called Deccanis) who had served the Tughluqs in Daulatabad rebelled and forced those loyal to the Tughluqs to flee back north to Delhi. This created a power vacuum in central and southern India that was largely filled by the Bahmanis in the Deccan and Vijayanagara in the south. As we shall see in the next chapter, these two kingdoms shared much in common as the history of southern India again diverged from that of the north.

Further Reading

Sunil Kumar and Richard Eaton offer rich overarching accounts of the early Delhi Sultanate. I rely on other scholars for work on specific features, including Peter Jackson (state), Alyssa Gabbay (Raziyya), Alka Patel (architecture), and Sunil Sharma (literature). Carl Ernst and Bruce Lawrence offer excellent work on the Chishtis. On medieval Indian Buddhism, I looked especially to Abhishek Amar, Jinah Kim, and the edited volume by Blain Auer and Ingo Strauch.

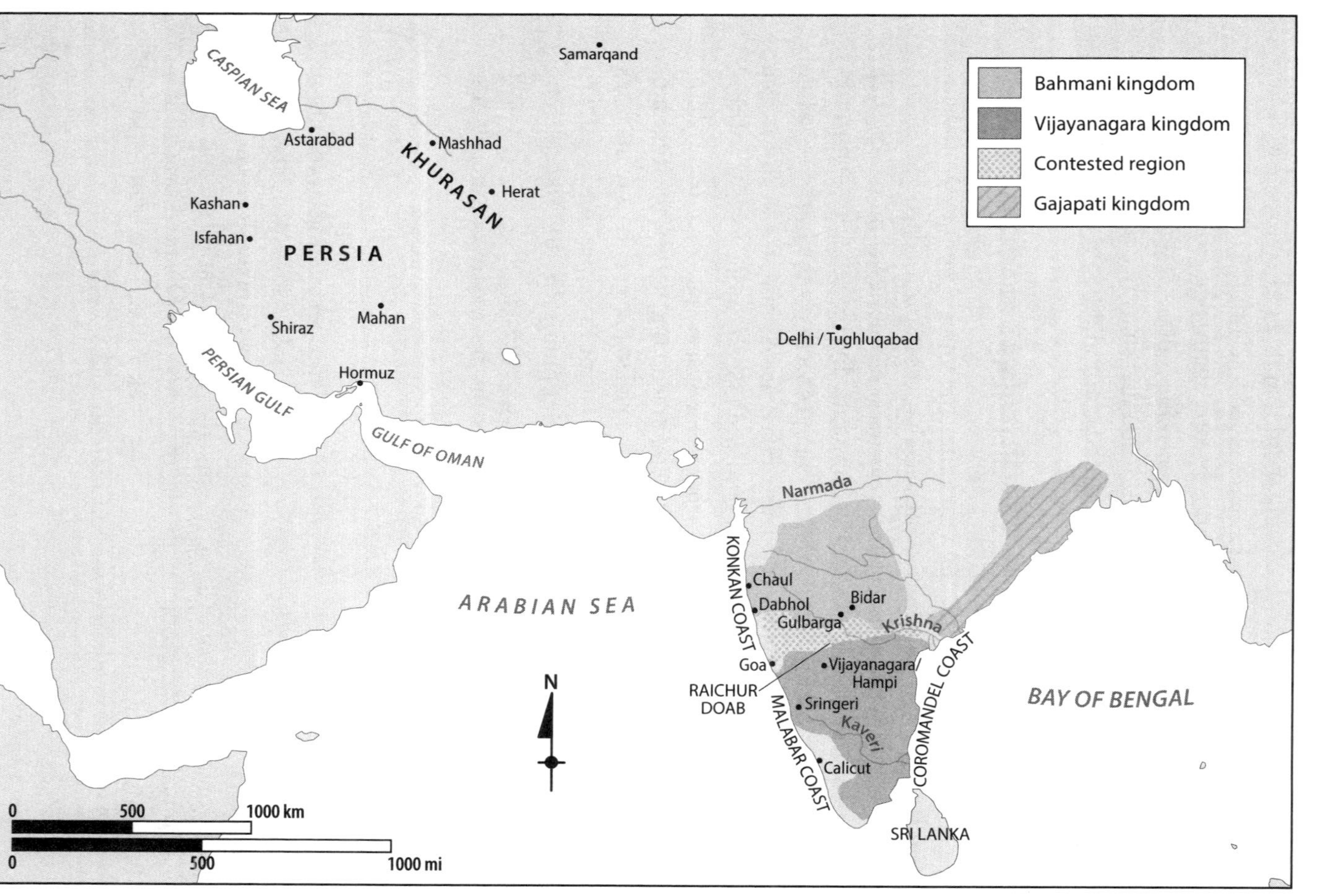

Peninsular India in the long fifteenth century.

11

The Long Fifteenth Century

Do not discriminate between a Hindu or a Musalman.

—Kashmiri Saint Lalla, fourteenth century (Kashmiri)[1]

In the 1440s, Abdul Razzaq traveled thousands of kilometers from Central Asia to Vijayanagara in southern India and found something quite familiar: paan. Paan is a popular Indian treat of areca nuts, lime water, and betel leaves that produces a mild narcotic buzz. Our earliest records of paan on the subcontinent date to the first millennium CE, which is probably when areca nuts began to be imported from their native environment of Southeast Asia.[2] Paan spread west from India, becoming a delicacy believed to offer health and virility across much of the premodern Islamic world by Abdul Razzaq's time.[3] In India, paan also offered an opportunity to consume across class lines, in an environment where many upper-caste elites refused to take meals with either lower castes or outsiders.[4] As a Sanskrit proverb goes: "Paan has lakhs of virtues, my friend, but one looming vice—After you're done sharing it, you have to part from friends."[5] Like paan, many aspects of cultural, political, and social life were shared across communities (including across religious groups) in parts of India and beyond from 1347 until the early 1500s, namely, "the long fifteenth century."[6] Here, I survey some shared, yet regionally manifested, developments from south to north, beginning with the twinned Vijayanagara and Bahmani kingdoms and ending with Kashmir.

Twinned Kingdoms of Vijayanagara and Bahmanis

The Bahmani and Vijayanagara kingdoms were founded in the same year, 1347, as two groups of elites capitalized on a power vacuum opened by the Tughluq retreat to northern India. As Richard Eaton and Phillip Wagoner put it, the kingdoms were "political twins, sharing remembered origins in Tughluq imperialism and a common experience of overthrowing Delhi's overlordship."[7] Bahmani and Vijayanagara similarities extended far beyond their founding stories. Over the better part of 200 years, the two kingdoms shared much in terms of court culture, diverse populations, investment in trade, administrative structures, and social realities. Both lasted into the sixteenth century, ruling on either side of the Krishna River and its fertile surrounding land, known as the Raichur doab. By considering them together here—the Bahmanis in the Deccan and Vijayanagara further south—and not primarily distinguishing them into "Muslim" and "Hindu," I recover some of their shared ruling culture and social norms.

Bahmani and Vijayanagara kings presented themselves similarly at court. Both rulers dressed in a culturally Islamic style, with the Vijayanagara kings wearing white tunics and tall conical hats. Numerous painted and sculpted images of Vijayanagara court attire survive in temples, with the best preserved at a Shiva temple in Lepakshi (in modern-day Andhra Pradesh).[8] This sartorial choice positioned Vijayanagara to easily participate in wider cultural exchanges, exemplified by the visit of the Timurid representative Abdul Razzaq Samarqandi in the 1440s. Abdul Razzaq was sent by Timur's son Shah Rukh (r. 1405–1447) to central India. Upon arriving he heard about the fabulous city of Vijayanagara, which housed 300,000 people in its heyday and was possibly the largest southern Indian metropole of its time.[9] Abdul Razzaq later compared Vijayanagara favorably with his home town of Herat in offering comfortable accommodations and formidable fortification walls.[10] He also found the physical court of Devaraya II (r. 1422–1446) familiar, with its north-facing multi-pillared hall like those of Bidar (the Bahmani capital), Tughluqabad (the Delhi Sultanate capital, i.e., Delhi), and Samarqand but without parallel among Hindu rulers.[11]

While the Vijayanagara kings worshipped Shiva and other Hindu deities, they often did not project themselves as Hindu kings but, rather, as sultans. For example, a 1347 inscription praised Marappa, a Vijayanagara founder, as a Sultan superior to Hindu kings: "Conqueror of the three kings, Lord of the eastern and western and southern oceans, Vanquisher of kings who break their word, Destroyer of the pride of hostile enemy kings, Lover of the courtesans of enemy kings, Sultan over Hindu kings (*hinduraya-suratala*), Victor over great enemy kings—Marappa is known by these titles."[12] These lines have been hailed as the first time that a Hindu used the Perso-Arabic term "Hindu," which often had a geographical or cultural sense (similar to how many use "Indian" today).[13] But, critically, the inscription claims that Marappa is a Sultan, not a Hindu. Instead, "Hindu kings" parallels conquered "enemy kings" in Marappa's surrounding titles and so appears to be a negative contrast, a status that the Vijayanagara rulers surpassed as "sultans" who frequently elected to participate in Indo-Muslim styles of royal presentation.

The Vijayanagara and Bahmani royalty intermarried. In the early 1400s, Tajuddin Firuz (r. 1397–1422) wed the daughter of Devaraya I (r. 1406–1422), thus becoming the "first Muslim king of the Deccan to marry the daughter of a neighboring non-Muslim monarch."[14] Moreover, Sultan Firuz went to Vijayanagara and spent days participating in lavish wedding celebrations.[15] Such revelry suggests a degree of comfort, which was perhaps borne of Firuz's being a polyglot. Indeed, his harem included women from many parts of India—Telangana, Maharashtra, Gujarat, Rajasthan, and Bengal—all of whom spoke different languages.[16] Princesses of other non-Muslim kings also married Bahmani royalty. For instance, Zeba Chahra, daughter of the Konkani king of Sangameshwar, wed Alauddin Ahmad II (r. 1436–1458) in the mid-1400s.[17] We do not know how these women adapted to life at Gulbarga and Bidar, the sequential Bahmani capitals, but perhaps—like the men they married—they found southern Indian court environments of their day similar in many respects.

The Vijayanagara and Bahmani nobility were diverse, populated by Muslims and Hindus. Devaraya II was especially welcoming of Muslims into Vijayanagara's military, reportedly incorporating hundreds as officers and thousands as cavalry and infantry.[18] This shrewd move aimed to gain knowledge about Bahmani weapons and war tactics, but it also had cultural implications. Ahmad Khan, one of Devaraya's Muslim

Figure 11.1. Horseman presenting as a Hindu on one side and a Muslim (facing page) on the other at the Varadharaja Perumal Temple in Kanchipuram, ca. sixteenth century CE, Tamil Nadu, India.

nobles, built a mosque in Vijayanagara in 1439 that was called a *dharmasale* (place of worship), a term more common for temples. Indeed, the mosque looks like nearby temples. Moreover, following Hindu ideas about transferring karma (chapter 7), an inscription proclaims that Ahmad Khan transferred the merit of having built the religious structure to King Devaraya.[19] The Vijayanagara trend of fluid cultural ex-

changes is similarly reflected in Hindu temple sculptures, such as a ca. sixteenth century statue in Kanchipuram that shows a horseman sporting Islamic-style clothes and a mustache on one side while donning Hindu-style clothes and a clean-shaven face on the other (figure 11.1).

Support of Brahmins also proved a point of connection for the Bahmanis, Vijayanagara, and those beyond the subcontinent. Like so many others from Central Asia, the traveler Abdul Razzaq knew of the Sanskrit Panchatantra stories in the Persian translation called *Kalila wa Dimna* (after the two jackals who narrate the tales; see chapter 8). Abdul

Razzaq connected these animal fables with the Brahmins he encountered at Vijayanagara, writing that such stories are the "results of the wisdom of the kingdom's learned men."[20] In terms of state administration, both kingdoms appointed Brahmins to high offices.[21] They also used similar land revenue systems. The kings assigned land to nobles, from which the nobles collected revenue to maintain troops and pay tribute to the king (called *nayamkara* by Vijayanagara and *iqta* by the Bahmanis).[22]

The twinned kingdoms diverged in how they treated lower-caste Hindus. Folks like Sitadu, a low-caste man born in an Andhra village called Rajapudi, worked for the Bahmanis. He migrated into the Deccan interior, adapted his name to Shitab Khan (he did not convert), and became a Bahmani officer.[23] Shitab Khan fell out of favor and fled Bidar when he was suspected of participating in a coup attempt again King Humayun (r. 1458–1461). He reentered the historical record nearly fifty years later under another permutation of his name, Chittapa Khana, capturing the former Kakatiya capital of Warangal.[24] We can only speculate about how Sitadu might have been received, or shunned, had he tried his luck at Vijayanagara, whose rulers fashioned themselves as upholders of caste and life-stage distinctions (*varnashramadharma*).[25] The most famous Vijayanagara king, Krishnadevaraya (r. 1509–1529), wrote a set of political maxims in Telugu that repeatedly recommend putting Brahmins in charge (see excerpt). In contrast, he described those of "low birth" as "untrustworthy" and warned that kings should "keep people from violating caste conventions."[26]

Putting the Right People in Charge: Excerpt from Krishnadevaraya's Telugu Political Maxims, ca. 1510

Employ Brahmins who are learned in statecraft,
who fear the unethical and accept the king's authority,
who are between fifty and seventy,
from healthy families,
not too proud, willing to be ministers,
capable of discharging their duties well.
A king with such Brahmins for just a day
can strengthen the kingdom in all its departments.

If such ministers are not available,
a king must act on his own,
and do whatever he can.
If not, a bad minister can become
like a pearl as large as a pumpkin—
an ornament impossible to wear.
The minister will be out of control,
and the king will live under his thumb.

For each task, appoint more than one person.
Then the work will be finished quickly.
If the numbers are reduced, it creates trouble,
but if they are increased, problems will be solved.

No job is done with money alone.
Many people should work at it with commitment.
If the king is generous, truthful, and fair,
such qualities may attract the best to the job.

Though you have money in your treasury and horses,
without the right sort of men
those assets will be ruined
and the kingdom will fall into enemy hands.
Haven't we heard of such kingdoms?

The king will often benefit by putting a Brahmin in charge,
for he knows both the laws of Manu and his own dharma,
and from fear of being mocked
by Kshatriyas and Sudras,
he will stand up to all difficulties.[27]

The Bahmanis and Vijayanagara valued sea-based trade. Overland trade with northern India was at a minimum, owing to the break with the Delhi Sultanate. The Reddi Kingdom of Kondavidu controlled access to the Coromandel coast, and so the Bahmanis looked west to the Konkan coast, with Goa, Dabhol, and Chaul among their chief ports (they lost all in later years).[28] They imported many items, such as warhorses that passed through Bahmani markets by the tens of thousands and were essential to state power.[29] Silk arrived raw from China and was reeled, dyed, and woven in Chaul and Thana before being exported west across the Arabian Sea.[30] Black glass beads circulated between East Africa and India, where they were perhaps relatively newly incorporated into mangalasutra necklaces worn by married Hindu women.[31] Indians also continue to export cotton, and fragments of Indian-woven cotton have been found in Egypt spanning more than a thousand years between the fifth and fifteenth centuries.[32] Vijayanagara kings such as Krishnadevaraya recommended that kings ought to "manage your ports well, and let commerce increase in horses, elephants, and gems, pearls, and sandal-paste."[33]

Like many premodern Indian kings, both the Bahmanis and Vijayanagara used slave labor, and I regret being unable to recover more of the stories of enslaved peoples. So often, historians follow the movements of elites, whose names and lives tend to be most prominent in historical documents. But nearly everywhere that Krishnadevaraya or Tajuddin Firuz traveled, slaves accompanied them. For example, after reveling at Vijayanagara for weeks to celebrate his wedding in 1407, Sultan Firuz brought 2,000 male and female slaves back to Gulbarga.[34] Slaves also traversed oceans. Mahmud Gawan (1411–1481), whose story I discuss below, brought slaves with him from Persia to India.[35] What was life like for those who were forced to sail the high seas? How did they perceive the different regions between which their masters moved freely? What could they tell us about their worries and dreams?

Enslaved and free people alike lived in a multilingual environment in medieval southern India. Telugu and Kannada were spoken in parts of the Bahmani and Vijayanagara kingdoms. In addition, Vijayanagara territory included Tamil-speaking regions, and the kings sponsored Sanskrit literature. The Bahmanis patronized Persian and Dakhni (also spelled Dakani and Dakhani), a dialect of Hindi with high amounts of Punjabi vocabulary spoken by the Deccanis (who were from northern India).[36] The Bahmanis also controlled Marathi-speaking areas, and one curious example shows how Vijayanagara was also lightly influenced by Marathi traditions. Starting in the eleventh century, gadhegal stones began to pop up in Maharashtra and Goa. Typically, the gadhegal (literally, ass-curse) was carved on a stone marking a space that should not be violated, such as a property line, temple, or mosque.[37] The curse warned that anyone who encroached would be "screwed by a donkey," which was typically written in vernacular and sometimes illustrated (literally, a donkey with an erect penis about to penetrate a woman).[38] The coarse ass-curse appears on both Bahmani and Vijayanagara inscriptions from ca. 1400.[39] Even in vulgar details, the twinned kingdoms demonstrated the high degree of cultural commonalities across central and southern India in the fourteenth and fifteenth centuries.

Deccan and Persia

From the late fourteenth to the late fifteenth centuries, the Deccan had robust ties with Persia across the Arabian Sea. Grasping these links requires, once again, highlighting the limitations of South Asian or Indian history as frameworks. The Bahmanis were effectively cut off from northern India following their break with the Tughluqs in the 1340s. The north-south divide was further enhanced by Timur's 1398 sack of Delhi, which the Bahmanis welcomed.[40] As northern and southern India followed distinct historical rhythms for decades, the Bahmanis actively solicited goods and talent from Persia and Central Asia. In so doing, they cultivated networks of people, architecture, literature, and ideas that traversed the medieval Arabian Sea and left significant legacies in the Deccan.

The Bahmani sultans began to pursue overseas ties and emigrees during the heyday of the Timurid Empire based in Persia, although their efforts paid off only later. Perhaps their most famous early target was the celebrated Persian poet Hafiz, whom Sultan Muhammad II (r. 1378–1397) invited to travel to the Deccan from Shiraz. Hafiz reached the port of Hormuz on the Persian Gulf before desisting and instead sent a poem to Gulbarga that explained:

> Though splendid promises were made
> how could I such a dotard prove,
> how could I leave my natal glade,
> its wines, and all the friends I love?[41]

Sultan Firuz continued trying to woo the Timurid Empire's best and brightest, regularly writing to Timur and sending ships.[42] The greatest influx of Iranian emigrees came to the Deccan in the decades after Firuz's death, between the 1420s and 1450s. No doubt, each new arrival had his own reasons for uprooting his life and moving to central India. But a strong enticement was the ability to reinvent oneself in the Bahmani state.[43] The Persian migrants also changed the Bahmani polity, especially shaping aesthetic tastes in calligraphy and architecture.

Mahmud Gawan (1411–1481) is perhaps the most well-known Persian emigree to the Bahmani Sultanate. His rise, fall, and legacy demonstrate some of the major dynamics in these migrations and their implications for high culture in the Bahmani Deccan. Mahmud Gawan alighted on the Konkan coast in 1453 as a middle-aged Persian merchant bearing silk, pearls, jewels, Arabian horses, and Turkish and Ethiopian slaves.[44] He intended to travel to Delhi but instead was enticed to Bidar, where he rose to considerable power in the Bahmani nobility. He wrote to people in Persia, Turkey, Syria, and Iraq, urging them to also journey to Bidar because "India is famous among all eminent persons of the world, and many learned persons live here."[45] He even invited the Persian poet Jami, who (like Hafiz) refused but noted that Gawan had made India the envy of the Persian-speaking world.[46]

Ultimately, Mahmud Gawan was executed in a case of political tension bubbled over between old Delhi elites (Deccanis) and newer-arrived foreigners (primarily Iranians and Central Asians). The two groups often clashed in the Bahmani Sultanate. There are even records of them being separated at court.[47] In Gawan's case, two men, one Deccani and one Ethiopian, grew jealous of his success and cooked up an entrapment plot. They forged a letter from Gawan that invited the Raja of Orissa to invade Bahmani lands and then bribed and tricked Gawan's seal-bearer into stamping it. Seeing the real stamp, Sultan Muhammad III (r. 1463–1482) took the forgery as truth and ordered Gawan beheaded for treason. While walking to his execution, Mahmud Gawan reportedly exclaimed: "The death of an old man like me is, indeed, of little moment, but to your Majesty it will be the loss of an empire, and the ruin of your character."[48] His bitter words proved prophetic, and the Bahmani kingdom began to fragment in the aftermath of Gawan's death in 1481.

Gawan's greatest legacy in the Deccan was a large school (*madrasa*) in Bidar, completed in 1472 and largely still standing today. Its outward tiles shimmered—and shimmer still—in shades of white, yellow, and the turquoise blue favored in Timurid design. Its architecture is so similar to fifteenth-century madrasas in Khurasan that it seems Gawan used imported plans.[49] Within this Central Asian-style school, a library held 3,000 volumes of Persian and Arabic texts. While in use, it accommodated more than 100 students and twelve professors, who lectured in

1,000-square-foot vaulted rooms. One imagines that those educated within its walls felt at home in the Deccan, even while their learning environment would also have blended into fifteenth-century Khurasan.

The Bahmanis also looked to a deeper Persian past for elements of their royal culture, borrowing symbols from the Persian Sasanian Empire (224–651). They copied a Sasanian royal emblem, a winged crescent, and placed it on Bahmani buildings.[50] The Bahmanis named themselves after Bahman, a Sasanian figure whose legendary life is celebrated in Firdawsi's popular *Shahnama* (Book of kings).[51] The Bahmanis even sat on a turquoise throne (*takht-i firuza*), evocative of the thrones of numerous pre-Islamic Persian kings described in the *Shahnama*.[52] However, in a reminder of how things can have multiple sources and resonances, the Bahmani's turquoise throne was fashioned by southern Indian craftsman. This story—showcasing the multiplicity of origins—is worth telling.

Telugu artisans fashioned the Bahmani's turquoise throne on the orders of a chieftain named Kapaya Nayaka, who originally intended the object for the Tughluqs. But the Tughluqs were gone from the Deccan by the time the throne was completed in 1361, and so Kapaya Nayaka gifted it instead to their Deccani successors, the Bahmanis.[53] The throne was framed in ebony, plated with pure gold, studded with precious gems, and enameled so it shone turquoise. Upon the presentation of this glorious object, the Bahmanis threw a party for forty days, during which, as the sixteenth-century historian Firishta delicately put it, "little attention was paid to the law of abstinence enjoined by our religion."[54] Traveling musicians came from Delhi, singing compositions by Amir Khusraw and Amir Hasan in a celebration of broad-based Indo-Persian culture.[55]

Ultimately, though, the turquoise throne turned from a symbol of Sasanian and Indian kingships into a sign of the inevitable withering of political power. Every Bahmani ruler added further gems to the throne, until the surface was completely covered and shone turquoise no more. Then, the last Bahmani king—losing power rapidly and strapped for cash—dismantled the throne for its precious gems.[56] The Bahmani kingdom, too, soon split apart, with its lands fragmenting into five separate sultanates based in Ahmadnagar, Bijapur, Berar, Golconda, and Bidar, respectively. Neither the Bahmanis nor their multivalent turquoise throne survived premodernity.

South Indian Hinduisms and Islams

Religious trends, too, were multi-sourced and cut across identities in medieval central and southern India. For example, in Calicut, the Muslim Mappila and low-caste Nair communities shared much in common. Calicut was a major commercial center along Kerala's Malabar coast, key for pepper exporting. Trade so defined Calicut that its rulers were known as Samudri Rajas, literally "Ocean Lords." Over time, Arab merchants intermarried, and some lower castes converted to Islam, constituting the Malayalam-speaking Mappila community. The Mappilas had little in common with Indian Muslim elites, such as Bahmani state officers and privileged travelers like Abdul Razzaq. But they shared numerous similarities with the Nairs, a group of Hindu castes in Kerala often considered as Shudras. For example, like the Nairs, the Mappila observed matrilineal inheritance, and the two communities wore similar clothing.[57] It is unclear how contemporaries perceived the Nairs to relate to other Hindu groups of the period, which were often viewed (and acted) as distinct more than unified. For example, when Abdul Razzaq visited Calicut in the 1440s, he remarked: "The infidels are of many sorts, Brahmins, yogis (*jogiyan*), and others. Although they all share the same polytheism and idolatry, every group (*qaum*) has a different system."[58]

The Virashaivas in Karnataka offer another example of a Hindu group that, even while remaining apart from other Hindu communities, intersected with Muslim peoples and practices. The Virashaivas (also known as Lingayats) originated in twelfth-century southern India as worshippers of Shiva who—unlike many other Hindu communities of the time—criticized temple-based worship and welcomed followers across caste and gender boundaries (chapter 9). By the early 1400s, they populated monasteries (mathas) in and around Vijayanagara. In the fifteenth century, they began to worship—alongside Muslims—at the shrine of Sultan Shihabuddin Ahmad I (r. 1422–1436), the ninth Bahmani ruler who was revered as a Sufi saint after his death. Lingayat priests attended the annual *urs* (death anniversary) commemorations, during which they participated in Hindu rituals such as offering pujas, singing shlokas, and distributing *prasad* (offerings).[59] Ahmad I's urs was calculated by the solar calendar (not by the lunar Hijri calendar, as is standard for Muslim Sufi saints) so that it coincided annually with the festive Hindu celebration of Holi.[60]

The Vijayanagara kings financed some Hindu groups, revealing how the resonances and interpretations of Vedic texts had shifted over time. In the fourteenth century, the Vijayanagara rulers supported the Smarta Shaivas at Sringeri, including Sayana who wrote an exhaustive commentary on the *Rig Veda* (ca. 1200 BCE). This was an extraordinarily intellectual achievement, and Sayana's commentary remains influential among Vedic interpreters today.[61] In terms of placing Sayana in history, two things are worth emphasizing. One, he wrote more than 2,500 years after the Rig Veda's composition and so grapples with an enormous amount of conflicting theological arguments that had been expressed over time. For example, he comments on the view promoted by some (but not all) Brahminical schools of thought that the Vedas are authorless (*apaurusheya*).[62] Two, Sayana enjoyed royal support in his project to claim "mastery over the whole of the Veda."[63] In this, we see another strand of Vijayanagara kingship that rests on reimagining a distant past to suit their present. While distinct in the details, this approach roughly parallels the Bahmani interest in Sasanian kingship discussed earlier.

The Vijayanagara rulers positioned themselves within a larger imagined Hindu landscape through invoking the Ramayana. As discussed in chapter 6, the Ramayana is a Hindu epic that tells the story of King Rama of Ayodhya triumphing over demons. Indian kings used the epic—including its rhetoric on kingship and its geography—to articulate political power, especially in the second millennium CE.[64] Accordingly, Vijayanagara rulers situated a Rama temple used for state rituals at the center of their capital city.[65] Rama worship had grown in that region during the early second millennium CE, and the area around the Vijayanagara capital was, by that point in time, associated with Kishkindha, the southern kingdom where Rama found the monkey army that helped him defeat the demon king.[66] Today, this sacred landscape is mainly of interest to pilgrims and tourists, who might visit Matanga Hill, where the deposed monkey king Sugriva is said to have hid from his brother and rival Vali. In Vijayanagara's heyday, the kings' claim to power was bolstered by such associations with the Ramayana story.

Vijayanagara rulers also used idioms of kingship associated with Shiva. They issued royal edicts as Virupaksha (Shiva), a signature that blurred the identities of sovereign and deity. In the early sixteenth century, Krishnadevaraya sponsored the construction of a towering gateway entrance to the Virupaksha Temple (figure 11.2). The gateway

Figure 11.2. Large gateway of the Virupaksha Temple complex at Hampi built by Vijayanagara king Krishnadevaraya (r. 1509–1529), ca. early sixteenth century CE, Karnataka, India.

honored Krishnadeva's coronation in a similar layering of divine and earthly claims to power.

Northern Indian Regional Centers

North of the Vindhya Mountains, events unfolded rather differently in the fifteenth century owing to Timur's bloody raid of Delhi in 1398. Timur was a Central Asian warlord-turned-king who targeted Delhi, not for conquest but rather to secure a tactical advantage.[67] In sacking Delhi, he also succeeded where his Mongol ancestors had failed upon being rebuffed by Delhi Sultanate forces in the thirteenth century.[68] For thinking about northern India, however, more critical than Timur's motivations is that his raid decimated the Delhi Sultanate capital. In December 1398 to January 1399, Timur's army plundered and killed indiscriminately in Delhi, leaving behind the rubble of many buildings and tens of thousands of bodies.[69] Those who survived faced the brutal reality that, after Timur left, Delhi was a shell of its former self.[70] Some Delhiites fled, either in advance of or after seeing Timur's destruction of their city, and resettled in regional urban centers. Delhi's loss, however, was others' gain, inaugurating a period of north Indian regional flourishing. Here, to give a sampling of this rich diffusion, I survey thriving multicultural traditions between 1398 and 1526 at Jaunpur, Gwalior, and Mandu.

In Jaunpur, about 700 kilometers southeast of Delhi, an Ethiopian descent slave of the Tughluqs established an independent Indo-Persian dynasty in the late fourteenth century. We call them the Sharqi dynasty since the founder, Malik Sarwar, was titled *malik-i sharq* (King of the East).[71] The Sharqis supported a growing population, fed by an increase in rice cultivation on newly deforested lands.[72] Their capital city of Jaunpur was home to diverse religious communities, described thus by Vidyapati, a poet who worked for a Sharqi dynasty subordinate, in the first decade of the 1400s:

> Hindus and Muslims (Turks) live together
> one's dhamma (dharma) funny to the other.
> One calls the faithful to prayer. The other recites the Vedas.
> One butchers animals saying bismillah. The other butchers animals in sacrifices.
> Some are called Ojhas, others Khojas.
> Some fast as per astrological signs, others fast in Ramadan.
> Some eat from copper plates, others from pottery.
> Some practice namaz, others do puja.[73]

Here, Vidyapati equates Hindus and Muslims (called Turks, a common ethnonym in Sanskrit and Prakrit texts) in terms of religious and cultural activities, saying that both recite things and ritually slaughter animals with only small details differing. Also, he posits that the two communities living together was a defining feature of the cosmopolitan metropolis of Jaunpur.[74] Noteworthy is that Vidyapati, writing in Apabhramsha, used the Perso-Arabic term "hindu." Over the next several hundred years, the word "hindu" slowly crept into South Asian vocabularies beyond Persian and Arabic, eventually coming to denote a broad-based religious community as most understand the category today.[75]

A little over 300 kilometers south of Delhi, Gwalior was a robust center of literary and artistic production during the fifteenth century, owing to Tomar rule and a prospering Digambara Jain community. The Tomar court patronized literature that looked to the deep mythological past and more recent political history. For example, in the 1430s, the Tomar ruler Dungarendra Singh challenged his court poet Vishnudas to explain how a mere five Pandava brothers defeated 100 Kaurava brothers in the epic Mahabharata battle. Dungarendra Singh initiated this challenge by handing Vishnudas a betel leaf, a use of paan memorialized in the Hindi expression *bida uthana* (to accept betel, i.e., to accept a challenge). Vishnudas completed his Hindi Mahabharata (*Pandav-carit*, Pandavas' exploits) in 1435, followed by a Hindi Ramayan in 1443.[76] The Gwalior court was also interested in political events, such as Alauddin Khalji's 1301 siege of Ranthambhor Fort (chapter 10), about which the Jain poet Nayachandra wrote in Sanskrit between 1402 and 1423.[77]

Outside of court, a robust population of Digambara Jains in Gwalior turned to stone to emphasize a different part of the imagined Indian past. Largely between 1440 and 1473, the local Jain community sponsored the carving, on the rock cliffs of Gwalior Fort, of more than 1,500 images of the twenty-four Tirthankaras (Jinas) said to have taught Jainism in our age. This massive devotional art project was overseen by Raidhu (1393–1489), a lay leader of the Padmavati-Puravada caste who also penned a wealth of poetry about the Jinas and other subjects.[78] This abundance of carved images also looked to the future. Raidhu and others believed that the Jina statues marked Gwalior as a sacred Jain locale that would survive the impending end of the world.[79]

Jain traditions also flourished, as did the arts more broadly, in Mandu, capital of the Sultanate of Malwa situated more than 800 kilometers south of Delhi. Two early surviving Indian illustrated manuscripts were produced in the Sultanate of Malwa, in 1411 and 1439, respectively. Both were of the revered Jain work *Kalpasutra*.[80] In 1469, Ghiyasuddin Shah (r. 1469–1501) came to power in Mandu, and he had a taste for the finer things in life, literally. He sponsored an illustrated cookbook titled *Nimatnama* (Book of delicacies, ca. 1500 CE) that is filled with mouthwatering recipes. For example, here is one recipe, for making the fried north Indian snack of samosas:

> Another kind of Ghiyas Shahi's samosas: take finely minced deer meat and flavor ghee with fenugreek and, having mixed the mince with saffron, put it in the ghee. Roast salt and cumin together. Having added cumin, cloves, coriander and a quarter of a ratti (a dash) of musk to the mince, cook it well. Put half the minced onion and a quarter of the minced dried ginger into the meat. When it has become well-cooked, put in rosewater. Take it off and stuff the samosas. Make a hole in the samosa with a stick and fry it in sweet-smelling ghee and serve it when tender. By the same method samosas of any kind of meat that is desired can be made.[81]

Food was considered medicinal (in addition to being enjoyable) in medieval India, and so the cookbook includes recipes for breaking a fever, reducing skin itchiness, and the like. The *Book of delicacies* even offers solutions to sexual problems, such as recommended foods for increasing semen potency.[82]

In both its text and many illustrations, the *Book of Delicacies* offers glimpses into the multiculturalism of Mandu court life around 1500. It has a lengthy section on paan, commending people to "chew it when indisposed as it helps indisposition, gets rid of sexual diseases, rheumatism and tonsillitis, and prevents all illnesses and flatulence."[83] "Tibetan musk" features among the ingredients in a recipe to cure premature ejaculation.[84] In the text's illustrations, the king appears alongside women of Ethiopian descent who served the court (figure 11.3). Reminiscent of the long history of kama (sensual pleasure) in India, the *Book of delicacies*' illustrations do not shy away from unclothed, erotic depictions when appropriate to the recipes being exemplified.

Premodern Kashmir

Looking north of Delhi, the region of Kashmir underwent similar trends of cultural sharing across religious lines and regional flourishing, even as it developed a bit apart from the rest of South Asia. Kashmir is largely surrounded by mountains. Owing to its relatively isolating topography, the region experienced a discrete rhythm of cultural and political development.[85] Still, Kashmiri history features many of

Figure 11.3. Ghiyasuddin Shah (ruler of Mandu 1469–1501) accepts a betel chew offered by an Ethiopian woman in the *Nimatnama* (Book of delicacies), ca. 1500 CE.

the trends formational to other parts of South Asia in the mid-second millennium, including Indo-Muslim rule that manifested in distinct ways in Kashmir.

In 1339, power in Kashmir was seized by the Shah Miris, who differed from Indo-Muslim dynasties elsewhere on the subcontinent in numerous ways. The Shah Miris had no practice of elite slavery, unlike the Delhi Sultanate. They employed Sanskrit as a language of state, including patronizing the Sanskrit-medium Brahmin historians Jonaraja (1459) and Shrivara (1486), both of whom followed Kalhana (ca. 1150) in writing chronicles of Kashmiri politics titled *Rajatarangini* (River of kings). The Shah Miris also used Sanskrit on royal tombstones and patronized some of the rare Sanskrit translations of Persian texts. Most notably, in 1505, Shrivara translated into Sanskrit Jami's *Yusuf va Zuleykha* (Joseph and Potiphar's wife), a premodern Persian bestseller written in 1483.[86] As late as the seventeenth century, sales deeds issued in Kashmir were sometimes bilingual Sanskrit and Persian.[87]

In other regards, the Shah Miris acted like other Indo-Persian dynasties. For example, Shah Miri royals were often ecumenical in their cultural and religious patronage. Queen Gul Khatun (d. fifteenth century) supported Hindu and Muslim communities, while Zain al-Abidin (r. 1420–1470) is often remembered for his liberal patronage of Sanskrit literature.[88] Additionally, the Shah Miris paved the way for Sufis to flourish in Kashmir, such as Nund Rishi (1379–1442) who criticized Hindu-Muslim divisions and spoke to both common people and elites.[89] Although such religious rhetoric was not unique to Sufis in Kashmir.

The fourteenth-century Kashmiri Shaivite Lalla (Lal Ded) also mocked the religiosity of those around her, including Brahmin pandits and icon veneration, which did not endear her to everyone. Lalla left behind our earliest known verses of Kashmiri poetry, such as:

> The thoughtless read the holy books
> as parrots, in their cage, recite "Ram, Ram."
> Their reading is like churning water,
> fruitless effort, ridiculous conceit.[90]

Lalla also warned against a strong division of Hindus from Muslims, as per this chapter's epigraph. While her words rang true for many in medieval South Asia as evidenced by earlier examples in this chapter of similar attitudes, her immediate audience of Kashmiri Brahmins proved more skeptical. Perhaps owing to her views—especially her criticisms of upper-caste practices—premodern Kashmiri Brahmins did not elect to remember Lalla in their texts.[91]

However, Kashmir's Sanskrit Brahmin historians did remember Suha Bhatta, a Brahmin who converted to Islam, and these records communicate their anxieties about conversion. Suha Bhatta features in Jonaraja's history as a caste-traitor who turned on his own (*sajati*) and allegedly persecuted Brahmins in the early fifteenth century.[92] We aren't sure about the truth of this account of Suha Bhatta, but Jonaraja perceived its moral thus:

> The hawk kills other birds.
> The lion hunts other animals.
> A diamond scratches other gems.
> The earth is dug by earth-digging tools.
> Planets, like flowers, fade in the sun.
> The rule is this: horrific harm comes from one's own kind.[93]

When Suha Bhatta chose to become Muslim, he took on new name (Malik Saifuddin), but Jonaraja never uses or even mentions it. Thereby Jonaraja denies Suha the agency to publicly signal adoption of a new religion. Only using his pre-conversion name also perhaps reflects Jonaraja's commitment to condemn Suha as a fellow Brahmin.

Conclusion: Power Always

In the fifteenth century, Kashmiri Muslim communities often fought with each other for political power. Shrivara detailed power struggles between Kashmiri Muslims and the Baihaqi Sayyids—a non-Kashmiri Muslim community that had migrated to the region—as both groups pursued state control in Kashmir. In the sense of experiencing tensions between internal and external Muslim communities, fifteenth-century Kashmir shared something in common with the Deccan, especially Bahmani power struggles. Still, at the dawn of the sixteenth century, India's many regions diverged from one another in numerous ways and that regionalism recurred in subsequent centuries.

Further Reading

On the Bahmanis, H. K. Sherwani's work remains a valuable reference, while Keelan Overton's edited volume adds context regarding links with Persia; I also drew on work by Richard Eaton and Emma Flatt. I found Phillip Wagoner's contextualization of Vijayanagara compelling, and I drew upon translations from Telugu by Velcheru Narayana Rao, David Shulman, and Sanjay Subrahmanyam. Eaton's work on both individuals and trends in the medieval Deccan is insightful. The edited volume by Francesca Orsini and Samira Sheikh covers much of northern India in the long fifteenth century.

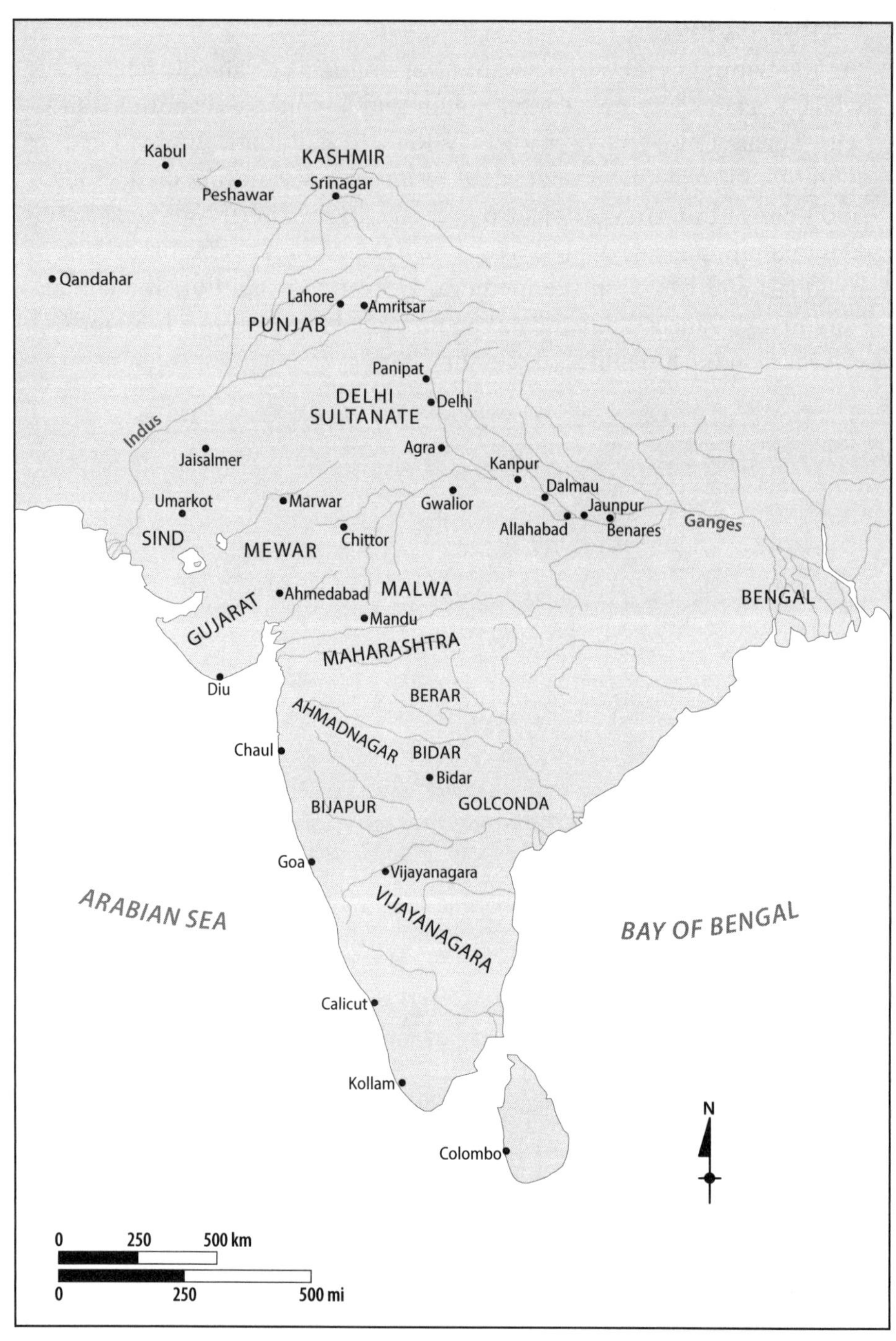

Regional centers in South Asia, ca. 1540.

12

Seeking God or Fame, 1500–1550

This diversity of creatures, castes, and colors
has all been written in a single stroke of the Pen.

—Nanak (d. 1539), founder of Sikhism (Punjabi)[1]

New political and religious leaders emerged in parts of the central and northern subcontinent between 1500 and 1550. The Portuguese seized Goa, initiating India's first brush with European colonialism. Meanwhile, the Mughals and Surs—from Central Asia and Afghanistan, respectively—became the most recent Muslim-led dynasties to vie for power around Delhi. Against this backdrop, Guru Nanak founded Sikhism, the newest of India's religious traditions, in the Punjab in the northwest. And bhakti—a Hindu tradition of personal devotion with roots in the central and southern subcontinent—blossomed in northern India. Mostly, these new players and trends were not interconnected, and some contrasted sharply with one another. For example, the Portuguese instituted colonial rule—a distinctive, new kind of political subjugation by a foreign state—whereas the Mughals carved out a premodern Indian kingdom as others had done for centuries. Even so, all the polities and individuals discussed in this chapter introduced novelty in areas ranging from trade networks to financial policies to spiritual practices. Also, all have recognizable legacies in modern-day South Asia, which is partly why some scholars identify 1500 as the beginning of India's "early modernity."[2] While some of these shifts prefigured modernity more than others, all changed South Asian political and religious possibilities in the first half of the sixteenth century.

India's First European Colonists

The Portuguese alighted on India's western coast in 1498, initiating the first subcontinental experience with European colonizers. In subsequent centuries, Indian communities faced additional colonization efforts by the Dutch, French, and British. Each group of Europeans operated in distinct geographical ambits within South Asia and left behind variegated cultural impacts. One commonality is that all European colonialists encountered the subcontinent as a politically fractured place. Accordingly, most strove to colonize a limited area that benefited their trade and political agendas. The Portuguese restricted their colonial efforts to a handful of cities along India's southwestern coast that ensured access to Indian Ocean trade routes. Due to specific policies and the longevity of Portuguese colonization—which lasted more than 450 years until 1961—this encounter was culturally transformative in and around Goa.

The Portuguese reached India's southwestern coast by sailing around the enormous continent of Africa, hitherto an insurmountable obstacle. In 1497, four ships set out from Lisbon—staffed with 148 to 170 men and three years of supplies—with the goal of rounding the Cape of Good Hope and sailing on to India.[3] The Portuguese king Manuel I (r. 1495–1521) bankrolled the mission with explorer Vasco da Gama as its leader.[4] At least some of the 150 or so men, including Vasco da Gama, reached India's western coast, although only with Indian assistance. After arriving at Africa's eastern side, the Portuguese found themselves in a world abuzz with established Indian Ocean traders and stopped at several places to take advantage of local knowledge. In Malindi (in modern-day Kenya), Vasco da Gama picked up a Gujarati pilot who helped him sail to Calicut, arriving in May 1498.[5]

Vasco da Gama stayed at Calicut for three months, leading an initial contact full of blunders and misunderstandings. He negotiated as a representative of Manuel I with Calicut's local dynasty, the Malayalam-speaking Samudri Raja (known as Zamorin in Portuguese sources). Vasco da Gama acted dishonestly from the start, exaggerating the Portuguese king's wealth and power. He was frustrated by local trade customs and, at one point, resorted to taking hostages.[6] The Portuguese left Calicut after three months thinking that all the Hindus they encountered were Christians and, moreover, that Asia was largely ruled by Christian kings. This erroneous view reflected European preconceptions about

India and attests to how personal experience does not always immediately overcome entrenched bias.[7] For his part, the Samudri Raja ruler perceived the Portuguese as funnily dressed Muslims who were strangely ignorant of the common Indian Ocean trading language of Arabic (this latter part being possibly true, given the general fiasco of this first contact).[8]

Both sides figured out their errors soon enough, as the Portuguese ramped up their intertwined trade and military activities in India. They sent additional missions to the coast around Goa in 1500, 1501, and 1502. Also, two Indian brothers, the Christian priests Joseph and Mathias, traveled to Lisbon in 1501. Mathias died en route, but Joseph went on to Rome.[9] The Portuguese soon established regular Lisbon-India voyages and began building fortifications along India's southwestern coast that served as the foundational infrastructure for the Portuguese State of India, formally established in 1505 and known as Estado da India. In subsequent decades, the Portuguese seized and fortified numerous southwestern coastal towns, including Goa (1510), Kollam (1519), Chaul (1521), and Diu (1530s).[10] The Portuguese found Indian allies, such as Timoja, the Hindu ruler of Kanara, who assisted in seizing Goa in 1510. They also made enemies, such as Bijapur, a Muslim-led Bahmani successor state that had controlled Goa. The Portuguese made Goa—which boasts natural defenses, was an established port for Arabian horses, and conveniently sits between Kerala and Gujarat—their home base on the subcontinent.[11] Many Portuguese men took local wives, resulting in a substantial population of Goanese Christians over the centuries.

The Portuguese Estado da India was a trade-based empire that tapped into Indian Ocean networks while introducing new goods that radically changed South Asian cultures. In terms of continuity, pepper—a staple of Asian trade for more than a millennium—remained a core Indian export.[12] To trade for pepper, the Portuguese brought gold, silver, and wine, all items for which Indians had a taste as far back as the Mauryan and Roman empires (chapters 4 and 6).[13] They ran open slave markets in Goa, where men and women of African and Indian descent were sold to perform household tasks, manual labor, and prostitution.[14] The Portuguese also carried new items to India, sourced from the Americas. They brought marigold flowers, which became common in Hindu rituals, including weddings and temple-based worship (puja).[15]

They introduced potatoes, tomatoes, cashews, and chilis, which are integral to many Indian cuisines today.

The Portuguese introduced a stark kind of religious intolerance to Goa. Whereas violent religious conflict in premodern South Asia was rare, it was a defining feature of premodern Europe whose kings regularly imposed their religion on their subjects and battled one another over religious differences. The Portuguese brought their prejudices with them. For example, upon seizing Goa from Bijapur in 1510, the Portuguese governor Afonso de Albuquerque massacred local Muslims, burning some alive in mosques.[16] He wrote to Manuel I: "I set fire to the city and put them all to the sword, and for four whole days your soldiers caused carnage among them; no Moor (Muslim) was left alive wherever he happened to be found; the mosques were filled with them and set fire to."[17] Afonso de Albuquerque's massacre interpreted the opposition of some Muslims—who had competing trade and political interests with Portugal—through the lens of Catholic crusading against Islam, a framework without parallel in earlier Indian thought.[18] Indian kings sometimes used religious rhetoric to express political conflict, but it rarely, if ever, guided state policy. In contrast, the Portuguese Estado da India grew more structurally intolerant in Goa throughout the sixteenth century. They introduced conversion incentives, such as excluding Brahmins from administrative posts.[19] Perhaps the starkest example of Portuguese prejudice introduced to Goa is the Inquisition.

The Inquisition operated in Goa between 1560 and 1812, targeting followers of Christianity, Hinduism, Islam, and Judaism. The Jesuits lobbied for its opening, with Francis Xavier advocating in 1546 for repressing "many who shamelessly and without fear of God live by the Mosaic Law and the Moorish (i.e., Muslim) sect."[20] Over the centuries, Indian Christians constituted the majority of those interrogated by the Goa Inquisition, which sought to root out lingering Hindu cultural practices including dress, songs, betel, and visiting temples.[21] Even as Jesuits encouraged Goans to adopt Catholicism and tried to accommodate local sensitivities, they simultaneously expressed anxieties about the purity of converts.[22] The Inquisition also targeted non-Indians, and I briefly consider Garcia de Orta's story because it highlights the acceleration of Portuguese intolerance against the backdrop of early modern Goa's multicultural society.

Garcia de Orta lived in Goa for thirty years between 1538 and 1568, during which he participated personally and professionally in a flourishing syncretic culture. He was a "new Christian," a person of Jewish heritage compelled by Portuguese intolerance to formally become Catholic.[23] Like many new Christians, he found greater religious freedom outside of Portugal. Indian Jewish communities had thrived for centuries along India's western coast, and Garcia de Orta "led a dual religious life in Goa for 30 years, without any major personal disruption from the Inquisition."[24] He ran a hospital, consulting freely with physicians from numerous ethnic and religious backgrounds. He wrote a dialogic book on medicine that was printed in Goa in 1563, six years after the first printing press was introduced to Goa.[25] Over and over, Garcia de Orta prized Muslim knowledge about India as especially authoritative, suggesting a strong degree of cross-cultural respect.[26]

Garcia de Orta died in Goa in 1568, without state challenge to his dual religious identities and syncretic approach to medicine. However, twelve years after his death, Portuguese authorities had grown more rigid, and the Inquisition found Garcia posthumously guilty of crypto-Judaism. They exhumed and publicly burned his remains in an act of potent vandalism that demonstrated the harsh results of European bigotries becoming part of Goan life.[27]

Loving God in Diverse Hindu Voices

While the Portuguese introduced new foods, flowers, and religious intolerance in Goa, northern India experienced a rather different trend: bhakti. Bhakti (devotion) is a strand of Hindu practice that emphasizes a personal connection between the devotee (*bhakta*) and the divine. The general idea pops up in many places in premodern India, including among first-millennium south Indian poet-saints (nayanars and alvars) (chapter 9). Another strand of the tradition flourished in Maharashtra, with literature written in Marathi, between the thirteenth and seventeenth centuries. Bhakti was especially robust in northern India between the fifteenth and seventeenth centuries, when numerous bhakti poet-saints composed poetry in vernacular languages, including Hindi.

Bhakti poets held various caste, class, and gender identities, and here we hear—arguably for the first time in northern Indian Hindu traditions—voices from across the social spectrum. Temple-based Hindu worship, controlled by Brahmins, continued. And upper-caste men also penned bhakti poetry, such as Surdas and Tulsidas (chapter 14). But some bhakti saints came from non-elite and underrepresented backgrounds, including Kabir (d. ca. 1518), Ravidas (d. 1520–1540), and Mirabai (d. 1557). They imagined the divine in distinct ways. Mirabai, a *sagun* bhakti saint, worshipped a named god (for her, Krishna), complete with his own tales and iconography. In contrast, Ravidas and Kabir, *nirgun* bhakti saints, praised a divine without a backstory or specific features (often called Ram, who should not be confused with the hero of the Ramayana story). All three appealed to an emotive religious experience that was open, in theory, to people of all social backgrounds.

Kabir and Ravidas were men from Benares whose lives we know more as hagiography than history. Hagiography contains its own truth of explaining charisma, and here I narrate what is popularly believed about these figures as insight into how and why they and their religious ideas have inspired many over the centuries. Both men are remembered as low caste, Kabir as a Muslim weaver widely believed to have taken a Hindu guru and Ravidas as a leather worker.[28] Despite their modest backgrounds and, for Ravidas, being polluted by working with animal skins, their poetry attracted people across the caste and class hierarchy. Even Brahmins flocked to them, so the stories say.

Still, neither Kabir nor Ravidas spared elites from harsh criticism. Kabir called out upper castes repeatedly, once writing: "Brahmins get tangled in the four Vedas and die."[29] Castigating Hindu and Muslim religious leaders alike for being attached to empty rituals, he said:

> Qazi, what book are you lecturing on?
> Yak yak yak, day and night.
> You never had an original thought.
> Feeling your power, you circumcise—
> I can't go along with that, brother.
> If your God favored circumcision,
> why didn't you come out cut?
> If circumcision makes you a Muslim,
> what do you call your women?
> Since women are called man's other half,
> you might as well be Hindus.

If putting on the thread makes you Brahmin,
what does the wife put on?
That Shudra's touching your food, pandit!
How can you eat it?
Hindu, Muslim—where did they come from?[30]

Ravidas, too, poked fun at the religious elites of his time, inviting listeners to laugh at upper castes who say the Ganges is pure, until its water is used to make liquor (see the excerpted poem). Instead of relying on one's birth status, he encouraged devotion to God:

A family that has a true follower of the Lord
is neither high caste nor low caste, lordly or poor.
The world will know it by its fragrance.
Priests or merchants, laborers or warriors,
halfbreeds, outcastes, and those who tend cremation fires—
their hearts are all the same.[31]

For both Kabir and Ravidas, disparaging religious rituals was also a recurrent theme in their poetry (see the excerpted poems).

These bhakti poets also impugned asceticism at times, which remained popular among numerous groups. For example, northern India's religious landscape included the Vishnu-focused Ramanandis and Shiva-worshipping Nath yogis, who used tantric approaches and pursued supernatural powers (*siddhi*s).[32] These groups sometimes denigrated each other. For instance, the Naths criticized Vishnu's various incarnations—some of whom were said to have married or otherwise pursued sexual relationships—as "overcome by lust."[33] Kabir spoke more generally against deprivation as a pathway to enlightenment.

Go naked if you want,
put on animal skins.
What does it matter till you see the inward Ram?

If the union yogis seek
came from roaming about in the buff,
every deer in the forest would be saved.

If shaving your head
spelled spiritual success,
heaven would be filled with sheep.

And brother, if holding back your seed
earned you a place in paradise,
eunuchs would be the first to arrive.

Kabir says: Listen brother,
without the name of Ram
who has ever won the spirit's prize?[34]

Kabir resisted being pigeon-holed into any broad religious identity, especially Hindu or Muslim, as the hagiographical story of his death underscores. After the saint died, his followers wrapped his body in a white shroud and processed through Benares. They came to a crossroads, where one path led to the Hindu cremation grounds and the other to the Muslim cemetery. A fight broke out among Kabir's Hindu and Muslim followers about which road to take, and his wrapped corpse was dropped in the scuffle. As the story goes, when his followers went to pick up Kabir's body, they found the white cloth to contain only rose petals.[35] Even in death, Kabir is remembered to have defied religious categorization, refusing to participate in either Hindu or Muslim rituals. Indeed, perhaps Abdul Haqq Muhaddis Dihlavi, a theologian and Sufi in the late sixteenth century, got it right when he said that Kabir was a monotheist but neither Muslim nor Hindu.[36]

Hindi Bhakti Poems of Kabir, Ravidas, and Mirabai, Fifteenth–Sixteenth Centuries

Kabir, "Saints, I see the world is mad"

Saints, I see the world is mad.
If I tell the truth they rush to beat me,
if I lie they trust me.
I've seen the pious Hindus, rule-followers,
early morning bath-takers—
killing souls, they worship rocks.
They know nothing.
I've seen plenty of Muslim teachers, holy men
reading their holy books
and teaching their pupils techniques.

They know just as much.
And posturing yogis, hypocrites,
hearts crammed with pride,
praying to brass, to stones, reeling
with pride in their pilgrimage,
fixing their caps and their prayer-beads,
painting their brow-marks and arm-marks,
braying their hymns and their couplets,
reeling. They never heard of soul.
The Hindu says Ram is the Beloved,
the Turk says Rahim.
Then they kill each other.
No one knows the secret.
They buzz their mantras from house to house,
puffed with pride.
The pupils drown along with their gurus.
In the end they're sorry.
Kabir says, listen saints:
they're all deluded!
Whatever I say, nobody gets it.
It's too simple.[37]

Ravidas, "Oh well born of Benares"

Oh well born of Benares, I too am born well known:
my labor is with leather. But my heart can boast the Lord.
See how you honor the purest of the pure,
water from the Ganges, which no saint will touch
If it has been made into intoxicating drink–
liquor is liquor whatever its source.
And this toddy tree you consider impure
since the sacred writings have branded it that way.
But see what writings are written on its leaves:
the Bhagavata Purana you so greatly revere.
And I, born among those who carry carrion
in daily rounds around Benares, am now
the lowly one to whom the mighty Brahmins come
and lowly bow. Your name, says Ravidas,
is the shelter of your slave.[38]

Mirabai, "He's bound my heart"

He's bound my heart with the powers he owns, Mother–
he with the lotus eyes.
Arrows like spears: this body is pierced,
and Mother, he's gone far away.
When did it happen, Mother? I don't know
but now it's too much to bear.
Talismans, spells, medicines–
I've tried, but the pain won't go.
Is there someone who can bring relief?
Mother, the hurt is cruel.
Here I am, near, and you're not far:
Hurry to me, to meet.
Mira's Mountain-Lifter Lord, have mercy,
cool this body's fire!
Lotus-Eyes, with the powers you own, Mother,
with those powers you've bound.[39]

Mirabai, a female bhakti saint, composed poetry about Krishna, often projecting herself as his lover. Krishna was a popular focus for this relational choice given the mythology about his many lovers, which was robust by the mid-second millennium CE. Krishna has a major paramour, Radha, who pines for him constantly, while he is often off playing romantic games and making love to *gopis* (cowherder women). Within bhakti, imagining oneself as a god's lover is a devotional path open to both men and women, although Mirabai's hagiography and poetry offer an unapologetically feminine perspective.

Mirabai is remembered as an indifferent wife who neglected her husband because of her deep devotion to Krishna. In one account, her in-laws were so dismayed by her flouting social conventions that they poisoned her (Krishna saved her, the story goes).[40] In her poetry, Mirabai offers herself to Krishna as "a virginal harvest for you to reap" and repeatedly writes about her body feeling on fire with longing for union with her divine lover.[41] The sensuality in her poetry is unmistakable and is meant to capture her spiritual devotion (see the excerpted poem). Today Mirabai is often celebrated as a vibrant female voice with the bhakti tradition and rightly so, in part, because she is unusual.[42] While more inclusive than earlier forms of north Indian Hinduism, north Indian bhakti still encompassed far more men than women among its most famous poets-saints of the sixteenth century.

Early Sikhism

Sikhism, one of India's newest religious traditions, was first articulated around 1500 in the Punjab and further codified in the following centuries. The founder was Guru Nanak (d. 1539), whose life is celebrated as a hagiography. As we have seen earlier in this chapter, hagiography was a popular genre more broadly in early modern India. Accordingly, stories of Nanak's life drew from a deep well of tropes to express pious leadership and, even when not historically accurate, explain his success as a charismatic leader.[43] In this broad sense, Nanak's life story is comparable to those of other Indian religious leaders in different eras, including the Gautama Buddha and Mahavira (chapter 3). Nanak was followed by nine successive gurus who continued to shape the Sikh path until the tenth guru's death in 1708. I highlight select moments from Sikh religious history here, starting with Nanak's initial epiphany, to flesh out some of some defining features of Sikh dharma.

Guru Nanak's life story, as recounted in later Sikh texts, mixes legend and truth, which I recount here as Sikhs have remembered it for centuries. Nanak was born to a Hindu couple of the Khatri class in a village near Lahore. His business-minded father emphasized financial and social success, but Nanak was attracted to spiritual pursuits. One day, he failed to return from his morning bath in a nearby river and was presumed drowned until he emerged from the waters three days later a changed man. Nanak pronounced his major insight—"There is neither Hindu nor Muslim"—and soon left his family, including a wife and two sons, to wander as a traveling teacher.[44] Years later, he settled in the Punjab, teaching a spiritual path that underscored service (*seva*), communal eating (*langar*), and community gatherings (*sangat*).[45] Nanak shared certain ideas with other nirgun bhakti saints, such as rejecting Hindu and Muslim rituals (e.g., Kabir), but he founded a distinct religious path.[46]

Nine sequential Sikh leaders followed Nanak, each adopting the honorific "guru," an appellation for teachers literally meaning "heavy." The Sikh gurus—we might call them heavyweights—were all from the

Khatri caste and mostly belonged to the same family.[47] Each further demarcated Sikh dharma. Arjan, the fifth guru, collected the writings of Nanak and others into the Adi Granth, an early iteration of the Sikh holy book. He installed the Adi Granth at Amritsar's Golden Temple, which has served since as a spiritual center of Sikh practices.[48] Guru Arjan was executed by the Mughal emperor Jahangir (r. 1605–1627) in punishment for supporting a princely rebellion, an early sign of Sikh involvement in political affairs.[49] The execution seems to have incentivized the next Sikh guru, Hargobind, to take up arms as a check on Mughal aggression.[50]

By the time of the ninth guru, Tegh Bahadur, armed bands of Sikhs wandered the Punjab and were perceived by the Mughal dynasty as a threat to imperial authority. Tegh Bahadur was arrested and executed by the Mughal king of his day, Aurangzeb (r. 1658–1707). Whereas the Mughals viewed these executions as minor affairs of state security, they developed into martyrdom tales among Sikhs.[51] Even amid such clashes, Sikhs adopted features of Mughal culture. Some Sikh writings are in Persian—a language promoted by the Mughal state—and early portraits of the ten gurus participate in a Mughal courtly painting style.[52]

The tenth guru, Gobind Singh (d. 1708), finalized the Sikh holy book, known thereafter as the Guru Granth Sahib, and appointed it in place of further earthly gurus. The book emphasizes the oneness of God. Its initial hymn, recited by many Sikhs daily, opens thus: "There is One Being, Truth by Name, Primal Creator, Without fear, Without enmity, Timeless in form, Unborn, Self-existent, The grace of the Guru."[53] The Guru Granth Sahib is dominated by poems attributed to the Sikh gurus, but it also includes verses by bhakti poet-saints like Kabir and Ravidas.[54] It is multilingual—with hymns in Punjabi, Persian, Braj Bhasha (a dialect of premodern Hindi), and Sanskrit—but written in a single script known as Gurmukhi, which Sikhs consciously developed to annunciate a separate religious identity. A parallel case of using script, rather than language, to demarcate a discrete religious community is the Khojki script used by Ismaili Muslims to write their multilingual religious texts known as the *ginans*.[55] There are later Sikh religious texts, including some that include legends about Nanak and the other gurus, but none challenge the Guru Granth Sahib's place among Sikh communities. In Sikh temples (originally called dharmashalas and today known as *gurdwaras*, doors to the Guru), the Guru Granth Sahib typically sits at the center of rituals and ceremonies.

One feature of Sikhism, worth dwelling on briefly, is its structural rejection of caste and the persistence of this social hierarchy nonetheless among Sikh communities. The Guru Granth Sahib disavows caste-based divisions, such as in these lines:

> What power has caste? It is righteousness that is tested.
> High caste pride is like poison held in the hand; from eating it one dies.[56]

Guru Gobind Singh wrote in another composition, the *Dasam Granth*, "Recognize: humanity is the only caste."[57] Guru Nanak is remembered for similar statements (see the epigraph of this chapter) and is believed to have rejected upper-caste markers, such as the sacred thread worn by Brahmin men (*upanayana*). Numerous Sikh practices are designed to break down caste-based barriers, such as communal eating (langar) at gurdwaras, where all sit together, eat the same food, and use the same plates. Many Sikhs assume caste-neutral surnames—Singh (lion) for men and Kaur (princess) for women—to break caste associations. If only the caste hierarchy could be dismantled by something as straightforward as changing one's name. The social draw of caste remains strong for some within Sikh communities today, and Dalit Sikhs experience ongoing oppression due to their low caste status.

Historically, the Mughals loom large in the background of Sikhism's initial formation. Nanak mentions Babur (the first Mughal king, d. 1530) in his writings.[58] As discussed, multiple Sikh gurus were executed by Mughal emperors who perceived Sikh political alliances and armed followers to undermine imperial control. In 1699, during peasant rebellions and ongoing tensions with the Mughals, a warrior community known as the Khalsa emerged within the Sikh tradition. The Khalsa formulated five Ks as membership markers: kesh (uncut hair), kanga (comb), kirpan (sword), kara (iron bracelet), and kachera (boxer-like underwear). While the Khalsa included only a minority of Sikhs, its emphasis on martial activities provides an important backdrop for the rise of Sikh militarism and ultimately a Sikh-led kingdom in the nineteenth century (chapter 18).[59] But we are getting ahead of our tour through Indian history. First, we must bring the Mughals into the foreground and understand how early members of this dynasty—which ultimately transformed much about Indian cultures and politics—fought their way to power in northern India.

Early Mughal and Sur Kingdoms

The Mughals began in 1526 as a small, fledging state founded by Babur, a failed Central Asian ruler who decided to try his luck in northern India. Babur had ascended the throne of Fergana, a valley in present-day Uzbekistan, at the tender age of twelve in 1494 when his father was killed in the collapse of a pigeon house (training pigeons was a royal pastime). Young Babur immediately faced challenges. He held a precarious sliver of power in a ruthless world where all male descendants—brothers, nephews, uncles, and cousins—had legitimate political claims. Warring largely against his own family, Babur took important Central Asian cities. He seized Kabul twice and Samarqand—famed for its soaring turquoise buildings—three times but lost both repeatedly. After a string of defeats, in his mid-thirties, Babur abandoned his political ambitions in Central Asia and instead set his sights on northern India.

When Babur looked south—to the Indus River, Lahore, and Delhi—he saw a land dominated by Muslim kings for centuries, often called Hindustan (northern India). In Babur's eyes, Hindustan was his birthright, because he was the great-great-great-grandson of Timur who had sacked Delhi in 1398. Also, India was a wealthy land that promised fertile farming, a flush treasury, and a fresh start. Babur's journey to Delhi took years, and he traveled with his army, male companions, and family members. The trek involved dangers as well as delights, recorded in Babur's memoirs, *Baburnama* (Babur's book), written in his native tongue of Chagatai Turkish.[60] For instance, outside of Peshawar, Babur got high on *majun* (a mild narcotic) and marveled at a field of purple and yellow wildflowers: "How strange the fields of flowers appeared under its influence. Nothing but purple flowers were blooming in some places, and only yellow ones in other areas. Sometimes the yellow and the purple blossomed together like gold fleck. We sat on a rise near the camp and just looked at the fields."[61] Babur's entourage crossed the Indus River in late 1525 and met the army of Ibrahim Lodi—the last Delhi Sultanate ruler—at Panipat, just north of Delhi, on a scorching hot April day in 1526.[62] Ibrahim boasted the larger army, but Babur was the better general and prevailed.

Babur spent the next four and a half years, between 1526 and 1530, carving out a small kingdom in northern India. He acquired further territory and embarked on building and beautification projects, such as installing gardens to domesticate a land he found alien. Babur chafed at north India's climate, writing in a section on Agra, a city around 230 kilometers south of Delhi, "We suffered from three things in Hindustan. One was the heat, another the biting wind, and the third the dust."[63] But even Babur proved susceptible to Hindustan's charms. He devoted chunks of his memoirs to cataloguing Indian plants and animals. Like so many who have traveled to India over the millennia, Babur loved a ripe mango, remarking "When the mango is good it is really good."[64] When Babur died in 1530, he left behind a modest kingdom that his son Humayun (r. 1530–1540, 1555–1556) soon lost to Sher Khan.

An Afghan upstart known as Sher Khan burst onto the north Indian political scene in the 1530s. He overtook Bengal in 1537–1538 and then posed a visceral threat to Humayun in Delhi. Sher Khan came from a modest background, and he caught many, including the Mughals, off guard with his well-trained soldiers.[65] Sher Khan's superior forces repeatedly beat the Mughal army, and Humayun soon began a multi-year exit from India, heading west and north. With the Mughals displaced, Sher Khan ruled as Sher Shah of the Sur dynasty for five years (1540–1545). He was succeeded by his son Islam Shah (r. 1545–1554) and then by a rapid series of Sur kings in 1554–1555. During these fifteen years, the stories of the Mughals and the Surs—who were both influential in Indian history—diverged.

Humayun's slow flight from India is usefully considered through the eyes of a woman he married along the way: Hamida Banu. In 1541, Humayun met Hamida, a young teenager to whom he was distantly related, and asked for her hand in marriage. Hamida refused the recently overthrown king for weeks but ultimately agreed at the Mughal family's urging and joined Humayun's retreating entourage.[66] She quickly became pregnant. We can only speculate about Hamida Banu's feelings during this time, but both her life and that of her unborn child were precarious. They were part of the fleeing cadre of a disempowered ruler, subjected to repeated attacks. At eight months pregnant, Hamida trekked across 250 kilometers of desert between Marwar (Jodhpur) and Jaisalmer, finding the wells en route filled with sand by Humayun's enemies.[67] Still a teenager, she gave birth to a son named Jalaluddin Akbar in October 1542 in Sind. In addition to the political turmoil, Hamida knew that Humayun's first-born son had died as a child years earlier, a common fate regardless of social status in premodernity.[68]

Akbar lived, but Hamida missed the first several years of her son's life. In 1543, Humayun's half-brother Askari kidnapped the baby and held him hostage in the Central Asian city of Qandahar, later transferring him to the control of another half-brother in Kabul.[69] Following long-standing Timurid tradition, Humayun vied with his brothers for political power, as did subsequent generations of the Mughals, and sometimes the most vulnerable were caught in the middle. In the meantime, Hamida traveled to Persia, where her husband spent a year (1544–1545) convincing the Safavid ruler Shah Tahmasp (r. 1524–1576) to back the Mughals' bid to reclaim Hindustan. Hamida was reunited with Akbar in late 1545, but Humayun's return march to Delhi took twice as long as he had spent leaving, and he again approached his capital city in 1555.

Back in northern India, the Sur dynasty ruled for fifteen years (1540–1555), during which they initiated political reforms and building projects. Sher Shah oversaw fiscal upgrades, including the introduction of a silver-based currency called the *rupee*, the namesake of most modern-day South Asian nations' currencies.[70] The Surs invested in roads and resting houses for travelers, including along the Grand Trunk Road, which had existed since Mauryan times and stretched from Kabul to Bengal (it still does, although interrupted by modern nation-state borders). The Surs built mosques and forts, including the huge Rohtas Fort (in modern-day Pakistan and a UNESCO World Heritage Site) and the Sher Mandal at Delhi's Purana Qila, where Humayun later died. When Humayun recovered his kingdom in 1555, the Mughals inherited this robust infrastructure and utilized all of it, thus ensuring that Sur ingenuity would shape Indian society for centuries. The Surs were also patrons and left a notable cultural legacy regarding Hindi literature.

Whereas many Indo-Muslim dynasties preferred Persian since it was a lingua franca across much of western and central Asia, the Sur rulers often used Hindi. Hindi (also called Hindavi and Hindustani) was spoken by many people in early modern northern India, including some bhakti poets and early Sikh leaders. Hindi literature also flourished in this period in numerous dialects, such as Braj Bhasha and Avadhi, and was commonly written in the Perso-Arabic script. Maulana Daud's *Chandayan* is the first known Hindi text, composed in 1379 at the military outpost of Dalmau (between Allahabad and Kanpur on the Ganges). It established the genre of *premakhyan* (love story), a book-length poem about earthly love and separation that serves as a metaphor for desiring union with God. Premakhyan romances mixed elements from Persian and Sanskrit literatures, weaving both together in a vernacular tale.[71] They are often associated with Sufism, a set of Islamic mystical approaches to God that proved broadly popular in premodern South Asia. During the first half of the sixteenth century, two Sufi poets dedicated Hindi romances to successive Sur rulers: Jayasi offered his *Padmavat* (1540) to Sher Shah, and Manjhan dedicated his *Madhumalati* (1545) to Islam Shah.

Both Jayasi and Manjhan imagined the bulk of their narratives, although Jayasi rooted his in the real historical event of Alauddin Khalji's 1303 siege of Chittor Fort. This episode was a popular subject, as were many Khalji assaults that premodern authors often reimagined with poetic license. Jayasi selected the myth that Alauddin desired Padmavati, wife of Chittor's ruler Ratansen, but failed to obtain her since everyone at Chittor sacrificed their lives during the Khalji-led assault. In reality, Padmavati is fiction, and Ratansen (also known as Ratan Singh) surrendered to the Khaljis.[72] But Jayasi promises a story, not of straightlaced political affairs but of a deeper Sufi truth that lauds self-sacrifice—as exemplified by the Kshatriya royalty of Chittor—as life's highest goal.[73] Here is how he imagined Padmavati and her co-wife Nagmati speaking as they, still alive, ascended their husband's funeral pyre:

> "Today the sun has set in the day, and the moon is sinking at night.
> Today let us give up our lives dancing for joy; today the fire for us is cool."
>
> They prepared the funeral pyre
> and gave generously in alms and charity.
> Seven times they circled the pyre.
>
> "There was one kind of circle at our wedding;
> now there is another as we go with you.
> In life, beloved, you embraced us.
> We will not leave your embrace in death.
> And the knot that you, our lover, tied,
> let it never be untied from beginning to end.
> What is this world but non-being in being?
> We and you, lord, will be together in both worlds."

They embraced him and lit the Holi fire.
They were burnt to ashes, but did not flinch.
They left this world, steeped in their love, and heaven glowed
ruby red.[74]

For Jayasi, these Hindu women exemplified the Sufi ideal of *fana* (self-annihilation) through the emerging Rajput practice—here projected back in time—of *jauhar*, where a defeated king's wives immolated themselves rather than be captured. Such mixing of symbolism across traditions is recurrent, even definitional, to the premakhyan genre.

One striking thing about Jayasi's romance is that Kshatriyas act as exemplars of good Sufi behavior. This made sense in early modern India, where religious identities were fluid. In fact, such praises of Kshatriya kings were common in other languages and textual genres of the period, as Kshatriya status emerged as a strong social currency. For example, a Sanskrit text titled *Rajavinoda* (King's play) praises Mahmud Begada (r. 1458–1511) of Gujarat's Muzaffarid (Indo-Muslim) dynasty by depicting him as a strong Kshatriya.[75] But such ideas fell away in later centuries. Soon the ideal of a Kshatriya ruler was interpreted to mean Rajputs, rulers in and around Rajasthan whose identity crystallized into an exclusive caste group around this time.[76]

Conclusion: Indian Kings Again

Humayun reconquered the Delhi throne from the Surs in 1555 and, less than a year later, plunged to his death down the stairs of the Sher Mandal. Some say that the king's foot caught on an askew carpet while he rushed to make the call to prayer. Others say he tumbled over in a drunken stupor. Maybe he just tripped. In any case, Humayun left behind a fragile kingdom. The remnants of the Sur dynasty lurked nearby, ready to strike, and there was no adult son to succeed Humayun. To avoid showing weakness, Mughal nobles kept Humayun's death a secret for two and a half weeks while they formulated a plan.[77] They agreed to crown thirteen-year-old Jalaluddin Akbar and appoint seasoned Bairam Khan as regent. Bairam Khan's regency lasted four years (1556–1560), during which he fought and gained territory for the teenage King Akbar. Most famously, Bairam Khan led Mughal forces in the second battle at Panipat, in 1556, where he defeated the Sur army led by the general Hemu, who happened to be Hindu. Fights for political power in South Asia continued to feature people of different religious backgrounds fighting on all sides. Even with that consistency, India's political scene changed dramatically in the coming decades as the Mughals grew from a small kingdom into an empire.

Further Reading

On the early Estado da India, I used the work of A. R. Disney and Sanjay Subrahmanyam. On Garcia de Orta, the volume edited by Palmira Fontes da Costa is enlightening. Purnima Dhavan, Louis Fenech, Nikky-Guninder Kaur Singh, and others trace early Sikhism. Jack Hawley, Linda Hess, and David Lorenzen provide insightful commentary and lovely translations of bhakti poetry; Patton Burchett's work was also helpful. Aditya Behl's scholarship on premakhyans remains unparalleled. On the early Mughals, Stephen Dale's work analyzes Babur in detail, and Wheeler Thackston's translation are invaluable.

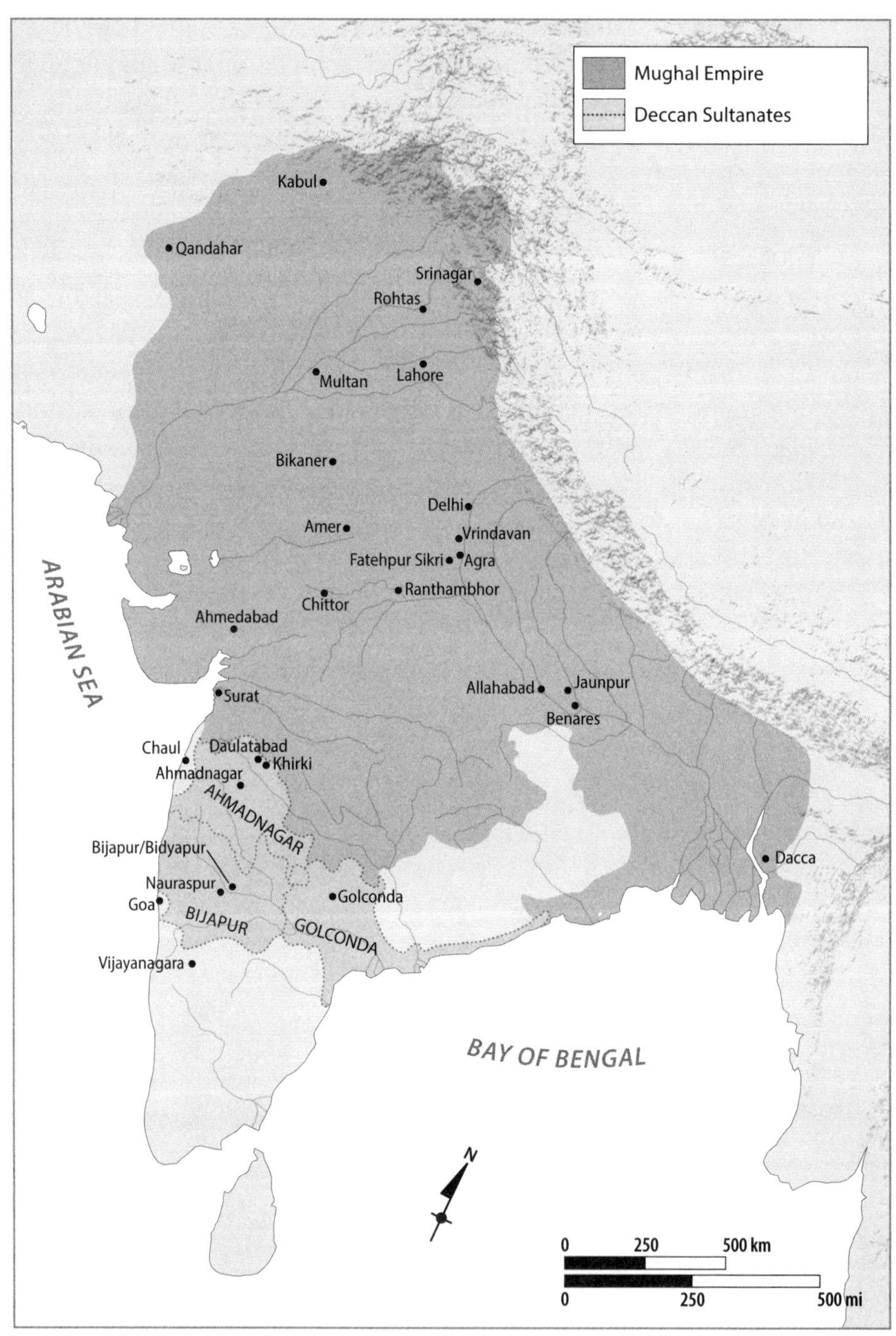

Mughal Empire and Deccan Sultanates, ca. 1600.

13

Ordinary and Extraordinary Lives in Early Modern India

I am infatuated with the Deccan and will never leave.

—Zuhuri (d. 1616), writing in Persian[1]

The Mughal emperor Akbar (1542–1605) was born under the ascendant Leo or Virgo. This astrological difference mattered to him and to many other early modern Indians who believed the stars exerted influence over human lives. In Akbar's case, his horoscope was cast four times, according to Persian, Greek, Ilkhanid (Mongol), and Brahminical methods.[2] The Brahmin astrologer declared Akbar's ascendant Leo, the better royal choice since it indicated "complete dominance, supremacy, power, and superiority."[3] He predicted that Akbar's "powerful fist will crush the hands of refractory malevolents, and the sound of his battle drums will turn the gall of lion-hearted warriors to water."[4] Indeed, Akbar presided over a successful land-based empire in northern India, but did he really fashion a kingdom with his own fists? Only in state propaganda. The king relied on elite groups (e.g., Rajputs) and non-elite groups (e.g., laborers) who collectively built and maintained the Mughal Empire. Mughal conquests paved the way for stunning cultural innovations, including one of the premodern world's most robust translation movements. During this time, the Deccan and southern India remained politically distinct and hosted discrete cross-cultural exchanges. I discuss both north and south India here, beginning with Mughal political and cultural achievements that are rightly credited to an array of groups.

Rajputs and Laborers Build Hindustan

The Mughal Empire expanded to cover much of northern India—that is, Hindustan—during Akbar's rule (1556–1605). Military conquest—through the blood and sweat of soldiers—provided the backbone of this imperial growth. As Muhammad Baqir (d. 1637), a Persian emigree to Mughal India, wrote in 1612:

> To those who seek an empire, the best dress is a coat of mail and the best crown is a helmet, the most pleasant lodging is the battlefield, the tastiest wine is the enemies' blood, and the charming beloved is the sword.
>
> Only that person who kisses the lip of the sword
> can embrace in a leap the bride of dominion.[5]

On the land they conquered, the Mughals and their allies built palaces, roads, caravanserais, tombs, mosques, temples, and more. As much as holding territory, these robust alterations to Hindustan's built landscape constructed the Mughal Empire.[6] Two groups—Rajputs and laborers—provide insight into these material and cultural changes in northern India.

Rajputs—Kshatriya rulers in and around Rajasthan—emerged as a defined caste group in early modern India and were key champions of the Mughal state. Politically, they were subdivided into lineages (e.g., Hada, Sisodiya, Kachhwaha, and so forth) with distinct capitals and kingdoms. The Mughals procured Rajput submission through diplomacy and, when that failed, force. All major Rajput lineages bowed to Mughal power eventually, even the Sisodiyas of Mewar who demonstrated the greatest resistance (they surrendered in 1615).[7] Other Rajputs, such as the Kachhwahas of Amer (near modern-day Jaipur), accepted Mughal authority early and so became principal architects of the empire.

The Kachhwahas of Amer forged Mughal ties during Humayun's reign (1530–1540, 1555–1556) and strengthened their imperial connection in 1562 with two events. A Kachhwaha princess married Akbar, at the suggestion of her father, Bharmal (r. 1548–1574).[8] At the same time, Akbar appointed Bharmal, his sons, and his grandsons as *mansabdar*s, ranked officers in Mughal imperial service.[9] The Kachhwahas had previously sought political gain through a marriage alliance with a Muslim political figure. In the 1540s, Bharmal had held onto his Amer throne by marrying another daughter to Haji Khan, a Sur-appointed Afghan governor in Rajasthan.[10] That alliance, too, was beneficial, although their Mughal links proved truly transformative. In 1569, Bharmal's daughter gave birth to Salim, who later ruled the Mughal Empire as Jahangir (r. 1605–1627). In 1572, when Akbar headed west to conquer Gujarat, he left Bharmal jointly in charge of Mughal state affairs in Agra.[11] Other Rajputs noticed the Kachhwahas's meteoric rise in status, and by 1580, dozens of Rajputs had joined Mughal service, and many had offered their daughters in marriage to Akbar.[12]

Mughal military strength—including through their early Rajput allies—compelled further Rajput lineages to join the Mughals. The 1567–1568 siege of Chittor, the Sisodiya capital city, was a watershed event. Akbar led Mughal forces in besieging Chittor for months while laborers dug tunnels and trenches to enable Mughal access to the city's defensive walls.[13] Between 100 and 200 laborers were killed daily by enemy fire, but the trenches enabled cannons to get close enough to breach Chittor's walls.[14] In the ensuing fighting, historians of the period report that Mughal forces massacred 30,000 people, including many civilians.[15] Whether that number is literal or not, it signals an extreme death toll. The Mughals meted out brutal treatment at Chittor as a shock-and-awe strategy, designed to instill fear in the hearts of any tempted to oppose imperial authority. To drive the point home, a Mughal "Victory Letter," written in Persian, celebrated the Mughals' "star of fortune" as "our royal presence descended upon the fortress of Chittor."[16]

In 1569, the Mughals took Ranthambhor from the Hada lineage in a less costly conflict. This made the Mughals the dominant power of western India, poised to conquer Gujarat (from a Muslim-led dynasty) a few years later.[17] By the 1570s, Rajputs numbered among the Mughals' chief warriors and commanders, including against recalcitrant Rajput lineages. For example, at the 1576 Battle of Haldighati, the Kachhwaha Man Singh (d. 1614) led the imperial army in inflicting high casualties on the Sisodiyas (although the Sisodiya leader, Rana Pratap, escaped).[18] In later decades, Man Singh fought on many Mughal frontiers, including in Kabul, Bengal, Bihar, and the Deccan.

Rajput-Mughal alliances had strong cultural effects. Many Rajputs learned Persian, required for all members of Mughal imperial service after 1582. In general, Indian knowledge of Persian grew over the coming decades, and, by the eighteenth century if not earlier, more Hindus knew Persian than Sanskrit.[19] In subsequent decades, many Indians—Hindu and non-Hindu—read Hindu religious texts such as the Ramayana and Bhagavadgita in Mughal-era Persian translations (discussed later in this chapter).

For their part, the Mughals incorporated non-Islamic Indian rituals of kingship. For example, the kings weighed themselves against silver, gold, and grain on special days and distributed the amount to the needy.[20] Mughal kings appeared to their subjects in a balconied window (*jharokha*, shown in figure 13.1), in a political appropriation of a darshan experience at a Hindu temple that projected the Mughal king as a near-religious icon. Akbar marked the heads of ruling Rajput lineages with a *tika* (vermillion mark) to incorporate them into Mughal service.[21] Further examples abound, and, by about midway through Akbar's reign (1580s), it is difficult to imagine Mughal culture without Rajputs, or, put another way, Rajputs accepted Akbar as a "Muslim Rajput."[22] Perhaps a simple hyphen is best in describing Mughal-Rajput ruling culture.

Rajput princesses who married into the Mughal family shaped court life. There was a power imbalance to Mughal-Rajput unions, as the Jain author Padmasagara explained in 1589:

> Upon hearing about his strength, some Rajputs (*hindunripa*) think it prudent
> to give him their daughters in the hopes that it would protect their kingdoms.
> Others give him presents, such as arrangements of moonstones, and fall before his feet.
> Others act like his followers. But all are devoted to serving him.[23]

In some ways, Rajput women probably found Mughal courts familiar, since Rajput and Mughal rulers alike maintained harems and practiced polygamy. Although they encountered greater religious diversity in Akbar's harem, where many women were practicing Muslims and some even took a hajj trip to Mecca in the 1570s–1580s.[24] In Akbar's time, Rajput princesses were not asked to convert and so maintained their own upper-caste Hindu practices, including celebrating Hindu festivals and engaging in icon-based veneration. Some Rajput Hindu women became mothers to Mughal princes and kings, including emperors Jahangir (r. 1605–1627) and Shah Jahan (r. 1628–1658) who were exposed from a young age to their mothers' religious traditions.

Figure 13.1. Mughal Emperor Jahangir (r. 1605–1627) at the jharokha window in the Agra Fort, ca. early seventeenth century CE.

Rajput men spearheaded building projects in Mughal India, such as Man Singh's Govindadeva Temple (a Krishna temple) in Vrindavan in 1590. This was the largest temple built in northern India since the 1200s.[25] The soaring structure altered the north Indian temple landscape, its monumentality likely inspired, in part, by Mughal monumental architecture.[26] There were further imperial connections with the Govindadeva Temple. Man Singh numbered among the highest-ranking Mughal mansabdars, and Akbar financially supported the temple's construction and maintenance.[27] A Sanskrit inscription at the Govindadeva Temple links Akbar's kingship with Vaishnava flourishing:

> When glorious Akbar naturally ruled the entire earth,
> good people followed their own dharma to the letter and so obtained great happiness.
> Virtuous worshippers of Vishnu always happily blessed him,
> because they said that this very place belongs to Lord Krishna and so is an auspicious home [under Akbar's rule].[28]

The temple's location in Vrindavan partakes in Hindu and Mughal traditions, being a site, respectively, associated with Krishna (Govinda is another name for Krishna) and where Akbar had a positive experience with Hindu spirituality. Visually, the Govindadeva Temple invokes Mughal aesthetics, boasting (notably for a Hindu temple) an icon-free facade.[29] The temple utilized red sandstone, common for local temples and emblematic of Mughal construction, especially at the capital city of Fatehpur Sikri.

Fatehpur ("city of victory") was the most extensive building project of Akbar's reign and offers an insightful vantage point for glimpsing another group, namely laborers, who built the Mughal state. Thousands of construction workers made Fatehpur Sikri rise in the early 1570s, and the city served as the Mughal capital from 1571 to 1585. Fatehpur is located about thirty-five kilometers from Agra and is built largely of sandstone that shimmers reddish pink in the sun. During its construction, skilled artisans cut wood and fashioned windows, while unskilled workers dug holes and laid bricks (earning more meagre wages than their skilled counterparts).[30] Illustrations produced for a ca. 1590–1595 *Akbarnama* (Akbar's book), although not strictly documentary, depict laborers hard at work building Fatehpur.[31] The skilled craftsmen operated in guilds, and some left their names written in Devanagari—Lakhman, Hamu, Khargu, Paigu, and so on—inscribed on stones and bricks. None of the guild names indicate a Muslim background, and that Akbar's city was built largely by Hindu laborers indicates how the Mughals fostered a multicultural polity at many levels.

Laborers also erected Mughal tent cities, which kings used as moving capitals as they journeyed to the far corners of their empire. Mughal emperors did not travel light. The royal entourage included the harem, princes, supporters, and servants, along with animals, furniture, and lots of luggage. Mughals and Rajputs also had domestic slaves, even as Akbar prohibited other forms of slavery such as enslaving war captives.[32] Forced labor was common, although Akbar tried to crack down on the practice in some areas such as Kashmir.[33] Mughal kings generally had two identical tent cities that were set up a day's ride from one another, so that the royal party could arrive and immediately settle in. In Akbar's time, it took 1,000 laborers, "natives of Iran, Turan (in Central Asia), and Hindustan (north India)" to correctly assemble the labyrinth of tents—including the red tents reserved for the king—and lay out carpets.[34] By the reign of Akbar's grandson, Shah Jahan, 3,000 were needed to raise the imperial tent city. Their jobs included hanging "strings of pearls" that gave the illusion of a "dome of the fixed stars."[35] Others had less flashy jobs, such as sweeping the floor.[36] Without laborers—who were often illiterate and almost never speak for themselves in historical texts—there would have been no Mughal Empire.

Translating Indian Knowledge

Akbar's court brimmed with painters, musicians, poets, philosophers, translators, and historians. Their intellectual and artistic output built upon Mughal land conquests, especially the concentration of wealth at imperial courts that attracted talent from across the subcontinent, Persia, and Central Asia. Many secured Mughal support to produce stunning paintings, participate in a large-scale translation movement, and more. Some of Akbar's courtiers' names are well known in South Asia even today, such as Tansen (musician), Abul Fazl (historian), Birbal (advisor), and Rahim (polyglot). For example, Indian children's comic books and television shows feature fanciful conversations between Akbar and Birbal, his Brahmin advisor. Other individuals are less famous now but important at the time, such as Urfi (poet), Naqib Khan (historian and translator), and the often-unnamed Brahmin translators. Among the many cultural achievements of Akbar's court, I focus on one here: the large-scale translation of Sanskrit texts into Persian. This extraordinary event—which continued during the reigns of Akbar's successors, Jahangir and Shah Jahan—numbers among Indians' chief intellectual achievements in premodernity, and it allows us to glimpse other aspects of Mughal cultural flourishing, including Persian literature and manuscript paintings.

Akbar's court was a multilingual space, where Persian and Hindi were regularly spoken and poets of both, plus Sanskrit, received lavish patronage. Among Persian-medium authors, the Mughal court earned a reputation as a utopia more tolerant of religious difference and richer than Safavid Persia.[37] Whereas the Bahmanis had solicited migration from Persia to the Deccan (chapter 11), Persians came to Mughal Hindustan of their own accord. For instance, Kausari, a Safavid poet, wrote:

> My life has become intolerable in Iran; I should go to India.
> All the poets like sweet parrots have made India their home.[38]

Indeed, Safavid Persia experienced a "brain drain" as poets decamped to Mughal India and embraced Indo-Persian culture.[39] Celebrating his new home, Urfi, a Shiraz native who joined Akbar's court in the 1580s, wrote:

> Abandon the customs of the Muslim people if you want
> to enter the temple of the Magis, where hidden secrets will be
>   revealed to you.
> You are from the land of Iran, change your old ways,
> if you want to see the beauteous splendor of India.[40]

North Indians, too, composed poetry in Persian and other languages under Mughal support. For instance, Lahore-born Abdur Rahim was among Akbar's chief military commanders, a multilingual poet (in Persian, Hindi, and Sanskrit), and a sponsor of Persian and Hindi literatures.[41] Agra-born Fayzi was Akbar's Persian-medium poet laureate (*malik al-shura*) and participated in the Mughals' seminal Sanskrit-Persian translation movement.

During the reigns of Akbar through Shah Jahan, a century in total (1556–1658), the Mughal court sponsored the translation of dozens of Sanskrit texts into Persian in what constitutes the most robust translation project of premodern India. In world history, large-scale translation movements often substantially changed cultures. Circa eighth–tenth century CE, the Abbasids translated Greek thought into Arabic, which "inspired the intellectual life of Muslim societies until modern times and affected the scientific and scholastic growth of the Latin West for centuries."[42] Also in the first millennium CE, Chinese intellectuals such as Xuanzang (chapter 8) translated Pali and Sanskrit Buddhist texts, which molded Chinese Buddhist traditions. Similarly, Mughal translations of Sanskrit works into Persian proved influential in Indian cultures, reshaping Indo-Persian literature, inspiring Indian painters, and informing Hindu identity.

The Mughal translation project had a broad scope. Members of Akbar's court translated Sanskrit story texts, philosophy, histories, and technical treatises. They often selected texts with long-standing import within Indian cultures, such as the *Panchatantra* (a story collection; chapter 8), the *Yogavasishtha* (esoteric Vaishnava ideas, chapter 10), and the epics Mahabharata and Ramayana (chapters 5 and 6). Akbar's court had a strong interest in history and so also translated Kalhana's *Rajatarangini* on Kashmir's kings (chapters 8 and 11). Drawing on numerous Sanskrit sources and informants, Abul Fazl described the major Brahminical philosophical systems, Buddhist and Jain thought, literary theory, and more in the *Ain-i Akbari* (Akbar's Institutes), part of his history of Akbar's reign.[43] Mughal translations continued under Jahangir and Shah Jahan, with a final flourishing under the Mughal prince Dara Shukoh (d. 1659) who had a more religious focus. He translated the Upanishads (chapter 2) and tried to find traces of Islamic ideas in early Hindu texts.[44]

Many Mughal translations were team efforts, where Brahmins read a Sanskrit text and verbally translated it into Hindi, intelligible to the Mughal translators who wrote down a Persian approximation. A manuscript illustration of this collaboration from Akbar's court depicts a book-heavy encounter. In the image, numerous horizontal Sanskrit manuscripts and vertical Persian manuscripts are strewn about as Brahmin and Mughal translator teams converse. The two groups appear rather similar in dress and appearance, a sign of their shared cultural milieu (figure 13.2).

The Sanskrit-Persian translation movement fed ideas about Mughal kingship. For example, Badauni, a curmudgeonly courtier and reluctant translator, wrote in his generally scathing history of Akbar's reign: "Cheating imposter Brahmins . . . told Akbar repeatedly that he had descended to earth, like Ram, Krishan (i.e., Krishna), and other infidel rulers who, although lords of the world, had taken on human form to act on earth."[45] Indeed, Mughal translators projected Akbar into the mythological universe of the Sanskrit epics. In the Persian Mahabharata, titled *Razmnama* (Book of war), Akbar is praised by name during a conversation between Yudhishthira and Bhishma, projected to have occurred thousands of years earlier.[46] That this appears out of time—incongruous with the plotline—underscores the universality of Akbar's kingship, a recurrent Mughal propaganda point. Illustrations of the Persian Mahabharata and Ramayana often bear strong similarities to depictions of the Mughal court, such that, for instance, Vishnu's incarnation Rama appears like an enthroned Mughal king (figure 13.3).

Figure 13.2. Brahmin pandits (*bottom*) and Mughal officials (*top*) collaborating on translating the Sanskrit Mahabharata into Persian at Akbar's court, 1598–1599 CE, ascribed to Dhanu, northern India.

Figure 13.3. Kusha and Lava recite the Ramayana to King Rama at his court in Ayodhya from an Akbari Persian Ramayana, ca. 1590s CE, northern India.

Sanskrit poets, too, cast Akbar as Vishnu on earth. In his Sanskrit grammar of Persian, the Brahmin Krishnadasa invoked caste-based ideas of Akbar protecting cows and Brahmins to advertise the Mughal king's alleged identity as a Vishnu avatar.[47] For centuries, Indian kings had been depicted as Hindu gods incarnate, especially Vishnu, and the Mughals, too, participated in this tradition.

Mughal artists painted lavish illustrations for translated Sanskrit texts, which number among the thousands of manuscript paintings that survive from Akbar's court. Akbar's atelier boasted artists from diverse regional, ethnic, and religious backgrounds. These artists collaborated with one another, and an individual's identity did not determine what or how he (or, rarely, she) painted.[48] Illustrations of the Persian Mahabharata and Ramayana involved the intriguing question of how to depict Hindu deities. Sometimes, Mughal artists used Persian imagery, such that the demigod bird Garuda appears as the Simurgh, a mythical Persian bird. Other times, they drew on India's long tradition of Hindu sculptures.[49] Such dynamism made for remarkable images, which inspired further creative projects.

The imperial copy of the Akbari Persian Ramayana (ca. 1580s) is the earliest surviving illustrated Ramayana in any language, and it soon spurred others. By the early 1600s, artists had fashioned numerous illustrated Persian Ramayanas, including one made for the polyglot Rahim and held today in Washington, DC's Freer Gallery of Art, part of the Smithsonian.[50] The trend soon crossed over languages. In the mid-seventeenth century, a Rajput court at Udaipur sponsored a lavish seven-volume manuscript of Valmiki's Sanskrit Ramayana that was inspired, in part, by Mughal manuscripts.[51] The Rajput Sisodiya patron, Jagat Singh, also followed the Mughal example of employing artists from diverse backgrounds. The Mewari Muslim Sahibdin produced more than one-third of the Mewar Ramayana's more than 400 images.[52]

Through Mughal translations, Sanskrit stories and texts became infused within broader Indo-Persian culture, often later feeding knowledge in other languages as well. One example is the love saga of Nala and Damayanti, first found in the Mahabharata and later told by Sanskrit poets as its own tale. Fayzi retold this romance as *Nal-Daman*, a Persian masnavi:

Tell that old tale anew,
of the love of Nal and the beauty of Daman.
Make a hundred songs of pain into poetry.
Fill the fresh goblet with an old wine.[53]

Likewise, the Ramayana proved as popular in Persian as it had long been in other Indian languages, and authors penned around two dozen discrete Persian versions of Rama's saga between the sixteenth and nineteenth centuries.[54] Later, in the nineteenth century, Persian *Nal-Daman*s and Ramayanas prompted Urdu retellings of both stories.[55] Other works proved foundational in introducing Europeans to Sanskrit philosophy, such as Dara Shukoh's Upanishads (titled *Sirr-i Akbar*, Greatest secret) that was later translated into French and Latin.[56]

Mughal translations provided many Hindus with access to their religious texts between the sixteenth and nineteenth centuries. Few early modern people knew Sanskrit, a language that was never a common vernacular and, even as a literary tongue, had long been limited to an educated elite. In contrast, many Indians of diverse religious backgrounds learned Persian to work for the Mughal state.[57] In the eighteenth and nineteenth centuries, Hindus voraciously read and copied Mughal-era translations of the Ramayana, Mahabharata, and other works, as evidenced by scores of surviving manuscripts. The Mughal translators had hoped to provide wider access to hitherto restricted texts. Abul Fazl's preface to Akbar's Persian Mahabharata names, among the reasons for the translation, clarifying the epic's contents since (Abul Fazl says) Brahmins often misled common people.[58] Still, Akbar's court likely did not imagine the expansive readership that developed in the following centuries as Persian became a key language of Hinduism with a veritable library of Mughal-era Persian translations of Sanskrit texts.

Political Religion at Akbar's Court

Akbar was eclectic regarding religion, with the consistency that he used religious symbolism and ideas for political gain. Mixing politics and religions was the norm among premodern Indian rulers, but two things are noteworthy about Akbar's endeavors. One, he concentrated power in his person and so made his religious practices relevant, in terms of Mughal culture and propaganda, for the broader empire.[59] Two, Akbar was remarkably polymorphous, even by the standards of generally polyvocal Indian kings. Still, there was a harsh edge to Akbar's political religion at times, which evolved throughout his nearly fifty-year reign.

Akbar was Muslim, and he invoked many Islamic ideas of kingship while challenging others. For instance, Akbar forged close ties with Sufi figures, as Indo-Muslim kings had for centuries (chapters 10–11), and especially honored the lineage of Chishti saints. He walked on foot to the shrine of Muinuddin Chishti in Ajmer numerous times and named his first-born son Salim, after Salim Chishti for whom he built a dargah at Fatehpur Sikri.[60] Anticipating the Islamic Hijri calendar reaching the year 1000 (1592), Akbar had himself celebrated as a messianic figure and sacred king from the late 1570s onward.[61] This ruffled some feathers, and, at times, Akbar's creative political adaptations of Islamic rhetoric cost him support. For instance, around 1580 the king rewrote the Islamic statement of faith (shahada) to insert himself as God's representative in place of the Prophet Muhammad. Following outrage, Akbar backtracked on this. He found greater success with ambiguous actions that endorsed standard Islamic ideas while also having a dual provocative connotation. For instance, texts from his court often begin with *allahu akbar*, which can mean "God is great" or "Akbar is God."[62] The phrase was also placed on seals given to initiates of an imperial discipleship program, known as *din-i ilahi*, that emphasized devotion to Akbar.[63]

Akbar held religious debates at court, at first between Muslim groups and later including Jains, Brahmins, and Jesuits. All these communities were part of the Mughal Empire, except Jesuits who visited from Portuguese Goa.[64] Akbar even designated part of Fatehpur Sikri the *ibadatkhana* (house of religious debate). Honest intellectual exchange was one goal, but Akbar also arbitrated between religious ideas, thereby enhancing his own imperial authority. For example, Akbar did not tolerate atheism, and so called on Jains (whose religion is often considered to be nontheistic) to prove that they believed in God.[65] He also ridiculed the ulama, the traditionally learned men of Islam who were accustomed to exercising influence within Indo-Muslim kingdoms. Akbar preferred to center power in himself, and so repeatedly acted against the ulamas' advice, such as by marrying more than four women.

Some communities told their own stories about religious exchanges at the Mughal court that offer a non-imperial perspective. For example, the Jain author Devavimala wrote about an exchange between Hiravijaya (a Jain leader) and Abul Fazl (Akbar's vizier) on Jain and Muslim ideas. The passage is noteworthy as a rare description of Islamic theology in a Sanskrit text that posits rough comparability between Islam and Jainism. It features a political figure, Abul Fazl, as articulating Muslim beliefs, thus attesting to the perceived interlinking of religion and politics in Mughal India. It also boasts that Hiravijaya sowed the seed of Jain dharma in Abul Fazl. Historically, this is unlikely, but the Jain audience for Devavimala's text may well have appreciated the imagination of their tradition as attractive to a powerful Indian ruler.

Hiravijaya and Abul Fazl Compare Jainism and Islam, Excerpt from Devavimala's Sanskrit *Hirasaubhagya*, 1580s

Abul Fazl said,

> O Suri, this was laid out by the ancient prophets in our scriptures—all Muslims (yavana) who are deposited on earth as guests of the god of death will rise at the end of the earth and come before the court of the Supreme Lord called *khuda*, just as they come to the court of an earthly king. He will cast good and bad qualities onto his own pure mind as if onto a mirror and bring about rightful judgment there, having refuted the false construction of mine versus another's. Having reflected, he will bestow the appropriate result of the yavanas' virtues and vices, like the fertile soil generates plentiful grain from different seeds. Some will be brought to heaven by him, just as boats are led to the edge of the ocean by a favorable wind. Then they will find joy, nearly overwhelmed with floods of suitable, amazing enjoyments. Others will be sent to hell by him because of sin. Like birds being crushed by hawks and pots being fired by potters, they will suffer great agonies at the mercies of hell's guards. O Suri, what is the validity of this Quranic speech (*kuranavakyam*)? Is it true, like the speech of great-souled people, or is it false like a flower sprouting in the sky?

Having spoken, Abul Fazl fell silent in the hopes of gaining wisdom from Hiravijaya's response. Then, the lord of sages spoke sweetly:

> He—who is free of dirt like a shell, devoid of defects like the sun, made of flames like fire, and without a body like the god of love—is the Supreme Lord. In what form does he attend court like a living being that adopts many appearances in his wanderings through existence? There he sets a person on the path to heaven or hell for what reason? A previous action, once ripened, has the power to grant both joys and sorrows. Thus, let action (karma) alone be recognized as the creator of the world, since otherwise God has no purpose.

When Hiravijaya, the lord of ascetics, fell silent after speaking, Shaykh Abul Fazl replied: "So you recognize that book [commentary: Quran] as false just as inconsistency is recognized in the speech of a garrulous, vile person." Lord Hiravijaya spoke again: "If the creator first made this world and then later destroyed it as if he were fire, he would have unparalleled distress. There is no creator or destroyer of the world whose variety is brought into being by its own karma. Therefore, the existence of a creator, like the birth of a son to a barren woman, appears false to me." Having enlightened Shaykh Abul Fazl with correct speech and cured him of his prior false opinion, Hiravijaya planted the dharma of compassion in the Shaykh's mind like a farmer plants a seed in the earth.[66]

Deccan Leaders Ibrahim Adil Shah II and Malik Ambar

South of Hindustan, the Deccan hosted five sultanates in the last half of the sixteenth century: three major polities (Ahmadnagar, Bijapur, and Golconda) and two weaker ones (Berar and Bidar) that were eventually absorbed by the others. A bit earlier, the Vijayanagara kingdom had also been a political player in southern India. That ended with the 1565 Battle of Talikota when four Deccan Sultanates combined forces and, like "demons of the Kali age" in the words of one Telugu poet, issued a crushing blow.[67] For months, Sultanate armies looted the Vijayanagara capital, which became a ghost town and remains so today.[68] Still, Vijayanagara ruling culture served as a common source of inspiration for the Deccan

Sultanates, which also shared other things. All were, in one scholar's phrase "non-imperial political organisations" that relied on negotiation, rather than expansion, to maintain power.[69] All faced pressure from the land-hungry Mughals, who repeatedly tried to conquer the Deccan (they succeeded a century later, in the 1680s; see chapter 15). Early modern Deccani culture was at once parallel to and distinct from that of Mughal Hindustan, as illustrated through the lives and patronage of two quite different leaders: Ibrahim Adil Shah II (d. 1627) and Malik Ambar (d. 1626).

Ibrahim Adil Shah II (r. 1580–1627) headed Bijapur's Adil Shahi dynasty and patronized an enviable lineup of Persian poets, historians, and artists. Zuhuri, perhaps the most famous Persian poet at Ibrahim's court, declined an invitation to travel north to Mughal India and instead, as per this chapter's epigraph, remained in the enthralling Deccan. The historian Firishta received Ibrahim's patronage to produce a history of India, known as *Tarikh-i Firishta* (Firishta's history), that shaped Indian and European historical knowledge of Indo-Muslim rule for centuries.[70] The artist Farrukh Beg (fl. ca. 1580–1619), an Iranian emigree, worked in Kabul, Lahore, and the Deccan during his life, including for Ibrahim.[71] In Adil Shahi domains, Farrukh Beg interacted with European travelers, and later in life copied a print of Dolor (Melancholy) designed by Flemish artist Marten de Vos.[72] Overall, Farrukh Beg's life embodied several key features—mobility, working for different patrons, and cross-cultural artistic enterprises—that characterized this period more generally in South Asia. Ibrahim Adil Shah II's court also hosted many musicians and a robust library, of which about seventy volumes survive today.[73]

Under Ibrahim, Adil Shahi cities prospered, including the cosmopolitan capital of Bijapur. Ibrahim renamed the city Bidyapur (city of knowledge, contrasting to Bijapur meaning "city of victory").[74] Bidyapur impressed everyone who visited. For instance, Asad Beg, a Mughal ambassador, described a Bidyapuri market in 1603–1604 as "full of rare items, such as are neither seen nor heard of in any other city."[75] Notable items on offer included Spanish wine, Arabian horses, and new world tobacco (Asad Beg brought some up north for Akbar).[76] Asad Beg concluded: "In summary, the entire bazaar seemed in motion, filled with wine and beauty, melodies and perfumes, paan and jewels, exquisite fabrics and delectable dishes. On one street, thousands of groups of people gathered—drinking, singing, falling in love, and reveling—without quarrelling. This seemed to go on forever. There is perhaps nowhere in the world that offers a more amazing sight to travelers."[77] Other visitors were similarly dazzled, such as the Bruges native Jacques de Coutre who visited in the same year (1604). He reported seeing palanquins with pearls as large as chickpeas and jewels adorning everything from drinking vessels to women's ears.[78]

Ibrahim Adil Shah II also built a new city known as Nauraspur, quite close to Bijapur, in 1599 that supported a robust syncretic culture. One historian of the time estimated that it took 20,000 workers to build Nauraspur, which was near fresh water and had space for gardens unlike the built-up and resource-strained Bijapur/Bidyapur.[79] The Dutch artist Cornelis Claesz (also known as Heda) was among its residents for more than a decade. He painted a three-by-two-foot image of the Roman gods Venus, Bacchus, and Cupid that reportedly entranced Ibrahim for hours.[80] This was hardly the first Indian introduction to Greco-Roman gods. A first-century-CE statue of Poseidon (Greek god of the sea) was brought to India shortly after its creation and found a home less than 200 kilometers west of Bijapur (chapter 6). Still, such encounters in the sixteenth century infused fresh ideas into Indian painters' repertoires. Mughal court artists, too, incorporated European imagery, such as angels that looked like they flew in straight from Rome.[81] At Ibrahim's court, Heda also represented Dutch East India Company (VOC) interests, as European trading activities in India continued to expand.[82]

Nauraspur was named for Ibrahim's concept of *nauras*, a compelling case study for syncretism in early modern India. "Nauras" has a dual sense, meaning "newly arrived" in Persian and the "nine aesthetic emotions" in Sanskrit (erotic love, tragedy, the comic, and so on) that are communicated through literature, theater, art, and music.[83] The phrase appears on Bijapuri seals and forts, in pen names and titles, to refer to wine and musical notes, and so forth.[84] Ibrahim even gifted in sets of nine.[85] Perhaps the most famous use of "nauras" is the striking collection of Dakhni songs attributed to Sultan Ibrahim: *Kitab-i Nauras* (Book of nine essences), which fuses aspects of Sanskrit and Persian literary cultures. Most of the songs praise Hindu deities, such as Saraswati and Ganesha, with briefer mentions of Muslim figures such as the Prophet Muhammad and Gisu Daraz (literally "long hair," a Sufi who died at the

Bahmani capital of Gulbarga in 1422).[86] Here's how one song praises Saraswati, the Hindu goddess of knowledge:

> There are different languages;
> but there is one emotional appeal,
> be he a Brahmin or a Turk [Muslim].
> He is only fortunate on whom
> the Goddess of learning smiles.
> O Ibrahim, the world only seeks knowledge—
> Serve and meditate upon with steadfast heart
> the power of words.[87]

The *Kitab-i Nauras* was written in a Deccani vernacular called Dakhni, similar to spoken Hindi of the time and written in Perso-Arabic script.[88] Like the text's contents and language, its illustrations, too, drew on multiple traditions. When there was no precedent to capture the text's novelty, artists innovated. For instance, Farrukh Beg painted a unique image of Saraswati sitting on a Bijapuri throne, resembling (as per the text) "an ivory statue" (figure 13.4).[89]

Not everyone who wound up on a Deccani throne, or close to it anyway, started life as privileged as Ibrahim Adil Shah II, and the story of Malik Ambar, a slave turned kingmaker, offers a different perspective on early modern Deccani pluralism. Malik Ambar was born in Ethiopia, enslaved, and taken to the Middle East where he converted to Islam. Ethiopian-origin slaves had been imported to India for centuries, where they were known as Habshis or Sidis (chapters 10–11). Malik Ambar was brought to India in the early 1570s among the 1,000 slaves purchased by Chinghis Khan, himself a former slave of African origin who had become the Nizam Shahi chief minister.[90] Upon Chinghis Khan's death, Malik Ambar gained his freedom, soon marrying and amassing political power.

Malik Ambar elected to rule from behind the throne. There was precedent for Habshi kings in India, such as Jaunpur's Sharqi dynasty (chapter 11) and the Habshi dynasty of Bengal that featured four rulers between 1486 and 1493.[91] But, instead, Malik Ambar fashioned himself a kingmaker. In 1600, when Ahmadnagar's Nizam Shahis appeared poised to crumble before Mughal aggression, Malik Ambar married his daughter to a twenty-year-old member of the Ahmadnagar ruling family

Figure 13.4. Saraswati enthroned, from a *Kitab-i Nauras*, 1604 CE, Farrukh Beg, Bijapur, India.

and installed his new son-in-law as a puppet king.[92] He then defended and rebuilt the Ahmadnagar Sultanate. Over the coming years, Malik Ambar served as *peshwa* (chief minister) for Ahmadnagar and integrated many Marathas (Marathi-speaking warriors) into state service and the military.[93]

While Malik Ambar's origins as a former slave did not prevent him from amassing power, his ethnicity came up at times. For example, the Mughal emperor Jahangir used colorism language to express his loathing of Malik Ambar, who defied Mughal state authority. He referred to the Habshi kingmaker as "black-fated" and "black-faced."[94] Jahangir never got the best of Malik Ambar, however, who died as an old man in bed.

Malik Ambar was a master builder whose water systems have survived the test of time. He oversaw the construction of canals, aqueducts, reservoirs, and more at his capital city of Khirki (later renamed Aurangabad).[95] He also directed construction of a series of cascading lakes at nearby Daulatabad, building on Yadava construction from the twelfth century. These water projects benefited both cities' populations. They included recreational features, such as an artificial waterfall at Daulatabad complete with a viewing platform. Much of this water infrastructure remains in use today, with locals at Daulatabad able to point to "malik ambar ki pipeline" (Malik Ambar's pipeline).[96] As the longevity of his achievements suggests, Malik Ambar was extraordinary. He offers a glimpse of what was possible, if rarely realized, in the dynamic society of the early modern Deccan.

Still, most Habshis led more ordinary lives in sixteenth-century India, as demonstrated by the sad story of Gabriel. Gabriel entered India about a decade later than Malik Ambar, in 1582, and soon found himself caught between worlds. Gabriel, too, had converted to Islam while enslaved in the Arab world. He was brought to the Portuguese Estado da India, where he converted to Christianity and was eventually manumitted.[97] In the 1590s, he went back and forth between the Ahmadnagar Sultanate and Portuguese India, acting as a Muslim in Ahmadnagar (known as Ali Handi) and a Christian in Chaul (known as Gabriel). Inhabiting multiple religious identities had precedent. For example, in the fifteenth century, the Russian Afanasii Nikitin had traveled to parts of western Asia and India, acting sometimes as a Christian and other times as a Muslim merchant (known as Khwaja Yusuf Khurasani).[98] But there was no European colonial presence to object to Nikitin code-switching religions as there was to Gabriel.

Gabriel was hauled before the Catholic Inquisition in 1595, confessed under duress to backsliding into Islam, and was given penance as punishment. Gabriel had spent most of his life in military slavery, but he only lasted a few months in the severe servitude conditions of Portuguese Goa.[99] Gabriel tried to escape back to Ahmadnagar but was caught and sentenced to hard manual labor in Lisbon. That is the last we hear of him in the historical record. Gabriel's saga is a reminder, among other things, that many premodern stories have unhappy endings.

Conclusion: Mughal Succession

The lives of ordinary and elite Indians sometimes intersected, such as when Akbar's death in October of 1605 sent shockwaves through north India. Writing in Hindi, Banarasidas, a Jain merchant, said that the news sent him tumbling down a flight of stairs and panic raged throughout the city of Jaunpur. "The whole town was in a tremor. Everyone closed the doors of their house in panic; shopkeepers shut down their shops. Feverishly, the rich hid their jewels and costly attire underground; many of them quickly dumped their wealth and their ready capital in carriages and rushed to safe, secluded places. Every householder began stocking his home with weapons and arms."[100] Meanwhile, the Mughals had to resolve the question of succession since all sons had equal claim to the throne.[101] Things were eased in this case since two of Akbar's three sons—Murad (d. 1599) and Danyal (d. 1605)—had predeceased their father, both dying of alcohol poisoning. The remaining son, Prince Salim, had rebelled against Akbar and set up a separate court in Allahabad between 1599 and 1604. But the two had reconciled, and, according to Banarsidas, people calmed down about ten days after Akbar's death, when they received news of Prince Salim's enthronement as Emperor Jahangir. Mughal succession did not always proceed bloodlessly, however, and so we return to the subject in subsequent chapters as the Mughal Empire thrived and grew for another century.

Further Reading

There is extensive scholarship on the Mughals, especially Akbar. Special mention ought to be made of Wheeler Thackston, who has single-handedly translated many Mughal-era Persian texts into English (his translation of the *Akbarnama* runs eight volumes. I drew on Catherine

Asher and Cynthia Talbot for Rajput history and Sunil Sharma for Persian poetry. For the Deccan, work by Keelan Overton, Roy Fischel, and Deborah Hutton was helpful. For scholarship on the Habshis Malik Ambar and Gabriel, I relied on Ananya Chakravarti, Richard Eaton, and Matteo Salvadore.

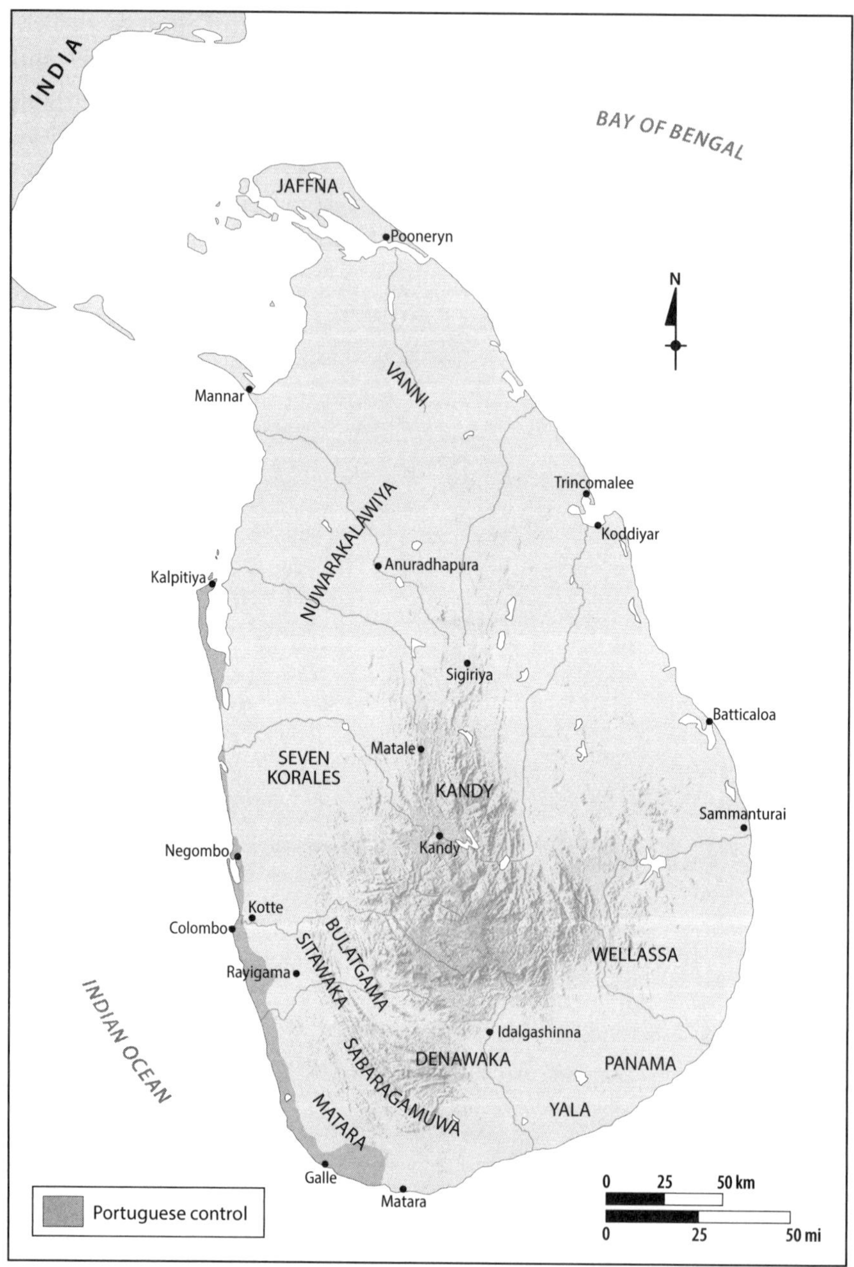

Ceylon, ca. 1600.

14

Religious Communities and Elite Culture, 1600–1650

Brahmin—put a fresh idea in a fresh refrain.
A fresh sprout appears more elegant in new dirt.

—Chandar Bhan Brahmin, Mughal Persian poet, ca. 1650 (Persian)[1]

As the seventeenth century dawned, Mughal rule was entrenched in northern India, Deccani Sultanates had divvied up much of the south, and European powers continued to gain ground. Many a historian has stopped at that, focusing on this period's political developments. I choose another, admittedly more narratively challenging, route in this chapter, namely analyzing how South Asian religious communities forged new ties and identities in response to early modern political shifts. I survey the social histories of four groups: Sri Lankan Buddhists, Bengali Muslims, Gujarati Jains, and Benares Brahmins. Several strands connect these groups' social developments, including increased travel and migration, interreligious contacts and contests, and greater production of wealth. That said, each community was based in a distinct region and underwent discrete processes of change. That dissimilarity—which showcases diverse reactions to broader historical shifts—makes it compelling to analyze them in succession. These case studies also embody some key South Asian social and cultural changes, such as large-scale conversions to Islam among Bengalis and a consolidation of Brahminical identity in northern India. In the chapter's second half, I turn to a more familiar story: Mughal artistic and architectural achievements in the seventeenth century, enabled by similar broad trends of robust migration and wealth concentration.

Buddhists in Colonial Ceylon

In the sixteenth and seventeenth centuries, Sri Lankans faced social and religious pressures from two European colonial powers. The Portuguese colonized parts of Sri Lanka—which was politically fragmented—between 1506 and 1658, and thereafter the Dutch took their place. Both the Portuguese and the Dutch pursued mercantile agendas, but some Portuguese—who were Catholic—also tried to gain Christian converts in what they called Ceilao (i.e., Ceylon). The Portuguese engaged in similar missionary activities in Goa (chapter 12), but there were substantial differences in the case of Ceylon. For one thing, the island was predominantly Buddhist, making it the first Buddhist society worldwide to experience European colonization.[2] Also, Portuguese colonial power proved more short-lived in Sri Lanka since they were expelled and replaced by the Protestant Dutch in the mid-seventeenth century (in Goa, the Portuguese remained until 1961). Portuguese proselytization provoked mixed responses among Sri Lankan communities that spurred new kinds of Christian and Buddhist religious identities.

Sri Lankans who converted to Catholicism often gained social and political standing. For example, most of the Karava caste of fishers became Christian under the guidance of Franciscans, who promised them material gain.[3] When five Karava leaders were publicly baptized in 1606, the Portuguese Captain-General "was pleased to grant them many favours and privileges in order to cause the envy of the other gentiles who might thus be led to follow their example."[4] Subsequent generations of the Karava rose in status as they expanded their expertise from fishing to making boats, carpentry, procuring raw construction materials, and more. Other early modern Sri Lankans gained freedom from indentured servitude or debt by changing their religion. In some cases, Christian converts avoided paying taxes to local Buddhist rulers.[5] Some kings, too, converted. Most famously, Dharmapala (r. 1551–1597) of the Kingdom of Kotte along Ceylon's southwest coast became Catholic in the 1550s and ruled, with Portuguese protection, as Dom Joao.[6]

Most Sri Lankans remained Buddhist, although they conceptualized their religion differently owing to their colonial experiences. Premodern Ceylon was a world of religious fluidity where it was common for followers of the Buddhist dhamma to honor Hindu gods.[7] In contrast, Portuguese missionaries argued that one needed to commit to a single set of religious practices (preferably Catholic). Stephen Berkwitz has argued that such sentiments inspired Sri Lankan Buddhists to articulate their religious identity in "more assertive, exclusive, and self-conscious" ways.[8] For example, the Sinhalese poet Alagiyavanna Mukaveti penned these lines around 1600–1610, criticizing Buddhists who engaged in Hindu or other practices:

> Like ignorant merchants who do not know the price of a gem,
> taking a lump of glass and greedily calling it a gem,
> ignorant beings, wishing for liberation, make offerings,
> venerating other gods besides the spotless Noble Sage.
> The effort made by ignorant beings that aspire to nirvana,
> serving other gods and forsaking the delightful Lord of Sages,
> is like pressing an oil machine on a sandy courtyard,
> while increasing in one's mind the desire to obtain oil.[9]

After the death of his Buddhist patron and amid an increase of Portuguese influence, Alagiyavanna converted to Catholicism. Other Sri Lankan Buddhists continued to engage with European Christian ideas—and articulated their own identity in fresh ways—for centuries, including during the British colonization of Ceylon (1796–1948).[10]

In the seventeenth century, encountering Portuguese and Dutch Christians prompted some Ceylonese Buddhists to bolster ties with their counterparts in Burma. In earlier centuries, Burma, especially the coastal kingdom of Arakan, had received Buddhist material items, such as copies of the Tipitaka (collection of Buddhist teachings) from Sri Lanka.[11] Ceylon-Arakan connections grew from the fifteenth century onward, piggybacking on the expansion of maritime trade.[12] Building on older links, an early seventeenth-century ruler of Kandy asked Arakan to send monks to help reconstitute the sangha (community of Buddhists renunciants).[13] Arakan agreed and honored similar requests going forward.[14] In the 1690s, the Dutch facilitated Arakan-Ceylon exchanges, transporting officials, documents, and monks between the two.[15] Through such activities, Arakan helped to preserve Buddhist practices in Ceylon, even as they were morphing during the island's long colonial encounter.

Bengali Muslim Converts

In Bengal, a rather different trend unfolded in early modernity as—quite unusually in South Asian history—much of the population converted to Islam. By 1600, Muslims had participated in South Asian life for 900 years as traders, Sufis, travelers, rulers, administrators, and more. Still, Muslims remained a minority within the subcontinent's crowded religious landscape. To be sure, many Muslims, especially rulers, were far more interested in political power than conversion. Certainly, this accurately describes the Mughals who never pursued any formal program of conversion, in Bengal or elsewhere.[16] Bengal was a frontier for the Mughals, integrated into the empire over several decades beginning in the 1570s.[17] In the seventeenth century, Bengal's local economy boomed and, relatedly, many Bengali communities began to adopt Muslim practices.

Both rice and textile trades flourished in seventeenth-century Bengal. Rice was newer in the region and depended on clearing forested land for cultivation. As agriculture grew, more forest dwellers became integrated into an agrarian economy. Early modern Bengal also exported textiles, a huge regional industry that added tens of thousands of jobs to meet the demand for fabrics across Eurasia.[18] Bengalis had excelled at textiles for centuries, with a notable uptick in production following the thirteenth-century Delhi Sultanate conquest of Bengal.[19]

Dacca muslin was Bengal's most famed textile. The fabric is so sheer and flowing that it was known as "running water" (*ab-i rawan*) and "woven air" (*beft hawa*) that, when thrown, would hang like a cloud in the sky.[20] The French traveler Tavernier, who visited India in the mid-seventeenth century, said he could scarcely even feel the fine fabric in his hands.[21] In a likely apocryphal story, the Mughal emperor Aurangzeb (r. 1658–1707) is said to have chastised one of his daughters for appearing naked when, in fact, she was clad in seven layers of fine Dacca muslin.[22] What is true is that the Mughal court kept the best Dacca muslin—only made in Bengal—for themselves.[23]

Even with the best kept aside for Mughal elites, nobody could get enough of early modern Bengali textiles. The Dutch East India Company established a trading post at Hooghly (Hugli) in 1636 that, by 1654, was purchasing 200,000 pounds of raw silk annually. At the same time, South Asian traders—especially Gujaratis and Punjabis—purchased ever greater quantities of Bengali textiles, often re-exporting them on the subcontinent and through Indian Ocean networks.[24] This trade was financed, in part, by new world silver that flooded into early modern Asia.[25]

Bengal's prospering trade and agriculture brought hitherto marginalized, forest-dwelling groups into mainstream society, and, as part of their social integration, many became Muslim. Weavers, loom makers, tailors, thick ribbon weavers, and dyers number among the earliest Bengali communities known to have adopted Islam. In trying to figure out why such communities converted, Richard Eaton has argued that it is important that they were not Hindu. Rather, Bengali forest communities had their own local religious practices, largely focused on goddess worship. And so, for these groups, becoming Muslim was part of becoming enmeshed in broader commerce patterns and social networks, similar to how forest dwellers in other regions adopted caste markers and Hindu practices throughout premodernity, often becoming Shudras.[26] As Eaton observes, it is paradoxical that much of "Bengal's Muslim population emerged under a regime that did not, as a matter of policy, promote the conversion of Bengalis to Islam."[27] Yet, this is only surprising if we overemphasize the role of state elites. Conversion trends among early modern Bengali Muslims are a potent reminder that economic forces often spur substantial social changes and that non-elite communities exercise agency over their religious identities.

Jains in Mughal Gujarat

On the other side of the subcontinent, Shvetambara Jains in and around Gujarat thrived under Mughal rule, in part owing to their imperial connections. Gujarat had featured in subcontinental and transregional trade networks since the Indus Civilization (chapter 1). In the seventeenth century, many Gujarati Jains capitalized on robust trade within South Asia, increased involvement from European merchants, and goods from the New World. Some Jains belonged to a caste group known as *bania*, which also included Hindus, and were reputed as businessmen. By the early sixteenth century, banias were known in Cairo as "great merchants and good account keepers."[28] In the mid-seventeenth century, members of this group traveled back and forth between Indian Ocean ports, such as from Basra (Iraq) to Surat, by the dozens.[29] The names and stories of individual early modern Jain merchants are mostly lost to time, except for the most successful who stand out as extraordinary exemplars of broader trends.

Two Gujarati Jains numbered among the richest private individuals of seventeenth-century India: Shantidas Jhaveri (d. 1659) and Virji Vora (d. ca. 1670). Shantidas lived in Ahmedabad and amassed wealth in the jewel trade and as a moneylender, including to Mughal princes. Virji Vora was a banker in Surat who comes up in English, Dutch, French, and Mughal sources as a "vastly rich" moneylender.[30] He was also a shrewd trader, often establishing a monopoly over a desirable item—such as Malabar pepper—and then jacking up prices.[31] Both men directed some of their material resources to their wider community. Shantidas helped his elder brother sponsor a Jain temple outside of Ahmedabad in the 1620s.[32] Virji Vora belonged to a Jain sect that rejected icon veneration, but he distributed food to the poor, such as during a famine in 1630–1632.[33] More generally, Gujarati Jain merchants also supported libraries and animal hospitals, thereby enacting Jain values of education and ahimsa (non-harm).[34]

Some Jains, including monks, also forged direct connections with Mughal elites. For example, in 1610, Jahangir granted Vijayasena, leader of the Gujarati-based Tapa Gaccha Jain sect, an imperial order (*farman*) banning animal slaughter during the Jain festival of Paryushan (observed in August–September). The farman advanced the central Jain concept of ahimsa to all living creatures. It also publicly advertised the strength of Jain imperial ties. Local lay Jains in Agra celebrated the achievement by commissioning a Mughal court artist, Shalivahana, to paint a lavish scroll illustration depicting white-clad Shvetambara monks among the diverse attendees at Jahangir's court.[35] The scroll illustration accompanied an invitation for Vijayasena to visit Agra and so was aimed at an internal Jain audience that wanted to celebrate their Mughal connections. Indeed, Jain monks wrote about their experiences at the Mughal court for decades after they had ceased in real life (around 1620). Some writers adopted Mughal imperial imagery for Jain communities, speaking of armies of monks who spread Jain teachings.[36] In so doing, they expressed a regional religious identity that made sense in Mughal-controlled Gujarat.

Brahmins in Mughal Benares

Mughal Benares attracted Brahmin migrants from across northern and central India whose activities had religious and social impacts far beyond the city. Benares, also known as Varanasi and Kashi (and also spelled Banaras), is associated with Shiva and situated along the Ganges River. It has been inhabited for thousands of years, but virtually nothing survives of the ancient city.[37] Benares underwent transformative changes in the seventeenth century, largely due to imperial patronage from Rajputs. Against this backdrop of largesse, Brahmins flocked to Mughal Benares, where they wrote new versions of Hindu stories and further delineated Brahminical identity.

In the 1570s, Tulsidas finished his new Hindi Ramayana, titled *Ramcharitmanas* (Holy Lake of Rama's Actions, often known as *Manas*), in Benares. Many Indians had retold the Ramayana story since the earliest version attributed to Valmiki a millennium and a half earlier (chapter 6). Generally, authors treated Rama with increased reverence over time. For example, Kamban's twelfth-century Tamil Ramayana emphasizes Rama's divinity, depicting him (unlike in Valmiki) as always aware that he is Vishnu incarnate.[38] Tulsidas takes this even further. His *Manas* is a bhakti work (in the sagun tradition) and presents Rama (i.e., Ram) as the perfect man and an unquestionable deity. Bringing both visions together was part of his innovation, captured in this line that also appears in a praise poem to Hanuman attributed to Tulsidas:

> Having corrected, with the dust of the guru's feet,
> the mirror of my heart,
> I narrate the stainless glory of Ram,
> which bestows the four blessed fruits.[39]

Tulsidas altered Rama's tale to bolster his image of an incarnate deity who should be universally worshipped. He even depicts Ravana, the story's villain, as fortunate in being slain by Rama, since this means the demon king can reach moksha.[40]

Arguably, Tulsidas's most stunning invention is an illusory Sita—literally a shadow (*pratibimba*)—who is stolen by Ravana while the real Sita remains safely ensconced in a purifying fire. Tulsidas's shadow Sita sought to answer Indians' long-standing discomfort with verifying Sita's sexual purity after she was held captive for months in Ravana's palace.[41] Earlier authors had relied on a fire test (*agni-pariksha*) to validate Sita's chastity.[42] Tulsidas retained the fire test, using it as the occasion for the real Sita to re-emerge from the purifying fire back into the world. But that Tulsidas does not even permit Sita to be in Ravana's custody signals that, 1,500 years into the written Ramayana tradition, doubt surrounding Sita's sexual purity had not been fully resolved.

In other ways, Tulsidas continued time-honored aspects of the Ramayana tradition. For example, he endorsed caste and gender privileges, depicting the ocean god Varuna as proclaiming, "Drum, rustic, Shudra, beast, and woman—all these are fit for beating."[43] For Tulsidas, Rama was an "exemplar of social propriety" (*maryada purushottama*) as an enforcer of proper caste and gender roles.[44]

Tulsidas's *Manas* shaped knowledge of the Ramayana saga across northern India, both in his time and today. Manuscripts of the text circulated in scripts used by different communities, including Devanagari, Persian, and Kaithi (a Kayasth script, associated with Mughal scribes).[45] Even more gained access to Tulsidas's rendition of Rama's saga through a multiday theatrical performance called *Ram Lila* (Rama's play). The Ram Lila, too, was developed in Benares, probably in the seventeenth century.[46] It was hardly the first staging of the Ramayana, but it alone became the early modern equivalent of a Bollywood blockbuster.[47] Today, Ram Lilas remain major cultural events, performed in autumn across northern India, and teach generations of northerners Rama's story in its bhakti version. Many who have never even heard of the *Manas* by name know Tulsidas's version of Rama's story. This sometimes leads to surprise and strong reactions when modern Indians consider sharper aspects of Valmiki's Sanskrit text.[48]

Another major activity of Brahmins, including Brahmin migrants, in Mughal Benares was producing judgments that defined Brahminness (*brahmanatva*, *brahmanya*). Generally, such letters concerned the status of specific caste groups and signaled an interest in defining community boundaries. For example, a 1583 letter sent from Benares to Konkan stipulates that Chiplunas, Devarsis, and Maharashtrian Brahmins can, in fact, eat together, and they should cease "hostilities with each other."[49] The letter was signed by Brahmins from Konkan, Maharashtra, Gujarat, western Bengal, and Mithila.[50] Later letters from Benares and elsewhere addressed the status of the Devarukhes and Shenvis (a subgroup of Goa's Sarasvat Brahmins), discussing as potentially relevant to considering whether they are Brahmins the groups' social mobility, fish-eating, and historic and current occupations.[51] The 1657 letter quoted here is one example. Others in seventeenth-century Benares took up the question of how one could perceive Brahminness in an individual, perhaps an issue that arose with increased mobility and contact between hitherto unacquainted Brahminical communities.[52] Brahmins often gathered for such discussions within the Vishveshvara Temple (mentioned specifically in the 1583 letter), rebuilt by the Bhatta family in the 1570s–1580s with support from Mughal-employed Rajputs.[53]

1657 Sanskrit Judgment Letter from the Council of Brahmins in Benares

Shiva conquers all. Now, at the Muktimandapa (in the Vishveshvara Temple) in Kashi (Benares), the truth as to whether the Devarshi Brahmins have Brahminness (*brahmanya*) is adjudicated by learned Brahmins and ascetics.

On this point, there is consensus in the assembly of learned householders belonging to all Brahmin lineages of Maharashtra, Karnataka, Konkana, Tailanga, Dravida, etc., and of the highest order of renouncers whose feet should be revered, on the basis of the Veda, shastras, and worldly evidence—The Devarshi Brahmins have learned the highest truth from the Veda, shastras, puranas, and itihasa [all Sanskrit texts typically restricted to upper-castes].

The Devarshis engage in the practices of good people (*sadacharana*), such as conducting and taking part in Vedic sacrifices. They purify those with whom they eat food, are worthy as family relations, and have as their nature unparalleled Brahminness (brahmanya).

Moreover, they have contracted marriages with the learned community. We have seen this. Shri Raghunatha Bhatta, a learned scholar of mimamsa philosophy, married the daughter of Anantabhatta Manikarni, who was a Devarukh, but he nevertheless performed the *vajapeya* sacrifice. And many others, who belong to that lineage, are also performers of the vajapeya, as are we.

Those who criticize this decision, which has been rendered by the learned, are denigrating Shiva and are murderers of Brahmins. This is what we say in this regard, though we could say more. This was written by Bhatta Lakshmana, learned in mimamsa philosophy. It was written with the permission of the learned. This was done in the Samvat year 1714 and the Shaka year 1579 (1657 CE). This joint letter has been approved by numerous learned men who have come together. [A list of signatories follows][54]

Some early modern Benaras Brahmins engaged more directly with Mughal culture by becoming imperial employees, often hired for their Brahminical cultural knowledge. For example, Kavindracharya Sarasvati received a stipend from Emperor Shah Jahan, at whose court he instructed Mughal princes in Sanskrit texts, likely including the *Yogavasishtha*, and sang vernacular *dhrupads*.[55] At one point, Kavindra convinced Shah Jahan to cancel a Mughal tax on Hindu pilgrims to Benares. His Brahmin contemporaries penned two sets of praise poems to commemorate the achievement, one in Sanskrit and one in Hindi.[56] In the 1650s and 1660s, Kavindra enjoyed the patronage of Danishmand Khan, a Mughal noble, and Francois Bernier, a French traveler who described Benares as the "Athens of India."[57] Kavindra's multiple identities—as a Sanskrit pandit, vernacular musician, Brahmin lobbyist, Mughal court star, and native informant for a European—indicate the overlapping possibilities for elite Brahmins in early modern north India.

Benares Brahmins who did not accept Mughal support were also influenced by residing within Mughal territory during the seventeenth century. For example, Nilakantha Chaturdhara produced a new edition of Vyasa's Sanskrit Mahabharata in which he added contemporary glosses, such as describing ancient mythological weapons as cannons and muskets (familiar from Mughal warfare). At times, Nilakantha Chaturdhara even used Perso-Arabic vocabulary, perhaps heard on the streets of Mughal Benares.[58]

Some Brahmins objected to engagements with Mughal culture, and the points of dispute indicate some of the contested boundaries of early modern Brahminical identity. For example, writing in Benares in the mid-1600s, Khandadeva warned against bilingual (*dvaibhashika*) Brahmins who might teach Sanskrit to Muslims and others theoretically ineligible by varna for such instruction.[59] The concern was real since Brahmins instructed multiple generations of Mughal elites in Sanskrit texts, and two full Sanskrit grammars of Persian survive, sponsored by Akbar and Jahangir, respectively.[60] The story of Jagannatha Panditaraja brings into sharp relief differing Brahminical approaches to seventeenth-century Indian multiculturalism.

Jagannatha Panditaraja, a Telangana-origin Brahmin, was one of the most accomplished Sanskrit intellectuals of the seventeenth century and spent his youth at the Mughal court, where he is widely believed to have learned Persian.[61] Reflecting his comfort in multiple cultural contexts, Jagannatha is also rumored to have taken a Muslim (*yavani*) wife, known in Sanskrit sources as Lavangi.[62] Jagannatha wrote Sanskrit verses about her that sound, in certain ways, closer to Persian poetry:

> That Muslim girl has a body soft as butter
> and if I could get her to lie by my side
> the hard floor would be good enough for me
> and all the comforts of paradise redundant.[63]

Jagannatha's interreligious love outraged many in his community, which widely practiced endogamy. Another Benares-based contemporary even reportedly maligned Jagannatha as an outcaste (*mleccha*) due to his disregard for social conventions.[64] Such responses reified a feature of caste communities dating back to the early first millennium CE, namely restrictive marriage controls, that endured in early modernity even as a select few bucked tradition.

Mughal Material Culture

As South Asian regional and religious communities redefined themselves, Mughal elites sponsored the arts and large-scale architectural projects in northern India. In some ways, Mughal material culture under Jahangir (r. 1605–1627) and Shah Jahan (r. 1628–1658) was shaped by similar trends of increased world connections. Consider, for example, the American turkey that visited King Jahangir's court. A Mughal courtier saw the bird in Portuguese Goa and dragged it overland to Agra. He unveiled the turkey at court, amazing Jahangir who marveled at how the strange animal kept changing colors (turkeys do this when stressed).[65] Jahangir ordered a court artist to draw the bird's likeness, and the image survives today as part of the considerable artistic output of Jahangir's atelier. Mughal elite culture flourished more broadly in the first half of the seventeenth century as patrons and artisans together produced stunning paintings, gardens, and buildings.

Mughal artists in Jahangir's workshop depicted real and imaginary scenes, often following the emperor's explicit directions. For instance, Balchand painted a deathbed portrait of Inayat Khan as he withered away from an opium addiction. Jahangir ordered the grim scene executed in a hyper-realistic style, describing his courtier's appearance thus: "He looked incredibly weak and thin. 'Skin stretched over bone.' Even his bones had begun to disintegrate. Whereas painters employ great exaggeration when they depict skinny people, nothing remotely resembling him had ever been seen. Good God! How can a human being remain alive in this shape?"[66] Jahangir also ordered artists to paint fictional events, such as the emperor alongside his Safavid rival, Shah Abbas (ruler of Persia, 1588–1629). The two men never met. But, in the painting, Jahangir towers over Shah Abbas and edges him off of Asia in an unsubtle projection of Mughal dominance (figure 14.1).[67] Some Mughal artists painted images that attested to cross-cultural connections. For example, images survive of Jahangir visiting with the Hindu ascetic (*sanyasi*) Jadrup (figure 14.2), part of ongoing Mughal relations with numerous Hindu communities.[68] As described in his memoirs, Jahangir visited this ascetic (rather than asking him to come to court) and was impressed, if slightly confused, by Jadrup's commitment to self-deprivation (see excerpt).

Visiting Jadrup, Excerpt from Jahangir's Persian Memoirs *Jahangirnama*, ca. 1616

It had been repeatedly heard that near the town of Ujjain an ascetic sanyasi named Jadrup Ashram had been living for several years in an out-of-the-way spot in the country far from civilization, where he worshiped the true deity. I very much desired to meet him and had wanted to summon him and see him while I was in Agra, but in view of the trouble it would have caused him I didn't do it. Now that we were in the vicinity,

Figure 14.1. Mughal Emperor Jahangir (r. 1605–1627) embracing the Safavid King Shah Abbas (r. 1588–1629), ca. 1618 CE, Abul Hasan.

Figure 14.2. Mughal Emperor Jahangir (r. 1605–1627) visiting with the Hindu ascetic Jadrup, ca. 1617–1620 CE, Govardhan.

> I got out of the boat and went an eighth of a kos [half a kilometer] on foot to visit him.
>
> The place he had chosen for his abode was a pit dug out in the middle of a hill. The entrance was shaped like a mihrab. . . . A skinny person would have great difficulty getting in. The length and width of the pit were the same. He had neither mat nor straw strewn underfoot as other dervishes do. He spends his time alone in that dark, narrow hole. In winter and cold weather, although he is absolutely naked and has no clothing except a piece of rag with which he covers himself in front and behind, he never lights a fire. As Mulla Rumi says, speaking in the idiom of dervishes: "Our clothing is the heat of the sun by day, and moonlight is our pillow and quilt by night."
>
> Twice a day he goes to make ablutions in the river nearby, and once a day he goes into Ujjain, enters the houses of only three Brahmins out of the seven married persons with children he has chosen and in whose asceticism and contentment he has confidence, takes in his hand like a beggar five morsels of food they have prepared for themselves, and swallows them without chewing lest he derive any enjoyment from the taste–this provided that no calamity has occurred in any of the three houses, no birth has taken place, and there be no menstruating women. This is how he lives.
>
> He desires no intercourse with people, but since he has acquired a great reputation, people go to see him. He is not devoid of learning and has studied well the science of the Vedanta, which is the science of Sufism.
>
> I held conversation with him for six gharis [around three hours], and he had such good things to say that he made a great impression on me. He also liked my company. When my exalted father had conquered the fortress of Asir and the province of Khandesh and was on his way back to Agra, he also paid him a visit in this very place and often mentioned it with fondness.[69]

Jahangir proudly claimed his Timurid ancestry, weaving it together with claims of Indian kingship. For instance, he had his Timurid heritage carved onto an Ashokan Pillar that he re-erected while still a prince at Allahabad in the early 1600s. Jahangir's inscription joined others on this pillar, including by the Gupta ruler Samudragupta (r. ca. 335–375), generations of pilgrims, and, of course, Ashoka.[70] Delhi Sultanate kings, too, had reused Ashokan pillars, thereby participating in the transcultural rhetoric of north Indian political power (chapter 10). Jahangir also made his own mark at times. For instance, he and his favorite queen, Nur Jahan, minted zodiac coins, cycling through the twelve signs by minting each during the appropriate month.[71] As Jahangir noted in his memoirs, "This method is peculiarly my own and has never been used before."[72]

Mughal paintings under Jahangir showed increasing Western influences as more Europeans visited Hindustan. For example, a famous image of Jahangir shows him preferring a Sufi shaykh to kings, including King James I whose image was copied from a European painting (European angels also adorn the scene). Paintings aside, however, European material culture did little to impress Mughal elites, who were often far wealthier than their Western counterparts. Sir Thomas Roe—who visited Jahangir's court in the 1610s to negotiate for the newly founded British East India Company—found that his English gifts were often rejected as paltry.[73] Even Roe's gifts that were accepted, such as a British coach, were spruced up by Mughal artisans before being presented at Jahangir's court.[74] Roe was aware that his gifts were seen as shoddy given opulent Mughal norms, but he and others appear less aware of their, by Mughal standards, low personal hygiene.[75] As Shah Jahan put it: "Truly, the Europeans (farangis) would be a great people but for their having three very bad aspects: first, they are Kafirs (i.e., unbelievers), secondly, they eat pork, and thirdly, they do not wash those parts from which replete Nature expels the superfluous from the belly of the body."[76] For their part, many Europeans were fascinated by Mughal art, even if they never traveled to the subcontinent. Rembrandt (1606–1669) and his school executed twenty-three surviving paintings of elite Mughal figures.[77]

The Mughals built many gardens in the first half of the seventeenth century, such as Nur Jahan's famed gardens in Kashmir. Kashmir had become integrated into the empire in the 1580s, with its conquest led by, among others, the Kachhwaha Rajput Bhagwant Das (Bharmal's son). In subsequent decades, Kashmir became a favorite royal haunt. Nur Jahan—Jahangir's favorite wife and the most powerful queen in the Mughal dynasty—traveled to the region frequently with her husband, and together they built Shalimar Bagh in Srinagar, a pleasure garden that also accommodated court business.[78] For Jahangir, visits to Kashmir were thought to be beneficial for his health, often rocky from his abuse of alcohol and opium. Also, Jahangir imagined Kashmir as a paradise for all, proclaiming: "For monarchs [Kashmir] is a garden that delights the eye, and for poor people it is an enjoyable place of retreat."[79] One wonders if all "poor people" would have agreed, however, since forced labor was known in the region for picking and cleaning saffron flowers and carrying wood.[80] Early modern Kashmiri villagers also suffered from periodic floods and famines.[81]

Shah Jahan, Jahangir's son and successor, engaged in substantial building projects, changing urban landscapes in ways still definitional to major South Asian cities today. He sponsored Delhi's Jama Masjid, a large congregational mosque, and much of the city's Red Fort. Chandar Bhan, a Brahmin who worked for Shah Jahan, described the Red Fort as a towering symbol of Mughal sovereignty along the Yamuna River thus:

> I take such pride in the emperor's palace
> from where it is only one step to the sky.
> Its lofty nobility transcends the firmament.
> The sun and moon arise from its threshold.
> So much pure gold was spent on it
> that it couldn't be counted even in a cosmic ledger.
> So how could I use mere words to describe its jewels and stones,
> which polish the rust off the mirror of dejected hearts?[82]

A verse found in the Red Fort's private audience hall (and often attributed to Amir Khusraw) is more succinct in proclaiming: "If there is paradise on earth—This is it! This is it! This is it!"[83] The same hall contained the exquisite Peacock Throne, commissioned by Shah Jahan. The throne was the most expensive item Shah Jahan ever patronized, costing a whopping ten million rupees (the Taj Mahal, discussed next, cost five million rupees).[84] The Peacock Throne was made of gold and adorned by some of the most famous stones of premodern Asia, including the Koh-i Noor diamond (from Golconda's diamond mines) and the Timur Ruby (which had belonged to Timur's grandson and upon which Jahangir had carved his and Akbar's names).[85] The Peacock Throne did not survive early modernity and was disassembled by Nadir Shah after his 1739 sack

Figure 14.3. Wazir Khan Mosque, ca. 1630s CE, Lahore, Pakistan.

of Delhi (chapter 16), but the Red Fort still stands and is used as a political backdrop by Indian political leaders in the twenty-first century.

Other Mughal elites followed Shah Jahan's example in large-scale construction. For example, between 1648 and 1650, Jahanara (Shah Jahan's eldest daughter) sponsored two mosques, one in Agra and another in Kashmir.[86] In the 1630s, Lahore's Mughal governor (who also worked as a physician) commissioned the exquisite Wazir Khan Mosque (figure 14.3) with a polychromed interior.[87] The Wazir Khan Mosque is a magnificent building, and yet it along with all other Shah Jahan-era structures are overshadowed in fame by Agra's Taj Mahal.

Shah Jahan built the Taj Mahal—easily the most famous Indian building from any historical period—for his favorite wife Mumtaz Mahal. Indeed, the couple had an extraordinary love story. They were married for nineteen years, and, according to the court historian Qazwini, it was a happy union for both. Discussions of marital bliss are unusual in Mughal sources and indicates that their love was likely genuine.[88] Still, their lives were punctuated by sorrows. Mumtaz bore fourteen children, of which only half survived. After the birth of her fourteenth child in 1631,

Figure 14.4. Taj Mahal mausoleum, mosque and mirror mosque, and grounds built for Mumtaz Mahal (d. 1631) by Mughal Emperor Shah Jahan (d. 1666), 1631–1648 CE, Agra, India.

a daughter named Gauharara, Mumtaz began to hemorrhage blood. She had time to say goodbye to Shah Jahan before dying, at the age of thirty-eight. To honor his dead beloved, Shah Jahan commissioned the white marble Taj Mahal (figure 14.4), which also became his final resting place in 1666.[89]

The Taj Mahal complex consists of a central mausoleum (with tombs underneath), a mosque and mirror mosque for symmetry, gardens originally filled with trees and water, and more. It was fashioned by thousands of artisans, and, among the mason marks (similar to those at Fatehpur Sikri, discussed in chapter 13), Hindu names outnumber Muslims ones.[90] Visitors often marvel at the inlaid multicolor stonework that covers the mausoleum's facade. Indeed, each flower is comprised of 100 individually laid stones.[91] Lavish inscriptions adorn the central mausoleum's entry, consisting of Quranic verses in black lettering inlaid on white marble.[92] The Taj Mahal is unambiguously Islamic, possibly an expression of paradise on earth, although it was not sectarian (Mumtaz was Shia, and Shah Jahan was Sunni).[93] About the stunning construction, Abu Talib Kalim (d. 1651), Shah Jahan's poet laureate, wrote:

> Upon her grave—may it be illumined until the Day of
> Resurrection!
> The King of Kings constructed such an edifice
> that since Destiny drew the plan of creation
> it has not seen such an exalted building.[94]

The stunning complex took more than a decade to build and required extensive maintenance. After Shah Jahan was overthrown in the late 1650s, Chandar Bhan Brahmin, a Mughal poet and state secretary (*munshi*), was appointed to care for the complex and its gardens.[95] He appears, like many Indians after him, to have valued the Taj's beauty and symbolism, saying that he would gain favor by looking after "the sacred illuminated tomb that is situated between this world and the hereafter."[96]

Conclusion: Threatened Heritage

The Taj Mahal complex is located in Agra, a long-standing site of Mughal construction that includes, among other notable buildings, Akbar's tomb.[97] Much of Mughal Agra is not preserved, however, and the Taj Mahal is currently under threat from two forces.[98] Some Hindu nationalists advocate for dismantling the final resting place of Mumtaz Mahal and Shah Jahan or converting it into a Shiva temple.[99] In so doing, they seek "to depreciate the Islamic contribution to India."[100] Also, environmental degradation imperils the Taj, including air and water pollution that have discolored its marble facade for decades.[101] Such dangers are a grim reminder that our access to the past is precarious and can be lost if we fail to value and preserve South Asia's diverse heritage.

Further Reading

I relied on the work of regional specialists, drawing especially on Stephen Berkwitz, Catherine Raymond, and Chandra de Silva for Sri Lanka; Richard Eaton for Bengali conversions; Shalin Jain for Gujarati Jains; and Rosalind O'Hanlon and Christopher Minkowski on Benares Brahmins. On the Mughals, Ellison Findly remains a solid resource on Nur Jahan, and Corinne Lefevre is a leading expert on Jahangir. Rajeev Kinra and Ebba Koch have written, in different ways, about Mughal culture under Shah Jahan.

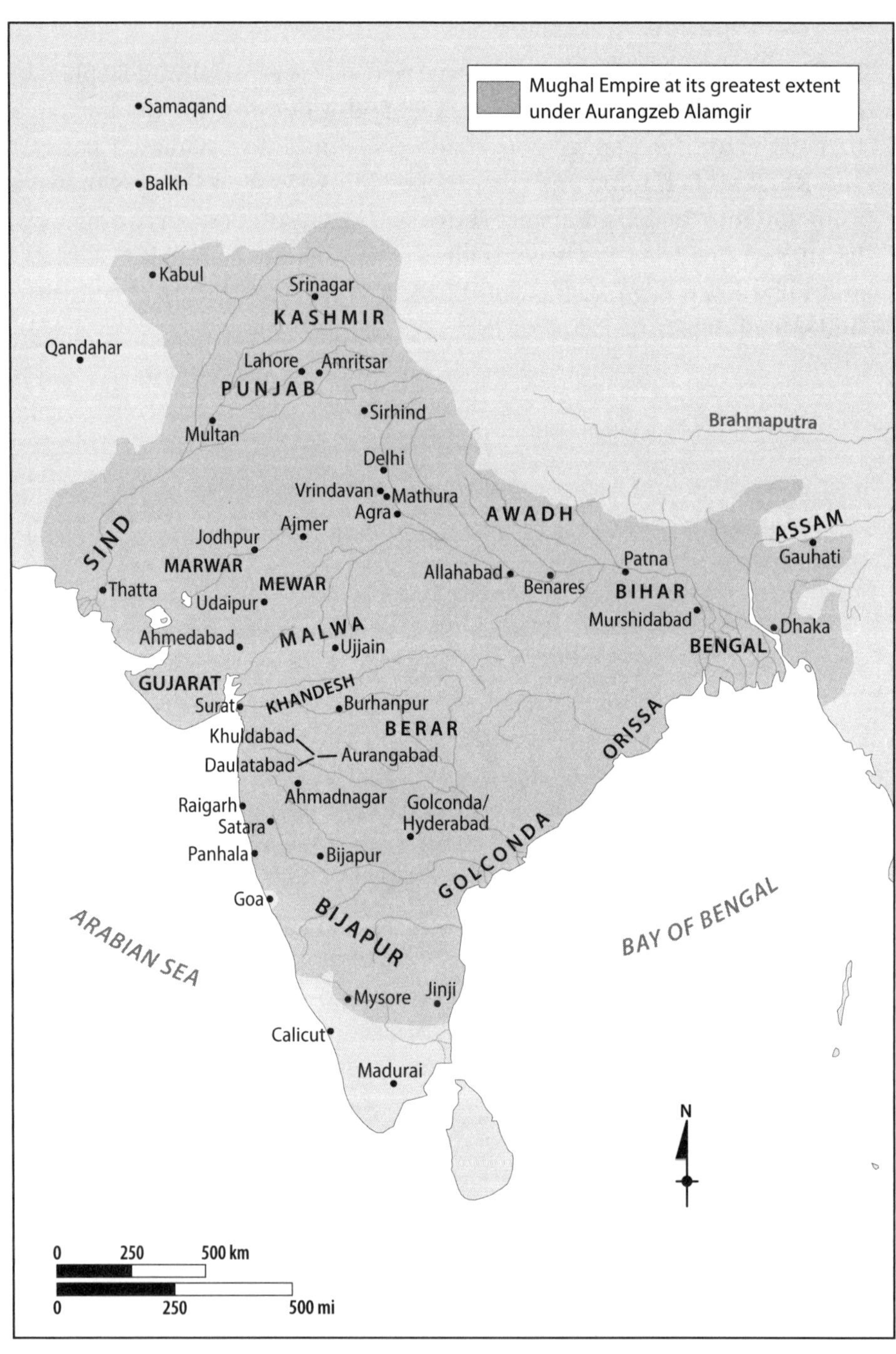

Mughal India, ca. 1700.

15

Aurangzeb's Empire and Two Shudra Lineages

It all happened so long ago,
in a different age,
another life.
Who is he to me, anyway?

—Kshetrayya, seventeenth century (Telugu)[1]

In the mid-seventeenth century, information flew across India. Informants, spies, and ambassadors gathered news—especially of political events—into daily reports (*akhbarat*) and letters that they dispatched to political centers, like Delhi, Raigarh (in Maharashtra), and Lahore. Professional runners transported these written missives up to 500 miles per week through tag-team sprinting.[2] For more urgent matters, mounted horses moved even faster. There was robust political drama in seventeenth-century India—featuring Mughal, Maratha, and Nayaka rule—and this chapter analyzes key events that no doubt perked up the early modern ears listening to news reports. But there are reasons for my foci here beyond narrating what captivated imaginations at the time. Under Aurangzeb Alamgir (r. 1658–1707), the Mughal Empire reached its zenith, constituting the largest Indian empire—in terms of land and population—up until that point in history. In analyzing Aurangzeb's reign, we consider events and policies that structured the lives of large numbers of early modern Indians. In central and southern India, Maratha and Nayaka rulers—both of Shudra lineages—offer an opportunity to see caste in action, including its negotiated relationship with kingship, in two very different ways. At the chapter's conclusion, I turn from kings to the social construct of caste, highlighting caste-oppressed communities that are often hard to glimpse in the historical record.

Aurangzeb's Indian Empire

Aurangzeb Alamgir (r. 1658–1707), the sixth Mughal monarch, presided over an Indian kingdom of unprecedented size and population. His armies expanded Mughal territory to encompass 3.2 million square kilometers, covering parts of modern-day India, Pakistan, Afghanistan, and Bangladesh. Roughly 150 million people lived within Aurangzeb's empire, double the number of Europeans alive at the time.[3] The Mughal cities of Agra and Delhi were each home to half a million people or more.[4] The head of such a massive, sophisticated polity merits substantial attention, both as the most successful exemplar of premodern Indian kingship and because Aurangzeb's decisions impacted the lives of many others. Aurangzeb's story as king began when he fought his three brothers for the Mughals' Peacock Throne.[5]

Fratricidal violence for political power is a recurrent theme in premodern India, featuring in myths like the Mahabharata (chapter 5) and historically from the ancient dynasties of Magadha in the sixth century BCE (chapter 3). The conflict between Aurangzeb and his three brothers—Dara Shukoh, Shah Shuja, and Murad—was notably intense. It began one fall day in 1657 when runners and riders fanned out from Agra with the news that Shah Jahan had fallen gravely ill. Shah Jahan's four adult sons all had equal claim to his throne, as per Timurid tradition, although family members tried to avert the expected bloodshed. The eldest royal sister, Jahanara, wrote to Aurangzeb warning that "the fruits of such actions [a succession war] can be only infamy and ruin." She pleaded with him, "Don't do this, don't do this!"[6] But the brothers sought, not infamy, but fame. None chose to voluntary forego the possibility of becoming the most powerful, richest king in India, and so they fought for nearly two years. Mughal nobles chose a prince to support, with Dara Shukoh and Aurangzeb proving the most popular contenders in a contest governed by the Persian proverb: *Ya takht ya takhta* (Either the throne or the grave).[7]

The lengthy succession struggle fascinated Mughal India, whose population followed its twists and turns through bazaar gossip and news reports. One dramatic moment came when Aurangzeb tricked his younger brother Murad, promising part of the empire in exchange for Murad's troops in the crucial 1658 Battle of Samugarh against Dara Shukoh. After winning at Samugarh (near Agra), Aurangzeb found an opportunity to pacify Murad with wine and arrested him. Aurangzeb later ordered Murad killed. Aurangzeb would have killed Shah Shuja, too, except that Shah Shuja escaped to Burma, dying in exile a few years later.[8] Dara Shukoh, the eldest brother, was the most formidable challenger in terms of political support, but he had never excelled at battlefield tactics, even when his life hung in the balance. Dara's troops mounted a last stand in March 1659 near Ajmer and were slaughtered by Aurangzeb's army. Dara fled, was arrested months later, and was soon beheaded in Delhi on Aurangzeb's orders.[9]

Aurangzeb followed Mughal tradition in meting out deadly treatment to his brothers-cum-political rivals. For example, Shah Jahan had murdered numerous brothers, nephews, and male cousins to secure his ascension.[10] But the Mughals dealt leniently with their adversaries' supporters. Aurangzeb integrated his brothers' backers into Mughal service without punishment and even repaid their debts, such as Murad's outstanding balance owed to the Gujarati Jain trader Shantidas Jhaveri (chapter 14).[11]

Aurangzeb's first major challenge as emperor was quelling opposition from Muslim leaders who viewed him as illegitimate. During the nearly two-year succession war, Shah Jahan had unexpectedly recovered from his illness, and so Aurangzeb had deposed his father. Whereas killing one's brothers was standard Timurid and Mughal practice, everyone at the time viewed overthrowing one's father as against Islamic law (*sharia*). This created real obstacles to ruling when the Mughal Empire's chief qazi (judge) refused to read the Friday sermon (*khutba*) in Aurangzeb's name, a critical mark of Indo-Muslim kingship. Aurangzeb fired him and appointed the more pliable Abdul Wahhab.[12] Aurangzeb's unmoving priority of political power—regardless of religious objections—pitted him against Muslim leaders and communities on several further occasions during his nearly fifty-year reign. When power and piety conflicted, Aurangzeb always chose power, living up to his regnal name of Alamgir (world-seizer).

Aurangzeb Alamgir largely followed multicultural Mughal kingship norms. Upon his lavish coronation in 1659, complete with musicians and poets (described in the excerpted text), Aurangzeb weighed himself against gold that was then distributed to the poor (originally a ritual associated with Hindu rulers, chapter 13).[13] He also displayed expected imperial generosity by abolishing taxes and opening dozens of almshouses across the empire. Aurangzeb continued to project himself as a paternalistic king in later decades. At various points, he tried to clean up prostitution, reduce opium consumption, and clamp down on theft at public festivals such as Holi.[14] Akbar had pursued similar goals, keeping prostitutes out of Fatehpur Sikri and trying to ban gambling and liquor.[15] Aurangzeb supported learned traditions, such as medicine (*tibb*), which had received state sponsorship from Akbar onward. Some Mughal physicians traveled to Persia to study and then brought their knowledge back to Aurangzeb's India.[16]

Description of Aurangzeb's May 1659 Coronation Ceremony, Excerpt from Persian *Maasir-i Alamgiri*, ca. 1710

[Aurangzeb Alamgir] ordered his officers to make preparations for the coronation celebrations, and they did their best. An eloquent preacher ascended the pulpit and read an impressive khutba, and he was rewarded to his heart's content. Such quantities of gold and silver coins were distributed in the name of the emperor that the wide bag of hope was filled by picking them up. The courtiers bowed to do honor and sang the praises of and prayed for the emperor. The doors of imperial treasuries were opened to all people, and the expectations of all, young and old, were fulfilled. . . . It was ordered that edicts should be issued announcing the accession and the happy news of protection and happiness to all parts of the empire. The emperor with open-handed liberality gave grand rewards to the princes, royal women, and imperial handmaids; every one of the nobles and faithful servants received promotion and the title according to his rank; pious and religious men, poets, musicians, and singers received suitable rewards and gifts.[17]

Like all other Mughal kings, Aurangzeb was Muslim and performatively used Islam, including its talismanic and Sufi aspects, to bolster his kingship. For example, faced with a threatening flood, he threw written prayers into the rising waters to cause them to recede.[18] He maintained ties with Chishti figures, visiting Muinuddin's shrine in Ajmer as Akbar had done (figure 15.1). Upon his death in 1707,

Figure 15.1. Mughal Emperor Aurangzeb (r. 1658–1707) visiting Muinuddin Chishti's shrine in Ajmer around 1680 CE, ca. early eighteenth century.

Aurangzeb was buried, as per his wishes, within a Chishti shrine in Khuldabad, Maharashtra.

Aurangzeb also placed his own mark on Mughal kingship, especially reflecting his obsession with justice (*'adalat*) as understood through his early modern Indo-Muslim lens. For example, recall that Akbar had directed extensive imperial patronage to translating Sanskrit texts into Persian, which required Brahmins and Mughals to collaborate (chapter 13). In contrast, the most robust intellectual product of Aurangzeb's court was the *Fatawa-i Alamgiri*, a massive synthesis of Hanafi legal judgments, written in Arabic and translated into Persian, compiled by dozens of ulama over eight years.[19] Aurangzeb's building agenda, too, marked new emphases for the Mughals. He built Lahore's Badshahi Masjid, the largest mosque in the world at the time and more ornate than major mosques sponsored by Shah Jahan.[20] In contrast, Aurangzeb generally declined to spend lavish sums on individual mausoleums, such that Aurangabad's Bibi ka Maqbara—built to house the remains of one of Aurangzeb's wives—pales in comparison to Shah Jahan's grand Taj Mahal (chapter 14).

Ten years into his reign, Aurangzeb pared down aspects of Mughal court ceremony. Some of his changes were prudent. For example, he eliminated appearing to his people at the jharokha, a practice that centered authority in the king but also advertised when Shah Jahan had fallen ill (which led to him being deposed). In other cases, Aurangzeb molded Mughal court proceedings to his personal tastes, such as when he reassigned court musicians (and, likely, court painters).[21] One result was to disperse artistic talent to the courts of princes and nobles, which proved a creative boon. Indo-Persian authors produced more treatises on music during Aurangzeb's reign than they had in the prior half millennium, largely working for sub-imperial patrons.[22]

Aurangzeb Alamgir conquered the Deccan, bringing a long-standing Mughal ambition into reality at great human cost. He relocated his court south in 1681 and, later that decade, successively assaulted Bijapur and Golconda, the two remaining Deccan Sultanates. The siege of Bijapur lasted fifteen months (1685–1686) and devastated the local population. The next year at Golconda, the Mughals deprived the fort of food, medicine, and water for eight months and then bribed a Qutb Shahi official to leave a door ajar one night. Fighting starved and cholera-stricken enemies, Mughal troops secured Golconda in mere hours (figure 15.2).[23]

Figure 15.2. Mughal Emperor Aurangzeb (r. 1658–1707) at the siege of Golconda in 1687 CE, ca. 1750.

During these brutal assaults, Bijapuri ulama pled for mercy, and Aurangzeb's own qazi, Abdul Wahhab's son, refused to sanction actions against other Muslim-led polities.[24] But Aurangzeb pursued political power relentlessly, changing his qazi (again) rather than his military strategy.[25]

Aurangzeb spent the next twenty years, between 1687 and 1707, wandering around southern India, trying to secure Maratha lands and forts. Both the Mughals and Marathas used scorched-earth tactics, literally burning crops, which led to hunger and disease.[26] Mughal territorial gains were modest, at best, in these final decades. One historian of the period described Aurangzeb, an old man in his seventies and eighties, unflatteringly as "very greedy" such that he "personally runs about panting for some heaps of stone."[27]

Governance problems beset the Mughal Empire in Aurangzeb's later years. Crooked tax collectors skimmed money—quite possibly a lot of money—off collections intended for the imperial treasury.[28] Bandits attacked travelers and traders on Mughal roads.[29] Aurangzeb wrung his hands about law-and-order problems in letters, such as lambasting his son Azam Shah as "indifferent to tyranny" in promoting corrupt officials. He warned that Azam Shah would have to explain his actions to God on the Day of Judgment, but the king did little to stop his wayward son. On a larger scale, the Mughal financial system entered a crisis as the Deccan conquests brought a flood of new mansabdars (ranked Mughal officials), for whom there was neither enough land nor money. Unable to pay his men, Aurangzeb would write on the slips of those claiming salaries, "There is only one pomegranate to serve a hundred sick men."[30] Even while Aurangzeb exercised unprecedented power over much of India, large cracks emerged in the Mughal state facade.

Hindus and Religious Minorities in Aurangzeb's India

Aurangzeb's empire included Muslims, Sikhs, Jains, Christians, and Hindus, many of whom thrived during Mughal rule. In the seventeenth century, "Hindus" typically did not use that Perso-Arabic term and instead identified themselves by caste, regional, or sectarian affiliations (e.g., as Brahmins, Marathas, southerners, Shaivites).[31] Forefronting distinctions between Hindu communities helps to capture their diverse experiences under Aurangzeb, who had no policy toward Hindus at large. Instead, following Mughal precedent and older Indian customs, Aurangzeb treated Hindu communities (and religious minorities) in different ways, depending on state interests.

Aurangzeb had personal connections with many elite Hindus. His family included Rajput women, who had intermarried with the Mughals for generations. Some of Aurangzeb's own most memorable lovers—at the beginning and end of his life—were Hindu women. In 1653, he saw Hirabai Zainabadi, a dancer and musician employed in his maternal aunt's home in Burhanpur, playfully pluck a mango from a tree and fell head over heels in love. The pair enjoyed a whirlwind romance, and Aurangzeb was heartbroken when she died less than a year later. He decided to go hunting to distract himself, proclaiming:

> Grieving at home gives no solace to the heart.
> In the lonely jungle I can cry out to my heart's content.[32]

Half a century later, Aurangzeb spent his final years in the company of Udaipuri, his son Kam Bakhsh's mother, who was also a musician and a Hindu.[33] In that case, Aurangzeb died first and Udaipuri soon followed in 1707.

Aurangzeb employed Hindus in state positions, which benefited Kayasths, Rajputs, and other elite Hindu groups. Aurangzeb positively gushed over his finance minister, Raja Raghunatha, repeating Raghunatha's wisdom on running the empire even decades after the minister's death.[34] Other contemporaries noted more generally that "there were no people better than the Hindus" for running imperial finances.[35] Under Aurangzeb, Rajput lineages thrived, even as the Rathors and Sisodiyas mounted a joint (ultimately unsuccessful) rebellion in 1679–1681.[36] New groups, especially Maratha elites, were integrated into state service owing to the Deccan conquests. Largely due to the Maratha influx, the percentage of Hindus in the Mughal imperial nobility surged by 50 percent under Aurangzeb as compared to his three predecessors.[37] Outside of court, too, Aurangzeb was often viewed positively by elite Hindus, being the dedicatee of two Hindu-authored Ramayanas.[38] Similarly, in his Mahabharata inspired by Tulsidas's *Manas*, Sabalsingh Chauhan repeatedly praised "Shah Aurang," the "Great lord of Delhi."[39]

The Mughal Empire included thousands of Jain and Hindu temples that were subject to twinned imperial policies of protection and destruction. Most commonly, Aurangzeb simply left temples alone. But he occasionally intervened in their affairs to exert paternalistic state protection. For example, one of Aurangzeb's early acts as emperor was ordering Mughal officials at Benares to ensure "that nobody unlawfully disturbs the Brahmins or other Hindus of that region, so that they might remain in their traditional place and pray for the continuance of the Empire."[40] Throughout his reign, Aurangzeb gave land and money to Brahmin communities.[41] He also personally appreciated the beauty of Indian temples, describing the Hindu, Jain, and Buddhist temples at Ellora as "one of the wonders of the work of the true transcendent Artisan (God)."[42]

Aurangzeb considered temples as legitimate targets in political disputes, an Indian stance dating back, at least, to the Chalukyas and Pallavas (seventh century CE) who had looted Hindu religious icons to express domination over political enemies (chapter 9). Following a long line of Indian kings—including the Pandyas, Pratiharas, Cholas, Chandellas, Delhi Sultanates, and his own Mughal predecessors—Aurangzeb ordered about a dozen Hindu and Jain temples damaged or destroyed during his reign, generally when temple affiliates undermined Mughal state interests. For example, he ordered Benares's Vishvanatha Temple destroyed after local landlords rebelled in 1669 (one wall of the temple still stands today, incorporated into a later mosque).[43] Aurangzeb leveled the Keshavadeva Temple in Mathura in 1670 amid Jat uprisings in the region.[44] Still, temple destructions were a relatively infrequent Mughal tool to compel submission and are perhaps most noteworthy because of their accompanying rhetoric.

Political motivations notwithstanding, early modern writers often invoked religious language to express violent displays of imperial authority carried out against religious targets. Mughal works spoke of hitting against the "infidels" and praised the spread of Islam through holy war (*jihad*).[45] Rajput texts sometimes followed a similar pattern of expressing political anger in religiously charged language, such as a ca. 1680 Hindi text that depicts Rana Raj Singh of Mewar (a Rajput who rebelled against Aurangzeb) decreeing:

> I spread the superior Veda and will preserve on earth the Puranas.
> The qazi's books and all the Qurans, I reduce all these to ashes.

I will grind down the Mughals and establish my own garrison in Delhi.
I maintain Hindu customs and uproot the demonic ways.
I will raise up the best holy temples and tear down the Muslim sites,
I will protect all the Rathors, the angry Rana Raj said.[46]

Like with Mughal rhetoric regarding Jain and Hindu temples, Rajput rhetoric on destroying Islamic sites and practices offers insight into propaganda. It allows us to see that early modern Indians—of various religious backgrounds—found it appropriate and useful to invoke heated religious rhetoric within conflicts. Even so, as noted earlier, we must forefront politics to recover the realpolitik causality behind targeting places of worship.

Aurangzeb broke with Mughal tradition by reinstating the jizya tax in 1679, which proved one of his most controversial decisions. Akbar had suspended the jizya—a discriminatory tax levied on most non-Muslims—across the Mughal Empire in 1564.[47] Aurangzeb brought back the tax, perhaps to address the Mughal Empire's financial difficulties or to employ the ulama, who served as special tax collectors for it. Many imperial elites opposed the policy, including Jahanara and Rajput leaders.[48] A letter survives, perhaps written by a Rajput, that lambasts the jizya as exacerbating the plight of the "famine-stricken" and reducing the once glorious Timurids to snatching "beggars' bowls."[49] The letter accuses Aurangzeb of reverting the Mughal disposition, articulated by Akbar, of universal civility (*sulh-i kull*) in favor of a more acrimonious stance.[50] Aurangzeb was unmoved by such arguments, although he later abated the jizya in deference to hardships, such as across the Deccan in 1704.[51]

Some religious groups were armed in early modern India, and Aurangzeb treated harshly those he perceived to threaten Mughal interests. For example, in 1672, Aurangzeb personally led Mughal troops against the Satnamis, a low-caste millenarian movement in eastern Punjab. The fierceness of Satnami, who were shaven-headed and led by a prophetess, astonished observers. Aurangzeb fought magic with magic, writing prayers and magical figures on banners to ensure Mughal victory.[52] Aurangzeb was not personally involved in assaults on Sikhs, another armed Punjab-origin group, but he sanctioned the Mughal assassination of Tegh

Bahadur, the ninth Sikh guru, in 1675.[53] Unsurprisingly, Sikh sources often promote a negative view of the Mughals. For example, the 1704 *Zafarnama* lambasts a Mughal leader as "fond of lucre, false in faith, unrighteous and unpractising, for God or Prophet without care."[54] In contrast, Aurangzeb left alone armed religious leaders who posed no threat to state interest and only fought among themselves, granting five armed Ramanandi commanders the ability "to move freely around the whole Empire" in the early 1690s.[55]

Aurangzeb treated certain Islamic communities harshly, even while maintaining equanimity in state employment. For example, he massacred a few dozen Mahdavis, a millenarian group in Gujarat in the 1640s, when he was a prince. He repeatedly harassed the Bohras, a Shia Ismaili group, even requiring their mosques to host five daily prayers in the Sunni style.[56] Still, such treatment did not bleed over into Mughal state service. This was put to the test when, in the late 1680s, a man from Bukhara petitioned Aurangzeb to ban Shias from Mughal service. Aurangzeb scoffed, saying: "What connection have earthly affairs with religion? And what right have administrative works to meddle with bigotry? 'For you is your religion and for me is mine.' If this rule suggested by you were established, it would be my duty to extirpate all the Rajahs (i.e., Rajputs) and their followers. Wise men disapprove of the removal from office of able officers."[57] Indeed, Aurangzeb ran a multicultural empire, like his predecessors, with no religious litmus test.

Shivaji's Caste Concerns

In central India, the Maratha Bhonsle family established itself as an independent power in the late seventeenth century and formulated a royal identity distinct from that of Indo-Persian rulers. The Bhonsle family first entered into the historical record in the early to mid-1600s when Maloji (d. 1622) and his son Shahji (d. 1664) served the Deccan Sultanates, including Malik Ambar.[58] The Bhonsles were widely considered to be Shudras, and they numbered among numerous Shudra groups gaining visibility around this time, including the Reddys in Andhra, Jats in and around the Punjab, Patels in Gujarat, and Nairs in Malabar.[59] As James Laine has noted, Shahji was likely perceived by his contemporaries as a "grateful beneficiary of his Muslim patrons."[60] But Shahji's son,

Shivaji (1630–1680), broke with his family heritage to declare himself a Kshatriya ruler of north Indian Rajput descent. Shivaji's decision underlined the ideological attraction of Rajput ruling identity, even in a world where all Rajputs were politically subservient to the Mughals. Shivaji's attempt to project himself as a Kshatriya also provides insight into the refinement of caste identities in the early modern Deccan.

Shivaji was a shrewd tactician and, like other political figures of his era, used every available means to gain power. One such moment came in 1659 when he met with Afzal Khan of Bijapur, ostensibly under a truce. Both men were distrustful and arrived secretly armed. Shivaji concealed an iron claw in his fist, which he used to disembowel Afzal Khan.[61] In battle, Shivaji's nimble troops practiced guerilla warfare and often outsmarted the bigger, bulkier Mughal army. In 1664, Shivaji astounded his contemporaries by raiding Mughal-controlled Surat. As the Mughal governor hid, Shivaji's men plundered royal assets and traders' homes in the lucrative port city for days.[62] In response, the Kachhwaha Rajput Jai Singh led Mughal forces to besiege Shivaji at Purandar Fort in 1665. Shivaji surrendered after a few months and was briefly pressured into Mughal service.[63] The arrangement did not last, however. After presenting tribute to Aurangzeb in Agra, Shivaji aroused suspicions by acting out of turn at court and so was placed under house arrest. He bribed the Mughal guards to release him and soon began carving out a slender Maratha kingdom across the Western Ghats.

In 1674, Shivaji crowned himself *chatrapati* (emperor) and faced a caste challenge. He needed to be a Kshatriya to perform the consecration (*rajabhisheka*) ceremony, but the Bhonsles did not number among the ninety-six "aristocratic Maratha families" that "claim Rajput descent."[64] As a result, they were grouped with "the remainder of Marathas" that "cannot claim twice-born status."[65] In other words, Shivaji's contemporaries considered him an "upwardly-mobile Shudra."[66] Like Aurangzeb, Shivaji did not let religion thwart his political ambitions, and so he engaged in a ceremony to advertise his self-purported Kshatriya heritage combined with a royal consecration, formulated and led by Gagabhatta, a Benares Brahmin.[67] Gagabhatta pitched the event as a caste recovery ceremony (since an individual cannot change castes[68]) and led Shivaji for weeks through ritual actions that featured time-honored markers of upper-caste Hindus. The king donned the sacred thread, was purified with water, and remarried his numerous wives using Vedic mantras. During the coronation, Shivaji ascended an ornate throne covered with skins of tigers, wild cats, and other animals.[69]

As a newly minted or recovered Kshatriya, Shivaji claimed to be kin of the Sisodiyas, the Sun-descended paragon of Rajput lineages. It was a bold claim, the boldest that Shivaji could have made.[70] But few if any early modern Rajputs were convinced. Jaswant Singh, leader of the Rathor Rajputs of Marwar, called Shivaji a "mere bhumia" (petty landholder).[71] Jai Singh of the Kachhwaha lineage would neither eat nor intermarry with the Bhonsle family.[72] Even today, Shivaji's Shudra origins are widely rumored in Maharashtra.[73] And yet that Shivaji went to such lengths to project himself as a Rajput attests to the importance of caste—a social category marked by hierarchy, ritual purity, and, for Shivaji, kingship—in the early modern Deccan.[74]

Even without persuading his Rajput contemporaries, Shivaji's caste recovery and coronation ceremony demonstrated his ability to compel Brahminical sanction. The ceremony's architect, Gagabhatta, hailed from a well-regarded learned family and was considered an expert on Shudras.[75] Perhaps Gagabhatta's views on Shivaji's caste were genuine; we have no way to know. We do know that Gagabhatta was extraordinarily well renumerated for his efforts, receiving more than 100,000 gold coins from the Bhonsle treasury along with other gifts.[76] During the ceremony, Shivaji also gave abundant gifts to Brahminical communities, including gold, silver, copper, ghee, food, and cows.[77] Such extravagance had economic ramifications for the kingdom, and Shivaji subsequently raided nearby territories and levied new taxes, including the *simhasan-patti* (coronation tax).[78] It attests to his political power that Shivaji was able to harness the wealth of his subjects and nearby kingdoms in support of his claim of Rajput ancestry.

Shivaji's coronation also served as a battlefield for contesting power between Brahminical communities, a broader feature of seventeenth-century India, when a group of tantric Brahmins objected to its efficacy. By the seventeenth century, tantra (a wide-ranging set of ritualistic practices) had been part of Hindu traditions for more than a millennium (chapter 8). Tantra had also become associated with royal power and, helpfully for Shivaji, often cut across caste lines.[79] Tantric Brahmins, led by Nishchala Puri, convinced Shivaji to undergo a second ritual, a do-over except performed according to tantric norms.[80] This second ceremony featured non-Vedic elements such as lions, which were important in Maratha imagery and purana texts (but not in the Vedas).[81] The Sanskrit manual for the tantric ceremony castigated Gagabhatta and his associates as incompetent priests who oversaw a ceremony "attended by numerous ill-omens and disasters."[82] Such passages indicate, among other things, Brahminical competition for access to royal resources.

In his final years on the throne, Shivaji (d. 1680) promoted neoclassical ideas about Sanskrit and caste, which created a new—if short-lived—ruling culture. He patronized the *Rajavyavaharakosha* (Lexicon of royal institutes), which provides Sanskrit synonyms for 1,500 Indo-Persian administrative words.[83] Sanskrit had never been a language of day-to-day state operations, and Persian was favored in the Mughal-Rajput ruling culture that dominated seventeenth-century northern India. But Shivaji sought to project a newly hardened version of Kshatriya rule.

Shivaji also encouraged depictions of himself and his enemies that used reified ideas regarding caste, such as in a Sanskrit court hagiography titled *Suryavamsha* (Sun's lineage, ca. 1675). The work depicts Shivaji as favoring Brahmins in a manner, in theory at least, definitional to Kshatriya kings.[84] In reality, Shivaji ran a multicultural polity, employing Muslims in his army and keeping qazis on payroll.[85] But none of this features in the propagandistic world of the *Suryavamsha*. Instead, the work couches Shivaji's actions in old Vedic narratives, such as referring to his killing of Afzal Khan as Indra facing Vrita.[86] Narratively, a closer parallel would have been Bhima ripping open Duhshasana's chest in the Mahabharata war, but this was not Vedic and so would not have provided the projected longevity that Shivaji desired. The *Suryavamsha* also claimed that Shivaji attacked Afzal Khan, in part, because the Bijapuri general was "hell-bent on obstructing the path of caste dharma (*varna-dharma*)."[87] This is unlikely on two scores. Shivaji attacked Afzal Khan as a political enemy, and Afzal Khan promoted no program of social equality so far as we know. But, for Shivaji, rulership involved claiming upper-caste status via its exclusionary privileges, eschewing the real-world examples around him of Rajputs who served the Mughals and Nayaka kings further south who ruled as Shudras.

Proud Shudra Nayaka Kings

From the mid-sixteenth century into the early eighteenth century, discrete Nayaka lineages ruled over parts of Karnataka and Tamil Nadu as Shudra sovereigns. The Nayakas were of Telugu origin and had originally served as military chiefs (*nayaka*s) under Vijayanagara rule. As Vijayanagara power waned in the 1500s, Nayakas founded their own ruling dynasties, with three major Tamil Nadu branches at Madurai, Thanjavur, and Jinji (also spelled Senji and Gingee), respectively. The Thanjavur and Jinji Nayakas both fell during the seventeenth century to other local powers, and the Madurai Nayakas were overthrown in the 1730s.[88] Even while in power, the Nayakas exercised limited political authority. Here I focus on Nayaka cultural policies and their political self-image, which offer windows into Shudra identity and Hindu practices in Madurai.

In contrast to Shivaji, Nayaka rulers celebrated their low-caste status. For example, Chemakura Venkatakavi wrote a Telugu poem for Raghunatha (r. 1612–1634) of Thanjavur exalting his patron as "born from the feet of incarnate Hari (Vishnu)."[89] This followed a widely known Vedic hymn on the origins of the four varnas, where Brahmins emerged from the head, Kshatriyas from the arms, Vaishyas from the legs, and Shudras from the feet (quoted in chapter 2). The original hymn indicated Shudras' inferiority and designated role as servants, but Chemakura twisted it in his patron's favor. He noted that being born in the "pure and brilliant class" of Shudra made the Nayakas kin of the Ganges, also born of Vishnu's feet.[90] The Nayakas still played into the caste hierarchy in many ways, such as by feeding Brahmins by the thousands.[91] In other ways, their ruling decisions had nothing to do with religion. For example, like their contemporaries, Nayaka rulers employed soldiers of various religious and ethnic backgrounds.[92] Their patronage, too, was broad-based, with the Nayakas of Thanjavur sponsoring Catholic churches and both the Thanjavur and Madurai lines supporting Sufi dargahs.[93] Still, few premodern Indian kings openly celebrated being Shudras, and the Nayaka rulers stood out in this regard.

In an exercise of royal authority, the Nayaka kings in Madurai restructured the spring Chittirai Festival, fusing together Vaishnava and Shaivite celebrations. When Tirumalai Nayaka (r. 1623–1659) took the throne, there were two discrete events: Vishnu's annual trek to the Vaikai River and celebrating Meenakshi and Sundareshvara (Shiva)'s marriage. In the new Nayaka version, the narratives were combined such that Vishnu is Meenakshi's brother and misses her wedding. The fused festival made Madurai's largest celebration focused on Meenakshi and Shiva's marriage, of which the Nayaka kings claimed to be the product.[94] The annual activities largely center on the Meenakshi Temple complex, which sprawls over fourteen downtown acres and was largely built under the Nayakas. Changing the festival demonstrated the ability of Nayaka kings to go against earlier ritual prescriptions regarding dates.[95] In a text written around when the new festival was debuted, Nilakantha Dikshita celebrated that Meenakshi's eyes—representing a younger, regional tradition—have replaced Vishnu's fish (*matsya*) incarnation, namely an older, transregional myth:

> There was this old Fish, exhausted
> from looking for all the Vedas.
> We don't think about him.
> What we praise,
> Mother,
> is what all the Vedas see,
> your two
> fish-eyes.[96]

Chittirai is still celebrated today as Madurai's largest annual Hindu festival.

Seeing Shudras and Dalits

In early modernity, caste-oppressed communities come into clearer focus, even beyond Shudra kings. Accordingly, I review here some features of the caste system in premodernity and focus attention, even if briefly, on those at the bottom of this social hierarchy. The construct of caste—both varna and jati—had been around for millennia by the seventeenth century. In Brahminical dharmashastra from the early first millennium CE and later, the caste system's inequality was theorized as a virtuous, unchangeable part of dharma, but this was always theoretical (chapter 7). In real life, caste was oppressive and dynamic as more communities were integrated into this hierarchy, most often in lower caste categories. Some premodern Indians pushed back against the social stratification of caste, including early Buddhists, Jains, Shaiva groups, and nirgun bhakti saints (including Guru Nanak, the founder of Sikhism).

Some even denied the inborn nature of varna and jati (standard Brahminical assertions). As a sixteenth-century Shaiva author put it: "Maya (Guru of the Asuras) created caste divisions (*jatibheda*) throughout the nine divisions of Bharata. It does not exist in other lands. Therefore, it is nothing but a fabrication."[97] But other early modern Indians found it impossible to imagine any subcontinental society absent caste distinctions. For example, the sixteenth-century *Rayavacakamu* (Tidings of the king) refers to "a Brahmin-caste demon," assuming that caste ordered even Indian demon society.[98] Those at the top of the hierarchy—especially Brahmins—are visible throughout premodern Indian history, but early modernity presents us with the evidence to take a closer look at those who populate the pyramid's bottom: Shudras and (beneath them) Dalits.

Between the fourteenth and seventeenth centuries, dozens of dharmashastra texts focused on how to admit Shudras into Hindu ritual life. This new emphasis responded to social changes, especially bhakti challenges to the relevance of caste to gaining liberation and the rise of wealthy, powerful Shudra communities.[99] The results were innovative while maintaining caste distinctions. For example, Krishnashesha (ca. sixteenth century) argued that Brahmins should open rituals to Shudras by reciting from a genre of sectarian Hindu texts known as puranas (chapter 7), since Shudras were prohibited from hearing the Vedas.[100] It was noteworthy to include Shudras, in any fashion, in Brahmin-led rituals. That said, early modern thinkers often distinguished between *asat* (bad) shudras who were servants and *sat* (good) shudras who were upwardly mobile, only affording limited ritual privileges to the latter. Even the "good Shudras" were still barred from hearing the sacred Vedas, a mark of belonging to the upper three varnas. And the new rituals were still under exclusive Brahminical control, which further entrenched the differential valuation of human worth within the caste hierarchy.

Dalits also come into view in this period, such as in a Telugu play that examines Dalit-Brahmin relations as well as the connection between gender and caste. Dalits (downtrodden; formerly called "untouchables") are a group below Shudras in the caste hierarchy and outside of the fourfold varna classification entirely. Around 1700, Shahaji composed a short Telugu drama titled *Take My Wife* (Sati-dana-suramu) about a Brahmin who lusts after a Dalit woman—to her horror as well as the consternation of his young Brahmin pupil—and eventually compels her husband's consent to have sex with her. Shahaji ruled from 1684 to 1712 at Thanjavur, where Shivaji's half-brother Ekoji (Shahaji's father) had established a Maratha-led polity in 1676. Shahaji's play *Take My Wife* was intended to be performed annually at a festival at the Rajagopalasvami Temple, about thirty kilometers south of Thanjavur.[101] The drama mentions many recurrent features of caste, including purity markers, diet, vocation, and marriage restrictions (see excerpt). In a part not included in the excerpt, the Brahmin (called "Guru," teacher) describes the Dalit woman (Matangi) as light skinned in a colorism compliment of her beauty.[102]

Excerpt from Telugu Drama *Take My Wife*, Attributed to Shahaji, ca. 1700

Guru [to the Matangi woman]:
May you have pleasure, and many children.
You have beautiful eyes. Listen to me.
Where are you from? What is your name?
What caste? Tell me, please.
Your charm has turned me to ashes.
Please talk to me.

Pupil: Why are you wasting your time on her? You're wearing a sacred thread,
a light-red *dhoti*, with sandal and sacred rice on your forehead.
She's disgusting. It's like an elephant talking to a goat.

Matangi: We're Untouchables. If you touch us, you become unclean.
Don't come close. We're Madigas, working with leather.
Our huts are to the east of the village.

Everybody insults us, and you're a Brahmin.
We eat beef, we drink liquor.
We don't know how to speak well.
Don't talk to me.

Pupil: My god! Why did you come here?
Come away.
Where have your Vedas and Puranas
and Shastras disappeared to?
I came to study with you because you
are a learned man,
and here you are deep in conversation
with a Matangi.

Guru: Wait, I have to respond to her.

Pupil: In that case, I don't want to be around. I'm off. I'm still young, unmarried.
If you hang out with Untouchables, and I'm close by, no one
will give me their daughter. I'll keep my distance.

Guru [to the Matangi woman]:
You said you're Untouchable, but there's no blame
in that. We are also Untouchable. Let me explain.
You said you shouldn't be touched, which means
you're pure as fire. All I want is to touch you.
You said you're beyond caste,
so you must be the highest of all.
You said nobody can touch you. I'm for that.
No one, that is, except me.
You said you deal in animal skins.
Are you any different from Lord Shiva?
We drink cows' milk, but you eat the whole cow.
You must be more pure.

Pupil: Do babies who drink their mother's milk eat the whole mother?

Guru: I'm feasting my eyes on your beauty.
(In Sanskrit) *Shall I paint your feet with lac,*
or bring you bracelets for your arms?

Shall I comb your hair?
Fondle your breasts?
Command me in honeyed tones.[103]

Shahaji designed his play to be provocative, and, indeed, it contains some harsh commentary on Brahmins. The Brahmin character is carnal and dishonest, citing Sanskrit verses in pursuit of his own lust. At one point, the wayward Brahmin confesses, "We Brahmins have made up all the rules, and invented religion. There is no better dharma than satisfying a Brahmin's need."[104] He then encourages the Dalit woman to give him her lips, breasts, and other sensual parts of her body. Provocative sexuality, itself, was not de facto problematic in early modern southern India. For example, in this chapter's epigraph, the seventeenth-century Telugu poet Kshetrayya imagines a courtesan expressing frustration at the long absence of her lover, the god Muvvagopala.[105] But any Brahmin-Dalit sexual relationship violated *varnadharma*, differential Hindu ethics by caste, a point driven home in the excerpt when the Brahmin expresses his lust in Sanskrit.

Take My Wife offers less airtime to the Dalit woman (and it is written by a dominant-caste person), but even its limited insights are noteworthy. She describes herself as "a woman without caste" and notes differences that should keep her away from the Brahmin and his sexual urges (see excerpt). Gender also plays strongly in the drama and deprives the Dalit woman of agency. Her husband—not her—resolves that she should sleep with the Brahmin and presents his wife, following a long-standing custom of gifting to upper castes.[106] The Brahmin comes to his senses at this point and refuses the Dalit woman, which avoids a sexual pairing across caste lines. But it also means that the Brahmin has refused a gift, which would result in "a bad name, and a load of sin" for the Dalit man.[107] Nobody asks what the woman wants, and in her final words in the drama she laments to Shiva: "A woman who has lost her honor is worse than dead. Save me, I'm in trouble."[108]

In the drama, the characters are Hindu, but caste was also practiced by non-Hindu communities in this period. For example, writing in 1595 for a Rajput patron, the Hindi poet Narottam attests that "the Muslims of the earth have many castes (jati)."[109] In Portuguese Goa, Christian groups vied with each other in a caste hierarchy by the early eighteenth century.[110] Indian Jewish communities, both in Kerala and Maharashtra, were organized by caste by the eighteenth century.[111] In such moments, the caste system emerges as an India-wide historical phenomenon that was articulated within Brahminical texts but practiced by communities of various religious backgrounds.

Conclusion: Dawn of the Long Eighteenth Century

In seventeenth-century India, social and cultural trends such as caste changed slowly, whereas politics was more volatile. The political world described in this chapter—where the Mughals consolidated control over much of the subcontinent and other kingdoms were more modest—fell apart quickly after the death of Aurangzeb Alamgir in 1707. News of the king's demise, at the age eighty-eight, was carried to the far corners of India by runners and horsemen, and, at first, things appeared to be business as usual. Aurangzeb's three living adult sons fought a war of succession. Muazzam won, killing his two brothers in battle and ascending the throne as Bahadur Shah (r. 1707–1712). But Bahadur Shah proved unable to fully pacify rebellions by Jats, Sikhs, and others who took advantage of the power vacuum created by Aurangzeb's death. A flurry of Mughal emperors followed Bahadur Shah, some ruling only for a few months, in a political mess reminiscent of the downfall of the Mauryan Empire after Ashoka's death in the third century BCE (chapter 4). While Aurangzeb's life had been dedicated to consolidating political power, his legacy in death was, ironically, its dispersal. This political fragmentation persisted throughout India's eighteenth century and was accompanied by a resurgence in regional flourishing.

Further Reading

Works by Richard Eaton, Katherine Brown, and Audrey Truschke proffer insights on Aurangzeb. Many earlier translations of Aurangzeb-period works are problematic, but I cite them nonetheless here where newer translations are unavailable. For Shivaji and caste, I relied on Ananya Vajpeyi, V. S. Bendrey, James Laine, and Richard Salomon (on the second coronation ceremony). Elaine Fisher, Velcheru Narayana Rao, David Shulman, and Sanjay Subrahmanyam have written about literature and politics in early modern Tamil Nadu.

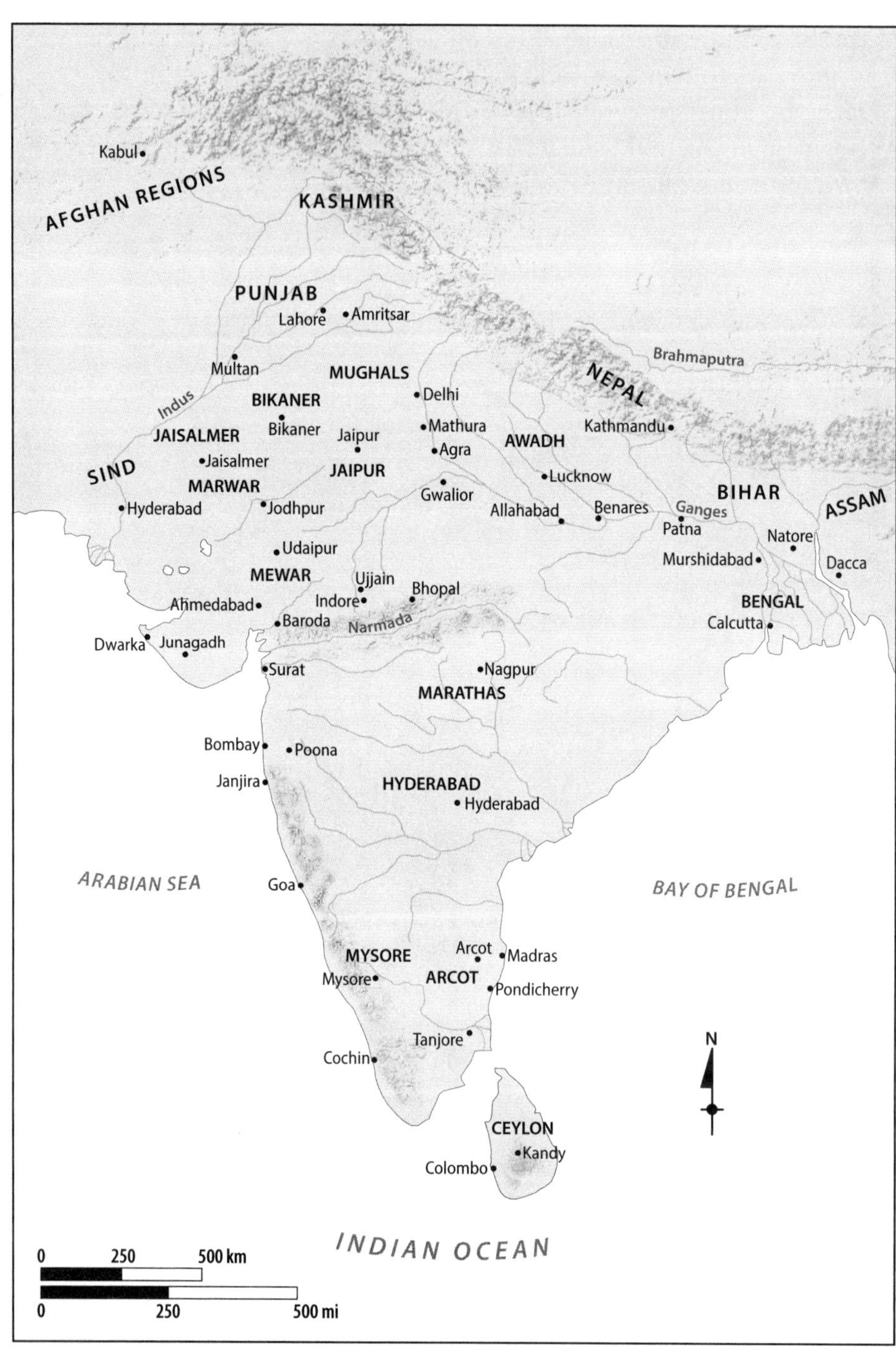

Regional rule in India, ca. 1755.

16

Regional Flourishing, 1720–1780

There is much illicit sex in the town and abortions are common. Keep an eye out especially for this.

—Rathor state official to Nagaur officials, 1776 (Marwari)[1]

Abortion was illegal in the eighteenth-century Rathor state of Marwar, situated in western India along the edge of the Thar desert. All the same, midwives and temple-dwelling Jain monks (*yatis*) dispensed herbs to terminate unwanted pregnancies resulting from adultery, intercaste affairs, and rape.[2] Stories of these medical interventions come down to us in Rathor archives because state officials sometimes investigated those involved, imposing punitive fines or banishment. Other regional Indian states of the period, too, interfered in social affairs, especially to control women's sexuality. For example, in 1735, the Peshwa-run Maratha state (central and northern subcontinent) decreed that Brahmin girls marry between the ages of seven and ten, before puberty.[3] These historical morsels encapsulate some of the broader changes in Indian life during the early to mid-eighteenth century, including increased state regulation of social activities and further crystallization of caste identities. They also attest to the rising visibility of marginalized groups, like unmarried pregnant women and child brides. But perhaps the most obvious feature that they demonstrate is local variation. Between 1720 and 1780, regions of the subcontinent experienced distinct rhythms of development and rule, even while sharing certain broad features and dynamic interregional contact.

Fracturing Mughal Political Authority

Eighteenth-century regional flourishing followed the collapse of Mughal political authority from 1707 forward. Five Mughal kings ascended the Peacock Throne between 1707 and 1720, as compared to four in the preceding 150 years. Amid this tumult, nobles gained unprecedented power, even deposing rulers, in intrigues that enraptured contemporary imaginations.[4] Stories circulated that seemed to convey the degradation of Mughal gravitas, such as when Farrukh Siyar (r. 1713–1719) had his hemorrhoids cut and cauterized, thus becoming impotent.[5] In the 1740s, a visitor from Hyderabad heard from Delhiites about Jahandar Shah (r. 1712–1713) sleeping off a hangover in a parked carriage.[6] Rapid-fire succession halted with Muhammad Shah Rangila (r. 1719–1748), but Mughal power continued to wither. Many parts of the empire broke away, and even in the imperial capital of Delhi, Mughal authority slipped. In 1729, a riot broke out among shoemakers and jewelers within steps of Delhi's Red Fort.[7] But that temporary loss of imperial control paled in comparison to events a decade later.

In 1739, Nadir Shah—a Turk who had overthrown the Safavid dynasty of Persia—looted Delhi and brutalized its population in a conclusive display that the Mughals were an empire no more. The Mughals saw Nadir Shah coming. In 1738 he hit Qandahar, captured Kabul, and crossed the Indus River, viewed for centuries as the northwestern boundary for entering Hindustan (northern India). The Mughal army confronted Nadir Shah's forces at Karnal, north of Delhi, but they were woefully mismatched. In short order, Nadir Shah captured Muhammad Shah Rangila and held the emperor hostage for weeks, while Nadir Shah's troops ransacked Delhi.[8] At one point, the people of Delhi violently resisted, and Nadir Shah ordered them massacred. Delhi's streets were littered with mangled corpses that were then thrown into the Yamuna River as food for the crocodiles.[9] When Nadir Shah and his men left Delhi, they took with them an incredible amount of Indian wealth, including the Peacock Throne, the Koh-i Noor diamond, elephants and horses, and lakhs of rupees, gems, and gold. In a painted image made decades later, Nadir Shah is bedecked with gold and jewels, literally wearing the spoils of the Mughal Empire.[10]

News of Nadir Shah's sack of Delhi spread like wildfire across the subcontinent, and many eighteenth-century Indians interpreted it as a ruinous, ill-boding act. In part, this reflects the invasion's brutality and the lawlessness it unleashed. Anand Ram, a high-ranking Mughal administrator, wrote about hiring private security to protect his property and assets.[11] Others noted the toll on Delhi's population, such as that the invasion drove women to commit suicide.[12] For many early modern Indians, the real punch of Nadir Shah's actions lay in humiliating the Mughals, a north Indian dynasty of unparalleled power for two centuries. As Ananda Ranga Pillai (1709–1761) lamented from French-controlled Pondicherry: "If such, indeed, be the fate that befell the Emperor of Delhi, need we wonder at the calamities that overtake ordinary men? Of what avail is the power and wealth of kings, on this earth? These are perishable. The Heaven of the All-merciful God is the only thing that endures. All others perish."[13] Subsequent decades witnessed further power struggles over Delhi, including between the Afghani Durranis and the Peshwa-led Marathas. In 1761, these two sides fought at Panipat, the site of battles that the Mughals dominated in 1526 and 1556, respectively. That the Mughals were not major contenders in the third battle at Panipat in 1761 signals their political sidelining.

Generations of historians have labored to explain the Mughal Empire's implosion, and no consensus has emerged. Among the more plausible theories are a land distribution crisis, financial pressures at multiple levels of production, and the inability of Mughal princes to garner support.[14] These proposed causes of Mughal political failure are not mutually exclusive, nor are they fully satisfactory. To be frank, I find the sole emphasis on *what* caused the Mughal kingdom to fracture misguided, since extinction is the sure end of all empires. As the Persian and Urdu poet Mir mused in the late eighteenth century:

> Every day there is a new master of the world—
> is Power a beggar, going from door to door?[15]

Also compelling, and little explored, is the question of *when* the Mughal Empire fell because the answers are multiple.

The Mughal state limped on in name for more than a century after Nadir Shah's sack of Delhi, coming to a formal end in 1858. It exerted robust cultural influence during its later decades and inspired political idioms for British colonialists and Indian princes. It even had an (albeit unsuccessful) eleventh-hour resuscitation as a political unifier during the Sepoy Rebellion of 1857 (chapter 18). And so, the obliteration of the

Mughals' land-based empire did not spark the evaporation of its cultural and social power or even political possibilities. The Mughals continued as part of South Asian history well into the nineteenth century.

Rise of Regional Political Powers

Delhi's cultural worlds thrived ca. 1710–1760, and some thinkers were even inspired by the surrounding political turmoil. Poets like Bedil (d. 1720) composed marvelous Persian verses, even as his dense "Indian style" (*sabk-i hindi*) of writing means that his brilliance is often lost in translation.[16] Bedil's younger contemporary, Arzu (d. 1756), was a renowned philologist who observed the historic link between Sanskrit and Persian, two etymologically related languages.[17] In a sign of shifting patterns of wealth, Arzu enjoyed the sponsorship of Mughal noble families, rather than royalty.[18] Still, pre-1739, Muhammad Shah Rangila liberally patronized painters who often showed the king engaged in recreation, such as smoking tobacco through a hookah pipe or throwing colored powder during Holi (figure 16.1).[19] Islamic thinkers flourished, such as Shah Wali Allah (1703–1762) who was preoccupied with synthesizing contradictions he perceived within and between Islamic jurisprudence, philosophy, Sufism, and *hadith* (sayings of the Prophet Muhammad). Wali Allah desired unity within the wide-ranging Islamic tradition, an impulse theorized by one scholar to stem from the social and political unrest that punctuated Wali Allah's life in Delhi.[20] Indeed, some intellectuals decamped from Delhi and moved to regional centers, such as Arzu who headed to Lucknow, ruled by the Nawabs of Awadh (Oudh), in 1754.

Politically, the Mughals' loss was many others' gain, with the Marathas—once Aurangzeb's disempowered detractors—being arguably the most direct inheritors of Mughal state power. Even in Aurangzeb's final years, some Marathas regained power under the leadership of Tarabai, whom the Portuguese dubbed "queen of the Marathas."[21] Shahu, Sambhaji's son, was released from a Mughal prison upon Aurangzeb's death in 1707 and declared himself the rightful Maratha chief, splitting off supporters from his aunt Tarabai. Ultimately, both branches of Shivaji's family lost power as a third party seized political control under the Maratha banner: Brahmin Peshwas. They came to prominence under Shahu, who appointed Balaji Vishwanath as royal advisor (peshwa) in

Figure 16.1. Holi celebration at the court of Mughal Emperor Muhammad Shah Rangila (r. 1719–1748), ca. 1720–1750 CE.

1713. Decades earlier, Balaji had worked as a clerk in Janjira, a fortified island off the coast of Maharashtra ruled by a Habshi dynasty (1621–1948).[22] But he ended life as a near king himself. Within decades, Balaji's line amassed enough clout to confine Shahu's descendants to a gilded prison at Satara Fort while the Peshwas ruled much of western India extending into the north.[23]

Some aspects of Peshwa Maratha rule followed Mughal customs, whereas others reflected their identity as Maharashtrian Brahmins. Maratha leaders after 1740 were, as Christopher Bayly has put it, "domesticated into a Mughal life style" in terms of dress, court paintings, architecture, and more.[24] However, drawing on their own religious tradition, they enforced caste rules about child marriage for girls (mentioned above). They also barred the casteless Mahars (Dalits, in modern terms) from entering Poona in the afternoon lest their long shadows pollute upper castes. They used bureaucratic and violent means to prohibit non-Brahmins from reciting the Vedas in Maratha territory.[25] As Anandibai, wife of a late eighteenth-century Maratha ruler, described it, the Peshwas instituted "Brahmin rule" (*brahmani daulat*).[26]

Outside of the Mughals' former heartland, political possibilities flourished. Many regional states rose around 1710–1760 centered in Awadh, Bengal, Hyderabad, Jaipur, Marwar, and elsewhere. New powers sometimes did not bother to formally declare separation from the Mughal state, since the Mughals were so unable to exert authority that it cost nothing to continue recognizing them as emperors in name. Amid the efflorescence of regional rulers in early to mid-eighteenth-century India, I find myself asking: Whose stories do we tell? We might investigate the infrequently discussed Wodeyar dynasty based in Mysore that, among other things, fought in the 1720s with the ruler of Arcot (who had broken away from Mughals) regarding tribute payment. Interestingly, we learn about the battle from writings by a Catholic Jesuit.[27] Elsewhere in southern India, the Nawabs of Savanur—a Pathan lineage from Afghan regions—established lucrative connections with European merchants in the early eighteenth century and patronized both Vaishnava temples and Shaivite (including Lingayat) monasteries (they became a princely state in British India and lasted until the mid-twentieth century).[28] Looking to eastern India, we might think about the Tungkhungia lineage in Assam's Brahmaputra valley that appointed two kings—one of whom was a woman—in the 1720s to avert astrologers' predictions of disaster.[29] Alas, here, these stories remain unexplored, if mentioned briefly to remind readers—as any responsible historian should do periodically in a sweeping history—that I cannot tell every tale. Instead, I narrate the founding of two of the era's most famous regional states in Hyderabad and Jaipur, respectively.

In 1724, Nizam al-Mulk established the Asaf Jahi dynasty in Hyderabad, near Golconda. Hyderabad had been founded in the 1590s by the Qutb Shahis, who built the iconic Charminar. Arguably, Nizam al-Mulk only launched a new state because he could not survive as a Mughal advisor.[30] Still, he proved more than adequate to the task and quickly recruited diverse supporters. For example, he convinced two branches of Marathas—led by competing grandsons of Shivaji—to back him against Mubariz Khan, a Mughal general who sought to crush the nascent Hyderabad state in 1724. From the late 1730s onward, many Marathas—alongside Afghans, Telugus, and others—entered state service under the Nizams of Hyderabad, finding robust opportunities for advancement.[31] Their presence cultivated state sensitivity to local needs, helping the dynasty to succeed. Simultaneously, the Nizams patronized Persian, attracting Iranian and north Indian intellectuals to Hyderabad and fashioning the city as a cosmopolitan center of eighteenth-century Indo-Persian culture.[32]

Up north, Sawai Jai Singh founded Jaipur in 1727 as the new Kachhwaha capital, which bore distinctive marks of Mughal imperial culture. Jaipur was built around a Mughal-style pleasure garden, called "Jai Niwas Bagh" and itself patronized by Jai Singh in 1713.[33] Jaipur's walls echo Mughal forts, and the decision to paint the planned city pink, a la Fatehpur Sikri, perfects the Mughal imitation.[34] It is unsurprising to find such architectural affinities, given that the Kachhwahas supported and intermarried with the Mughals for the better part of two centuries. Strong overlaps with Mughal culture also came out in Kachhwaha patronage. For example, Jai Singh sponsored a large-scale astrological park in Jaipur and employed both Brahmin and Muslim astrologers, as had the Mughals (even as Jai Singh favored Islamic astrology and employed Brahmins who did likewise).[35] Following many Indian kings, including the Mughals, Jai Singh ecumenically patronized religious institutions, making gifts to Hindu temples as well as Catholic priests.[36] Jaipur was planned to provide for Hindu religious needs, with plenty of Hindu temples tucked away in courtyards as per common north Indian building trends.[37] Rather than religious buildings, shops were given places of prominence in Jaipur. A 1739 Hindi poem celebrates some of the trans-regional goods available in bustling Jaipur, such as Kutch camels, Arab horses, and jewelry from across the world.[38]

Birth of Modern Benares

Eighteenth-century India witnessed significant development of urban centers and Hindu religious practices, which came together in Benares. The city of Benares had been inhabited for at least 2,000 years prior, with devotional activities centered around staircases descending into the Ganges River (*ghat*s). But, as mentioned (chapter 14), virtually nothing of early Benares survives. Even oft-cited Sanskrit accounts of the city date to the mid-second millennium CE.[39] The architectural foundations of modern Benares were laid in the 1600s by Mughal Rajput officials who often drew heavily on imperial fashions. For example, the Kachhwahas built *haveli*s (mansions) at two ghats—Man Mandir and Panchaganga—with Mughal-style windows.[40] During the 1700s, Benares underwent more dramatic shifts due to changing religious practices, wealth from new sources, and revivalist building projects.

In the early to mid-eighteenth century, new rulers emerged in Benares. Regionally, it became part of Awadh, whose Nawabs broke away from the Mughals in the 1720s. Locally, the Brahmin Bhumihar family seized control in the 1730s, becoming Benares zamindars. Much about the Bhumihars' takeover was quite ordinary for the time, including that they used force, forged marital alliances, and relied on a caste-defined base of support.[41] Also conventional was that the Bhumihars submitted to regional rulers, in their case the Nawabs of Awadh, and ruled under their auspices. For Benares's lower classes, life probably changed little during the forty-odd years that the Bhumihars exercised power. Many lower-caste groups worked the land, such as Chamars (a Dalit community) who were paid in grain by higher-caste Brahmins and Rajputs. Segregated living was a reality, with Chamars and other casteless groups relegated to village outskirts.[42] But for higher castes in Benares, the period of Bhumihar rule proved transformative.

Between the 1730s and 1770s, upper-caste Hindu rituals blossomed in Benares, led by Brahmins and financed by devotees. Some Brahmins consciously advertised Benares as a pilgrimage site, such as Nagesha Bhatta who was born into an established lineage of Benares Brahmins. He wrote a Sanskrit text marketing Benares as a sacred space where devotees could engage in religious activities, like charity meals, that required the oversight of Brahmin priests (and financially benefited the priests).[43] Nagesha Bhatta also helped to popularize Benaras as a virtuous place to die. The Maratha-affiliated Narayan Dikshit Patankar zeroed in on Manikarnika Ghat as Benares's premier cremation site.[44] In the twenty-first century, Brahmin priests burn at least 100 bodies daily at Manikarnika Ghat.[45] Some eighteenth-century visitors to Benares were prominent persons, such as Radhabai (widow of the Maratha Peshwa ruler Balaji) who set off much ritual feasting across the city in 1735.[46] More common were humbler devotees, who collectively pumped money into the local pilgrimage economy. As more worshippers visited eighteenth-century Benares, more Brahmins migrated to work as ritual specialists in the city.[47]

New patrons bolstered eighteenth-century Benares's growing reputation as a ritual pilgrimage center. These patrons are noteworthy, in part, because they were transregional—based in Delhi, Maharashtra, Bengal, and Madhya Pradesh—and so placed Benares in a wider subcontinental context. The Maratha Peshwas were the keenest supporters, investing so extensively that modern historians have described eighteenth-century Benaras as "almost an extra-local centre of the Maratha state" and "largely a creation of the Marathas."[48] Other regional rulers, too, sponsored building projects, and some cases featured female agency. Rani Bhawani (r. 1748–1789) of Natore in Bengal—known for popularizing Durga Puja in Bengal—built and endowed Benares temples dedicated to Shiva and Durga.[49] Ahilyabai Holkar (r. 1767–1795) of Indore in central India rebuilt Benares's Vishvanatha Temple—destroyed as political retaliation by the Mughals a century earlier—at an adjacent site.[50] Many building projects sought to resurrect styles attested in early second-millennium temples, such as the use of *shikharas* (temple towers).[51] Like all revivalist projects, they created a tradition rooted in their own historical moment, connected with a burgeoning eighteenth-century Benares economy of pilgrimage and ghat-centered rituals (figure 16.2).

Figure 16.2. Palace of the maharaja of Indore along Benares's ghats, Varanasi, India, photograph ca. 1890s CE.

Benares was also a trade hub, even before 1700, and those commercial networks intersected with religious trends such that Shaivite renunciants emerged as key merchants in the eighteenth century. Early modern Benares was known for producing textiles (so is modern Benares, especially silk). And the city is well connected by water and roads with other regions of the subcontinent.[52] In the 1700s, Shaivite ascetics used those routes to move goods, exporting silk and cotton and importing items ranging from Kashmiri shawls to Nepali drugs. They sold imports locally in Benares and re-exported to other Indian regions, such as Bengal.[53] A few general points help to explain why Shaivite ascetics were well-positioned to succeed as traders. Their mathas (monasteries) offered organizational support in making business arrangements. Also, some sanyasis traveled in armed bands, and both their weapons and numbers were conducive to protecting merchandise.[54]

Benares's politics changed in the 1760s–1780s, when the Bhumihars secretly allied with the British who used their foothold to take over the city's administration. This is the first instance we have encountered of an Indian ruler partnering with British colonialists but will hardly be the last. The Bhumihars originally gained British support under Balwant Singh, who sought to balance the Nawabs of Awadh.[55] In part, the Bhumihar-British alliance followed time-honored Indian practices of forging political ties without consideration for origin or religion. But the British exercised a different kind of power, namely colonial power, which the following chapters explore in detail. Here it suffices to say that Indian rulers often allied with the British at the price, sooner or later, of their own independence. In Benares, the British amassed enough power by 1781 to exile Balwant's son, Chetan Singh. While political control changed abruptly, culture did not. The British soon made themselves part of Benares by patronizing Brahmin learning and established Benares Sanskrit College in 1791.[56] As of 1810, a census of homes indicated that 40,000 Brahmins, as much as 20 percent of the city's population, lived on alms and charity.[57]

While Benares was made, throughout the eighteenth century, into "a self-consciously Hindu city," it was also home to non-Hindu religious groups. For example, a small Jain community thrived, including temple-dwelling Shvetambara Jain monks from 1778 forward.[58] Muslims, too, lived in eighteenth-century Benares. Although we do not have population numbers for the 1700s, today Muslims constitute more than a quarter of Benaras residents.[59] In general, peace prevailed among Benares's many religious communities, although there were periodic cases of interreligious tension nearby. For example, at Jaunpur (about 70 kilometers north of Benares), a group of Hindus erected a temple between two mosques in 1776, thus upsetting local Muslims in a conflict that led to the involvement of Chetan Singh as well as violence and destruction of religious buildings on both sides.[60] In literary terms, it is worth noting that Benares—reputed as a center for Sanskrit literature—also hosted Braj Bhasha and Persian poets in the eighteenth century.[61]

Hindu and Caste Identities

Hindu and caste identities were forged through various mechanisms in parts of the eighteenth-century subcontinent, and the Rathor state of Marwar (modern-day Jodhpur) offers a compelling case study for both, including use of the term "Hindu." Here it bears reminding that "hindu" is a Perso-Arabic word that was scarcely used self-referentially in premodern India. Between 1200 and 1800, "Hindu" mostly surfaced in Persian texts and often had a geographic sense of someone from Hind (i.e., India).[62] The sense of "Hindu" as a religious descriptor appeared only fitfully for centuries, but one rich source of precolonial materials on the point are Rathor state archives from the 1700s. As Divya Cherian has shown, the emergence of "Hindu" in Rathor documents was accompanied by discussions of a contrasting category of *achhep*s (literally, "untouchables").[63] Accordingly, Rathor archives also provide insight into crystallizing caste identities—both for those at the top and bottom of this social hierarchy—before the advent of British colonialism. We cannot responsibly generalize from this regional case study to all of India. To introduce some comparison, however, I turn briefly at the end of this section to a discussion of caste in eighteenth-century Pondicherry.

In Marwar, two big changes—one political and one social—help explain the context in which a regional Marwari "Hindu" community defined itself by upper-caste norms. First, in 1765, Vijai Singh (r. 1752–1793) of Marwar joined a Krishna-focused vegetarian movement known as the Vallabha-sampradaya.[64] This initiation marked a move away from Rajput kingship built upon Mughal patronage and heralded a rulership rooted in Vaishnava ritual and practices. Second, upper-caste merchants emerged as critical state actors in eighteenth-century Marwar and used their new positions to enshrine their caste practices—sometimes drawn from Jain as well as upper-caste Hindu traditions—into law.[65] This gave the merchants an "aura of virtue" that they imposed on lower castes.[66] In part, these two trends manifested in morally focused laws that Indian kings of various religious backgrounds had tried to enact for centuries, such as bans on gambling and alcohol (similar bans were also tried, unsuccessfully, by numerous Mughal rulers). They also resulted in using legal mechanisms within the Rathor state to enforce upper-caste practices, such as not harming animals to the extent of outlawing the killing of lice, spiders, and scorpions.[67]

The Rathor state used coercion to force lower castes to bow to upper-caste norms while enforcing social separation between communities. In a move reminiscent of the Brahmin theorist Manu who recommended differential punishments by caste in the first millennium CE (chapter 7), the Rathor state instituted—in theory and practice—harsher consequences for lower castes who illegally slaughtered animals as compared to upper castes guilty of the same crime.[68] But living by vegetarian upper-caste norms did not raise the social standing of casteless groups. If anything, social separation increased under Rathor rule. In 1775, the state forcibly relocated leather workers to put greater distance between them and Brahmin homes. In the 1780s, Marwar officials mandated that "upper castes" (*utam jat*) such as Brahmins and Mahajans have separate water sources from "untouchables" (*achhep jat*).[69]

Still, not everyone thought about caste and religion—and the relationship between the two—the same way in eighteenth-century India, as two examples from Rajasthan demonstrate. In the 1770s, barber and shoemaker communities, separately, disagreed internally about whether one of their own, who had converted to Islam, could still be considered within their caste. The shoemaker community spanned the Rathor and Kachhwaha kingdoms, indicating that caste identity and debates were not restricted by states.[70] In the case of the barbers, there were extenuating circumstances. Starving parents had sold their son, as a boy, into slavery with itinerant Muslims. The boy had converted during his enslavement and later escaped and reunited with his family in Rathor.[71] The barber community argued about the convert's status for at least twenty years, and we do not know how (or whether) they resolved the issue. But the robust internal disagreement testifies to the importance of caste boundaries for these communities.

Ananda Ranga Pillai's Tamil Account of an Intercaste and Interreligious Event near Pondicherry, from His Private Diary, Eighteenth Century

Tuesday, 30th November 1745, or 19th Karttigai of Krodhana—This day, there was an event worthy of record. In the village of Reddipalaiyam, to the east of Ozhukarai, a church has been constructed by Kanakaraya Mudali, and he has placed some images therein. In honour of this, he invited, without distinction, all the Brahmins, Vellazhas, Komuttis, Chettis, goldsmiths, weavers, oil-mongers, and people of other castes; and all Europeans and Christians, and entertained them with a feast at Ozhukarai.

Choultries (resting places) and gardens were allotted for the preparation of food by Brahmin cooks, and meals for Vellazhas were cooked in the house of Agambadaiyans. All the arrangements were made in strict conformity with the religious scruples of each caste, and the people who attended received every attention. Meals for Europeans were prepared at Pondichery and brought over to Ozhukarai. Tables were procured for them to dine at, and every comfort was provided for them. The Governor M. Dupleix, and his consort, in company with all the members of Council, repaired thither, and partook of the banquet. He remained until five in the evening, and then returned to Mortandi Chavadi.

All the people of Pondichery who went to Ozhukarai enjoyed themselves and proceeded homewards in the evening. Neither in the arrangements which Kanakaraya Mudali made, nor in the supplies which he procured, was there anything wanting. Nevertheless, despite the heavy cost of the entertainment, and the elaborate nature of the preparations, there was something which detracted from the splendour, grace, and excellence of the hospitalities. Persons of every persuasion should abide by the rules prescribed for them: their conduct, so regulated, would look consistent. Although of a different persuasion, he followed the practice of a Hindu; assembled people of that religion; and gave them a treat which afforded room for dispraise and derision, and every man gave vent to his criticisms as he saw fit.

If he wished to conform to the rules of his church, and the commands of his scriptures, he should have entertained only the Europeans, Native Christians, Pariahs, and such others; whose associations brought them in touch with his religion. Even this would be considered derogatory to one of his position and reputation. However magnificent may be the style of any social act in which one indulges; if it be at variance with the established practice of the community concerned, it cannot redound to one's credit. If a man who has forsaken his religion, and joined another, reverts to the manners and customs of his former belief, he must inevitably draw upon himself contempt.[72]

While caste groups were often regional, the social hierarchy of caste spanned India by well before the eighteenth century and had also come, in practice, to encompass non-Hindus. That said, memory persisted that caste is theorized in Hindu (really, Brahminical) texts alone, a point that arises in Ananda Ranga Pillai's diary. In the mid-eighteenth century, Ananda Ranga served Joseph-Francois Dupleix, who oversaw French colonial holdings in India from 1742 to 1754. Ananda Ranga wrote a Tamil account of his experiences from Pondicherry (established in 1673) that is wide ranging and includes numerous passages on caste, including within Christian communities.[73] In the excerpt given here, he chastises Kanakaraya Mudali (admittedly, a professional rival) for including Hindus and their caste customs in a Christian setting where they do not belong. Caste aside, another important point of this passage is that such cross-cultural social events happened near Pondicherry in 1745, bringing together Europeans and Indians from diverse communities (albeit with food cooked separately as per caste restrictions).

Urdu, Sindhi, and Punjabi Vernacular Literatures

Vernacular literatures thrived across the subcontinent in the eighteenth century, and the case of Urdu is notable for its transregional context. At the time, Urdu was called *rekhta*, literally "mixed" because it swirled together Hindavi and Persian (often Hindavi grammar and Persian vocabulary).[74] Scholars do not fully agree on Rekhta's origins, but one key moment, ca. 1720, was when the poetry collection (divan) of Vali Dakhni was brought from the Deccan to Delhi.[75] This spurred a wave of Urdu poetry in Delhi and smaller northern cities as many poets followed Vali's advice that:

> The road of fresh ideas is never closed.
> Until the end of days, the gate of poetry remains open.[76]

Vali's language was informed by Dakhni, a southern dialect of Hindi itself born of transregional interaction when northerners migrated to southern India in the fourteenth century (chapters 10–11). Dakhni was boosted in the late seventeenth century when Aurangzeb Alamgir relocated the Mughal court to southern India for more than twenty years.[77] In a reversal of these trends, Urdu was birthed—or at least popularized—when a southerner's poetry was received up north.

Early Urdu poets drew on many Indian cultural and literary traditions. From the beginning, they acknowledged a strong debt to Persian even while contrasting the two languages. For example, Sauda (1713–1781) wrote:

> Whatever the tongue, what counts is an idea's excellence.
> Poetry is not confined to Persian alone.[78]

Persian poetry thrived in India into the nineteenth century, even as Urdu rose in popularity. Some eighteenth-century poets used Urdu as a language of devotion (bhakti) to the Hindu god Krishna.[79] For example, Savant Singh Nagridas (1699–1764) wrote in his *Ishq Caman* (Garden of love):

> Hearing of his fame in whatever tongue,
> the one of mighty wonderful beauty must be called Krishna.[80]

In other cases, a single author drew on multiple traditions, such as Muhammad Afzal in the *Bikat Kahani* (Dire tale, 1625) that draws on folk Indian traditions and Persian poetry in describing a woman separated from her lover through a twelve-month period.[81] In one delightful verse, the author plays on the poetic conceit that the monsoon rains ought to cool but, for a lover, burn and chafe:

> My friend, the rainy season burns me severely;
> my entire body is aflame.
> Dark clouds have spread everywhere and surrounded me—
> my beloved has not come yet.[82]

More well known are Urdu poets, such as Mir (d. 1810), who penned Sufi devotional poetry as part of a wider flourishing of this genre.

Sufi poetry thrived in many north Indian vernaculars, including Urdu, Punjabi, and Sindhi, during the eighteenth century. For example, the Punjabi poets Bullhe Shah (d. 1758) and his younger contemporary Waris Shah (b. ca. 1730) both told the romance of Hir pining for her lover Ranjha as a metaphor of Sufi longing for the divine. Ranjha also has similarities to Krishna, in a manifestation of long-standing overlaps between Sufi and Hindu traditions that comes out even more powerfully in Sindhi poetry.[83] Sind had been home to Muslim communities for a millennium as of the early eighteenth century, including Sufis who were not formally affiliated with a specific lineage.[84] One such poet, Shah Abdul Latif (1689–1752), wrote a Sindhi poem that revered Hindu yogis, presenting them as models to be emulated. His descriptions were likely based on real-world experiences, perhaps with a group of tantric Shaivite ascetics known as Nath yogis who had enjoyed Mughal patronage and themselves drew on Sufi practices.[85] In Abdul Latif's admiring lines, we glimpse a layered mix of appreciation and borrowing between premodern South Asian religious traditions that had a "shared but not syncretic grammar of asceticism."[86]

Excerpt from Shah Abdul Latif's Sindhi Poem on Hindu Yogis, ca. 1750

In this world there are yogis of light and yogis of fire. Their company is alight with love; I will not survive without them.

In this world yogis dwell in the warmth of love. They have parted company with ease and keep distant from comfort. They have created havoc in me; I will not survive without them.

Oh, do not forget the yogis for a moment. Search desperately for the footprints of the ascetics. Look for the path they have followed and go after them. Pursue them by night and day; I will not survive without them.

The sound of the yogis' instruments is precious to me. Their horns are all made of gold, but regard their detachment and do not speak of their wealth. Having gained your trust, they will suddenly leave for the east. Come, they have signaled to us; I will not survive without them.

The instruments of the yogis are precious to me. They are beyond conversation, they do not engage in discussion. They have attained ecstasy; I will not survive without them.

. . .

The ascetics have got rid of their ego. The naked ones possess the entire treasury of love. They are as fragrant as sandalwood; I will not survive without them.

The naked ones have gone to Hinglaj (in Balochistan) to behold the goddess. The devotees of Shiv rejoice at the sight of Dwaraka (in Gujarat). Their guide is Ali (Prophet Muhammad's son-in-law); I will not survive without them.

Sitting by themselves, they take private counsel. The masters set out on their journey, deserting the place where they stayed. Their departure made me weep; I will not survive without them.

The yogis have destroyed their separate existence, their business is with the universal. The lodge where they stay is nonexistence; I will not survive without them.[87]

Conclusion: Fracture and Flourishing

As of the mid-eighteenth century, India was ruled by dozens of regional kingdoms that provided a variegated backdrop for social and cultural changes. To be sure, there were plenty of transregional networks through trade, patronage, and languages. This period also witnessed shared trends of urban development and shifts in religious and caste identities. Politically, however, it was a moment of fracture, and it is critical to cognize that, as of about 1750, India did not exist as a unified political entity. To be sure, nobody in India's premodernity ever ruled the entire subcontinent. A few premodern kings came somewhat close, most notably Ashoka of the Mauryan Empire and Aurangzeb of the Mughal Empire. But these men were mere memories by 1750, when India was defined by political fragmentation and accompanying regional flourishing.

Further Reading

Meena Bhargava edited a volume on Mughal decline that remains the best overview of arguments on the topic. Satish Chandra's work is solid on Mughal events of the early decades of the eighteenth century, while other scholars offer insight on rising regional centers (e.g., Muzaffar Alam on Awadh). I drew on work by Vasudha Dalmia, Madhuri Desai, and Kamala Mishra on Benares. Divya Cherian's book on the Rathor state of Marwar is a treasure trove. Many have written about early Urdu, and I rely here especially on the scholarship of Imre Bangha, Purnima Dhavan, Francesca Orsini, and Heidi Pauwels. Christopher Shackle has translated eighteenth-century Sufi poetry from Sindhi and Punjabi. On Sufism-Hinduism connections, I found insightful scholarship by Patton Burchett, Carl Ernst, and Annemarie Schimmel.

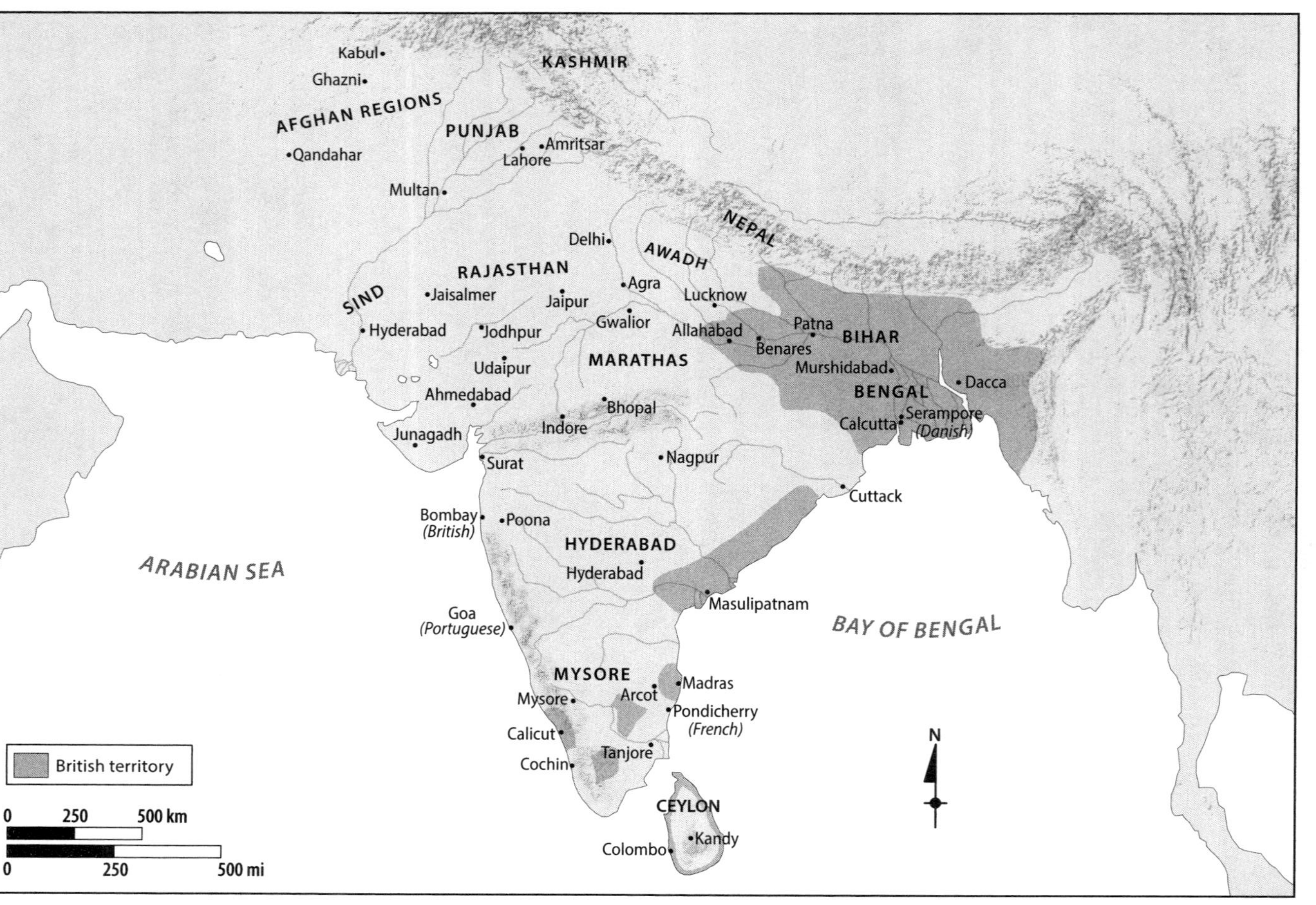

South Asia, 1798.

17

Company Bahadur

He who used to sell reed and whittle wood
now commands the army, having raised a flag on that reed.

—Qalandar Bakhsh, d. 1810 (Urdu)[1]

> On January 1, 1809, Rammohan Roy passed—and did not salute—a local British collector in Bhagalpur, a city along the Ganges River in Bihar. Roy was a cosmopolitan man of his time. He was born in the 1770s into a Brahmin family that had long served the Mughals and was educated in Sanskrit, Persian, and Arabic before taking employment with the British East India Company. That afternoon in Bhagalpur, Roy was seated in a palanquin, its door nearly closed to keep out dust, and did not see the collector. All the same, the British collector was angered at perceived impertinence and responded with abuse that Roy deemed "too gross" and "indecorous" to repeat in a later English letter he wrote to India's Governor-General seeking redress "for the injury which [Roy's] character has sustained."[2] Roy got his wish, and the British collector was mildly censured.

Roy's run-in with a British collector encapsulates key features of Indian life during the rise of the British East India Company, including Indian elites seeking Company employment, disdainful British attitudes toward Indians, Indians using British systems to pursue justice, and the many contradictions within this growing web of connections. British colonialism had two major phases in South Asia: Company rule (1757–1858) and the British Raj (1858–1947). This chapter focuses on the first phase through roughly 1835, during which Company power slowly spread out from modest coastal holdings in a fractious pattern, cannibalizing some of eighteenth-century India's many small independent kingdoms. Throughout I emphasize the roles that discrete Indian communities played in facilitating and, alternatively, opposing British colonial rule. Orientalist knowledge and Hindu reform movements also dawned during this period, stemming from Indian encounters with the British and shaping Indian society going forward.

Presidencies through Mofussil

The British were late bloomers among European colonial powers in South Asia, and readers are familiar from prior chapters with the advents of Portuguese rule in Goa (1510), Dutch rule in Sri Lanka (1658), and French rule in Pondicherry (1673). The British East India Company was founded in 1600 when Elizabeth I (a contemporary of the Mughal emperor Akbar) granted a conglomeration of English merchants a charter for Asian trade. From the start, the Company's trade mission was accompanied by asserting its right to govern its employees, engage in diplomacy, and pursue other actions associated with states.[3] Still, the British East India Company did not take off until the eighteenth century.

Like other Europeans, the British sought Indian wealth and pursued a colonial form of power, where the colony (India) was exploited to serve the metropole (England). Some Indians perceived the Company's intertwining of trade and empire early on, such as Ramachandrapant Amatya. Writing for a Maratha court in 1717, he distinguished European traders—naming the Portuguese, English, Dutch, and Danes—as "not like other merchants" because "each of them has a king for a master. It is at his command and on his account that they come to these lands."[4] Ultimately, the British achieved unmatched political and mercantile influence in India, directly ruling about three-fifths of the subcontinent by the mid-1850s. But things did not start out that way.

In the early eighteenth century, the Company was largely limited to select Indian ports, three of which later became centers of presidencies: Madras (founded in 1639), Bombay (seized from Portuguese control in the 1660s), and Calcutta (founded in the 1680s). Company traders sought the usual items, such as pepper and textiles, whose sale enriched shareholders back in Europe. Indian calicos proved so popular in England during the late 1700s that they threatened the British wool industry.[5] The

Company was also, from the get-go, a military operation with a standing army, willing to use force to ensure favorable trade arrangements. For example, angered by not receiving custom duty exemptions, the British attacked the Mughals at Hugli in the 1680s with a robust fleet, the largest to sail to Asia until the 1790s.[6] The Company lost badly and so retreated to a town that soon became a foundational part of Calcutta.[7] After this loss, Company men began to fortify their few Indian land holdings with increasing haste.

Bombay, Calcutta, and Madras all grew under Company rule, attracting many Indians to urban life. By 1800, Calcutta boasted a population of roughly 250,000, and Madras and Bombay were home to between 150,000 and 200,000 people apiece.[8] Of these growing populations, the British were a mere fraction and often fared poorly. As early as 1664, Company officials complained that "Englishmen dropp away like doggs," and, indeed, for the next century European officers died more often than not while serving in Bengal.[9] It is appropriate that South Park Street Cemetery (founded in 1767) is among modern Calcutta's tourist sites associated with the British, some of its headstones attributing deaths to the "pressure of the climate."[10] Within these fortified cities, the Company relied on Indian intermediaries, who pursued their own wealth and power. In Calcutta, the Jagat Seths, Bysakhs, and others served as Company brokers from the early eighteenth century onward, negotiating with the Mughals, giving loans, and handling debts.[11] By the 1750s, the Seths were the biggest bankers in Bengal, with unparalleled economic and political influence.

A watershed moment for the Company was securing the right to collect revenue in Bengal, a lucrative province, in the 1750s and 1760s. The first step was overthrowing the region's ruler (*nawab*), Sirajuddaulah, in a plot hatched by local merchants, including the Jagat Seths, and the disgruntled general Mir Jafar. The Seths found Sirajuddaulah unconducive to their trade interests, and Mir Jafar stood to take Sirajuddaulah's place.[12] For their part, the British desired to avoid paying customs and sought revenge for Sirajuddaulah's attack on the British settlement of Fort William in Calcutta in 1856 (occasioned by a disagreement over customs fees).[13] These distinct mercantile and political ambitions came together in dethroning Nawab Sirajuddaulah.

The overthrow happened on a battlefield in June 1757, about 150 kilometers north of Calcutta, although we might justly put scare quotes around what is called the "Battle of Plassey" and usually said to mark the advent of Company rule in India. Mir Jafar stood aside with his troops, while Robert Clive—an aggressive British man with a knack for self-aggrandizement—led an army of 3,000 men, two-thirds of whom were Indian soldiers known as *sepoys*. It rained, dampening the Nawab's cannon powder. That, plus poor training, sent his army of 50,000 scattering, and Clive's sepoy-dominated forces won, earning millions of rupees and land for the Company (and for Clive personally).[14]

In 1764, Company soldiers—6,000 sepoys and 1,000 Europeans—met with the combined armies of the nawabs of Bengal and Awadh, plus Mughal troops, at Buxar (Baksar) and engaged in a far bloodier conflict. A quarter of Company soldiers died or were gravely injured, but their side prevailed.[15] The next year, the Mughals signed a treaty that granted the Company the right to revenue collection (*diwani*) in Bengal. This treaty—in which the Mughals granted diwani to the Company—gave the British incentive to keep the Mughals alive in name, even echoing them through the nickname "Company Bahadur." Over the next several decades, the Company overhauled Mughal financial and administrative systems to ensure British access to a steady stream of Indian wealth.[16]

Colonial rule, by design and definition, benefited the metropole by exploiting the colony. Between the 1770s and 1813, the Company enforced trade monopolies in India. In Bihar and Bengal, they established a salt monopoly in 1772 and an opium monopoly in 1773, shipping large quantities of opium to China.[17] Their trade was not always sustainable and in the 1780s even required a bailout from London that prompted the establishment of an oversight Board of Control. Still, that very decade, one Indian observed of the British presence in Bengal, "Lacs piled upon lacs [millions] have therefore been drained from this country."[18] The same writer worried that, in the future, "the distresses of the people, and the depopulation and desertion of the land, will go hand in hand, until they are come to their height, and the desolation is become complete and general."[19]

Indeed, the Company viewed their obligations to Indians differently than prior rulers of Bengal, which came out painfully in reactions to famines. Monsoon rains were light across Bengal in 1768 and failed entirely in 1769. During the ensuing famine and accompanying smallpox epidemic, which lasted from 1769 to 1770, the Company did nothing to alleviate human suffering. Writing only a few years later in the 1780s,

Ghulam Hussain Khan lamented that "vast multitudes were swept away" by starvation and illness.[20] Modern historians estimate that 15 to 20 percent of Bengal's population died during the 1769–1770 famine, a starkly different outcome than after earlier failed harvests. For example, 1737 and 1738 witnessed poor harvests in Bengal, but the Mughals and local rulers helped alleviate conditions by buying grain, making loans, and permitting late revenue payments.[21] In contrast, thirty years later, the British did none of those things and, in fact, still tried to collect revenue from starving farmers. No wonder that one Indian officer (ca. 1820) likened a Company collector to a tiger, advising it safest "to shun his fearful presence."[22] The British oversaw—and contributed through inaction to—dozens of famines during two centuries of colonial rule, culminating in the 1943 famine (also in Bengal) that cost two million Indians their lives (chapter 22).

Beginning in the 1790s, the British instituted two major shifts to Company policy. They began sending British officers from cities into the *mofussil* (country regions) as judges or revenue collection officials and stationed British officers as "residents" in princely states. The idea behind both was to gain a firmer grasp on political power in India, perhaps partly inspired by a desire to prevent uprisings of the sort seen in the American Revolution (begun in 1775) and the French Revolution (begun in 1789).[23] All the same, in the early decades of the 1800s, the British enacted oppressive policies similar to or worse than those in colonial America, such as requiring stamped paper for official documents akin to the 1765 Stamp Act in America.[24] More immediately, the dispersal of the British throughout India in the 1790s placed many in more regular, direct contact with Indians.

Company rule involved racist attitudes and structural barriers, even while enabling interracial relationships. British writings of the period frequently contain insulting depictions of Indians, which some used for their political advantage. For example, Company employee J. Z. Holwell spread exaggerated stories of the "Black Hole" of Calcutta, in which a few dozen British soldiers suffocated to death while imprisoned by the Nawab of Bengal in 1756. British anger over the incident—largely known through Holwell's writings that used fictional elements designed to make Indians appear as savages—fed a desire for Company conquest in Bengal leading into the Battle of Plassey.[25] Indians noted "the aversion which the English openly shew for the company of the natives."[26] Sympathetic

British concurred, such as Judge Frederick John Shore who described his countrymen's "haughty superciliousness, arrogance, and even insolence of behaviour" toward Indians in the 1830s.[27] Still, especially in big cities, elites of Indian and European communities mixed in the initial decades of Company rule. They attended the same auctions and estate sales in late eighteenth-century Calcutta, and travelers noted the cross-cultural "soiree" culture of Madras into the 1810s.[28]

Many British men lived with or married Indian women in the eighteenth century. We lack formal numbers but consider that the majority of children baptized at St. John's Church in Calcutta between 1767 and 1782 were Eurasian and one-third of European wills in Bengal between 1780 and 1785 contained provisions for Indian companions or children.[29] Indian wives gave British men access to family networks, helpful for information gathering and trade. Early on, their Eurasian children could work for the Company, but advancement options became limited after 1793 when the British barred those with Indian ancestry from higher-level appointments.

As the nineteenth century dawned, British-Indian love affairs became less popular and more risky. Perhaps the most famous love story is that of Khair-un-Nissa, part of the local Shia elite of Hyderabad, and James Achilles Kirkpatrick, the British resident in the city from 1798 to 1803. She got pregnant, and the pair married in a private Muslim wedding ceremony (he under his Indian name of Hushmat Jang). Richard Wellesley, the governor-general of India, disapproved, and Kirkpatrick's career never recovered.[30] Kirkpatrick died in 1805, and, as per his will, his two children by Khair-un-Nissa were given English names and sent to London.[31] They never saw their mother or India again.

The Company was resourceful and relentless when it came to extending its political power. It deployed sepoy-majority armies against recalcitrant Indian rulers, engaging in multiple battles against Mysore, the Marathas, and other foes.[32] The British used whatever means they could to exert influence over Indian rulers, even adopting the local strategy of hunger strikes (*dharnas*) in the late eighteenth century to compel the Nawab of Arcot to act in Company interests.[33] They gobbled up the land holdings of European colonial powers and South Asian rulers alike, such as when they took over Dutch territories in Ceylon (Sri Lanka) in 1796 and subsumed the interior Kingdom of Kandy in 1815.[34] Sometimes, the Company annexed conquered areas to a presidency (Bombay, Calcutta, or Madras), and other times, they returned land to local rulers in a colonial version of vassal states. We generally call these quasi-independent Indian rulers "princes" to mark their subservient relationship (also called a "subsidiary alliance").

As of the late eighteenth century, British Company rule and influence was uneven, even as securing profit for the metropole was a consistent driving force. Further standardization came after Britain passed the Charter Act in 1813, which dissolved the Company's trade monopolies (with a few exceptions, such as opium) and formally expressed British crown sovereignty over its Indian holdings, which were expanding.

Indians in the Company

During more than a century of Company rule (1757–1858) over parts of the subcontinent, Indians were involved in many aspects of the colonial enterprise, including as soldiers, informers, revenue collectors, slaves, and traders. To be sure, many British men took actions with real effects on Indian lives, and I mention some individuals in the prior and subsequent sections. But I resist the path, walked by so many modern historians, of a British-centric narrative for colonial rule in India. Perhaps forefronting British agency makes sense if one is thinking about British history (of which colonialism is a critical component), but, in my view, it is a poor way to approach Indian history.[35] It is also inaccurate and top-heavy, leading scholars such as Anand Yang to call for greater attention to local society within what he dubs a "limited Raj."[36] Here I center Indian decisions and positions, focusing on the many Indians who helped or, alternatively, opposed British rule.

Regional Indian rulers and communities had divergent reactions to the Company, sometimes flip-flopping. For example, the ruler of Vittala on the Malabar coast supported Mysore's Haidar Ali (r. 1761–1782) against the British but, by the fourth and final Anglo-Mysore battle (1799), had become a British ally. The next year, Vittala's ruler used the guns he had received from the Company to destroy a temple in Manjeshwar, which prompted local Brahmins to petition for British intervention. The British agreed and hanged Vittala's ruler.[37] Other groups, too, viewed the British as offering protection, with decidedly mixed results. For example, in 1784, the Burmese Konbaung dynasty conquered the Arakan Mrauk U Kingdom, prompting thousands of Arakanese refugees to flee to Bengal and seek British shelter. These Arakanese escaped capture and enslavement in Burma but, a decade later, the Company delivered some of the refugees to Burmese authorities.[38]

Tipu Sultan (r. 1782–1799) of Mysore is perhaps the most famous Indian ruler to have militarily opposed the British East India Company. His father, Haidar Ali, had staged a successful coup against Mysore's Wodeyar dynasty in 1761. Tipu's rule was largely in line with long-standing Indian customs, including that he forged links with Sufi lineages and financially supported Hindu temples (he even mediated a dispute between two sects at a Visnu temple).[39] More unusually, Tipu—whose name means "tiger"—staunchly opposed British influence. And so, at a time when Hyderabad's Nizams and Maratha Peshwas were bowing to pressure to accept British residents at their courts, Mysore's ruler had standing orders to arrest any uninvited European who crossed into his territory.[40] Tipu even dreamed of the British being defeated—dreams being a medium for accessing higher truths in Islamic traditions—writing in his dream diary in 1797: "In the early hours of the morning, I had a dream: Raghunath Rao, the Maratha agent, who had been to me before, appeared before me and said, 'The English have suffered a crushing defeat in Europe and are now on the verge of leaving Bengal voluntarily.' On hearing his statement, I said, 'That is fine, I will despatch troops as well as money; if God wills, the Nazarenes [Christians] will be expelled from India.'"[41] But Tipu's dreams did not become reality, and the story of his defeat is worth narrating.

Company troops killed Tipu Sultan in 1799 and overran his kingdom. From a British perspective, most noteworthy is that they found one of the world's great war trophies in the Mysore palace, namely a life-size tiger mauling a British soldier. If one plays the in-built organ, the soldier's arms move in distress while he moans in agony. Intended to project Tipu's prowess, Tippoo's Tiger (figure 17.1) was sent to England where it remains on display today at London's Victoria and Albert Museum.[42] Regarding Indian history, two things about this episode exemplify larger trends. One, while Tipu fought the British, he allied with the French and even sent an embassy to Versailles in 1788.[43] Eighteenth-century Indian rulers were regional in terms of land control, but many enjoyed global connections and called on European rulers to help their causes. Two, Indian sepoys fought for the Company in the 1799 battle, a point deserving of further explanation.

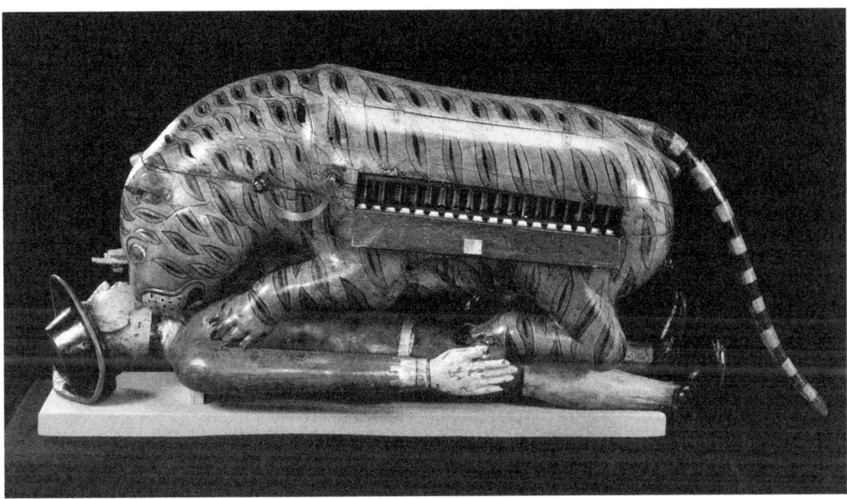

Figure 17.1. Tippoo's Tiger, semi-automaton and organ built into an almost life-sized image of a tiger mauling a British soldier, ca. 1790 CE, Mysore court of Tipu Sultan (r. 1782–1799), wood.

Indian soldiers—known as sepoys from the Persian *sipahi* (soldier)—constituted the vast majority of Company armies. To be sure, Europeans also served the Company as officers and foot soldiers (and the British Crown maintained royal troops on Indian soil from 1778 onward).[44] But Indians outnumbered the British in all major Company battles, a point we should remember when talking about "British" casualties in India, which were typically overwhelmingly sepoy. For instance, one of the Company's bloodier setbacks was the First Anglo-Afghan War (1839–1842), which ended in a massacre of around 16,000 Company soldiers and camp followers, of which more than 95 percent were Indians.

In thinking about Indian agency and choice, it is valuable to ask—Why did Indians fight for the British East India Company? Some did it for job security and to support their families, as the Company paid decently and reliably, more so than many contemporary Indian rulers.[45] For others, it was a family profession. In Madras Presidency, some sepoy soldiers were accompanied by their families and trained their children young.[46] In the nineteenth century, the British typecast certain groups—such as Nepali Gurkhas and Punjabi Sikhs—as good fighters, and that projection was embraced over time by some within those respective communities. Youthful striving—an old standby in military recruitment—also played a role, such as when Dean Mahomed joined a regiment in Patna as a preteen in 1770, against his mother's wishes.[47]

Sepoys were attracted to Company armies, in part, by British willingness to accommodate religious, cultural, and regional preferences. British officers generally acquiesced to caste-based requests concerning eating and living arrangements, which allowed for the robust participation of Brahmins and Rajputs.[48] As one scholar has put it, "There was a deliberate attempt to build a kind of upper caste Hindu sanctuary within the army."[49] Sepoys were encouraged to celebrate holidays, such as Holi and Dussehra, as per regional preferences. For example, regiments from (modern-day) Himachal Pradesh observed the fall festival of Dussehra by sacrificing goats and buffaloes (also, by firing cannons), whereas sepoys from elsewhere preferred vegetarian celebrations.[50] Sepoy units had Indian doctors from 1786 onward, and different treatments were sometimes preferred by sepoy versus European soldiers.[51] For instance, as of 1840, European regiments used five times the number of leeches monthly as sepoy regiments.[52] At other times, health care required Indian-European collaboration, both in training and in sourcing medicines like aloe and mercury from as far away as China via Bay of Bengal trading networks.[53]

Indian runners and spies provided British Company men with politically useful information. These networks drew on old Mughal ties (chapter 15), merchant connections, and families. For instance, Eurasian James Skinner (1778–1841) said that his chief spy was raised by his family.[54] Many runners came from lower castes, such as Mahars in Rajasthan and Chamars in Benaras. In contrast, spies were often more elite, ideally literate in numerous languages and scripts. Kashmiri Brahmins served as informers for competing employers, including Company and Sikh leaders.[55] Even while these information networks served Company interests, they constitute an example of British integration into older Indian means of knowledge sharing.

In other regards, too, the British were happy to benefit from continuing established Indian practices, such as slavery. Going back to Chola times or earlier, slaves had worked southern lands, and this arrangement did not change for decades within Madras Presidency. Generally, human bondage followed caste hierarchies with lower castes and Dalits being exploited by upper-caste landowners. The British were not squeamish about enslaving people, having built large parts of the global slave trade for decades. They argued that slavery in southern India was "mildest," even "benign."[56] The British also bought house slaves, just like Indian rulers before them such as the Marathas, Mughals, and Rajputs.[57] The Company formally banned slavery within their subcontinental domains in 1843, although conditions on the ground—where upper castes used violence to compel lower castes to work and even included Dalits on property deeds of sale—were slower to change.

One thing that never changed during Company rule is that Indians participated in British-led colonialism. This, in turn, shaped how the British ruled. Such dynamics also featured in the production and reception of Orientalist knowledge, which had widespread ramifications for Indian identities and thought.

Orientalist Knowledge

During Company rule, British officers and intellectuals—in consultation with Indians—produced Orientalist knowledge that shaped aspects of life in colonial India. The British held a range of views about Indian learning, from earnest interest to arrogant dismissal. On one extreme, some men like Robert Clive (d. 1774) never bothered to learn any Asian languages. Most infamous, perhaps, is Thomas Macaulay's "Minute on Education" delivered to the British parliament in 1835 in which he argued for English-medium education in India and made the astonishingly ignorant statement:

> I have no knowledge of either Sanscrit or Arabic. But I have done what I could to form a correct estimate of their value. I have read translations of the most celebrated Arabic and Sanscrit works. I have conversed, both here and at home, with men distinguished by their proficiency in the Eastern tongues. I am quite ready to take the oriental learning at the valuation of the orientalists themselves. I have never found one among them who could deny that a single shelf of a good European library was worth the whole native literature of India and Arabia. The intrinsic superiority of the Western literature is indeed fully admitted by those members of the committee who support the oriental plan of education.[58]

I am more interested here in British men who actually read Indian texts and worked with Indian intellectuals, such as Warren Hastings (d. 1818), who spoke Persian and Urdu, and William Jones (d. 1794), who worked with Indian pandits to translate Sanskrit and Persian texts. These men brought their own assumptions to studying Indian knowledge, and so we dub them and their works "Orientalist." Colonial-era Orientalist knowledge is part of the history of studying South Asia in the modern academy, and it shaped parts of colonial-era Indian society.

Toward the end of the eighteenth century, British Orientalists became enamored with Brahminical Sanskrit literature. They produced English translations of first-millennium CE texts—such as the Bhagavadgita (1785), *Hitopadesha* (1787), and Kalidasa's *Shakuntala* (1789)—as well as later lyrical poems like Jayadeva's *Gitagovinda* (1792).[59] Readers have encountered all these works in prior chapters, in discrete historical contexts. But in the 1780s–1790s, Orientalists clubbed them together to create a canon of classical Sanskrit literature. The focus on premodern Sanskrit literature itself stems from antiquarianism. They also translated to accommodate their own cultural norms, such as prudishness that prompted Jones (and many Europeans after him) to elide the more sensuous bits of *Shakuntala* and *Gitagovinda*.[60] As a result, the early Orientalists recreated Sanskrit literature within the confines of their cultural taboos, to great impact. Jones's *Shakuntala*, for example, was translated into more than a dozen European languages in subsequent decades and so became one of the first Indian cultural products that many Europeans encountered.[61]

As more Indians learned English in the nineteenth century, they too read Orientalist translations of what, by then, had been demarcated as their classical literature (i.e., Brahminical Sanskrit texts largely from the first millennium CE). Sanskrit had never been a commonly used language in South Asia and instead was restricted to select elites. And so, in a sense, colonial-era English translations echoed older Indian translation movements—such as Mughal Persian translations of Sanskrit texts—in making previously restricted works more accessible (chapter 13). But the Orientalist prism on Sanskrit literature is unmistakable, in its narrow selections and translation decisions, and those distortions shaped Indians' knowledge just as it shaped that of Westerners. Even today, many Indians are surprised at the embrace of eroticism in premodern Sanskrit poetry and are more aware of Brahminical texts than other premodern materials.

The British investment in Sanskrit Brahminical texts also came out in legal treatises, which had wide-ranging social consequences. Nathaniel Halhed—supported by Hastings and working with eleven Brahmin pandits from Bengal—authored the *Code of Gentoo Laws* in 1776 based on the dual assumptions that there was Hindu (i.e., Gentoo) law applicable to everyday situations and that it was articulated in Sanskrit texts. Really, the book created a code of Brahminical law that was strictly divided from Islamic law and divorced from Mughal judicial contexts.[62] The British-enacted Hindu-Muslim law divide permeated every area of legal life in colonial India, with courts in 1825 searching for distinct precedents on subjects as mundane as dealing with alluvions (land created by silt deposits).[63]

When the British thought about Hindus and Muslims together, they put them in a historical chronology of "Hindu rule" through about 1200 CE, followed by "Muslim rule" through the 1750s, and capped by "British rule." In writing Indian history, they relied partly on premodern Indian texts, like Firishta's sweeping history written in the 1600s for the Deccan-based Adil Shahi dynasty.[64] But the British were responsible for substantial innovations that doubled as colonial propaganda in works such as Alexander Dow's *History of Hindostan* (1772) and (Scottish) James Mill's *History of British India* (1817). Over and over, they demonized Indo-Muslim rulers—their immediate predecessors in ruling large parts of the subcontinent—so that the British might look good by comparison. More broadly, the British reduced Indian rulers to religion, writing about "Hindu rulers" and Muslims rulers" and suggesting that the British alone could rise above religious divisions. It proved a compelling dogma and was disseminated widely among British officials in India.[65]

Misguided colonial readings of Indian history also gained traction with Indians. Similar ideas surfaced in vernacular histories such as Mrityunjay Vidyalankar's *Rajabali* (Royal lineage, 1808), the first printed Bengali history of India, which offers a biased image of Aurangzeb and depicts Company rule as divinely sanctioned.[66] But such propaganda should not be mistaken for historical reality. Bucking earlier trends, Orientalist knowledge was instrumental in creating Hindu-Muslim division as a major feature of Indian society beginning in the nineteenth century.[67]

Both Orientalists and missionaries were interested in Indian vernaculars, and their interventions changed these traditions. Numerous Indian vernaculars were printed for the first time at Serampore, a Danish colony north of Calcutta where missionaries were free to operate (they were banned in Company-ruled areas until 1813). Between 1800 and 1830, the Serampore Press published more than 210,000 volumes in forty languages.[68] In Company-controlled areas, some British developed an interest in Hindi, sometimes called Hindustani in this period, with John Gilchrist publishing the first English-Hindoostanee (his spelling) dictionary in the 1780s.[69] Gilchrist was later appointed Professor of Hindustani at Calcutta's College of Fort William (1800–1854), founded to teach Indian vernaculars to British soldiers. Gilchrist is also credited with an idea that ultimately reshaped the linguistic politics of northern India, namely that we ought to divide Hindi and Urdu into separate languages by script, using Devanagari for Hindi and Perso-Arabic for Urdu.[70] Still, following Mughal precedent, Persian remained the official language of the Company until 1837, some seventy years into Company rule.

The British also developed knowledge about India through traveling. For example, Colin Mackenzie (1753–1821) traversed parts of southern India and relied on native assistants like the three Kavali brothers for a mixture of translations, ethnographic observations, and practical arrangements.[71] In Rajasthan between 1799 and 1822, James Tod learned about Rajput history and ultimately published his three-volume *Annals and Antiquities of Rajast'han*. He was assisted by Ghasi, an artist who also worked for Udaipur's rulers, and Gyanchandra, a Jain yati who helped him read the *Prithviraj Raso*, a Hindi work of Rajput legends that has informed much popular knowledge.[72] British women, too, traveled India, and some wrote about their experiences. For instance, Jemima Kindersley accompanied her husband, an artillery officer in the Bengal army, between 1764 and 1768.[73] She was perhaps the first European woman to visit Allahabad, along with her four-year-old son, where she noted a cockroach infestation at the British-run fort and large bats "fixing their claws in [people's] hair."[74] Several decades later, a standard tourist itinerary began to emerge. For instance, between 1809 and 1811, Maria Graham visited Elephanta Island near Bombay, Mamallapuram south of Madras, Bombay's Parsi temples, and the Buddhist Karle caves in Maharashtra. She also wrote about experiences still associated with tourism in India today, such as riding an elephant.[75]

It is hard to overstate the influential legacy of the early Orientalists and others involved in creating knowledge as part of the colonial effort. Some of that legacy is negative, and many modern people hold ill-informed ideas about South Asia whose origins can be traced to the 1770s–1830s. But Orientalist knowledge is also foundational to the modern study of history, in India and the West. For example, James Prinsep deciphered the Brahmi and Kharoshthi scripts (which had long ago been forgotten) in the late 1830s, which gave us access once again to Ashokan inscriptions. Prinsep published his findings in the *Journal of the Asiatic Society of Bengal*, founded in 1784 and still published today to foster research on India. Later Indologists, including Indians, built upon Prinsep's work, such as Bhau Daji (1821–1874) who finished deciphering the rock inscriptions at Junagadh (chapter 4).[76]

In 1785, William Jones noted the similarities between Sanskrit, Greek, and Latin in his Second Anniversary Speech to the Asiatic Society of Bengal. He was not the first in India to note the language connection (Arzu preceded him; chapter 2). But Jones popularized knowledge of the links, which spurred further linguistic study. In the 1810s, a clear theory of Dravidian languages emerged, and so scholars understood, for the first time, that there are two major language families in South Asia with Indo-European languages dominating the north (e.g., Hindi, Bengali, Gujarati, Punjabi, Urdu) and Dravidian languages common in the south (e.g., Malayalam, Tamil, Kannada, Telugu).[77] These discoveries—and many others made during the early colonial period—remain foundational to our collective understanding of South Asian history.

Hindu Reform Movements

Orientalist knowledge changed how Indians thought about themselves, including their religions. Responding to a mix of new ideas, European criticisms, and their own shifting sentiments, some Hindus called for robust changes to religious practices starting in the late eighteenth century. These Hindu reform movements began in Bengal, owing to the region's robust British presence and its emerging *bhadralok* (Hindu urban elite).[78] The Hindu reformers championed modifications that, in their view, would make Hinduism more rational, equitable, and modern. For example, early Hindu reformers advocated for rejecting icon veneration, ridding Hindu communities of caste, eliminating sati (widow burning), and increasing access to education. They also argued for the unity of God, influenced by Christian Unitarian ideas.[79] Many Hindus alive in the colonial period saw no need for their religion to be "reformed," and some defended their existing traditions. But the Hindu reform movements had widespread effects, changing the terms of internal Hindu religious debates.

The early Hindu reform movements coincided with the advent of the term "Hindooism" (using that spelling), first attested in the 1780s. This emerging category subsumed groups—like the Lingayats and Vaishnavas—that had long considered themselves distinct and so gave rise to competing visions of proper Hindu ideas and practices. Rammohan Roy (1772–1833)—a Company man, Brahmin, and key reformer whom we met in the introduction—was quite possibly the first Hindu to write about "Hindooism."[80] He founded the Brahmo Samaj in 1828, and it continued after his death (and continues today) to advocate for its ideal "reforms" to Hindu traditions. Roy and other Bengali Hindu reformers faced competition, especially from popular Vaishnava movements in Bengal.[81] Their "reforms" were sometimes opposed by other bhadralok societies, such Calcutta's Dharma Sabha founded by Radhakanta Deb in 1830 that promoted a more conservative vision of Hindu practices. There was also pushback from other quarters. In rural areas of eastern Bengal, villagers refused transport and housing to Brahmo Samaj missionaries and desecrated their prayer halls. Brahmo Samaj converts often faced stiff family opposition.[82]

Hindu reformers such as Rammohan Roy responded to European Christian criticisms of Hinduism and engaged with Hindu theology, and we cannot separate the two projects. Rammohan Roy, for example, cited the Upanishads as easily as the Bible. He wrote an immense amount—in Bengali, English, Persian, Arabic, and Sanskrit—on his desired changes to Hindu practices and beliefs (see excerpt). Roy's language can be harsh at times, rejecting staunchly both the Christian Trinity and Vishnu's multiple avatars (incarnations) as inappropriately polytheistic (Roy embraced monotheism).[83] Still, Roy believed that ancient Hindu texts outlined a moral path, which he encouraged his brethren to embrace while they rejected contemporary corruptions. Roy traveled to England in 1831, formally as a Mughal representative (the name "Roy" was adapted from a title given to his great-grandfather, Krishnachandra, by a Mughal official during Aurangzeb's reign).[84] The trip pushed back against Hindu caste norms, since by crossing the *kala pani* (ocean, literally "black waters") one lost one's caste in common thinking of the day. Roy died in 1833 among Unitarian friends in Bristol where, in a final rejection of common Hindu customs, he is buried.

Rammohan Roy, Excerpt from Introduction to the *Ishopanishad*, 1816

For the chief part of the theory and practice of Hindooism, I am sorry to say, is made to consist in the adoption of a peculiar mode of diet; the least aberration from which (even though the conduct of the offender may in other respects be pure and blameless) is not only visited with the severest censure, but actually punished by exclusion from the society of his family and friends. In a word, he is doomed to undergo what is commonly called loss of cast.

On the contrary, the rigid observance of this grand article of Hindoo faith is considered in so high a light as to compensate for every moral defect. Even the most atrocious crimes weigh little or nothing in the balance against the supposed guilt of its violation.

Murder, theft, or perjury, though brought home to the party by a judicial sentence, so far from inducing loss of cast, is visited in their society with no peculiar mark of infamy or disgrace.

A trifling present to the Brahmin, commonly called *Prayaschit*, with the performance of a few idle ceremonies, are held as a sufficient atonement for all those crimes; and the delinquent is at once freed from all temporal inconvenience, as well as all dread of future retribution.

My reflections upon these solemn truths have been most painful for many years. I have never ceased to contemplate with the strongest feelings of regret, the obstinate adherence of my countrymen to their fatal system of idolatry, inducing, for the sake of propitiating their supposed Deities, the violation of every humane and social feeling. And this in various instances, but more especially in the dreadful acts of self-destruction and the immolation of the nearest relations, under the delusion of conforming to sacred religious rites. I have never ceased, I repeat, to contemplate these practices with the strongest feelings of regret, and to view

> in them the moral debasement of a race who, I cannot help thinking, are capable of better things; whose susceptibility, patience, and mildness of character, render them worthy of a better destiny. Under these impressions, therefore, I have been impelled to lay before them genuine translations of parts of their scripture, which inculcates not only the enlightened worship of one God, but the purest principles of morality, accompanied with such notices as I deemed requisite to oppose the arguments employed by the Brahmins in defence of their beloved system. Most earnestly do I pray that the whole may, sooner or later, prove efficient in producing on the minds of Hindoos in general, a conviction of the rationality of believing in and adoring the Supreme Being only; together with a complete perception and practice of that grand and comprehensive moral principle—Do unto others as ye would be done by.[85]

The Hindu reform movements solicited British intervention in certain matters, such as sati (widow burning). Sati was rare in colonial India, but it captured British imaginations because they perceived it as a gruesome practice. Hindu reformers agreed, and they worked with the Company to ban sati in the early nineteenth century. Other Hindus fiercely opposed this move (such as members of Calcutta's Dharma Sabha), and the debate raised a question that would recur throughout British colonial rule in India: Should the colonial government regulate socio-religious practices? Eighteenth-century Indian rulers had sometimes done so, such as the Marathas mandating child marriage for Brahmin girls and the Rathors enforcing caste-based segregation (chapter 16). But many Indians felt that it was different for colonial British rulers to interfere with Indian religions (especially other than Christianity). The British often agreed, at least until Indian customs conflicted with their own notions about civilized conduct. This thorny issue arose repeatedly in subsequent decades, including regarding child marriage, female infanticide, and anticolonial rhetoric at religious festivals.

The Hindu reform movements continued throughout the colonial period, and I return in chapters 19 and 20 to other strands of the movements that transformed aspects of Hinduism. As an early reformer, Rammohan Roy responded, creatively and robustly, to his changed environment. This included embracing Hinduism as a broad-based tradition, internalizing certain British colonial criticisms, and articulating a way forward through critically reading Hindu religious texts.

Conclusion: Empires Lost and Gained

Amid shifting Indian social realities and the rise of the British East India Company, the Mughals persisted in a shabby state. They were confined to an area of Delhi known as Shahjahanabad and served as living museum pieces, largely of interest to traveling Europeans. Emma Roberts wrote about visiting Akbar Shah II (d. 1837), describing the king as shrunken and bereft of dignity. She noted that the "throne or pavilion of the great Moghul is of white marble, beautifully carved, inlaid with gold."[86] In contrast: "The king is seated, cross-legged, upon cushions, and, except upon occasions of state, does not affect great splendour of attire, being frequently entirely wrapped up in shawls, and shewing only a few valuable jewels to the eager eyes of European strangers. The court is, in fact, shorn of all its grandeur, and the monarch, painfully conscious of his own degradation, can only be reconciled to the exhibition of himself, for the sake of the revenue afforded by the gold mohurs, which are offered as *nuzzurs* at every presentation."[87] In part, the Company kept Akbar Shah II and his successor, Bahadur Shah Zafar, around to highlight, by contrast, alleged British "modernity."[88] In other regards, the Company drew on Mughal ruling culture, such as minting coins in the Mughal ruler's name (and in Persian) until the mid-1830s. Even if they were has-been kings, the Mughals and their Indo-Persian ruling culture informed Company rule. Capturing something of these social and political dynamics, the Delhi town crier is reported to have shouted as his refrain in the mid-nineteenth century: "People belong to God, rule to the King, and control to the Company Bahadur."[89] This division of authority did not last, however, and the saying soon became obsolete.

Further Reading

For overviews of Company rule, I used C. A. Bayly and Jon Wilson (both also extend into the British Raj). I turned to other scholars for specific topics, such as Seema Alavi on sepoys and the Company, Kate Brittlebank on Tipu Sultan, and Durba Ghosh on interracial relationships. Brian Hatcher has written on the Hindu reform movements, and Bruce Robertson has edited and analyzed some of Rammohan Roy's writings. So many have written about the early Orientalists, of which Manan Ahmed Asif's work stands out for its robust engagement with premodern sources as well.

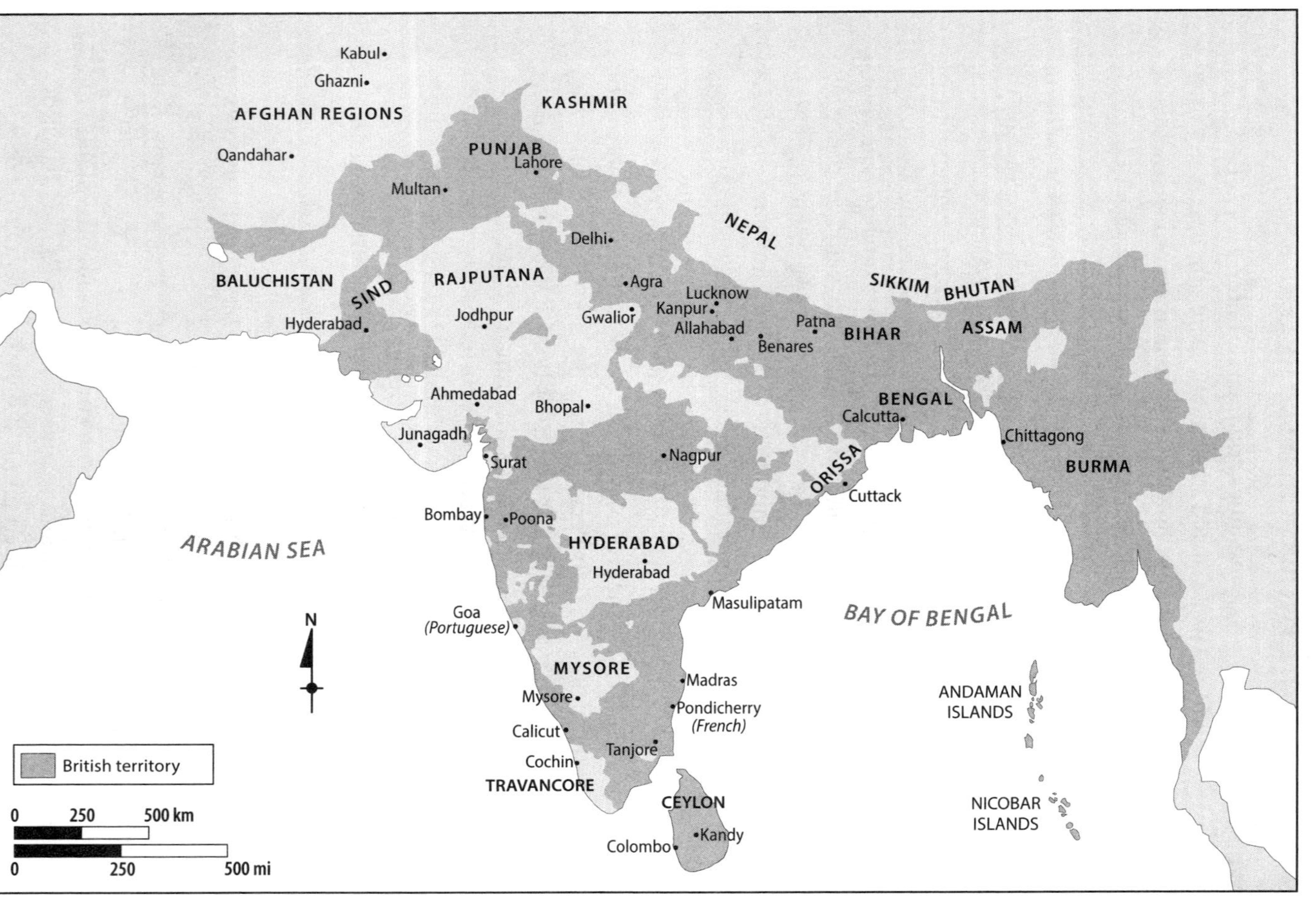

British India and princely states, 1857.

18

Sepoy Rebellion and Dawn of the British Raj

Everything is to become red.

—Ominous saying reported by Anglo-Indian press, Calcutta, 1857[1]

In 1857, Calcutta's press reportedly printed a prediction that everything would soon redden, a warning or a promise perhaps. It might refer to blood, foretelling an Indian rebellion against British colonial rule. Alternatively, it could imply sepoy military uniforms or the pink color that typically denoted British territory on nineteenth-century maps, meaning that British rule would soon prevail across India.[2] Both predictions held truth, and yet few—if any in India—saw coming two sequential events that reshaped South Asian politics: the Sepoy Rebellion in 1857 and the dawn of the British Raj in 1858. I contextualize these watershed moments by first discussing the final decades of British East India Company rule (1835–1857) when British leaders exhibited increasing aggression. As the Company devoured Indian territory, local society experienced social shifts fueled by the spread of English-medium education and press technology. Then, a rebellion broke out that, while ultimately quashed, changed the British colonial enterprise in South Asia.

Company Territorial Aggression, 1835–1857

The gloves came off during the final decades of Company rule on the subcontinent. British colonialists accelerated time-worn tactics, such as warring for territory, using residents to pressure Indian princes, and allying with merchants to overthrow local rulers. An example of the last mechanism is the British annexation of Sind in 1843, which was bankrolled by Seth Naomul, a local trader. Naomul ran duty-free stores in the Company's Karachi cantonment and procured supplies for sepoy and British troops headed northwest to the First Anglo-Afghan War (1839–1842).[3] Still, his pro-Company actions may have been "ultimately self-defeating" since he and other merchants lost access to the region's lucrative opium trade after 1843 as the British enforced their monopoly on the drug.[4] The Company's 1843 annexation of Sind is most often remembered in the apocryphal tale that Charles Napier sent a pun dispatch announcing his victory: "Peccavi," Latin for "I have sinned." In reality, a teenage girl named Catherine Winkworth invented this multilingual wordplay, which was published by London's humorous *Punch* magazine and mistakenly attributed to Napier.[5] The cavalier attitude was spot on to describe many British who schemed, swindled, and fought to swell Company landholdings and wealth from the 1830s through the 1850s.

The British also deployed new strategies to seize further Indian territory, such as the doctrine of lapse from 1834 to 1857 whereby they took over Indian kingdoms lacking an acceptable bloodline male heir. The doctrine is often associated with the Marquis of Dalhousie, James Ramsay, governor-general of India from 1848 to 1856. Dalhousie annexed a quarter of a million square miles of the subcontinent, more than any British officer who preceded him, including the kingdoms of Satara (1848), Nagpur (1853), Jhansi (1854), and numerous smaller princely states.[6] The threat or reality of violence loomed behind each land acquisition. Here I delve further into two large-scale territorial seizures: the Sikh Kingdom, annexed through cruel politicking and war in 1849, and Awadh, annexed due to misgovernance claims in 1856. These cases demonstrate how South Asians contended with an increasingly bellicose Company under Dalhousie and offer an opportunity to see broader social and cultural shifts.

The Sikh Kingdom was founded in 1799 by teenaged Ranjit Singh (1780–1839) and soon stretched across the Punjab and beyond. Ranjit Singh was born into a relatively privileged family that already controlled substantial land in Punjab.[7] They belonged to a group of Sikhs who embraced a martial identity through the Khalsa (Sikh warrior community established in 1699) and used religious language to articulate political ambitions, such as calls to fight a *dharamyudh* (religious war).[8] Ranjit

Singh rose to prominence by conquering Lahore, formerly a Mughal capital, from another Sikh family in 1799.[9] He declared himself *maharaja* (emperor) of the Punjab in 1801 and ruled much of the region for the next thirty-eight years, also conquering Kashmir around 1820.

Ranjit Singh acted similarly to earlier Indian rulers, including the Mughals, while also incorporating Sikh cultural norms. He was ecumenical in state patronage and marriage practices, wedding Sikh, Hindu, and Muslim women.[10] He built a mosque and madrasa in Lahore to honor one of his Muslim wives, Moran (so called because she danced like a peacock, *mor* in Urdu and Hindi).[11] Ranjit Singh spoke approvingly of Aurangzeb at times, such as admiring the Mughal emperor's ferocity in facing down a mad elephant.[12] He came to possess the Koh-i Noor diamond, once a symbol of Mughal sovereignty that had been looted from India nearly a century earlier by Nadir Shah (chapter 16). Ranjit Singh also drew on Sikh ideas to express sovereignty, such as using turban exchanges to forge political alliances. Turbans signified a fraternal link as per Rajput traditions since the sixteenth century, and, for Sikh men of the era, the turban "was a symbol of martial prowess" owing to kesh (uncut hair) being among the markers of Khalsa warriors.[13] Known as *sher-e punjab* (Lion of the Punjab), Ranjit Singh generously patronized Amritsar's Golden Temple, sponsoring extensive adornments still visible today.

The Sikh Kingdom contended with internal and external political challenges, with the Company proving the most ferocious. Like other Indian rulers (see chapter 17), Ranjit Singh forged agreements with the Company that helped temporarily solidify his political position. For example, the 1809 Treaty of Amritsar declared Company recognition of Ranjit Singh as the sole ruler of the Punjab, which gave him license to cement his dominance over other Sikh and Afghan leaders.[14] But the Company outlasted Ranjit Singh (d. 1839), whose successors fell into infighting as three adult sons and grandsons cycled through as heads of the Sikh Kingdom between 1839 and 1843.[15] In 1843, a fourth successor came to power: Ranjit Singh's youngest son Duleep Singh (r. 1843–1849), who was only four years old and so ripe for exploitation. As a British lord put it, this child-prince "must do our bidding."[16]

At first, Duleep Singh's mother, Maharani Jind Kaur (known as Jindan), served as regent and frustrated British designs on the Sikh throne, but she was soon sidelined. British resident Henry Lawrence suggested in summer 1847 that Jindan should observe purdah, only conducting business periodically from behind a screen "as do the Princesses of other courts, such as Jodhpore, Jyepore, and Nepal." Jindan rejected the gendered suggestion made to minimize her influence, proclaiming: "So long as the Maharajah is sovereign of his own kingdom, it is the same as if I was sovereign myself."[17] Unable to solicit her compliance, Lawrence forced Jindan into exile in August 1847, separating her from her then nine-year-old son.[18]

In 1849, the Company won a military confrontation with Sikh forces, after which they compelled the child-prince Duleep Singh to sign a treaty of annexation. This "treaty" included a list of loot that the British took home to England, including the famed Koh-i Noor diamond and Ranjit Singh's golden throne. They also took Duleep Singh to England, giving the child a 17,000-acre estate in Suffolk but cutting him off from his homeland (I finish his story below).[19] In the early 1850s, the British commissioned a Dutch firm to recut the Koh-i Noor, thereby making the diamond conform to British tastes of appearing more lustrous but shaving off 80 carats.[20] Both the reduced Koh-i Noor and Ranjit Singh's empty throne remain in London today, the former as part of the crown jewels and the latter on display as a war trophy opposite Tippoo's Tiger (chapter 17) at the Victoria and Albert Museum.[21]

The last Indian kingdom that the Company annexed was Awadh (Oudh), which stretched across the fertile Gangetic plain. Awadh was ruled by Shia nawabs from 1722 to 1856, who, like many other early eighteenth-century rulers, had de facto broken away from the Mughals. They shifted their kingdom's capital from Faizabad to Lucknow in 1775, at which point the nawabs of Awadh ruled around 89,000 square miles, a kingdom nearly the size of modern-day Uttar Pradesh (independent India's largest state).[22] The British annexed half of Awadh in 1801, after which the Company kept a British resident at court in Lucknow. Dalhousie described the nawab's remaining kingdom in 1851 as "a cherry which will drop into our mouths some day."[23] Despite such dismissive fruit metaphors, local culture thrived in Awadh during the first half of the nineteenth century.

Awadh's elites supported literary, artistic, architectural, and technological endeavors through the mid-1800s. Perhaps most famously, *tawaifs* (female entertainers skilled in dance and music) flourished in nineteenth-century Lucknow, and some were quite wealthy. Men participated in poetry symposiums (*mushairas*), where one could hear the latest Urdu verses. Crowds of Muslims and Hindus honored Shia festivals, such as Muharram that commemorates Husayn's martyrdom at the Battle of Karbala in 680 CE.[24] Poetic elegies (*marsiyas*) narrated this event and were sometimes shared in labyrinth-like *imambara* buildings, sponsored by the nawabs.[25] Imambaras also had prosaic features, and the nawabs sponsored one such building in the 1780s to provide famine relief.[26] Awadh's last nawab, Wajid Ali Shah (1822–1887), patronized the arts liberally, including dance and music (interests he continued into the 1880s as a deposed ruler living in Calcutta).[27] Awadh's rulers also invested in public works, such as substantially expanding their road networks from the late eighteenth century forward.[28] They installed a typographic press in Lucknow in 1817 and brought the first steamboat to India in 1819.[29] In brief, Awadh thrived, culturally and technologically, prior to its colonial takeover.

Dalhousie annexed Awadh in 1856 on the pretense that Wajid Ali Shah had failed to implement urgently needed reforms, especially to reduce crime. The move met with rejoinders in India and England. Wajid Ali Shah (or somebody writing in his name) published *Reply to the Charges against the King of Oude* in Calcutta in 1856, and Samuel Lucas (possibly a pseudonym) published *Dacoitee in Excelsis, or, The Spoliation of Oude, by the East India Company* in London in 1857. Lucas's criticism is harsh, such as these opening lines: "It will be seen how falsely a pretended care for a native race can be made the excuse for thwarting their inclinations, while appropriating their substance; and how, consulting our own objects alone, we can enforce a revolution to which they were adverse, and can thrust upon them our rule because we coveted their rupees."[30] Wajid Ali Shah was more circumspect, perhaps because he sought to persuade the British to reinstate him. Still, he ended by pointing out that the Company's pretext of combating crime did not hold water since "crimes committed in my dominions" are "in the proportion of one to ten to those committed in the Company's territories."[31] Such works testify to the persuasive limits of colonial propaganda. Wajid Ali Shah's text also participates in a development so ordinary today that it can be easy to overlook in history, namely that Indians began writing and publishing in English.

Printing Presses, Speaking English, and Changing Religion

Print technologies expanded rapidly on the subcontinent starting in the 1830s, especially with the introduction of lithography. Typographic presses had been used in India for a few centuries already, but lithography—which prints from a flat surface—was cheaper and more portable. It also allowed for calligraphy, which was culturally preferable for Persian and Urdu printing. Over the next few decades, communities in Agra, Benares, Bombay, Calcutta, Delhi, Kanpur, Lucknow, Madras, and elsewhere used printing presses to spread their ideas, with educational and theological works outpacing other genres.[32] Both Hindi and Urdu texts were lithographed, including Tulsidas's Ramayan (1832) and an Urdu translation of the Quran (1848).[33] European Christian missionaries printed evangelical materials, and Indians of various religious backgrounds published sharp responses in what one scholar describes as "tract warfare."[34] Print could also be used for political challenges, a possibility that alarmed some Indian rulers. For example, Ranjit Singh (d. 1839) licensed two lithographs in the hopes of disseminating the Guru Granth Sahib, the central Sikh holy book, but he later shackled the presses out of fear that they might print seditious materials.[35]

Indian presses churned out works in many languages, but one was still fairly new to most Indians: English. From the early nineteenth century forward, English spread as a new kind of cosmopolitan language in South Asia. It was never adopted by most South Asians but—like Persian for earlier generations—served as an elite tongue that also gave access to government employment opportunities. Unsurprisingly, given the history of Company rule stretching out from Calcutta, Bengalis were among the earliest to make the English language their own.

Indian demand for English education was robust. The first secretary of the Madras School Book Society, Vennelacunty Soob Row, estimated that 500 schools advertised to teach English on Madras's Mount Road alone in the 1820s.[36] The Company began introducing English-medium education in Indian colleges, such as Benares Sanskrit College and Old Delhi College, in the late 1820s to early 1830s. At the same time, book societies in the three Company presidencies' capitals (Bombay, Calcutta, and Madras) opened schools and printed English-medium literature, as did missionary groups.[37] In 1835, the British passed the English Education Act that pulled official support from Indian classical languages, such as Persian and Sanskrit, and prioritized teaching and using English in India. In 1839, a petition to open an English-medium high school in Madras attracted 70,000 signatures from inhabitants of the city.[38]

Some English-speaking Indian elites adopted new ideas and habits, along with a new language, in the early nineteenth century, and these changes often prompted intracommunity discord. We encountered one example with the early Hindu reformers who founded the Brahmo Samaj and received pushback (chapter 17). Another Hindu example is Mohan Lal Zutshi, a Kashmiri Brahmin who was among the first students to study English at Old Delhi College in the late 1820s. This positioned Mohan Lal to travel with the explorer Alexander Burnes in Central Asia and, later, to visit England. But upon returning to Delhi, Mohan Lal was rejected by other Kashmiri Brahmins who accused him of losing his caste due to dining with the British (he denied this) and having left the Brahminical sphere of aryavarta ("land of the pure," i.e., India).[39] He asked the British to intervene on his behalf, but they considered it an internal community matter. Faced with living the rest of his life as a religious outcaste, Mohan Lal instead chose to convert to Islam.[40]

In some cases, English-medium education created opportunities for European Christian missionaries to proselytize to Indians. For instance, at a Madras school run by the Free Church Mission of Scotland, three upper-caste Hindu boys converted to Christianity in 1841, against their parents' wishes.[41] The episode prompted other parents to withdraw their children from the school.

Perhaps the most famous nineteenth-century Indian convert to Christianity was Duleep Singh, the deposed child-prince of the Punjab, who ultimately reconverted to Sikhism in an attempt to resist British colonialism. After being deposed in 1849, Duleep Singh lived as a rich, land-owning Christian in England for thirty years. Then, in the 1880s, prophesies flew around the Punjab about a man who would lead Sikhs in revolt against the British, and some thought the promised one was Duleep Singh.[42] He agreed and attempted to return to India to be initiated into the Khalsa in 1886. Seeing a threat to their colonial power, the British police arrested Duleep in Aden. He performed the Amrit initiation there, taking on the five markers of the Khalsa, although this lacked the challenge to British authority that the same action might have had on Indian soil. Duleep Singh moved to continental Europe and pursued anticolonial activities until his death in 1893.[43] He even solicited Russian help in aspiring, as he put it in 1887, "to deliver some 250,000,000 of my countrymen from the cruel yoke of the British Rule."[44] Duleep Singh was not alone in being discontent with British colonialism, a point made forcefully by the Sepoy Rebellion of 1857.

Armed Rebellion

The Sepoy Rebellion constituted the greatest armed threat that Indians ever posed to the British colonial enterprise. It began in spring 1857 when a handful of sepoys turned on their British commanders in northern India, and soon sepoys across Bengal Presidency joined in violent pushback to Company rule. Within weeks, the Rebellion also attracted civilian support from across the social spectrum, including from deposed rulers, tribal communities, convicts, and courtesans.[45] Noticing this transition from military revolt to broader uprising, one English-medium Calcutta newspaper declared on May 21, 1857: "It is no longer a mutiny, but a rebellion."[46] Some put stock in the curious timing, with both Indians and British citing astrologers' predictions that British rule would end a century after the Battle of Plassey (1757).[47] The British and loyal sepoys quelled the unrest through force, putting down most of the rebellion within months and stamping out the remnants by early to mid-1858. Still, the Sepoy Rebellion had extensive social ramifications, especially for Indian Muslim communities (chapter 19), and was a politically transformative event, prompting the end of Company rule and the dawn of the British Raj.

The Sepoy Rebellion had antecedents in that many Indian communities had used force to resist British colonialism in prior decades. Perhaps the closest precedent was the 1806 Vellore Revolt in Madras Presidency, in which rebel sepoys killed about 100 British.[48] The years leading up to the 1857 Rebellion saw numerous tribal and Adivasi uprisings, including among Bhils in central India (1852), Santhals in eastern India (1855–1856), and Savaras in Odisha (1856–1857). The British generally met armed resistance with brutal violence of their own, such as summarily shooting rebels and Indian civilians, hanging them, and blowing them apart with cannons. After seeing British "undistinguishing vengeance" at Vellore, some sepoys predicted, "If another insurrection shou'd occur in the army, all the men will be united in the sentiment and action."[49] Indeed, most Bengal sepoys rebelled in spring of 1857, with only 8,000 left loyal to the British as of September 1858 (out of 120,000 a mere eighteen months earlier).[50]

Rumors of religious and caste offenses were the immediate spark for sepoys to rebel. The British planned to introduce Enfield rifles to sepoy troops, who began to whisper in early 1857 that the accompanying cartridges—which had to be bitten open to load the gun—were greased with pig lard and beef tallow. This alarmed Muslims and upper-caste Hindus for analogous reasons. Mangal Pandey, a Brahmin sepoy in Barrackpore, was the first to object that ingesting such animal products would cause him to lose his caste. After taking up arms against a British officer in March 1857, he was quickly tried and hanged.[51] More than a month later, in May 1857, Muslim cavalrymen in Meerut rebelled, upset at consuming pork against standard Islamic proscription, and this time the violence spread. Nobody has ever quite worked out if the rumors of tallow and lard held any truth, but regardless many of the 230,000 sepoys who worked for the Company as of 1857 believed that their jobs suddenly meant breaking religious and caste taboos and thus facing social ostracization.

Broader disaffection with British colonialism helps to explain why so many in northern India rebelled in 1857. Nineteenth-century Indians had a legion of grievances against Company rule, including British racism against Indians, draining wealth from the subcontinent, overseeing famines, humiliating Indian rulers, coercive takeovers of princely territories, interfering in religious practices, and aggressive European Christian missionaries. There were additional reasons for sepoy discontentment in the 1850s, including being sent to die in foreign wars and attempts to diversify caste representation in sepoy regiments.[52] This last issue was especially threatening to the predominantly upper-caste Bengal army, the main muscle of the Sepoy Rebellion. Brahmins were the largest group among Bengal Presidency sepoys, followed by Rajputs and Bhumihars.[53] The myriad Indian grievances played out differently in specific places, with more prosaic causes for violence also thrown into the mix. For instance, Mangal Pandey was reported to be under the influence of *bhang*, a cannabis-based narcotic, when he took up arms against his British commander.[54]

In May 1857, rebel sepoys congregated in northern cities—especially Kanpur, Delhi, and Lucknow—to fight under regional leaders, and the movement proceeded distinctly in each place. In Kanpur, the rebels were led by Nana Sahib, one of three adopted sons of the last Maratha Peshwa and inheritor of his property; they held Kanpur until July 1857. In Delhi, rebel sepoys turned to Bahadur Shah Zafar, the octogenarian Mughal emperor, as a nominal leader and staved off British forces until September 1857. In Lucknow, where the Rebellion stretched into March 1858, rebels enthroned the eleven-year-old Birjis Qadr (son of the deposed nawab Wajid Ali Shah) with his mother Hazrat Mahal serving as regent.[55] These political figures all had complaints against the British, but it is not clear that they wanted to support armed resistance, at least initially. None had realistic means to refuse the gun-toting sepoys who demanded their support. One testimony remembers that the sepoys made Nana Sahib an offer he couldn't refuse: "A kingdom awaits you if you join our cause but death if you side with our enemies."[56] Similarly, Rani Lakshmibai of Jhansi—a much celebrated female leader in the Rebellion who had lost her kingdom due to Dalhousie's doctrine of lapse—had little choice when rebels surrounded her and her own guards joined them.[57]

Amid nominal political leadership, the sepoys retained significant autonomy throughout the Rebellion. The British believed that the rebel sepoys communicated via chapatis, a round flat bread, that maybe held meaning themselves or perhaps were used to conceal messages.[58] That delightful tidbit is contested. But there is no doubt that the rebels used recently expanded print technology, including lithography, to spread their message.[59]

Excerpts from Azamgarh Proclamation, September 1857, Published in the *Delhi Gazette*

It is well known to all, that in this age the people of Hindustan, both Hindoos and Mahommedans [Muslims], are being ruined under the tyranny and oppression of the infidel and treacherous English. It is therefore the bounden duty of all the wealthy people of India, especially of those who have any sort of connexion with any of the Mohammedan royal families, and are considered the pastors and masters of their people, to stake their lives and property for the well-being of the public . . .

. . .

Section III.—Regarding Public Servants.—It is not a secret thing, that under the British government, natives employed in the civil and military services, have little respect, low pay, and no manner of influence and all the posts of dignity and emolument in both the departments, are exclusively bestowed upon Englishmen . . .

Natives, whether Hindoos or Mohammedans, who fall fighting against the English, are sure to go to heaven; and those killed fighting for the English, will, doubtless, go to hell, therefore, all the natives in the British service ought to be alive to their religion and interest, and, abjuring their loyalty to the English, side with the Badshahi government and obtain salaries of 200 or 300 rupees per month for the present, and be entitled to high posts in future. If they, for any reason, cannot at present declare openly against the English, they can heartily wish ill to their cause, and remain passive spectators of passing events, without taking any active share therein. But at the same time they should indirectly assist the Badshahi government and try their best to drive the English out of the country.

All the sepoys and sowars who have for the sake of their religion, joined in the destruction of the English, and are at present, on any consideration in a state of concealment, either at home or elsewhere, should present themselves to me without the least delay or hesitation.

Foot soldiers will be paid at the rate of three annas, and sowars at eight or twelve annas per diem for the present, and afterwards they will be paid double of what they get in the British service. Soldiers not in the English service, and taking part in the war against the English, will receive the daily subsistence-money. According to the rate specified below for the present; and in future the foot soldiers will be paid at the rate of eight or ten rupees, and sowars at the rate of twenty or thirty rupees, per month and on the permanent establishment of the Badshahi government, will stand entitled to the highest posts in the state, to jagheers [land grants] and presents—

Matchlockmen	2 annas a-day.
Riflemen	2½ do.
Swordsmen	1½ do.
Horsemen, with large horses	8 do.
Do. with small do.	6 do.[60]

Many rebels claimed to protect Hindu and Muslim religious sentiments. Numerous documents spoke of Hindus and Musalmans in tandem, including the Mughals' Azamgarh Proclamation (excepted here) that was issued in August and published in September in the *Delhi Gazette*. Some sepoys spoke more generally about religion (din) as the uniting reason for their fight.[61] An Urdu pamphlet printed in Lucknow exhorted: "For the defence of their respective religions (*din aur dharam*), all Hindus and Muslims, women and men, should devote themselves to the slaughter of the English."[62] Adding in a racial dimension, one rebel reportedly proclaimed: "All black men are one. It is a matter of religion (din). Why should we lose our religion?"[63] Such proclamations carried force, in large part, against the backdrop of a growing emphasis on religious identities stoked by British colonial ideas, including Orientalist scholarship (chapter 17). Rebels also used practical means to recruit people to their cause. Nana Sahib promised a lifetime pension to the surviving female relatives of any man who died in battle, while the Azamgarh Proclamation included a pay scale for rebel fighters.[64]

Violence was definitional to the Sepoy Rebellion, which included civilian casualties from the start. In Kanpur, Nana Sahib ordered the slaughter of several hundred evacuating British in June and then in July directed the remaining British women and children hacked to pieces and thrown into a well, even as British forces were advancing to retake the city.[65] In Lucknow, many British and loyal sepoys took refuge in a set of buildings called the Residency, where they were besieged for months with some dying slow, painful deaths. Unsurprisingly, the British zeroed in on such violence as emblematic of alleged Indian brutality, an old point of prejudice, while ignoring their own barbarity.

The British mercilessly suppressed the Sepoy Rebellion and collectively punished the Indian population in its aftermath, as events in Delhi exemplify. In September of 1857, British soldiers and Sikh sepoys retook the city, along with assistance from Punjabi, Gurkha, and Kashmiri troops.[66] They soon began killing rebel soldiers and civilians. They lined up people in Delhi's streets and shot them in what one Company commander described as "literally murder."[67] Some Indians, including Mughal princes, were beheaded, and others were hanged on British gallows erected throughout the city.[68] Rebels that survived were sometimes sent across the *kala pani* (ocean, literally "black waters") to the Andaman Islands, where the British resurrected a previously abandoned penal colony.[69] The act of crossing the ocean prompted a loss of caste as per common beliefs at the time, which was a further humiliation. In Delhi, the British and their allies desecrated Delhi's Jama Masjid (congregational mosque) by cooking pork and (separately) urinating therein.[70] In the words of Urdu writer Muhammad Zakaullah (1832–1910), "Delhi turned hellish."[71]

Even in the midst and immediate aftermath of the Sepoy Rebellion, Indian allies supported the British. Loyal sepoys constituted about two-thirds of troops who retook Delhi for the British, and they articulated their own reasons for acting. For example, some Sikhs had recently been beaten by north Indian sepoys in two Anglo-Sikh wars (1845–1846 and 1848–1849) and so sought revenge.[72] Some invoked older pseudo-historic memories, such as the Punjabi poet Khazan Singh who, writing in 1858, cited Tegh Bahadur's alleged curse of Aurangzeb (who had the Sikh leader executed in 1675): "The Sikhs will come and despoil your city."[73] Some Indian princes helped track down rebels for money. For instance, Maulavi Ahmadullah, a south Indian elite and a Sufi martial leader, was wanted by the British for advocating *jihad* (righteous war) against the Company. He fled from Awadh in 1858 and sought refuge with the Raja of Rohilkhand who, instead, blew him up via cannon and cut off his head to claim the British reward of 50,000 rupees.[74]

The Sepoy Rebellion and its aftermath were defining acts in the history of British colonialism in India. The storyline is messy, since sepoys fought on both sides of the conflict. Additionally, most Indians (especially in Madras Presidency) sat out these bellicose events that rocked the northern subcontinent. Still, the Sepoy Rebellion changed political affairs for all Indians moving forward.

Advent of the British Raj

The Sepoy Rebellion compelled drastic changes to British colonialism in South Asia. In 1858 alone, the British took three major decisions: they ended the Mughal dynasty, dissolved Company rule, and instituted direct rule of the British crown over the majority of India. Formally, three sequential actions enacted these changes: respectively, the trial and exile of Bahadur Shah Zafar in January–March 1858, the Government of India Act of 1858, and Queen Victoria's Proclamation of 1858 (printed below). The net effect was that the British crown tightened its grip on India. The British royalty had been involved in governance and war on the subcontinent for decades and had taken over increasing decision-making powers from the Company. Still, things were different under the British Raj (1858–1947), beginning with dethroning the Mughal emperor.

The Mughal dynasty was ended via a sham trial of the infirm and elderly Bahadur Shah Zafar. The British held the mock proceedings within Delhi's Mughal-built Red Fort for theatrical effect and blamed Bahadur Shah as a Muslim.[75] The prosecutor argued that Bahadur Shah was "head of the Mahommedan faith in India" and so responsible for the "Mussalman intrigue and Mahommedan conspiracy [to which] we may mainly attribute the dreadful calamities of the year 1857."[76] Even during the Rebellion, the British exhibited what E. A. Reade, a lieutenant-governor, described as "mussulmanophobia" (i.e., Islamophobia), and such sentiments still ran high a year later.[77] The British projection of Bahadur Shah as an evil mastermind contrasted sharply to the deposed emperor's sickly appearance, seen in a final surviving photograph from May 1858 (figure 18.1). As art historians have noted: "[The photograph] presents the last Mughal emperor devoid of the accouterments of court and ceremonial, in plain clothes and without his crown, his only solace a huqqa pipe lingering in the foreground, an echo of the conventions of eighteenth-century Mughal painting. The photograph forms a poignant bookend to the visual narrative of Mughal rule."[78] Bahadur Shah was convicted, of course, and exiled to Burma, thereby clearing the path for there to be one sovereign—a British sovereign—declared as ruler of India.

Queen Victoria outlined the basic structure of the British Raj in her November 1858 Proclamation, which was published in English and numerous Indian vernaculars. Her vision prioritized British culture and control. For instance, the proclamation is laced with Christian rhetoric, reflecting contemporary British ideas of their cultural and religious superiority. The queen endorsed violence against rebel Indians to ensure British domination in South Asia. She positioned the Raj as successor to "honorable" Company rule. Additionally, she skirted, or at least simplified, the truth at times. For instance, she promised industry and public works for the benefit of Indians without mentioning that building Indian roads, railways, irrigation canals, and the like enriched the Brit-

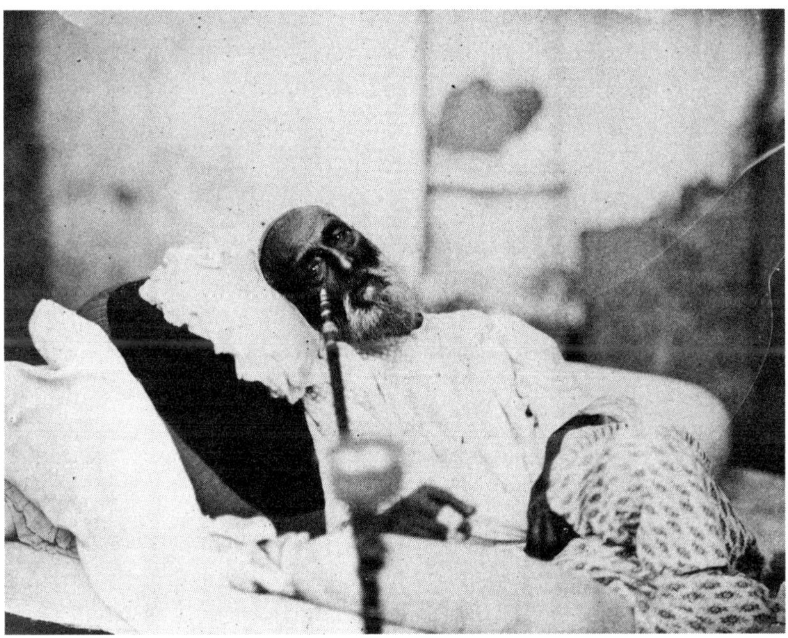

Figure 18.1. Mughal Emperor Bahadur Shah Zafar II (d. 1862) awaiting British deportation in Delhi, May 1858 CE.

ish. I reproduce this lengthy document in full (and with its original capitalization) because it sets the tone for how the British Empire proceeded in India for the next ninety years.

Queen Victoria's Proclamation to Princes, Chiefs, and People of India, November 1858

Victoria, by the Grace of God, of the United Kingdom of Great Britain and Ireland, and of the Colonies and Dependencies thereof in Europe, Asia, Africa, America, and Australasia, Queen, Defender of the Faith.

Whereas, for divers weighty reasons, We have resolved, by and with the advice and consent of the Lords Spiritual and Temporal, and Commons, in Parliament assembled, to take upon Ourselves the Government of the Territories in India heretofore administered in trust for Us by the Honorable East India Company:

Now, therefore, We do by these Presents notify and declare that, by the advice and consent aforesaid, We have taken upon Ourselves the said Government; and We hereby call upon all Our Subjects within the said Territories to be faithful, and to bear true Allegiance to Us, Our Heirs, and Successors, and to submit themselves to the authority of those whom We may hereafter, from time to time, see fit to appoint to administer the Government of Our said Territories, in Our name and on Our behalf:

And We, reposing especial trust and confidence in the loyalty, ability, and judgement of Our right trusty and well beloved Cousin and Councillor, Charles John Viscount Canning, do hereby constitute and appoint him, the said Viscount Canning, to be Our first Viceroy and Governor-General in and over Our said Territories, and to administer the Government thereof in Our name, and generally to act in Our name and on Our behalf, subject to such Orders and Regulations as he shall, from time to time, receive from Us through one of Our Principal Secretaries of State:

And We do hereby confirm in their several Offices, Civil and Military, all Persons now employed in the Service of the Honorable East India Company, subject to Our future pleasure, and to such Laws and Regulations as may hereafter be enacted.

We hereby announce to the Native Princes of India that all Treaties and Engagements made with them by or under the authority of the Honorable East India Company are by Us accepted, and will be scrupulously maintained; and We look for the like observance on their part.

We desire no extension of Our present territorial Possessions; and while We will permit no aggression upon Our Dominions or Our Rights, to be attempted with impunity, We shall sanction no encroachment on those of others. We shall respect the Rights, Dignity and Honour of Native Princes as Our own; and We desire that they, as well as Our own Subjects, should enjoy that Prosperity and that social Advancement which can only be secured by internal Peace and good Government.

We hold Ourselves bound to the Natives of Our Indian Territories by the same obligations of Duty which bind Us to all Our other Subjects; and those Obligations, by the Blessings of Almighty God, We shall faithfully and conscientiously fulfil.

Firmly relying Ourselves on the truth of Christianity, and acknowledging with gratitude the solace of Religion, We disclaim alike the Right and the Desire to impose our Convictions on any of Our Subjects. We declare it to be Our Royal Will and Pleasure that none be in any wise favored, none molested or disquieted by reason of their Religious Faith or Observances; but that all shall alike enjoy the equal and impartial protection of the Law: and We do strictly charge and enjoin all those who may be in authority under Us, that they abstain from all interference with the Religious Belief or Worship of any of Our Subjects, on pain of Our highest Displeasure.

And it is Our further Will that, so far as may be, Our Subjects, of whatever Race or Creed, be freely and impartially admitted to Offices in Our Service, the Duties of which they may be qualified, by their education, ability, and integrity, duly to discharge.

We know, and respect, the feelings of attachment with which the Natives of India regard the Lands inherited by them from their Ancestors; and We desire to protect them in all Rights connected therewith, subject to the equitable demands of the State; and We will that generally, in framing and administering the Law, due regard be paid to the ancient Rights, Usages, and Customs of India.

We deeply lament the evils and misery which have been brought upon India by the acts of ambitious Men, who have deceived their Countrymen by false reports, and led them into open Rebellion. Our Power has been shewn by the Suppression of that Rebellion in the field; We desire to shew Our Mercy, by pardoning the Offences of those who have been thus misled, but who desire to return to the path of Duty.

Already in one Province, with a view to stop the further effusion of blood, and to hasten the Pacification of Our Indian Dominions, Our Viceroy and Governor-General has held out the expectation of Pardon, on certain terms, to the great majority of those who, in the late unhappy Disturbances, have been guilty of Offences against our Government, and has declared the Punishment which will be inflicted on those whose Crimes place them beyond the reach of forgiveness. We approve and confirm the said act of Our Viceroy and Governor-General, and do further announce and proclaim as follows:–

Our Clemency will be extended to all Offenders, save and except those who have been, or shall be, convicted of having directly taken part in the Murder of British Subjects. With regard to such the Demands of Justice forbid the exercise of mercy.

To those who have willingly given asylum to Murderers, knowing them to be such, or who may have acted as leaders or instigators in Revolt, their lives alone can be guaranteed; but, in apportioning the

Penalty due to such Persons, full consideration will be given to the circumstances under which they have been induced to throw off their allegiance; and large indulgence will be shewn to those whose Crimes may appear to have originated in too credulous acceptance of the false reports circulated by designing Men.

To all others in Arms against the Government, We hereby promise unconditional Pardon, Amnesty, and Oblivion of all Offence against Ourselves, Our Crown and Dignity, on their return to their homes and peaceful pursuits.

It is Our Royal Pleasure that these Terms of Grace and Amnesty should be extended to all those who comply with their Conditions before the First Day of January next.

When, by the Blessing of Providence, internal Tranquility shall be restored, it is Our earnest Desire to stimulate the peaceful Industry of India, to promote Works of Public Utility and Improvement, and to administer its Government for the benefit of all Our Subjects resident therein. In their Prosperity will be Our Strength; in their Contentment Our Security; and in their Gratitude Our best Reward. And may the God of all Power grant to Us, and to those in authority under Us, Strength to carry out Our Wishes for the good of Our people.[79]

Queen Victoria's 1858 proclamation conceded to pressures laid bare by the Sepoy Rebellion. Most notably, it froze British territorial expansion on the subcontinent, a reversal of Dalhousie's policy of aggressively taking over princely states. British territory remained stable in India for the next ninety years, with direct rule over about 63 percent of the subcontinent's land and 78 percent of its population (Indian princes controlled the rest).[80] In a nod to the power of rumor concerning greased cartridges, Queen Victoria promised that the British would not interfere in South Asian religious practices going forward. As explored in later chapters, colonial officials found this promise difficult to keep. They faced pressure from Indian reformers who, like Rammohan Roy regarding sati earlier (chapter 17), solicited state intervention on social issues with religious implications, such as child marriage and sending girls to school. In such cases, it was hotly contested what, exactly, noninterference in religion meant. The 1858 proclamation was clearer on Queen Victoria's position as ruler over the subcontinent. From this point forward, Victoria projected herself as sovereign of India, formally adopting the title "Empress of India" in 1876.[81]

Conclusion: Remaking Identities

The advent of the British Raj (1858–1947)—the second major phase of British colonialism in India—impacted all Indians. About two-fifths of the subcontinent's land remained under the discrete control of hundreds of local princes (and a few princesses). In princely territories, British influences were generally more subdued. Still, even they experienced the technological and cultural changes that accompanied colonial governance (e.g., printing presses and English-language schooling, as discussed). In the next chapter, I turn to further developments in the early decades of the British Raj in which Indians produced and negotiated new kinds of information about themselves and in so doing reshaped Indian identities.

Further Reading

On the Sikh Kingdom and its aftermath, I relied on scholarship by Priya Atwal, Tony Ballantyne, Purnima Dhavan, and J. S. Grewal. Michael Fisher's work on Company annexation is strong, and I consulted others on specific regions (e.g., Matthew Cook on Sind). Ulrike Stark's work on early publishing and lithography is excellent. Many scholars have written on the Sepoy Rebellion, and I found especially compelling work by Ilyse Morgenstein Fuerst, Rudrangshu Mukherjee, Kim Wagner, and essays in the seven volumes edited by Crispin Bates and others. Pramod Nayar and K. C. Yadav offer solid resources on the trial of Bahadur Shah Zafar.

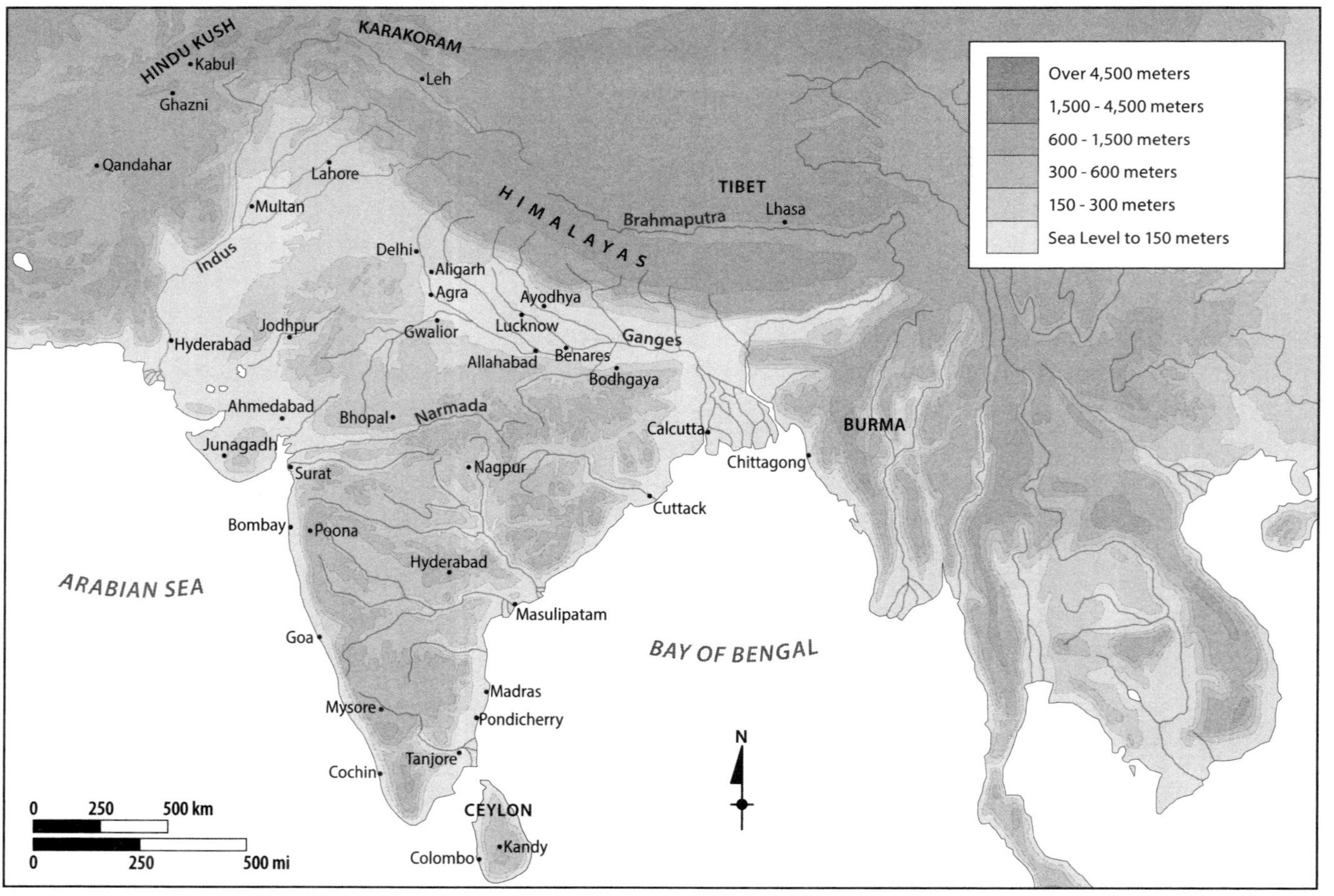

Topographical map of South Asia.

19

Knowing India and Indians, 1860–1900

Every few miles the water changes,
every eight miles, the language too.

–Hindustani maxim[1]

Between 1864 and 1877, Nain Singh—a schoolteacher from the Himalayan region of Kumaon—visited Tibet four times, mapping the region from Lhasa to Leh for the Great Trigonometrical Survey of India. He was one of many Indians to participate in British-led efforts to produce unprecedented knowledge about the subcontinent, its surrounding areas, and South Asian peoples during the early decades of the British Raj (1858–1947).[2] During the Raj, the British crown directly ruled three-fifths of the subcontinent and oversaw the remainder via Indian princes. The colonial apparatus ca. 1860s–1890s changed features of everyday life and social organization, especially as new kinds of information informed what and how Indians thought about themselves. I cover key shifts here, focusing on how Indians participated in producing such knowledge and then used and contested it to transform their society.

Counting Indians in the Colonial Census

In the initial decades of the Raj, British colonialists spearheaded projects to learn about India and Indians using statistical, scientific metrics. For example, the Great Trigonometrical Survey of India, begun in 1802, triangulated distances by measuring the subcontinent and beyond, stretching into Burma and Tibet. A rash of additional surveys followed, including cadastral (land) surveys in the 1860s–1870s, the Botanical Survey in 1890, the Linguistic Survey in 1894, and so forth. These surveys produced copious amounts of knowledge—following scientific standards of the time—about colonial-era Indian society, which nobody had known previously. For example, the Linguistic Survey results were published in twenty-one volumes and documented 723 linguistic varieties.[3] Indians had long been aware that they spoke many languages, but there is a gulf of difference between a general lived experience of linguistic diversity, as per this chapter's epigraph, versus the Linguistic Survey's statistical documentation of subcontinental dialects and languages. While all colonial surveys had social effects, one stands out as especially transformative: the census, begun in 1871–1872 and thereafter repeated every decade.

The British Raj was the first government to carry out a statistical census of any South Asian population. A handful of earlier rulers—including the Mughals (late sixteenth century) and the Rathors of Marwar (mid-seventeenth century)—had attempted to sketch out basic features of their subjects, but their efforts were representative (not comprehensive), allowed for plural categories, and did not furnish comparative data.[4] In contrast, the British counted and compared every single Indian. They used mutually exclusive categories that objectified and quantified difference regarding religion, caste, languages spoken, literacy, marital status, and more.[5] The first census of British India was conducted in 1871–1872 and counted over 200 million Indians. In 1881, the census was expanded to most princely states, swelling the number surveyed to 250 million.[6] The census was notable both as an exercise of state power and for producing and reifying social categories, and I consider each in turn.

The British devoted resources to the census because it served their political interests. In the counting itself, the exercise displayed colonial control by imposing state wishes on every Indian. Furthermore, the census was a "conquest of knowledge" through which colonial rulers defined the identities of their Indian subjects.[7] More practically, the "epistemic regime" of the census furnished information that informed military and administrative objectives, such as more accurate taxation schemes.[8] Indian communities understood that the census empowered the colonial state. Reflecting this, the 1871–1872 census report included a chapter on the "demeanour of the people during the census, and the various rumours that were current at the time."[9] These included imaginative concerns, such as that the British sought to locate blood sacrifice victims for railway bridges.[10] However, perhaps the most common fear was an accurate one, namely that the census would serve as a "tax ticket."[11]

Misgivings aside, many Indians were involved in conducting the census, as in nearly all facets of colonial state governance. Roughly half a million Indians, mainly volunteers, collected data for the 1881 census.[12] By 1901, more than 1.3 million enumerators participated in the counting that was completed in a single day.[13] Where possible, the British recruited locally, which helped reach more challenging populations. For example, in 1871–1872, a village leader conducted a preliminary count of hill tribes in the Vizagapatam District of southern India by going village to village and making a knot in a rope for each person.[14] Seen from the ground up, then, the census was a social experiment performed jointly by the British and Indians that—through its process and the data it produced—accentuated certain social categories, especially religion and caste.

The census proved a powerful tool in forging modern Indian religious identities. By asking about religion at all (a subject not included on censuses of Britain at the time), the colonial state projected religion as a central Indian social category.[16] Additionally, census officials limited each Indian to a single religious identity. The cumulative results are seen on the subcontinent today, where religious identity is often socially vital and exclusive. In the late nineteenth century, this was a notable shift that departed from earlier, sometimes more fluid, forms of religious identity. While the stated goal of the census was to document Indian society as it already existed, in practice it in equal measure brought new realities into being.

The census reified the religious category of "Hindu" in particular ways. In the late nineteenth century, many "Hindus" did not think of themselves as part of the same tradition, either by that or any other label. For example, Brahmo Samaj member Pratap Chandra Mazumdar said of the spiritual teacher Ramakrishna in 1879: "What is there common between him and me? I, a Europeanized, civilized, self-centred, semi-sceptical, so-called educated reasoner, and he, a poor, illiterate, shrunken, unpolished, diseased, half-idolatrous friendless Hindu devotee?"[17] Both were counted as Hindu on the colonial census, along with others who had long used discrete identifiers such as Vaishnavites, Shaivites, Shakta

Enumerator Schedule from the 1881 Census of India[15]

FORM OF ENUMERATOR'S SCHEDULE

***District*______, *Sub-division*______, *Tháná*______, *Circle No.*______, (*Circle officer*______), *Village*______, (*No.*______),**

***Enumerator of Beat No.*______.**

***House No.* (______).**

1	2	3	4	5	6	7	8	9	10	11	12
					RELIGION						
Serial number of each inmate.	Name.	Condition, i.e., whether married or unmarried, widow or widower.	Sex.	Age last birthday.	Religion.	Caste if Hindu; sect if of other religion.	Mother-tongue.	* Place of birth. † ‡	§ Occupation of men, also of females who may do work.	*Education.* 1. Under instruction. 2. Not under instruction, but able to read and write. 3. Not under instruction and not able to read and write.	*Infirmities.* 1. Unsound mind. 2. Deaf-mutes from birth. 3. Blind. 4. Lepers.

* If a European British subject, add "British subject."

† If of mixed European and Asiatic parentage, add "Eurasian."

‡ If a foreigner, state of what country.

§ Boys at school, small children, and women who perform no regular work, should not be shown at all under column 10.

worshippers, Lingayats, Satnamis, Ramanandis, bhaktas, and Brahmins. Census officials slotted many Indians into the broad category of "Hindu," including those who articulated mixed religious identities to enumerators. For instance, those who identified as "Brahmin Christian" or "Kshatriya Christian" in the 1871–1872 census were likely recategorized as "Hindoo."[18] Such acts rendered the category of "Hindu" more prevalent, important to contest, and politically powerful.

Caste, too, was emphasized in the census, which ultimately altered and entrenched this social hierarchy. Caste had operated as a premodern system of Indian social stratification for millennia, as detailed throughout this book (especially chapters 2, 5, 7, 9, 11, 12, and 14–18). Additionally, Brahminical thinkers had long justified caste as part of their dharma. One colonial innovation was to bring together practice and theory, even before the census. For example, in 1825, Eurasian James Skinner wrote the Persian work *Tashrih al-aqvam* (Account of peoples) that described and illustrated caste groups based on ethnographic observations but using categories drawn from Brahmin-authored dharmashastra texts.[19]

Half a century later, colonial census officials similarly tried to club together the Brahminical theory of caste and its messy social realities. For example, during the 1881 census, colonial officials consulted the Bengali Brahmin thinker Rajendra Lal Mitra (d. 1891), who gave a ranked list of castes based on old Sanskrit texts. As Mitra put it: "[The census's] duty is clearly to follow the textbooks of the Hindus and not to decide on particular claims."[20] But census officials had to adjudicate claims when caste communities contested census categories, such as when a group classified as Vaishyas objected that the census did not recognize them as equal to Rajputs (who are Kshatriyas).[21] The census also innovated in treating caste as a pan-Indian social reality (rather than as a feature of local life). The end result of repeated categorizing, ranking, and contestation regarding castes from different parts of India was substantial innovation to an old social order.

Beyond British India, others, too, documented caste groups as a way of describing Indian society at this time. For example, Nanjundayya's *Ethnographical Survey of Mysore*, published beginning in 1906, categorizes communities in that large princely state by caste. Nanjundayya treats religion as a relatively minor feature of each caste group, mentioned after a host of others, including marriage norms, puberty ceremonies, birth and death rituals, origin, and language(s) spoken.[22] Photography also offered a way to capture snapshots of Indian communities around 1900, from Kashmiri peasant women to Brahmin elites (figures 19.1 and 19.2).

Economics, Education, and Law

The British Raj developed a robust state apparatus that altered the possibilities of life—and the arenas of contestation—for many Indians. Perhaps more than any other, Thomas Macaulay's ideas shaped the colonial state, including the Penal Code that was drafted in the 1830s and implemented in 1860. Also following Macaulay, the British Raj promoted English in higher education, thus producing an elite Indian upper class positioned to mold their own English-medium public sphere. Still, in many areas, colonial administration was haphazard at best.[23] While the British administered India to benefit themselves, their decisions most immediately impacted Indians and enabled new kinds of imagined Indian communities. Here I investigate both aspects, analyzing how colonial state policies changed, or inspired changes, regarding economics, education, and law.

The British Raj followed its colonial predecessor, the British East India Company, in setting trade policies that enriched Britain and impoverished India. For example, under the British Raj, cotton imports to India skyrocketed. In the 1830s, India imported sixty million yards of cotton from Britain annually, rising by 1870 to more than a billion yards annually, more than three yards for every living Indian.[24] This was a powerful legacy of the Western-based Industrial Revolution (1760–1840) that shifted manufacturing in favor of Europe. These global trends undercut India's native cotton industry, and especially female weavers were unable to compete with global prices. Decades later in the 1930s, the human cost of exploitative British Raj economic policies was painfully clear to Gendun Chopel, a Tibetan monk who traveled in India and Ceylon between 1934 and 1946: "As for the lowly, their small livelihoods that provide the necessities for life are sucked like blood from all their orifices. Such a wonderous land as India appears to be filled with poor people who are like hungry ghosts."[25]

Figure 19.1. Kashmiri women under the watchful eye of an overseer, 1895 CE, photographer unknown.

Figure 19.2. Three Brahmins writing out manuscripts in Kashmir, 1895 CE, photographer unknown.

Opium continued to rank high among colonial Indian exports. Britain fought two wars—in 1839–1842 and 1856–1860, respectively—to enforce its ability to export Indian opium to China. Opium's addictive powers drive people to poison themselves with the drug, and such social ills were widely, painfully known at the time. Dadabhai Naoroji, who was involved in British and Indian politics at different points, repeatedly criticized the interlinked vice and profit of the British-led opium trade. His 1901 bestselling book included one such excoriating analysis (excerpted here), pointing up how the British materially benefited from knowingly poisoning the Chinese.[26] To break for a moment into stark presentism, his sharp words hold special salience given the opioid epidemic that has ravaged both the United States and parts of India, especially the Punjab, since the 2010s.[27]

Criticism of the Opium Trade, Excerpt from Dadabhai Naoroji's *Poverty and Un-British Rule in India*, 1901

There is the opium trade. What a spectacle it is to the world! In England, no statesman dares to propose that opium may be allowed to be sold in public houses at the corners of every street, in the same way as beer or spirits. On the contrary, Parliament, as representing the whole nation, distinctly enacts that "opium and all preparations of opium or of 'poppies,' as 'poison,' be sold by certified chemists only, and every box, bottle, vessel, wrapper, or cover in which such poison is contained, be distinctly labelled with the name of the article and the world 'poison,' and with the name and address of the seller of the poison." And yet, at the other end of the world, this Christian, highly civilised, and humane England forces a "heathen" and "barbarous" Power to take this "poison," and tempts a vast human race to use it, and to degenerate and demoralize themselves with this "poison"! And why? Because India cannot fill up the remorseless drain; so China must be dragged in to make it up, even though it be by being "poisoned."

It is wonderful how England reconciles this to her conscience. This opium trade is a sin on England's head, and a curse on India for her share in being the instrument. This may sound strange as coming from any Natives of India, as it is generally represented as if India it was that benefited by the opium trade.

> The fact simply is that, as Mr. [Grant] Duff said, India is nearly ground down to dust, and the opium trade of China fills up England's drain. India derives not a particle of benefit. All India's profits of trade, and several millions from her very produce (scanty as it is, and becoming more and more so), and with these all the profits of opium, go the same way of the drain–to England. Only India shares the curse of the Chinese race. Had this cursed opium trade not existed, India's miseries would have much sooner come to the surface, and relief and redress would have come to her long ago; but this trade has prolonged the agonies of India.[28]

One group of Indians—English-educated, upper-caste, wealthy elites—capitalized on the opportunities within the British Raj to claim new social privileges. This group was a severe minority. The 1881 census indicated that less than 1 percent of Indian men were literate in any language. Among Indian women, only four out of every 1,000 were able to read, at most.[29] Literacy—a rarity in all premodern societies—was concentrated among the privileged in British India. Brahmins accounted for 69 percent of graduates from Madras University in 1894 and boasted higher percentages at other colleges.[30] Also, only the wealthy could afford Indian universities, with Presidency College in Calcutta charging nearly five times the fees of Oxford University in 1870.[31] Still, for the select group able to use their preexisting caste and wealth privileges, English-medium instruction offered promising possibilities.

Some English-educated Indian graduates pursued newer professions such as journalism, thereby participating in India's broad transition from a premodern oral society to a modern world reliant on mass-produced written materials to circulate political and social news. Six college graduates, all Brahmin men, founded the English-medium newspaper *The Hindu* in 1878 as a weekly paper, making it a daily paper—the first Indian-owned daily—in 1889. One of *The Hindu*'s founders later articulated their goals as follows: "We knew that public feeling, not only politically and morally, but socially, is influenced in all countries by the tone of their public journals, as the community is bound however unconsciously to imbibe the spirit of the newspaper which its members daily read; and realised the responsibility of the undertaking, and the immense evil that would be inflicted on the community if we failed to develop those qualities of political moral and social well-being which are so essential for the advancement of the nation."[32] Indeed, the archives of *The Hindu* and other newspapers serve today as key sources for accessing debates within Indian society during the British Raj.

Many Indian princes—an ultra-elite group—knew or learned English in this period and integrated themselves to a great degree socially with the British, with whom they shared ruling interests. Some princes were part of the Order of the Star of India, established by Queen Victoria in 1861.[33] In 1875–1876, the Prince of Wales spent six months touring India, and princes competed to present him with lavish textiles, weapons, and jewels. In return, he gifted them copies of Max Muller's English translation of the Rig Veda, completed in England, which seemed to echo the colonial strategy of importing raw goods from the colony, processing, and re-exporting.[34] The flashiest displays of allyship between the British monarchy and Indian princes came at three imperial durbars in Delhi in 1877, 1903, and 1911, respectively (figures 19.3 and 19.4). Displaying "medieval mania," British imperial durbars drew extensively on Mughal imagery while communicating a very different, colonial ruling relationship.[35]

Despite an emerging English-educated class of Indians, the British Raj remained fiercely racist, and this came out powerfully in controversies over judgeships. An early test case arose when Muthuswamy Iyer was appointed to the Madras High Court in 1878, which prompted bigoted objections in the English-medium press, such as "Subordination to a Brahmin is an outrage which makes the blood boil in the veins of a European."[36] Racial tensions recurred during early 1880s debates about the Ilbert Bill, which proposed to give qualified Indian judges authority over British defendants—men and women—in court proceedings.[37] Whereas Iyer's appointment had held, the British Raj bowed to pressure over the Ilbert Bill by gutting most of the legislation before it passed.[38]

To some, the Ilbert Bill controversy highlighted the limits of any reform of British colonial rule. As a Poona publication put it in 1883: "We can never hope or deserve success if we foolishly rely upon the personal magnanimity of those who rule India."[39] To others, the lesson was to build up civil society, as *The Hindu* argued: "Had [voluntary] Associations existed, would not the united voice of two hundred millions of India's people drowned even the London Thunderer [*The Times*], and rendered it unavailing against Ilbert's Bill or any other useful reform in India?"[40] The Ilbert Bill affair ultimately prompted the founding of the

Figure 19.3. Begum of Bhopal during the 1911 CE British royal tour of India, printed in 1914.

Indian National Congress, a transformative group that later led India's independence movement (chapter 21).

The colonial legal system regulated all manner of behavior, and a set of debates about child marriage allows us to glimpse frequently overlooked figures in British India, namely Indian women. The issue was correlated with female education since, as Rukhmabai powerfully argued in 1885, women were rarely allowed to continue their education after marriage (see excerpt). Rukhmabai herself had been married at the age

Figure 19.4. Nizam of Hyderabad bowing to King George V and Queen Mary at the Delhi Durbar, 1911 CE, Delhi, India.

of eleven, but, unusually, she continued her education. When she reached her twenties, her husband wanted to enforce his conjugal rights, she refused, and they wound up in court. A colonial judge ruled in his favor, prompting reformer Pandita Ramabai to write in 1887 about the decision: "They [the government] have promised to please the males of our country at the cost of women's rights."[41] Rukhmabai chose prison over forced sex with her husband, and her case raised awareness about the plight of Indian women compelled to marry before puberty.

Criticism of Child Marriage, by a Hindu Lady (Rukhmabai), Excerpt from *Times of India*, June 26, 1885

The general apathy towards social improvements which characterizes our people has been telling upon the whole community, but tells most heavily upon the female sex. Hindu social customs do not entail on men half the difficulties which they entail upon women. Excepting the two principal difficulties resulting from infant marriage, they enjoy full mental and physical freedom. Religion or social custom does not, in any way, interfere with their liberty. Marriage does not interpose any insuperable obstacle in the course of their studies. They can marry not only a second wife, on the death of the first, but have the right of marrying any number of wives at one and the same time, or any time they please. If married early, they are not called upon to go to the house and to submit to the tender mercies of a mother-in-law; nor is any restraint put upon their actions because of their marriage. But the case with women is the very reverse of this. If the girl is married at the age of eight (as most of them are), her parents are at liberty to send her to school till she is ten years old; but, if they wish to continue her at school longer, they must obtain the express permission of the girl's mother-in-law. But even in these advanced times, and even in Bombay—the chief centre of civilization—how many mothers-in-law are there who send their daughters to school after they are ten years old!

Thus, Mr. Editor, when we are just beginning to appreciate education, we are taken away from school, and therefore you can imagine what progress, if any, we could make in our studies in the scanty time at our disposal. Nothing tangible need be expected from the efforts of our reformers, whose number even in Bombay is insignificantly small—who have dared to oppose the prejudices of their community, and sent their daughters and daughters-in-law to school after the age mentioned above. For even a girl, who is so exceptionally blessed as to have parents holding the most liberal views on education, can only prosecute her studies for three or four years longer, for she is generally a mother before

> she is 14, when she must of sheer necessity give up the dream of mental cultivation, and face the hard realities of life. It seems, therefore, hopeless to expect any advancement in the higher female education, when the custom of infant, or rather early marriage continues as rife as ever. Unless the state of things is changed, all the efforts at higher female education seem like putting the cart before the horse. . . .
>
> As men among Hindus have much more freedom of action than women, they are indifferent to the social reforms which prejudicially affect the other sex. If this defect of theirs is pointed out by strangers (i.e., non-Hindus) instead of being ashamed of it they lose their temper, or at least make a great show of losing it. . . .
>
> Sir, I am one of those unfortunate Hindu women, whose hard lot it is to suffer the unnameable miseries entailed by the custom of early marriage. This wicked practice has destroyed the happiness of my life. It comes between me and that thing which I prize above all others—study and mental cultivation. Without the least fault of mine I am doomed to seclusion; every aspiration of mine to rise above my ignorant sisters is looked upon with suspicion, and is interpreted in the most uncharitable manner.
>
> We have a proverb, which says the "we can philosophically (lit. coolly) bear the misfortunes of our neighbours." This is quite true. To realize other's misery you must feel it yourself. Men cannot, in the least, understand the wretchedness which we Hindu women have to endure.[42]

Following the Rukhmabai decision, reformers advocated for the Age of Consent Bill, which proposed to raise the age of sexual consent for girls from ten to twelve. Indians debated the proposal from the perspective of Hindu religious customs and women's rights. For example, B. G. Tilak (1856–1920) opposed raising the age of consent, as (he argued) it encouraged female independence and infringed on Hindu religious practices (specifically, consummating marriages early).[43] Tilak's view that child marriage for girls was a Hindu custom was backed up by some Orientalists, such as Max Muller, who never traveled to South Asia but nonetheless depicted child marriage as idyllic for Indians at times (notably, not for Europeans).[44] Many Indian women disagreed. This scathing comment was published in a Marathi-medium women's magazine in 1891: "Max Muller saheb is living in a foreign country and will do so forever. He has no first-hand knowledge of an average Indian nor of the behaviour and conduct of our men. Therefore the statements made by the saheb are not uniformly applicable to everyone of us. Among cases of child marriage only around four or five couples out of a hundred live in a state of mutual love and harmony. And around ninety couples do not experience this state of love and affection: instead there is constant bickering and quarrelling in the home."[45] Some of Tilak's arguments favoring child marriage were answered directly by Rukhmabai in two letters that she published in the *Times of India* under the pseudonym "Hindu Lady" (one is excerpted here). Still, the debate was not entirely along gender lines. The male-run *The Hindu* and *Swadesamitran* (a Tamil-medium newspaper founded in 1882) endorsed the Age of Consent Act, as did social reformers like Mahadev Govind Ranade (although Ranade personally engaged in child marriage by marrying an eleven-year-old when he was thirty-one).[46] The Age of Consent Act passed into law in 1891 and was one case where social activism compelled legal changes in British India, over the objections of religious conservatives.

Religious Reforms and Communal Conflict

British India hosted a crowded religious landscape, and many communities underwent immense changes during this period. As the Lahore *Tribune* noted on the former point in March 1889: "Street preaching is very much in vogue here now-a-days. All along Anarkali [Bazaar], Hindu, Mohamedan, Christian, Arya and Brahmo preachers may be seen earnestly expatiating on the excellences of their respective creeds, surrounded by crowds of apparently attentive listeners."[47] In addition to these groups, Parsi, Sikh, Jain, and tribal traditions comprised the Indian social fabric in the late nineteenth century. All Indian religious communities necessarily engaged with the British Raj, and some changed rather substantially, both in connection with colonial pressures and otherwise. In this section, I cover key shifts within late nineteenth-century Muslim and Hindu communities, respectively, turning at the end to interreligious conflict, which grew out of colonial pressures to reify religious identities.

Islamic reform movements of the early British Raj tended to respond, in various ways, to the British blaming Muslims for the 1857 Sepoy Rebellion and ongoing suspected disloyalty (on the rebellion, see chapter 18). For example, in 1871, William Hunter published a book whose title indicates its general tenor: *The Indian Musalmans: Are They Bound in Conscience to Rebel against the Queen?*[48] Syed Ahmad Khan (1817–1898), a notable thinker of the period, responded with his own tract in 1872 that proclaimed the existence of modern Muslims, such as himself, who were loyal to the British and keen to embrace aspects of Western culture. As he put it, "God save me from my friends!"[49] Khan was knighted in 1888 to honor his pro-British participation in the Sepoy Rebellion (leading to his common appellation "Sir Syed").[50] In South Asia, perhaps his greatest legacy was founding Aligarh Muslim University in 1875, which still numbers among India's premier intellectual institutions today.

Other Indians carved out Muslim identities that were more focused on theological innovation. For instance, the Ahmadiyya emerged as a distinct messianic tradition in the Punjab during the late nineteenth century. Their leader, Mirza Ghulam Ahmad (ca. 1839–1908), claimed to be the promised messiah and a prophet. At an 1892 meeting, 500 attendees gathered from Aligarh to Mecca and declared that Ahmadiyya goals included spreading Islam and working with the British.[51] But the group clashed with other Muslims, including many ulama, in part because the Ahmadiyya accepted a new prophet (most Muslims consider Muhammad to be the final prophet). Also, Mirza Ghulam had a knack for accurately predicting the death of his critics, which unnerved people. In one case in 1899, the British intervened by brokering a legal settlement wherein Muhammad Husain, a prominent member of the ulama, promised to cease verbally abusing Mirza Ghulam. In exchange, Mirza Ghulam agreed to stop foretelling the demise of Muhammad Husain and other detractors.[52] The Ahmadiyya continue to face persecution from other Muslim communities today (chapter 23).

Hindu self-identity also underwent robust changes during the British Raj as thinkers responded to ongoing dialogues with Orientalist scholars and European Christian missionaries. One big shift was that some Hindus began to use "arya" or "aryan" as a racial category for upper-caste Hindus. "Arya" is an old Sanskrit word meaning "pure" or "noble" that is used as a cultural and linguistic descriptor in the Vedas, the oldest extant Indian texts (chapter 2). In the late nineteenth century, it was coopted into a burgeoning theory of biological difference—categorized as science in its day—to represent upper-caste Hindus as a superior race.

British and German Orientalists are most well known for this radical redefinition of "arya" based on a crude application of Darwinian theory to human races.[53] The idea was also current in India, where the racially-mixed Theosophy movement based in Madras praised "Aryan moral regeneration."[54] Writing in vernacular languages, some Hindus, too, adopted this racial sense of "arya" to speak of "arya dharma" and thereby constructed a new form of pseudo-ethnic Hindu identity.[55] Some spoke interchangeably about the "Hindu race" and the "aryan race."[56] One group even put the newly racialized word into their name: the Arya Samaj.

The Arya Samaj was a high-caste Hindu reform movement founded in 1875 in the Punjab. Its leader, Dayanand Saraswati (1824–1883), in the words of one scholar, "rejected the popular Puranas, polytheism, idolatry, the role of Brahman priests, pilgrimages, nearly all rituals, and the ban on widow marriage—in short, almost all of contemporary Hinduism."[57] One of Dayanand's major early opponents was Bharatendu Harishchandra, a Vaishnava monotheist who advocated for bhakti and icon veneration.[58] In contrast, Dayanand viciously attacked the Bhagavata Purana, a key Vaishnava text.[59] He also liked to bring up the Maharaja Libel Case from the 1860s, which involved claims of Krishna bhakti leaders exploiting followers financially and (female followers) sexually.[60] Dayanand made other enemies as well, such as Jains who threatened to sue the Arya Samaj leader for his inflammatory representations of Jainism.[61] Among Dayanand's many harsh ideas, two were taken up more widely within Hindu communities and so merit further discussion: conversion and cow protection.

Premodern Hindu practices had not included mechanisms for individual conversion, which the Arya Samaj changed by introducing *shuddhi* rituals to "purify" (i.e., convert) individuals to upper-caste Hinduism. In part, anxiety about British India census numbers and the perception that other religious communities were growing faster than Hindus fed the desire for a conversion program.[62] At first, in the late 1880s, the Arya Samaj targeted Hindus who had converted to Islam or Christianity to be "purified" back into Hinduism. But within a few years, they expanded to evangelize to Sikhs, Dalits, and tribal communities, mimicking the tactics of Western Christian missionaries.[63] The Arya Samaj's conversion activities upset many. For example, members of the Sikh community were outraged in 1900 when the Arya Samaj converted

200 Sikh Dalits in Lahore, including shaving their previously uncut hair (a mark of Sikhism).[64] Some upper-caste Hindus remained unconvinced that shuddhi ceremonies could purify casteless or low-caste peoples and took up weapons in the 1920s to prevent members of the Chamar community (a Dalit group) who had undergone shuddhi from using public wells or entering temples.[65] Despite detractors, shuddhi rituals persisted, and today efforts to convert individuals to upper-caste Hindu practices are predominantly associated with Hindu nationalists.[66]

Cow protection was another Arya Samaj interest that gained traction and, in so doing, popularized upper-caste norms and projected Muslims as an enemy. Not consuming beef had been a marker of certain upper-caste communities since the first millennium CE (earlier, Vedic peoples sacrificed and ate cattle).[67] The Arya Samaj transformed this caste practice into a broad Hindu social and political activity. They established the first *gaurakshas* (cow protection) center in 1879 in Rajasthan, and such sites proliferated in the 1880s and 1890s.[68] Many agitations to "save" cows in the late nineteenth century were led by low-caste groups, such as Ahirs and Kurmis, who aspired to upper-caste attitudes as a means of social advancement.[69] As part of their aspiration to upper-caste behavior, some also assaulted Dalits, specifically Chamars, who came under scrutiny for their work in the leather trade alongside Muslims.[70]

Hindus of various caste backgrounds projected Muslims, who sometimes ate beef and sacrificed cows during religious festivals, as an enemy from whom cows required protection. A shared foe can bring a community together, and the Hindu community was in formation during this period. A 1917 chain letter expresses some of the Hindu unity that was fomented by demonizing Muslims over the prior several decades:

> This letter comes from the world of the cow. It brings an entreaty to brother Hindus. The religion of the cow is being destroyed. What crime has she committed that she should be killed by non-believers? Hindu brothers are entreated to watch over the cow in every village and every house. If they do not, the cow will sadly breathe its last and disappear from the villages. If you see a Musalman with a cow, it is your duty and religion (dharma) to take it from him. It is also your dharma to write and send on

> five letters. If you do not, you bear the sin of cow-slaughter. If you do, it is equivalent to the gift of five cows.[71]

Cow protection activities often involved violence against Muslims (and still do).[72] In the late nineteenth century, such cases were part of a larger trend of accelerating communal tensions.

Hindu movements increasingly demonized Muslims in the late nineteenth-century, which followed the lead of British colonialists and gave the Raj more grist for its propaganda mill. For instance, Dayanand Saraswati blamed Muslims for the alleged decline of Hindu traditions over centuries in his *Satya Prakash* (Light of truth, 1875): "During the rule of the Aryans (i.e., Vedic times), no slaughter was allowed of cows or other serviceable animals. Then men and other creatures lived happily in the Aryavartha (aryavarta) and other countries of the world. Milk, butter, oxen and other animals were in abundance and supply of food articles was up to the mark. From the time the flesh-eating foreigners have come to India and begun slaughtering cows, etc., and the rule has passed to wine-drinking officials, the miseries of the Aryans are gradually increasing."[73] The ancient history imagined by Dayanand is false, but his anti-Muslim sentiments were real and increasingly prevalent. For instance, an 1860s textbook by Benares elite Siva Prasad employed Islamophobic stereotypes about the Mughals, following some British writings on premodern Indian history.[74] Growing sentiments against Muslims also manifested in real-world violence. For instance, the 1800s are the first time that some Hindus attempted to claim the site of the Babri Masjid, a ca.-1528 mosque in Ayodhya in northern India, as the alleged birthplace of Rama, a Hindu god and mythological hero.[75] The Ayodhya issue remains contentious today (chapter 24).

Public festivals were potentially volatile situations amid rising communal tensions in the British Raj. Nineteenth-century Hindu communities cultivated large public celebrations of events that had been smaller or confined to homes previously, such as Ram Lila and Ganesh Chaturthi (Ganesha's birthday), respectively. Violence sometimes erupted, especially when these celebrations overlapped with Muslim holidays, often a cyclical occurrence every several decades since the Muslim lunar calendar rotates major holidays around the solar year.[76] While Hindu-Muslim conflict surfaced largely in the north, parallel (albeit less deadly) clashes in the south sometimes occurred during coinciding Hindu and Christian holidays. For example, in 1891, the Malabar Puram festival and Easter overlapped, prompting conflict between the Nayars and Thomas Christians.[77]

The British benefited from tensions between Indian religious communities by upholding colonial institutions as neutral intermediaries. Section 153A of the Indian Penal Code outlawed "attempts to promote feelings of enmity or hatred between different classes."[78] Every time the British found occasion to use that provision regarding interreligious conflict, it strengthened their argument that colonial rule was needed to keep the peace. Of course, the British conveniently ignored that they held substantial responsibility for cultivating the conditions of large-scale interreligious conflict in South Asia in the first place. In the end, communal tensions far outlived their original colonial context, and Hindu-Muslim conflict is a major feature of modern India.

Showcasing Indian History

British colonialists financed efforts to recover Indian history and protect important sites, which was part of their ruling strategy and shaped general knowledge of South Asian history. As early as 1813, the British East India Company directed repairs to the Taj Mahal and Akbar's Tomb in Agra, noting: "We admit that the credit of our administration is, in some degree, connected with the preservation of these Memorials of the former splendour and majesty of the Indian Empire."[79] This link between preservation and state authority strengthened under the British Raj. Alexander Cunningham, who was especially interested in Buddhists sites in northern India, wrote in 1861: "It will not be to our credit as an enlightened ruling power, if we continue to allow such fields of investigation, as the remains of the old Buddhist capital in Behar, the vast ruins of Kanouj, the plains round Delhi studded with ruins more thickly than even the Campagna of Rome, and many others, to remain without more examination than they have hitherto received."[80] I am more interested here in *how* colonial-era institutions treated and displayed historical sites and artefacts, because those decisions molded everyone's views of premodern India. Colonial-era museums, for example, curated what many Indians knew about their history, and colonial preservation efforts determined the state and status of monuments moving forward. Both left

Figure 19.5. Great stupa and eastern gate at Sanchi constructed ca. third century BCE–first century CE, photograph by James Waterhouse, 1861–1862.

a mix of helpful and problematic legacies with which historians still grapple today.

The Archaeological Survey of India (ASI) was founded 1861 to survey and preserve monuments. British men ran the survey and relied on Indian assistants for labor at dig sites and as translators, while being slow to grant Indians more authority. Raja Rajendralal Mitra (d. 1891) was a notable exception and did critical work at Bodhgaya, where the Gautama Buddha is said to have been enlightened.[81] In its early decades, Archaeological Survey of India officials relied on premodern travelers—such as Faxian and Xuanzhang (chapters 7 and 8)—to identify sites to be considered for surveying and preservation.[82] The organization emphasized spaces, not living people. Even Archaeological Survey of India photographs of monuments trended toward showing few to no people, as if sites like Sanchi (figure 19.5) were timeless markers of a lost past rather than physical monuments within colonial Indian society.[83]

Colonial biases shaped the work of the Archaeological Survey of India. For example, archaeologists divided architecture by religion into "Hindu" and "Muslim" and then projected those categories to be sequential. This was illogical and ahistorical but accorded with the general colonial assumption that everything Indian could be categorized by religion.[84] A striking consequence of this bad assumption concerned the Taj Mahal, an obsession of Lord Curzon, Viceroy of India 1899–1905. Because the Mughal Emperor Shah Jahan built the Taj Mahal, Curzon imagined that the structure must be "Saracenic" (i.e., Islamic) in style but somehow failed to present properly. And so, he made it look more Islamic (in his view) by buying and installing a lamp from Cairo that still hangs in the inner mausoleum chamber today.[85]

The British created museums to showcase Indian cultures and histories. Museums were often known by the Hindustani terms "ajaib ghar" or "ajaib khana" (wonder house) and were wildly successful, judging by the crowds they drew.[86] In 1864, more than 100,000 Indians passed through the Calcutta Museum, and by 1913, 800,000 annually visited major museums in Calcutta and Bombay.[87] Male visitors outnumbered women, although many of the museums had "zenana days" for women in purdah to come, during which even the staff on duty were all women.[88] Some colonial-era Indians even visited museums as part of wedding celebrations or holidays, such as during Pongol in Madras.[89] One curatorial practice developed in this period and still widely used today is displaying artefacts by a mix of dynastic and religious labeling.[90]

Perhaps the largest oversight of archaeologists in the early British Raj concerned the 1872–1873 excavation of Harappa in the northwest. The railway had preceded the excavation at Harappa, and many Indus Civilization bricks were removed to be used as track ballast over a 100-mile stretch between Lahore and Multan.[91] But nobody knew about the Indus Valley Civilization, yet. Alexander Cunningham oversaw the 1872–1873 excavation and uncovered an Indus seal but misidentified it as "foreign to India."[92] Overall, he concluded that he had "found very little worth preserving."[93] Another half century elapsed before anyone understood that the seal was one of many produced by an ancient, indigenous, pre-Vedic Indian civilization. Like many Indian identities and social structures, Indian history was still in formation during the initial decades of the British Raj.

Conclusion: More to Know

As the British Raj ruled much of the subcontinent, they introduced conditions that enabled robust changes within Indian society. Indians helped produce new kinds of information about themselves through the census, museums, and other venues. Then they contested the shifts in identity such knowledge inspired in a thousand ways, via petitions, courts, vigorous debate, education, theological innovations, newspapers, and communal conflict. No consensus arose out of such negotiations, but the terms of engagement changed in ways—especially the forefronting of religious identities—that are still visible in the modernity we inhabit today.

Further Reading

On the census in British India, I used scholarship by Bernard Cohn, Arjun Appadurai, and Peter Gottschalk. Thomas Metcalf's work on British Raj ruling ideologies has withstood the test of time, and I also found the work of Peter van der Veer and R. Suntharalingam helpful on north and south India, respectively. Vasudha Dalmia's scholarship is excellent on late nineteenth-century Hindu reform and early nationalist movements. On museums and archaeology, I relied on work by Tapati Guha-Thakurta, Kavita Singh, and Upinder Singh.

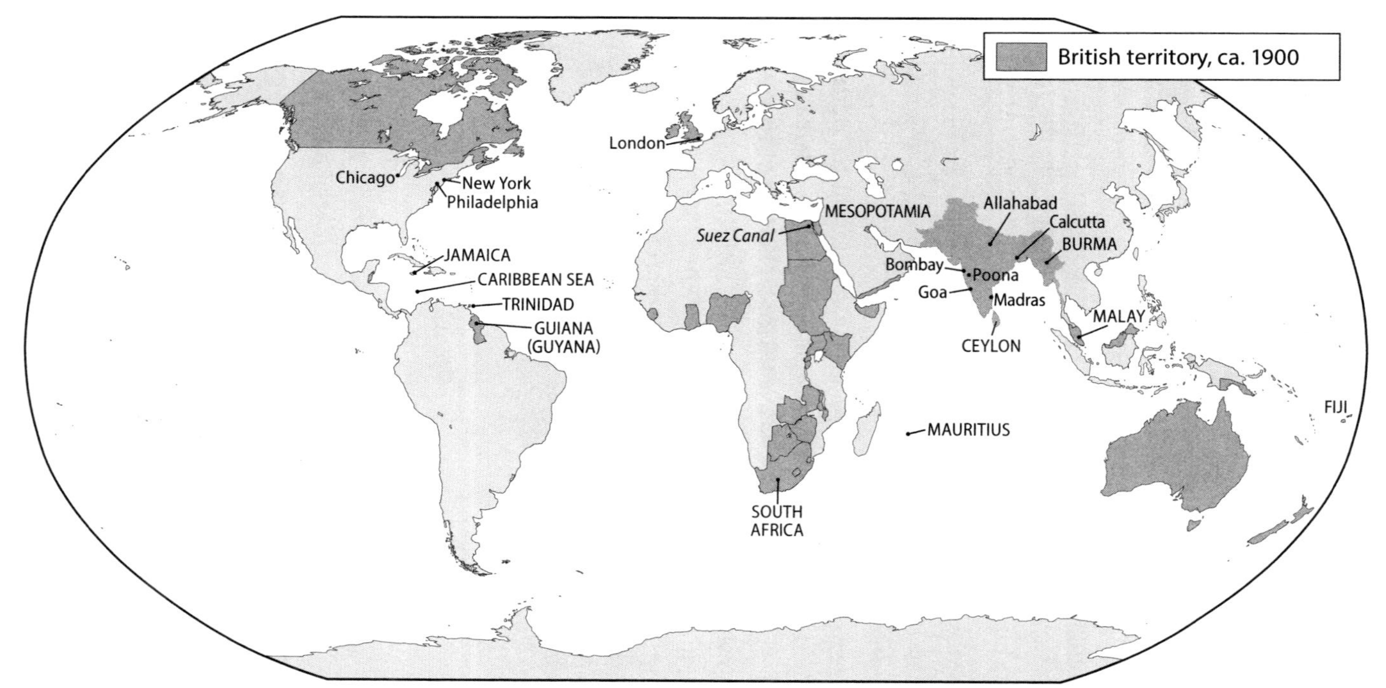

British Empire, ca. 1900.

20

Indians on the Move, 1880–1920

Education is indestructible wealth. He who possesses it is happiest in this world.

—Pandita Ramabai, 1882 (Marathi)[1]

In Ramabai's case, *she* possessed education, and this was unusual in the 1880s when most Indian men—and even more Indian women—were illiterate. Ramabai lived an extraordinary life. In 1883, a year after writing these words praising education, she boarded a steamer at Bombay and headed for London with her two-year-old daughter. They traveled around the globe during the next six years, alighting in Britain, the United States, Canada, Japan, and Hong Kong before returning to India in 1889, where Ramabai (d. 1922) promoted her chief cause: girls' education. Ramabai's remarkable travels and educational activism built upon accelerating trends of Indian migration and social reform around the turn into the twentieth century. Indeed, shifts in domestic and international migration patterns at the height of the British Raj affected millions of Indians, for some leading to new homes forever and for others providing novel experiences that changed their outlooks upon returning to India. Indians also began to travel to the United States, a new phenomenon, in the late nineteenth century. Those who stayed at home, too, found fresh ways to strive for better lives, and Dalit and Shudra activism grew in this period. Overall, the possibilities of human life—including in far-flung locations—expanded for many Indians between 1880 and 1920.

Domestic Travelers and Migrants

Indians traversed the subcontinent in unprecedented numbers and with previously unimaginable speed from the late nineteenth century forward, especially for employment and pilgrimages. New infrastructure—especially the railways that crisscrossed British India and princely states—enabled this surge in mobility. The British first invested in Indian railways in the 1850s, a few decades after having done so in England, to move military troops and supplies. British selfish intentions notwithstanding, the railways soon became widely used by the Indian public. The first line opened in April 1853, connecting Bombay to Thane with twenty-one miles of track, and building accelerated thereafter. By 1875, 6,500 miles of track had been laid, and twenty-six million Indians rode the railways annually. By 1900, 25,000 miles of track transported 175 million Indian passengers every year. By 1920, multiple annual rides had become the norm, and 520 million passengers (out of 318 million Indians) rode 36,000 miles of track per year.[2]

Indians of all socioeconomic backgrounds found their lives changed by the railways. Many worked for railway companies, with an estimated eight million South Asians employed in laying tracks between 1853 and 1900.[3] As of 1900, more than 330,000 Indians were on regular payroll.[4] Far more Indians experienced the railways as riders, most often traveling third class, the most economical and uncomfortable option. Before the 1900s, there were no toilets, water provisions, or food available in third class carriages, which were often overcrowded. In theory, passengers disembarked at stations to use the facilities, although railway employees sometimes kept third-class carriage doors locked to prevent this. Such ill treatment prompted outrage in local papers, and ensuing discussions involved the airing of standard British racism about the "habits" of Indians.[5] Still, colonial insolence did little to dissuade Indian railway travelers, who grew more numerous every year.

Religious pilgrims used India's expanding railway system to attend new religious gatherings fashioned in this age of increased mobility. Perhaps the most famous example is the Kumbh Mela, held every twelve years at the confluence of the Ganges and Yamuna rivers in Allahabad.[6] The Kumbh was developed in the nineteenth century, which saw a broad expansion of large-scale public Hindu celebrations (chapter 19). Colonial Kumbh Melas drew millions of pilgrims and so were massive economic affairs, generating income for local communities ranging from Brahmins who performed rituals for fees to food and trinket sellers.

The Kumbh's crowds posed a dilemma for the colonial state. On the one hand, the British preferred to not interfere in religious affairs as per Queen Victoria's promise designed to avert rebellion (chapter 18). On the other hand, a gathering of millions of Indians stoked colonial fears about infectious disease outbreaks and anticolonial political organizing.[7] Both fears were realized at various colonial Kumbhs. On the latter point, Indian independence leaders found it useful to mix politics and religion, rhetorically and to shield themselves from state oppression.

As some Indians moved around, others stayed home—especially women—and experienced changes in their domestic lives. For instance, in the 1880s, the wives of migrant workers often received money orders containing their husbands' earnings.[8] In some districts, like Saran in Bihar in eastern India, so many men migrated for work that sex ratios became skewed in favor of women.[9] Among upper classes, some men worked for the British Raj and were stationed far from home. One wife, Rokeya Sakhawat Hossain (1880–1932), wrote a remarkable piece of feminist fiction while her husband was away in Bamka, a small town in Bihar.[10] She published the short story, titled "Sultana's Dream," in 1905 in the Madras-based *Indian Ladies' Magazine*. In it, she imagines a matriarchy, Ladyland, where educated women preside over a crime-free utopia while men are kept indoors, "in their proper places" in the mardana ("men's quarters," a play on zenana, women's quarters).[11] Rokeya's interest in promoting women's empowerment also fueled her activism, and in 1909 she opened a school for girls.[12]

Not all domestic travelers were welcomed by the British colonial state, which criminalized entire peripatetic communities. An "itinerant underworld" had come under British scrutiny since Company rule, especially *thuggee*—from which we get English "thug"—a sort of institutionalized banditry.[13] Seeking to restrict itinerant communities, the British applied the Criminal Tribes Act in northern India in 1871 and expanded it across British India in subsequent decades.[14] The Sansi were the largest targeted group in the Punjab, where they were forced into resettlement and labor camps.[15] By independence in 1947, three and a half million Indians—about 1 percent of the total population—had been categorized as belonging to criminal tribes.[16] The major thing that united this set of groups was a historical tendency toward being itinerant, independent of railways or the colonial economy.

Journeying Overseas

Looking beyond the subcontinent, millions of Indians traveled overseas during the British Raj, and several trends characterized this explosion of global travel. First, in a parallel to domestic trends, the sheer scale of movement was unprecedented in world history. One scholar estimates that thirty million Indians braved the high seas between 1834 and 1937, with six million never returning home.[17] The most common destinations, such as Ceylon, Burma, and the Malay Peninsula, had long attracted Indian traders and travelers (albeit in smaller numbers).[18] Some settled further abroad and formed the first large-scale Indian diaspora communities in the Caribbean, Mauritius, Fiji, and South Africa. Some Indian migrants, especially indentured laborers, were coerced. Whether fully voluntary or not, overseas travel changed the horizon of possibilities for South Asians and gave rise to new imagined Indian and diaspora communities.

Indians were able to journey abroad in great numbers and further from home during the British Raj because of technological advances. Some still used sailboats, the time-honored way that Indians had crossed oceans for two millennia. But many traveled on steamboats, which reduced voyage times substantially. Indians also benefited from Egypt's Suez Canal, a 120-kilometer human-made channel that opened in 1869 and connected the Mediterranean Sea to the Red Sea, thus rendering it unnecessary to round the horn of Africa to reach Europe from South Asia via sea.[19] Whereas a sailboat took seven or eight months to travel from India to Britain in the late eighteenth century, a late-nineteenth-century steamboat completed the same journey in a mere three weeks.

With these technological leaps, international trade expanded twenty-five times in volume between 1850 and 1914, and Indians were among the traders and seamen involved in that economic boom. Maybe a quarter of a million Indian traders resided outside of South Asia by 1930.[20] Even while benefiting from prosperous trade, some experienced rising restrictions beginning in the 1880s due to anti-Asian bills in white settler colonies, such as South Africa.[21] Indians also worked as seamen, known as *lascars*, on British ships, where they were paid less in comparison to their European, Chinese, and Arab counterparts.[22] Eventually, abysmal working conditions and low pay incentivized seamen to form trade unions in the 1910s, making them among the first organized labor in India. Seamen used strikes at key ports, like Bombay and Goa, to gain robust wage increases.[23]

Indentured laborers suffered exploitative working conditions when they traveled abroad during the nineteenth century. Indentured labor was invented when the global slave trade ended.[24] The British, once active participants in buying and selling human beings, prohibited overseas sales of slaves in 1807 and abolished slavery in most British colonies through the Slavery Abolition Act (1833) and the Indian Slavery Act (1843). This negatively impacted some elite Indians' business interests, such as Gujarati merchants who financed slave ships that carried shackled Africans and traded textiles to slavers.[25] More broadly, ending the worldwide slave trade created labor shortages that India was well-positioned to fill. As Charles Darwin wrote in Mauritius, a sugar plantation colony off Africa's southeast coast, in the 1830s, employers were "feeling confident in a resource in the countless population of India."[26]

The system of indenture lasted about eighty years, from 1838 to 1917, during which one million or more Indians left South Asia permanently. Indian indentured laborers typically signed three- to five-year contracts to perform agricultural work abroad. They were called "coolies" (figure 20.1), and most departed India from Calcutta or Madras, with smaller numbers leaving from Bombay and French India ports.[27] As per their contracts, indentured laborers had a right to return to India, but relatively few did from more far-flung destinations such as the Caribbean and West Indies. Many Indians stayed where they landed in Guyana, Trinidad, Suriname (a Dutch colony), Jamaica, and so forth.[28]

Indians signed up for back-breaking agriculture labor, an ocean or more away from home, for a host of reasons. Some sought greener pastures, such as migrants from lower-caste and Dalit backgrounds. These constituted most Indian agricultural labors who traveled to Southeast Asia in the late 1800s, and Chamars were more likely than caste Hindus to emigrate as families.[29] Among individual migrants, far more men participated than women. Some men were probably rebel sepoys in the 1857 Rebellion (and perhaps later participated in labor uprisings on plantations).[30] Often, women entered indentured labor contracts due to desperate circumstances. Some had no family or had been disowned, like Manharni and Rojha, both from Bihar, who left India in 1872–1873.[31] Some women ran away, escaping abusive husbands. Others turned up pregnant under unexplained circumstances, like Sujaria, who sailed from Calcutta at four months pregnant and listed no father for her unborn child on her emigration pass.[32] Not everyone chose to leave, and there are reports of Indians being kidnapped into indentured labor, although

Figure 20.1. Indentured men and crew on the deck of a vessel recently arrived in Georgetown, British Guiana (Guyana), ca. 1890 CE.

adjudicating the veracity of such claims is difficult and there are sometimes contradictory stories.[33] Some who left never arrived at their destinations, such as Maharani who sailed to British Guiana (Guyana) in 1885 and was raped on board, soon dying.[34] Violence, including domestic and sexual violence, was a huge part of the collective experience of Indian indentured laborers.[35]

I leave the story of indentured laborers here, since, once they reached their destinations, they became part of the histories of Guyana, Trinidad, and so forth. But indenture again intersected with Indian history. Mohandas Gandhi—leader of India's independence movement—spent formative years in South Africa in the 1890s–1910s and met descendants of the "evil" indenture system that many saw as an extension of slavery.[36] After his return to India, Gandhi successfully campaigned to abolish indenture for good in 1917.[37] As mentioned, few indentured laborers returned from the Caribbean to India. Those who did return often discovered that they no longer fit into Indian society.[38] Some faced the same social problems that had driven them to leave in the first place, and others found that India had changed in their absence, leaving some unable to even find their ancestral villages that had washed away in floods.[39] Today, Indians are most likely to encounter descendants of indenture in diaspora populations in Western nations, such as the United States, where the

Figure 20.2. Sikh sepoy soldiers marching with the Guru Granth Sahib, Mesopotamia (modern-day Iran), 1918.

South Asian community broadly construed includes Guyanese and Trinidadians along with Pakistanis, Bangladeshis, and so forth.

Sepoys constitute a final group of Indians who went abroad in substantial numbers during this period, specifically to fight in World War I (1914–1918). By this point, the British had concentrated their military recruitment within certain Indian communities, whom they saw as "martial races." Sikhs, for example, constituted 1 percent of the Indian population during World War I but 20 percent of sepoys (figure 20.2).[40] Hundreds of thousands of sepoys participated in the brutal fighting of what was called, at the time, the Great War, largely in Mesopotamia.[41] As one soldier, Luddar Singh, lamented in a letter home in 1915 from a hospital bed: "This is not a war. It is a Mahabharat or the end of the world."[42] Around 73,000 sepoys died in the conflict, and, of those who came home, some inadvertently brought a deadly influenza with them.

In total, an estimated twelve to twenty million Indians died in the 1918–1919 influenza pandemic, also called the Spanish Flu, the biggest disaster in recorded Indian history.[43] The deaths were so rampant that they brought parts of the colonial state—from Calcutta's High Court to the Forestry Service—to a screeching halt, illustrating the power of disease as an unexpected peril of increased global travel.

Indians in America

The United States was among the more distant places that South Asians traveled in the late nineteenth century. Material goods had moved between the subcontinent, Sri Lanka, and the Americas for several centuries, with new world items ranging from silver to tobacco to chilis changing South Asian economies and routines (chapter 12). But individual travelers had rarely traversed these great distances. As new technologies and global networks enabled greater travel, two distinct groups of Indians alighted on American shores in the late 1800s: manual laborers who worked on farms or in lumber yards and elites who sought spiritual, intellectual, and business connections with their American counterparts. These two groups came from different socioeconomic and religious backgrounds. The migrant workers were largely Punjabi Sikhs and Muslims, whereas elite travelers were often Brahmins. They also traveled to different parts of America, with the laborers working on the West Coast and elites visiting the East Coast and Midwest. Together they constituted the first trickle of Indian immigrants and visitors to the United States and, concomitantly, the initial introduction of Americans to embodied South Asian cultures.

Between 1889 and 1914, several thousand Indian laborers, predominantly Punjabi Sikhs and some Muslims, migrated to the United States. They encountered racist pushback, such as when hundreds were driven out of Bellingham, Washington, in 1907 by a white mob.[44] Somewhat confusingly for modern readers, these Indian migrants—Sikhs and Muslims—were described, in American parlance of the period, as "Hindu" in a racialized sense of the term meaning "Indian."[45] The migrants were nearly all men, and many settled in southern California's agriculture-focused Imperial Valley and married Hispanic women.[46] Their children constituted a biethnic Punjabi-Mexican community of several thousand that, while their fathers generally did not convert, were largely raised Catholic.[47] In encountering racism, intermarrying, and practicing accommodation, these early Indian migrants participated in enduring aspects of American pluralism.

More well known are prominent Indians who visited America in the 1880s–1900. For example, Jamsetji Tata (a Parsi) toured America in 1900 and later relied on American (and European) supervisors to oversee South Asia's first large steel plant (it opened after his death, in 1911, in Jamshedpur).[48] Here, I focus on three other elites who offered contrasting representations of Indian society, beginning with Anandibai Joshee.

Anandibai Joshee (1865–1887) traveled to Philadelphia in 1883, at the age of eighteen, to attend medical school. This was a highly unusual decision for a woman of her time, especially as her early life had been conventional.[49] She was a Chitpavan Brahmin married at age nine to an older man and gave birth at age fourteen. But the child died, and Anandibai was unable to conceive thereafter, experiences that perhaps motivated her medical interests (and her husband's interest in having his wife pursue medicine).[50] As she wrote to the Woman's Medical College of Pennsylvania in 1883 requesting admission: "That determination which has brought me to your country against the combined opposition of my friends and caste ought to go a long way towards helping me carry out the purpose for which I came, i.e. to render to my poor suffering country women the true medical aid they so sadly stand in need of, and which they would rather die for than accept at the hands of a male physician. The voice of humanity is with me and I must not fail."[51] Anandibai graduated in 1886 as the first Indian woman to earn a medical degree abroad.

Anandibai Joshee blazed a new trail for Indian women by pursuing higher education in the West, but she also defended patriarchy, and male violence shaped her life. Her husband, Gopalrao, beat her at times.[52] Recalling this from America, oceans away and years later, she wrote to Gopalrao about the psychological impact of his abuse and her understanding of its cultural and religious roots: "I pleaded with you to end my existence. There is nothing in the law to stop such things against women. If there are any laws they work against women. Therefore I had no option but to bear everything silently. A Hindu woman has no right to speak even a word against her husband or to advise him. She has only the 'right' to allow her husband to do what he wants and remain silent."[53] I read Anandibai's words as twinged with sorrow, but the gender dynamics she described were promoted by others without remorse. For example, the ultra-conversative Marathi newspaper *Kesari*, owned by B. G. Tilak, proclaimed proudly in 1888:

> If a Hindu husband sees his disobedient wife walking on the street or entering some house, he may drag her home or enter a stranger's house to bring her home; in neither case is he liable to a lawsuit according to the Hindu religion. . . . A man who finds his cow wandering about and puts a rope around her neck and brings her home is not liable to a lawsuit according to English law. The Hindu religion considers a woman to be on par with property and cattle. The only distinction is that as a human being she is entitled to food and clothing.[54]

Anandibai may have had private regrets about how her husband treated her, but she publicly endorsed patriarchal practices. For instance, while in America, she defended child marriage for Hindu girls.[55] Even on her deathbed, she preserved Brahminical norms, including untouchability, and thereby demonstrated that "well schooled Hindu wives were in no danger of losing their religion or their values."[56] She died shortly after returning to India, in 1887, and was lauded in obituaries for combining academic achievements and conservative values, in acclamations such as "her perseverance, undaunted courage and devotion to her husband were unparalleled."[57]

Some of Anandibai's contemporaries ruffled more feathers—taking sharper progressive stances and rejecting traditional customs—such as Pandita Ramabai (1858–1922). Ramabai's upbringing in India was a mix of traditional and innovative.[58] Her father was a Brahmin Sanskrit intellectual, but, unusually, he taught her mother Sanskrit, and Ramabai learned the classical language from both her parents (her knowledge of Sanskrit led to her appellation "pandita," learned woman). When Ramabai was sixteen and still unmarried, her parents and sister died in a famine, and Ramabai—as per her own later writings—began to lose her commitment to Hindu practices, which she experienced as tied to caste norms.[59] After the death of her brother, her sole surviving family member, in 1880, she married outside her caste. As she put it, "Having lost faith in the religion of my ancestors I married a Bengali gentleman of the Shudra caste."[60] Her husband died a year and a half later, leaving her widowed at the age of twenty-three with an infant daughter. As mentioned, the pair became world travelers.

Pandita Ramabai advocated for female education, including for child widows, over several decades through writings, public talks, fundraising, and opening schools. Even before she left India in 1883, Ramabai encountered fierce conservative pushback, especially from B. G. Tilak whose newspaper *Kesari* maintained that "women cannot interfere" in reform attempts and instead "have to submit to male control."[61] Ramabai converted to Christianity in Britain in the early 1880s and arrived in America in 1886 to attend Anandibai's graduation from medical school (the two were distant cousins). Thereafter, she stayed in the American northeast for a few years to raise awareness of, from her perspective, the plight of Indian women.[62]

In Philadelphia, Ramabai wrote a manifesto and caste critique titled *The High-Caste Hindu Woman*. Parts of the book use statistics to argue that American women had gained measurable social progress through education, legal rights, and voluntary associations.[63] Ramabai sought comparable gains for Indian women, and in so doing she offered a clear-eyed account of the challenges facing Indian women, especially widows. She gained support from some American groups, such as the Woman's Christian Temperance Union that helped finance the book's publication.[64] But other Indian travelers to America disliked Ramabai's unvarnished representation of Indian social realities, including Vivekananda who pursued a distinct agenda.

Vivekananda was the first Hindu religious leader to popularize Hinduism to Americans. He debuted in this role at the 1893 World's Parliament of Religions in Chicago, held during the World's Fair, and thereafter traveled on a lecture circuit across the United States for several years. Vivekananda advanced, as Hinduism, a clean-cut, masculine version of Vedanta uncoupled from many historic practices. In this sense, Vivekananda was part of the Hindu reform movements and sought to present Hinduism as he thought the religion should be, rather than its full range of diverse Indian realities. For instance, Vivekananda's guru Ramakrishna (d. 1886) had participated in tantric rituals and worshipped Kali, often depicted in Bengali images of the era with necklaces of severed human heads and striding atop Shiva's corpse (figure 20.3). Ramakrishna also endorsed bhakti and personally embraced the role of Radha, Krishna's lover.[65] Vivekananda, however, turned away from what he saw as "effeminate" practices and used the phrase "women and eunuchs" to mean loathsome people.[66] Instead, he presented himself as a handsome, well-spoken "Hindoo monk of India."[67]

Vivekananda embraced the Orientalist stereotype that the East abounds in religious wisdom and mysticism, while the West dominates in science and rationality. As he put it in a speech in New York, "Asia

Figure 20.3. Goddess Kali with a necklace of severed human heads and limbs striding atop Shiva's corpse, ca. 1879 CE, West Bengal, India, lithograph.

produces giants in spirituality just as the Occident produces giants in politics, giants in science."[68] In part, Vivekananda wanted Westerners to adopt Eastern (specifically his neo-Vedantic) religious precepts, advocating "Up, India, conquer the world with our spirituality."[69] He founded Vedanta societies in America (some still function today) and attracted Western disciples, which marked Vivekananda as a modern popular guru when he returned to India.[70] Vivekananda also wanted India to benefit from an infusion of Western ideas—such as American "grit" and "manhood"—and this put him at odds with other Hindu reformers.[71] For example, Vivekananda encouraged Hindu men to eat meat, including beef, since "the competition of this world must of necessity take meat."[72] As one scholar has put it, summarizing Vivekananda's position, "Beef, biceps and the Bhagavadgita" would help move Hindus forward.[73]

Vivekananda gave a well-received address at the 1893 World's Parliament of Religions that showcased how he chose to present Hinduism to Americans. Vivekananda was one of several Indian religious leaders at the event, including representatives of Muslim, Christian, Jain, Brahmo Samaj, and Theosophist traditions.[74] Jainism was represented by a lawyer, Virchand Gandhi, since the monk Atmaram would not break his vow of ahimsa (nonviolence) to travel abroad.[75] Anagarika Dharmapala (1864–1933) from Ceylon represented Buddhism, chastising the largely Christian American audience for their ignorance of Gautama's life: "You call yourselves a nation—a great nation—and yet you do not know the history of this great teacher. How dare you judge us!"[76] Out of the South Asian contingent, Vivekananda made the biggest impression. His speech, to a crowded room, earned thundering applause with its opening line: "Sisters and Brothers of America."[77] I reproduce the rest of the lecture in full as a key early document in early American encounters with Hindus.

Vivekananda's Speech at the World's Parliament of Religions, Chicago, 1893

It fills my heart with joy unspeakeable to rise in response to the warm and cordial welcome which you have given us. I thank you in the name of the most ancient order of monks in the world; I thank you in the name of the mother of religion, and I thank you in the name of the millions and millions of Hindu people of all classes and sects.

My thanks, also, to some of the speakers on this platform who have told you that these men from far-off nations may well claim the honor of bearing to the different lands the idea of toleration. I am proud to belong to a religion which has taught the world both tolerance and universal acceptance. We believe not only in universal toleration, but we accept all religions to be true. I am proud to tell you that

I belong to a religion into whose sacred language, the Sanscrit, the word seclusion is untranslatable.

I am proud to belong to a nation which has sheltered the persecuted and the refugees of all religions and all nations of the earth. I am proud to tell you that we have gathered in our bosom the purest remnant of the Israelites, a remnant which came to southern India and took refuge with us in the very year in which their holy temple was shattered to pieces by Roman tyranny. I am proud to belong to the religion which has sheltered and is still fostering the remnant of the grand Zoroastrian nation. I will quote to you, brethren, a few lines from a hymn which I remember to have repeated from my earliest boyhood, which is every day repeated by millions of human beings: "As the different streams having their sources in different places, all mingle their water in the sea, Oh, Lord, so the different paths which men take through different tendencies, various though they appear, crooked or straight, all lead to Thee."

The present convention, which is one of the most august assemblies ever held, is in itself a vindication, a declaration to the world of the wonderful doctrine preached in Gita. "Whosoever comes to me, through whatsoever form I reach him, they are all struggling through paths that in the end always lead to me." Sectarianism, bigotry, and its horrible descendant, fanaticism, have possessed long this beautiful earth. It has filled the earth with violence, drenched it often and often with human blood, destroyed civilization and sent whole nations to despair. Had it not been for this horrible demon, human society would be far more advanced than it is now. But its time has come, and I fervently hope that the bell that tolled this morning in honor of this convention will be the death-knell to all fanaticism, to all persecutions with the sword or the pen, and to all uncharitable feelings between persons wending their way to the same goal.[78]

What Vivekananda omitted from his 1893 speech is critical, perhaps more than what he said, to understanding how he wanted to represent his religion and culture abroad. He made no mention of Muslims, either as contributors to Indian culture or as targets of rising communal tensions. Instead, for Vivekananda, India and Vedantic Hinduism were close to synonymous. He excluded all of what are sometimes dubbed Hinduism's "left-hand" practices, such as antinomian tantric rights, and in fact refers to no rituals whatsoever. He likewise mentions no specific Hindu deities, and his language suggests a monotheistic approach, a feature of Hindu reform movements since Rammohan Roy (chapter 17) that was likely more palatable to a predominantly Christian Chicago audience. Vivekananda ignored caste. He spoke about caste in other contexts, sometimes opposing it but also calling it "a natural order" and proclaiming "Caste is good. That is the only natural way of solving life."[79] He omitted women's rights, an issue of considerable debate in his day in India. In subsequent talks in the United States, Vivekananda affirmatively denied the challenges faced by Hindu widows, contradicting and thereby arousing the ire of Ramabai who had firsthand experience on this score.[80]

Vivekananda and Ramabai both returned to India in the 1880s–1890s and pursued their respective priorities. Vivekananda started the Ramakrishna monastery (math) at Belur in Bengal to train Hindu boys, house ascetics, and spread Vedantic ideas.[81] One of the institution's founding guidelines was "the Math will not pay much attention to social reform," with the logic being that "those evils will die out of themselves" given education and food.[82] In contrast, Ramabai opened a school for girls, largely child widows, as well as the Mukti Mission to help vulnerable women during famines.

Back in India, Ramabai continued to endure vicious attacks by conservative upper-caste men. In public talks, they sometimes shouted her down, and the celebrated Bengali polymath and poet Rabindranath Tagore witnessed one such occasion in Poona.[83] Tilak and his paper *Kesari* showed special vitriol for Ramabai's reform efforts. The paper referred to the thousands of women saved from starvation at the Mukti Mission and elsewhere as locked in "prison-houses" by "Ramabai the Jailer."[84] In 1904, Tilak himself wrote that Ramabai should abandon her Hindu title of "pandita" (learned woman) and instead call herself "reveranda." The proposed title is a nod to her conversion to Christianity and a misogynist play on the vernacular term *rand* (also *randa* and *randi*) for prostitute.[85] This vulgar, gendered attack indicates the sorts of cultural resources available to Tilak, who apparently thought such a barb compromised neither his dignity nor his nationalist politics. Analyzing what, exactly, about Ramabai made men like Tilak see red, Jyotirao Phule, a low-caste reformer, wryly noted, "Small wonder then that the Brahmins are bawling at Ramabai on account of her having utterly demolished their artificial religion!"[86]

Dalit and Shudra Activism

During the late nineteenth and early twentieth centuries, Dalit and lower-caste leaders emerged as vigorous advocates for their communities. One early intervention, made by Jyotirao Phule (1827–1890), a Mali Shudra, was introducing a new name for those at the bottom of the caste hierarchy: *dalit*, meaning downtrodden or oppressed.[87] "Dalit" gradually replaced the unkind, Brahminical term "untouchable" and is the preferred nomenclature today. A standard history of Dalit and lower-caste activism in this period has yet to be written, a sign of ongoing casteism and our proclivity to focus on upper-caste voices. Here, I cover three major issues that Dalit activists prioritized between roughly 1880 and 1920 (i.e., before the heydays of Ambedkar and Periyar). They worked to increase access to education (and through that, access to employment and jobs), confront social norms around caste, and forge community identity through engagements with Indian history.

Dalit and lower-caste Indians faced formidable roadblocks to gaining education in British India. Brahmins dominated many universities (chapter 19). In primary and secondary government schools, upper-caste parents organized to bar lower-caste children and would sometimes withdraw their offspring if even a single Dalit student was admitted.[88] Missionary schools offered one solution for caste-oppressed communities. For instance, Jyotirao Phule studied at a Scottish missionary school, where he forged formative friendships across caste lines.[89] His wife, Savitri (d. 1897), was illiterate when they married, but Jyotirao taught her to read, and she later trained as a teacher in Ahmednagar at a school run by a female American missionary.[90]

Both Phules advocated for girls' education and opened schools. Many of their contemporaries disapproved, especially of Savitri bucking the interlinked norms of gender and caste by teaching. Legend says that she wore an old sari on her walk to school each morning, since people would throw things at her en route, and changed into fresh clothes after arriving.[91] Later in life, Savitri participated in famine relief efforts and started a home for widows and illegitimate children. She and Jyotirao adopted a Brahmin widow's son. The boy grew up to become a doctor and joined Savitri in spearheading plague relief efforts in the 1890s, during which Savitri caught the disease and died.[92] Savitri's Marathi poetry articulates her conviction that education could radically change the future for lower castes and Dalits, freeing them from a history of upper-caste oppression.

Savitri Phule's Marathi Poetry on the Power of Education, Late Nineteenth Century

"Go, Get Education"

Be self-reliant, be industrious
Work—gather wisdom and riches.
All gets lost without knowledge
We become animals without wisdom.

Sit idle no more, go, get education
End misery of the oppressed and forsaken.

You've got a golden chance to learn
So learn and break the chains of caste.
Throw away the Brahmin's scriptures fast.

"Rise to Learn and Act"

Weak and oppressed! Rise my brother
Come out of living in slavery.

Manu-follower Peshwas are dead and gone
Manu's the one who barred us from education.

Givers of knowledge—the English have come
Learn, you've had no chance in a millennium.

We'll teach our children and ourselves learn
Receive knowledge, become wise to discern.

An upsurge of jealousy is in my soul
Crying out for knowledge to be whole.

This festering wound, mark of caste
I'll blot out from my life at last.

In Baliraja's kingdom, let's beware
Our glorious mast, unfurl and flare.

Let all say, "Misery go and kingdom come!"

Awake, arise and educate
Smash traditions—liberate!

We'll come together and learn
Policy–righteousness–religion.

Slumber not but blow the trumpet
O Brahmin, dare not you upset.

Give a war cry, rise fast
Rise, to learn and act.[93]

Colonial-era Dalit and lower-caste leaders found a limited British appetite for addressing caste-based disenfranchisement. For instance, the British acquiesced to requests for caste segregation in some cases (e.g., among sepoys), whereas they denied them in others (e.g., in railway carriages).[94] In addition, an older set of caste prejudices persisted in villages where upper castes often owned land and exploited lower-caste bonded laborers. In some such cases, lower castes and Dalits used missionary and state pressures to pursue limited relief.[95] Upper-caste groups often eschewed even limited reforms. For instance, the Madras Mahajana Sabha declined to address land disenfranchisement and other forms of oppression among Parayars in the 1890s, noting that the British had already taken up the issue.[96] Western missionaries sometimes advocated on behalf of Dalits in princely states such as in Cochin and Travancore where enslavement and sale of Dalits was legal and widespread until 1855.[97] But both the colonial state and Western missionaries viewed caste as a religious issue, which disinclined them to intervene beyond the most egregious cases.

Anti-caste activists were able to use the threat of British involvement to save individuals from caste-based violence at times. For instance, Savitri Phule wrote to her husband Jyotirao in 1868 about an intercaste Dalit-Brahmin relationship:

> One Ganesh, a Brahmin, would go around villages, performing religious rites and telling people their fortunes. This was his bread and butter. Ganesh and a teenage girl named Sharja who is from the Mahar (untouchable) community fell in love. She was six months pregnant when people came to know about this affair. The enraged people caught them, and paraded them through the village, threatening to bump them off. I came to know about their murderous plan. I rushed to the spot and scared them away,

pointing out the grave consequences of killing the lovers under the British law. They changed their mind after listening to me. Sadubhau angrily said that the wily Brahmin boy and the untouchable girl should leave the village. Both the victims agreed to this. My intervention saved the couple who gratefully fell at my feet and started crying. Somehow I consoled and pacified them. Now I am sending both of them to you.[98]

Among other things, this episode highlights community enforcement of caste segregation, including endogamy, in British India. Even after Savitri saved the lives of Sharja and Ganesh, she could not salvage their social standing and instead helped them start anew elsewhere.

In addition to pursuing education and freedom during the British Raj, Dalits and Shudras began to consider how they fit into the emerging story of Indian history. Community thinkers proposed a few different, conflicting narratives. None of these are strictly historically accurate, but I recount them here as part of India's rich intellectual history. These narratives all, in distinct ways, attempted to claim agency and dignity for historically oppressed communities.

Some thinkers proposed that Shudras, Dalits, or both were fallen upper castes who could find liberation in reasserting their elite identities. For example, a series of Chamar thinkers in the 1910s and 1920s claimed Kshatriya origins, such as U.B.S. Raghuvanshi, who argued in a 1910–1916 publication that Chamars were a royal lineage descended from the Sun God.[99] For some, a logical step toward social progress, then, was adopting upper-caste practices, such as abstaining from alcohol and meat. Activists distributed pamphlets such as "Madhupishachi" (Devil of intoxication) and wrote *bhajans* (devotional songs) against drinking.[100] Caste associations—such as Chamar sabhas in northern India and the first All-India Adi-Hindu conference in 1922 in Hyderabad—passed resolutions calling for habit changes to reclaim a higher-caste identity.[101]

Taking a different approach, some argued that lower castes and Dalits were indigenous to India and had been historically oppressed by invading upper-caste aryans. This line of thought invoked the Aryan Invasion Theory, current among Indologists of the period (now rejected).[102] For instance, a Marathi tract titled *Jatibhed Viveksar* (Criticism of caste divisions) was published in the 1860s under the pseudonym "Ek Hindu" (a Hindu) and argued that indigenous Shudras were heroes for proudly facing the invading aryans.[103] Jyotirao Phule similarly argued that

Shudras and Dalits were among India's original inhabitants, whereas aryans were not.[104] He took mythological figures, such as Parashurama who is imagined to have slaughtered Kshatriyas over and over, as historical figures who committed genocides of indigenous Indians.[105] Then, Phule contended, Brahmins invented caste to justify their oppressive behavior: "In order to fulfil their plan that those people should remain perpetually in slavery, and that they should be able to live comfortably on what the Shudras earned by the sweat of their brow, the Brahmans set up the fiction of caste divisions, and made up several books on it for their own selfish ends."[106] Such arguments diverged sharply from classic Brahminical thought in which lower castes and Dalits were held responsible for their low social positions owing to karma (chapter 7).

In a southern twist on Dalit interpretations of the nineteenth-century Aryan Invasion Theory, some anti-caste thinkers saw ancient Brahmin migrations south as tyrannical. For instance, Iyothee Thass (1845–1914) argued that northern aryan invaders had corrupted southern Buddhists.[107] As with the ideas of Phule and others, Thass built on scholarship of his time while imputing moral judgments specific to his activism. Foreshadowing Ambedkar several decades later, Thass converted to Buddhism in the late nineteenth century. This enabled him to reject Hindu traditions that he experienced as oppressive and to assert a Tamil identity, which he projected as "original Dravidian culture."[108] In so doing, Iyothee Thass participated in formulating both a larger religious community and a thoroughly regional identity.

Conclusion: Vaccinating Indians

I have largely focused throughout this chapter on Indians who left South Asia, and so it seems appropriate, in closing, to highlight a society-altering import to India during the British Raj: vaccines. Waldemar Haffkine, a Russian Jewish scientist, is a major figure here, sent by Louis Pasteur to northern India in 1893 to test a cholera vaccine.[109] The inoculation proved so successful that Calcutta slum dwellers lined up all day to receive a jab.[110] When the plague struck in 1896, Haffkine developed a vaccine in record time and began administering it in Bombay slums, saving countless lives (figure 20.4). Older vaccines, such as against smallpox (debuted in 1796), were also widely distributed. The Begum of Bhopal, a princely state with a succession of female rulers, offered rewards

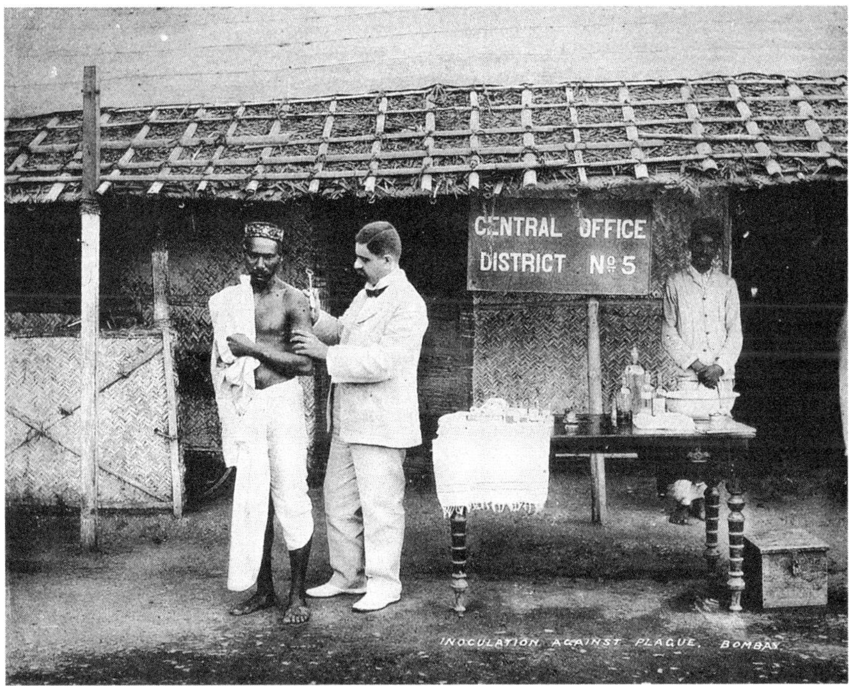

Figure 20.4. Inoculation against the plague, Bombay, 1896–1897 CE.

to parents who vaccinated their children against smallpox.[111] We cannot know exactly how many millions of lives were saved by vaccines in British India. But it is a safe bet that some individuals who, absent vaccines, would have died participated in India's independence struggle, which occupied center stage in the 1920s–1940s.

Further Reading

Chinmay Tumbe offers a broad take on migration patterns, and I turned to others for specifics, including Claude Markovits on business, Ritika Prasad on railways, and Kama Maclean on the Kumbh Mela. Gaiutra Bahadur and Hugh Tinker offer detailed, nuanced takes on indentured labor. For early Indian travelers to the United States, Karen Leonard covers Punjabi farmers, Uma Chakravarti and Meera Kosambi analyze Ramabai, and many have discussed Vivekananda. For Dalit and lower-caste movements in this period, I used work by V. Geetha, Chinnaiah Jangam, Rosalind O'Hanlon, S. V. Rajadurai, Ramnarayan Rawat, Rupa Viswanath, and others.

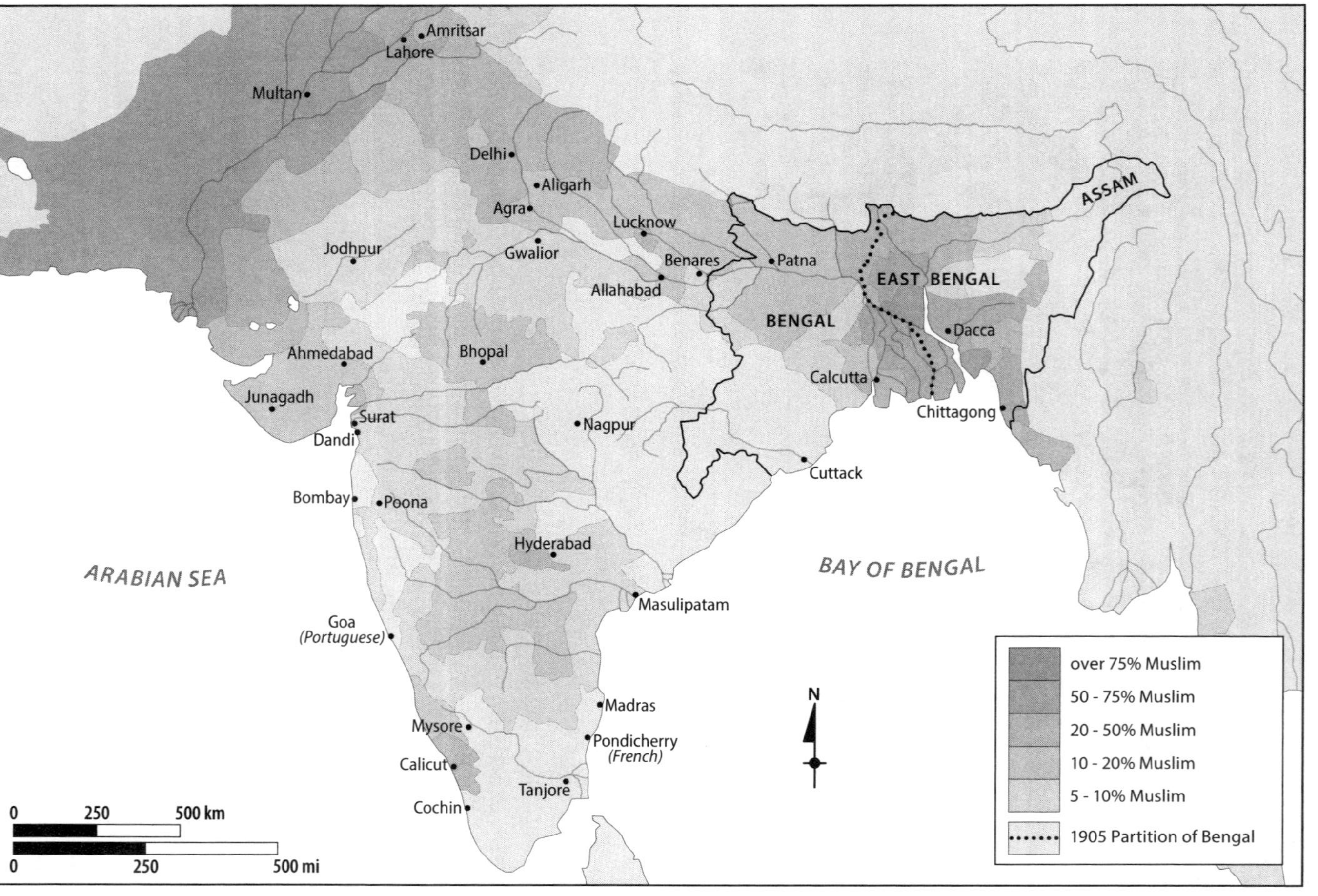

Muslim population in British India, ca. 1910.

21

Advocating for Independence, Nationalism, and Equal Rights

Born as humans, why should we lead a life of slaves? There is no sin in losing life in defending our rights. Come forward and claim your birthright.

—Kusuma Dharmanna, Telugu Dalit intellectual, 1923[1]

On December 26, 1927, 25,000 Dalits marched through Allahabad to inaugurate the first all-India Adi-Hindu Mahasabha conference. Among other things, the conference declared that Dalits (i.e., "Adi-Hindus," original Hindus) were distinct from caste Hindus and should have separate electorates.[2] Both ideas recurred throughout the 1920s and 1930s as debates about caste, religion, and political representation animated a generation of Indians who sought to remake their society. The most famous Indian movement of the era was the push for independence from British colonial rule led by the Indian National Congress. I cover this at some length, including circling back to the late nineteenth century to provide critical background. Other discrete movements also flourished in subsequent decades, including early Hindu nationalism and (separately) the quest for liberation from caste oppression led by B. R. Ambedkar. These sociopolitical agendas were incongruous with one another, but all invoked distinctly modern ideas of independence, nationalism, and equal rights.

Indian Political Organizing, 1885–1919

The Indian National Congress (i.e., Congress) was formed in 1885 in Bombay to advocate for increased Indian participation in the British colonial government. It came on the heels of the Ilbert Bill controversy over Indian judges, which had pointed up the difficulties of reforming the British Raj given the systematic exclusion of Indians from positions of power (chapter 19). Seeking greater political influence (although not independence, yet), a group of elites organized. The founding Congress assembly numbered seventy-two delegates (including the retired Indian civil servant and British reformer Allan Octavian Hume). Although far from representative of the general Indian population, these delegates sought to overcome other social divides—including region, language, and religion—to advocate on behalf of all Indians.[3] Congress's vision of pan-India advocacy was starkly new, and it debuted with in-built limitations.

Even at Congress's founding, tensions arose about the possible exclusionary role of religion in forging a common Indian political identity, something that was without precedent in Indian history. For instance, the north Indian *Tribune*—founded by a Punjabi and edited by a Bengali—emphasized the high-caste Hindu markers of the strong Madras contingent at Congress's 1885 inaugural session:[4]

> Madras sent the greatest number of delegates, all of good education and high social standing. They completely enchanted the audience with their liberal views and impressive eloquence. Clad in conservative Hindu garments, with their shining foreheads rubbed with sandal after the orthodox Hindu fashion, and speaking in eloquent English about the various ways in which India should improve her political statue, they exhibited a spectacle at once charming and instructive; charming in as much as it was a glorious sight to behold genuine Hindus (preserving intact ancient custom of their great race) holding the most radical views about politics; instructive in as much as it was capable of infusing a belief that India could improve, to the highest extent desirable, its political status without becoming *Anglicized*.[5]

In contrast, only two of Congress's founding seventy-two delegates were Muslim.[6] A couple of Muslim presidents led Congress during its initial twenty years, but many in the community kept aloof. For instance, Syed Ahmad Khan, founder of Aligarh Muslim University, compared Congress's proposal of representative electorates to a rigged dice game that Muslims were destined to lose since, being outnumbered by Hindus four-to-one in the general population, "there will be four votes for the Hindu to every one vote for the Mohammedan."[7] In 1886, Syed Ahmad established the All India Muhammadan Educational Conference to advocate for Indian Muslim interests.[8]

Religious tensions resurfaced in the early 1900s, when the British partitioned Bengal Presidency into a Hindu-majority western half and a Muslim-majority eastern half. Like many British Raj decisions, Bengal's partition projected religion as the defining feature of Indian society. Announced in 1903 and formalized in 1905 by George Curzon (Viceroy of India 1899–1905), the experiment did not last, and the British canceled Bengal's partition in 1911. But it provided proof of concept that British India could be severed to create Hindu and Muslim majorities in different areas. That idea of division stuck around and became central to the twin births of the Indian and Pakistani nations through partition in 1947 (chapter 22). More immediately, in the initial decade of the 1900s, Curzon's partition of Bengal sparked Indian political organizing.

Congress fashioned the swadeshi movement (1903–1908), encouraging Indians to boycott British goods in favor of purchasing Indian (swadeshi) items to protest Bengal's partition. The boycott constituted a shift in Congress's hitherto mild advocacy efforts and was partly organized in religious spaces. For instance, during Durga Puja in the fall of 1905, 50,000 Bengalis gathered at Calcutta's Kalighat Temple where priests led them in swearing off British goods.[9] Even today, Durga Puja is a recurrent site of political statements and dissent.[10] The swadeshi boycott boosted some Indian business families, such as the Tatas who had made their initial fortune in opium and cotton but turned to steel in 1907 (Tata Steel remains a leading steel company today, and the Tata family also has other business ventures).[11] Critically, the swadeshi movement worked. It gained support for Congress and compelled the British to reverse the partition of Bengal, thereby demonstrating the power of economic boycotts, a mainstay of the Indian independence struggle.

Some Muslims broke with Congress during the swadeshi movement and formed the All-India Muslim League (i.e., League) in 1906. The

League was the next incarnation of Syed Ahmad's Muhammadan Educational Conference and aimed "to protect and advance the political rights and interests of the Musalmans of India."[12] Congress remained the most powerful Indian political group over the next several decades, but the League's early organization helped them gain concessions. Most notably, in the 1916 Lucknow Pact, Congress agreed to support League demands for separate electorates for Indian Muslims.

During the swadeshi movement, some Congress leaders drew on a Hindu lexicon to articulate a pan-Indian national identity, which others found exclusive. Among the movement's nationalist cries was Bande Mataram (also called Vande Mataram), a mixed Bengali-Sanskrit poem by Bankimchandra that Rabindranath Tagore set to music in 1896.[13] Invoking Mother India as an armed goddess to be worshipped, Bande Mataram fused Hindu religious imagery with nationalist longings. Congress leaders used the song as an anthem for decades, over objections raised by Muslims who periodically pointed out its discomfort for many in their religious community. Later, both Mohandas Gandhi and Jawaharlal Nehru admitted to seeing their point. Nehru wrote about Bande Mataram in 1937, "It does seem that the background is likely to irritate the Muslims," and the same year Congress issued guidelines to only use the first two verses (which do not mention specific Hindu deities by name) and granting permission to substitute other patriotic songs.[14] The mitigated embrace of Bande Mataram indicates the willingness of many nationalist leaders to invoke Hindu imagery, even as some attempted to strike a balance given India's religious diversity.

Aurobindo Ghose's Translation of "Hymn to the Mother" (Bande Mataram)

Mother, I bow to thee!
Rich with thy hurrying streams,
Bright with thy orchard gleams,
Cool with thy winds of delight,
Dark fields waving, Mother of might,
Mother free.
Glory of moonlight dreams
Over thy branches and lordly streams,—

Clad in thy blossoming trees,
Mother, giver of ease,
Laughing low and sweet!
Mother, I kiss thy feet,
Speaker sweet and low!
Mother, to thee I bow.

Who hath said thou art weak in thy lands,
When the swords flash out in twice seventy million hands
And seventy million voices roar
Thy dreadful name from shore to shore?
With many strengths who art mighty and stored,
To thee I call, Mother and Lord!
Thou who savest, arise and save!
To her I cry who ever her foemen drave
Back from plain and sea
And shook herself free.

Thou art wisdom, thou art law,
Thou our heart, our soul, our breath,
Thou the love divine, the awe
In our hearts that conquers death.
Thine the strength that nerves the arm,
Thine the beauty, thine the charm.
Every image made divine
In our temples is but thine.

Thou art Durga, Lady and Queen,
With her hands that strike and her swords of sheen,
Thou art Lakshmi lotus-throned,
And the Muse a hundred-toned.
Pure and perfect without peer,
Mother, lend thine ear.
Rich with thy hurrying streams,
Bright with thy orchard gleams,
Dark of hue, O candid-fair
In thy soul, with jewelled hair
And thy glorious smile divine,
Loveliest of all earthly lands,

> Showering wealth from well-stored hands!
> Mother, mother mine!
> Mother sweet, I bow to thee,
> Mother great and free![15]

Some upper-caste Hindus wanted a more starkly homogenous nationalist ideal, forming the Hindu Mahasabha under the leadership of Madan Mohan Malaviya (1861–1946), a Sanskrit-educated Brahmin, in 1915. The Hindu Mahasabha gained more power in the 1920s, building on earlier consolidations of upper-caste Hindu identity through cow protection movements (chapter 19) and slogans like "hindi, hindu, hindustan" that encapsulated one vision of the critical identity markers of being Indian.[16] The Hindu Mahasabha actively encouraged the use of Khari Boli Hindi, which is a dialect of the language common today but was less widespread in the early twentieth century. They also supported using Devanagari script in an explicit attempt to distinguish Hindi from Urdu and to link the languages with being Hindu and Muslim, respectively, contrasting Hindi as an *aryabhasha* (aryan language) with Urdu as an "alien implant."[17] Such agendas did not go over well with many Indians, including southerners who resented the imposition of a north Indian language (the Dravidian movement had roots around this time) and non-Hindus who rejected the proposed fusion of Indian and Hindu identities.[18] But the Hindu Mahasabha's ideas—including its anti-Muslim rhetoric—proved influential, in part, because Hindu Mahasabha and Congress leadership overlapped for decades.

Heading into the 1910s, discrete factions in Congress held incongruous views about the goals and methods of political agitation, with B. G. Tilak (1856–1920) heading up the *garam dal* (hot faction). Tilak is best known for his pronouncement "Home Rule is my birth-right, and I shall have it."[19] He endorsed violence in pursuit of self-rule, approvingly stating that "Shrimat Krishna's teaching in the *Gita* is to kill even our teachers, our brothers."[20] Tilak often grounded his ideas in Hindu religious texts and rhetoric, even comparing bombs used by nationalists to mantras (Hindu invocations).[21] The British Raj arrested, tried, and convicted Tilak of sedition twice, in 1897 and 1908, both times citing his support for violence.[22] Tilak did not reform in prison and spent his second sentence of six years in Burma composing a commentary on the Bhagavadgita that expands his view of the text as a call to action (karma), including condoning killing one's enemies.[23] Many disagreed with Tilak's ideas during his life, including Gopal Krishna Gokhale (1866–1915) who led a moderate wing of Congress, the *naram dal* (soft faction). Still, violence surfaced throughout the Indian independence movement, including long after nonviolence became the headline principle under the leadership of Mohandas Gandhi—who was mentored by Gokhale—from 1920 forward.[24]

In 1919, the British Raj conceded, albeit in a limited way, to nationalist pressures by passing the Government of India Act. Also called the Montagu–Chelmsford Reforms after the British pair who fought for the bill, the 1919 Act introduced dyarchy (split government), wherein elite Indians participated in elections and their representatives wielded limited local governing powers.[25] But two problems presented. First, the 1919 Act fell short of self-rule and offered no clear timeline for proceeding toward that goal. This left unchallenged attitudes, such as that ascribed to the Earl of Birkenhead who was the secretary of state for India in the mid-1920s, that Indians would be prepared for self-rule in 600 years.[26] Second, the 1919 Government of India Act was accompanied, the same year, by the Rowlatt Acts, also known as "Black Acts," that suspended habeas corpus for sedition cases. This created ripe conditions for massive British infringement on Indian political expression. Indians protested with a *hartal* (general strike) on April 6, 1919, following which the British executed the single bloodiest massacre in Indian colonial history.

On April 13, 1919, a peaceful crowd of 10,000 or 20,000 gathered at Jallianwala Bagh in Amritsar. Trying to stem protests over the oppressive Rowlatt Acts, the British had forbidden large gatherings, but some Indians were unaware of the prohibition and others sought to challenge it. The crowd featured a mix of protestors and those celebrating the Sikh holiday of Baisakhi. General Reginald Dyer commanded several hundred Gurkha sepoys who were to keep order at Jallianwala Bagh, and, instead, he commanded them to fire into the peaceful gathering. In numbers, Dyer's troops fired 1,650 bullets, wounding more than 1,200 and killing 379 Indian civilians, in the span of ten minutes.[27] An unrepentant Dyer later testified that he wanted to "reduce . . . the morale of the rebels."[28] He was disciplined, but many agreed with his tactic of massacre. Six months later, a senior British officer in Delhi proclaimed, "Force is the only thing that an Asiatic has any respect for."[29] Quite to the contrary, in this moment, Indian Congress leaders were beginning to embrace nonviolent resistance as their primary weapon against British colonial rule.

Gandhi's Congress and Its Discontents

Mohandas Gandhi (1869–1948) was the architect of Congress's nonviolent resistance strategy that showed the world the inhumanity of British colonialism and secured Indian and Pakistani independence. Gandhi was born in Gujarat but spent his young adult years abroad, studying law in London and honing organizing strategies over more than two decades in British colonial South Africa.[30] He returned to India in 1915, at the age of forty-five, and soon became the pivotal figure of India's independence movement. Gandhi joined an illustrious lineup in Congress, including Motilal Nehru (1861–1931) and his son Jawaharlal Nehru (1889–1964), while others, such as Vallabhbhai Patel (1875–1950), were attracted to the cause by Gandhi's leadership. Mohandas Gandhi wrote a staggering amount in his lifetime, including several books and regular columns in weekly papers titled *Navjivan* (1919–1931), *Young India* (1919–1931), and *Harijan* (1933–1948). Here I focus on Gandhi's key political actions, with some consideration of his influential (and, often, controversial) social ideas.

When Gandhi returned as somewhat of a prodigal son to India in 1915, he brought with him critical experiences. He had led acts of nonviolent resistance (*satyagraha* in his terminology) in South Africa, learning the value of good discipline among followers and the power of female participation in political actions.[31] He used both practices to good effect in India. While abroad, Gandhi also developed a specific—far from universal—idea of what true Indian independence (*swaraj*) entailed. He articulated in his *Hind Swaraj*, published in 1909, that swaraj meant freedom from the British imperial infrastructure and economies, in addition to freedom from colonial rule, and had to be achieved on a personal level before society-wide success. He railed against the British railways in India because "they propagate evil" and wanted Indians to cultivate a controlled, self-sustained lifestyle rather than build a powerful state.[32] When questioned by those who wanted "the same powers" for India as any other nation, including "our navy, our army" and "our own splendour" that could make "India's voice ring through the world,"

Gandhi responded that such views "want English rule without the Englishman." He bluntly stated: "That is not the Swaraj that I want."[33]

Gandhi cultivated a strict personal regime and public persona that granted him social clout and charisma. He took a vow of chastity in 1906 (after having fathered five children) and deliberately engaged in caste-violating work for a Vaishya, like cleaning latrines. Shortly after returning to India, he shed his Western suits in favor of an Indian dhoti whose handspun cloth (*khadi*) he made on a spinning wheel (*charkha*). Gandhi sought to convince others to adopt similar habits, and his emphasis on khadi also tied into an economic boycott of British cotton. Indeed, in 1921, Gandhi's charkha was put on Congress's flag—sometimes called the "tricolour" after its bands of orange, white, and green—as emblematic of the independence movement.[34] But, overall, Gandhi's rigid choices set him apart, as the *mahatma* (great-souled) for whom people would travel miles for a religious glimpse (darshan).[35] Gandhi cautioned "I am not God," but he benefited all the same from public displays of religiosity that made him superhuman in the eyes of many, closer to a divine avatar than a mere mortal.[36]

In 1920, Gandhi persuaded the Congress Party to adopt noncooperation as its official policy, organizing a general boycott of British industries and institutions as well as strikes over the next eighteen months. This move was enabled by an alliance between Congress and Muslim supporters of the Khilafat movement, who wanted to preserve the Ottoman Caliphate that was under threat in the aftermath of World War I. The Khilafat movement failed when independent Turkey abolished the caliphate in 1924, but meanwhile Hindu-Muslim unity in India—as Congress supported the Khilafat movement in exchange for their buy-in on noncooperation—inspired many. As Gandhi put it: "If I had not joined the Khilafat movement, I think, I would have lost everything. In joining it I have followed what I especially regard as my dharma. I am trying through this movement to show the real nature of non-violence. I am uniting Hindus and Muslims. I am coming to know one and all and, if non-co-operation goes well, a great power based on brute force will have to submit to a simple-looking thing. The Khilafat movement is a great churning of the sea of India."[37]

The noncooperation movement came to a sudden, violent head in February 1922 when a mob murdered several dozen Indian policemen in the town of Chauri Chaura. In response, Mohandas Gandhi called off the entire movement, which emboldened the British Raj to arrest him. Gandhi was convicted of sedition and received a six-year sentence (the judge cited as precedent Tilak's six-year sentence in 1908).[38] Gandhi remained imprisoned only about two years, being released in 1924 due to ill health after having his appendix removed in a surgery conducted via torchlight.[39]

While Gandhi was incarcerated and recovering, 1923–1925 saw a rash of terrorist activities in British India. Numerous men—especially upper-caste Bengalis—had renounced political violence to join Gandhi's non-cooperation movement, and, after that was suspended, they returned to their old ways.[40] Arguably, we should not strictly separate the nonviolent and violent aspects of the Indian independence struggle. After all, Congress leaders lobbied on behalf of violent political prisoners during the 1920s–1930s and benefited from the pressures that violence can place on governments.[41] Still, Gandhi personally eschewed using force his entire life, and his influence shaping Congress was unmatched until his death in 1948. Gandhi spent the last half of the 1920s working with volunteers to ensure organizational discipline in ways later emulated by U.S. Civil Rights leaders such as Martin Luther King Jr.[42]

In 1929, Congress passed the purna swaraj (full independence) resolution, calling for India to break away from British rule, and leaders soon embarked on a series of civil disobedience actions. In 1930, Gandhi led his Salt March, where he and a group of eighty followers walked to a Gujarati coastal town called Dandi and picked up salt. This simple action violated the British Salt Act, which taxed the common staple, and its deliberate illegality was underscored by the poet and activist Sarojini Naidu, who addressed Gandhi, on the beach, as "Law Breaker" (figure 21.1).[43] Many imitated this satyagraha, and Gandhi initiated follow-up actions, including a nonviolent raid on a salt factory at Dharasana in 1930 that was timed to coincide with the mobilization for the 1931 British-led census of India.[44] Congress's push for independence coupled with Gandhi's salt satyagraha led to numerous roundtables between Indians and British officials, one of which occasioned the slur from Winston Churchill that Gandhi was a "half-naked fakir" whom he found "nauseating."[45] One outcome of this set of meetings was the 1935 Government of India Act that abolished dyarchy and significantly expanded Indian political participation at various levels of the British Raj.

Figure 21.1. Mohandas Gandhi and Sarojini Naidu during the salt satyagraha, 1930 CE, Gujarat.

As the Indian independence movement grew, Congress's upper-caste leadership faltered in gaining support from anti-caste activists. Some Dalit leaders had been suspicious of Congress early on, such as the Tamil thinker Iyothee Thass who condemned the pride in caste, religion, knowledge, and wealth that he saw as animating the 1903–1908 swadeshi

Figure 21.2. Mother India from the title page of Kusuma Dharmanna's *Nalladoratanamu*, published in 1923 CE (Telugu writing reads: Equality is Independence).

movement.[46] In 1923, Kusuma Dharmanna published a Telugu book with an image of Mother India weeping as she holds unbalanced scales of justice over starving Dalits (figure 21.2). An inscription on the image reads "Equality is Independence."[47] This image was reprinted by several later anti-caste thinkers, and Kusuma Dharmanna—who encouraged Dalits to not accept a life of slavery (see the chapter epigraph)—further clarified his views on Congress, writing: "In the name of *Swarajya* they organise meetings! Always praise Gandhi, preach Hindu-Muslim unity and advocate wearing *Khaddar* [khadi]. They claim peace as *Swarajya* and organise peace volunteers! But they bury our issues."[48] Another anti-caste advocate, E. V. Ramasamy (often known by the appellation Periyar, "big man"), left

Congress in 1925 after a disagreement over segregating schools on caste lines. He declared his new agenda to be: "No god; no religion; no Gandhi; no Congress; and no brahmins" and founded the Self-Respect Movement in 1926 to focus on anti-caste social reform.[49] In 1928, Congress further alienated Dalits by publishing the Nehru Report, which failed to offer any reserved seats for the caste-oppressed in a proposed central legislature.[50]

As of the early 1930s, Mohandas Gandhi had an uneven history regarding caste, with the three pillars of his approach being opposition to untouchability, defense of caste divisions, and a focus on upper-caste redemption. Condemning the treatment of Dalits, he wrote, "Hinduism has sinned in giving sanction to untouchability."[51] He even equated the practice with the horrors wrought by the British Raj: "What crimes for which we condemn the Government as Satanic have not we been guilty of towards our untouchable brethren? We are guilty of having suppressed our brethren; we make them crawl on their bellies; we have made them rub their noses on the ground; with eyes red with rage, we push them out of railway compartments—what more than this has British Rule done?"[52] At the same time, Gandhi defended the caste distinctions of varnadharma, including a division of labor and reverence for Brahmins. In Gandhi's own words: "Regarding a Brahmana [Brahmin] and a bhangi (scavenger) as equals does not mean that you will not accord to a true Brahmana the reverence that is due to him."[53] Last, Gandhi focused on "upper-caste penance," believing that Dalit upliftment would come if upper castes "purged ourselves of the sins we have committed against our weaker brethren."[54] Many Dalits found Gandhi's views on caste wrong-headed and insultingly paternalistic, including his proposed renaming of untouchables as *harijans* (God's children). Ultimately, Ambedkar (1891–1956) showed the fallacies of Gandhi's ideas—especially the hubris that caste can be humane—in his pioneering *Annihilation of Caste*, published in 1936. But first, Ambedkar, like many others, was compelled to bend to Gandhi's will.

In 1932, Mohandas Gandhi leveraged his own life to oppose B. R. Ambedkar's demand for separate electorates for the caste-oppressed (i.e., "depressed classes," as they were called at the time). Ambedkar's idea had precedent since Congress had agreed with the League to back separate electorates for Muslims in the 1916 Lucknow Pact. In this case, Ambedkar negotiated directly with the British, who gave his desired result in the 1932 Communal Award. Echoing decades of upper-caste fears that they would lose a Hindu majority if cleaved from Dalits (chapter 19), Mohandas Gandhi began a hunger strike, until his death or the award was rescinded. Gandhi's literal "over my dead body" approach—which modern thinkers have described as "harshly coercive" and "barefaced blackmail"—worked.[55] The hunger strike inspired many upper-caste Hindus to undertake solidarity actions with Dalits, such as sharing meals and providing temporary access to temples, which split off support from Ambedkar. Gandhi even earned the support of Dalit leaders such as Madras-based M. C. Rajah, who said to Ambedkar:

> For thousands of years we had been treated as Untouchables, downtrodden, insulted, despised. The Mahatma is staking his life for our sake, and if he dies, for the next thousands of years we shall be where we have been, if not worse. There will be such a strong feeling against us that we brought about his death, that the mind of the whole Hindu community and the whole civilised community will kick us downstairs further still. I am not going to stand by you any longer. I will join the conference and find a solution and I will part company from you.[56]

Seeing the writing on the wall, Ambedkar responded: "I am willing to compromise."[57] He then negotiated the Poona Pact with Gandhi, whereby "depressed classes" received reserved seats but not separate electorates. The compromise offered too little for some within the Dalit community, and north Indian Dalit leaders coordinated protests in 1933–1934.[58]

Gandhi alienated other communities, too, in the push for independence, even as he strove to bridge social boundaries. As one modern scholar has put Gandhi's faltering problems among Indian Muslims, "To many Muslims, [Gandhi] was a Hindu Mahatma who stood for majoritarian Hindu rule."[59] Trying to overcome dissent, some Congress leaders attempted to position their party as the anti-British option, but some Muslim leaders were unconvinced. For instance, in January 1937, Jawaharlal Nehru argued that Indians faced a binary choice between the Congress and the British, to which Muhammad Ali Jinnah (1876–1948), head of the Muslim League, replied, "I refuse to line up. There is a third party in the country, and that is Muslim India."[60] In chapter 22, I further discuss conflicts between the League and Congress, which became pronounced in the 1940s. Meanwhile, another movement was underway in India in the 1920s–1930s that stood apart from the quest for independence but introduced a virulent set of political ideas: Hindu nationalism.

Birth of Hindu Nationalism in a Fascist Age

Hindu nationalism or Hindutva—a political ideology of Hindu supremacy[61]—had roots in the late nineteenth century but was formally articulated in the 1920s. Critically, Hindu nationalism was not predominantly a religious movement, even as it used Hindu imagery. V. D. Savarkar (1883–1966), a key early Hindutva ideologue, was an atheist who was dismissive of pious Hindus and considered Hinduism a "limited, less satisfactory and essentially sectarian" religion, even a "dogma," that perhaps "should be dropped altogether."[62] Instead he advocated embracing the political ideology of Hindutva, popularizing this term coined by Bengali thinkers in the 1890s.[63] Hindu nationalism was distinct from the Indian independence movement in that Hindutva ideologues projected Indian Muslims, rather than British colonialism, as their primary enemy.[64] Two major events mark the advent of Hindutva ideology: the publication of Savarkar's *Hindutva* in 1923 and the founding of the Rashtriya Swayamsevak Sangh in 1925.

In his *Hindutva* (1923), Savarkar advanced a series of startling arguments about the nature of Hindu identity, largely borrowing from European ideas. Conscious of his innovation and debt to Western thought, Savarkar opened with a Shakespeare quote: "What is in a name?"[65] Savarkar then redefined the "Hindu" community using three major factors, all familiar from European nationalisms of the period: geographical unity, racial features, and common culture.[66] Savarkar's language is highly affective, whipping up emotions regarding the projected wrongs of Muslims in India's past.[67] Savarkar's views on Indo-Muslim history are ahistorical but rhetorically attractive to some, positing vague "recollections" of Muslims attacking Hindus in Indian history: "Does not the blood in your veins, O brother of our common forefathers, cry aloud with the recollections of the dear old scenes and ties from which they were so cruelly snatched away at the point of the sword?"[68] Savarkar saw Hindus as the subcontinent's original colonizers, and he advocated for bringing back their glorious days of domination.[69] For Savarkar, Indian Muslims were to be the dominated group, and speaking to a *Los Angeles Times* reporter in 1944, Savarkar invoked Jim Crow America in stating that he intended to treat “Mohammedans” “as a minority in the position of your Negroes.”[70]

From the start, V. D. Savarkar embraced violence as a defining part of Hindutva ideology. This proved a point of sharp disagreement between Savarkar and Mohandas Gandhi when the two met in London during Dussehra in fall 1909. Both men spoke in front of a crowd about the Ramayana epic, with Gandhi arguing that it could unite Indians of all faiths and that the epic’s violence was a metaphor for conquering the beast within. In contrast, Savarkar celebrated Rama’s conquest of Lanka as a literal example of what he later pitched as aryan colonization, whereby massacre ensured Hindu freedom.[71] A British surveillance report of the meeting indicates that Savarkar’s views swayed the audience but not Gandhi.[72] Savarkar was arrested in 1910 for participating in the assassination of British officer William Curzon Wyllie. He spent more than a decade in prison, during which he wrote and smuggled out his treatise titled *Hindutva* that argues, among other things, that violence is critical to Hindu supremacy, his end goal.[73] In later texts, he clarified that Hindu men should commit “super-savage cruelty” at times, including raping Muslim women to punish Muslims as a community. He saw this as justified since Hindus ought “to be arch-devils against the devils.”[74]

In 1925, K. B. Hedgewar (1889–1940) met Savarkar and soon put his ideas—about violence, the Hindu community, and European models—into action by founding the RSS (Rashtriya Swayamsevak Sangh) as a paramilitary organization to promote Hindu nationalism.[75] The early RSS imitated the organization and program of European fascist movements. For instance, RSS recruitment methods were similar to those of Balilla (Italy’s fascist youth group), and even today the RSS recruits young boys and gives them arms training and ideological indoctrination within local branches (*shakhas*).[76] Throughout the 1930s, RSS leaders maintained connections with fascist movements in Mussolini’s Italy.[77] Fascist groups generally have an enemy that they hate and use as a foil for themselves. Whereas the hated other was Jews in European fascism of the 1920s–1940s, the RSS followed Savarkar in considering “as its foremost enemy India’s minority Muslim community.”[78]

Both Savarkar and RSS leaders “openly admitted owing their ideological and organisational inspiration to Mussolini’s Italy and Hitler’s Germany,” even as the staggering harms of Hitler’s Third Reich became evident in Europe.[79] For example, the Nazis and Savarkar published approvingly of one another in November 1938, the month of the Kristallnacht Pogrom.[80] At the same time, speaking in Nagpur, Savarkar proclaimed: "If we Hindus grow stronger in time these Moslem friends of the league type will have to play the part of German-Jews."[81] A year later, the RSS's second leader, M. S. Golwalkar (1906–1973) wrote that Germany's "purging the country of the semitic Race—the Jews" was "a good lesson for us in Hindusthan to learn and profit by."[82] Savarkar and the RSS also intersected with the Hindu Mahasabha, whose leadership Savarkar took over in the 1930s (this prompted a break between the Hindu Mahasabha and Congress).[83] At the group's 1939 meeting, one speaker, Bhai Parmanand, exhorted the audience, "Make Savarkar your Fuehrer. And in no time your nation [will] rise to the pinnacles of glory."[84]

In the period from the 1920s through the 1940s, Hindu nationalism attracted only a minority of Indians. The RSS had about 600,000 members (called *swayamsevak*s, volunteers) when India gained independence in 1947.[85] Its modest momentum was soon disrupted when RSS-affiliate Nathuram Godse assassinated Mohandas Gandhi in 1948, leading to a temporary India-wide ban of the RSS (chapter 22). For decades thereafter, many Indians considered Hindutva ideology to be toxic. But things change, and I end this section on a presentist note.

In the 2020s, Hindu nationalism defines the Indian political mainstream, with its widespread attraction constituting a defining phenomenon over the past decade. Hindutva ideology has not substantively changed in the last century, and its recent dominance in India is usefully considered part of a larger global turn to far-right politics.[86] Hindutva's current popularity builds upon decades of work spearheaded by the RSS from the 1940s onward of forming additional Hindu nationalist groups in India and abroad, which number in the thousands today and are collectively known as the Sangh Parivar (RSS's family).[87] Hindutva's popularity in our times relies on an extensive "propaganda machine" that, among other things, actively attempts to cover up unsavory parts of Hindutva's history and to erase that most Indians over the last hundred years have rejected Hindu nationalism.[88] Given this latter point, it may be hard for readers, maybe especially younger readers, to imagine a time when Hindutva was a minority position, supported only by the most extreme. Such was the world of the 1920s–1940s, when Hindu nationalism was largely overshadowed by other trends.

Advocating Caste Abolition

Some Indians sought liberation from forms of oppression other than colonialism, and one of the defining fights of the era targeted caste-based discrimination. In this, B. R. Ambedkar stood as a towering figure, whose activism and intellectual contributions are still felt today. Ambedkar was born in 1891 as a Mahar, numerically the largest untouchable community in Bombay Presidency.[89] Both of his parents were literate, which was unusual, and as the son of an army-employed school headmaster, he attended a cantonment school.[90] This gave Ambedkar a leg up, but his caste pulled him down. Again and again, he was subjected to privations at school, not given water and forced to sit on the floor.[91] Still, he excelled, catching the eyes of some teachers and ultimately the prince of Baroda, who funded Ambedkar's graduate work at Columbia University in New York City from 1913 to 1916.[92] Ambedkar also studied abroad in London, and when he returned to India, he found casteism as forceful as ever.

In the 1920s, Ambedkar led a series of satyagrahas at Mahad to advocate for Dalit access to roads and drinking water in tanks. Often these were near temples, and so Dalits were prohibited, Brahmin religious leaders said, on purity grounds. Notably, Ambedkar approached Dalit access to public facilities as a civil rights issue of reclaiming shared spaces, rather than as a religious concern primarily.[93] He faced fierce opposition, including from some Congress leaders. Ambedkar also departed from Congress leaders, especially Gandhi, on an important point of nomenclature, using the term "dalit" (oppressed, coined by Jyotirao Phule) from 1928 onward, as opposed to Gandhi's paternalistic "harijan" (God's children).[94] At times, Ambedkar undertook acts designed to vigorously condemn casteism in high-caste Hindu thought, such as burning the *Manusmriti*, whose harsh views on caste we encountered in chapter 7.

Excerpts from B. R. Ambedkar's *Annihilation of Caste*, 1936

The Hindus often complain of the isolation and exclusiveness of a gang or a clique and blame them for anti-social spirit. But they conveniently forget that this anti-social spirit is the worst feature of their own caste system. One caste enjoys singing a hymn of hate against another caste as much as the Germans enjoyed singing their hymn of hate against the English during the last war [World War I]. The literature of the Hindus is full of caste genealogies in which an attempt is made to give a noble origin to one caste and an ignoble origin to other castes. The Sahyadrikhand [part of the *Skanda Purana*] is a notorious instance of this class of literature.

This anti-social spirit is not confined to caste alone. It has gone deeper and has poisoned the mutual relations of the sub-castes as well. In my province the Golak Brahmins, Deorukha Brahmins, Karada Brahmins, Palshe Brahmins, and Chitpavan Brahmins all claim to be subdivisions of the Brahmin caste. But the anti-social spirit that prevails between them is quite as marked and quite as virulent as the anti-social spirit that prevails between them and other non-Brahmin castes. There is nothing strange in this. An anti-social spirit is found wherever one group has "interests of its own" which shut it out from full interaction with other groups, so that its prevailing purpose is protection of what it has got.

. . .

Now this gradation, this scaling of castes, makes it impossible to organise a common front against the caste system. If a caste claims the right to inter-dine and intermarry with another caste placed above it, it is silenced by mischief-mongers—and there are many Brahmins amongst such mischief-mongers—that it will have to concede inter-dining and intermarriage with castes below it! All are slaves of the caste system. But all the slaves do not suffer equally.[95]

Ambedkar had many sharp insights on caste that animated his activist work and inform current academic ideas. He saw caste as a social phenomenon that ranked people, writing, "The caste system is not merely a division of labour. It is also a division of labourers." He understood and argued in the excerpt given here that caste had seemingly endless divisions, grading even those of similar rank against each other and dehumanizing everyone. While caste bound all Indians, Ambedkar pointed out repeatedly that its negative consequences were unequally experienced by Dalits who suffered from the scourge of untouchability. He saw endogamy as the main mechanism by which caste was perpetuated, stating bluntly: "The real remedy for breaking caste is intermarriage."[96]

Ambedkar's thinking on Hinduism, too, had long-standing repercussions, especially within Dalit communities where some followed him in rejecting the religion. Ambedkar declared his intention to leave Hinduism in 1935, stating in Maharashtra after failed Dalit activism to enter some Hindu temples: "Because we have the misfortune to call ourselves Hindus, we are treated thus. If we were members of another faith, none dare treat us so. . . . We shall repair our mistake now. I had the misfortune of being born with the stigma of an untouchable but I will not die a Hindu for this is in my power."[97] On another occasion, Ambedkar reiterated: "To the Untouchables Hinduism is a veritable chamber of horrors."[98] Ambedkar saw no path forward for himself as a Hindu, arguing that the chasm "between the Hindus and the Untouchables is both religious and social," superseding all other divisions in Indian society of his day, including between Hindus and Muslims.[99] Ultimately, Ambedkar chose Buddhism as his new religion and converted in a near deathbed public ceremony in 1956 along with close to half a million other Mahars all dressed in brilliant white for the occasion.[100] Ambedkar's Buddhism was largely his own creation, in which he reimagined the Buddhist dhamma as a social justice program.[101] In this, too, Ambedkar had a substantial impact, and India's eight million or so Buddhists today are largely followers of Ambedkar's Navayana (innovative) branch of Buddhism.

B. R. Ambedkar was a founding father of the modern Indian nation-state, and chapter 23 covers his critical role in writing the Indian constitution and serving as India's first law minister. Yet, early on, Ambedkar saw the contradiction embedded in fighting for freedom amid unequals. He ended his 1936 *Annihilation of Caste* with the following paragraph, directed to anti-caste activists:

> Yours is more difficult than the other national cause, namely, swaraj. In the fight for swaraj you fight with the whole nation on your side. In this, you have to fight against the whole nation—and that too, your own. But it is more important than swaraj. There is no use having swaraj, if you cannot defend it. More important than the question of defending swaraj is the question of defending the Hindus under the swaraj. In my opinion, it is only when Hindu society becomes a casteless society that it can hope to have strength enough to defend itself. Without

> such internal strength, swaraj for Hindus may turn out to be only a step towards slavery. Goodbye, and good wishes for your success.[102]

As for Ambedkar, he did not choose between India's independence and anti-caste activism, instead pursuing both with vigor and agility.

Conclusion: Almost Independent

Divisions shot through the Indian independence movement as the 1940s dawned and it became clear that ending British colonialism in India was on the horizon, but the terms of self-rule were not yet articulated. Not everyone wanted freedom from British rule, or even saw it as freedom, given the internal rifts within Indian society based on language, caste, region, and politics. Some Indians were focused on issues other than independence, such as articulating Hindutva ideology. Still, the big story leading into the violent birth of modern-day India and Pakistan—both carved out of British India in 1947—was division between Hindus and Muslims as well as within each broad-based community as multiple visions for the future competed for Indian attention.

Further Reading

The writings and speeches of India's core founding fathers have been collated into collected works, and I cite here from those of B. R. Ambedkar, Mohandas Gandhi, and Aurobindo Ghose. I also cite some of their central monographs, such as Ambedkar's *Annihilation of Caste* (1936; cited in the 2014 edition with Arundhati Roy's insightful introduction) and Gandhi's *Hind Swaraj* (1909). Rajmohan Gandhi and David Arnold are astute biographers of Mohandas Gandhi's life, and I found helpful work on Ambedkar by Anupama Rao and others. Durba Ghosh's work on violence in the Indian independence movement is compelling. On early Hindutva, I used scholarship by Janaki Bakhle, Vinayak Chaturvedi, Christophe Jaffrelot, and Tanika Sarkar.

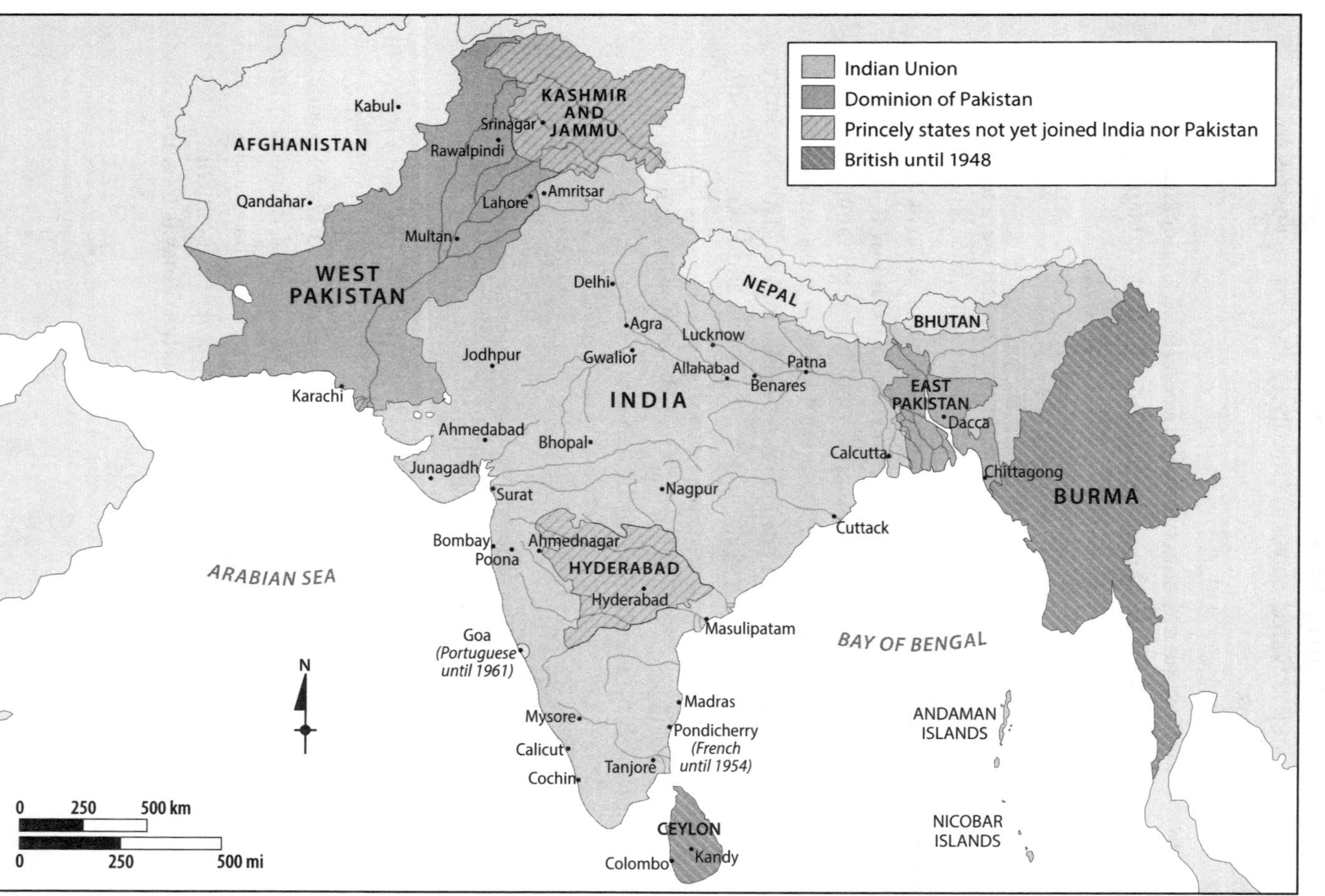

Post-partition South Asia, 1947.

22

Dividing India in 1947

Over there, behind the barbed wires, was Hindustan.
Over here, behind identical wires lay Pakistan.

—Saadat Manto, Toba Tek Singh, 1955 (Urdu)[1]

At a basilar level, the Indian independence movement succeeded in ending British colonial rule in 1947, but freedom came with vicious caveats. On their way out, the British broke India, partitioning their colony into three land areas divided, unevenly, between two nations. The newly minted Pakistani and Indian states exploded with mass migration and violence, especially impacting Hindus, Sikhs, and Muslims in Punjab and Hindus and Muslims in Bengal. One to two million South Asians died at each other's hands in riots, pogroms, interstate conflict, insurgent uprisings, and ethnic cleansings between 1946 and 1949. Additionally, princely states such as Kashmir and Hyderabad were left in dispute, which resulted in invasions, wars, and, for some who survived, denial of political self-determination. Relations remain rocky between India and Pakistan today, separated by literal barbed wire in sections, as per the Urdu author Saadat Hasan Manto. Surveying a mix of political events, social trends, and personal stories enables us to capture the bloody twin births of independent India and Pakistan.

Hindu-Muslim Tensions and World War II

By 1940, Hindu-Muslim tensions were part of the South Asian social fabric. This was a radical shift from a mere two centuries earlier, when Hindu identity was still unarticulated as such and conflict between broad-based religious communities was not a major subcontinental dynamic. Equally new in South Asian history was a politically cohesive India forged through colonial violence (really, semi-cohesive, given that British India was punctured by hundreds of princely states). Violence also proved definitional to the next phase of Indian politics, namely a division creating what the *New York Times* dubbed "two Indian nations" on their front page for Friday August 15, 1947.[2] It was neither fated nor obvious that Indian independences, plural, would be secured via the deleterious violence of partition.[3] Last-minute decisions and unforeseen consequences are critical to explaining the sequence of events.

The idea of splitting British India to create two states—with a Muslim-majority one dubbed Pakistan—was articulated only in the 1930s through two key moments. In December 1930, statesman and philosopher-poet Muhammad Iqbal (1877–1938) endorsed a split into two states during his address to the All-India Muslim League in Allahabad: "I would like to see the Punjab, the North-West Frontier Province, Sind and Baluchistan amalgamated into a single State. Self-government within the British Empire, or without the British Empire, the formation of a consolidated North-West Indian Muslim State appears to me to be the final destiny of the Muslims, at least of North-West India."[4] Notably, Iqbal disavowed "religious rule in such States," defining Islam in the same address as "an ethical ideal plus a certain kind of polity."[5] In 1933, an Indian student at the University of Cambridge, Choudhary Rahmat Ali (1897–1951), published a pamphlet introducing the proposed name of "Pakistan," meaning "land of the pure" and also an acronym of its five projected western provinces: **P**unjab, **A**fghan (North-West Frontier Province), **K**ashmir, **S**ind, and Baluchi**stan**.[6] The concept of a religious-based partition had precedent, most notably in the 1905–1911 British split of Bengal into Muslim-majority and Hindu-majority areas (chapter 21). But, as of the early to mid-1930s—when Pakistan was a wild-card idea—its basic proposed features remained unclear. Would it have an eastern portion? Would it be a distinct nation or loosely federated with the rest of India? What role would Islam play in the government? What would happen to Sikhs, who were spread across the Punjab?

With minimal clarification on Pakistan's proposed contours, the Muslim League advocated its creation from 1940 forward under the leadership of Muhammad Ali Jinnah. The League overall underwent huge growth between 1927, when it had a mere 1,330 card-carrying members, and 1944 when it counted two million members.[7] This came nowhere close to representing all Indian Muslims, a community ninety-five million strong and constituting roughly 25 percent of Indians, as per the 1941 census.[8] In fact, the 1937 Indian elections were a resounding rejection of Jinnah's leadership with the League receiving a measly 4.4 percent of votes cast by Indian Muslims.[9] But Jinnah was undeterred, and, in 1940, he successfully lobbied for the League to pass the Lahore Resolution that prioritized advocating for Pakistan (without using the name):

> Resolved that it is the considered view of this Session of the All-India Muslim League that no constitutional plan would be workable in this country or acceptable to the Muslims unless it is designed on the following basic principles, viz., that geographically contiguous units are demarcated into regions which should be so constituted, with such territorial readjustments as may be necessary, that the areas in which the Muslims are numerically in a majority, as in the North-Western and Eastern zones of India, should be grouped to constitute Independent States in which the constituent units shall be autonomous and sovereign.[10]

That same year, 1940, Jinnah wrote to Mohandas Gandhi: "Let me say again that India is not a nation, nor a country. It is a sub-continent composed of nationalities, Hindus and Muslims being the two major nations."[11]

Throughout the early to mid-1940s, the League gained momentum, even while many Indian Muslims disavowed Muslim nationalist rhetoric. For instance, when Maulana Azad became Indian National Congress president in 1940, he proudly proclaimed his intertwined Muslim and Indian identities. "I am a Musalman and am proud of that fact. Islam's splendid traditions of thirteen hundred years are my inheritance. I am unwilling to lose even the smallest part of this inheritance . . . I am proud of being an Indian. I am a part of the indivisible unity that is Indian nationality. I am indispensable to this noble edifice and without me this splendid structure of India is incomplete. I am an essential element which has gone to build India. I can never surrender this claim."[12] The president of the Jamiat-ul-Ulema, a Congress-friendly Muslim political party in northern and central India, rebuked Jinnah in 1945 as "Kafir-i-Azam" (Great heathen), a play on his honorific title "Quaid-i-Azam" (Great leader).[13] Some Shias worried about their religious rights being trampled in any state fashioned by the League's Sunni leadership, warning in a 1946 newspaper that Pakistan "is going to be Sunnistan."[14] Still, the League amassed significant political clout, and Pakistan—a new state defined, for the first time in South Asian history, along religious lines—proved a powerful ask.[15]

Amid the push for Indian and (for some) Pakistani independence, World War II broke out in September 1939, which interrupted the independence movement (and, accordingly, my narrative thereof). The Indian National Congress did not offer clear support for the British. This contrasted sharply with World War I (1914–1918), when Mohandas Gandhi had recruited sepoys to fight.[16] However, Jawaharlal Nehru's view as of October 1939, articulated in the Lucknow-based *National Herald*, was that Congress opposed German fascism and British imperialism: "The world moves and India moves with it and the methods and language of a generation ago are singularly out of place everywhere, and nowhere more so than in India. Our faces are set forward, not backward, and forward we shall march. We have no intention of shouting *Heil Hitler*; neither do we intend to shout *British Imperialism Zindabad*."[17] In addition to Congress withholding support, Britain found itself stretched thin by the war effort, and their most powerful ally—America's Roosevelt administration—favored Indian independence.[18] Winston Churchill, who became Britain's prime minister in May 1940, authorized Stafford Cripps to travel to India in early 1942 and bargain for Congress backing the Allies in exchange for Indian self-government at the war's conclusion. But the Cripps mission failed, and, in response, in summer 1942, Mohandas Gandhi initiated the Quit India movement. As Gandhi enunciated the movement's thrust in Bombay in August 1942: "The *mantra* is: 'Do or Die.' We shall either free India or die in the attempt; we shall not live to see the perpetuation of our slavery."[19]

Pressured on many sides, the British Raj reacted as it had time and again: with brute force and widespread crackdowns. In 1942, British officials arrested all Congress's leadership—including Jawaharlal Nehru, Maulana Azad, and Mohandas Gandhi—imprisoning them, along with 60,000 to 90,000 additional Indian political prisoners.[20] Some Congress leaders used the time behind bars to outline their views. Nehru penned his *Discovery of India*, on nationalism and Indian history, while jailed at Maharashtra's Ahmednagar Fort.[21] But the mass imprisonments smothered Congress's ability to organize during the war years. Meanwhile, the

Quit India movement proceeded and, in the absence of political leadership, was undisciplined and violent. British Raj officials were given a "free hand . . . to use force" in response and killed thousands of protestors.[22] Additionally, colonial policies produced a famine in Bengal in 1943 in which two million died, a bleak demonstration of the British-made reality, in the words of the Anglo-Indian writer George Aberigh-Mackay, "Famine is the horizon of the Indian villager."[23]

Congress's lack of support notwithstanding, millions of Indians fought for the Allies. The Indian army more than doubled in size between 1941 to 1945, with two and a half million Indian sepoys joining Allied forces and 24,000 sacrificing their lives.[24] This rapid militarization fed into some of the partition violence in the later 1940s. It also illustrates the diversity of viewpoints, even at the tail end of the British Raj, on how Indians ought to relate to colonial rule. Some Indians fought because they were loyalists to the British, whereas others pursued pragmatic career goals or stable employment.

Taking a different tack, a small number of Indians collaborated with Nazi Germany and Imperial Japan, following the logic that their enemy's enemy (i.e., Britain's enemy) was their friend. Most famously, Subhas Chandra Bose escaped house arrest in British India in 1941 and fled to Berlin. In 1942, he was photographed meeting with Heinrich Himmler, head of the SS, and Adolf Hitler, whom Bose viewed as "an old revolutionary."[25] In 1943, after realizing that Hitler would not help India achieve independence, Bose decamped to Imperial Japan. He spent the next two years recruiting Indian prisoners of war to train for the Japanese-sponsored Indian National Army that theoretically fought for the Axis powers (in reality, many defected back to the Allies at their earliest opportunity).[26] At the war's conclusion, the British court-martialed a handful of Indian National Army leaders, but Bose never had to face the consequences of allying with fascists. He was killed in a plane crash in East Asia on August 18, 1945, three months after Nazi Germany capitulated to the Allies and mere days after the Japanese announced their unconditional surrender.[27]

World War II ended in the Pacific with the dropping of two atomic bombs, whose development had a curious intersection with Indian history. Robert Oppenheimer headed the Manhattan Project that developed the destructive weapon. Oppenheimer had taught physics at Berkeley in the 1930s, where he studied Sanskrit under Arthur Ryder and read the Bhagavadgita in its original language.[28] By this point, elite American universities had followed European institutions in studying and teaching Sanskrit literature.[29] When Oppenheimer saw the atomic bomb's test explosion in the New Mexico desert in July 1945—a flash of light followed by an ominous mushroom cloud—he quoted two Sanskrit lines from the Gita in his own translation: "If the radiance of a thousand suns were to burst at once into the sky / that would be like the splendor of the Mighty One" and, quoting Krishna, "I am become Death, the shatterer of worlds."[30] Indeed, the atomic bomb shattered Imperial Japan, killing tens of thousands instantly at Hiroshima and Nagasaki and ending World War II. A weakened Britain emerged from the war ready to offload its Indian colony.

Sunset on British India

From mid-1945 through 1946, India experienced accelerating social and political turmoil as it became clear that the British would leave, but nobody agreed on the terms. After Germany surrendered in May 1945, the British released the bulk of Indian political prisoners incarcerated during the war years, including Congress leaders, and canceled many warrants for violent activists who had gone underground. The British Raj then tried to elicit a consensus on how, precisely, to transfer political power to Indians. They brought Congress and League leaders together at Simla (Shimla), a northern hill station, in summer 1945, but the conference fell apart over disagreement about appointing representatives.[31] A frustrated Archibald Wavell, India's Viceroy, complained in his diary, "Gandhi and Jinnah are behaving like very temperamental prima donnas."[32] The British tried again in 1946 to elicit consensus among India's fractured political parties, that time for a tiered federation system, but that too failed. Much ink has been spilled on the to-and-fro of Indian independence leaders in these months (and I cover some of it in this chapter). But events on the ground also offer a fruitful perspective for grasping the environment leading up to an event so well known and cataclysmic that it is sometimes capitalized: Partition.

Wavell called for general elections in India, held December 1945–March 1946, and the results attested that many Indian Muslims had changed their minds about Jinnah and the League. Whereas less than one in twenty Indian Muslim voters endorsed for the League in the 1937 elections, nearly 75 percent did so in 1945–1946, which handed the League all thirty central legislature seats reserved for Muslims and almost 90 percent of reserved provincial seats.[33] There are limits to what this data indicates. The 1945–1946 election was electorally restrictive, with only about 10 percent of Indians eligible to vote, and the process was riddled with fraud. Still, these elections were the most democratic exercise on the subcontinent ever, and they indicated a sea change in Muslim support for Jinnah's idea of Pakistan.[34]

Overall, 1946 witnessed social instability across India. There were seemingly endless strikes across industries as more than 1,600 industrial disputes involved close to two million workers. Princely states, too, saw uprisings.[35] But by far the violence most calamitous—that had never been witnessed on such a scale before in South Asia—was communal violence along religious lines. Some saw this coming, such as Vallabhbhai Patel, who wrote in January 1946, "If Pakistan is to be achieved the Hindus and Muslims will have to fight. There will be a civil war."[36]

The Calcutta killings were the first large massacre, exacted over five days, August 16–20, 1946. Groups had anticipated clashes for months, and the spark—which explains why things began on August 16—was when Jinnah, frustrated by the latest machinations in political negotiations, called for a day of "direct action," meaning a hartal (strike). Hindu Mahasabha and Congress leaders in Bengal characterized the strike as targeting Hindus.[37] On August 16, 1946, the League ran advertisements in major newspapers in Punjab and Bengal:

> Today is Direct Action Day
> Today Muslims of India dedicate their lives and all they possess to the cause of freedom
> Today let every Muslim swear in the name of Allah to resist aggression
> Direct action is now their only course
> Because they offered peace but peace was spurned
> They honoured their word but they were betrayed
> They claimed Liberty but were offered Thraldom
> Now Might alone can secure their Right[38]

The violence began in the early morning between Hindu and Muslim communities, and organized groups on both sides fanned the flames. Within a week, 5,000 Indians were murdered, and tens of thousands were injured or rendered homeless.[39]

Several features of the 1946 Calcutta killings recurred in subsequent cases of communal violence in India, during partition and until today.

First, the violence was organized by militias and political groups, with perhaps the most efficient being the Hindu Mahasabha, a Hindu nationalist party.[40] As discussed next, both the Mahasabha and the Hindu nationalist RSS took advantage of partition's chaos to enact violence against religious minorities. Second, more Muslims died than Hindus.[41] As Vallabhbhai Patel wrote in October 1946, "In Calcutta, Hindus had the best of it. But that is no comfort."[42] Communal violence has generally disadvantaged religious minorities in independent South Asian nations as well. Third, in 1946, the violence spread as events in Calcutta inspired aggressions in Bengal and Bihar, some of which raged for months. As Hindus and Muslims blamed each other for specific acts, a spiral effect unfolded driven by compounding calls for revenge.[43]

By early 1947, it was painfully clear that violence and independence would go together for Indians, and the British appointed a new leader, Louis Mountbatten, to serve as their final Viceroy of India. When Mountbatten arrived in Delhi in March 1947, parts of Punjabi cities were aflame, including Amritsar, Multan, and Rawalpindi.[44] Indian independence leaders—including Nehru (Congress), Baldev Singh (Sikh leader), and Jinnah (League)—were no closer to agreeing *to whom* the British should transfer political authority. After a few months of back and forth, all four leaders—Mountbatten, Nehru, Jinnah, and Baldev Singh—spoke in succession on June 3, 1947, at 7:00 p.m. on All India Radio to announce that British India would be split into two dominions roughly according to religious majorities: Pakistan and India.[45] Mountbatten soon declared that independence would commence, not in mid-1948 as originally scheduled, but rather on August 15, 1947. In the rush to meet that rapid deadline, as the Indian Urdu writer Ismat Chughtai (1915–1991) later put it, "Communal violence and freedom became so muddled that it was difficult to distinguish between the two."[46]

Colonial Endgame of Partition

By mid-June 1947, Indians knew that they would be split into two protonations in two months, but the details remained fuzzy. The public was unaware until after the last minute—two days post-independence—of the boundary lines separating India and Pakistan.[47] The uncertainty led to wild speculation and fear, especially for those in Punjab and Bengal (the states to be carved apart), which in turn fueled migration and violence.[48] As a large-scale population transfer began in summer 1947, no government intervened, and British political elites carried on as usual with their social calendars. The Mountbattens even celebrated their silver wedding anniversary (twenty-five years) in India in July 1947, hosting Jinnah, Nehru, and numerous Indian princes at a dinner party.[49] While the elites toasted, the calamity of partition began to unfold between late June and mid-August 1947 through two processes: legalistic decisions by political leaders and growing communal conflict amid large-scale migrations.

The lines partitioning Punjab and Bengal were decided by British barrister Cyril Radcliffe through a politicized legal process. Radcliffe relied on reports produced by eight Indian high-court judges who were divided between the Bengal Boundary Commission and the Punjab Boundary Commission. Every judge was affiliated with either the League or Congress and pushed his party's political agenda.[50] The judges-cum-political representatives held hearings in Calcutta and Lahore, respectively, for eight to ten days in July. During this time, they listened predominantly to Congress, League, and other political representatives present maps and legalistic arguments.[51] This followed general British colonial practices of relying on judicial authority (rather than geographic or civil service expertise) for boundary making, but it is worth underscoring what that choice omitted.[52]

The boundary commissions did not conduct fieldwork, failing to even survey the land they hacked into two nations, which led to numerous oddities, even absurdities. The partition lines cut through villages, factories, and shrines. At times the boundary relied on shifting geographical features, such as rivers that dried up annually. Even in their legalistic approach, the boundary commissions made mistakes by using old maps. For instance, part of the eastern border through Bengal followed the Mathabhanga River, which had changed course from its placement on the outdated map used by the Bengal Boundary Commission. As a result, about 500 square miles that Radcliffe and his team thought they were earmarking for India went to Pakistan.[53]

Cyril Radcliffe had the final say on the Punjab and Bengal partition lines, and he understood that his primary job was to finish quickly. Radcliffe arrived in India on July 8, 1947—his first and only visit to South Asia—and was given five and a half weeks to draw a line delineating roughly 3,800 miles of border.[54] He attended neither boundary commission's hearings, nor did he view most of the land that he cleaved apart (he took one plane trip to see part of rural Punjab).[55] Mountbatten heralded Radcliffe's lack of familiarity with India as proof of his impartiality.[56] The real push, noted by Oskar Spate—a British geographer hired to represent the Ahmadiyya community—was for a "quick decision" above all else.[57] Indeed, Radcliffe completed his task a few days early, by August 13, exactly five weeks and one day after he landed in Delhi.

Mountbatten delayed announcing the partition lines for several days. He informed Indian and (by that point) Pakistani political leaders of the details on August 16, 1947 and released the line publicly on August 17, 1947.[58] Pakistan comprised 23 percent of British India's land mass and 18 percent of its population, split between two noncontiguous eastern and western portions that were separated by 1,000 miles of independent India.[59] One newspaper described it as "territorial murder."[60] The partition award did not explain Radcliffe's decision-making process, and in later years Radcliffe simply said, "All leaders like Jinnah, Nehru and Patel told me that they wanted a line before or on 15th August. So I drew them a line."[61]

When the British transferred power at the stroke of midnight on August 15, 1947, to the dominions of India and Pakistan, their respective leaders—Nehru and Jinnah—gave parallel speeches. Jawaharlal Nehru opened with these well-known lines at India's Constituent Assembly: "Long years ago we made a tryst with destiny, and now the time comes when we shall redeem our pledge, not wholly or in full measure, but very substantially. At the stroke of the midnight hour, when the world sleeps, India will awake to life and freedom."[62] Muhammad Ali Jinnah inaugurated the Pakistan broadcasting service on August 15 with: "It is with feelings of greatest happiness and emotion that I send you my greetings. August 15 is the birthday of the independent and sovereign State of Pakistan. It marks the fulfilment of the destiny of the Muslim nation which made great sacrifices in the past few years to have its homeland."[63] Nehru and Jinnah's speeches overlapped substantially, which seems to reflect the intertwined independence of India and Pakistan. Both leaders marked a historical break, looking ahead to a "future that beckons" (Nehru) and "the beginning of a new and a noble era" (Jinnah). Both used the language of "responsibility" and held up their brand-new nations as examples for the world. Both acknowledged violence in the transition but promised peace, which seemed implausible but desirable given the harsh realities in Bengal and Punjab.[64]

Partition's Bloodshed

Even at the shared moment of Indian and Pakistani independence, violence raged (described below) and more was feared. Oskar Spate wrote in Karachi on August 15 that the "idea seems to be to get the celebrations over and then have the shooting."[65] Indeed, Vallabhbhai Patel warned Mountbatten regarding rumors about the Bengal line on August 13: "If the award confirms the worst fears entertained by the public, it is impossible for me to predict the volume of bitterness and rancour which would be let loose and I am certain that this will create a situation which both you and I may have to regret."[66] Regrets about partition are individualistic, but many agreed that it was not the freedom they wanted. As the Pakistani Urdu poet Faiz Ahmed Faiz (1911–1984) wrote in a poem published on August 14, 1947:

> This leprous daybreak, dawn night's fangs have mangled—
> This is not that long-looked-for break of day.[67]

East and West Pakistan were majority Muslim, whereas independent India was majority Hindu, but tens of millions found their ancestral homes and themselves, strangely, in the wrong state. Despite vocalizing their concerns, the Sikh population and holy sites were divided between Pakistan and India. One million South Asians had already left their homes as of mid-August 1947 to migrate to where they thought they could live in peace, and eleven million more fled in the following months, constituting the largest migration in known human history. For both those who became refugees and those who stayed behind, communal violence reached unprecedented levels, tearing across Punjab and Bengal and impacting large cities across India and Pakistan.

Survivors of partition struggled with capturing its horrors and insanity, with many turning to historical fiction. In India, Khushwant Singh (1915–2014) penned a novella in 1956, *Train to Pakistan*, memorializing the trains that traveled between young India and Pakistan exchanging Muslims for Hindus and Sikhs. These included "ghost trains" where all on board were slaughtered. The writings of Saadat Hasan Manto (1912–1955)—who grew up in Amritsar and migrated from Bombay to Lahore in 1948—have struck many as uniquely insightful regarding partition's pain.[68] Among his more famous stories, "Toba Tek Singh" focuses on the exchange of asylum patients between India and Pakistan through the eyes of Toba Tek Singh, who is named after his village and confused by the new geopolitical reality. Manto wrote "Khol Do" (Open It) and "Thanda Gosht" (Cold meat) within a few days of each other, both about rape as a weapon of communal terror.[69] I give an excerpt here from a more biographical piece by Manto, *Stars from Another Sky*, along with excerpts from an essay by Ismat Chughtai. Both question if partition really brought freedom and struggle to articulate its horror. In my own commentary, I stay closer to the facts, inadequate as they are to capture the brutal experience.

Saadat Hasan Manto (d. 1955), Excerpt from *Stars from Another Sky* (Urdu)

Fourteenth August, the day of independence, was celebrated in Bombay with tremendous fanfare. Pakistan and India had been declared two separate countries. There was great public rejoicing, but murder and arson continued unabated. Along with cries of "India Zindabad," one also heard "Pakistan Zindabad." The green Islamic flag fluttered next to the tricolour of the Indian National Congress. The streets and bazaars reverberated with slogans as people shouted the names of Pandit Jawaharlal Nehru and Quaid-i-Azam Muhammad Ali Jinnah.

I found it impossible to decide which of the two countries was now my homeland—India or Pakistan. Who was responsible for the blood which was being mercilessly shed every day? Where were they going to inter the bones which had been stripped of the flesh of religion by vultures and birds of prey? Now that we were free, had subjection ceased to exist? Who would be our slaves? When we were colonial subjects, we could dream of freedom, but now that we were free, what would our dreams be? Were we even free? Thousands of Hindus and Muslims were dying all around us. Why were they dying?

All these questions had different answers: the Indian answer, the Pakistani answer, the British answer. Every question had an answer, but when you tried to look for the truth, none of those answers was any help.

Some said if you were looking for the truth, you would have to go back to the ruins of the 1857 Mutiny. Others said, no, it all lay in the history of the [British] East India Company. Some went back even further and advised you to analyse the Mughal empire. Everybody wanted to drag you back into the past, while murderers and terrorists marched on unchallenged, writing in the process a story of blood and fire which was without parallel in history.[70]

Ismat Chughtai (d. 1991), Excerpt from "Communal Violence and Literature" (Urdu)

The flood of communal violence came and went with all its evils, but it left a pile of living, dead, and gasping corpses in its wake. It wasn't only that the country was split in two—bodies and minds were also divided. Moral beliefs were tossed aside and humanity was in shreds. Government officers and clerks along with their chairs, pens and inkpots, were distributed like the spoils of war. And whatever remained after this division was laid to waste by the benevolent hands of communal violence. Those whose bodies were whole had hearts that were splintered. Families were torn apart. One brother was allotted to Hindustan, the other to Pakistan; the mother was in Hindustan, her offspring were in Pakistan; the husband was in Hindustan, his wife was in Pakistan. The bonds of human relationship were in tatters, and in the end many souls remained behind in Hindustan while their bodies started off for Pakistan.

Communal violence and freedom became so muddled that it was difficult to distinguish between the two. After that, anyone who obtained a measure of freedom discovered violence came alongside. The storm struck without any warning so people couldn't even gather their belongings. When things cooled down a bit people collected themselves and had a chance to observe what was going on around them.

With every aspect of life disrupted by this earth-shaking event, how could poets and writers possibly sit by without saying a word? How could literature, which has close ties with life, avoid getting its shirtfront wet when life was drenched in blood? Forgetting the struggles of love and separation, people concentrated on saving their skin and bones . . .

> As soon as the writers and poets had a moment to breathe, they turned towards their objective. A variety of viewpoints and sentiments, some progressive, some reactionary, and still others that were neither of these but some mysterious entity in the middle, could be observed. Some writers, armed with plaster and mortar, threw themselves headlong into laying this mortar and whitewashing.[71]

Partition's carnage was perpetrated by everyday people, make-shift militias, and law officers who chose communal over professional loyalties. In some cases, neighbors turned on neighbors, such as Harjit who attested decades later, "One day our entire village took off to a nearby Muslim village on a killing spree. We simply went mad. And it has cost me fifty years of remorse, of sleepless nights—I cannot forget the faces of those we killed."[72] In other cases, the violence was organized by groups such as the Hindu Mahasabha and the RSS. The British tracked RSS activities and noted in a mid-June 1946 report that the group had a "long term policy of steady preparation for the attainment of its ultimate goal of Hindu supremacy."[73] The RSS and the Hindu Mahasabha led ethnic cleansing in the princely states of Alwar and Bharatpur in Rajasthan in 1947, killing around 30,000 Muslims and largely forcibly converting or driving out the rest.[74]

Partition refugees traveled by trains (figure 22.1), steam ships, cars, and planes, but most—millions of people—walked. The columns, called *kafilas*, were miles long as Hindus and Muslims took what they could carry and left behind jobs, property, wealth, and family. The American photographer Margaret Bourke-White photographed some of the refugees for *Life* magazine, and her photos became the defining images of these events.[75] Once they reached their destinations, the migrants constituted huge refugee populations. In Pakistan, one in ten was a refugee (*muhajir*) by late 1947.[76] In India, the largest refugee camp was Kurukshetra, named after the location of the legendary Mahabharata conflict, although its battles in 1947 were against disease, housing shortages, and unwanted pregnancies.[77] Many refugees were traumatized, such as the man who slapped Nehru during the prime minister's tour of a camp and demanded: "Give my mother back to me! Bring my sisters to me!"[78]

Some partition violence was gendered, following on patriarchal ideas shared by many Indian and Pakistani communities that family honor de-

Figure 22.1. Refugees crowding on a train during the partition of British India, 1947 CE, Punjab. Photographer unknown.

pends on controlling women's bodies. Tens of thousands of women were abducted, on both sides.[79] Many were raped, had their breasts cut off, were subjected to genital mutilation, murdered, or some combination thereof. Indians and Pakistanis branded women's bodies with freedom slogans, marking their breasts and faces with "Pakistan Zindabad" or "Jai Hind" (long live Pakistan or India).[80] To avoid such crimes, some women committed suicide or were murdered by their own kin.[81] Many who experienced sexual violence were unable to recover their lives, even years later. Trying to reintegrate abducted women into society, Indian campaigners cited the example of Rama taking back Sita, despite her having lived in the demon Ravana's palace for months. This argument overlooked the part of the Ramayana story where Sita endures a fire test, jumping into the flames to prove her sexual purity. In any case, many mid-twentieth century Indians were unable to look past the children born of rape.[82]

In addition to waves of violence, partition left behind administrative loose ends. It took years, but India and Pakistan divided literally everything in the end, including armies, records, and even paperweights.[83] Still, as many have observed, aspects of partition remained unfinished. People traveled back and forth between the two nations without official hindrance for years. Travel became more restricted in the 1950s when "India-Pakistan passports" were introduced, ironically, to facilitate travel.[84] Parts of the border remained disputed and unmarked for more than a decade, with a 1960 agreement settling outstanding disputes along the Punjab boundary.[85] In the meantime, additional challenges confronted the new nation-states.

Dust Unsettled

Newly independent India and Pakistan faced immediate challenges (beyond partition), beginning with uncertainty about some princely states. British India's 565 princely states were omitted from the partition decision. There was a fiction that each state would revert to independence with its prince deciding his territory's post-British Raj position. In reality, most princely territories were engulfed within either India or Pakistan, and so joined almost by default one of these two nations. Still, a few princes with larger domains hesitated. For instance, Tonk—a Rajasthan principality of 300,000 people spread across 2,500 square miles—maintained nominal independence for seven months before its nawab acceded to India.[86] For two princely states—Hyderabad and Kashmir—things grew more complicated and bloody.

Hyderabad established itself as an independent state for more than one year before Indian forces invaded. Congress had designs on Hyderabad going into partition, but its nizam—landlocked in "India's belly"—decided to remain independent.[87] For a while, Hyderabad and India negotiated. But then, in September 1948, India initiated what it called a "police action," invading independent Hyderabad and killing perhaps 50,000 Muslim supporters of the nizam.[88] Congress politicians publicly denied the war's human cost for decades, but they knew the truth. The officially commissioned Sunderlal Report—written in 1948 but not declassified by India until 2013—confirmed death numbers in the tens of thousands.[89] Taking over Hyderabad in 1948 was not the last time that independent India invaded to gain territory (e.g., Goa in 1961). The withholding of information, too, became a trend, also witnessed in the dispute over Kashmir.

Owing to quirks of geography and history, it was unclear whether Kashmir would join India or Pakistan, and both states desired the territory. As of 1947, Kashmir was a Muslim-majority region with Hindu leadership under the Dogra dynasty. Kashmir had substantial borders with Pakistan and India, as well as China, which enabled a real choice for accession and made the territory of strategic importance. Additionally, Kashmir held symbolic value for both new nations, as a Muslim-majority area for Pakistan and as a site of ancient Sanskrit learning (emphasized by the Dogra regime) for India.[90] To top it off, Kashmir boasts natural resources, including key parts of the Indus River system.[91] For both India and Pakistan, the political will of Kashmiris was a subsidiary concern overshadowed by the region's attractive features.

In fall 1947, Pakistan-based tribesmen invaded to preempt the Dogra maharaja agreeing to join India. Kashmiris had suffered from an oppressive state and communal conflict before this point. The Dogra regime (rulers of Kashmir 1846–1947) cultivated support among Kashmiri pandits—Hindu Brahmins who constituted about 5 percent of the population—and discriminated against Kashmiri Muslims.[92] This had prompted Hindu-Muslim conflict, such as the July 1931 unrest in which Muslims pushed back against Dogra oppression.[93] But, violence escalated to unprecedented levels in 1947–1948 as India and Pakistan fought their first war, over Kashmir, with a death toll of around 7,500.[94] The war ended with a ceasefire in 1949 brokered by the United Nations, a new institution itself, with the promise of a future plebiscite in which the people of Kashmir would vote to decide their political future. The plebiscite has never occurred.[95] As of the time of writing (August 2024), Kashmir remains partly administered by India and has the most militarized border in the world along the Line of Control, effectively the ceasefire line from 1949.

While these civil and international conflicts unfolded in 1948, Pakistanis and Indians lost two of their key founding fathers: Jinnah and Gandhi, respectively. Jinnah died in September 1948 of health problems that stemmed from tuberculosis, whereas his fellow independence leader, Mohandas Gandhi, had a rather different death.

Gandhi was at a prayer meeting on January 30, 1948, at Delhi's Birla House, when Nathuram Godse—a Hindu nationalist and Maharashtrian Brahmin affiliated with the RSS and V. D. Savarkar[96]—shot him at point-blank range. Several features of this brutal murder reflect defining aspects of Hindutva ideology and its followers. Godse shot Gandhi at a prayer meeting, a reminder of Hindutva's disregard for piety.[97] It was an act of deadly violence, a virtue in Hindutva ideology (chapter 21). Last,

Godse used a Beretta semiautomatic pistol, made by one of Europe's oldest companies, a physical incarnation of Hindutva's debt to European thought.[98]

Gandhi was no friend of the RSS. A few months earlier, he had confronted M. S. Golwalkar, the group's head from 1940 to 1973, about the RSS's violent activities in Delhi.[99] Still, as detailed in chapter 21, Congress had tolerated soft Hindu nationalism for decades and shared leaders with the Hindu Mahasabha. In killing India's most celebrated independence leader, Nathuram Godse shined a harsh light on Hindu nationalist ideology such that it was no longer possible, at least for a while, for most Indians to overlook "the violence of Hindutva."[100] Indeed, as one scholar has put it, whether Savarkar offered an "explicit plan of instructions" that motivated Godse or not, "Godse's assassination of Gandhi . . . was both prefigured and justified in [Savarkar's] writings."[101] In brief, Godse's murder of Gandhi posed a choice for Indians between embracing Hindu nationalist violence or upholding Gandhi's pluralistic values, and they overwhelmingly chose the latter.

Gandhi's death united the Indian nation in grief. Addressing his people on the radio, Jawaharlal Nehru spoke in Hindi and thereafter in English: "The light has gone out of our lives and there is darkness everywhere. I do not know what to tell you or how to say it. Our beloved leader, Bapu as we called him, the Father of the Nation, is no more."[102] Harivansh Rai Bachchan (1907–2003) wrote poems to capture his thoughts, and one began, "Today our Bapu has passed on / Today our flag is lowered in shame."[103] But communal violence soon reduced, and in the coming months, thousands of Muslim refugees returned to Delhi.[104] In retrospect, Gandhi's death served as a turning point, after which the worst of partition violence was behind the new Indian state. As Yasmin Khan has put it, Gandhi's "assassination proved a cathartic experience which enabled and embodied the beginning of the new nation."[105]

Critical to this new beginning for the new Indian nation was rejecting Hindu supremacy. India tried and convicted Gandhi's assassin Nathuram Godse in 1948–1949. Godse gave a fervent speech at trial, testifying that he was angry because Gandhi had tried to "appease" (Godse's term) Muslims and in so doing advocated views "prejudicial and detrimental to the Hindu Community."[106] Godse admitted that, watching Gandhi, "my blood boiled, and I could not tolerate him any longer."[107] Newly independent India decided not to tolerate such fanaticism, and so—going against pleas for mercy by two of Mohandas

Gandhi's sons—the Indian state executed Godse in 1949.[108] The RSS and Savarkar were also implicated in Gandhi's assassination.[109] Nehru, believing that the RSS was "definitely proceeding on the strictest Nazi lines," banned the group for a year.[110] Savarkar (d. 1966) was formally acquitted of Gandhi's murder, but he was widely believed then and now to have been involved, a point even mentioned in his obituary.[111] For decades thereafter, Congress—the party of Gandhi—dominated Indian politics, and few Indians wanted to touch Hindutva.[112]

Conclusion: Remembering Horrors We Would Rather Forget

After 1947, an eerie silence persisted for decades regarding the violent births of India and Pakistan. For many, the memories were too painful. Even major scholarly projects to collect oral histories of partition did not emerge until the 1990s, when people realized that all those who could tell the stories would soon die.[113] Survivors who wrote about partition immediately after the event, such as Manto, sometimes faced obscenity charges and trials. All in all, as Krishna Sobti (1925–2019), a Hindi writer and partition refugee, later put it, "Partition was difficult to forget but dangerous to remember."[114] For a historian, the matter is more straightforward if equally brutal: partition redefined the political contours of the Indian subcontinent, further entrenched religious-based conflict, and left behind human trauma, all of which have visible legacies in present-day South Asia.

Further Reading

There is extensive scholarly literature on partition, of which I found the work of Urvashi Butalia and Yasmin Khan invaluable. I relied on other scholars for specific aspects, including Lucy Chester on the boundary commission and Suranjan Das and Joya Chatterji on Bengal. Ayesha Jalal's work on Jinnah and the Muslim League has shaped historical thinking. For Subhas Chandra Bose, I used Leonard Gordon's biography, which avoids the inappropriate whitewashing that mars some modern biographies of this figure.

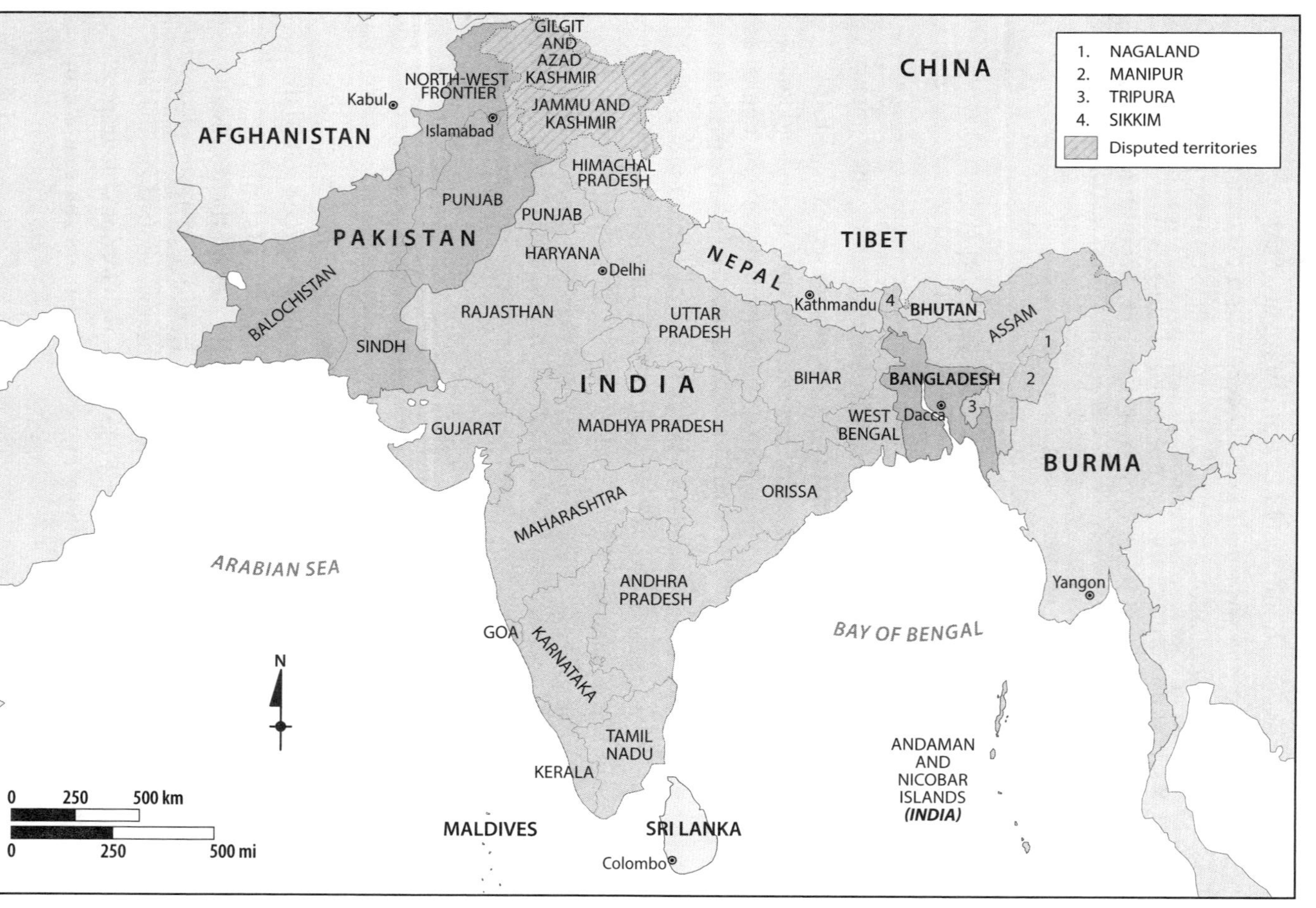

South Asian political divisions, 1972.

23

New Nation-States, 1947–1990

We are reshaping the world my dear. Shattering it to bits and remoulding it closer to the heart's desire.

—Mumtaz Shah Nawaz, *Heart Divided*, 1957 (English)[1]

During the early decades of independent nation-states, between 1947 and 1990, South Asians forged national identities. The anticolonial movement faded in salience after the British had departed, and, in fact, South Asian political elites benefited from integrating much of the colonial apparatus into their own governments. Each nation sought distinct ways to unite and govern their citizens, and I cover major developments by decade. From 1947 into the 1950s, postcolonial nation-states wrote constitutions and established themselves as independent political powers. In the 1960s, especially India and Pakistan positioned themselves in wider global networks. Challenges were persistent, including threats to state power (such as in Bangladesh and Sri Lanka) during the 1970s and 1980s and the rise of conservative movements in Pakistan and India in the 1980s. Throughout these various trends, people outlined the contours of national belonging, negotiating what it meant to be citizens of Pakistan, India, Sri Lanka, and (a bit later) Bangladesh.

Forging National Identities

As of the early 1950s, there were six South Asian states—Afghanistan, Bhutan, Ceylon (renamed Sri Lanka in 1972), India, Nepal, and Pakistan—and each developed on its own timeline. Afghanistan was among the older states, gaining independence in 1919 after the third Anglo-Afghan war. Afghani leadership spent the 1930s–1940s enmeshing their nation in global financial networks.[2] The late 1940s–1950s were a period of rapid political change in South Asia as India and Pakistan gained independence in 1947, Ceylon became independent in 1948, Bhutan became a protected state under India in 1949, and Nepal's Rana autocracy was overthrown in an internal revolution in 1951. Two states emerged later: the Maldives (a series of islands southwest of the subcontinent) gained independence from Britain in 1965, and Bangladesh broke off from Pakistan in 1971 (discussed in this chapter). As South Asians became siloed into discrete states, national boundaries proved to be harder than those of earlier political formations.

Sri Lanka—still called Ceylon until 1972—transitioned to independence relatively smoothly but did not conceive a cohesive national identity. Sri Lankans became independent after more than four centuries of colonialism, sequentially, by the Portuguese (1506–1658), Dutch (1658–1796), and British (1796–1948). The transfer of power was bloodless, and Ceylon elites celebrated their freedom on February 4, 1948, with an imperial ceremony that largely replicated Queen Victoria's Golden Jubilee of 1887.[3] But political and ethnic fractures soon emerged. And eight years later, much of Sri Lanka's Tamil minority boycotted Independence Day celebrations, fearing that the Sinhalese-speaking majority (about 70 percent of the population) would impose their language and try to minimize Tamil culture. As G. G. Ponnambalam, a Tamil member of Sri Lanka's parliament, asked rhetorically in 1956: "Is this all that independence is to mean to the Tamil community? That from white masters we are to turn to a lot of brown masters?"[4] His fears were warranted. Within the year, the Sinhalese majority passed the Sinhala-Only Act, and anti-Tamil riots soon followed; Sri Lanka spiraled into civil war in the 1980s (discussed later in this chapter).[5]

Other South Asian nations, too, faced questions of how to forge national unity, and India pursued a path of embracing pluralism. Newly independent India was staggeringly diverse by many metrics—language, culture, ethnicity, and religion—and celebrated this with nationalist pride. For example, in late 1948, Delhi's Government House hosted the "Masterpieces of Indian Art" exhibition where, for four annas (1/4 of a rupee), an Indian citizen could participate in "an event of national value," and see a "representative . . . display of India's art," stretching from the Indus Civilization to Mughal, Rajasthani, and Pahari paintings.[6] The exhibition catalogue contended: "There is no argument which carries greater persuasion with it in favour of a country's ideals and way of life than its art and Indian art richly documenting the past culture of India has a unique position in this respect as revealing the mind of the Indian people."[7] The exhibition formed the core collection for Delhi's National Museum, which opened in 1949.[8] That same year, India issued sixteen stamps with images of heritage sites across the nation that represented nearly every religion, including Gujarat's Shatrughna Temple (Jain), Amritsar's Golden Temple (Sikh), Orissa's Konarak Temple (Hindu), and Bijapur's Gol Gumbaz (Muslim, an Adil Shahi mausoleum).[9] The message was clear—independent India would find her unity in diversity.

India's national symbols, adopted in the state's early years, heralded pluralism. These included India's tricolor flag, adapted from Congress, with bands of saffron (for Hindus), green (for Muslims), and white (for everyone else). At the flag's center sits the dharmachakra (wheel of dharma) of the premodern Mauryan emperor Ashoka, whose subcontinental empire outstripped most others in premodernity (chapter 4). The Indian state also adopted the Mauryan lion capital, drawing from a past so distant it could be reimagined (ahistorically) as proto-national.

On the ground, Indian nationalism remained more fractured, including along linguistic lines. Acquiescing to southern pressure, Nehru redrew the internal state lines of India to follow linguistic divisions in the mid-1950s, even as he pleaded for his countrymen to prioritize unity:

> We should not become parochial, narrow-minded, provincial, communal and caste-minded, because we have a great mission to perform. Let us, the citizens of the Republic of India, stand up straight, with straight backs, and look up at the skies, keeping our feet firmly planted on the ground and bring about this synthesis, this integration of the Indian people. Political integration has already taken place to some extent, but what I am after is something much deeper than that—an emotional integration of the Indian people so that we might be welded into one, and made into one strong national unit, maintaining at the same time all our wonderful diversity. I do not want this diversity to be

regimented and taken away, but we must be wary of losing ourselves in petty quarrels.[10]

Nehru's call for integration despite disagreement panned out in many ways in independent India, including the constitution.

Indians drafted their constitution during the first few years of independence, defining citizens' rights and key contours of the state. B. R. Ambedkar, an attorney and Dalit rights advocate, was appointed law minister by Jawaharlal Nehru in 1947 and oversaw India's Constituent Assembly of several hundred men and seventeen women.[11] The success of Ambedkar's assembly in drafting a constitution—which is the world's longest at well more than 100,000 words and still governs India today—is remarkable.[12] Many former British colonies inherited British-authored constitutions (e.g., Malaysia and Ceylon), and others encountered crippling internal dissension (e.g., Pakistan).[13]

Moreover, the Indian constitution—which took effect on January 26, 1950, known thereafter as Republic Day[14]—contains ambitious liberal interventions. Its preamble promises "equality of status and of opportunity" to all Indian citizens.[15] Fleshing out that promise, the constitution grants universal suffrage, free and compulsory education, and robust reservations for historically oppressed communities, while outlawing caste-based and gender-based discrimination. The Indian state has not always delivered its constitution's promises. But even in recent years, Indians have invoked this founding document as a blueprint for democratic rights.[16]

For all its aspirations, the Indian constitution's lofty values came with disquieting restrictions. Article 370 gave special protections to Kashmiris, while falling short of ensuring them political self-determination. The Indian Constitution's core is rooted in British colonial law, reproducing parts of the 1935 Government of India Act and retaining emergency powers for the state to abrogate the constitution and all its liberal rights.[17] In general, emergency powers, favorite tools of British colonialists, increased in postcolonial India as political leaders clamped down on critics.[18]

Additionally, two social trends—inequality and Hindu majoritarianism—pressed against the Indian constitution's embrace of human rights and social progress. Regarding inequality, Ambedkar warned the

Constituent Assembly in late 1949 of the limits of prescribing "equality of status and of opportunity" to a deeply unequal society:[19]

> On the social plane, we have in India a society based on the principle of grade inequality which means elevation for some and degradation for others. On the economic plane, we have a society in which there are some who have immense wealth as against many who live in abject poverty. On the 26th of January 1950, we are going to enter into a life of contradictions. In politics we will have equality and in social and economic life we will have inequality. In politics we will be recognizing the principle of one man one vote and one vote one value. In our social and economic life, we shall, by reason of our social and economic structure, continue to deny the principle of one man one value. How long shall we continue to live this life of contradictions? How long shall we continue to deny equality in our social and economic life? If we continue to deny it for long, we will do so only putting our political democracy in peril.[20]

Also, the Indian constitution is uneven regarding religion. Article 25 guarantees free practice of religion but also subsumes Buddhists, Jains, and Sikhs under the umbrella of "Hindu," an erasure of independent religious identities. A nonbinding directive section charges the Indian state to work toward prohibiting cow slaughter, an upper-caste Hindu concern beginning in the late nineteenth century (chapter 19) that has fueled anti-Muslim violence in recent decades (chapter 24). The directive section also encourages the state to spread Hindi, another Hindu nationalist cause that is often perceived as imperialist by south Indians who speak Dravidian languages.

The inclusion of Hindu nationalist objectives in India's constitution reflected long-standing disagreement among Indian political leaders about whether majoritarian ideas had any place in a pluralistic republic. Nehru took great pride in crafting "a secular state with complete freedom for all religions and cultures."[21] But leaders like Lajpat Rai (d. 1928), a Hindu Mahasabha and Congress member at various points, advocated prioritizing "Hindu rights."[22] India's constitution, contradictorily, does both.

India's twin state, Pakistan, faced parallel issues regarding national identity, compounded by its unusual geography. East and West Pakistan were separated by 1,000 miles and even further apart culturally. East Pakistan was largely delta land barely above sea level, a strong contrast to the arid lands of West Pakistan. East Pakistan was geographically smaller than West Pakistan but more densely populated, containing more than half of the nation's population. The two portions had different levels of religious diversity. In the 1951 census, 23 percent of East Pakistanis were non-Muslims as compared to only 3 percent of West Pakistanis.[23] East and West Pakistanis spoke various languages, sharing none in common save Urdu (spoken by less than one in ten as a mother tongue).[24] Most East Pakistanis never traveled to West Pakistan and vice versa, and those who did felt alienated. East Pakistani Ataur Rahman Khan confessed during a debate in Pakistan's Constituent Assembly in early 1956: "I feel a peculiar sensation when I come from Dacca to Karachi. I feel physically, apart from mental feeling, that I am living here in a foreign country. I did not feel as much when I went to Zurich, to Geneva or Switzerland, or London as much as I feel here in my own country that I am in a foreign land."[25] Differences alienated residents of Pakistan's two major land areas from each other, rather than offering them a basis for national identity.

Pakistanis were—in the theory behind the state's founding—to be united by Islam, but in practice they found no consensus about this polychromatic tradition or its political role. Jinnah, Pakistan's great champion who enjoyed whiskey and pork, issued uneven statements about Islam.[26] He declared in August 1947 that religion, caste, and creed "has nothing to do with the business of the State," whereas in January 1948, he urged members of the Sind Bar Association to prepare to "sacrifice and die in order to make Pakistan [a] truly great Islamic State."[27] For some Pakistanis, Islam was a way to distinguish their nation from other governmental systems, such as Liaquat Ali Khan (1895–1951), Pakistan's first prime minister, who encouraged his countrymen to "follow the teachings of the Prophet and not those of Marx, Stalin or Churchill."[28] Still, Liaquat Ali Khan rejected a theocratic state, stating unequivocally in 1949: "Islam does not recognise either priesthood or any sacerdotal authority; and, therefore, the question of a theocracy simply does not arise in Islam. If there are any who still use the word theocracy in the same breath as the polity of Pakistan, they are either labouring under a grave misapprehension, or indulging in mischievous propaganda."[29] Indeed, many of Pakistan's ulama advocated a theocracy in which Allah was sovereign, which would grant the ulama immense power since they alone (the ulama argued) were Allah's representatives on earth.[30] Still, even the ulama did not agree on a basic definition of Islam, as noted in a 1954 Pakistani government report.[31]

In the absence of agreement, contestations around Islam—its definition, state role, and social position—were formational in Pakistan's early years and often led to lived contradictions. Alcohol consumption is a case in point. Prohibited by most readings of Islamic teachings, alcohol sales were restricted in most of Pakistan by 1949 in deference to conservative sensibilities. But Murree Brewery, founded in 1860 and still a profitable company today, operated throughout by serving a customer base of predominantly Pakistani Muslims.[32]

In 1949, Pakistan's Constituent Assembly passed the Objectives Resolution as a guiding national document, and it split the difference on Islam in the state. The Objectives Resolution endorsed democracy (eschewing theocracy) but specifically "as enunciated by Islam."[33] The resolution directed that "Muslims shall be enabled to order their lives in the individual and collective spheres in accordance with the teachings and requirements of Islam as set out in the Holy Quran and the *Sunnah*" and "adequate provision shall be made for the minorities freely to profess and practise their religions and develop their cultures."[34] Still, Pakistan's national symbols tend to emphasize Islam, such as the crescent moon and star on a predominantly green flag.

As Islam was invoked, again and again, as central to Pakistani identity, some tried to define, at the very least, who was not Muslim, and one bitter dispute centered around the Ahmadiyya. With origins in the late nineteenth-century Punjab, the Ahmadiyya espouse views on prophethood that differ from those of most Muslims and consequently had long faced harassment (chapter 19). In 1953, numerous Muslim religious and political groups targeted the Ahmadiyya community in Lahore, killing at least 200 Ahmadis and displacing many more. The 1953 anti-Ahmadiyya riots were quelled by three months of martial law in Lahore, although systemic anti-Ahmadiyya violence persisted in Pakistan for decades. This hostility bottomed out in a 1974 constitutional amendment—passed unanimously and still in effect today—that bars the Ahmadiyya from identifying as Muslim.[35]

Elections, Self-Sufficiency, and Diplomacy

In terms of democracy, India and Pakistan took different paths in the 1950s and 1960s. Indians participated in four general elections during these decades—in 1951–1952, 1957, 1962, and 1967—with the Indian National Congress Party winning all four. Each election was the largest democratic exercise in history, owing to India's growing population. Many Indians went to great lengths to vote, including women (figure 23.1). One candidate observed in rural south India of women who kept purdah: "Looking down in the darkness at a cluster of nearby villages, I saw a picturesque and strange sight: hundreds of little lights were moving in orderly fashion through the coconut groves towards the town. . . . They were Moslem women determined to vote before the men crowded round the polling booths. . . . The women gravely walked through the streets in rows of two, each holding the end of a white cotton sheet over her head."[36] The Indian state made accommodations to enable suffrage for all, including using pictures for political parties since most voters were illiterate (figure 23.2).

In contrast, Pakistani politics featured no general elections through the 1960s and were volatile. The Muslim League, Jinnah's party that had won Pakistan's existence, collapsed. The Constituent Assembly managed to produce a constitution in 1956, but it was abrogated by General Ayub Khan's coup in 1958. Ayub cited the Munir Doctrine, a doctrine of necessity articulated in a 1954 court judgment by Judge Muhammad Munir (previously of the Punjab Boundary Commission). The doctrine stipulated that the governor general could dissolve Pakistan's Constitutional Assembly by "necessity" and has been cited in military coups led by Ayub Khan (1958), Zia-ul-Haq (1977), and Pervez Musharraf (1999).[37] Ayub Khan served as Pakistan's president until 1969 and oversaw his nation's attempt to stake out its place in global networks of finance, trade, and diplomacy.

Pakistan inherited a weak economic position. Independent India contained nearly all British India's industries, including most cotton mills.[38] West Pakistan even had few urban centers, and the port town of Karachi served as its first capital city. Working from a largely agrarian economy base, Pakistan averaged annual economic growth rates of 5.5 percent throughout Ayub's rule (1958–1969).[39] Islamabad was built in this period, a planned city that serves as the nation's capital today.

Figures 23.1 and 23.2. Indian villagers voting in the 1952 general election.

What of this growth trickled down to help common people is another matter, however, an issue shared with India.

Prime Minister Jawaharlal Nehru (1947–1964) cultivated India's initial economic strategy in a series of five-year plans. He prioritized economic self-reliance, aiming to reduce imports, build up heavy industry such as steel production, and exercise active state interference and control (sometimes called the "license raj").[40] Nehru's economic policies delivered moderate growth, with India's GDP rising nearly every year from 1950 forward as, like Pakistan, India recovered from colonial-era stagnation.[41] Nehru also devoted resources to India's water infrastructure, forging irrigation schemes and building dozens of high dams. Upon showing the Bhakra Nangal Dam—the second highest dam in the world at the time—to his Chinese counterpart, Zhou Enlai, in 1956, Nehru proclaimed, "These are the new temples of India where I worship."[42] Not everyone agreed, as the contemporary Adivasi poet Jacinta Kerketta wrote about a local farmer displaced by such dams: "Today Soma starves, / For his fields are now massive reservoirs."[43]

Independent India avoided famines, no small feat given that dozens of famines had claimed millions of victims under the British Raj, with one of the most deadly occurring in 1943. In contrast, China was rocked by the great famine of 1958–1961 that killed fifteen to thirty million people.[44] As economists have noted, democracies "where the government tolerates opposition" are most successful in avoiding mass starvation of their people.[45] Put more directly, early independent India's commitment to a healthy elections and dissent saved lives.

Moving into the 1970s and 1980s, India and Pakistan became enmeshed in global economic trends. Both benefited from the green revolution in farming that introduced new strains of wheat and rice, along with innovative farming technology, to increase yields.[46] Indians and Pakistanis began traveling as migrant workers to oil-rich Gulf states and sending money home that stimulated both nations' economies.[47] Additionally, the Indian economy overall began to liberalize in this period and opened to foreign investment even more after 1991, which stimulated wealth production.

Two interrelated factors held back, and continue to hold back, Indian and Pakistani economic growth: low levels of primary education, including gender inequity, and low levels of female participation in the workforce.[48] In both nations, a minority of adult women could read as of the 1990s (adult female literacy was 44 percent in India in 1999 and 11 percent in Pakistan in 1993).[49] Both rates have risen since, with 65 percent of Indian women being literate as of the last census and 50 percent of Pakistani women.[50] But literacy rates pale in comparison to nearby nations (e.g., 91 percent of Sri Lankan women are literate), and low rates persist along caste and class lines and in rural areas.[51] As of 2002, only 2–3 percent of Dalit women ("Scheduled Castes" in the parlance of the modern Indian state) could read in some districts of Bihar and Rajasthan.[52] Female literacy correlates with a host of other quality-of-life improvements for men and women, including lower child mortality, higher vaccination rates, and reduced gender inequality.[53] Indian and Pakistani societies struggle with patriarchal norms, which vary by region and class but overall trend against women joining the workforce. In both nations, only about one in four women worked in the formal economy as of the early 2020s, and the percentage of women in India's workforce dipped sharply between 2005 and 2020.[54]

Newly independent India and Pakistan pursued different paths in international relations, especially regarding the Cold War between the United States and the Soviet Union (late 1940s–1991). India chose nonalignment. Still, the United States numbered among India's largest trading partners during the Nehru years (1947–1964), sold India arms, and gave India significant aid.[55] Relations between the two nations soured in the 1970s after India supported Bangladesh against American-allied Pakistan in the 1971 war (discussed next) and then in 1974 tested nuclear weapons. The American company Coca-Cola withdrew from the Indian market in 1977 (absent foreign competition, the Indian brand Campa Cola flourished). All the while, Russia and India maintained good relations, and India became reliant on Soviet-supplied weapons.[56]

In contrast, Pakistan allied with the Western Bloc. Pakistan even, alongside the United States, supported the Afghan mujahideen against Soviet invasion from 1979 onward (Pakistan also hosted many Afghan refugees). In its early decades, Pakistan also developed close relations with China. In contrast, Indian-Chinese ties were harmed by India welcoming the Dalai Lama as a refugee from Chinese-occupied Tibet in 1959 and by the Chinese humiliation of Indian defenses during a 1962 border dispute in Kashmir.[57] In brief, India and Pakistan developed different allies, which further complicated their already fraught diplomatic relations with each other.

India and Pakistan disagreed on plenty in their early decades, including how to share use of the Indus River waters. The Indus River, really a set of connected rivers and major fresh water source, snakes across the Punjab (which means "five rivers," referring to the Indus tributaries Jhelum, Chenab, Ravi, Sutlej, and Beas). Foreseeing future problems, Cyril Radcliffe, who drew the partition lines, suggested an India-Pakistan joint venture to regulate the Indus as a shared resource, but Nehru and Jinnah brusquely rejected the idea.[58] And so, Radcliffe drew the western partition line splicing through the Indus River and its tributaries, such that major branches go through or begin in India or Kashmir before emptying into branches in Pakistan. India and Pakistan negotiated use of the Indus waters with a 1960 treaty that they negotiated with World Bank assistance. Sensibly, the treaty largely devoted the west rivers to Pakistan and the east rivers to India.[59] The 1960 Indus Water Treaty remains in effect today and demonstrates the benefits of cooperation between independent India and Pakistan.[60]

State Crises, 1970s–1980s

Numerous South Asian nations experienced internal state crises in the 1970s and 1980s as they continued to negotiate, often violently, over questions of national identity and belonging. Here I cover four such crises: Bangladeshi Independence (1971), India's Emergency (1975–1977), Operation Blue Star and its bloody aftermath (1984), and the Sri Lankan Civil War (1983–2009). Three of these events feature groups of citizens objecting that they were not adequately included within their state and thus demanding a new one (only Bangladeshis succeeded). The Emergency stands apart as a story of state power grabbing that set a dangerous precedent in India. All four crises left behind trauma in specific communities that is still felt today.

In 1971, East Pakistan broke away from West Pakistan in a bloody conflict and became Bangladesh. The prior year, 1970, Pakistan held its first general election since partition.[61] Zulfikar Ali Bhutto of the Pakistan People's Party carried the vote in West Pakistan, and Mujibur Rahman of the Awami League won in East Pakistan. When the two failed to agree on whether or how to share power, Bangladesh declared independence in March 1971, and Pakistan's army began a slaughter. Almost immediately, the Indian government led by Indira

Gandhi[62] (Jawaharlal Nehru's daughter) intervened quietly, providing Bangladesh with "material assistance" of arms, bullets, and more.[63] It was a risky move for Indian leaders—who were vocal about their own right to deny political self-determination in Kashmir and to quash insurgents in the northeast—to back violent secessionists next door. But the prospect of a weakened Pakistan—no longer "moth-eaten" but split altogether—proved tempting, and Indian leaders thought they could keep their involvement secret.[64] As Indira Gandhi told K. F. Rustamji, head of India's Border Security Force, in March 1971: "Do what you like, but don't get caught."[65]

Months later, neither side had gained the upper hand, and so the Indian army publicly intervened in December 1971, hitting East and West Pakistan over two weeks. The assault cost thousands of lives. And it ensured independence for Bangladesh, whose first prime minister was the 1970 election winner: Mujibur Rahman (d. 1975).

Bangladesh's India-assisted birth was accompanied by a genocide and massive displacement. In total, the Pakistani army and its associates killed a few hundred thousand Bangladeshis and prompted ten million to flee across the border to India. Bengalis were targeted in the killing, and one U.S. official noted "evidence of selective singling out" of Hindu professors, settlements, and students.[66] Indira Gandhi argued to international leaders as early as May 1971 that Pakistan was looking to "chang[e] its communal composition through an organised and selective programme of eviction."[67] Both Indian and U.S. diplomats referred, in 1971, to Pakistan's actions in Bangladesh as a genocide, as did newspapers.[68] But the international community did not intervene, including the United States, an ally of Pakistan. Both Pakistan and Bangladesh emerged from the conflict with severely reduced minority populations, Pakistan due to the loss of its eastern wing where religious minorities were concentrated and Bangladesh primarily due to mass forced migration.[69]

In India, Indira Gandhi emerged from the 1971 conflict over Bangladesh a national hero. Even members of the Bharatiya Jana Sangh, a Hindu nationalist political rival of Congress, praised Indira's success, such as Atal Bihari Vajpayee who hailed her as an incarnation of the goddess Durga.[70] Over the next four years, Indira Gandhi delivered numerous accomplishments. In 1971, India abolished the privy purses, annual funds paid by the Indian state to former princely rulers (Pakistan still pays the privy purses). In 1972, her government passed the Wildlife Protection Act.[71] In 1974, India successfully tested a nuclear bomb, detonated on the Gautama Buddha's purported birthday in a bit of dark irony given his teachings on liberation from suffering.[72]

But trouble brewed in the background for Indira Gandhi and India. Throughout the early 1970s, charges were winding their way through the Indian courts that Indira Gandhi had committed electoral malpractice in the 1971 election. On June 12, 1975, the Allahabad High Court found Indira Gandhi guilty and barred her from politics for six years.[73] Indira is rumored to have said, on multiple occasions, "My father was a saint in politics. I am not."[74] Indeed, she responded the Allahabad High Court judgment by ordering supporters to draw up "arrest lists," and two weeks later, on June 25, 1975, her government declared an "internal Emergency" and suspended the Indian Constitution.[75]

India's Emergency lasted twenty-one months and featured authoritarian state conduct, including mass civil and human rights violations. For all Indians, Indira Gandhi's government suspended habeas corpus and electoral rights, rendering India no longer a functioning democracy. For some, the assaults were more severe. Indira jailed her political opponents, and the police subjected many to obscene torture, including rape, inserting chili powder in their rectums, urinating in their mouths, and rolling wood on their thighs until the ligaments tore from the bones.[76] Sanjay Gandhi, Indira's younger son, was given a free hand to pursue his interest in demolishing lower-income dwellings (i.e., "slums"). He bulldozed the homes of 700,000 in Delhi alone.[77] Some Indians knew little about these activities while they occurred, aside from rumors, since the Emergency also meant India's press was gagged.

During the Emergency, under Sanjay Gandhi's direction, the Indian state sterilized eleven million people—targeting the poor and Muslims—through degrees of compulsion. Some of these measures predated the Emergency, such as financial incentives for sterilization (and IUD insertions) that had been Indian policy since the 1960s.[78] But the Emergency offered tools to accelerate coercion drastically. By early 1976, health minister Karan Singh openly sanctioned "compulsory sterilisation" measures by state legislatures.[79] On the ground, gangs terrorized families, cutting electricity to villages and rounding up men to "volunteer" to be sterilized.[80] In all cases, coerced sterilization took away reproductive rights, which was the goal of this eugenics experiment. Some victims were inflicted with additional injuries or died since procedures were often performed under unsanitary conditions.[81]

The Emergency ended with a snap election in 1977, which Congress—the party of Mohandas Gandhi and Jawaharlal Nehru—lost for the first time since independence. The opposition Janata Party comprised a short-term alliance of those opposed to the Emergency and hit hard on claims that Congress was "guilty of murdering democracy" and "should never be elected to power again."[82] But the voters' rebuke did little to dissuade subsequent Indian prime ministers from using emergency powers. Two scholars have even referred to Indira Gandhi's suspension of the constitution from 1975 to 1977 as India's "first dictatorship," suggesting that, in its second incarnation, "Hindu nationalist authoritarian populism is accentuating, in the manner that the Emergency did, the illiberal aspects of Indian democracy that have been present all along."[83] As for Indira, she regained power in India's 1980 election, after the Janata alliance disintegrated, and soon faced a secessionist challenge that proved her undoing.

In the early 1980s, a Sikh separatist movement gained steam in India, wherein some Sikhs demanded a separate homeland carved out of the Punjab. The idea of a Sikh state called "Khalistan" (land of the pure) had been around since the 1940s when Sikh groups found their concerns over partition falling on deaf ears (chapter 22).[84] The idea of Khalistan resurfaced post-independence, championed nonviolently by Sikhs in the diaspora and supported by armed insurgents in India loosely led by Jarnail Singh Bhindranwale (1947–1984). Their desire to secede, especially the movement's violent wing, challenged Indian state sovereignty. In June 1984, Indira Gandhi ordered Indian troops to assault Bhindranwale and his supporters at Amritsar's Golden Temple, where they had taken refuge. Indian troops killed hundreds, maybe thousands, of militants (including Bhindranwale) and civilians in what they dubbed Operation Blue Star, led by General Kuldip Singh Brar.

Operation Blue Star decimated the security threat of the Sikh separatist movement, but it also initiated a series of brutal events for Indira Gandhi and the Sikh community. Many Sikhs—including many who did not support Khalistan—were horrified by the government's violation of their holy temple. Seeking retaliation, two Sikh bodyguards of Indira

Gandhi shot her at point-blank range in October 1984. The murder seemed to fulfill Bhindranwale's prediction, made shortly before his death as Indian troops surrounded the Golden Temple, that "if the authorities enter this temple . . . the throne of Indira will crumble. . . . They will be forced to chew iron lentils (bullets)."[85] Indira Gandhi's assassination set off a wave of anti-Sikh riots, centered in and around Delhi, in which several thousand Sikhs were slaughtered. The Congress government did not intervene and may have assisted the communal violence.[86] The perpetrators of the 1984 anti-Sikh riots have largely gone unpunished, and the Indian state has not grappled with its own role in the violence.

Sri Lanka also faced separatist movements, with the most long-lived prompting a civil war from 1983 to 2009 in which a minority strove to create an independent Tamil homeland in northeastern Sri Lanka. As mentioned, Sri Lanka's Sinhalese majority attempted to undermine the Tamil minority from the 1950s onward, through the Sinhala-Only Act and other measures. This sparked the creation of numerous Tamil rights groups in 1970s, which were ultimately dominated by the Liberation Tigers of Tamil Eelam (LTTE), also known as the Tamil Tigers with "tiger" being a nod to the Cholas who had ruled northern parts of Sri Lanka in the eleventh century (chapter 9).[87] The Tamil Tigers were militant. Their suicide bombers assassinated former Indian prime minister Rajiv Gandhi (d. 1991) and Sri Lankan president Ranasinghe Premadasa (d. 1993), the former on the heels of India's failed attempt to broker a diplomatic solution to Sri Lanka's conflict.[88] In the end, the civil war was resolved militarily when Sri Lanka's army crushed the Tamil Tigers and killed their leader, Velupillai Prabhakaran, in May 2009.[89]

Like the other state crises surveyed here, Sri Lanka's civil war featured a government unleashing brutal violence on its own people. This sort of muscular state, a mainstay of the nation-state world, has fueled internal pushes to homogenize multiple South Asian nations. Even Bhutan, a small Himalayan nation of less than one million people, has engaged in ethnic cleansing, denationalizing and expelling more than 100,000 members of its Nepali-speaking minority, known as the Lhotshampas, in the 1980s and 1990s.[90] South Asians continue to reshape their worlds, as per this chapter's epigraph, although we should be precise when thinking about who desires such changes and their human cost.

In the crises surveyed here, South Asian political elites acted brutally to preserve state sovereignty, by which they meant the sovereignty of some—usually, although not always, the majority—at the expense of other members of their societies.

Right-Wing Turns

Both India and Pakistan experienced right-wing surges in the 1980s. In Pakistan, Muhammad Zia-ul-Haq (d. 1988) oversaw the institution of patriarchal and discriminatory laws that he described as "Islamic." Zia, a military officer, overthrew Prime Minister Zulfikar Ali Bhutto in July 1977 and declared in a televised speech on the day of his military coup: "Pakistan, which was created in the name of Islam, will continue to survive only if it sticks to Islam. That is why I consider the introduction of Islamic system as an essential prerequisite for the country."[91] Zia's ambitions regarding Islam were perhaps better articulated by Pakistani human rights defenders Asma Jahangir and Hina Jilani, who charged that Zia "used Islam as an instrument to consolidate his power."[92] Notably, Islam was a singular tradition for Zia, which put him at odds with the plurality of overlapping Muslim communities—Sunnis, Sufis, Shias, ulama, Ahmadiyya, and others—who called Pakistan home. Zia soon began his Islamization program, targeting four major areas: the judiciary, penal code, economic activity, and education policy.[93]

Many Zia-era laws reduced women's rights in the Pakistani state. For instance, the Hudood Ordinances introduced public whippings for women who had extramarital sex (including rape victims). They were commonly used to retaliate against women who had married against their fathers' wishes, divorced their husbands, or had run away, seeking escape from abusive fathers, brothers, or partners.[94] Thousands of women were arrested under these laws, increasing Pakistan's female prisoner population from seventy in 1979 to six thousand in 1988.[95] Women found it difficult to defend themselves in court, especially after the 1984 Law of Evidence reduced women's testimony to worth half that of men. Pakistani women formed groups to push back against these discriminatory laws, such as the Women's Action Forum founded in 1981. Some women's groups protested, and on February 12, 1983, the police attacked one such nonviolent protest with batons and tear gas. The date is commemorated annually as Pakistan Women's Day.[96]

Zia-era laws also had bad results for Pakistani religious minorities. Zia instituted stricter blasphemy laws (some of which dated from the colonial period and were also inherited by modern India). Among other things, Zia introduced the death penalty for those who besmirched the honor of the Prophet Muhammad. Even in theory, this law is problematic since no religious communities, except for Muslims, recognize Muhammad as a prophet. In reality, Zia's blasphemy laws were weaponized against political critics and religious minorities, especially Christians, and more recent public debate on changing them has been chilled by deadly violence against reformers.[97]

Across the border, India began its own right-wing political turn with the founding of the BJP in 1980, although its fruits were slower to mature. At first, the BJP—a Hindu nationalist party with ties to the paramilitary RSS—took a moderate approach and performed poorly.[98] Their 1984 election manifesto praises the "positive concept of secularism to which BJP is committed" but warns that "secularism should not be allowed to become a euphemism for appeasement."[99] The language of "appeasement" echoes an objection to Indian pluralism made most famously by Nathuram Godse, the RSS man who assassinated Mohandas Gandhi.[100] Using this platform, the BJP won a measly two seats in the Lok Sabha in the 1984 election. Soon enough, the BJP abandoned its milder stance, instead publicly endorsing Hindutva in the 1990s and declaring its commitment to Hindu nationalist causes like the Ram Mandir (chapter 24).[101]

Pursuing Caste Equity

Caste privilege and possible remedies thereof arose anew in the 1980s–1990 as Indians struggled with enduring social inequality. In 1979, the Janata Party initiated the Mandal Commission to produce a report on what they termed "Other Backward Classes" (OBCs), namely low castes that constituted 52 percent of the population as per the commission's report.[102] The majority of Mandal Commission members were themselves from OBC backgrounds, including the group's namesake B. P. Mandal (d. 1982). The commission noted that caste restrictions had lightened in some areas of Indian social life but had strengthened in politics (see excerpt). As a corrective, the commission recommended introducing 27 percent reservations among government jobs for OBCs, in addition to the 22.5 percent already reserved for Scheduled Castes (SCs) and Scheduled Tribes (STs).[103] To quote the commission report's own epigraph, "There is equality only among equals. To equate unequals is to perpetuate inequality." The Mandal Commission's proposed reservations were unpopular with some upper castes, and the Indian government sat on the commission's results, doing nothing, for a decade.

Mandal Commission's 1980 Report, Summary of Chapter V—Social Dynamics of Caste

Caste system has been able to survive over the centuries because of its inherent resilience and its ability to adjust itself to the ever changing social reality. The traditional view of caste system, as contained in Chapter IV, is based more on Hindu Shastras than the actual state of social reality. Moreover, caste restrictions have loosened considerably as a result of the rule of law introduced by the British, urbanisation, industrialisation, spread of mass education and, above all, the introduction of adult franchise after independence. But all the above changes mark only shift of emphasis and not any material alteration in the basic structure of caste.

It is generally agreed that whereas certain caste taboos have weakened as a result of the above changes, the importance of casteism in Indian politics is on the increase. This perhaps, was inevitable. Caste system provided the political leadership with readymade channels of communication and mobilisation and, in view of this, the importance of caste was bound to increase in Indian politics. As Rajni Kothari [an Indian political scientist] has observed, "those in India who complain of 'casteism' in politics are really looking for a sort of politics which has no basis in society."

The pace of social mobility is no doubt increasing and some traditional features of caste system have inevitably weakened. But what caste has lost on the ritual front, it has more than gained on the political front. In view of this it will be unrealistic to assume that the institution of caste will wither away in the foreseeable future.[104]

While the Indian government ignored the Mandal Commission, lower-caste groups and individuals spearheaded their own ways of combating caste-based discrimination. Phoolan Devi was active from 1979 to 1983 as a sort of Robin Hood figure, who robbed from the high-caste rich and gave to the low-caste poor.[105] The Dalit Panthers, founded in the 1970s and inspired by America's Black Panthers, were active into the 1980s and focused on grassroots education and protests. The Bahujan Samaj Party was formed in 1984 to represent lower-caste interests and continues to contest elections today.[106] Some involved in these movements rejected Hinduism and converted to the Navayana branch of Buddhism outlined by B. R. Ambedkar that focused on social justice.

In 1990, the Indian government announced that they would implement the Mandal Commission's recommendations, and urban-dwelling upper-caste communities balked. Fearing that they would lose their dominance in public life, upper-caste students protested in numerous cities, especially in the north. For example, women college students in Delhi held signs proclaiming, "We don't want unemployed husbands," a sentiment that encoded their belief that upper-caste flourishing depended on oppressing lower castes and their unwillingness to marry across caste lines.[107] One of the protests' lasting impacts was the emergence of women alongside men as a key demographic group for the Hindu far right.[108]

Conclusion: Nation Building and Dissent

In their initial decades, South Asian nations faced pressing questions of national identity. What did it mean to be Indian once India was a nation-state, something without precedent in subcontinental political history? What defined being Pakistani, an identity imagined for less than two decades prior to independence? Indians, Pakistanis, Bangladeshis, Sri Lankans, and other South Asian nationals formulated multiple answers to such questions regarding their respective states. And some of their answers—centered around language, religion, and culture—lent themselves to pluralistic realities more easily than others. Debates about national identities and tolerance continue today, as South Asian nation-building remains an ongoing set of projects that features dissent as much as consensus.

Further Reading

Scholarship on modern South Asia, especially political history, is vast. Often, historians focus on a specific nation, and accordingly I rely on Nira Wickramasinghe regarding modern Sri Lanka; Ian Talbot, Ayesha Jalal, and others regarding Pakistan; and a host of scholars for India. I found Jean Dreze and Amartya Sen's work to helpfully connect economic trends and numbers back to people. I also use state archives and reports as primary sources throughout this chapter.

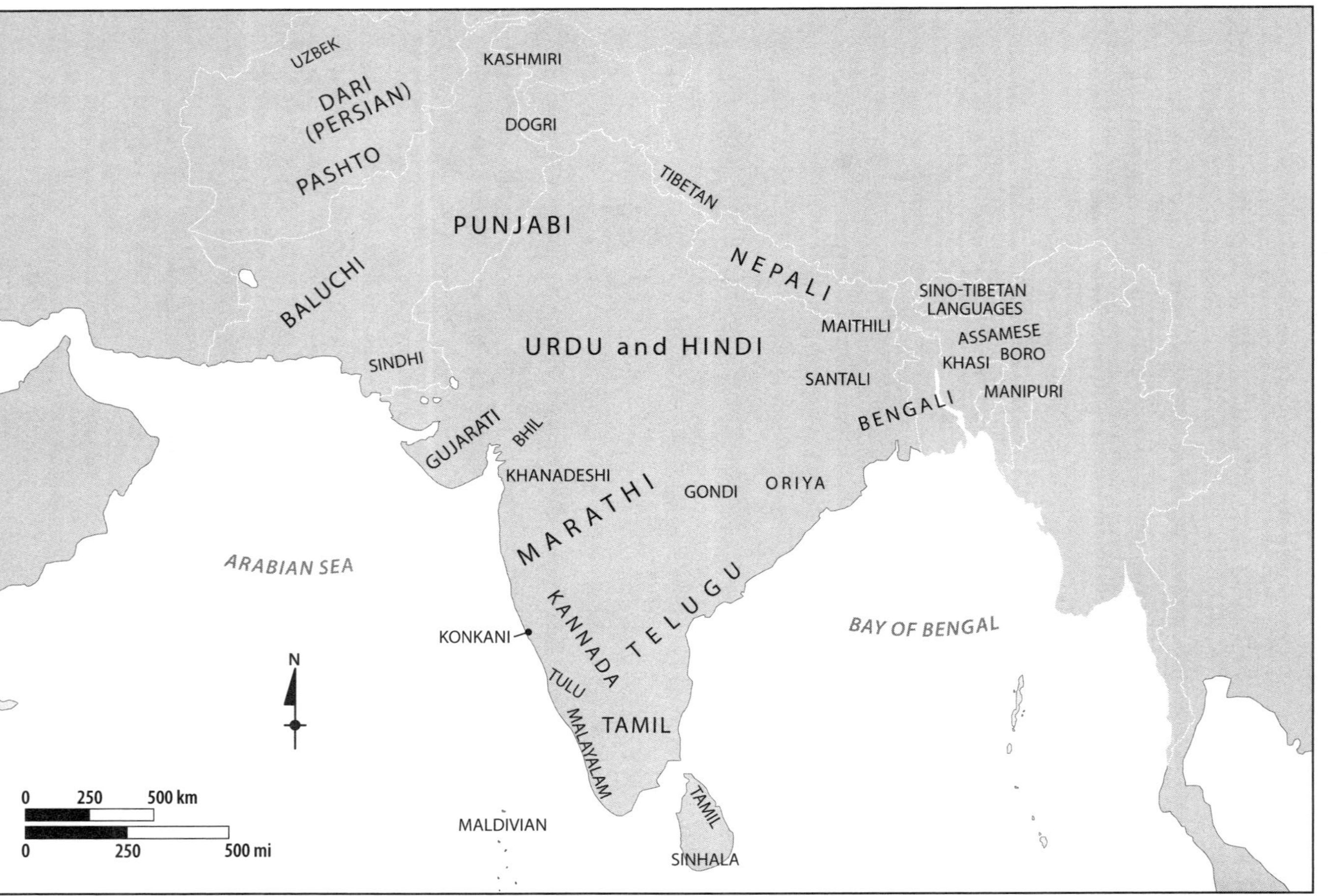

Prevalent languages by region in contemporary South Asia.

24

Everyday Life in Contemporary South Asia

Water! Forest! Land!–*Jal, Jangal, Jamin*

–Adivasi slogan against displacement by coal mines, 2010s (Hindi)[1]

Since 1990, South Asian communities—and, through their actions, the land of South Asia—have changed more rapidly than in prior eras. Here, I focus on shifts to daily life and society. This emphasis moves away from the "identity and freedom" themes of politics that have dominated the prior several chapters.[2] Many of the topics discussed in this chapter—including standards of living, performing arts, and social intolerance—cross over South Asian national boundaries and so afford a transnational perspective. Some subjects also touch on broader shifts that this book has traced since ancient India, especially regarding economic and social trends. I end with a challenge that is facing all contemporary South Asian communities and stands to accelerate in future decades: climate change.

Living Standards and Social Trends

The population of South Asia—especially the Indian subcontinent—is booming and youthful. Newspapers took note in 2000 when the one-billionth Indian was born and in 2023 when India overtook China as the world's most populous nation.[3] South Asia's growing population skews young, with more than 40 percent of Indians, Pakistanis, and

Bangladeshis being under the age of twenty-five.[4] Such demographics help South Asian economies grow, even as the region's large nations continue to struggle to meet citizens' needs. As the economists Jean Dreze and Amartya Sen wrote in 2002 about India: "As India enters the twenty-first century, the lives of a majority of its citizens continue to be blighted by endemic poverty, undernutrition, ill health, educational deprivation, environmental degradation and wide-ranging social inequalities."[5] Many of these problems have improved substantially over the last twenty years. Although hunger still persists, and, due to malnutrition, around one in three Indian children has stunted growth.[6] Such realities shape the possibilities of life, especially for underprivileged communities, along with other social shifts.

Bangladesh, India, and Pakistan are all majority rural nations that are urbanizing rapidly as their citizens move to cities seeking jobs and opportunities. Consequently, some urban centers have become megacities with populations exceeding ten million. South Asia now houses four of the world's twelve largest cities: Delhi, Mumbai (renamed from Bombay in the mid-1990s), Dhaka, and Karachi.[7] Dhaka has grown the most quickly among this quartet, expanding from one million inhabitants in 1971 to over twenty million in 2023, and in general Bangladesh is urbanizing slightly faster than its South Asian neighbors.[8] Delhi is poised to become the biggest city worldwide by 2030.[9] South Asian leaders across nations have found it difficult to manage rapid urbanization, and residents of Delhi, Dhaka, Karachi, and other South Asian cities often suffer from bad housing, poor waste management, and suffocating air pollution. The air quality worsens in certain seasons owing to weather patterns and holidays, with Diwali fireworks proving especially harmful and difficult to curb in Indian cities.[10] Air pollution also threatens sites of Indian heritage, such as by discoloring the marble of the Taj Mahal (chapter 14).

Indian cities are hubs of wealth and poverty, with the contrast demonstrating the extremity characteristic to contemporary South Asian economic growth. Mumbai (formerly Bombay) is a good example. Mumbai hosts the Ambani family home, where four to seven members of India's richest family have resided since 2011, enjoying 400,000 square feet across twenty-seven stories. Some of the private complex's more eye-popping perks including nine high-speed elevators, a swimming pool, a movie theater, and a snow room whose walls spit out snowflakes.[11] Mumbai's average temperature is 82 degrees Fahrenheit (27.5 degrees Celsius). In contrast, about half of Mumbai's residents live in densely packed areas like Dharavi, one of the world's largest slums that houses perhaps a million people in roughly one square mile.[12] One way that Mumbai's less fortunate make money is by waste picking, gathering litter and garbage to sell to recyclers, work that poses severe health risks. Concentrations of elite wealth in cities like Mumbai have fueled such difficult jobs and poor living conditions, rather than reducing them. That these two realities coexist underscores what much data confirms: wealth creation by Indian elites does not automatically trickle down to the nation's less well-off.[13]

South Asians of all socioeconomic means have found themselves enmeshed in global economic trends in recent decades, often centered around consumption abroad. Multiple South Asian nations export workers to far richer countries in the Gulf, where they labor in construction, hospitality, and domestic settings (see the afterword). At home, too, South Asian states host industries aimed at foreign markets, especially in the West, such as India's call centers and software companies. South Asian nations also export material items, including oil, gems, jewelry, rice, and—surprising to many—beef.[14] The United States is the biggest importer of Indian goods and a popular destination for Indian immigrants, who arrive through legal and undocumented channels.[15]

Garment industries provide a robust example of how safety protocols, and thus the lived experiences of workers, differ radically between South Asian nations. Bangladesh is the second largest apparel exporter worldwide after China.[16] This industry provides employment, especially to low-skilled women who have few other options to work outside the home.[17] But workers were subjected to hazardous factory conditions for decades, as brutally demonstrated in 2013 when Dhaka's Rana Plaza building—which hosted numerous garment factories—collapsed, killing more than 1,100 Bangladeshis.[18] The previous day, visible cracks had developed in the building, whose upper floors had been constructed illegally. But workers faced losing their jobs if they failed to meet production deadlines and so came to work despite the risk.[19]

The Rana Plaza disaster prompted wider analyses of Bangladeshi garment factories. These revealed that few factories had passed safety inspections and that millions of workers were not covered by existing safety programs.[20] Safety standards in the industry have improved substantially in the past decade, although survivors of the Rana Plaza collapse (mainly women) have still received little to no compensation.[21] In contrast, largely owing to labor organizing and strikes in the 1980s–1990s, Sri Lanka's garment industry has boasted better safety measures for decades, captured by the tagline "garments without guilt."[22]

South Asian communities, both rural and urban, have experienced an increased standard of living over the last several decades, although specific claims can be complicated to assess and sometimes misleading. Bathrooms in India are a case in point. More than 10 percent of Indians still practiced open defecation as of 2022, a rate far lower than at independence but still higher than rates in neighboring Pakistan or Bangladesh.[23] To address this sanitation issue, India's BJP launched the Swachh Bharat Abhiyan (Clean India Mission) in 2014 that has subsidized the construction of millions of home and public toilets. However, most of these toilets are not connected to sewage lines, instead largely depositing into pits, and so require manual scavenging to clean.[24] Manual scavenging is generally performed by Dalit communities and, despite legislation formally outlawing the practice, remains common throughout India. India's BJP government had tried to deflect attention from these issues, especially the casteism embedded in manual scavenging, pursuant to making the Swachh Bharat campaign appear successful.[25]

South Asian nations continue to contend with the social hierarchy of caste as well as the intersecting issue of colorism, favoring lighter over darker skin tones. Worldwide, the skin whitening industry was estimated at eight billion dollars in 2020, projected to rise to more than twelve billion by 2027, and includes large markets in America and Africa. In India, "Fair and Lovely" has long been a bestselling brand, which changed its name to "Glow and Lovely" in 2020 but continues to sell the same allegedly skin-whitening products. In South Asian marriage ads, descriptions like "fair" and "wheatish complexion" are common to denote the desirability of light-skinned brides. Many Indians participate in arranged marriages (which generally ensures caste endogamy), and one study showed that parents perceived potential mates for their children, both women and men, more favorably if they had lighter skin.[26] Conversely, darker-skinned groups often report discrimination, including both African and darker-skinned South Asian athletes who have played for Indian cricket teams, a favorite pastime in many commonwealth nations.[27]

Some South Asian groups face unique challenges in contemporary times, such as India's Adivasi (indigenous) communities that are at risk of physical and cultural displacement. For instance, coal mining in Chhattisgarh in central India threatens large-scale deforestation, thereby infringing on the homes of the region's Adivasis who comprise about 10 percent of all Indian Adivasi communities.[28] Adivasi leaders have responded vocally, demanding "Water! Forest! Land!" (see chapter epigraph), which they perceive as under threat from India's Hindu majority. Adivasis have long seen themselves as a separate community with values not shared by other Indian communities. As Jaipal Singh, a member of the Munda tribal community, said in response to Jawaharlal Nehru during constituent assembly debates of the late 1940s: "There is little you are offering us. The constitution is yours. The borders are yours. The sovereignty is yours. The flag is yours. What is ours? What is it that is both tribal and Indian in the constitution? What is the shared legacy, the common weave? You have defined rights, the isms, the industry, the science, let something be ours."[29] Still, as of the time of writing (summer 2024), India's Hindu nationalist government is resisting Adivasi calls to have the option of a distinct religious category on India's next census.[30]

National and Transnational Art

Art flourishes as a medium of human expression in everyday life in contemporary South Asia. For example, driving on the roads of India and Pakistan, one glimpses periodic explosions of colors on commercial trucks that are adorned with intricate designs. Truck art has reached unique heights in Pakistan, where the decoration of a single vehicle can cost a driver the equivalent of thousands of U.S. dollars. Pakistanis expend such resources to participate in what one scholar has described as "[Pakistani] society's major form of representational art."[31] In brief, art matters to contemporary South Asians, both in its aesthetic and social dimensions.

Some South Asian states boost specific art forms in pursuit of creating nationalist identities. For example, in 1953–1954, Indians founded multiple national academies, including the Sangeet Natak Akademi (drama, music, dance), Sahitya Akademi (literature), and Lalit Kala Akademi (fine arts).[32] All still function today, often popularizing arts that are presented as products of "classical India." Like the idea of "classical India" itself, many modern forms of Indian dance, music, and so forth were far more recent products of twentieth-century nationalism.[33] Still, the pretense of classicism arguably helped to foster national pride by projecting a deep cultural history for the quite new Indian nation.

In the invention of Indian neo-classical arts, lower castes were often purged from the ranks of practitioners in favor of upper-caste dominance. Many early modern Indian performance traditions were centered in low-caste communities. This includes devadasis and tawaifs, female entertainers who hailed from Hindu and Muslim communities, respectively, and were often affiliated with courts, part of guilds, or (for devadasis) associated with Hindu temples (chapters 15 and 18). In the nineteenth century, many British colonialists and Indian reformers maligned these women, who sometimes engaged in sex work alongside their performances.[34] Both devadasis and tawaifs found it hard to continue working under such pressures in colonial India, and indeed, the birth of modern Bharatanatyam dance—widely celebrated today—involved replacing devadasi practitioners with middle-class dancers, under Brahmin stewardship.[35] Modern Bharatanatyam dancers are often taught an invented history, in which their artistic form is said to stretch back to ancient Sanskrit texts, a narrative that, by design, eschews most references to devadasis.

Artists have challenged religious and state identities in contemporary South Asia, which has prompted backlash. For instance, in the past few decades, extremists in northwest Pakistan have killed dancers, artists, and singers perceived to break social norms, especially women.[36] India, too, has experienced growing problems with intolerance of art, exemplified by Hindu nationalist pressure on M. F. Husain that ratcheted up over several decades.[37] In the 1950s, the Lalit Kala Akademi hosted national exhibitions of modern art and awarded one of its early cash prizes to M. F. Husain, a prolific artist sometimes called "India's Picasso."[38] The Indian state subsequently bestowed numerous prestigious awards on Husain, including the Padma Shri (1966), Padma Bhushan (1973), and Padma Vibhushan (1991).[39] Throughout his long career, M. F. Husain commonly depicted mythical figures, sometimes naked to represent purity. Some such images—of Durga and Saraswati (Hindu goddesses) and of India personified as a woman—upset Hindu nationalists, whose right-wing political movement grew stronger from the 1980s forward (see the next section). Reacting to the art and its maker as an Indian Muslim, members of India's far right filed lawsuits against Husain, vandalized his shows and home, and even put a bounty on his head.[40] In 2006, M. F. Husain fled India, fearing for his safety, and lived in exile until his death in 2011.

Not all Indians have heard of M. F. Husain, but probably every single one is aware of India's booming film industry known as Bollywood. Bollywood—so-named because it is centered in Bombay (now Mumbai)—is a booming economic enterprise that produces Indian blockbusters. India also has other film industries, including Tollywood (Telugu cinema) and robust independent filmmakers. Bollywood films reflect contemporary values and sometimes provide a backdrop for India's culture wars. Common areas of contestation include cultural and religious depictions, and film censorship is common (censorship of television shows is also on the rise).[41] In the past decade, India's BJP has pressured Bollywood into "belting out more films aligned with the government's Hindu supremacism."[42] This includes films that "villainize Muslims, liberal intellectuals, and past secular governments."[43]

One place to see the shift in Bollywood toward far-right politics concerns the treatment of history, a perennial film subject. Contemporary Bollywood films on historical subjects include *Asoka* (2001, on the third-century-BCE Mauryan emperor), *Mangal Pandey* (2005, on the 1857 Sepoy Rebellion), *Jodhaa Akbar* (2008, on the sixteenth-century Mughal emperor), and *Mohenjo Daro* (2016, on the Indus Civilization 2600–1900 BCE). Other Bollywood films center on historical legends, such as *Umrao Jaan* (1981, on nineteenth-century Indo-Muslim culture), *Lagaan* (2001, on British colonial exploitation), and *Padmaavat* (2018, on an invented love affair of the fourteenth-century ruler Alauddin Khalji, discussed in chapter 12). A Telugu film worth mentioning is *RRR* (2022), which was among the highest grossing Indian films ever and advances a "Hindu-nationalist fantasy" through a story set during British colonialism.[44] Following suit, the 2023 film *Gandhi Godse* "valorizes the Hindu extremist who killed Mahatma Gandhi" (chapter 22).[45] Bollywood's embrace of Hindu nationalism, especially in the last decade, is also visible in the poignant contrast between earlier and more recent films. For instance, *Jodhaa Akbar* (2008) celebrates the Mughals and upholds the aesthetics of Indo-Persian rule as a contribution to Indian culture, whereas *Padmaavat* (2018) applies crude Islamophobic stereotypes to the past. The two films offer a microcosm reflection of two distinct visions for how Muslims fit into Indian society, further elaborated in the next section.

Hindutva Intolerance and Iconoclasm

Of the eight modern nations that comprise South Asia, seven are "partly free" as per Freedom House rankings (Afghanistan is "not free"). For one nation, this designation stands out because it is relatively new: India, which was downgraded from "free" to "partly free" in 2020 after six years of BJP rule.[46] The V-Dem Research Institute agrees and has characterized India as an "electoral autocracy" since 2020.[47] The BJP practices Hindutva, also known as Hindu nationalism, and thereby seeks to "redefine the Republic of India as a Hindu Rashtra or Hindu Nation" (chapter 21).[48] Hindutva's implementation harms many people, including—as outlined in annual reports from human rights watchdog groups—journalists, scholars, students, human rights activists, women, Adivasis, and religious minorities.[49] Among these, Hindu nationalists' primary enemy—"infiltrators" as per Narendra Modi—are Indian Muslims, who bear the lion's share of Hindutva harassment, violence, and oppression.[50] India houses the world's third largest Muslim population (after Indonesia and Pakistan), and India's embrace of Hindu nationalist ideology has negatively impacted Indian Muslim communities.

Hindutva ideologues accumulated the political and social capital that enabled their 2014 takeover of India's central government largely through stoking anti-Muslim sentiments and violence. A key movement was Hindu nationalist agitation from the 1980s onward to destroy the Babri Masjid in Ayodhya, a town in northern India, and erect a Hindu temple in its place. The Babri Masjid was built in the early sixteenth century and posed no issues for more than three centuries.[51] In the mid-1800s, amid the colonial emphasis on religious difference, Hindus first laid claim to this Islamic religious space as the alleged site of the Hindu god Rama's birth (chapter 19). In the 1980s, Hindu nationalist groups such as the VHP (Vishva Hindu Parishad) and Bajrang Dal, both connected to the RSS,[52] organized a large-scale campaign to replace the Babri Masjid with a Rama Temple. These groups amplified false claims that a Ram Temple had once stood on the mosque's location.[53]

In the autumn of 1990, BJP and RSS leader L. K. Advani performed a self-styled yatra (procession) to Ayodhya across northern and central

India to try to draw attention to the cause of replacing the Muslim mosque with a Hindu temple. As widely predicted, he inspired Hindu-Muslim riots in dozens of towns along his journey (he was also jailed briefly).[54] Throughout, Advani pitched himself as an inheritor of the hero and god Rama, even decorating his air-conditioned Toyota—a notable status symbol given Indian import restrictions and poverty at the time—to look like Rama's chariot. In so doing, he played on public displays of Hindu piety popularized in the late nineteenth century (chapter 19). Advani and many others repeated a Hindi cry to build the temple where the mosque stood: *mandir vahi banayenge* (the temple will be built right here!).

In 1992—after years of far-right agitation—a Hindu mob tore down Ayodhya's Babri Masjid brick by brick, thereby committing a major act of anti-Muslim iconoclasm and destroying a piece of Indian cultural heritage. This was precisely the point, namely, to decimate Indian heritage associated with Muslims. Even decades later, Muslim minorities in Ayodhya recall feeling "panic-stricken" and "terrified" for their safety on the day the Babri Masjid was destroyed. Some sought refuge with neighbors, and others fled to nearby fields to try to escape "a frenzied mob running amok in the streets."[55] Their fears were justified. Following the destruction, riots broke out across India, and a few thousand Muslims were murdered.[56] As one scholar wrote about these horrific events, "The colonial notions of India's enduring division into Hindu and Muslim, and of 'history' as a mode of validation for one's actions in the present, had borne bitter fruit."[57]

By destroying the Babri Masjid, Hindu nationalists gained prominence for their cause, and they later repeated the tactic of unleashing anti-Muslim violence. Notably, in 2002, Narendra Modi, then–chief minister of Gujarat and a lifelong RSS member, oversaw three days of Hindu-led violence against Muslims in his state.[58] In that instance, about 2,000 Indians were murdered (mostly Muslims), and hundreds of thousands were displaced by Hindu mobs.[59] Some rioters placed images of Hanuman in mosques, enactments of Hindu supremacy over India's Muslim minority akin to events in Ayodhya in targeting Muslim religious sites.[60] International investigations have concluded that the Gujarati police acted on Modi's orders by assisting the violent mobs in targeting Muslims and later engaged in a brutal cover-up.[61]

The 2002 Gujarat pogrom played differently abroad versus at home. Narendra Modi was banned from entering the United States for more than a decade thereafter because of his role in "severe violations of religious freedom."[62] The United Kingdom similarly banned Modi for ten years.[63] But the Gujarat pogrom solidified Modi's reputation in India as a "strongman who stands as a muscular defender of the Hindu majority" and serves, in the vein of many populist leaders, as "the right conduit for expressing revenge."[64] Attractive, in part, precisely because he never apologized for the 2002 anti-Muslim Gujarat pogrom, Narendra Modi led the BJP's campaign in India's 2014 general elections.[65] He also promised accelerated economic growth under BJP leadership (this did not pan out).[66] Modi became India's prime minister in 2014, thereby making the Hindu nationalist BJP India's dominant political party.

During BJP rule from 2014 to 2019, anti-Muslim violence accelerated in India and become part of daily life. Muslims faced attacks for praying (as did Christians, another Indian religious minority disfavored by Hindu nationalists).[67] Interfaith couples were persecuted by Hindu far-right groups, who sometimes focused on the Muslim individual involved.[68] Indian reporters who happen to be Muslim were singled out for attack.[69] Some Indian Muslims were assaulted, even killed, over accusations of eating beef in an enforcement of upper-caste Hindu purity norms.[70] In many cases, well-armed vigilante groups like the Bajrang Dal enacted these crimes, with tactic or explicit support from the Indian government.[71] Often, they focused on moral policing, and their networks constituted a "deeper state" that, not being subject to elections, subverts India's democracy.[72]

The world noticed India's plummeting human rights record—especially for religious minorities—under BJP leadership between 2014 and 2019, along with sharp declines in the health of Indian democracy, freedom of the press, and other metrics. So did India and, while some Indians were appalled, others liked what they saw.[73] Modi led the BJP to victory again in India's general elections of May 2019. As an astute reporter observed, "For many, Modi's reelection suggested that he had uncovered a terrible secret at the heart of Indian society: by deploying vicious sectarian rhetoric, the country's leader could persuade Hindus to give him nearly unchecked power."[74]

In November 2019—with an Indian mainstream increasingly defined by Hindu nationalist ideology—India's Supreme Court handed down its decision in the Babri Masjid destruction case, awaited since 1992. The court decided that, despite the Babri Masjid being illegally destroyed by Hindu assailants, a Hindu Ram Temple could be built in its place.[75] The decision lacks any legal basis and is incoherent at times.[76] This reflects Hindutva ideology itself being a mix of "garbled mantras" that are only consistent in hatred of Muslims.[77]

The 2019 Ayodhya judgment was also symptomatic of a larger issue, namely that Hindu nationalists had eroded the Indian judiciary's independence. As a result, courts no longer provided checks on Hindutva challenges to Indian democracy, freedom of religion, and rule of law.[78] Practically, the 2019 Ayodhya judgment initiated the construction of the Ram Temple, whose foundation stone was laid by Prime Minister Modi and was opened (still incomplete) in January 2024, as the *New York Times* put it, as "a triumph for India's Hindu nationalists."[79] Indian media was considerably more positive in its reporting of the opening of Ayodhya's Ram Temple, and relevant to making sense of this disparity is that India ranked 161 out of 180 nations regarding press freedom as of 2023.[80] As Reporters Without Borders (Reporters sans Frontieres) has put it, "India's media has fallen into an 'unofficial state of emergency' since Narendra Modi came to power in 2014 and engineered a spectacular rapprochement between his party, the BJP, and the big families dominating the media."[81] Amid intense dispute about Ayodhya's Ram Temple, one thing is agreed upon by all parties: the temple will always lay upon the rubble of a mosque.

In making sense of contemporary India's hard-right swerve, over several decades, from a secular democracy striving for equality to a Hindu state with shrinking human and civil rights, observers hold different views. Some, such as historian Sunil Khilnani, see a "blurring, even dissolving, [of] the idea of India."[82] Others, such as the head of Amnesty International in India, Aakar Patel, consider it "unclear what the idea of India is, was or if any such construct existed."[83] Some from nearby states hear echoes of the intolerance they fled. Fahmida Riaz, an Urdu Pakistani poet who lived in exile in India for decades, suggests a parallel between Modi's India and Zia's Pakistan (chapter 23), exclaiming "turned out you were just like us" and wondering if Hindus will soon pass fatwas (Islamic legal judgments that often promote hardline views; see excerpt).

Fahmida Riaz's 2014 Urdu Poem "Turned Out You Were Just Like Us"

So it turned out you were just like us!
Where were you hiding all this time, buddy?

That stupidity, that ignorance
we wallowed in for a century–
look, it arrived at your shores too!
Many congratulations to you!

Raising the flag of religion,
I guess now you'll be setting up Hindu Raj?
You too will commence to muddle everything up.
You, too, will ravage your beautiful garden.

You, too, will sit and ponder–
I can tell preparations are afoot–
who is [truly] Hindu, who is not.
I guess you'll be passing fatwas soon!

Here, too, it will become hard to survive.
Here, too, you will sweat and bleed.
You'll barely make do joylessly.
You will gasp for air like us.

I used to wonder with such deep sorrow.
And now, I laugh at the idea:
it turned out you were just like us!
We weren't two nations after all!

To hell with education and learning.
Let's sing the praises of ignorance.
Don't look at the potholes in your path:
bring back instead the times of yore!

Practice harder till you master
the skill of always walking backwards.
Let not a single thought of the present
break your focus upon the past!

Repeat the same thing over and over—
over and over, say only this:
How glorious was India in the past!
How sublime was India in days gone by!

Then, dear friends, you will arrive
and get to heaven after all.
Yep. We've been there for a while now.
Once you are there,
once you're in the same hell-hole,
keep in touch and tell us how it goes![84]

The contemporary illiberal thrashings of Hindutva are just that, contemporary, and this makes any conclusion elusive because we do not yet know how this far-right trend of the last few decades will fit into India's broader history. Certainly, in the short term, India's future looks bleak, especially for the 20 percent of citizens that are religious minorities facing a "deteriorating human rights situation" owing to aggressions by "government officials, political leaders, and supporters of the Bharatiya Janata Party (BJP)."[85] In the long term, perhaps democratic India will emerge out of its current embrace of Hindutva, with pluralists poised to recover their nation's higher ideals of justice, equality, liberty, and fraternity as outlined by Ambedkar in the Indian Constitution.[86] Alternatively, Hindutva could define the Indian political and cultural mainstream for the foreseeable future. Either way, this far-right political trend has compounded an issue facing the entire region of South Asia that will undoubtedly prove definitional for the next few generations: climate change.

Climate Change

Owing to its combination of geography, poverty, and dense population, the subcontinent is uniquely vulnerable to the deleterious effects of climate change. Indeed, owing to human activities, South Asians have suffered from shifts in weather patterns and temperatures for decades, and many trends stand to worsen substantially in the coming years. Key issues include contaminated drinking water, flooding, cyclones, scorching temperatures, rising ocean levels, and food insecurity. South Asians have contributed to environmental degradation in contemporary times, such as through resource mismanagement. But, overall, South Asians suffer because of worldwide trends of climate change that are imperiling their home and ways of life.

South Asians largely rely on Himalayan-fed rivers—including the Indus, Ganges, and Brahmaputra—for drinking water and to irrigate crops, but water flow patterns stand to shift. Snowfall patterns are already changing in the Himalayas, and the melting of snow and ice is accelerating. As a result, by 2050, South Asia's major rivers will likely see reduced flows in the dry season.[87] Drinking water has long been a pressure point due to its relative scarcity on the subcontinent. India, for example, houses one-sixth of the world's population but boasts only 4 percent of its freshwater.[88]

India's rivers are compromised by pollution, such as the Ganges River that provides fresh water to more than 40 percent of India's population. Many Hindus consider the Ganges to be a holy river and goddess who descended from heaven, which has led to the idea that pollution is impossible. A 1982 citizens' report explains: "The oldest myth about the Ganga river is ensconced in the tale of Bhagirath who was able to persuade the goddess Ganga to come down from heaven to earth and of Shiva who had to capture the torrential fall in his hair so that the earth would not get destroyed. The newest myth was created by a courageous Union Cabinet Minister who foolhardily declared before Parliament that the Ganga could never be polluted."[89] In reality, the report notes, "The Ganga river system has been converted into a network of cesspools and drains by the industries and municipalities in the region" and numbers "among India's most polluted rivers."[90] The report wryly posits, "Shiva is no longer required to protect the Earth from the Ganga; now the Ganga itself requires protection from the violence of people."[91] Indeed, in 1984, two years after the citizens' report was published, chemical pollutants became so concentrated that a stretch of the Ganges literally went up in flames.[92] In the past few decades, various international projects have attempted to clean up the Ganges. Still, as recently as January 2023, Indian government monitoring revealed alarming levels of bacterial contamination.[93]

Flooding affects millions in India, Pakistan, and Bangladesh annually. Human activities, such as deforestation, have increased the risk of flooding in certain areas. For instance, in the early to mid-twentieth century, Bombay's mangrove forests were chopped down, eliminating a natural buffer between the ocean and shore.[94] A large mangrove forest, known as the Sundarbans, spans both Bangladesh and parts of India's Bengal, although it has shrunk to about half its former size over the last 200 years.[95] Bangladesh is largely low-lying delta land and so notably prone to cyclones and floods, which impact up to 70 percent of the land and population.[96] Notably disastrous floods occurred in Dhaka in 1987, 1988, 1998, 2004, and 2007.[97] While such events have become more intense in recent decades, death tolls have reduced due to better planning and forecasting that enables people to be evacuated. For instance, a 1970 cyclone killed 500,000 Bangladeshis, a 1991 cyclone killed 150,000, and a 2007 cyclone killed less than 5,000.[98]

In parts of South Asia, rising temperatures imperil human life. By 2050, global warming and associated aspects of climate change are projected to reduce wheat production in the region by 16 percent, which would be catastrophic given projected South Asian population growth over the same period.[99] By the late twenty-first century, parts of South Asia may become too hot for human beings to survive.[100] Some of South Asia's cooler regions—especially in Afghanistan and Nepal, along with nearby Burma—could see an increase in fertile land due to rising temperatures, but this will prove little consolation to those scorched out of hotter climes.

Adivasi communities number among those most at risk of climate change in South Asia and, they argue, best equipped to address it due to their ecologically friendly values. As mentioned (chapter 23), Adivasi perspectives are rarely valued by the Indian government. Even in cases where Indian officials try to address climate or ecological issues, they often run afoul of Adivasi communities. For example, in the 1990s, the World Bank canceled funding for Odisha's Simlipal Tiger Reserve and National Park due to the Indian government's poor treatment of the forest dwellers displaced therein.[101] Still, Adivasi activists are outspoken advocates for themselves and all Indians. As Dayamani Barla, a journalist and member of an Indian tribal community from Jharkhand, said in 2022: "The mantra to control the impacts of climate change lies within the tribal lifestyle that is built around the culture of humans coexisting with the forests. This is the key to fighting against climate change and global warming."[102]

Conclusion: South Asian Futures

As of today, in the early twenty-first century, there is little consensus in South Asia about the likely future of the region and its diverse communities. Each nation is taking its own path and hosts robust internal divisions within its population. Still, South Asians remain connected with other parts of the world and subjected to broad shifts. Although neither of these trends is new historically, the impacts of global links on South Asia have grown more robust and, regarding climate change, challenging. In a sense, we might say that South Asia's future stands to bear a similarity to its past in being multifaceted, contested, and connected to the rest of the world. Amid uncertainty, one thing is clear—there is not one South Asian future laying ahead but many.

Further Reading

Given the contemporary focus of this chapter, I relied extensively on modern news reporting alongside scholarship. For data, United Nations agencies proved useful, and for human rights reporting, I especially recommend Human Rights Watch and Amnesty International. Sunil Amrith's work on water deserves special mention. I salute and commend that many South Asian reporters, investigative journalists, and activists that have produced critical data about various aspects of their nations in recent decades, often at great risk to themselves.

Afterword: Now

It is just a moment in history. *Kya kar sakte hain.* (What can one do?)

—M. F. Husain, Indian artist who died in exile (d. 2011)[1]

Any scholarly work that traces history into its own contemporary moment faces the challenge of lacking historical distance. In writing the final chapters of this book on events post-1947, I was clear-eyed about misleading framings for modern South Asia that I wished to avoid. These bad ideas include, discretely, nationalist cheerleading for any modern South Asian state, an India-centric storyline (in the sense of India as the modern-nation state), and clash-of-civilizations theses concerning religious and ethnic conflicts. Still, I struggled to identify a desirable way—meaning a historically honest and intellectually fruitful approach—to conclude this survey of nearly 5,000 years of South Asian history. My uncertainty about the best emphasis in conclusion was compounded by the banal reality that the book's end point is arbitrary. After all, the publication date merely reflects when I happened to write this tome. We are not the end point of history, or its culmination, or even its nadir. We live in "just a moment in history," as per M. F. Husain, except that our moment is not yet the past. Given that we all stand in history, some presentism is unavoidable, and, in this afterword, I comment on three issues that I declined to interject into the main narrative but loomed in my mind, especially when writing the last few chapters: the growing South Asian diaspora, exclusive nationalist claims on history, and declining human rights in India post-2019.

Modern South Asia is partly defined by its growing diaspora, meaning South Asians who left their homeland and pursued new lives elsewhere.

As of spring 2024, the South Asian diaspora was roughly forty-five million people strong and growing daily.[2] Many South Asian migrants travel to the Middle East, with Saudi Arabia being a popular destination. Several Middle Eastern nations rely so strongly on migrants, from South Asia and elsewhere, that collectively they constitute a majority in each state (e.g., United Arab Emirates, Bahrain, Kuwait, and Qatar).[3] The United States is home to more than five million people of South Asian descent, and the United Kingdom is home to more than three million.[4] One thing shared by South Asian migrants, across discrete destinations, is that many contribute to their home nations' economies through remittances, sending money back to family in Nepal, Pakistan, India, and so forth.[5] Some migrants eventually return, whereas others elect to make a new home abroad. For example, 225,000 Indians renounced their citizenship in 2022, a number that had nearly doubled over the prior decade.[6] In their new nations, each diaspora is unique in its composition and cultures.

When I teach contemporary South Asian history, I typically include a section about the formation of the South Asian American diaspora. This is not, strictly speaking, on topic since it is part of American history rather than South Asian history. But covering the local diaspora helps contextualize the lived experiences of many of my students (and, in this case, many of my readers). Emigration from South Asia to the United States was rare before the 1960s owing to racist laws. That changed with the 1965 Hart-Celler Immigration Act, which opened the door to South Asian migrants of a rarified class. Since 1965, millions of South Asians have emigrated to the United States through a process of "triple selection," meaning (1) having access to elementary and secondary education in South Asia, (2) completing higher education in South Asia, and (3) being deemed "skilled" by U.S. immigration authorities.[7] Amid this large group of elite South Asian migrants, smaller groups are also represented. Some of South Asian descent moved to the United States from the Caribbean or other former locations of indenture. Other South Asians have entered the United States through unofficial channels (and are more likely to engage in unskilled labor). There are also small pockets of older migrants, especially the children of Punjabi Sikhs and Muslims, dating back to late nineteenth-century America (chapter 20). Even given such diversity, formal U.S. structures favoring skilled South Asian migrants have shaped the general contours of the diaspora, and the average South Asian American is far more elite—wealthy, educated, and enjoying access to opportunities—than the average South Asian.

The South Asian American diaspora skews overwhelmingly in favor of upper castes (whereas, in South Asia, upper castes are a minority). This diaspora demographic tilt is due to the "triple selection" process outlined above, especially the first two steps of educational opportunity in India, which have privileged upper castes since British colonialism and earlier (chapter 20).[8] Moreover, as a scholar of the South Asian diaspora has put it, "Caste permeates the society of Indians living abroad."[9] Many diasporic social groups and business organizations are organized along caste lines.[10] Having an upper-caste concentration changes the tenor of social debates and perceptions of mainstream opinion within South Asian American communities. Caste-based discrimination is an enduring issue, now part of American social life, and raised more recently especially by Dalit minorities within the diaspora who seek caste equity.

There are additional inequalities, beyond caste, within the South Asian American diaspora. In the United States, Indians dominate numerically over Pakistanis (this is far less the case in the United Kingdom). Also, within the South Asian American community, Hindus arguably enjoy greater freedom to express their views and practice their religion as compared to South Asian Muslims who report far higher religious discrimination rates.[11] There are tensions between Hindus and Muslims in the diaspora, which broadly reflect communal tensions in contemporary South Asia and derive from a specific movement within the diaspora, namely Hindu nationalism.

The Sangh Parivar—the family of Hindu nationalist groups centered around the RSS—began replicating itself abroad in 1948 and entered the United States around 1970. Many U.S.-based Hindu nationalist groups are foreign wings of their Indian counterparts, such as the HSS (the overseas RSS), VHP-America (American branch of India's VHP), and their respective student groups (Hindu Yuva and Hindu Students Council).[12] Such organizations work alongside American Hindu nationalist groups without exact parallels in India to promote Hindutva objectives. In the United States context, that often means claiming that Hindus alone can speak as authentic Indian voices, undermining South Asian Muslim Americans, arguing against diversity and civil rights initiatives, and whitewashing India's worsening human rights record under BJP rule.[13] The Hindu far right constitutes one of the loudest, fiercest set of voices within the South Asian American diaspora, and analyzing them helps us to understand Hindutva—which was intercontinental even in its founding since it imported strategies and techniques from early twentieth-century European fascist movements[14]—as an ongoing transnational phenomenon.

Widening out to the diaspora more broadly, South Asian Americans tend to relate to their heritage along two broad tracks. In part, they adapt their cultural and religious traditions to accommodate their new home context, which produces distinct South Asian American traditions. For example, there is a marked emphasis on Gujarati Garba dance on American college campuses (Gujaratis are around 6 percent of Indians but 20 percent of Indian Americans).[15] Hindu temples in the United States are often ecumenical, featuring numerous Hindu deities, and celebrate holidays from multiple South Asian regions (in India, temples are typically devoted to a single deity and festivals are often celebrated regionally).[16] The diverse traditions of South Asian Americans constitute an academic subfield in their own right, within American Studies. As a historian of South Asia, however, I tend to intersect more with the second track, namely diasporic claims over aspects of traditions located within South Asia, including history.

Some South Asian migrants who become citizens of other nations—whether of the United States, United Kingdom, Canada, Australia, or so forth—continue to embrace South Asian history as their own. Insofar as such claims are matters of cultural heritage, I find them wonderful. One of the great pleasures and honors of my academic career has been teaching a diverse undergraduate student body at Rutgers University-Newark, which has strong representation from members of the South Asian American diaspora. I commend those who pursue knowledge of their historical heritage: you all enrich my classrooms and those of many other professors across the United States.

In some cases, personal claims over South Asian history can be exclusive, and here things become problematic. Some advance the view that specific pasts can only be discussed and understood by those of a certain background or bloodline. I address this as a South Asia phenomenon in the Historiography essay, and I summarize my views here in the context of parallel diasporic claims that only South Asian Americans (rather than Americans of other immigrant heritages, like me) ought to study, write, and teach South Asian history. Such identity-based approaches fall outside of historical method, which underscores training and recognizes that everyone has positionality. I decline to give credence to diasporic takes on nativism that discredit historical rigor in favor of identity-based ownership.

I decided to end this book, in chapter 24, with an emphasis on everyday life and challenges, which resulted in omissions of some political events. For example, I failed to mention that Pakistan became a nuclear power in 1998, India and Pakistan fought over Kashmir in the 1999 Kargil conflict, Nepalis overthrew their Hindu monarchy in 2008, and the Sri Lankan civil war ended in 2009 (I snuck a mention of this last point into chapter 23). I made comparable choices—selecting one narrative lens over others—at numerous prior points in this book. But readers are more likely to notice lacuna in contemporary times, especially events that are within living memory. In my mild defense, chapter 23 largely focuses on political history. Also, as mentioned in the introduction, I invite readers to see what omitting much-discussed political events allowed me to include in chapter 24: female literacy rates, urbanization trends, contemporary art and dance, and climate change. I contend that these issues are critical to understanding modern South Asia and perhaps especially deserving of attention owing to our collective inclination to privilege political history.

I covered Indian political movements related to Hindu nationalism only through about mid-2019, declining to comment on events after the reelection of the BJP in that year (with a few exceptions), because this is a rapidly changing situation. Overall, Indian rights and democracy have plummeted since 2019 through BJP assaults on Kashmir's autonomy, attempts to strip Indian Muslims of citizenship, the 2020 Delhi Riots, use of internet blackouts and other authoritarian tools to reduce the visibility of dissent, a tightening grip on Indian media and social media, and accelerating restrictions on the economic, religious, and social participation of Indian religious minorities.[17] Especially alarming is the extreme Hindutva othering of Indian Muslims who are subjected to increasing hate crimes in Modi's "partly free" India.[18] As of the time of writing in summer 2024, this situation is worsening as per human rights watchdog groups.[19]

I elected not to cover these events, except briefly in this afterword, because it is a story not yet fully written. The obvious counter to that position is that many historians write about the present, including myself in prior publications. Still, I found writing about ongoing events—whose conclusion is still undetermined—to sit uneasy within a book anchored in done and dusted history. I am clear on one thing, namely that India's Hindutva fever will break, as fascist fevers always do.[20] But as of when I write these words, Hindutva's demise remains in the future. And this book is, fundamentally, about the past. In response to M. F. Husain's (admittedly rhetorical) question *kya kar sakte hain* (What can one do?), my answer, out of many possible answers, is as follows—we can learn about history, understand what South Asian realities have been, and displace ourselves and the constricting biases of our times from center stage.

Historiography

There are rules for professional historians, and there is leeway within disciplinary boundaries. I cover both here, striving to give a forthright account of how I approached recovering and narrating the South Asian past. In contrast, I elected to keep historiography out of the substantive chapters of this book, instead focusing there on recovering the past and showcasing South Asian history. Still, I recognize the need for historians (and historians-in-training) to work through our own intellectual baggage. Accordingly—and in the interest of transparency—I give frank explanations in this essay of the decisions I made to distill into a single tome a history that can, and justly should, fill libraries. My starting point for this analysis is a rather basic one, namely that the possibilities of writing history are constrained by scholarly ethics and facts.

What Indian History Is and Is Not

I wrote this book as a scholar of South Asian history and so take an academic approach. Of course, there are non-academic ways to recall and narrate the past. As one historian has noted, history "belongs to everyone and to no one, whence its claim to universal authority."[1] But not all historical narratives are equally valid, and mine adheres to rigorous standards of scholarly ethics, historical method, and accuracy. In this, my approach differs from common strategies in more popular historical narratives. Less dramatically, my methods also vary in certain regards from those of other historians, and I elaborate on both distinctions here.

I do not soft-pedal the more difficult angles of South Asian pasts, meaning that I elect for historical faithfulness above modern comfort. As some readers will know, politics are fast and furious in several twenty first-century South Asian nations that incentive historians to whitewash aspects of history that sit ill with modern majoritarian movements.[2] I analyze some of these movements, such as Hindu nationalism in India and Islamization in Pakistan, as part of modern history (chapters 23–24).

But scholarly ethics prohibit me from bowing to their pressures, no matter how fierce or violent, to tamper with the past.[3]

Arguably more insidious is pressure for a monocausal narrative in South Asian history. As the historian Harbans Mukhia explained in early 2021, British colonialists used religion to craft a history of India with a sole driving force, and modern thinkers have corrected that misguided idea by arguing for a multifaceted approach. Now, India's far-right Hindu nationalist movement—the major intellectual inheritor of British colonialism—wants, once again, a simplistic Indian history centered on Hindu-Muslim conflict alone.[4] The idea is narratively attractive since it offers cohesion to tie together a messy past, but it is inaccurate. Even when it is narratively inconvenient, I remain firmly committed to accurate Indian history, which includes a plethora of trends and a great degree of religious pluralism.[5]

Historians are killjoys at times, and I often provide real-world explanations for phenomena that many prefer to experience as more magical, even timeless. For example, I shave off later, celebrated additions to the life story of the Gautama Buddha to recover him as a historical figure (chapter 3). I analyze how the eighteenth-century pilgrimage economy transformed Benares into a major religious destination and enriched specific local communities (chapter 16). On an individual level, readers will find no unmitigated heroes in these pages, not even the likes of Mohandas Gandhi, a visionary Indian independence leader who had a decidedly mixed record on caste (chapter 21). Some of my positions are bound to raise eyebrows, such as showing how Indian literature and art in the mid-first millennium CE relied on inequality (chapter 7). Historians must follow the evidence, even when it shatters a beloved illusion.

History is not a glory story, nor is it a lineup of wonderful things we all like, but it is even darker since the sublime and horrific often coexist. As the philosopher Walter Benjamin wrote: "There is no document of civilization which is not at the same time a document of barbarism. And just as such a document is not free of barbarism, barbarism taints also the manner in which it was transmitted from one owner to another."[6] In India, this is evidenced in premodern Brahminical Sanskrit texts, which contain stunning intellectual and literary achievements while encoding harsh bigotries. To give a material example, Chola temples are gorgeous places of worship as well as sites of slavery (chapter 9). It ought not to be surprising that human history is filled with exploitation, prejudices, and horrors. But even those who intellectually acknowledge this reality sometimes feel the tendency to celebrate what certain contemporary communities continue to honor. In my view, historians ought to guard against the whitewashing that familiarity—both superficial and real—can make all too tempting.

Throughout the book, I address many contentious issues that a premodern Sanskrit intellectual might term *goshpade yuddham* (battle in a cow's hoofprint), meaning tempest in a teapot. In this, I stand on the shoulders of many historians before me who have covered contemporary controversies about the past. But I make one major departure from prior historians, namely, I cover polemics when they come up in history, not when initially discussing the subject on which they focus. Accordingly, I cover British exaggerations of Hindu-Muslim conflict during Mughal rule when discussing the eighteenth and nineteenth centuries, not the sixteenth century (chapters 17 and 19). I mention idealizations of Vedic India by upper-caste Hindu groups when discussing the nineteenth century, not the second millennium BCE (chapter 19). I outline the British obsession with dividing premodern Indian architecture by religion when covering colonialism, not premodernity (chapter 19). I discuss Alauddin Khalji's imaginary love affair with Padmavat when it was popularized in the sixteenth century, not its projected dates of the thirteenth–fourteenth centuries (chapter 12). When a controversy or a popular misunderstanding is so widespread that it will likely pop into some readers' minds, I resort to explanatory endnotes.

I make two limited exceptions to my emphasis on historical facts. At times, I repeat hagiographies (imagined life stories)—always clearly identified as such—for religious leaders. This choice enables me to capture what made millions of Indians follow the Gautama Buddha, Mahavira, Kabir, Nanak, and others (chapters 3, 11, and 12). This approach is especially valuable when we have limited historical information on certain individuals. Still, hagiography ought never to be confused with historical truth. Additionally, I use literature throughout the book, drawing on myths such as the Mahabharata and poetry from a range of time periods and authors. Literature is, itself, part of history, and I further use some works to identify values, ideas, and points of contestation for the communities that produced and cherished specific works of fiction. As with hagiography, I overtly alert readers when I use literature and am forthcoming about how to do so responsibly as a historian.

Our History Problems

Historians have our own history of thinking about the South Asian past dating back to the eighteenth and nineteenth centuries, but reviewing that *parampara* (tradition) can be risky. Many historians introduce major South Asian historical topics (e.g., the Gupta Kingdom or Buddhism's decline in the Indian heartland) by repeating our discipline's bad, outdated ideas on the subject and then explaining why we think differently now. The impulse is virtuous in trying to educate students about progress in historical thinking. But the problem is that this approach introduces historically inaccurate ideas anew to generation after generation of history students. To rub salt in the wound, students sometimes remember the outdated ideas better than their more sound replacements, thus perpetuating colonial-era misconceptions for several further decades. To avoid this vicious cycle, I focus throughout this book on history, not historiography, seeking to offer a better narrative of the past rather than first filling readers' minds with discarded ideas. I concentrate my historiographical thoughts here, working through the nuances of a series of bad ideas that fall under the catch-all category of Orientalism—stereotypical ideas about South Asia, typically dating to colonialism—but benefit from more precise consideration.

For a start, we all have Sanskrit problems. Sanskrit is an ancient elite Indian language, initially used only by Brahminical communities and then, starting in the first millennium CE, by many others, including Jains, Buddhists, kings, and diverse intellectuals and poets. Sanskrit texts offer a myriad of insights into premodern Indian lives and intellectual ideas, but some colonialists took this too far in the eighteenth and nineteenth centuries. They projected Sanskrit texts as straightforward descriptions of Indian social life, past and present, to the exclusion of works in other languages (chapter 17). These colonial-era Orientalist scholars focused on Brahmin-authored works, constituting a "Brahminical archive" of Sanskrit texts as the major archive for studying Indian history.[7] This narrowed interpretation of Indian life to Sanskrit intellectuals and further narrowed Sanskrit intellectuals to Brahmins, a small sliver of the Indian population at any point in time. Here, I offer three major corrections, beginning with drawing on a broader range of Sanskrit texts whose authors include Jains, Buddhists, and Muslims. I also interpret Sanskrit texts more contextually, as products of their time and elite ideations (rather than assuming their accuracy). Last, I displace Brahminical Sanskrit texts by introducing other sorts of textual evidence as well as forefronting archaeological evidence at times (e.g., chapter 3).

A foundational Orientalist idea that still rears its ugly head is that India has no history and so has not changed over time. Originally, timeless India—unchanging in its spiritual traditions, system of government, or culture (usually imagined as singular, in Orientalist thought)—was a demeaning notion that served to justify European colonial rule. These days, an implausible Indian immutability continues to be embraced both within and outside the subcontinent as what makes India special.[8] In both incarnations, "India lacks history" is a toxic idea that removes the entire region from the broad narrative of human history, and accordingly I reject it here. I do not reject that India is special in many ways, and I locate its uniqueness in the vibrancy, mutability, and diversity of specific South Asian communities.

Colonial-era thinkers introduced a strong religious lens to the study of Indian history, along with a tripartite temporal division into Hindu, Muslim, and British periods. I cover this briefly as a point of intellectual history (chapter 17), but I otherwise find little use for it. This triptych framework is wildly inaccurate. Premodern Indian governments are not usefully identified by religion, were pluralistic in their composition, and did not institute anything approaching theocratic rule (that is an exclusively modern South Asian phenomenon). Premodern India never witnessed "Hindu rule" or "Muslim rule," as most modern people imagine those things. And the transition from religion to nationality with "British rule," the final period in this formulation, is colonial propaganda. Other scholars have taken a range of approaches to replacing this harmful tripartite chronology, the most common of which is renaming. Thus, "Muslim" becomes "Persianate," "British" is dubbed "colonial," and so forth. I find substituting terms to be an ineffective cure, since it fails to confront the underlying disease of demarcating historical periods by religion and does not address the exceptions so numerous they disprove the rule (e.g., numerous Maratha, Rajput, and Nayaka lineages ruled during so-called Muslim rule).

Instead, I shy away from a scaffolding of political divisions altogether. I refer to ancient, early, premodern, medieval, early modern, and modern time periods, with their contours deliberately left fuzzy and overlapping. Such flexibility is a nod to regional differences and a signal to take these categories as general indicators rather than strict timeframes. My refusal to demarcate hard historical time periods may unmoor some readers, but I find the benefits of usefully reconceptualizing time in South Asian history to outweigh the discomfort of losing familiar markers.

My narrative centers on South Asians, which is important to underscore given the state of scholarship. Some corners of the academy have found it strangely difficult to forefront South Asian individuals and communities in historical narratives, even when this is precisely what they set out to accomplish. For instance, the subaltern school launched in the early 1980s with promising case studies of peasants, workers, and others often overlooked in history. But soon the movement collapsed in a heap of Western theory as scholars argued in convoluted language about colonialism and postcolonialism until they were blue in the face, leaving the stories of "subaltern" South Asians, once again, untold in English-medium scholarly circles.[9] Overall, I agree with Margaret Atwood when she opined that "there might be a bit too much theory kicking around in the world."[10] I remain unimpressed with scholarly movements within South Asian history that have allowed theory (nearly always Western-dominated and male-dominated theory) to supplant space that ought to be devoted to South Asian stories.[11] A corollary issue is that some scholars strive to recover *only* larger trends, sans individual stories or even names. In my estimation, this cannot be done responsibly or accurately, as a point of historical method. Moreover, I deliberately crafted a narrative about South Asians and so incorporated a robust emphasis on individuals alongside the greater historical trends in which they participated.

For British colonialism in South Asia, we face the peculiar problem that some historians forefront Europeans, projecting them as the main movers and shakers of this multi-century event. So often, once Company rule (1757–1858) comes into the picture, Indian names evaporate from modern narratives and are replaced by the likes of Kirkpatrick, Halhed, Jones, and Clive at center stage.[12] My objection to this approach is straightforward: A European-centered narrative does not constitute accurate Indian history. Perhaps a European focus is appropriate if one is narrating British history since, as the Indian American novelist Salman Rushdie wrote in his *Satanic Verses*, "The trouble with the English is that their history happened overseas, so they don't know what it means."[13] I agree that a sizeable amount of British history occurred in India, but I leave that rich subject for British historians to explore. As a South Asia historian, I maintain a focus on South Asian individuals, societies, and agency during British colonialism and throughout this book (down to the chapter epigraphs, with few exceptions). I still mention many Europeans—including all the names given earlier in this paragraph—but I do not position them as dominating a story that, rightly for a book of South Asian history, centers South Asians.

As mentioned, with limited exceptions, I do not bring up specific points of historiography throughout this book, restricting my methodological comments to considering different kinds of evidence and predominantly offering what I judge to be better narratives. I recognize that some historians may object to my decision to prioritize history over historiography. I would gently point out that plenty of historians have done this differently, by first articulating bad history before offering their own corrective, and so there are many books to sate tastes for a historiography-first approach.[14] For me, I felt it was best to stop beating dead horses and simply let them decay. In contrast, I explicitly discuss the merits of different kinds of evidence (e.g., written, literary, material, even genetic) at several points, especially in some of the early chapters. My intention is to demystify some of the historian's craft and impart some basics of historical thinking. At a narrative level, my conscious and persistent focus on history and evidence, rather than modern historiography, marks this book as a work about South Asia's past, not our present.

Your History Problems

As I wrote this book, the good-faith objections of some readers and colleagues echoed in my ears. Sometimes, I heard challenges through feedback kindly provided on chapter drafts, and other times, I anticipated questions, based on years of experience teaching South Asian history. In this section, I address what, I think, will be some common objections to the content and narrative of this book. In answering imagined and real objectors, I draw inspiration from premodern Indian philosophers, who commonly stated the opponent's view (*purvapaksha*) followed by the author's own position (*uttarapaksha*). I adjust the writing style of this approach in accordance with modern English norms, but I honor the force of my objectors all the same. Even so, I hope my clarifications explain what we stand to gain from my version of the historian's craft.

I cut many things from this book, condensing parts of Indian history that other historians have elaborated at greater length (e.g., the Gupta Kingdom, the Ramayana, tantra, Shah Jahan's rule) and cutting some subjects altogether (e.g., the development of most Indian literatures). I made these choices to accommodate other, under-told stories. For example, as compared to many historians, I dwell less on the Guptas and other first-millennium-CE dynasties but offer more analysis of trade, caste-based oppression, and pilgrimage networks in early India (chapters 6–8).[15] I talk less about Shah Jahan's rule but cover developments within Sri Lankan Buddhist and Bengali Muslim communities in early modernity (chapter 14). Such emphases produce a narrative that is more unexpected and, I think, more compelling and balanced. My chapters are succinct by design, and it was never an option to sacrifice brevity, simply adding additional sections to avoid the criticism that I omitted certain topics. No doubt, there will be readers miffed that I did not offer enough detail on their favorite nugget of South Asian history. My hope is that this is not the only book you read about the South Asian past, and I include brief bibliographic essays at the end of each chapter as a jumping off point for readers hungry to learn more.

Political history is rightly seen as one subfield of history, and it should not dominate our view of South Asia. The conflation of South Asian history and dynasties is quite old, and even the Roman author Pliny (d. 79 CE) expressed India's antiquity by noting that it had 153 kings over 6,451 years.[16] Really, Pliny meant north India, which indicates that a king-heavy view of Indian history tends to be north India-centric. Modern historians ought to know better. More than forty years ago, a South Asia art historian noted that "even political historians today recognize that the genealogy of rulers governs only superficially the events of ancient India."[17] I include plenty of kings and queens in these pages and, for later periods, presidents and prime ministers. But, to offer a concrete example, I chose to focus less than many historians on the Delhi Sultanate in the twelfth and thirteenth centuries and more on the spread of Sufism in this period (chapter 10). Similarly, for post-independence South Asia, I write less about India's first and longest-standing prime minister, Jawaharlal Nehru (d. 1964) and instead offer more detail on literacy rates and the Mandal Commission (chapter 23).[18] In brief, I focus less on the few rulers and more on the plurality of South Asian communities.

Some points of South Asian history lack scholarly consensus, and this put me, a single historian, in a difficult position. After assessing the evidence, I took many stands on substantive arguments, such as the origins of farming (chapter 1), the dating of the Mahabharata (chapter 5), how the British East India Company gained Indian territory (chapter 17), and relations between Gandhi and Ambedkar (chapter 21). Good-faith disagreement is part of scholarship, and I generally flag alternative viewpoints in the endnotes. In some cases, I found the current state of scholarship too paltry or conflicting to state a viewpoint responsibly and so remain agnostic, such as regarding the genesis of the Brahmi script (chapter 4) and the origins of tantra (chapter 8).

I embrace flexibility regarding dates in two distinct ways that is somewhat unusual for a historian but, in my view, ought to be more widely adopted in the field. One, I often consider texts in the centuries after their composition, to account for and center their reception. In contrast, many historians of ancient India consider texts tied to their composition date, estimated or actual. That approach may be useful for literary analysis, but I consider it best historical practice to look at major Indian texts, like the Bhagavadgita, through different moments of reception in ancient through modern times (e.g., chapters 5, 10, and 21). This means that I deliberately consider texts at multiple moments of impact that significantly postdate their composition dates. Two, some developments in South Asian history—including some that touched and changed many peoples' lives—are hard to date or occurred over expansive periods of time. Examples include the caste system, the rise of sectarian Hinduism, and the dispersion of Panchatantra tales. I cannot responsibly offer specific, narrow dates for these trends, and so I use broad time frames to capture these processes of change.

On the level of language, I often elect for more intelligible or common words and phrasings in this book, bucking trends among specialists. For example, I use the common "Islamic" eschewing "Islamicate" and speak of the "Indus Valley Civilization" and "Indus Civilization" interchangeably, even though some scholars are staunch advocates of only using the latter. I often explain specific choices in endnotes, and here I underscore more generally the importance of legibility and how specialist terminology can limit the reach of scholarship. That trade-off may be worthwhile in some contexts, but I found it an ill fit for an overview history book. I agree with religious studies scholar Jon Keune when he wrote: "Highly specialized technical language can function as guild-speak, policing the gates to the scholarly profession, even if unintentionally, so that only the properly acculturated and high-born may enter. I do not want to reinforce this."[19] I also caution that technical terms can only paper over, and cannot solve, our substantive and analytical problems. For example, the issue with writing about India's "Islamic dynasties," as some term them, is over-emphasizing religion, a proclivity that is often still present among those who use the protracted term "Islamicate." I encourage specialists to focus more on analysis, in my work and in others, and less on pedantic phrasing.

A subsidiary terminology issue is that I use a mix of emic (South Asian) and etic (non–South Asian and often anachronistic) terms. For emic terms, I draw from South Asian languages ranging from Sanskrit to Persian to Prakrits to Tamil, and these words are defined in the book's glossary. But ultimately, history is largely about analysis, and so there is nothing inherently detrimental about anachronism given the historian's goal to *interpret* the past.[20] In some cases, using modern terms enables us to succinctly name a phenomenon for investigation (e.g., Hinduism and caste, both English terms coined during European colonialism). Even the word "hindu" itself is not emic since it is a Perso-Arabic term that first appeared in India around the tenth century CE. No "Hindu" called themselves such until centuries later, and the appellation was not commonly used self-referentially until the nineteenth century.[21] Still, "Hindu" remains a useful catch-all category for followers of one of South Asia's major religious traditions. "Caste" has a more recent origin from Portuguese, although it describes an older social hierarchy (incidentally, the Portuguese helped coin and popularize other useful terms for South Asian phenomena, such as "monsoon").[22] I use terms like Hinduism and caste, anachronistically, to track changes in religious and social trends over centuries.

On the other hand, emic terms are not always useful. For instance, "aryan" is used in the earliest surviving Indian texts, the Vedas composed beginning ca. mid-second millennium BCE. But the term has gained a newer, menacing meaning owing to nineteenth and twentieth century racial theories and twentieth-century German history. Aware that many readers are likely knowledgeable about those events, I avoid "aryan" to prevent possible misunderstanding. In summary, rather than following strict rules on using emic versus etic terms, I chose language that best conveys meaning to contemporary readers regarding South Asian history.

Glossary

Adi Granth	Early version of the central Sikh holy book Guru Granth Sahib.
Adi-Hindu	Lit. "first Hindu," category used by early twentieth-century Dalit activists to forefront their indigeneity.
Adivasi	Lit. "first-dweller," indigenous or autochthonous peoples of South Asia, many in modern-day India are politically categorized as "Scheduled Tribes."
agamas	Hindu texts composed beginning in the late first millennium CE, often associated with Shaiva worship.
agni	Lit. "fire"; Hindu god, central to Vedic rituals.
ahimsa	Nonviolence, opposite of *himsa* (violence); set of political strategies associated with Mohandas Gandhi.
Ahmadiyya	Islamic messianic tradition founded in the late nineteenth century, frequently persecuted in modern times.
Ajivika	Religious group that emerged in the fifth century BCE alongside Jainism and Buddhism; they are extinct today.
Allah	God, most often in Islamic traditions.
amrit	Initiation ceremony that marks entry into the Sikh Khalsa.
Anglo-Indian	British person born or residing in India; people of mixed British and Indian descent (especially post-independence).
Apabhramsha	Lit. "degenerated," a Prakrit language.
apsara	Female celestial being.
ardhanarishvara	Half-male and half-female form of Shiva combined with Parvati.
artha	Power or wealth, among the three aims of Brahminical life in the mid-first millennium CE along with dharma and kama.

arya (aryan)	Lit. "noble" or "pure"; self-referential term used by Brahmin authors of the Vedas and later; a racialized category of upper-caste Hindus used in the late nineteenth century; in nineteenth- and twentieth-century European racial theories, a white non-Jewish person; used by some modern scholars for Indo-European speakers as a linguistically defined category.
Arya Samaj	Upper-caste Hindu reform movement founded in the Punjab in 1875.
aryavarta	Lit. "land of the pure," area where Brahmins live (geographically this expanded from the north Indian heartland in premodernity to all of India by colonial rule).
asceticism	Self-deprivation practices, associated with many South Asian religions.
ashrama	Life stage with four sequential stages articulated for a Brahmin male, paired with caste observances with phrase *varnashramadharma*.
ashvamedha	Horse sacrifice ritual, part of Vedic religious practice and later adopted as a mark of Indian kingship.
asura	Demon.
atman	Soul or self, discussed in the Upanishads.
avatar	Incarnation.
Avesta	Zoroastrian religious text whose language is closely related to Vedic Sanskrit.
Ayodhya	Town in northern India; believed by some Hindus to be the birthplace of Rama (an incarnation of the god Vishnu).
ayurveda	Pseudoscientific medical tradition that often cites Sanskrit texts.
Bangladesh Genocide	1971 genocide of Bengalis in East Pakistan.
bania	Caste of traders.
baptism	Religious immersion in water, arises in South Asia contexts as a Christian sacrament and as part of Sikh Khalsa rites.

bhadralok	Hindu urban elites in Bengal, often English-educated and employed by the British colonial state.
Bhagavadgita	Hindu religious work that features Krishna, part of the Mahabharata and often read separately, also known as Gita.
bhajan	Devotional song.
bhakta	Follower of bhakti.
bhakti	Tradition of religious devotion often considered part of Hinduism, characterized by writing in vernaculars and some broader participation from women and lower castes.
Bharata	Part of northern India (especially in early texts); the subcontinent.
bhikkhu	Buddhist monk.
bhikkhuni	Buddhist nun.
BJP	Bharatiya Janata Party, Hindu nationalist political party in India founded in 1980.
bodhisatta	"Bodhisattva" in Sanskrit; prior life of the Gautama Buddha; person who delays nirvana to assist others on the Buddhist path.
brahmacharin	Celibate student, one of four life stages (ashramas) prescribed for Brahmin men.
brahmadeya	Tax-free land gifted to Brahmins.
brahman	Ultimate reality discussed in the Upanishads, not to be confused with Brahmana (a group of Sanskrit texts) or Brahmins (the uppermost of the four varnas).
Brahmi	Early Indian script, popularized by the Mauryan Empire, ancestor of most known Indian scripts today.
Brahmin	First of four hierarchical social classes (*varna*), traditionally priests (sometimes spelled Brahman or Brahmana in English).
Brahminical	Related to Brahmins.
Brahmo Samaj	Hindu reform movement founded in Bengal in the 1820s.
British Raj	British colonial rule in India 1858–1947, directly ruled three-fifths of the Indian subcontinent and 80 percent of

	its population while ruling the remainder indirectly through the princely states.
buddha	Lit. "enlightened person"; a Buddhist who has achieved enlightenment; the Gautama Buddha.
caravanserai	Resting place for travelers.
caste	A discriminatory social hierarchy based on birth; in South Asia, caste includes the four-fold varna system and endogamous jatis.
Ceylon	Name for Sri Lanka during European colonialism until 1972.
chaitya	Buddhist hall or cave with a stupa.
Chamar	Dalit community, predominantly in northern India.
Chandala	Group outside of the four-fold varna system, stock character in premodern Sanskrit texts.
charkha	Spinning wheel on which one makes khadi, on Indian National Congress Flag 1921–1947 and replaced by Ashokan wheel on the Indian nation-state's flag.
colonialism	Exploitative political and commercial relationship in which the colony serves the metropole.
commonwealth	Voluntary association largely comprised of former British colonies.
communal	Pertaining to relations between religious communities, especially Hindus and Muslims in modern South Asia.
Company	British East India Company (also known as EIC, EEIC, and BEIC), operated in India ca. 1600–1858 with 1757–1858 constituting the first phrase of British colonialism in South Asia, at its height the Company ruled just over 60 percent of the subcontinent.
Congress	Indian National Congress, also known as INC, a political party formed in 1885, spearheaded the Indian independence movement.
coolie	Unskilled Indian worker, often used for indentured laborers.
Coromandel coast	Southeastern coast of the Indian subcontinent.

Dakhni	Indo-European vernacular of the early modern Deccan, inspired Rekhta.
Dalit	Lit. "downtrodden" or "crushed," those outside the four-fold varna system including Mahars and Chamars, preferred nomenclature for those formerly called "untouchable."
dargah	Shrine associated with a Sufi saint.
darshan	Lit. "seeing," mutual sight of devotee and god, most often in a Hindu temple.
dasa	Opposite of "arya" in the Vedas, autochthonous groups in northwestern India when Indo-European migrants arrived in the second millennium BCE.
devadasi	Courtesan dancers sometimes affiliated with temples, typically lower caste.
dhamma	Prakrit for Sanskrit "dharma"; Buddhist practices; recurrent subject in inscriptions by Mauryan emperor Ashoka.
dharma	Morality; Hindu concept of differential ethics by caste and life stage that became a major subject post-Vedas; genre of Brahminical legal literature; one of the three Brahminical goals of life in the mid-first millennium CE along with artha and kama.
dharmashala	Lit, "place of worship," used for premodern Hindu temples, Jain temples, Sikh gurdwaras, and mosques.
dharmashastra	Genre of ideal-based legal treatises, usually authored by Brahmin men.
dhoti	Loincloth.
Digambara	Lit. "sky-clad" referring to naked monks, one of two main branches of Jainism.
din	Religion (Persian term).
divan	Persian or Urdu poetry collection.
Diwali (Dipavali)	Festival of lights, celebrated by Hindus and Jains.
diwani	Revenue collection rights.

Dravidian	Language family, today centered in southern India; a person who speaks a Dravidian language.
dyarchy	Split government introduced by 1919 Government of India Act.
Emergency	A twenty-one-month stretch between 1975 and 1977 when Prime Minister Indira Gandhi suspended India's constitution.
Estado da India	Portuguese State of India centered in Goa.
Eurasian	Person of mixed European and South Asian descent.
fakir	Ascetic, can be Hindu or Muslim.
farman	Imperial order.
fatwa	Islamic religious judgment.
gadhegal	Ass-curse stone, found in central India in the second millennium CE.
Gaur	Bengal.
gaurakshas	Lit. "cow protection," set of movements founded by the Arya Samaj in the late nineteenth century that encouraged adherence to upper-caste norms and spread anti-Muslim sentiment.
Gautama Buddha	Historical founder of Buddhism, also known as Siddhartha, Shakyamuni, and Gotama; considered by some Hindus to be an incarnation of Vishnu.
Gentoo	Used by Europeans for Hindus in the eighteenth and nineteenth centuries, derived from *gentile*.
ghat	Stone steps leading into a holy river (often the Ganges).
Gita	Bhagavadgita, Hindu religious text featuring Krishna that is part of the Mahabharata and often read separately.
gopis	Cowherder women who are lovers of Krishna.
gotra	Patrilineal Brahmin lineages, generally exogamous.
Gurdwara	Sikh temple, earlier known as "dharmashala."
Gurmukhi	Script developed by early Sikh community and traditionally used for Sikh texts.

guru	Lit. "heavy"; a teacher; one of ten Sikh religious leaders; a Hindu religious leader with many followers in colonial and modern times.
Guru Granth Sahib	Central Sikh holy book.
Habshi	Ethiopian-origin person, many came to India as military slaves, synonym "Sidi."
hajj	Muslim pilgrimage to Mecca.
Harappan	Related to the Indus (Valley) Civilization which is sometimes called "Harappan Civilization" after its first major city uncovered in the nineteenth century.
harem	Female quarters of an elite household, common to both Muslim and Hindu rulers in premodern South Asia, synonym "zenana."
hartal	General strike, tactic used during the Indian independence movement.
haveli	Mansion.
Hijri	Islamic lunar calendar.
Hindavi	Synonyms "Hindi" and "Hindustani."
Hindi	Modern umbrella term used for a wide variety of vernacular dialects in the northern and central subcontinent (including Braj Bhasha, Avadhi, and Khari Boli), synonyms "Hindavi" and "Hindustani"; in modern times associated with the Devanagari script.
Hindu	Persian term; in premodernity denoted "Indian" in a geographic or cultural sense; in modern times a religious community; a racialized category for Hindu nationalists.
Hindu Mahasabha	Hindu nationalist political party founded in 1915.
Hindu nationalism	Far-right political ideology of Hindu supremacy first articulated in the late colonial period, synonym "Hindutva."
Hindu reformers	Hindu thinkers in the late eighteenth to early twentieth centuries who sought to alter aspects of Hindu traditions; they typically responded to a mix of European

	Christian missionary criticisms and changing social norms.
Hindustan	Northern India; the Indian subcontinent.
Hindustani	Common term for the language of Hindi / Urdu, especially in the nineteenth century.
Hindutva	Far-right political ideology of Hindu supremacy first articulated in the late colonial period, synonym "Hindu nationalism."
hookah	Waterpipe, used for tobacco in premodern India.
imambara	Structure used for Shia rituals, often associated with the Nawabs of Lucknow (1722–1856 CE).
India	Pre-1947 the Indian subcontinent (including what is now Pakistan, Bangladesh, and parts of Afghanistan); post-1947 the modern nation-state of India.
Indian National Army	Japanese-sponsored army comprised primarily of Indian-descent prisoners of war in World War II.
Indian Ocean	Oceanic area that connected long-distance traders in parts of the subcontinent, other parts of Asia, and Africa.
Indo-Aryan	Group of Indo-European languages that includes most north Indian languages, Sanskrit, and Prakrits; linguistically defined group who used Vedic Sanskrit.
Indo-European	Language family that encompasses most north Indian vernaculars, Sanskrit, and Prakrits.
inscription	Words etched onto stone.
Islamicate	Culturally Islamic but not specifically theological.
itihasa	Mythology or lore, genre of Sanskrit literature that includes the Mahabharata.
jati	Endogamous social group within the Indian caste system, theorized in Hindu religious texts beginning in the first millennium CE. Today there are thousands of jatis that are often regionally specific, also "jat."
jauhar	Early modern practice of self-immolation typically by the wives of a Rajput ruler.

jharokha	Balconied window, used by some Indian kings in a political appropriation of darshan.
jihad	Religious struggle, deployed metaphorically and literally at different points in South Asian history.
Jina	One of the twenty-four founders of Jainism of which the last (Mahavira) is historically verifiable, synonym "Tirthankara."
Kali Yuga	Final and worst of four eras in Hindu thought.
kama	Lit. "pleasure"; Hindu god; one of the three aims of Brahminical life in the mid-first millennium CE along with artha and dharma.
Kapalika	Ascetic tantra community.
karma	Lit. "action"; an idea shared by many South Asian religions but conceptualized differently in each one; ritual activity in the Vedas; results of all actions that guides one's status in rebirth in Upanishadic Hinduism and later; black sticky substance that adheres to one's soul in Jainism.
karuna	Tragedy, an aesthetic emotion in Sanskrit rasa theory.
Kashmir	Northwestern area of the subcontinent.
Kashmiri pandits	Brahmin community in or from Kashmir.
kavya	Sanskrit poetry and literary prose.
Kayasth	Caste of scribes.
khaddar	Khadi.
khadi	Homespun Indian cloth, associated with the Indian independence movement.
Khalsa	Community of Sikh warriors founded in 1699.
Kharoshthi	Oldest known Indian script, derived from Aramaic.
Khuda	God, Persian term.
khutba	Friday sermon typically given in a mosque; reading the khutba in a king's name was a sign of rulership in premodern India.

Krishna	Hindu god, incarnation of Vishnu.
Kshatriya	Second of four hierarchical social classes (*varna*), traditionally rulers and warriors.
Kubera	Hindu god of wealth, said to live on Mount Kailash in the Himalayas.
Kumbh Mela	Hindu religious festival held every twelve years at Allahabad, the largest religious gathering on earth.
lakh (lac)	100,000, used colloquially in Indian English similar to "million" in American English to denote a large sum.
langar	Communal eating, part of Sikh religious tradition.
lascar	Indian seaman on a British ship.
League	All-India Muslim League, a political party founded in 1906.
Line of Control	Border separating Azad Kashmir from India-occupied Kashmir, effectively the 1949 ceasefire line.
linga	Aniconic representation of Shiva, a rounded cylinder often paired with a yoni.
madrasa	School, usually in Islamic traditions.
Mahabharata	Epic myth centered around a Great War between the Kauravas and Pandavas, first written in Sanskrit about 2,000 years and retold in countless versions and languages.
maharaja	Lit. "great king."
Mahatma	Lit. "great-souled," appellation for Mohandas Gandhi (among others).
Mahavira	Twenty-fourth Jain ford-maker and historical founder of Jainism.
Mahayana	Branch of Buddhism.
Mahomedan	Older English term for "Muslim," considered inaccurate and offensive today.
Malabar coast	Southwest coast of India from the Arabian Sea to the Western Ghats.
mandir	Temple.

mansabdar	Ranked officer in Mughal imperial service.
mantra	Verse or formula used in ritual or meditation.
Maratha	A jati in central India; rulers of a state in eighteenth-century India.
Marathi	Indo-European vernacular spoken in central India.
masjid	Mosque.
masnavi	Book-length rhyming poem, usually in Persian or Urdu.
matha (math)	Monastery, often associated with Shaivas.
Middle Way	Buddhist path, characterized by moderation regarding asceticism.
mimamsa	school of Vedic interpretation and philosophy.
mleccha	Lit. "barbarian"; often "Muslim" in second-millennium CE Sanskrit sources.
mofussil	Countryside.
moksha	Liberation from the cycle of rebirth (samsara).
moor	Muslim, used by medieval and early modern Europeans.
Mughal	Indo-Muslim dynasty 1526–1858.
Muharram	Shia festival honoring Husayn's martyrdom at the 680 Battle of Karbala.
Munda	Group of Austroasiatic languages.
Musalman	Muslim, used in Hindi and Urdu.
nauras	"Nine aesthetic emotions" in Sanskrit and "newly arrived" in Persian, key concept at the court of Ibrahim Adil Shah II (d. 1627).
Navayana	Branch of Buddhism founded by Ambedkar (d. 1956).
nawab	Ruler, especially used for post-Mughal Indo-Muslim rulers.
nayaka	Lit. "hero"; Shudra royal lineages in southern India in the second millennium CE.
nirvana	Liberation from the cycle of rebirth (samsara), often associated with Buddhism.

nizam	Ruler, especially used for post-Mughal Muslim rulers.
OBC	Other Backward Class, a category used by India's Mandal Commission in 1980 to describe low-caste communities.
Occident	The West.
om	Sanskrit syllable, imbued with sacredness in much Hindu thought.
Operation Blue Star	Code name for a 1984 Indian government assault on Sikh separatists within Amritsar's Golden Temple.
Orient	The East.
Orientalism	Stereotypical and dismissive attitudes to understanding the East.
Orientalist	Eighteenth- or nineteenth-century Western scholar who studied India.
paan	Indian treat of areca nuts, lime water, and betel leaves that one chews.
Pahlavi	Language spoken in the first millennium CE in Persia, also called "Middle Persian."
Paishachi	Allegedly lost Prakrit language, said to be the language of the *Brihatkatha*.
Pakistan	Nation-state founded in 1947 with two non-contiguous portions, of which East Pakistan broke off to become Bangladesh in 1971.
Pali canon	Three-part collection of Buddhist teachings, synonym "Tipitaka."
Panchatantra	Famous collection of Indian animal fables.
pandit	Lit. "learned," female version "pandita."
Parashurama	Lit. "Rama with an axe," incarnation of Vishnu known for having slaughtered several generations of Kshatriyas.
pariah	Low-caste jati; general slur for outcastes.
parinibbana	Final enlightenment of the Gautama Buddha, "parinirvana" in Sanskrit.
Parsi	Follower of Zoroastrianism, commonly used in India.

partition	Split of British India into two dominions in 1947 that became the nation-states of India and Pakistan.
Persian	An Indo-European language and the language of most Indo-Muslim dynasties; cultural descriptor; the people of Iran.
Persianate	Culturally Persian.
peshwa	Royal advisor, title used by multiple early modern central Indian states including the Marathas.
plebiscite	Referendum, usually referring to the promised political referendum in Kashmir that has yet to occur.
Prakrit	Set of Indo-European languages related to Sanskrit, used by early Buddhist and Jain communities to avoid Brahminical Sanskrit.
prasad	Offering to a god, usually in Hinduism.
prashasti	Sanskrit praise poem to gods or kings.
premakhyan	Genre of Hindi Sufi romance stories.
presidency	Area of land under the control of the British East India Company, there were three presidencies centered respectively in Bombay, Calcutta, and Madras.
princely states	Semi-autonomous areas of British India that were ruled by discrete princes (and, occasionally, princesses) under the auspices of the British Raj.
puja	Hindu worship.
purana	Lit. "old"; a genre of Hindu religious texts dating from the first millennium CE through modern times, often associated with gods popular in later versions of Hinduism such as Vishnu and Shiva.
purdah	Female seclusion, practiced by royal and elite women in India from diverse religious backgrounds in the second millennium CE.
qasida	Persian or Arabic praise poem.
qawwali	Genre of popular Sufi devotional music, its origins are often associated with Amir Khusraw (d. 1325).
qazi	Judge in Islamic traditions.

raja (raj)	King.
Rajput	Kshatriya rulers in and around Rajasthan, crystallized into a caste group in the second millennium CE.
rakshasa	Demon.
Rama (Ram)	Kshatriya hero of the Ramayana, incarnation of Vishnu.
Ramayana	Epic myth of the warrior king Rama (Ram), first written in Sanskrit about 2,000 years and retold in countless versions and languages.
Ram Lila	Performance of Tulsidas's Hindi Ramayana, invented in Benares in the seventeenth century and now popular across northern India.
rasa	Aesthetic emotion in Sanskrit literary theory; invoked in "nauras" concept of Bijapur's Adil Shahi dynasty.
Rekhta	Lit. "mixed," early name for Urdu.
resident	British man stationed at the court of an Indian ruler during British colonialism.
RSS	Rashtriya Swayamsevak Sangh, a paramilitary group that advocates Hindutva (Hindu nationalist ideology).
sabha	Assembly.
samadhi	Meditation practice aimed at union with a higher being.
samsara	Cycle of rebirth, assumed to be part of reality in Hinduism, Buddhism, Jainism, and Sikhism.
Sangam	Collection of old Tamil literature.
sangat	Sikh community gathering.
sangha	Community of Buddhist ascetics.
Sangh Parivar	Lit. "RSS's family," the loose coalition of Hindu nationalist groups in India and abroad.
Sanskrit	Indo-European language that exists in two major sequential registers: Vedic Sanskrit and classical Sanskrit; in BCE times, Sanskrit was often associated with Brahminical practices alone; in the early centuries CE, Sanskrit went viral and became a widespread (if elite)

	literary and political language; today, Sanskrit is largely limited to scholars and Hindu religious contexts.
sanyasi	Mendicant; the final of four life stages (ashramas) prescribed for Brahmin men.
sati	The Hindu practice of widow burning.
satyagraha	Lit. "grasping truth," Mohandas Gandhi's philosophy of nonviolent resistance.
Scheduled Castes	Dalit communities, a legal category in modern India.
sepoy	Indian soldier who fought for the British, cavalry men are also sometimes included in this category (technically, they were called *sowars*).
seva	Lit. "service"; value articulated in the Sikh tradition.
shahada	Muslim statement of faith.
Shahnama	"Book of kings," Persian-language epic written around 1000 CE.
Shaiva	Related to or worshipper of Shiva.
Shakta	Related to or worshipper of the Goddess.
sharia	Islamic law, which is neither singular nor stable.
shastra	Sanskrit genre of specialized knowledge and technical treatises.
shaykh	Sufi teacher.
Shia	One of the two main branches of Islam.
shishta	Sanskrit-speaking educated Brahmin men.
Shiva	Hindu god post-Vedas.
shloka	Sanskrit verse.
shraddha	Ancestral rite.
shramana	Renunciant.
shringara	Erotic love, an aesthetic emotion in Sanskrit rasa theory.
shuddhi	Lit. "purification"; Hindu conversion ritual popularized by the Arya Samaj.

Shudra	Fourth of four hierarchical social classes (*varna*), traditionally servants and laborers.
Shvetambara	Lit. "white-clad" referring to the simple white clothing of monks, one of two main branches of Jainism.
Sidi	Ethiopian-origin person, many came to India as military slaves, synonym "Habshi."
Sikh	Follower of Sikhism.
Sinhala	An Indo-European language spoke in Sri Lanka; person from a Sinhala-speaking region.
soma	Edible plant with mind-altering qualities, important within Vedic practices.
South Asia	Indian subcontinent and some adjacent regions; in modern terms "South Asia" encompasses eight nations: Afghanistan, Bangladesh, Bhutan, India, Maldives, Nepal, Pakistan, and Sri Lanka.
sowar	Cavalry man who fought for the British.
stupa	Rounded mound that houses relics of the Gautama Buddha.
Sufi	Follower of the mystical branch of Islam, generally combined with other Islamic identities such as being a jurist, ulama, Shia, or Sunni.
sulh-i kull	Universal civility as articulated under the Mughal king Akbar (r. 1556–1605).
Sunni	One of the two main branches of Islam.
svadharma	Lit. "one own dharma," Hindu idea of ethical behavior that differs by caste and gender (and, sometimes, life stage).
swadeshi	Lit. "made in one's own place," part of the Indian independence movement.
swaraj	Lit. "self-rule," independence.
Tamil	Dravidian language spoken in southern India, among the oldest written languages in South Asia (along with Sanskrit and Prakrits); person from a Tamil-speaking region.

tantra	Lit. "system"; a wide-ranging set of ritual practices including antinomian and anti-caste activities, often associated with worshippers of Shiva; texts of the tantra religious movement.
tarikh	Historical work, usually in Persian.
tawaif	Female dancer and singer, usually Muslim.
Telugu	Dravidian language spoken in parts of southern India; person from a Telugu-speaking region.
Theravada	Branch of Buddhism, sometimes referred to by the diminutive term "Hinayana."
theris	Buddhist nuns who authored the *Therigatha*.
Thomas Christians	South Indian Christians who (apocryphally) trace their origins to the Apostle Thomas.
thuggee	Institutionalized banditry, from which the English word "thug" is derived.
tika	Red mark on the forehead used in Indian religious, cultural, and political contexts.
Tipitaka	Tripartite collection of Buddhist Pali texts, "tripitaka" in Sanskrit, synonym "Pali canon."
Tirthankara	Lit. "ford-maker," one of the twenty-four founders of Jainism of which the last (Mahavira) is historically verifiable, synonym "Jina."
Treta Yuga	Second of four worsening ages in Hindu thought, mythical time period for the Ramayana.
tricolour	Flag of Congress or independent India with bands of orange, white, and green.
turk	Muslim or a pseudo-ethnic category in premodern Sanskrit texts.
ulama	Traditionally learned men of Islam.
untouchable	Those outside the four-fold varna system, the preferred modern nomenclature is "Dalit."
upanayana	Ceremony of adopting the sacred thread worn by caste-observant Brahmin men.

Upanishads	Sanskrit texts, earliest of which were composed in the sixth century BCE.
Urdu	Persianized register of Hindi, also called Rekhta; in modern times, associated with the Perso-Arabic script.
urs	Death anniversary of a Sufi saint.
uttarapaksha	Argument in Sanskrit philosophy that is advanced as an answer ("uttara") to an imagined objector.
vairagya	Grief and detachment in Sanskrit aesthetic theory, proposed by ninth-century thinker Anandavardhana as the emotion produced by reading the Mahabharata.
Vaishnava	Related to or worshipper of Vishnu.
Vaishya	Third of four hierarchical social classes (*varna*), traditionally farmers and traders.
varna	Lit. "color"; social class of which there are conventionally four in a ranked hierarchical order: Brahmin, Kshatriya, Vaishya, and Shudra.
varnadharma	Hindu ethics divided by caste and class (varna).
varnashramadharma	Lit. "ethics according to class and life stage," a Brahminical ideal.
Vedas	Oldest Brahminical religious texts, four in total, traditionally transmitted orally.
vihara	Buddhist monastery.
vira	Heroism, an aesthetic emotion in Sanskrit rasa theory.
Vishnu	Hindu god who gained popularity post-Vedas, has multiple incarnations.
vizier	Royal advisor.
yajna	Sacrifice (including of animals), central to Vedic religious traditions.
yaksha	Male tree spirit, some are said to serve Kubera.
yakshi	Female tree spirit, seen on Hindu temple architecture.
yati	Temple-dwelling Shvetambara Jain monk.
yavana	Greek, foreigner, or Muslim in Sanskrit.

yoga	Lit. "union"; multiform and multisource ascetic and meditative practice; in modern times, a series of physical movements.
yogi	Practitioner of yoga.
yoni	Lit. "vagina" or "vagina and womb," often the base for a Shiva linga.
zenana	Female quarters, synonym "harem."
zindabad	"Long live," often used with a country name in modern political chants.
Zoroastrianism	Religion in ancient Persia, cognate with Vedic traditions, followers are called Zoroastrians or Parsis.

Illustrations and Sources

Figure 10.2. Shvetambara Jain monk instructing a king, ca. 1300 CE, Gujarat, India, opaque watercolor on palm leaf. The San Diego Museum of Art, public domain.

Figure 11.1. Horseman presenting as a Hindu on one side and a Muslim on the other at the Varadharaja Perumal Temple in Kanchipuram, ca. sixteenth century CE, Tamil Nadu, India. Photograph by Audrey Truschke, 2019.

Figure 11.2. Large gateway of the Virupaksha Temple complex at Hampi built by Vijayanagara king Krishnadevaraya (r. 1509–1529), ca. early sixteenth century CE, Karnataka, India. Photograph by Alexander John Greenlaw, 1856.

Figure 11.3. Ghiyasuddin Shah (ruler of Mandu 1469–1501) accepts a betel chew offered by an Ethiopian woman in the *Nimatnama* (Book of delicacies), ca. 1500 CE. London: British Library, public domain.

Figure 13.1. Mughal Emperor Jahangir (r. 1605–1627) at the jharokha window in the Agra Fort, ca. early seventeenth century CE. Toronto: Aga Khan Museum, public domain.

Figure 13.2. Brahmin pandits and Mughal officials collaborating on translating the Sanskrit Mahabharata into Persian at Akbar's court, 1598–1599 CE, ascribed to Dhanu, northern India. Philadelphia: Free Library, public domain.

Figure 13.3. Kusha and Lava recite the Ramayana to King Rama at his court in Ayodhya from an Akbari Persian Ramayana, ca. 1590s CE, northern India. Doha: Museum of Islamic Art, public domain.

Figure 13.4. Saraswati enthroned, from a *Kitab-i Nauras*, 1604 CE, Farrukh Beg, Bijapur, India. Jaipur: City Palace, public domain.

Figure 14.1. Mughal Emperor Jahangir (r. 1605–1627) embracing the Safavid King Shah Abbas (r. 1588–1629), ca. 1618 CE, Abul Hasan. Washington, DC: Smithsonian Institution, public domain.

Figure 14.2. Mughal Emperor Jahangir (r. 1605–1627) visiting with the Hindu ascetic Jadrup, ca. 1617–1620 CE, Govardhan. Paris: The Louvre, public domain.

Figure 14.3. Wazir Khan Mosque, 1630s CE, Lahore, Pakistan. Photograph by Audrey Truschke, 2007.

Figure 14.4. Taj Mahal mausoleum, mosque and mirror mosque, and grounds built for Mumtaz Mahal (d. 1631) by Mughal Emperor Shah Jahan (d. 1666), 1631–1648 CE, Agra, India. Photograph by John Edward Sache, 1865–1875.

Figure 15.1. Mughal Emperor Aurangzeb (r. 1658–1707) visiting Muinuddin Chishti's shrine in Ajmer around 1680 CE, ca. early eighteenth century. Amherst: Mead Art Museum, public domain.

Figure 15.2. Mughal Emperor Aurangzeb (r. 1658–1707) at the siege of Golconda in 1687 CE, ca. 1750. Providence: Brown University Library, public domain.

Figure 16.1. Holi celebration at the court of Mughal Emperor Muhammad Shah Rangila (r. 1719–1748), ca. 1720–1750 CE. Los Angeles County Museum of Art, public domain.

Figure 16.2. Palace of the maharaja of Indore along Benares's ghats, Varanasi, India, photograph ca. 1890s CE.

Figure 17.1. Tippoo's Tiger, semi-automaton and organ built into an almost life-sized image of a tiger mauling a British soldier, ca. 1790 CE, Mysore court of Tipu Sultan (r. 1782–1799), wood. London: Victoria and Albert Museum, reproduced under CC BY-SA 3.0.

Figure 18.1. Mughal Emperor Bahadur Shah Zafar II (d. 1862) awaiting British deportation in Delhi, May 1858 CE. London: British Library, public domain.

Figure 19.1. Kashmiri women under the watchful eye of an overseer, 1895 CE. Photographer unknown. London: British Library, public domain.

Figure 19.2. Three Brahmins writing out manuscripts in Kashmir, 1895 CE. Photographer unknown.

Figure 19.3. Begum of Bhopal during the 1911 CE British royal tour of India, printed in 1914. Sourced from K. K. Venugopal's *The Historical Record of the Imperial Visit to India, 1911* (1914). Public domain.

Figure 19.4. Nizam of Hyderabad bowing to King George V and Queen Mary at the Delhi Durbar, 1911 CE, Delhi, India. Sourced from F.G.H. Salusbury's *King Emperor's Jubilee, 1910–1935* (1935), public domain.

Figure 19.5. Great stupa and eastern gate at Sanchi constructed ca. third century BCE–first century CE, photograph by James Waterhouse, 1861–1862. London: Victoria and Albert Museum, public domain.

Figure 20.1. Indentured men and crew on the deck of a vessel recently arrived in Georgetown, British Guiana (Guyana), ca. 1890 CE. Houghton Library, Harvard University, public domain.

Figure 20.2. Sikh sepoy soldiers marching with the Guru Granth Sahib, Mesopotamia (modern-day Iran), 1918. London: Imperial War Museum.

Figure 20.3. Goddess Kali with a necklace of severed human heads and limbs striding atop Shiva's corpse, ca. 1879 CE, West Bengal, India, lithograph. New York: Metropolitan Museum of Art, public domain.

Figure 20.4. Inoculation against the plague, Bombay, 1896–97 CE. Photograph attributed to Clifton & Co. London: Wellcome Collection, public domain.

Figure 21.1. Mohandas Gandhi and Sarojini Naidu during the salt satyagraha, 1930 CE, Gujarat. Photograph attributed to Agence de presse, public domain.

Figure 21.2. Mother India from the title page of Kusuma Dharmanna's *Nallado-ratanamu*, published in 1923 CE (Telugu writing reads: Equality is Independence). Public domain.

Figure 22.1. Refugees crowding on a train during the partition of British India, 1947 CE, Punjab. Photographer unknown, public domain.

Figures 23.1 and 23.2. Indian villagers voting in the 1952 general election. Photographs attributed to Ministry of Information & Broadcasting, Government of India, public domain.

Postscript and Acknowledgments

A scholar seeking knowledge stoops and is lofty.
  The ignorant never stoop and are low.

—Tamil *Kural*, ca. fifth century CE[1]

My investment in South Asian history has defined my professional life. It began when, as an eighteen-year-old undergraduate at the University of Chicago, I fell head over heels in love with Sanskrit literature. That love grew—as true love tends to do—and eventually encompassed significant swathes of the premodern South Asian past. My love was always intellectual and embraced, rather than prohibited, critical thought. When I found dark corners and skeletons in the closet (history is full of such things), I was further driven to understand and unpack the complexities of Indian cultures, traditions, religions, and social processes. I soon realized, however, that the India that endlessly fascinates and excites my mind—premodern India—is long gone. I do not mourn the loss of premodernity, but I confess to being upset that so few modern people seem to know much about South Asian pasts. And I am aggrieved by those who feel shame about Indian history and so seek to supplant it with their preferred modern mythology. This book grew out of my intellectual appreciation and curiosity regarding Indian history, coupled with a staunch commitment to accuracy about that past.

Some may read these lines, note my name, and object: Why you? After all, I am a *vaideshika*, a *firangi*, a foreigner, a non-Indian, a non–South Asian, who writes about Indian and South Asian histories. One response is to point out, gently, that we are all outsiders to history. As the Kerala-origin poet Meena Alexander put it, "History is maquillage. No homeland here."[2] That said, some of us feel more comfortable than others in the past, or at least long for inclusion across the gulf of time. Like so many historians, I inhabit a disjointed, multitemporal reality where the past—specifically, for me, South Asian history—is sometimes more alive than the present. Its accurate recovery is viscerally important to me and serves as a source of ongoing motivation as well as a reward in itself. But, as Sanskrit dramatists say: *alam ativistarena*, Stop prattling on! Affective feelings, no matter how genuine, do not qualify me or anyone else to write about South Asian history. For that, I turn to my academic credentials.

I have the training needed to write a sweeping history of India that cuts across several millennia. I am an early modernist, who was trained as a Sanskritist (Sanskrit is a premier language of ancient India) and has been dragged into ferocious debates about modern Indian politics. I read, to varying degrees, Sanskrit, Persian, Hindi, Urdu, Braj Bhasha, and English, all of which are important languages at specific points in South Asia history. In short, in my own training and research, I cut across ancient, early modern, and contemporary South Asia, and I have access to a robust amount of primary source material in its original languages.

I teach the entire history of South Asia, from ca. 2600 BCE until the current year, over two semesters annually at Rutgers University in Newark, New Jersey. And so, I have worked out with hundreds of students how to narrate the messy story—really stories, plural—of Indian history in a semi-coherent manner. One thing I have learned is that there are lots of ways to approach the past that each appeal to a different palate. I try to give a taste of many discrete historiographical methods in these pages as I incorporate social, micro, transregional, religious, political, and literary histories.

Still, writing such a sweeping, variegated book was challenging, to put it mildly. Any missteps are my own. But to the extent that I progressed toward my goal—to accurately recover and narrate the history of the Indian subcontinent with some attention to surrounding regions of South Asia—I owe many thanks to those who, like me, are scholars seeking knowledge and lent a helping hand.

I warmly thank my generous colleagues who contributed to this book project. Many read draft chapters, batted around ideas, or otherwise shaped this work, including Blain Auer, Gaiutra Bahadur, Stephen

Berkwitz, Debjani Bhattacharyya, Johannes Bronkhorst, Benjamin Brose, Sheetal Chhabria, Matthew Adam Cobb, John E. Cort, Vidya Dehejia, Purnima Dhavan, Wendy Doniger, Richard Eaton, Roy Fischel, Ilyse R. Morgenstein Fuerst, Rajmohan Gandhi, Laurence Gautier, Finnian M. M. Gerety, Kashi Gomez, Peter Gottschalk, Linda Hess, Christophe Jaffrelot, Ayesha Jalal, Sonam Kachru, Gwendolyn Kelly, Jonathan Mark Kenoyer, Nayanjot Lahiri, James Laine, Anubhuti Maurya, James McHugh, Andrew Ollett, Sohini Sarah Pillai, Sheldon Pollock, Ramnarayan Rawat, Yael Rice, Tamara Sears, McComas Taylor, Chinmay Tumbe, Steven Vose, Phillip B. Wagoner, Nira Wickramasinghe, and Taymiya Zaman.

Many additional colleagues answered points of inquiry from me, recommended readings, provided permission to reproduce images or translations, or otherwise contributed to this intellectual project. For this, I thank Michael Allen, Leyla Amzi-Erdogdular, Daniel Asen, Manan Ahmed Asif, Yaqoob Khan Bangash, Ananya Chakravarti, Sally J. Sutherland Goldman, Chinnaiah Jangam, Prashant Keshavmurthy, Pasha M. Khan, Jagjeet Lally, Julie Lockwood, Shabana Mir, Sangay Mishra, Sara Mondini, Christian Novetzke, Luther Obrock, Kristian Petersen, Daniel Ramirez, Ayesha Ray, Sugata Ray, David Reich, Jason Schwartz, Hamsa Stainton, and Dheepa Sundaram.

In these acknowledgment lists are old friends and advisors who have seen me through multiple phases of my scholarly career. There are also some scholars whom I have never met. I appreciate all those generous enough to respond to my inquiries, even when it was our first acquaintance. Additionally, I thank the anonymous reviewers of the book whose serious engagement sharpened my ideas and writing.

Special thanks are due to the team at Princeton University Press, beginning with my fabulous editor Priya Nelson. I owe much to Priya, including formulating the idea for this book in the first place and convincing me to write it (especially after, the first time she asked, I said no). Emma Wagh, Dimitri Karetnikov, and others have worked hard on polishing and editing, and this book would be in much poorer shape without them. I thank Ron Draddy for transforming my chaotic notes into beautiful maps that complement and extend the arguments I make in these pages.

My students at Rutgers University-Newark have been formational to this book in several ways. They inspired me to confront sexism and casteism, which are entrenched in the discipline of South Asian history and which I strive to minimize here. Every time I taught underheard voices from the Indian past, my students' eyes lit up. Many Rutgers-Newark students further encouraged me in this direction by posing astute questions about women, lower castes, and other historically marginalized groups in South Asian history. At times, I could not answer my students' questions, but I later dug up information and wove those marginalized voices into this book's narrative of the past. I am grateful for the students who pushed (and continue to push) me to be a better professor and scholar. Additionally, some individual students offered feedback on drafts of specific chapters, and for this I thank Darsh Patel and Megan Tomaselli.

I wrote a large portion of this book with the support of a Public Scholars Fellowship from the National Endowment for the Humanities. I also benefited from a Global Equity Grant from Princeton University Press. I am grateful for the support provided by both grants that enabled me to produce this work.

The bulk of this book is based on secondary sources and published primary sources, as is appropriate for an overview work. Still, I dipped my toe into archival materials from time to time. I thank the archives, libraries, and museums whose collections I drew upon for this aspect of my research. These include the Aga Khan Museum in Toronto, British Library in London, British Museum in London, Brown University Library in Providence, Free Library in Philadelphia, Houghton Library in Cambridge, Institute for the Study of Ancient Cultures in Chicago, Lahore Museum, Los Angeles County Museum of Art, Louvre in Paris, Mead Art Museum in Amherst, Metropolitan Museum of Art in New York, Museum of Islamic Art in Doha, San Diego Museum of Art, Smithsonian Institution in Washington, DC, and the South Asian American Digital Archive. Thanks to Veerta Ali Ujan for permission to reproduce a poem by her late mother, Fahmida Riaz.

A special word of appreciation goes to the Rutgers University Library staff. They tracked down many books and articles and offered superb support throughout the years of researching this book. I also thank Rutgers University more broadly, especially those who have contributed to fostering a diverse, multicultural, intellectual environment on campus that has proven a wonderful habitat for me as a scholar.

I saved the best for last: my family. My mom has been a rock of support, always. My three children partially grew up while I was writing this book, and they are my pride and joy. My husband, Thane, is my beating heart. Asking him to marry me, two decades ago, was the best decision of my life. It is to Thane that I dedicate this book.

My narration of South Asian history, no doubt, falls short at times. To quote a bit of Indo-Persian poetry from the sixteenth century, "Alas, I am no seller of words to expect approval from people."[3] All shortcomings are my own, and, on this score, I look forward to the thoughtful criticisms of my colleagues and other readers. I also have a challenge for each group. For historians of South Asia who find things wanting in these pages, I propose to you: Do it better. We need more books that render South Asian history accessible to broader audiences. I salute my predecessors and allies in this endeavor, and I invite the rest of you, my esteemed colleagues, to enter the collective project of producing public-facing, accessible scholarship. For everybody else, your challenge is this: Whether this is the first book you've ever read on South Asian history or the one-thousandth book, don't let it be the last.

Notes

STARTING POINTS

1. Quoted in Kanaganayakam, *Lutesong and Lament*, 47 (Kanaganayakam's translation).

2. Murphy, "Utility of 'South Asia.'"

3. Asif, *Loss of Hindustan*, 32 (on the internal illegibility of "South Asia"); Nandy, "Idea of South Asia" (on the circumscribed history of "South Asia" and the problems with the term). Other terms, such as Bharata (or Bharat), Bharatavarsha, Jambudvipa (or Jambudvip), and Hindustan are more localized in South Asian history, and so I do not consider them here.

4. Ramanujan, "Is There an Indian Way of Thinking?," in his *Collected Essays*.

5. Reich, *Who We Are*, 146.

6. Abu-Lughod, *Before European Hegemony*, 261.

7. I borrow "provincializing" from Chakrabarty, *Provincializing Europe*.

8. Farge, *Allure of the Archives*, 97.

9. Klein, "Looking for Slavery in Colonial Archives," 114.

10. Wujastyk, "Indian Manuscripts," 161 (on manuscript preservation).

11. Noboru Karashima quoted in Ali, "Death of a Friend," 36.

12. Yaa Gyasi, *Transcendent Kingdom: A Novel* (New York: Knopf, 2020), 253.

13. Amanda Gorman, *Call Us What We Carry: Poems* (New York: Penguin, 2021), 2.

14. Merutunga, *Prabandhachintamani*, v. 6 (the text is dated 1305).

15. Anuk Arudpragasam, *A Passage North: A Novel* (New York: Random House, 2021), 5.

1. INDUS VALLEY CIVILIZATION, 2600–1900 BCE

1. Sumerian myth of "Enki and Ninhursaga," adapted from *Electronic Text Corpus of Sumerian Literature*.

2. Ray, *Archaeology of Seafaring*, 87.

3. We do not know what the Indus Civilization peoples called themselves or even what languages they spoke. As a result, all names for the Indus Valley Civilization ("Meluhha" aside) are anachronistic and date at the earliest to the rediscovery of this ancient culture in the 1920s. Still, there are conflicting opinions regarding which modern nomenclature is best. The two oldest (still quite modern) names were coined by Europeans in the early twentieth century: (1) Harappan Civilization, after the first city discovered by modern archaeologists and (2) Indus Valley Civilization (along with its acronym, IVC), after the valley where its largest cities are located. Some scholars still use "Harappan Civilization" in a nod to modern archaeological tradition, but "Indus Valley Civilization" is by far more common, especially outside of India. In recent decades, some scholars have preferred "Indus Civilization," arguing that this phrase includes the many Indus Civilization cities not in the Indus Valley (Chakrabarti, introduction to *Indus Civilization Sites*, 7). I find this argument flawed given that "Indus" still refers to the valley, river, or basin. That said, I appreciate the attempt at a more geographically accurate title for this civilization (even as I think it falls short), and "Indus Civilization" has the virtue of relative brevity. Here, I use both the more common "Indus Valley Civilization" and the more succinct "Indus Civilization" interchangeably. I reject the inappropriate Hindu nationalist appendage of Saraswati (a mythical river and Hindu goddess) to any variation of the Indus Civilization's name.

4. I follow here the dominant model of human origins, backed by robust archaeological and genetic evidence. There is limited evidence of rock flakes and tools indicating that hominins (although not necessarily *Homo sapiens*) may have traveled to South Asia far earlier (Fisher, *Environmental History*, 22).

5. Joseph, *Early Indians*, 17.

6. Joseph, *Early Indians*, chap. 1. Most South Asians today owe part of their genetic ancestry to these "first Indians," with ancestral south Indians overall having stronger genetic links than ancestral north Indians (many Indians also have genetic links to other populations; Reich, *Who We Are*, chap. 6). Genetic analysis over the last few decades has been helpful for clarifying basic migration patterns of prerecorded human history. Although it is perhaps better known in the public sphere for giving rise to political controversies (on how geneticists negotiate this, e.g., see Reich, *Who We Are*, 134–135).

7. Barley (from southwest Asia) and wheat (from the near east) are both found in Baluchistan during the Neolithic period (i.e., roughly after 7,000 BCE) and further east and south later (Boivin, "Proto-Globalisation and Biotic Exchange," table 14.1). Sugarcane, from Papua New Guinea, was grown in India by the late first millennium BCE (Boivin, "Proto-Globalisation and Biotic Exchange," table 14.5). On new world crops, see chapter 13. Sandalwood is widely assumed to be native to southern India, but archaeobotanical evidence suggests a second-millennium BCE introduction from Southeast Asia (Asouti and Fuller, *Trees and Woodlands of South India*, 116–117).

8. For an argument on the benefits of hunter-gatherer lifestyles as compared to sedentary agriculture, see Scott, *Against the Grain*.

9. Fisher, *Environmental History*, 20–21 (with considerably more detail than my admittedly brief description here).

10. Joseph, *Early Indians*, 13–16.

11. Mathpal, *Prehistoric Rock Paintings of Bhimbetka*.

12. Chakrabarti, *Oxford Companion to Indian Archaeology*, 15 (skeletal evidence); Ray, "Axial Age," 307 (beads).

13. Coningham and Young, *Archaeology of South Asia*, 46–53. On plant and animal domestication going together, see Zeder, "Origins of Agriculture."

14. Singh, "Environmental Changes in Southern Asia," 286–288.

15. Bellwood, *First Farmers*, 94–97; Fuller, "Agricultural Origins," 22.

16. Fuller, "Agricultural Origins," 37–46, 48–55. It is not surprising that farming has multiple points of origin in South Asia; indeed, it likely has multiple points of origin in the fertile crescent as well (Bellwood, *First Farmers*, 53–56).

17. Jarrige et al., *Mehrgarh*, 120 (p. 151 on dates).

18. Jarrige et al., *Mehrgarh*, 135 (molar crowns).

19. Francis, *Asia's Maritime Bead Trade*, 7.

20. Durrani, Ali, and Erdosy, "Introduction," 1–6; Durrani, Ali, and Erdosy, "New Perspectives," 86–87; Durrani, Ali, and Erdosy, "Further Excavations at Rehman Dheri," 66 (population estimate).

21. At times, the dates for "early Harappan" have become expansive, stretching back as far as 5500 BCE (e.g., Kenoyer and Meadow, "Excavations at Harappa," table 10.1).

22. Mughal, "Early Harappan Period."

23. Possehl, *Indus Civilization*, 6 (size).

24. Some call the Ghaggar-Hakra the "Saraswati River"; I decline to follow suit since this anachronistically and confusingly projects Brahminical ideas onto the Indus Civilization.

25. Scholars vary considerably in their population estimates for Mohenjo Daro, with some going as high as 80,000 (Kenoyer and Meadow, "Excavations at Harappa," 156). Lakhanjo Daro is comparatively less well known and was only discovered in the 1980s (Kenoyer, "Archaeology of Indus Urbanism").

26. For an overview of key sites, see Kenoyer, *Ancient Cities*; on sites in modern-day India specifically, see Chakrabarti, *Indus Civilization Sites*.

27. Possehl, *Indus Civilization*, 79–82.

28. E.g., the Harappan "granary," misnamed based on superficial similarity to Roman granaries (https://www.harappa.com/slide/granary-harappa).

29. Kenoyer, "Integration and Diversity," 17.
30. Wright, *Ancient Indus*, 240.
31. Kenoyer, "Households and Neighborhoods," 400.
32. Kenoyer, *Ancient Cities*, 52–56.
33. Kenoyer, "Integration and Diversity," 8.
34. Chase, "Meat Provisioning," 247–249.
35. I speak here of popular misunderstandings. For a provocative academic argument on Indus Civilization egalitarianism that centers around the question of a ruling class, see Green, "Killing the Priest-King."
36. Kenoyer, "Integration and Diversity," 14 (bronze saw).
37. Most commonly called "Priest King," this statue is held by Karachi's National Museum. I decline to use its conventional title since it projects much onto the statue, sans evidence.
38. Most commonly called "Dancing Girl," this statue is held by Delhi's National Museum.
39. E.g., the toy cart of Nausharo, Baluchistan (https://www.harappa.com/slide/toy-carts-nausharo).
40. In this paragraph and the next, I draw on Kenoyer, *Ancient Cities*, chap. 4. For an exhaustive look at the seals, see the five volumes of *Corpus of Indus Seals and Inscriptions*, edited by Asko Parpola and others (Helsinki: Suomalainen Tiedeakatemia 1987–2022).
41. Kenoyer, *Ancient Cities*, 87.
42. Kenoyer, "Iconography of the Indus Unicorn."
43. Kenoyer, "Integration and Diversity," 11–12.
44. Wright, *Ancient Indus*, 163.
45. Kenoyer, "Integration and Diversity," 15.
46. E.g., consider the fanciful idea of the early to mid-twentieth century that the Indus Civilization people knew no state violence or warfare. This has been largely abandoned, especially since finding defensive walls (e.g., see D. H. Gordon's 1946 letter to Mortimer Wheeler about the impossibility of the Indus peoples being "flabby pacifists," quoted in Ray, *Colonial Archaeology*, 148–150).
47. Farmer, "Claims Concerning the Longest Indus 'Inscription.'"
48. Witzel and Farmer, "Horseplay in Harappa."
49. This idea that the Indus Civilization people spoke a Dravidian language(s) has political implications for some today (Ramaswamy, "Remains of the Race"). This being a modern and not a historical issue, I do not delve into it further here. Those interested should note the (admittedly, thin) theories that Dravidian speakers, too, may have migrated to South Asia (Krishnamurti, *Dravidian Languages*, 3–5).
50. Kenoyer, *Ancient Cities*, 78.
51. Chakrabarti, *Oxford Companion to Indian Archaeology*, 487.
52. Farmer, Sproat, and Witzel, "Collapse of the Indus-Script Thesis."
53. Parpola, *Deciphering the Indus Script*, 65–67.
54. In China, Longshan culture (3000–2000 BCE) is the closest temporal parallel to the Indus Civilization, although comparable civilizational achievements were not achieved until Shang rule in the second millennium BCE (Tanner, *China*, 23–27).
55. Thapar in Thapar et al., *Which of Us Are Aryans?*, 69–70.
56. Rao, "Shipping and Maritime Trade," 36 (copper).
57. Kenoyer, "Archaeology of Indus Urbanism."
58. Fisher, *Environmental History*, 36.
59. Kenoyer, Price, and Burton, "New Approach to Tracking Connections," 2286.
60. Leemans, *Foreign Trade*, 159–164.
61. Many have written on this, and harappa.com also contains a wealth of information on transregional trade in this period.
62. Kenoyer, *Ancient Cities*, 97 (royal cemetery at Ur).
63. Quoted in Kramer, *Enmerkar*, 7 and 9 (Kramer's translation).
64. Thornton, "Mesopotamia, Meluhha," 601–603.

65. Possehl, "Shu-ilishu's Cylinder Seal."

66. Parpola, Parpola, and Brunswig, "Meluhha Village," 160.

67. Vidale, "Growing in a Foreign World."

68. Possehl, *Indus Civilization*, 131.

69. Parpola, *Deciphering the Indus Script*, 53 (Parpola notes that the source could also be an unknown variant of proto-Elamite script, and he notes evidence against the idea); cf. Kenoyer, "Origin and Development" (he argues for indigenous origins of the Indus script in the northwestern subcontinent).

70. I borrow "bulging loincloth knot" from Doniger, *Hindus*, 34. Many have seen a proto-vision of Shiva in this seal, which is incorrect (Srinivasan, "Unhinging Siva," 78–83). That said, it is possible that later Hindu communities borrowed aspects of Indus Civilization iconography, such as "yogic postures, phallic representations, and narrative scenes" (Kenoyer in Metropolitan Museum of Art, *Art of the First Cities*, 403).

71. Parpola, *Deciphering the Indus Script*, 247–250.

72. Possehl, "Transformation of the Indus Civilization," 458 (Great Bath). In general, on Indus Civilization decline, see Lahiri, *Decline and Fall.*

73. Kenoyer, "Uncovering the Keys," 75.

74. Possehl, *Indus Civilization*, 67–71 (Dholavira).

75. Possehl, "Transformation of the Indus Civilization," 455.

76. Staubwasser et al., "Climate Change."

77. Possehl, "Transformation of the Indus Civilization" (Indus); Wright, *Ancient Indus*, 37–38 (Ghaggar-Hakra).

78. Menon in Thapar et al., *Which of Us Are Aryans?*, 97.

79. Claudia Glatz on Bragg, "Hittites"; Wang et al., "Holocene Asian Monsoon" (China).

80. Robbins Schug et al., "Infection."

81. Scott, *Against the Grain*, xii.

82. Johansen, "Issues and Problems of Ashmound Research."

83. Johansen, "Landscape, Monumental Architecture, and Ritual," 316.

84. Coningham and Young, *Archaeology of South Asia*, 132.

85. Paddayya, "Problem of Ashmounds."

86. Johansen, "Landscape, Monumental Architecture, and Ritual," 312.

87. Witzel in Thapar et al., *Which of Us Are Aryans?*, 22.

88. Kenoyer, "Iconography of the Indus Unicorn," 122.

2. ANCIENT MIGRANTS AND VEDIC PRACTICES

1. *Rigveda* 5.44.13 (book 5, hymn 44, verse 13).

2. Thapar in Thapar et al., *Which of Us Are Aryans?*, 167–168.

3. Witzel in Thapar et al., *Which of Us Are Aryans?*, 1 (on uparishyena).

4. Jamison and Brereton, introduction to *Rigveda*, 1:5.

5. As an emic term, "aryan" is attractive. That said, I avoid it where other descriptors are adequate substitutes to head-off confusion with the racialized sense of "aryan" rooted in nineteenth- and twentieth-century European thought. This racialized meaning of "aryan" also arises in colonial India and so is discussed in chapter 20.

6. E.g., Brereton, Bronkhorst, Jamison, Witzel, and others cited in this chapter.

7. The understanding of ancient migrations laid out here is sometimes called the Aryan Migration Theory, which replaced the older Aryan Invasion Theory that was formulated during British colonial rule (chapters 20 and 21). The theory of Aryan invasion was abandoned by scholars decades ago due to lack of evidence for large-scale violence. Also, there was no large political entity to invade in India in the mid second millennium BCE; so far as we can surmise, there were not polities beyond the village level. Specific clans no doubt took land by force at times in skirmishes, including fights between aryan clans, but "invasion" is not an apt characterization. Today, the discarded theory

of an Aryan invasion arises predominantly in Hindu nationalist discussions, where they invoke it as a straw man argument. Their obsession with beating this dead horse, pun intended, stems from their investment in claiming a narrow kind of indigeneity, premised on denying ancient India's history of migrations. This is a modern issue pertaining to far-right politics and has no bearing on a historically grounded understanding of Vedic culture.

8. Dudney, *India in the Persian World of Letters*, chap. 2 (we don't know if Arzu wrote the text in Delhi or Lucknow, p. 55).

9. Thapar, *Early India*, 107–108.

10. Kellens, "Avesta" (on the collection of Zoroastrian texts and dating).

11. Witzel, "Rgvedic History," 322.

12. Reich et al., "Reconstructing Indian Population History."

13. Narasimhan et al., "Formation of Human Populations"; Shinde et al., "Ancient Harappan Genome." Still, we have no way of genetically identifying members of a linguistic group, and so the genetic evidence remains consistent but not authoritative at present (in contrast, the linguistic evidence is iron-clad).

14. Cf. Bellwood, *Early Farmers*, chaps. 4 and 10. Bellwood theorizes Indo-European speaking migrations thousands of years before the dates I give here, based on the assumption that farming spread in ancient times primarily via migration, rather than adoption, and that other Indian groups did not develop farming technology on their own. I find both assumptions to be speculative, to put it mildly. Bellwood also dismisses skeletal evidence that contradicts his views (257–258).

15. Witzel in Thapar et al., *Which of Us Are Aryans?*, 28.

16. Each name has a meaning (Staal, *Discovering the Vedas*, xvi).

17. Jamison and Brereton, introduction to *Rigveda*, 1:4.

18. Jamison and Brereton, introduction to *Rigveda*, 1:59.

19. *Sarvasammatashiksha*, cited in Deshpande, "From Orality to Writing," 64.

20. Mahabharata 13.24.70. All Mahabharata citations refer to the critical edition using the standard convention of book, chapter, verse(s).

21. UNESCO, "Tradition of Vedic Chanting," 2008, https://ich.unesco.org/en/RL/tradition-of-vedic-chanting-00062.

22. Jamison and Brereton, introduction to *Rigveda*, 61–62.

23. Jamison and Brereton, introduction to *Rigveda*, 61.

24. *Rigveda* 6.25.2.

25. Deshpande, "Vedic Aryans," 69.

26. *Rigveda* 6.45 and 8.46.

27. Thapar in Thapar et al., *Which of Us Are Aryans?*, 76 (textual evidence); Reich, *Who We Are*, 137–138 (genetic evidence). My proposed connection between these two pieces of information is, admittedly, limited by the general challenges of correlating genetic and textual evidence.

28. Krishnamurti, *Dravidian Languages*, chap. 1. There is debate about the origins of Dravidian and Munda languages, with theories for both that place their origins outside the subcontinent (e.g., in eastern Iran and southwest China, respectively as per Bellwood, *First Farmers*, 246–247 and 274; cf. to east of the subcontinent as per Anderson, "Introduction," 1, on Munda). I do not include the subcontinent's fourth major language family, Sino-Tibetan, since those languages are limited to mountain regions (Southworth, *Linguistic Archaeology*, 52).

29. Krishnamurti, *Dravidian Languages*, section 1.7.

30. On the lack of domesticated horses in the Indus Valley Civilization (and disingenuous modern attempts to fabricate evidence to the contrary), see Witzel and Farmer, "Horseplay in Harappa."

31. E.g., Chase, "Meat Provisioning," 257–258.

32. E.g., Patton, *Bringing the Gods to Mind*, 103.

33. Jamison, *Ravenous Hyenas and the Wounded Sun*, 17.

34. *Rigveda* 7.88.

35. *Rigveda* 10.129, Doniger's translation in *Rig Veda*, 25–26.

36. *Rigveda* 8.48.3 (Jamison and Brereton's translation; quotes in prior sentence verses 9 and 6, respectively).

37. These two paragraphs draw on Jamison, *Sacrificed Wife*, 65–72.
38. Brown and Rasmussen, "Bestiality," 173n12.
39. Jamison, *Sacrificed Wife*, 65.
40. Witzel, "Vedas and Upanisads," 90.
41. Witzel, "Vedas and Upanisads," 73.
42. Hawley, "Naming Hinduism," 27, discussing Robert Frykenberg's work.
43. Plofker, *Mathematics in India*, chap. 2.
44. *Rigveda* 10.90.11–12 (my translation).
45. Some have tried to extract political history from the Vedas, with the most notable result being Michael Witzel's theory of the ancient Kuru State (Witzel, "Early Sanskritization"; Witzel, "Realm of the Kuru"). In my estimation, this premise rests on scant evidence, at best, and risks mistaking mythology for political reality. I do not pursue it here for that reason as well as for two additional reasons. One, even if the theory of an ancient Kuru State is true, in whole or part, we know precious few details about this speculative polity. It remains undefined in nearly all aspects of the exercise of political power, and so it offers, in my estimation, little insight into Vedic life. Two, quite separately, scholars have focused too much, not too little, on states in standard narratives of Indian history. Against this state-heavy backdrop, I find the Vedas—in not readily providing information about political authority—to constitute a welcome opportunity to focus on other aspects of the South Asian past. Whereas the Vedas obscure political history, they offer us riches in thinking about the development of sacrifice and ritual, detailed on a granular level, to a specific society.
46. *Satapatha-Brahmana* 3.7.3.1–6.
47. Jamison, *Sacrificed Wife*.
48. Jamison, "Secret Lives of Texts," 4–5.
49. E.g., *Rigveda* 10.162 (miscarriage) and 10.184 (birth).
50. *Rigveda* 10.61.
51. *Rigveda* 10.145; translation lightly adapted from Doniger, *Rig Veda*, 290.
52. *Rigveda* 7.55.
53. Staal, *Discovering the Vedas*, xv–xvi (on the anachronism of *shruti* and *apaurusheya*).
54. Olivelle, introduction to *Early Upanisads*, 13.
55. Olivelle, introduction to *Early Upanisads*, 10 (numbers and sixteenth century).
56. Olivelle, introduction to *Early Upanisads*, 27 (childbirth); Doniger, *Hindus*, 178 (impotence).
57. Olivelle, *Early Upanisads*, 74–76 (my translation); for this and subsequent quotes I consulted Olivelle's translation.
58. Olivelle, *Early Upanisads*, 276 (my translation).
59. Olivelle, *Asrama System*, chaps. 3–5.
60. Tull, "Karma."
61. Olivelle, *Early Upanisads*, 90 (my translation).
62. Olivelle, introduction to *Early Upanisads*, 11.
63. Witzel, "Vedas and Upanisads," 88.
64. Olivelle, *Early Upanisads*, 158.
65. Brough, *Early Brahminical System*, 2.
66. Olivelle, *Early Upanisads*, 218 (my translation); I consulted translations by Doniger in *Hindus*, 164, and by Olivelle.
67. Olivelle, *Early Upanisads*, 92.
68. Brahman (ultimate reality) should not be confused with Brahmin (uppermost varna).
69. Olivelle, *Early Upanisads*, 100 (my translation).
70. Brereton, "*Tat tvam asi*."

3. BUILDING AND RENOUNCING CITIES, 550–325 BCE

1. Mutta in Hallisey, *Therigatha*, 2 (my translation; see Hallisey's translation on p. 3).
2. Chakrabarti and Lahiri, "Iron Age in India," and Lahiri, "Archaeology and Some Aspects of the Social History," 6 (early iron use); see also Chakrabarti, *India*, 353.

3. Chakravarti, *Social Dimensions*, 27.

4. Singh, *Discovery of Ancient India*, 70–71.

5. Thapar, *From Lineage to State*, 99.

6. Marshall, *Taxila*, 1:89–91.

7. Marshall, *Taxila*, 1:101–102.

8. Magee et al., "Achaemenid Empire in South Asia."

9. Sinopoli, "Human Representation in the South Indian Iron Age."

10. Kelly, "Megalithic Bleached Carnelian Beads," 112 (color); Kelly, "Craft Specialization, Technology and Social Change," 388 (quantity).

11. Kelly, "Craft Specialization, Technology and Social Change," 207–211.

12. Rajan, "Kodumanal Excavations," 76.

13. Kelly, "Craft Specialization, Technology and Social Change," 259–265.

14. This paragraph draws on Chakrabarti, "Rajagriha."

15. Chakrabarti, "Rajagriha," 263; Harding, "Rajgir and Its Hinterland," 6.

16. Chakrabarti, "Rajagriha," 263.

17. Singh, *Political Violence in Ancient India*, 19.

18. Gupta and Hardaker, *Punchmarked Coinage of the Indian Subcontinent*, 19.

19. Gupta and Hardaker, *Punchmarked Coinage of the Indian Subcontinent*, 51.

20. Gupta and Hardaker, *Punchmarked Coinage of the Indian Subcontinent*, 24–25.

21. Jha, *Ancient India*, 78; Singh, *Political Violence in Ancient India*, 20.

22. Singh, *History of Ancient and Early Medieval India*, 261.

23. Magee et al., "Achaemenid Empire in South Asia," 711.

24. Herodotus, *Histories*, 234.

25. Herodotus, *Histories*, 278.

26. Magee et al., "Achaemenid Empire in South Asia," 713.

27. Strauch, "Character of the Indian Kharosthi Script," 133–134. By this point, the Indus script had been forgotten in India, as best we can tell.

28. Singh, *Political Violence in Ancient India*, 54.

29. Singh, *Political Violence in Ancient India*, 21; Thapar, *Early India*, 154–155.

30. Thapar, *From Lineage to State*, 114–115.

31. Gethin, introduction to *Sayings of the Buddha*, xxiv.

32. Singh, *Political Violence in Ancient India*, 20.

33. On the implications of this dating of Gautama's death, see Prebish, "Cooking the Buddhist Books."

34. Etienne Lamotte cited in Gethin, introduction to *Sayings of the Buddha*, xv; Harrison, "Some Reflections on the Personality of the Buddha," 19.

35. Hallisey, introduction to *Therigatha*, xxxiiin4; Norman, "Introduction," xxxi.

36. Hallisey, introduction to *Therigatha*, vii.

37. Hallisey, introduction to *Therigatha*, vii.

38. *Anguttara Nikaya*, quoted in Kaushik, *Women and Monastic Buddhism*, 98.

39. Mutta in Hallisey, *Therigatha*, 11 (Hallisey's translation).

40. Vasetthi in Hallisey, *Therigatha*, 77.

41. Addhakasi in Hallisey, *Therigatha*, 22–23.

42. Sona and Chanda in Hallisey, *Therigatha*, 63 and 71, respectively

43. Norman, "Introduction," xxxi–xxxii.

44. Gutta in Hallisey, *Therigatha*, 87.

45. Hallisey, introduction to *Therigatha*, xxix–xxx.

46. Hallisey, *Therigatha*, 71 (Hallisey's translation).

47. Hallisey, *Therigatha*, 77 (Hallisey's translation).

48. Dundas, *Jains*, 23.

49. *Acharangasutra* 1.4.1.1–2 (Hermann Jacobi's translation), cited in Dundas, *Jains*, 41–42.

50. Cf. to view that the twenty-third Tirthankara, Parshvanatha, is historical (Kelting, "Jain Traditions," 73).

51. Dundas, *Jains*, 56.

52. Dundas, *Jains*, 46.

53. Kelting, "Jain Traditions," 90.

54. Basham, *History and Doctrines of the Ajivikas*, 55. I draw on Basham throughout this and the following paragraphs.

55. Basham, *History and Doctrines of the Ajivikas*, 228; Bronkhorst, *Greater Magadha*, 40–41; Dundas, *Jains*, 29.

56. Basham, *History and Doctrines of the Ajivikas*, 190–191.

57. Bhattacharya, "Carvaka Fragments," 612 and 616, respectively.

58. For a collection of fragments, drawn from other sources, see Bhattacharya, "Carvaka Fragments."

59. Abul Fazl, *Ain-i Akbari*, 2:114 (my translation).

60. Gethin, *Sayings of the Buddha*, 15–16 (Gethin's translation).

61. Thapar, *Early India*, 158–159.

62. Singh, *Political Violence in Ancient India*, 246.

63. Green, *Alexander of Macedon*, 399–402; Bronkhorst, "Plagues and Brahmins," 194 (on diseases).

64. Bronkhorst, *How the Brahmins Won*, 36.

4. ASHOKA'S MAURYAN EMPIRE

1. Hultzsch, *Inscriptions of Asoka*, 190 (my translation).

2. For a succinct defense of "great man" history, see MacCulloch, "Is There Still Value in 'Great Man' History?"

3. Singh, *Political Violence in Ancient India*, 55.

4. Olivelle, *Ashoka*, xxv ("singular").

5. Kosmin, *Land of the Elephant Kings*, 33; Lahiri, *Ashoka*, 164.

6. Thapar, *Asoka and the Decline of the Mauryas*, 104.

7. Singh, *Political Violence in Ancient India*, 13.

8. Thapar, *Asoka and the Decline of the Mauryas*, 103.

9. Quoted in Lahiri, *Ashoka*, 53; see Kosmin, *Land of the Elephant Kings*, 41–42 for a different translation.

10. Lahiri, *Ashoka*, 57–58.

11. Olivelle, *Ashoka*, 10, citing Dieter Schlingloff.

12. Lahiri, *Ashoka*, 58.

13. Kosmin, *Land of the Elephant Kings*, 47.

14. Kosmin, *Land of the Elephant Kings*, 47–48; Lahiri, *Ashoka*, 53.

15. Kosmin, *Land of the Elephant Kings*, 37–53.

16. Thapar, *Asoka and the Decline of the Mauryas*, 73.

17. Lubin, "Asoka's Disparagement of Domestic Ritual," 31–32.

18. Kosmin, *Land of the Elephant Kings*, 3 (uses); Trautmann, "Elephants and the Mauryas," 165–166 (supply).

19. Kosmin, *Land of the Elephant Kings*, 35.

20. Kosmin, *Land of the Elephant Kings*, 35.

21. On these stories, see, e.g., Lahiri, *Ashoka*, 101–108; Thapar, *Asoka and the Decline of the Mauryas*, chap. 2.

22. Some count only six major pillar inscriptions (e.g., Tieken, *Asoka Inscriptions*, 23); note that Tieken's book came out too late for me to incorporate more fully into this chapter.

23. Falk, *Asokan Sites and Artefacts*, 139.

24. Gillespie et al., "Predictive Modelling for Archaeological Sites."

25. Thapar, *Asoka and the Decline of the Mauryas*, 9.

26. Olivelle, "Asoka's Inscriptions," 157.

27. Lahiri, *Ashoka*, 8–9. Many scholars have suggested that Brahmi was invented by the Mauryan state chancellery (e.g., Olivelle, "Asoka's Inscriptions," 170, citing Falk). In this narrative, some have suggested that Brahmi's inventors were perhaps inspired by Kharoshthi, a script derived from Aramaic and attested in northwestern India as early as the fourth century BCE (Salomon, *Indian Epigraphy*, 46; Salomon, "Origin of the Early Indian Scripts," 276, citing Falk on the Aramaic point). However, archaeologists point to Brahmi found on rock shelters and pot shards in southern India and Sri Lanka slightly earlier (Rajan, "Situating the Beginning," 51; Ray, "Colonial Archaeology"). Currently, the dating of these southern specimens is suggestive but not, in my view, strong enough to definitively overturn the Mauryan narrative. There is also no current explanation of how this writing system traveled from Sri Lanka to northern India. In brief, the current evidence on the invention of the Brahmi script is somewhat conflicting and perilously incomplete. As a result, I decline to take a position on the point and look forward to future work, especially archaeological work, to clarify this issue. For a similar assessment, see Olivelle, *Ashoka*, 61–62.

28. Singh, *Political Violence in Ancient India*, 54–55.

29. Translation lightly adapted from Thapar, *Asoka and the Decline of the Mauryas*, 46; see also translation in Lahiri, *Ashoka*, 132; Prakrit in Hultzsch, *Inscriptions of Asoka*, 166.

30. Lubin, "Asoka's Disparagement of Domestic Ritual," 35.

31. Thapar, "Ashoka—A Retrospective," 33.

32. Schopen, *Bones, Stones, and Buddhist Monks*, 115.

33. Lahiri, *Ashoka*, chap. 4.

34. Lubin, "Asoka's Disparagement of Domestic Ritual," 36–38.

35. Falk *Asokan Sites and Artefacts*, 255–269.

36. Hultzsch, *Inscriptions of Asoka*, 5, 53, 73 (spelling varies).

37. Singh, *Political Violence in Ancient India*, 268, citing the tenth rock inscription.

38. The five kings named here are likely, respectively, Antiochus II Theos of Seleucid Empire (r. 261–246 BCE), Ptolemy II Philadelphus of Egypt (r. 285–247 BCE), Antigonus Gonatas of Macedon (r. 276–239 BCE), Magas of Cyrene (r. ca. 300–250 BCE), and Alexander of Corinth (d. 247 BCE) or Alexander II of Epirus (d. ca. 255 BCE).

39. Prakrit and English in Hultzsch, *Inscriptions of Asoka*, 66–70 (at Shahbazgarhi; my translation); I consulted translations in *Longman Anthology of World Literature*, A874–875 (N. A. Nikam and Richard McKeon's translation) and Thapar, *Asoka and the Decline of the Mauryas*, 382–384 (along with Hultzsch's translation). "Among the Greeks" sentence borrows from this line as it appears in another copy of the same inscription at Kalsi (Hultzsch, *Inscriptions of Asoka*, 44).

40. Olivelle offers a succinct list in "Asoka's Inscriptions," 171.

41. Quoted in Kachru, "Ashoka's Moral Empire" (Kachru's translation).

42. In Prakrit and English translation in Sircar, *Asokan Studies*, 14.

43. Falk, *Asokan Sites and Artefacts*, 56–57.

44. *Satapatha-Brahmana* 3.1.2.21.

45. Quoted in Olivelle, *Ashoka*, 315.

46. Kachru, "Ashoka's Moral Empire."

47. E.g. *Arthashastra* 1.12.23, 2.29.7, and 2.35.11; Parasher-Sen, "Tribes," 133–134. On the *Arthashastra*'s date, see Olivelle, introduction to *Arthashastra* (*King, Governance, and Law*), 25–31.

48. *Corpus Inscriptionum Indicarum*, 3:203–220, lines 22–23.

49. Lahiri, *Ashoka*, 271–272.

50. Thapar, "Perceiving the Forest," 108–109.

51. Lal, "Iron Tools," 66–68.

52. Wahab and Youngerman, *Brief History of Afghanistan*, 35.

53. Shaffer, "Later Prehistoric Periods," 149.

54. Carratelli and Garbini, *Bilingual Graeco-Aramaic Edict*; Olivelle, *Ashoka*, 65 (on rulership theory).

55. Lahiri, *Ashoka*, 175.

56. Lahiri, *Ashoka*, 144–149; Jha, "Chemical Industries," 124 (on gold mining in Maski).

57. Adapted from *Longman Anthology of World Literature*, A:876–877 (N. A. Nikam and Richard McKeon's translation).

58. Quoted from Thapar, *Asoka and the Decline of the Mauryas*, 396 (Thapar's translation).

59. Singh, *Political Violence in Ancient India*, 95.

60. Falk, *Asokan Sites and Artefacts*, 287–288.

61. Falk, *Asokan Sites and Artefacts*, 257 and 280–282.

62. Falk, *Asokan Sites and Artefacts*, 113–115; Thapar, *Asoka and the Decline of the Mauryas*, 399.

63. GH 591 in http://coinindia.com/galleries-maurya.html, accessed April 25, 2024; suggested identification in Singh, *Political Violence in Ancient India*, 90.

64. Hultzsch, *Inscriptions of Asoka*, 161–164 (Sarnath); Lahiri, *Ashoka*, 255–257.

65. Lahiri, *Ashoka*, 251.

66. Lahiri, *Ashoka*, 44.

67. E.g., on Lumbini, see Tremblay, "Mauryan Horizon."

68. Schopen, *Bones, Stones, and Buddhist Monks*, 126.

69. Schopen, *Bones, Stones, and Buddhist Monks*, chap. 1.

70. Falk, "Owners' Graffiti on Pottery from Tissamaharama," 62–63.

71. Falk, "Owners' Graffiti on Pottery from Tissamaharama," 88.

72. Deshpande, "Interpreting the Asokan Epithet *devanampiya*," 34–35.

73. Kachru, "Ashoka's Moral Empire"; Lahiri, *Ashoka*, 5.

74. Quoted in Olivelle, "Asoka's Inscriptions," 169.

75. Olivelle, "Semantic History of Dharma," 505.

76. Singh, *Political Violence in Ancient India*, 55.

77. Falk, *Asokan Sites and Artefacts*, 148.

78. E.g., Falk, *Asokan Sites and Artefacts*, 164, 166.

79. Lahiri, *Ashoka*, 263; Rezavi, "Antiquarian Interests in Medieval India," 996 (laborers), quoting Shams Siraj Afif.

80. Falk, *Asokan Sites and Artefacts*, 149.

81. Falk, "Remarks on the Minor Rock Edict of Asoka at Ratanpurwa"; Lahiri, *Ashoka*, 17.

5. MAHABHARATA

1. Mahabharata 5.139.55–56a (my translation).

2. Khilnani, "Panini."

3. Deshpande, "Changing Perspectives in the Sanskrit Grammatical Tradition," 219–220; Deshpande, *Sanskrit and Prakrit*, 27–30.

4. Pollock, *Language of the Gods*, 67–69.

5. Quoted in Ollett, "Making It Nice," 271.

6. Pollock recounts this process in detail in *Language of the Gods*.

7. Joseph, *Early Indians*, 211–213; Moorjani et al., "Genetic Evidence for Recent Population Mixture in India."

8. Reich, *Who We Are*, 144.

9. For decades, scholars estimated the composition date of Vyasa's Mahabharata between 300 BCE and 300 CE. Some still cite these dates (e.g., Doniger, *Hindus*, chaps. 9–10), but I find little compelling evidence pointing to the earlier part of that date range. A more precise accounting is as follows: Some version of the core Mahabharata battle narrative was verbally narrated, roughly 2,000 years ago. This oral transmission may have preceded a written version (by either centuries or a briefer time period), or it may have arisen concomitantly; there is no way to know for sure. The Mahabharata was first written down, most likely, between 150 BCE and 150 CE (I favor closer to the later date; cf. to the former in Witzel, "Vedas and the Epics," 67 concurring, as he notes, with Alf Hiltebeitel). In any case, the earliest written version of the Mahabharata does not survive today. The epic underwent a vigorous set of changes during Gupta rule ca. 300–450 CE (Fitzgerald, "Mahabharata," 52–53; Obrock, "*Mahabharata*," 6). We can glimpse the contours of the Gupta redaction but only in

general terms. The critical edition of the Mahabharata—a twentieth-century invention—strips away more recent additions, especially from the second millennium CE, but text critical practices do not and cannot recover, in precise detail, the epic as it existed 1,500 years ago (Sukthankar, prolegomena to vol. 1 of Mahabharata, lxxxvi and cii–civ; Brockington, *Sanskrit Epics*, 56–63).

10. McCrea, "Hierarchical Organization of Language," 430; Pollock, "Mimamsa and the Problem of History," 607–609.

11. Fitzgerald, "Great Epic of India," 613.

12. Olivelle, introduction to *Arthashastra* (*King, Governance, and Law*), 70. *Itihasa* is widely mistranslated as "history."

13. Monius, "*And We Shall Compose a Poem.*"

14. Hawley and Pillai, "Introduction to the Literature of the Mahabharata," 3.

15. Obrock, "*Mahabharata*," 2; Ramanujan, *Collected Essays*, 168–169 ("Repetition in the *Mahabharata*").

16. Mahabharata 1.56.33 and 18.5.38.

17. Fitzgerald, "Mahabharata," 52–53; Obrock, "*Mahabharata*," 6.

18. Mahabharata 2.71.14–15.

19. The four yugas are, in order: Satya, Treta, Dvapara, and Kali.

20. Mahabharata 6.23.1.

21. Mahabharata 6.23.

22. Mahabharata 6.23.28–31 (my translation); I consulted translations by Miller (*Bhagavad-Gita*) and van Buitenen (*Bhagavadgita in the Mahabharata*).

23. Mahabharata 6.24.8 (van Buitenen's translation in *Bhagavadgita in the Mahabharata*).

24. Mahabharata 6.24.9.

25. Dhand, "Paradigms of the Good," 273–274.

26. Mahabharata 6.25.35.

27. Mahabharata 6.24.47.

28. Davis, *Bhagavad Gita*.

29. *Jnaneshvari*, mentioned in Davis, *Bhagavad Gita*, 7.

30. Brodbeck, *Krishna's Lineage*.

31. Mahabharata 6.33.5–12, 6.33.15–18, 6.33.30–34 (my translation); I consulted translations by Miller (*Bhagavad-Gita*) and van Buitenen (*Bhagavadgita in the Mahabharata*).

32. Smith, introduction to *Mahabharata*, xiv; Mahabharata 11.26.9–10.

33. On sacrifice as a motif in the Mahabharata, see Bronkhorst, "Sacrifice in the *Mahabharata*," and Reich, "Sacrificial Violence and Textual Battles."

34. E.g., several of the dramas found in Kerala in 1910 and originally attributed to Bhasa, including *Dutaghatotkacha* (Ghatotkacha the Messenger), *Karnabhara* (Karna's burden), and *Urubhanga* (Shattering the thighs). Also, e.g., *Binding of the Braid* (*Venisamhara* of Narayana Bhatta, ca. eighth century CE, Bengal) and *Slaying of Kichaka* (*Kichakavadha* of Nitivarman, ca. seventh–tenth century CE, Kalinga).

35. Mahabharata 12.1.8 (*shokavyakulacetasam*).

36. Mahabharata 12.1.15.

37. Mahabharata 12.7.4–8; I consulted translations by Bowles, *Dharma, Disorder and the Political*, 140, and Fitzgerald, *Mahabharata*, 180.

38. Mahabharata 11.25.36–42.

39. Fitzgerald, "Great Epic of India," 622.

40. Mahabharata 12.15.15–16 and 12.15.49 (virtuous violence).

41. Mahabharata 12.55.14.

42. Fitzgerald, introduction to *Mahabharata*, 82.

43. Quoted in Tubb, "*Santarasa* in the *Mahabharata*," 143–144; see also Hudson, *Disorienting Dharma*, chap. 1.

44. Bronkhorst, *How the Brahmins Won*, 27.

45. Hala, *Poems on Life and Love*, 176 (Khoroche and Tieken's translation).

46. Courtright, *Ganesa*, 151–153. Fitzgerald, "India's Fifth Veda," 128; I thank Sohini Pillai for the Tamil insight.

47. Mahabharata 12.181.11–13.

48. Doniger, *Hindus*, 287.

49. Doniger, *Hindus*, 674–676; Kanjilal, "Excluded to Exceptional," 352–359.

50. Mahabharata 1.215.

51. Mahabharata 1.217.1–6 (my translation); I consulted translations by Framarin ("Environmental Ethics and the *Mahabharata*," 186) and van Buitenen (*Mahabharata* 1:417–418).

52. Mahabharata 1.217–19.

53. On philosophical explanations, see Framarin, "Environmental Ethics and the *Mahabharata*."

54. Mahabharata 2.43–65 (full dice game episode).

55. Pillai, "Mahabharata as Krsnacarita," 261–262.

56. Mahabharata 2.58–64 (Krishna explains his absence in Mahabharata 3.14).

57. Jamison, *Sacrificed Wife*, 12 and 15.

58. E.g., Chitra Divakaruni, *The Palace of Illusions: A Novel* (New York: Doubleday, 2008); on this novel and other modern reimaginations of Draupadi, see Lothspeich, "Draupadi."

59. Quintanilla, "Closer to Heaven than the Gods."

60. Asher, "Early Indian Art Reconsidered," 52–57.

61. Salomon, *Ancient Buddhist Scrolls from Gandhara*, 25–26.

62. Mahabharata 3.186–88.

63. Bailey, "*Sthavirabuddhayah* in the Markandeyasamasyaparvan," 687–688 (stupas); Hegarty, *Religion, Narrative and Public Imagination*, 68–69 (pillars).

64. Cort, *Framing the Jina*, 127–128.

65. Obrock, "*Mahabharata*," 7.

66. Franco, *Spitzer Manuscript*, 314.

67. Witzel, "Brahmins of Kashmir," 31–34.

68. Mahadevan, "Southern Recension of the *Mahabharata*," 4–6.

6. SOUTH ASIANS TRAVELING, 200 BCE–300 CE

1. Hart and Heifetz, *Four Hundred Songs*, 147 (Hart and Heifetz's translation).

2. See Strauch, *Foreign Sailors on Socotra*, 122–158 on the forty-seven surviving inscriptions on this wall (p. 132 on Vishnudhara).

3. Chew, *Southeast Asia Connection*, 63–64; Rajan, "Emergence of Early Historic Trade," 187.

4. Francis, *Asia's Maritime Bead Trade*, 9 and 20.

5. Casson, "Ancient Naval Technology," 8–9; Cobb, *Rome and the Indian Ocean Trade*, 142–144.

6. Acri, Blench, and Landmann, "Introduction," 1–2.

7. Sidebotham, *Berenike*, 75.

8. Cobb, *Rome and the Indian Ocean Trade*, 155.

9. Asher, "India Abroad," 159 (Asher says that Brahmi and Sanskrit had reached Vocanh, while also noting a "distinctively Indian name"); Sakhuja and Sakhuja, "Rajendra Chola I's Naval Expedition," 80.

10. Abeydeera, "Geographical Perceptions of India and Ceylon." For a thorough account of Greek and Roman sources on Sri Lanka, see Weerakkody, *Taprobane*.

11. Scholars have not always acknowledged the actives roles of South Asians in traversing the sea routes and the Silk Roads. Most scholars have privileged a Western perspective when writing about this period, even when discussing, say, archaeologic digs in India (Coningham, "Beyond and before the Imperial Frontiers"). This has led them to assume, wrongly, that the Roman Empire spearheaded ancient commerce, Westerners dominated the high seas, and we do not even need to mention trade east of the subcontinent across the Bay of Bengal and beyond. I seek to tell a different, more accurate story here.

12. Quoted in Sarkar, "Chinese Texts," 272.

13. Casson, "Ancient Naval Technology," 10. On the variable size of boats, see De Romanis, *Indo-Roman Pepper Trade*, 70.

14. On horses, see de Saxce, "Local Networks and Long-Distance Trade," 58.

15. Francis, *Asia's Maritime Bead Trade*, chaps. 4–5.

16. For other lists and overviews, see, e.g., Cobb, *Rome and the Indian Ocean Trade*, chap. 6 and Parker, "Ex Oriente Luxuria." On pottery, Ford et al., "Geochemical Investigation of the Origin of Rouletted," 918.

17. Cobb, *Rome and the Indian Ocean Trade*, 196–197; Parker, "Ex Oriente Luxuria," 52.

18. Quoted in Boehrer, *Parrot Culture*, 5 (Boehrer's translation of Pliny's *Natural History*, 10.58.117); see also Pliny, *Natural History*, 3:367.

19. Olson et al., "Drinking Songs"; Tryjanowski et al., "Birds Drinking Alcohol."

20. Cobb, *Rome and the Indian Ocean Trade*, 198–200.

21. Guy, *Tree and Serpent*, 182–183.

22. Parker, "Ex Oriente Luxuria," 53–54; Weinstein, "Indian Figurine from Pompeii," 194.

23. De Pume, "Roman Bronzes from Kolhapur"; Guy, *Tree and Serpent*, 184–185; McLaughlin, *Rome and the Distant East*, 47.

24. Pliny, *Natural History*, 6:475–477.

25. Frankopan, *Silk Roads*, 21 (examples of frankincense and myrrh).

26. Francis, *Asia's Maritime Bead Trade*, 20; Francis, "Beads," 451 (on process).

27. Parker, *Making of Roman India*, 151–152. Pepper was also grown in parts of Southeast Asia.

28. Sidebotham, *Berenike*, 225.

29. Cobb, *Rome and the Indian Ocean Trade*, 213 (private residences); Van der Veen and Morales, "Roman and Islamic Spice Trade," 60 (*De Re Coquinaria*).

30. Cobb, "Black Pepper Consumption."

31. Selby, *Tamil Love Poetry*, 24 (Selby's translation).

32. Davis, *Global India*, 11.

33. The first find was in 1786 at Nellore in Andhra Pradesh; see the list (from 1989) in Turner, *Roman Coins from India*, appendix 1; on Roman coins in Sri Lanka, see Weerakkody, *Taprobane*, 151–170.

34. Cobb, "Mediterranean Goods in an Indian Context," 170–173; Gurukkal, "Forms of Production," 160–162.

35. Davis, *Global India*, 13–16 (also *suvarnanagara* and *suvarnadvipa*).

36. Falk, "Indian Gold Crossing the Indian Ocean," 109–110.

37. The modern Indian nation-state imported about 1,000 tonnes of gold in 2021; Rajendra Jadhav, "India Spends Record $55.7 Bln on Gold Imports in 2021," Reuters, January 4, 2022, https://www.reuters.com/business/indias-spends-record-557-bln-gold-imports-2021-govt-source-2022-01-04/.

38. Hart and Heifetz, *Four Hundred Songs*, 195–196 (Hart and Heifetz's translation).

39. Doniger, *Winged Stallions and Wicked Mares*, 8–13.

40. Karttunen, *Yonas and Yavanas*, 361; Mahabharata 2.47.13.

41. Cobb, *Rome and the Indian Ocean Trade*, 50–51; cf. Moore, "When Not Just Any Wine Will Do," 104–105.

42. Hart and Heifetz, *Four Hundred Songs*, 43 (Hart and Heifetz's translation).

43. McHugh, *Unholy Brew*, 54.

44. Bollee, *Cultural Encyclopaedia of the Kathasaritsagara*, 460–461.

45. Wen, *King's Road*, 99–111.

46. Parker, "Ex Oriente Luxuria," 49–50.

47. Cobb, *Rome and the Indian Ocean Trade*, 195–196; Hall, "Iphigenia in Oxyrhynchus and India," 413–414.

48. Casson, *Periplus Maris Erythraei*, 81 (Casson's translation).

49. Klijn, *Acts of Thomas*.

50. One of the best resources is Chatterjee and Eaton, *Slavery and South Asian History*, although it scarcely covers ancient India.

51. Anderson, "Four Noble Truths."

52. Harvey, "*Dukkha*."

53. *Epigraphia Indica* 7:52.

54. Ray, "Ethnographies of Sailing," 73 (now part of Mumbai, due to British colonial land reclamation projects).

55. Norman, *Pali Literature*, 110–112 (the Chinese translation may be based on a Sanskrit original); translated by I. B. Horner in two volumes as *Milinda's Questions* (London: Pali Text Society, 1963–1964).

56. Davis, *Global India*, 38–39.

57. Salomon, *Ancient Buddhist Scrolls*, 81–84 and chap. 7.

58. Asher, *Bodh Gaya*, 6–7.

59. Asher, *Sarnath*, 83–86.

60. Schopen, *Bones, Stones, and Buddhist Monks*, 245–247.

61. Lopez, *Lotus Sutra*, 17 (pp. 21–22 on the *Lotus Sutra*'s date).

62. Schopen, *Bones, Stones, and Buddhist Monks*, chaps. 5–7.

63. *Epigraphia Indica* 7:52–54.

64. Fogelin, "Ritual and Presentation," 143.

65. Davis, *Global India*, 42.

66. Rhys Davids and Oldenberg, *Vinaya Texts*, 1:112–113 (Rhys Davids and Oldenberg's translation); I removed a "ye" from the English translation.

67. Geiger and Bode, *Mahavamsa*, 82–83.

68. Baums, "Inventing the *Pothi*," 343–344.

69. Lopez, *Lotus Sutra*.

70. Ramanujan, "Three Hundred *Ramayanas*," in *Collected Essays*, 131–160; Richman, *Many Ramayanas*; Richman, *Ramayana Stories in Modern South India*.

71. Thapar, *Past before Us*, 215–216 (*Dasaratha Jataka*) and 248 (*Paumachariyam*).

72. Scholarly estimates for the initial date of the composition of Valmiki's Ramayana vary between 500 BCE and 200 CE, but scholars have moved toward the later end of that range in recent decades (e.g., Robert Goldman's estimate in 1984 of sixth century BCE [introduction to *Ramayana of Valmiki*, 1:22] versus Robert and Sally Goldman's estimate in 2004 of "the first half of the first millennium BCE" for some parts while agreeing with Brockington that other parts were composed later ["Ramayana," 76]). I concur with many scholars who see Valmiki's Ramayana as likely having been solidified in a form we could recognize in the early centuries CE (e.g., Monius, "*And We Shall Compose a Poem*," 151; Thapar, *Past before Us*, 220–222). Most scholars date the Ramayana to later than the core story of the Mahabharata, although this gets messy since both texts were fluid (Brockington, *Sanskrit Epics*, 26–27). The epics project themselves as occurring in the reverse order, with the Ramayana happening first.

73. Hess, "Rejecting Sita" (on Rama's "cruelty," Hess's term). Hess addresses Sita's harsh words to Rama during the fire test; also note Sita's words to Lakshmana when they argue about him following Rama in pursuit of the golden deer (Ramayana 3.43). All Ramayana citations refer to the critical edition, published under the title *Valmiki Ramayana*.

74. See Pollock, "Divine King" on how Rama's divinity is part of Valmiki's text.

75. Robert Goldman, who has devoted his life to studying the Ramayana, describes it as an "elaborate fairy tale" (introduction to *Ramayana of Valmiki*, 1:28); see also Davis, *Global India*, chap. 4.

76. *dharme pitrpaitamahe* (Ramayana 4.18.39).

77. Pollock, "Ramayana and Political Imagination," 264.

78. Ramayana 1.2.9–18 (my translation): I consulted Goldman's translation (*Ramayana of Valmiki*, 1:127–128).

79. Monius, "*And We Shall Compose a Poem*," 151.

80. Pollock, "Literary Culture and Manuscript Culture," 87; Wujastyk, "Indian Manuscripts," 159–160.

81. Pollock, *Language of the Gods*, chaps. 1–2.

82. The *Buddhacharita* (Life of the Buddha) and *Saundarananda* (Handsome Nanda), both translated in the Clay Sanskrit Library series.

83. Ollett, *Language of the Snakes*, chaps. 2–3; Pollock, *Language of the Gods*, 61–62.

7. INEQUALITY, PLEASURE, AND POWER IN EARLY INDIA

1. Quoted in Andrew Ollett, "Selections from *Seven Centuries*," http://prakrit.info/prakrit/reader.html?r=4, #227, accessed July 24, 2024 (my translation); for Tieken and Khoroche's translation, see Hala, *Poems on Life and Love*, 199–200. On the date range of the *Sattasai* (also known as *Gathasaptashati*), see Lienhard, *History of Classical Poetry*, 81. "Outcaste" is *pana*, understood to indicate "chandala," a caste-less group, by most commentators (Ollett, "Selections from *Seven Centuries*," commentary on #227).

2. A tricky challenge confronts us throughout this chapter: fuzzy dates. This chapter covers roughly 300 to 600 CE but with significant and repeated deviations on both ends. This is for two reasons. One, I seek to trace specific phenomena that push beyond this timeframe, including substantial changes in Hindu religious practices, growing social stratification, and a surge of elite cultural production. Two, we remain uncertain about precisely when some key texts were composed. One solution to the problem of temporally uncertain evidence is to ignore it and instead to focus on inscriptions, the one unambiguously dated archive from this period (see Ali, "Royal Eulogy as World History" and, for an earlier period, Thapar, *Past before Us*, chap. 7). I give inscriptions their due in the section on statecraft, but limiting ourselves to the inscriptional archive—which largely focuses on dynasties, property, and taxes—severely circumscribes our access to premodernity. I want to know about many other aspects of premodern South Asian life as well, and, accordingly, I also use literary and material evidence to trace religious, cultural, and social developments. As a mild defense of blurring dates, I remind readers of a methodological point covered in the Historiography essay, which is that we should not be unduly attached to moments of genesis for specific ideas but rather invest our attention in recovering their subsequent circulation and impacts on South Asian societies.

3. The *Devimahatmya* (maybe sixth century CE) is part of the *Markandeyapurana* (Erndl, "Sakta," 147). Cf. to views of the puranas as partially historical texts (Thapar, *Past before Us*, chap. 6).

4. Erndl, "Sakta," 149–150.

5. Doniger, *Siva*.

6. Clooney and Stewart, "Vaisnava," 164–165.

7. Doniger O'Flaherty, "Myths Depicted at Elephanta," 33–34 (on scenes mentioned); Collins, *Iconography and Ritual of Siva at Elephanta*.

8. Willis, *Archaeology of Hindu Ritual*, 8.

9. Bakker, "Royal Patronage and Religious Tolerance," 462, citing Michael Willis.

10. Davis, "Origin of Linga Worship," 639.

11. My summary; see discussion and variants in Doniger, *Siva*, 302–306.

12. Davis, "Origin of Linga Worship" translates the relevant sections.

13. The Gudimallam Lingam is still in situ, in an active temple.

14. Willis, *Archaeology of Hindu Ritual*, chap. 2.

15. For a primer on Hindu worship practices in temples, see Eck, *Darsan*.

16. Manu, *Manu's Code of Law* 2.21–22; also discussed in Bronkhorst, *Greater Magadha*, 1.

17. Flood, *Introduction to Hinduism*, 129–131; Shulman, *Tamil*; Zvelebil, *Smile of Murugan* (on Tamil deities and literature generally); Clothey, *Many Faces of Murukan* (on Murugan).

18. Mahadevan, "Southern Recension of the *Mahabharata*," 4–5.

19. Clothey, *Many Faces of Murukan*, 71.

20. Mann, *Rise of Mahasena*, 2–3.

21. Olivelle, "Semantic History of Dharma."

22. Olivelle, "Introduction," 18.

23. Olivelle, introduction to Manu, *Manu's Code of Law*, 3.

24. Lubin, "Writing and the Recognition of Customary Law," 227 (see also Davis, "Introduction," 3).

25. Aktor, "Social Classes," 65.

26. Ramanujan, *Collected Essays*, 39 notes Manu's "extraordinary lack of universality."

27. Manu, *Manu's Code of Law* 8.267 (Olivelle's translation).

28. Manu, *Manu's Code of Law* 8.270–272 (adapted from Olivelle's translation).

29. Manu, *Manu's Code of Law* 8.268.

30. Jamison, "Women," 199 (summarizing the *Vasishtha Dharmasutra* 21.1–4).

31. Davis, "Seeing through the Law," 20–21.

32. Yajnavalkya, *Treatise on Dharma*, 1.70.

33. Manu, *Manu's Code of Law* 5.147–149 (Olivelle's translation).

34. Tull, "Karma," 323 and 328.

35. Translated in Doniger, *Hindus*, 402–403.

36. Manu, *Manu's Code of Law* 12.1.

37. Manu, *Manu's Code of Law*, chap. 12.

38. The four *ashramas* were initially conceptualized as options more than a sequence (Olivelle, *Asrama System*, 74).

39. Parasher-Sen, "Naming and Social Exclusion," 420–424.

40. Legge, *Record of Buddhistic Kingdoms*, 43 (I adjusted the grammar and borrowed at one point from the translation in Deeg, "Has Xuanzang Really Been in Mathura?," 57–58).

41. Thapar, "Asokan India and the Gupta Age," 49.

42. Ali, *Courtly Culture*, chaps. 4–5; McHugh, *Sandalwood and Carrion*.

43. Mazzarella, "Cultural Politics of Branding."

44. Vatsyayana, *Kamasutra*, 16 (Doniger and Kakar's translation).

45. Vatsyayana, *Kamasutra*, 18 (Doniger and Kakar's translation).

46. *Moksha* (liberation) was added later as the fourth aim.

47. Hala, *Poems on Life and Love*, 15 (Khoroche and Tieken's translation).

48. Vatsyayana, *Kamasutra*, 3 (Doniger and Kakar's translation).

49. Hala, *Poems on Life and Love*, 73 (Khoroche and Tieken's translation).

50. Hala, *Poems on Life and Love*, 193 (Khoroche and Tieken's translation). More broadly, see Dehejia, *Body Adorned*, chap. 2.

51. Pollock, "Introduction" to *Literary Cultures in History*, 1; on Prakrit literature, see Ollett, *Language of the Snakes*. On the *Brihatkatha* possibly never existing, see Taylor, *Fall of the Indigo Jackal*, 17. On Paishachi as a lost language, see Ollett, "Ghosts from the Past."

52. Sheldon Pollock has written extensively on this, especially in *Language of the Gods*.

53. Respectively, *Abhijnanashakuntala* (Recognition of Shakuntala), *Vikramorvashiya* (How Urvashi was won), and *Raghuvamsa* (Raghu's lineage); the first two were translated into English as part of the Clay Sanskrit Library Series, and the last within the Murty Classical Library of India.

54. Bakker, "Theatre of Broken Dreams," 197–199.

55. Kalidasa's *Meghaduta* is available in many translations, including in Mallinson, *Messenger Poems*.

56. On the date, see Thapar, *Past before Us*, 356.

57. Pollock, *Rasa Reader*.

58. Bailey, *Love Lyrics*, 274 (my translation, with thanks to Sheldon Pollock for his comments on this verse; for Bailey's translation, see p. 275). The fifth line could be more literally translated as "Poor mind! You have no nature of your own." This verse also has a philosophical dimension, playing on non-dualistic Vedanta.

59. *Nitishatakam*, v. 84 in Bhartrhari, *Subhashitatrishati* (my translation).

60. Kalidasa, *Recognition of Shakuntala*, 296–299.

61. Hart, *Poems of Ancient Tamil*, 7; Shulman, *Tamil*, 66–67 (eighteen minor works are often also included).

62. Quoted in Tharu and Lalita, *Women Writing in India*, 72–73 (George Hart's translation).

63. Ollett, "Making It Nice," 273–274 (on earlier dates); Tieken, *Kavya in South India*, 128–139 (on later dates). On anthologizing dating to a later period, see Zvelebil, *Smile of Murugan*, chap. 3.

64. Mahadevan, "Southern Recension of the *Mahabharata*," 25 and 32.

65. Parthasarathy, *Cilappatikaram*, chap. 30 (also mentioned in the introduction, 7).

66. Also summarized in Hart, *Poems of Ancient Tamil*, 104–107; Shulman, *Tamil*, 98–100.

67. For overviews of Gupta historiography, see Bisschop and Cecil, "Primary Sources and Asian Pasts" and Lorenzen, "Historians and the Gupta Empire."

68. Gupta-Vakataka relations are often thought to have been friendly, but the evidence suggests a more complicated picture involving armed conflict (Bakker, "Theatre of Broken Dreams").

69. Some specific examples are given in Bakker, "Theatre of Broken Dreams."

70. Lorenzen, "Historians and the Gupta Empire," 52.

71. Willis, "Later Gupta History," 131.

72. Vasudeva, introduction to Kalidasa, *Recognition of Shakuntala*, 16.

73. Willis, *Archaeology of Hindu Ritual*, 5 (citing Fred Virkus on fragmented power).

74. Olivelle, introduction to *Arthashastra* (*King, Governance, and Law*), 38.

75. Olivelle, introduction to *Arthashastra* (*King, Governance, and Law*), 25–31 (dates); McClish, *History of the Arthasastra*, chap. 5 (multiple authors).

76. Olivelle, introduction to *Arthashastra* (*King, Governance, and Law*), 33–34.

77. Olivelle, introduction to *Arthashastra* (*King, Governance, and Law*), 51–53; Pollock, *Ends of Man*, 63–64.

78. *Corpus Inscriptionum Indicarum*, 3:203–220.

79. Pollock, *Language of the Gods*, 240.

80. Asher, "India, Magadha, Nalanda," 58.

81. Pollock, *Language of the Gods*, 240–248.

82. Pollock, *Language of the Gods*, 143 (Pollock's translation with light emendations).

83. Willis, *Archaeology of Hindu Ritual*, 244.

84. Asher, *Nalanda*, 11–12.

85. Dundas, "Floods," 231.

86. Dundas, "Floods."

87. Dundas, "Floods," 237.

88. Jha, *Ancient India*, 153–154; Thakur, "Forced Labour in the Gupta Period."

89. Jha, *Ancient India*, 159.

90. *Corpus Inscriptionum Indicarum*, 5:5–9.

91. Mishra and Pradhan, "Sati Memorials and Cenotaphs," 1014.

92. Verma, *Women and Society*, 69–78.

93. Hala, *Poems on Life and Love*, 130 (Khoroche and Tieken's translation).

94. Verma, *Women and Society*, 218, citing Romila Thapar.

95. Jamison, "Marriage and the Householder," 135–136; Verma, *Women and Society*, 63–66.

96. Dharmashastra literature, discussed earlier in this chapter, is more theoretical and did not reflect legal codes in daily use.

97. Lubin, "Writing and the Recognition of Customary Law," 231; he translates the charter on pp. 232–238.

98. E.g., Lubin, "Writing and the Recognition of Customary Law," 242–244.

99. Adapted from translation in Lubin, "Writing and the Recognition of Customary Law," 232–233.

100. Klijn, *Acts of Thomas*.

101. Frykenberg, *Christianity in India*, 99–100.

102. Malekandathil, "Sassanids and the Maritime Trade," 161–162.

8. INDIA IN THE WORLD, CA. 700 CE

1. Edgerton, *Panchatantra Reconstructed*, 1:396 (my translation); for Olivelle's translation, see *Pancatantra*, 155.

2. Adapted from translation in Olivelle, *Pancatantra*, 157–158.

3. Blackburn, "Brahmin and the Mongoose."

4. Xuanzang's biography has been translated by Li Rongxi under the title *Biography of the Tripitaka Master*; for an account of additional biographies of Xuanzang, see Deeg, "Many Biographies," 922–927.

5. Deeg, "Has Xuanzang Really Been in Mathura?," 35–43.

6. Xuanzang, *Biography of the Tripitaka Master*, 42–43; Brose, *Xuanzang*, 24–25; Gordon, *When Asia Was the World*, 11–13.

7. For overviews of Xuanzang's experiences I rely primarily on Brose, *Xuanzang*, and Gordon, *When Asia Was the World*, chap. 1.

8. Gordon, *When Asia Was the World*, 14.

9. Brose, *Xuanzang*, 32–34.

10. This issue in interpreting travelogues of premodern Chinese pilgrims to India is noted in Deeg, "Describing the Own Other," 137n25; on this trope, see Nattier, *Once upon a Future Time*.

11. Kalhana, *Kalhana's Rajatarangini* 1.289–317. See also Xuanzang's comments in *Buddhist Records of the Western World*, 1:167–172.

12. Kalhana, *Kalhana's Rajatarangini* 8.1184 (adapted from Stein's translation).

13. *Record of the Western Regions*, quoted in Brose, *Xuanzang*, 140 (Brose's translation).

14. *Record of the Western Regions*, quoted in Brose, *Xuanzang*, 140 (Brose's translation).

15. *Record of the Western Regions*, quoted in Brose, *Xuanzang*, 140–141 (Brose's translation).

16. *Record of the Western Regions*, quoted in Brose, *Xuanzang*, 141 (Brose's translation).

17. Brose, *Xuanzang*, 52. Most likely, Xuanzang did not have access to the commentary of Dharmakirti (ca. seventh century CE), if it had even been written yet (Tillemans, "Dharmakirti," n3).

18. Harsha is also known as Harshavardhana, which distinguishes him from the eleventh-century Harsha of Kashmir.

19. Lorenzen, *Kapalikas*, 20–22, and Thapar, *Past before Us*, 483 (on Shaiva ritual); Bana, *Harsa-carita*, 66 (quotation; Cowell and Thomas's translation).

20. Harsha himself wrote three Sanskrit dramaturgical works, one of which recounts a Buddhist story (*Nagananda*); all are translated in the Clay Sanskrit Library.

21. *Record of the Western Regions*, quoted in Brose, *Xuanzang*, 150–151 (Brose's translation).

22. Eck, *India*.

23. Amar, "Buddhist Responses to Brahmana Challenges," 163–171.

24. Amar, "Buddhist Responses to Brahmana Challenges," 156.

25. Amar, "Buddhist Responses to Brahmana Challenges," 178–179.

26. Hyecho, *Hye Ch'o Diary*, 39–40; on Hyecho's travelogue, which survives in fragments today, see Lopez, *Hyecho's Journey*.

27. Brose, *Xuanzang*, 1; Gordon, *When Asia Was the World*, 16.

28. Felbur, "Kumarajiva," 6.

29. Deeg, "Chinese Buddhist Travelers."

30. Olivelle, introduction to *Pancatantra*, xliv.

31. Taylor, "Panchatantra," 2.

32. Taylor, *Fall of the Indigo Jackal*, chap. 1 goes over the *Panchatantra*'s messy textual history.

33. Taylor, *Fall of the Indigo Jackal*, 23–25.

34. Discussed in Edgerton, *Panchatantra Reconstructed*, 2:3.

35. Taylor, *Fall of the Indigo Jackal*, 50; Olivelle, introduction to *Pancatantra*, xxxvi.

36. Olivelle, *Pancatantra*, 137–139 (Taylor discusses this story in *Fall of the Indigo Jackal*, 88–91).

37. Taylor, *Fall of the Indigo Jackal*, 39–41.

38. Taylor, *Fall of the Indigo Jackal*, 184.

39. E.g., see the discussion in Davis, "Seeing through the Law."

40. Ferdowsi, *Shahnameh*, 3:339–342.

41. For overviews of this transmission, see, e.g., Blankinship, "Tales of Two Jackals"; Taylor, *Fall of the Indigo Jackal*, 3–4.

42. Respectively, Olivelle, *Pancatantra*, 22 and 30–31.

43. Olivelle, *Pancatantra*, 156–157.

44. Floyd, "Engaging Imperfect Texts," 118 (on the milkmaid).

45. Blackburn, "Brahmin and the Mongoose," 494.

46. Appleton, *Jataka Stories*, especially chaps. 1–2 and 8.

47. Dehejia, *Discourse in Early Buddhist Art*, 21–24.

48. Dehejia, *Discourse in Early Buddhist Art*, 21.

49. Elverskog, *Buddhism and Islam*, 73 (Muslim communities); Shaw, "Introduction," liii (Chaucer and *Arabian Nights*).

50. Ferdowsi, *Shahnameh*, 3:331–335.

51. About 70 percent of the adult population of the United States, the United Kingdom, and India has played chess (United Nations, "World Chess Day: 20 July," https://www.un.org/en/observances/world-chess-day). Even today, differences remain between Indian chess and chess elsewhere in the world; for example, traditional Indian rules disallow the two-square initial pawn move and en passant.

52. van Bladel, "Eighth-Century Indian Astronomy," 259; Wujastyk, "Balkh to Baghdad" (ayurveda works).

53. van Bladel, "Eighth-Century Indian Astronomy," 264–285.

54. Plofker, *Mathematics in India*, 97–102 (eclipses) and 127–128 (pi); as Plofker notes, it is possible that Indian mathematicians had calculated pi accurately a few generations before Aryabhata.

55. Gutas, *Greek Thought, Arabic Culture*, 136–141.

56. Pollock, *Language of the Gods*, chap. 3.

57. Pollock, *Rasa Reader*, 59.

58. Bronkhorst, "Spread of Sanskrit in Southeast Asia."

59. Doniger, *Hindus*, 186.

60. I do not take a position on the "origins" of tantra, which strikes me as an impossible query at present. For a review of scholarship on this and an argument for seeing tantra in a wider Asian context, see Acri, "Tantrism 'Seen from the East.'"

61. Gerety, "Between Sound and Silence," 210–213 gives an overview of the scholarly debate here.

62. For a summary of this position and scholarly alternatives, see White, *Yoga Sutra*, chap. 13.

63. Gerety, "Between Sound and Silence," 210 ("patchwork"). Popular memory likes to point back to the Indus Civilization as the source for yoga, which has been discredited by scholars (Mallinson and Singleton, "Introduction," x and xxxiii n8).

64. Gerety, "Whole World Is OM," 11 and 107–109, discusses Parpola's thesis on the Dravidian etymology of "om" and objections to it; see also Gerety, "Between Sound and Silence" on early Brahminical uses of the term.

65. Gerety, "Whole World Is OM" (multiform), and Gerety, "Between Sound and Silence," 210 (malleable), quoting Andrea Jain.

66. Isayeva, *Shankara and Indian Philosophy*, 14.

67. On "om" in this, see, e.g., Gerety, "Whole World Is OM," 2.

68. Rambachan, *Advaita Worldview*, 3.

69. E.g., Rambachan, *Advaita Worldview*.

70. Sanderson, "Saiva Age."

71. For useful discussions of how to define tantra in South Asian history, see, e.g., Gough, *Making a Mantra*, 8–9; Padoux, *Hindu Tantric World* (mainly on Hindu tantras), 7–17; Urban, *Power of Tantra*, 4–22 (dealing with Orientalist issues); White, "Tantra in Practice," 7–31. Also note Wendy Doniger's prudent warning: "How you define Hindu Tantra is largely predetermined by what you want to say about it" (*Hindus*, 407).

72. Lorenzen, *Kapalikas*, chaps. 2–3.

73. For some accounts, see, e.g., Padoux, *Hindu Tantric World*, chaps. 5–10 and Sanderson, "How Public Was Saivism?"

74. E.g., Sanderson cites numerous royal inscriptions from the mid-first millennium, as far north as Nepal, of kings upholding caste norms ("Saiva Age," 41n1); Xuanzang records practices such as keeping those of certain classes outside of the city and maintaining segregation, not sharing utensils, and Kshatriyas and Brahmins dressing distinctly (Brose, *Xuanzang*, 106–108).

75. Eck, *India*, 287–292.

76. Urban, *Power of Tantra*, 37–38 (citing the Buddhist *Hevajratantra* and a royal land grant); Bernier, *Himalayan Architecture*, 23 (citing the Archaeological Survey of India).

77. Translation adapted and summarized from the *Kalikapurana* in van Kooij, *Worship of the Goddess* 57.1–4.

78. Urban, *Power of Tantra*, 58 and 62–63.

79. Ferstl, "Bana's Literary Representation"; cf. in his *Harsa-Carita*, Bana notes a Shaiva who conducts a ritual atop a corpse.

80. Quoted in Brose, *Xuanzang*, 36 (Brose's translation).

81. White, *Kiss of the Yogini*, 158–159, citing Alexis Sanderson.

82. Sanderson, "Saiva Age," 179.

83. Gough, *Making a Mantra*.

84. Davis, "Story of the Disappearing Jains," 220–221.

85. Dundas, *Jains*, 127.

86. Peterson, *Poems to Siva*, 244, 249, and 278–279.

87. Quoted in Peterson, *Poems to Siva*, 141 (Peterson's translation).

88. Quoted in Peterson, *Poems to Siva*, 286 (Peterson's translation with small emendations).

89. One tradition credits Appar with converting Mahendravarman from Jainism; other sources do not mention his original religion (Lorenzen, *Kapalikas*, 49–50; Peterson, *Poems to Siva*, 9 on the Appar story; Davis, "Story of the Disappearing Jains," 215 on the earliest account of Mahendravarman's conversion by Appar).

90. Lorenzen, "Parody of the Kapalikas."

91. Hinnells, "Parsi Communities" (citing dates from the early 700s forward).

92. Patel, "Mosque in South Asia," 3–4.

93. Dale, "Trade," 157.

94. Maclean, *Religion and Society in Arab Sind*.

95. *Record of the Western Regions*, quoted in Brose, *Xuanzang*, 106–107 (Brose's translation).

9. MEDIEVAL SOUTH INDIA

1. Paranavitana, *Sigiri Graffiti*, 2:260, no. 421 (Paranavitana's translation).

2. My description is based on Mahalingam, *Topographical List of Inscriptions*, 7:54 (no. 228).

3. Dehejia, *Thief Who Stole My Heart*, 70–71.

4. E.g., Mahalingam, *Topographical List of Inscriptions*, vol. 7, nos. 100, 205, 321, 412, 413, 554, 788, and 1267 (an additional issue in no. 1267 is intermingling freely with Vaishnavas).

5. Dehejia, *Thief Who Stole My Heart*, 9; Mahalakshmi, "Chola (Cola) Empire," 1–2.

6. Ali, "Death of a Friend," 41.

7. Rajendran et al., "Geoarchaeological Evidence."

8. Dehejia, *Thief Who Stole My Heart*, 69–70 (temple inscriptions); on the south Indian inscriptional archive, see Subbarayalu, *South India under the Cholas*, 15–24.

9. Ali, "Royal Eulogy as World History," 197–203.

10. *Epigraphia Indica* 16:74–75; also cited in Davis, *Lives of Indian Images*, 82.

11. Geiger and Rickmers, *Culavamsa* 55.21 (Geiger and Rickmers's translation).

12. Bilhana, *Vikramankadevacharita*, 3.61 (my translation); also quoted in Chattopadhyaya, *Studying Early India*, 199.

13. Abraham, *Two Medieval Merchant Guilds*, 174 (pearls); Dehejia, *Thief Who Stole My Heart*, 171 (copper).

14. Dehejia, *Thief Who Stole My Heart*, 167.

15. Manatunga, "Sri Lanka and Southeast Asia," 196.

16. Eaton, "Temple Desecration in Pre-Modern India," 65.

17. Davis, *Lives of Indian Images*, 57–59; Eaton, "Temple Desecration in Pre-Modern India," 66.

18. Eaton, *India in the Persianate Age*, 29; Eaton, "Temple Desecration in Pre-Modern India," 66.

19. *Varahamihira's Brihatsamhita* 46.8 (my translation); see also translation in Davis, *Lives of Indian Images*, 53.

20. Eaton, "Temple Desecration in Pre-Modern India," 66; Davis, *Lives of Indian Images*, 76.

21. Quoted in Eaton, "Temple Desecration in Pre-Modern India," 65; see also Davis, *Lives of Indian Images*, 52. Some scholars date Rajadhiraja's reign from 1018, which puts him overlapping with his father's reign by more than two decades.

22. Karashima, *Concise History of South India*, 126.

23. Eaton, *India in the Persianate Age*, 19.

24. Davis, *Lives of Indian Images*, 73.

25. Davis, *Lives of Indian Images*, 71–76.

26. Davis, *Lives of Indian Images*, 55–57.

27. Eaton, "Temple Desecration in Pre-Modern India" and Eaton, "Temple Desecration in Indo-Muslim States."

28. Eaton, "Temple Desecration in Pre-Modern India," 63; for more extensive comparison of Ghaznavid and Chola raids, see Eaton, *India in the Persianate Age*, chap. 1.

29. Flood, *Objects of Translation*, 34 (Islamic texts); Eaton, *India in the Persianate Age*, 21 (Shiva icon).

30. Eaton, "Temple Desecration in Pre-Modern India," 63.

31. Ollett, "Attempted Iconoclasm"; Thapar, *Somanatha*, 105.

32. Flood, *Objects of Translation*, 41–42.

33. Flood, *Objects of Translation*, 38–40.

34. Meisami, "Ghaznavid Panegyrics," 34–35 (quote; Meisami's translation); see also Thapar, *Somanatha*, 45–48.

35. Al-Utbi's *Tarikh-i Yamini* (1031 CE) doesn't mention the raid (Thapar, *Somanatha*, 43–44).

36. Hardy, *Historians of Medieval India*; see also discussion in Kumar, *Emergence of the Delhi Sultanate*, 20–29.

37. Biruni, *Kitab al-Biruni*, 13 (al-hind); my translation adapted from Sachau's translation in Biruni, *Alberuni's India*, 1:17.

38. Ernst, "Muslim Studies of Hinduism?," 177–178.

39. E.g., Bronner, *Extreme Poetry*, 92–99; Rabe, *Great Penance*.

40. Dehejia, "Chola Bronzes," 17 (italics in original).

41. Dehejia, "Chola Bronzes," 17.

42. Mahalakshmi, "Chola (Cola) Empire," 4.

43. Dehejia, *Thief Who Stole My Heart*, 69–70.

44. Smithsonian Collection F1929.84, https://asia.si.edu/object/F1929.84/, accessed July 25, 2024. Dehejia argues to identify the image as a queen, most recently, in *Thief Who Stole My Heart*, chap. 4.

45. Dehejia, *Body Adorned*, 4.

46. Davis, *Ritual in an Oscillating Universe*, 3–21.

47. This comes up repeatedly in inscriptions; I am also grateful to Tamara Sears for this insight.

48. Dehejia, *Body Adorned*, 2–4.

49. Sakhuja and Sakhuja, "Rajendra Chola I's Naval Expedition," 85.

50. Karashima, *Concise History of South India*, 129; Subbarayalu, *South India under the Cholas*, 65–68.

51. Bhimsen, *Tarikh-i-Dilkasha*, 193 (still, they grow strong on such food as per Bhimsen).

52. E.g., Mahalingam, *Topographical List of Inscriptions*, 7:21 (no. 94).

53. Mahalingam, *Topographical List of Inscriptions*, 7:267 (no. 1130); see also 7:432 (no. 1864) on women sold to a temple as *devaradiyars*.

54. Mahalingam, *Topographical List of Inscriptions*, 7:452 (no. 1949).

55. Davis, "Slaves and Slavery," 306, citing the *Smritichandrika* of Devannabhatta.

56. Dehejia, *Thief Who Stole My Heart*, 252–253.

57. Quoted in Subbarayalu, *South India under the Cholas*, 157; cf. Stein, "South India," 30.

58. Dehejia, *Thief Who Stole My Heart*, 93–95 (on Chola support of rice cultivation).

59. Ali, "War, Servitude, and the Imperial Household," 45.

60. On political dynasties, note Nakka Madambi, who left a ca. 800 inscription at Sigiriya referring to himself as "superintendent of slaves" for the Pandyan ruler (Paranavitana, *Sigiri Graffiti*, 2:401–402, no. 652). On female slaves owned by temples, see Orr, *Donors, Devotees, and Daughters of God*, 116–121.

61. Subbarayalu, *South India under the Cholas*, 157.

62. Karashima, *Concise History of South India*, 92–93.

63. Subbarayalu, *South India under the Cholas*, 120.

64. Karashima, "Allur and Isanamangalam."

65. Subbarayalu, *South India under the Cholas*, 128; Sastri describes this in different terms in *Colas*, 578–579.

66. E.g., Karashima, *Concise History of South India*, 180–181; Subbarayalu, *South India under the Cholas*, 170.

67. Orr, "Jain and Hindu 'Religious Women,'" 190–194.

68. Sears, *Worldly Gurus and Spiritual Kings*.

69. *Epigraphia Indica* 32:45–55; see also Chakravarti, "Monarchs, Merchants and a Matha," 265–270.

70. Dehejia, "Chola Bronzes," 12.

71. Dehejia, *Thief Who Stole My Heart*, 23.

72. Dehejia, *Thief Who Stole My Heart*, 32.

73. On this form's origins, see Srinivasan, "Shiva as 'Cosmic Dancer.'"

74. Dehejia, *Thief Who Stole My Heart*, 247.

75. Dehejia, *Thief Who Stole My Heart*, 180.

76. Davis, "Chola Bronzes in Procession."

77. Eck, *Darsan*, 6–7.

78. The 954 Lakshmana Vishnu temple of King Dhanga, the 1011 Vishvanatha Shiva temple of King Yashovarman, and the ca. 1050 Kandariya Mahadeo Shiva temple (Dehejia, *Body Adorned*, 101).

79. Desai, *Religious Imagery of Khajuraho*.

80. *Shilpaprakasha* 2.502 (translated in Rabe, "Secret Yantras," 442).

81. Rabe, "Secret Yantras," 434–449 (yantras); Desai, *Religious Imagery of Khajuraho*, 196–197 (higher union, also mentions yantras); Dehejia, "Reading Love Imagery," 112 (alleviating need).

82. *Lilavati*, 29n4 (translation as quoted in Thapar, *Early India*, 472).

83. *South-Indian Inscriptions*, 3:418; also cited in Dehejia, "Reading Love Imagery," 98.

84. Nagaraj, "Critical Tensions," 336.

85. Nagaraj, "Critical Tensions," 348.

86. Nagaraj, "Critical Tensions," 348.

87. Ramanujan, *Speaking of Siva*, 111–142 (on Akka).

88. Ramanujan, *Speaking of Siva*, 127 (Ramanujan's translation).

89. Ramanujan, *Speaking of Siva*, 134 (Ramanujan's translation).

90. Quoted in Tharu and Lalita, *Women Writing in India*, 81–82 (Susan Daniel's translation with small emendations).

91. Pollock, *Language of the Gods*, chap. 9.

92. Rao, "Multiple Literary Cultures in Telugu," 391–397.

93. Pollock, *Language of the Gods*, part 2.

94. Abraham, *Two Medieval Merchant Guilds*, chaps. 2–3; Lee, "Constructing Community," chap. 1.

95. Quoted in Ali, "Between Market and Court," 192 (Ali's translation following Barnett, lightly adapted). See also *Epigraphia Indica* 19:30–35.

96. *Epigraphia Indica* 19:33 and 35.

97. Abraham, *Two Medieval Merchant Guilds*, 92–98.

98. Lee, "Constructing Community," 39.

99. Ali, "Between Market and Court," 197.

100. Sen, "Military Campaigns of Rajendra Chola," 67–72 (misrepresenting); Sakhuja and Sakhuja, "Rajendra Chola I's Naval Expedition," 79 (levy).

101. Kulke, "Naval Expeditions of the Cholas," 9.

102. For an overview of major theories behind this Chola aggression, see Kulke, "Naval Expeditions of the Cholas," 1–2.

103. Sakhuja and Sakhuja, "Rajendra Chola I's Naval Expedition," 77.

104. Lee, "Constructing Community," 2.

105. Lee, "Constructing Community," 162–165.

106. Ming troops destroyed most or all these structures in a xenophobic moment in the mid-fourteenth century (Lee, "Constructing Community," 149–151).

107. Dewaraja, "Cheng Ho's Visits to Sri Lanka"; Green, "Introduction," 24.

108. Lien, "Hindu Deities in Southern Vietnam."

109. Kulke, "Naval Expeditions of the Cholas," 12. The Chola king at the time was Kulottunga; for an account of him, see Cox, *Politics, Kingship, and Poetry*.

110. Fallon, "Introduction," xxxi; Hooykaas, *Old-Javanese Ramayana*, 5.

111. Pollock, *Language of the Gods*, 390.

112. Paranavitana, *Sigiri Graffiti*, 1:ccx–ccxv; Hallisey, "Works and Persons in Sinhala Literary Culture," 721–727.

113. Paranavitana, *Sigiri Graffiti*, nos. 162, 174, and 197 (crowds) and no. 316 (quote).

114. E.g., Paranavitana, *Sigiri Graffiti*, no. 68 (contesting a woman's identity), no. 76 (lamenting poor preservation), no. 559 (complimenting the artist), and many verses praising the frescoes.

115. E.g., Paranavitana, *Sigiri Graffiti*, nos. 185 and 366, nos. 96 and 426, and nos. 231 and 621 (plagiarism) and no. 676 (improving). Premodern standards of copying without attribution were different. But students are well advised to ponder how seriously modern scholars take plagiarism today, to the extent of identifying it in writing from more than a millennium ago.

116. Paranavitana, *Sigiri Graffiti*, no. 134; also translated and discussed in Hallisey, "Works and Persons in Sinhala Literary Culture," 723.

117. E.g., Paranavitana, *Sigiri Graffiti*, no. 652.

118. Subbarayalu, "Anjuvannam," 160–161; see the Pahlavi, Hebrew, and Arabic (Kuffic) signatures on a ninth–tenth century copper plate, now held by a Syrian church in Kerala (*Travancore Archaeological Series*, 2:61 and 2:70).

119. Champakalakshmi, *Trade, Ideology and Urbanization*, 217.

120. Goitein and Friedman, *India Traders of the Middle Ages*, 55–57.

121. Goitein and Friedman, *India Traders of the Middle Ages*, 58.

122. Goitein and Friedman, *India Traders of the Middle Ages*, 73–76.

123. Goitein and Friedman, *India Traders of the Middle Ages*, 70.

124. Dehejia, *Thief Who Stole My Heart*, 251–252. Also note the example given in this chapter's introductory paragraph.

125. Dehejia estimates that 2,000 bronzes or more have been recovered over the last fifty years (*Thief Who Stole My Heart*, 261).

10. INDO-PERSIAN RULE AND CULTURE, 1190–1350

1. Lawrence, *Morals for the Heart*, 159 (Lawrence's translation).

2. Quoted in Newman, "Islam in the Kalacakra Tantra," 317 (my translation). The Brahmin sage quotes are from the *Yajnavalkyasmriti* (quote 1), *Panchatantra* (quote 2), and *Garudapurana* (quote 2) (Truschke, *Language of History*, 37).

3. Singh, *Political Violence in Ancient India*.

4. Gommans, "Warhorse and Gunpowder in India," 109–110.

5. Quoted in translation in Eaton and Wagoner, *Power, Memory, Architecture*, 39.

6. Talbot, *Last Hindu Emperor*, 2n5.

7. Eaton, *India in the Persianate Age*, 43.

8. Ibn al-Athir, *Chronicle*, 3:48–49.

9. Eaton, *India in the Persianate Age*, 39–41.

10. Eaton, *Rise of Islam*, 33–34.

11. Jackson, "Turkish Slaves on Islam's Indian Frontier," 70; Kumar, *Emergence of the Delhi Sultanate*, 95–96.

12. Kumar, *Emergence of the Delhi Sultanate*, 82–84, on Turkish slaves.

13. Davis, "Slaves and Slavery."

14. Eaton, *India in the Persianate Age*, 44–46.

15. As quoted by Juzjani, quoted in translation in Kumar, *Emergence of the Delhi Sultanate*, 116.

16. Eaton, *India in the Persianate Age*, 45.

17. Gabbay, "In Reality a Man," 46–47.

18. Asif, *Book of Conquest*, chap. 5 (on women); on the *Chachnama* as a transcreation of an eight-century CE Arabic text, see Habib, "Linguistic Materials from Eighth-Century Sind"; cf. to argument for the book being authored in thirteenth-century Sind in Asif, *Book of Conquest*, chap. 2 (see Habib's response in, "Review of Asif").

19. Quoted in translation in Gabbay, "In Reality a Man," 53 (I removed brackets).

20. Gabbay, "In Reality a Man," 48.

21. Quoted in Persian from Isami in Haeri, *Unforgettable Queens*, 115 (my translation).

22. Bano, "Acquisition and Trade of Elite Slaves," 232.

23. Isami, *Futuhus-Salatin*, 134; also quoted in translation in Haeri, *Unforgettable Queens*, 129.

24. Patel, "Mosque in South Asia," 8.

25. Patel, "Historiography of Reuse," 2, citing Michael Meister.

26. Patel, "Expanding the Ghurid Architectural Corpus."

27. Sarvananda, *Jagaducharita*, 58–65.

28. Chakravarti, *Trade and Traders*, 220–239.

29. Truschke, *Aurangzeb*, 102.

30. The Qutb Minar used to stand 242 feet tall, before some nineteenth-century changes (Asher, *Delhi's Qutb Complex*, 40–41).

31. Welch, Keshani, and Bain, "Epigraphs," 19–23 (Arabic and Persian); Prasad, *Sanskrit Inscriptions of Delhi Sultanate*, 2–3 (corrupt Sanskrit).

32. Flood, "Pillars," 107.

33. Flood, "Pillars," 110.

34. Asher, *Delhi's Qutb Complex*, 59.

35. Sadi, *Gulistan*, 39 (Thackston's translation).

36. Bharadwaj, "Migration," 225; Kumar, *Emergence of the Delhi Sultanate*, 333–336.

37. Obrock, "Uddhara's World"; Prasad, *Sanskrit Inscriptions of Delhi Sultanate*, 3–15.

38. Prasad, *Sanskrit Inscriptions of Delhi Sultanate*, 9 (v. 12, my translation).

39. Prasad, *Sanskrit Inscriptions of Delhi Sultanate*, 8 (v. 3).

40. Quoted in translation in Gabbay, "Language of Tolerance," 210n95.

41. Eaton, *India in the Persianate Age*, 47.

42. Flood, "Pillars," 111n62.

43. Eaton, *India in the Persianate Age*, 59.

44. Eaton, *India in the Persianate Age*, 58–59.

45. Digby, "Before Timur Came," 300–301.

46. Eaton, *India in the Persianate Age*, 71.

47. Barani, *Tarikh-i Firuzshahi*, 475 (my translation).

48. Ernst and Lawrence, *Sufi Martyrs of Love*.

49. Auer, "Chishti Mu'in al-Din."

50. Ernst and Lawrence, *Sufi Martyrs of Love*, 85.

51. Quoted in Digby, "Sufi Shaykh," 72.

52. Digby, "Sufi Shaykh."

53. Translated by Bruce Lawrence under the title *Morals for the Heart*.

54. Hafiz, *Divan*, #218.

55. Sharma, *Amir Khusraw*, 59.

56. Phukan, "Through a Persian Prism," 216.

57. Losensky and Sharma, *Bazaar of Love*, 93–94 (Losensky and Sharma's translation; from *Qiran al-Saadain*).

58. Jayanaka, *Prithvirajavijaya* 10.43–46 (my translation); translated in Pollock, "Ramayana and Political Imagination," 276–277.

59. Gangadevi, *Madhuravijaya* 8.12.

60. Jalali and Ansari, "Persian Translation of Varahamihira's Brhatsamhita" (on *Brihatsamhita*); Ernst, "Islamization of Yoga" (on *Amritakunda*). On other fourteenth-century Persian translations of Sanskrit texts, see Sarma, "Translation of Scientific Texts," 70.

61. Hamza, "Hakim's Tale."

62. Vose, "Making of a Medieval Jain Monk," 224–240.

63. Balbir, "Propos des Hymnes."

64. Losensky and Sharma, introduction to the *Bazaar of Love*, xxxvii.

65. Sharma, *Amir Khusraw*, chap. 4.

66. Ollett, *Language of the Snakes*, 9 and 134. Following Ollett, I consider Apabhramsha within the family of Prakrit languages.

67. Abdur Rahman, *Samdesarasaka*, 41 (Mayrhofer's translation).

68. Nair, *Translating Wisdom*, 31 and 194–195n4.

69. See chap. 5; see also Davis, *Bhagavad Gita*, on the "circumscribed and erudite" audience for the Gita in medieval India (44).

70. Novetzke, *Quotidian Revolution*, 237.

71. Novetzke, *Quotidian Revolution*, 239.

72. Novetzke, *Quotidian Revolution*, 209–210.

73. Novetzke, *Quotidian Revolution*, 267 (and I borrow "quotidian" from Novetzke).

74. Knutson, *Into the Twilight*, chap. 3; Miller, "Jayadeva," 7.

75. I am indebted to Richard Eaton for the observation that some Buddhist monasteries, like Vikramashila, were likely viewed as projecting the political authority of their royal patrons.

76. Elverskog, *Buddhism and Islam*, 1–3; Truschke, "Power of the Islamic Sword."

77. Amar, "Reassessing the Muslim Attacks," 57–59 (focusing on through the twelfth century).

78. Dharmasvamin, *Biography of Dharmasvamin*, chaps. 5 and 10 (Bodhgaya and Nalanda) and 64–65 (unrest).

79. McKeown, *Guardian of a Dying Flame*, 20–22.

80. Amar, "Reassessing the Muslim Attacks," 67.

81. Known as the Zhenjue Temple; McKeown, *Guardian of a Dying Flame*, 261–262.

82. Kim, *Receptacle of the Sacred*, 225.

83. Kim, *Receptacle of the Sacred*, 270.

84. Slaje, "Buddhism and Islam in Kashmir," 139.

85. Chatterjee, "*Adivasis*," 19–20.

86. Basham, *History and Doctrines of the Ajivikas*.

87. Gail Omvedt, Giovanni Verardi, and others have attempted to explain the end of Indian Buddhism. I find most of the current explanations somewhere between unsupported by the evidence (e.g., Buddhism was absorbed into Vaishnava practices) and factually incorrect (e.g., Muslims killed all the Buddhists).

88. Gommans, "Warhorse and Gunpowder in India," 112; Khan, "Coming of Gunpowder" (on the early introduction of gunpowder in northern India).

89. Amir Khusraw, *Khazainul Futuh*, 107 (Habib's translation).

90. Kakka, *Nabhinandanajinoddhara*, 3.1–9 (my translation); also translated in Truschke, *Language of History*, 229–230.

91. Truschke, *Language of History*, 91.

92. Flood, *Objects of Translation*, 257.

93. Some scholars have mistaken Malik Kafur as Ethiopian owing to the name of Malik, but Isami is quite clear that he is *marhathah-nijhad* (Isami, *Futuhus-Salatin*, 319). I thank Richard Eaton for consultation on this point.

94. Ibn Battuta, *Rehla*, 44.

95. Kumar, *Emergence of the Delhi Sultanate*, chap. 4.

96. Sarma, "Jain Assayer" (Thakkura Pheru).

97. Ibn Battuta, *Rehla*, 165.

98. Ibn Battuta, *Rehla*, 58.

99. Sears, "Ibn Battuta's Buddhists," 117.

100. Ibn Battuta, *Travels*, 4:788.

101. Sears, "Ibn Battuta's Buddhists," 102.

102. Ibn Battuta, *Rehla*, 212 (Husain's translation).

103. Metcalf, "Ibn Battuta as a Qadi in the Maldives."

104. There are competing opinions about whether the Black Death hit India. If it did, it happened before it ravaged Europe and does not appear to have resulted in a comparable scale of human death. Cf. Sussman, "Black Death" (no plague in India) and Digby, "Sufi Shaykh," 80n30 (maybe the plague hit northern India in the 1320s).

11. THE LONG FIFTEENTH CENTURY

1. Quoted in translation in Kaul, *Lal Ded*, 107.

2. McHugh, *Unholy Brew*, 64–65 and 74; Gode, *Studies in Indian Cultural History*, 1:113.

3. Thackston, "Kamaluddin Abdul-Razzaq Samarqandi," 311.

4. McHugh, *Unholy Brew*, 70–73 and personal correspondence.

5. Bhatavadekar and Ainapure, *Subhashitaratnakara*, 286 (my translation); also cited and translated in Gode, *Studies in Indian Cultural History*, 1:145.

6. Most, possibly all, earlier scholars have used the phrase "long fifteenth century" to refer to the period between 1398 (Timur's sack of Delhi) and 1555 (Humayun's return to India) (Orsini and Sheikh, "Introduction," 1–2). This periodization is north India-centric and ignores events south of the Vindhya Mountains. In pursuit of more fully incorporating southern India and the Deccan into the narrative of South Asian history, I adapt this useful concept of a long fifteenth century but use dates that also reflect realities across the north-south divide. Accordingly, I date the "long fifteenth century" as beginning in 1347, when the Tughluqs retreated to Delhi and both the Bahmani and Vijayanagara kingdoms were established. Its end point is not especially critical to how I have written this chapter, but it would be reasonable to place this in the 1520s. In that decade, three events occurred in different parts of the subcontinent: the end of the Bahmani dynasty in 1528, Babur's entry into Delhi in 1526, and Krishnadevaraya's death in 1529.

7. Eaton and Wagoner, *Power, Memory, Architecture*, 30.

8. Wagoner, "Sultan among Hindu Kings," 856–858.

9. Asher and Talbot, *India before Europe*, 73.

10. Thackston, "Kamaluddin Abdul-Razzaq Samarqandi," 307–310.

11. Eaton, "Persian Cosmopolis," 79. I follow Phillip Wagoner on Devaraya II's regnal dates ("Sultan among Hindu Kings," 858).

12. University of Mysore, *Annual Report*, 161 (my translation slightly adapts from p. 166).

13. Talbot, "Inscribing the Other," 700 (slightly earlier is the Prakrit "himdu" in the *Vividhatirthakalpa*, 97).

14. Eaton, *Social History of the Deccan*, 48.

15. Eaton, *Social History of the Deccan*, 48–50.

16. Firishta, *History*, 2:368–370.

17. Eaton, *Social History of the Deccan*, 74; Sherwani, *Bahmanis of the Deccan*, 233–234.

18. Asher and Talbot, *India before Europe*, 65–66; Wagoner, "Harihara," 317–318, citing Firishta.

19. Wagoner, "Fortuitous Convergences," 249–260.

20. Thackston, "Kamaluddin Abdul-Razzaq Samarqandi," 307 (Thackston's translation).

21. Sherwani, *Bahmanis of the Deccan*, 143–144.

22. Eaton, *India in the Persianate Age*, 88.

23. Eaton and Wagoner, *Power, Memory, Architecture*, 166–167.

24. Eaton and Wagoner, *Power, Memory, Architecture*, 167–172.

25. Asher and Talbot, *India before Europe*, 74.

26. Quoted in Rao, Shulman, and Subrahmanyam, "New Imperial Idiom," 91 and 104.

27. Translated in Rao, Shulman, and Subrahmanyam, "New Imperial Idiom," 91–92 (they translate the political maxim section in full; I adjust some spellings and grammar).

28. Alam and Subrahmanyam, "Iran and the Doors to the Deccan," 78.
29. Nikitin, "Travels of Athanasius Nikitin," 12–13.
30. Eaton, *Social History of the Deccan*, 75.
31. Varadarajan, "Konkan Ports and Medieval Trade," 13.
32. Barnes, "Introduction," 4 (fifth century); Eaton, *Social History of the Deccan*, 75 (fifteenth century).
33. Quoted in Rao, Shulman, and Subrahmanyam, "New Imperial Idiom," 98.
34. Eaton, *Social History of the Deccan*, 50.
35. Flatt, *Courts of the Deccan Sultanates*, 103.
36. Eaton, "Rise of Written Vernaculars," 116–117.
37. Wirkud, "Discussing the Importance of the Ass Curse Steles," 131.
38. Novetzke, *Quotidian Revolution*, 79.
39. Wirkud, "Discussing the Importance of Ass Curse Steles," 131–132 (Bahmani); Wirkud, "Gadhegals from Goa," 203–205 (Vijayanagara).
40. Sherwani, *Bahmanis of the Deccan*, 158–159.
41. Quoted in Firishta, *History*, 2:349 (Briggs's translation).
42. Overton, "Introduction," 9.
43. Overton, "Introduction," 6–9.
44. The next two paragraphs draw on Eaton, *Social History of the Deccan*, chap. 3; Flatt also describes Gawan's execution in *Courts of the Deccan Sultanates*, 135.
45. Quoted in Eaton, *Social History of the Deccan*, 66.
46. Sherwani, *Bahmanis of the Deccan*, 346n19.
47. Eaton, *Social History of the Deccan*, 69.
48. Firishta, *History*, 2:508 (Briggs's translation).
49. Blair and Bloom, "From Iran to the Deccan," 186–187.
50. Shokoohy, "Sasanian Royal Emblems."
51. Alam and Subrahmanyam, "Iran and the Doors to the Deccan," 78.
52. Khazeni, *Sky Blue Stone*, 57 (*Shahnama* comparison).
53. Eaton, *Social History of the Deccan*, 50n47.
54. Firishta, *History*, 2:307–308 (Briggs's translation).
55. Firishta, *History*, 2:308.
56. Eaton, *Social History of the Deccan*, 50n47.
57. Eaton, *India in the Persianate Age*, 187–188.
58. Quoted in translation in Alam and Subrahmanyam, *Indo-Persian Travels*, 66.
59. Mondini, "Architectural Heritage and Modern Rituals," 135.
60. Sherwani, *Bahmanis of the Deccan*, 195.
61. Jamison and Brereton, introduction to *Rigveda*, 19.
62. Galewicz, *Commentator in Service of the Empire*, 209.
63. Galewicz, *Commentator in Service of the Empire*, 81.
64. Pollock, "Ramayana and Political Imagination."
65. Dallapiccola et al., *Ramachandra Temple*.
66. Pollock, "Ramayana and Political Imagination," 268.
67. Digby, "After Timur Left," 48.
68. Eaton, *India in the Persianate Age*, 102–103.
69. There are multiple subsequent accounts of Timur's sack of Delhi; note that Timur's alleged memoir, *Tuzuk-i Timuri*, is a later invention (Manz, "Timur Lang," 512).
70. Orsini and Sheikh, "Introduction," 3.
71. Eaton, *India in the Persianate Age*, 107.
72. Eaton, *India in the Persianate Age*, 107–108.
73. Vidyapati, *Kirttilata*, 2.45–46 (my translation, borrowing from Jha, *Political History of Literature*, 216, and Lorenzen, "Who Invented Hinduism?" 651).
74. Jha, *Political History of Literature*, 215–217.
75. Truschke, "Hindu," 253–266.
76. Bangha, "Early Hindi Epic Poetry," 365–370.

77. Truschke, *Language of History*, 89–96; Hens, "Beyond Power and Praise."

78. Granoff, "Mountains of Eternity"; de Clercq, "Apabhramsha as a Literary Medium," 347 (on caste).

79. Granoff, "Mountains of Eternity," 44–46.

80. Beach, *Mughal and Rajput Painting*, 8–9.

81. Titley, *Ni'matnama Manuscript*, 2 (Titley's translation, lightly adapted).

82. Titley, *Ni'matnama Manuscript*, 38 (Titley's translation).

83. Titley, *Ni'matnama Manuscript*, 50 (Titley's translation).

84. Titley, *Ni'matnama Manuscript*, 62 (Titley's translation).

85. Eaton, *India in the Persianate Age*, 88–92; Slaje, "Buddhism and Islam in Kashmir," 128–129.

86. Obrock, "Muslim *Mahakavyas*," 67–70.

87. Stein, "Sanskrit Deed of Sale."

88. Kaul, *Rajatarangini of Shrivara*, 3.216.

89. Khan, "Rishi Movement."

90. Quoted in Kaul, *Lal Ded*, 104 (Kaul's translation).

91. Khan, "Rishi Movement," 132–133.

92. Jonaraja, *Rajatarangini*, vv. 596–682.

93. Jonaraja, *Rajatarangini*, v. 651 (my translation).

12. SEEKING GOD OR FAME, 1500–1550

1. Singh, *Verses of the Sikh Gurus*, 56 (Singh's translation lightly adapted).

2. O'Hanlon, "Contested Conjunctures," 771–774; Pollock, "Introduction" to *Forms of Knowledge*, 2–4; Richards, "Early Modern India."

3. Saraiva, *Marrano Factory*, 342; Subrahmanyam, *Career and Legend of Vasco da Gama*, 79–80 (Saraiva says three ships).

4. Disney, *History of Portugal*, 119–120.

5. Subrahmanyam, *Career and Legend of Vasco da Gama*, 121–128.

6. Disney, *History of Portugal*, 123–124; Subrahmanyam, *Career and Legend of Vasco da Gama*, 139–145.

7. Subrahmanyam, *Career and Legend of Vasco da Gama*, 150–154 and 161.

8. I draw heavily on this paragraph on Disney, *History of Portugal*, 122–125.

9. Vallavanthara, *India in 1500 AD*, 62–63.

10. On the Estado da India as an "empire," see Subrahmanyam, "Written on Water."

11. Disney, *History of Portugal*, 129–130.

12. Disney, *History of Portugal*, 150.

13. Pescatello, "African Presence in Portuguese India," 38 (wine).

14. Pescatello, "African Presence in Portuguese India," 37–41.

15. Mir, Ahanger, and Agarwal, "Marigold," 310.

16. Disney, *History of Portugal*, 130.

17. Quoted in Robinson, "Cross," 94.

18. Disney, *History of Portugal*, 133–134.

19. Disney, *History of Portugal*, 165.

20. Quoted in Saraiva, *Marrano Factory*, 348.

21. Saraiva, *Marrano Factory*, appendix 4.

22. Chakravarti, *Empire of Apostles* (on *accommodatio*).

23. da Costa, "Introduction."

24. Katz, "South Asian Judaisms" (Jewish communities); Arrizabalaga, "Garcia de Orta," 15–16 (quote).

25. Cagle, "Cultures of Inquiry," 107; da Costa, "Introduction," 4 (first printing press). On the text, see Zupanov, "Garcia de Orta's *Coloquios*."

26. Pearson, "Locating Garcia de Orta," 44.

27. Arrizabalaga, "Garcia de Orta," 19; Saraiva, *Marrano Factory*, 346–347n3.
28. Hawley in Hawley and Juergensmeyer, *Songs of the Saints*, 9–11 (on Ravidas).
29. Kabir, *Kabir Granthavali*, 17.10 (my translation).
30. Kabir, *Bijak*, 69–70 (Hess and Singh's translation).
31. Hawley and Juergensmeyer, *Songs of the Saints*, 25 (Hawley and Juergensmeyer's translation).
32. Burchett, *Genealogy of Devotion*, chap. 5.
33. Discussed and quoted in Burchett, *Genealogy of Devotion*, 189–190.
34. Quoted in Hawley, *Three Bhakti Voices*, 275 (Hawley's translation).
35. Note some variants of this story as per Hawley, *Three Bhakti Voices*, 322–323.
36. Moosvi, "World of Labour," 261; Abdul Haqq Muhaddis was allegedly reporting on an earlier conversation between his father and grandfather.
37. Kabir, *Bijak*, 42–43 (Hess and Singh's translation).
38. Ravidas in Hawley and Juergensmeyer, *Songs of the Saints*, 25 (Hawley and Juergensmeyer's translation).
39. Mirabai quoted in Hawley, *Three Bhakti Voices*, 105 (Hawley's translation).
40. Hawley, *Three Bhakti Voices*, 128.
41. Quoted in Hawley, *Three Bhakti Voices*, 126 (Hawley's translation).
42. Hawley in Hawley and Juergensmeyer, *Songs of the Saints*, 119–122.
43. On Nanak's hagiography, see Singh, "Life of the Puratan Janamsakhi."
44. McLeod, *B40 Janam-Sakhi*, 21 (McLeod's translation).
45. See accounts based on the *Janamsakhi*s in Shackle and Mandair, introduction to *Teachings of the Sikh Gurus*, xiii–xiv; Singh, *Sikhism*, 4–7.
46. On nirgun poets and their criticisms of society, see Lorenzen, *Praises to a Formless God*.
47. Shackle and Mandair, introduction to *Teachings of the Sikh Gurus*, xv; I am indebted to Sheldon Pollock for the translation of "guru" as "heavyweight."
48. Mann, *Making of Sikh Scripture*, chaps. 4–5, on Arjan's compilation and the subsequent history of editing the Adi Granth.
49. Balabanlilar, *Emperor Jahangir*, 56; Fenech, "Martyrdom and the Sikh Tradition," 629; Jahangir, *Jahangirnama*, 59.
50. Fenech and McLeod, *Historical Dictionary of Sikhism*, 6.
51. Fenech, "Martyrdom and the Sikh Tradition."
52. Singh, "Sikh Art," 423.
53. Singh, *Verses of the Sikh Gurus*, 51 (Singh's translation; this is known as the *mul mantar*). Sikhs use many names for God, with *vahiguru* being the most common today.
54. Singh, "Guru Granth Sahib," 127.
55. Asani, "At the Crossroads," 623–624; Shackle and Moir, *Ismaili Hymns*, chap. 3.
56. Quoted in Cole, "Sikh Interactions with Other Religions," 253.
57. Singh, *Sikhism*, xv.
58. Singh, *Sikhism*, 17.
59. Dhavan, *When Sparrows Became Hawks*.
60. Dale, *Garden of the Eight Paradises*.
61. Babur, *Baburnama*, 285 (Thackston's translation).
62. It is generally scorching hot in April around Delhi, even allowing for some temperature variation as per the so-called Little Ice Age 1550–1850 that was characterized by monsoon failures in South Asia (Ray, *Climate Change*, 14–16).
63. Babur, *Baburnama*, 360 (Thackston's translation).
64. Babur, *Baburnama*, 343 (Thackston's translation).
65. Kolff, *Naukar, Rajput and Sepoy*, chap. 2.
66. *Humayunnama* of Gulbadan Begum in Thackston, *Three Memoirs of Homayun*, 36–37.
67. Wink, *Akbar*, 6–7.
68. Fisher, *Short History of the Mughal Empire*, 65.
69. Fisher, *Short History of the Mughal Empire*, 65.
70. Wink, *Akbar*, 65.

71. Behl, *Love's Subtle Magic*, chap. 3.

72. Chandra, *Medieval India*, 89–90.

73. Eaton, *India in the Persianate Age*, 135.

74. Quoted in Behl, *Love's Subtle Magic* (Behl's translation), 214. On *Padmavat*, see also de Bruijn, *Ruby in the Dust*.

75. Kapadia, *Praise of Kings*, chap. 4.

76. Kolff, *Naukar, Rajput and Sepoy*, chap. 3 (on the Rajput labor market).

77. Richards, *Mughal Empire*, 12.

13. ORDINARY AND EXTRAORDINARY LIVES IN EARLY MODERN INDIA

1. Quoted in Sharma, "Nizamshahi Persianate Garden," 160 (my translation).

2. Abul Fazl, *History of Akbar*, 1:80–145; Orthmann, "Circular Motions," 104–105.

3. Abul Fazl, *History of Akbar*, 1:93 (Thackston's translation).

4. Abul Fazl, *History of Akbar*, 1:93 (Thackston's translation); on the Brahmin astrologer, known by title as *jotik rai* from Sanskrit *jyotisharaja*, see Minkowski, "Learned Brahmins."

5. Baqir, *Advice on the Art of Governance*, 48–49 (Alvi's translation).

6. On "Hindustan" as Mughal north India, see Sohoni, *Architecture of a Deccan Sultanate*, 5; cf. Asif, *Loss of Hindustan*.

7. Joffee, "Art, Architecture and Politics in Mewar," 34–37; Talbot, "Mewar Court's Construction of History," 23.

8. On Humayun, see Richards, *Mughal Empire*, 20.

9. On the Mughal mansabdar system, see Fisher, *Short History of the Mughal Empire*, 100–107 (on its messiness in practice, see Chatterjee, *Negotiating Mughal Law*, 118–120).

10. Khan, *Kachhwahas*, 7.

11. Khan, *Kachhwahas*, 11–12.

12. Richards, *Mughal Empire*, 21.

13. *Tabaqat-i Akbari* quoted in Nath, *Climate of Conquest*, 40.

14. Nath, *Climate of Conquest*, 46; Talbot, "Justifying Defeat," 338.

15. Kolff, *Naukar, Rajput and Sepoy*, 10 (number 30,000); Richards, *Mughal Empire*, 26 (Chittor's fall). I am indebted to Roy Fischel for the phrase "shock and awe" to describe Mughal actions at Chittor.

16. Zaman, "Mughal Conquest of Chittor," 293 (Zaman's translation).

17. Talbot, "Justifying Defeat," 338–339 (Ranthambhor); Nath, *Climate of Conquest*, 31 (Gujarat).

18. Talbot, "Mewar Court's Construction of History," 22.

19. On Hindus reading religious works in Persian, see Gandhi, *Emperor Who Never Was*, 249–250.

20. Wade, *Imaging Sound*, 232–233n22.

21. Richards, *Mughal Empire*, 21; Sarkar, *History of Jaipur*, 12.

22. Richards, *Mughal Empire*, 23.

23. Padmasagara, *Jagadgurukavya*, v. 88; also translated in Truschke, *Language of History*, 233. The gender dynamics of Rajput-Mughal unions were never reversed, and so Mughal princesses did not wed Rajput kings.

24. Lal, *Domesticity and Power*, 208–213.

25. Asher, "Architecture of Raja Man Singh," 184.

26. The imperial connections mentioned in this paragraph and more are outlined in Asher, "Kacchavaha Pride and Prestige," and Asher, "Architecture of Raja Man Singh."

27. Asher, "Architecture of Raja Man Singh," 183–184 (mansabdar); Asher, "Mapping Hindu-Muslim Identities," 123 (Akbar's support).

28. Quoted in Bahura, "Sri Govinda Gatha," 201 (my translation).

29. Ray, *Climate Change*, 75–76 on visual similarities.

30. This paragraph draws on Rezavi, *Fathpur Sikri Revisited*, chaps. 2 and 11.

31. Victoria and Albert Museum IS.2:91–1896 and IS.2:86–1896.

32. Eaton, "Introduction," 11–12; Eaton notes that banning slaves was primarily a practical (not an ethical) move, designed to prevent nobles from "building up independent power bases" of captured fighters (12).

33. Moosvi, *World of Labour*, 251.

34. Quoted in translation in Nath, *Climate of Conquest*, 125.

35. Chowdhury, "Imperial Mughal Tent," 673.

36. Nath, *Climate of Conquest*, 125, quoting Abul Fazl.

37. Dale, "Safavid Poet," 200; Sharma, *Mughal Arcadia*, 20–27.

38. Quoted in Sharma, *Mughal Arcadia*, 22 (Sharma's translation).

39. Sharma, *Mughal Arcadia*, 193 ("brain drain").

40. Quoted in Sharma, *Mughal Arcadia*, 31–32 (Sharma's translation).

41. Lefevre, "Court of 'Abd-ur-Rahim"; Naik, *'Abdu'r-Rahim*. On Rahim's Hindi poetry, see Busch, "Hidden in Plain View," 282–284, and Busch, "Riti and Register," 108–114.

42. Yucesoy, "Translation as Self-Consciousness," 523.

43. The *Ain-i Akbari* is the third volume of the *Akbarnama*.

44. Gandhi, *Emperor Who Never Was*, chap. 8 (Upanishads); Gandhi, "Prince and the *Muvahhid*" (on Dara Shukoh's engagements with Hindu ideas more broadly).

45. Badauni, *Muntakhab al-Tavarikh*, 2:326 (my translation); also translated in Truschke, "Padshah like Manu," 14. In contrast, Abul Fazl was a laudatory historian (Hardy, "Abul Fazl's Portrait").

46. Truschke, *Culture of Encounters*, 123–125.

47. Krishnadasa, *Parasiprakasha*, vv. 2–4; translated in Truschke, *Culture of Encounters*, 39–40.

48. Rice, "Workshop as Network" (Mughal artistic collaboration); Verma, *Mughal Painters*, 25 (scarce female Mughal artists).

49. Adamjee and Truschke, "Reimagining the 'Idol Temple of Hindustan,'" 152–153 (on both examples).

50. Seyller, *Workshop and Patron*.

51. Joffee, "Art, Architecture and Politics in Mewar," 66–77.

52. The Mewar Ramayana manuscript is dispersed. It was digitally unified but, as of the time of writing (summer 2024), remains inaccessible due to a 2023 cyber-attack on the British Library; it is unclear when or if the digitally unified manuscript will be available again, and it serves as a grim reminder that digital resources, too, are often ephemeral.

53. Quoted in Alam and Subrahmanyam, "Love, Passion and Reason," 111 (Alam and Subrahmanyam's translation).

54. Mujtabai, *Aspects of Hindu Muslim Cultural Relations*, 68–71.

55. Phillips, "Garden of Endless Blossoms" (Ramayana); Alam and Subrahmanyam, *Writing the Mughal World*, chap. 5 (*Nal-Daman*).

56. Gandhi, *Emperor Who Never Was*, 251.

57. Alam, "Culture and Politics of Persian," 162–163.

58. Abul Fazl's preface in *Razmnama*, 1:xviii; relevant portion translated in Ernst, "Muslim Studies of Hinduism?" 181.

59. O'Hanlon, "Kingdom, Household and Body" (concentrated power in his person).

60. Richards, *Mughal Empire*, 30–31; on Sufi-royal connections and contestations, see Alam, *Languages of Political Islam*.

61. Moin, *Millennial Sovereign*, 132–146.

62. Richards, *Mughal Empire*, 72 (on ambiguous meaning).

63. Lefevre, "Din-i Ilahi," 82–83; the din-i ilahi remains widely misunderstood and mischaracterized in modern times. It was not a new religion, and indeed Akbar never renounced Islam. Rather, the din-i ilahi was a small-scale discipleship program with a handful of elite followers.

64. Maclagan, "Jesuit Missions to the Emperor Akbar."

65. Truschke, *Culture of Encounters*, 174–180.

66. Devavimala, *Hirasaubhagya* (ca. 1590–1610), 13.137–151 (my translation; also in Truschke, *Language of History*, 235–236). Also see Dundas's translation in "Jain Perceptions of Islam," 38–39.

67. The phrase is from the seventeenth-century *Rajavacakamu* (Wagoner, *Tidings of the King*, 113; Wagoner's translation).

68. Eaton, *India in the Persianate Age*, 167.

69. Fischel, *Local States in an Imperial World*, 14 (pp. 166–175 on Vijayanagara inspiration).

70. Asif, *Loss of Hindustan*, chap. 1.

71. Overton, "Farrukh Husayn."

72. Skelton, "Farrukh Beg," 13.

73. Overton, "Book Culture," 116.

74. Fischel, *Local States in an Imperial World*, 165.

75. Asad Beg Qazvini, *Waqai*, 82 (my translation).

76. Hutton and Tucker, "Dutch Artist in Bijapur," 230n23.

77. Asad Beg Qazvini, *Waqai*, 83 (my translation).

78. Overton, "Vida de Jacques de Coutre," 234–235.

79. Hutton, *Art of the Court of Bijapur*, 107–108, citing Shirazi.

80. Hutton, *Art of the Court of Bijapur*, 116–117; Hutton and Tucker, "Dutch Artist in Bijapur," 205.

81. Koch, "Solomonic Angels."

82. Hutton and Tucker, "Dutch Artist in Bijapur," 216.

83. *Nava-rasa* in Sanskrit. Fischel, *Local States in an Imperial World*, 164; Hutton, *Art of the Court of Bijapur*, 110 (quoting Zuhuri).

84. Hutton and Tucker, "Dutch Artist in Bijapur," 212–213.

85. Joshi, "Asad Beg's Mission to Bijapur," 188.

86. On Gisu Daraz, see Alam and Subrahmanyam, *Indo-Persian Travels*, 48–54; Eaton, "Gisu-Daraz."

87. Quoted in translation in Hutton, *Art of the Court of Bijapur*, 70.

88. Sharma, "Forging a Canon," 414n1.

89. Ibrahim Adil Shah II, *Kitab-i-Nauras*, 140 (Ahmad's translation); Haidar, "*Kitab-i Nauras*," 34.

90. Eaton, "Rise and Fall of Military Slavery," 116.

91. Czekalska and Kuczkiewicz-Fras, "Africans in India," 198–201 (Bengal's Habshi dynasty).

92. Eaton, "Rise and Fall of Military Slavery," 125.

93. Eaton, *Social History of the Deccan*, 122–123.

94. Quoted in Eaton, "Rise and Fall of Military Slavery," 127.

95. Also called Khadki.

96. I draw heavily in this paragraph on Mubayi, "Malik Ambar ki Pipeline."

97. For Gabriel's life, see Chakravarti, "Mapping 'Gabriel,'" and Salvadore, "Between the Red Sea Slave Trade."

98. Alam and Subrahmanyam, *Indo-Persian Travels*, 85.

99. Chakravarti, "Mapping 'Gabriel,'" 29.

100. Banarasidas, *Ardhakathanaka*, 165–167 (Lal's translation).

101. Faruqui, *Princes of the Mughal Empire*.

14. RELIGIOUS COMMUNITIES AND ELITE CULTURE, 1600–1650

1. Quoted in Kinra, *Writing Self*, 222 (my translation).

2. Berkwitz, *Buddhist Poetry and Colonialism*, 1.

3. Berkwitz, *Buddhist Poetry and Colonialism*, 135 and 266n22.

4. Quoted in Roberts, *Caste Conflict*, 31.

5. Bhuvanekabahu's letters in de Silva, *Portuguese Encounters with Sri Lanka*, 54–55 and 57–58.

6. de Silva, *Portuguese Encounters with Sri Lanka*, 73.

7. Berkwitz, *Buddhist Poetry and Colonialism*, 27.

8. Berkwitz, *Buddhist Poetry and Colonialism*, 2.
9. Quoted in Berkwitz, *Buddhist Poetry and Colonialism*, 154 (Berkwitz's translation).
10. For an overview of this scholarship, see Berkwitz, *Buddhist Poetry and Colonialism*, 5–7; Blackburn analyzes such processes during British colonialism in Sri Lanka (*Locations of Buddhism*).
11. Raymond, "Religious and Scholarly Exchanges," 94–95.
12. Charney, "Where Jambudipa and Islamdom Converged," 87–92.
13. Geiger and Rickmers, *Culavamsa*, 94.15–21; Raymond, "Religious and Scholarly Exchanges," 96.
14. Although, on occasion, Arakan declined such requests (Charney, "Where Jambudipa and Islamdom Converged," 212).
15. Raymond, "Religious and Scholarly Exchanges," 97.
16. Fisher, "Islam in Mughal India." Note that much modern disinformation concerns the Mughals and conversion, falsely attributing large-scale, state-sponsored conversion efforts to this land-based empire. Such narratives are best understood as part of modern Hindu nationalist discourse, growing out of Hindutva reliance on British colonial ideas about religious divisions in South Asian history as well as deep Islamophobia (see chaps. 17, 21, and 24).
17. Gommans, *Mughal Warfare*, 170–179.
18. Prakash, *Dutch East India Company*, 234–248.
19. Eaton, *Rise of Islam*, 97.
20. Menon and Uzramma, *Frayed History*, 10.
21. Tavernier, *Travels in India*, 2:7.
22. The story dates back, at least, to 1772 (Bolts, *Considerations on India Affairs*, 206n).
23. Houghteling, *Art of Cloth*, 46 (46–47 on the process of creating Dacca muslin).
24. Eaton, *Rise of Islam*, 203.
25. Moosvi, "Silver Influx," 79–80.
26. Benke, "Sudracarasiromani of Krsna Sesa," 233–244, drawing on D. D. Kosambi, R. S. Sharma, Irfan Habib, and others.
27. Eaton, *Rise of Islam*, xxv; on these processes, see also, more recently, Eaton, *India in the Persianate Age*, 361–368.
28. Quoted in translation in Subrahmanyam, "Imarat and Tijarat," 764.
29. Mehta, *Indian Merchants*, 28.
30. Thevenot in Sen, *Indian Travels*, 22.
31. Akhtar, "Mercantile and Financial Operations of Virji Vora," 316–317; Gopal, *Jains in India*, 148.
32. Commissariat, "Imperial Mughal Farmans," 12.
33. Jain, "Jain Elites," 221.
34. Speziale, "Introduction," 12 (animal hospitals).
35. Sastri, *Ancient Vijnaptipatras*, 19–42.
36. Dundas, *History, Scripture and Controversy*, 24, citing Meghavijaya's *Digvijayamahakavya*.
37. Desai, *Banaras Reconstructed*, 3.
38. Narayan, *Ramayana*.
39. Quoted in Lutgendorf, *Life of a Text*, 105 (Lutgendorf's translation).
40. Richman, *Ramayana Stories in Modern South India*, 175.
41. Lutgendorf, *Life of a Text*, 7 and 344–346; on shadow Sita being unknown in Valmiki, see Goldman and Goldman, introduction to *Ramayana of Valmiki*, 6:104.
42. P. L. Vaidya, who critically edited book 6 of Valmiki's Ramayana, argued that the agnipariksha was Valmiki's innovation (6:xxxvi). In any case, it did not fully assuage concerns, and so subsequent authors introduced the narrative of Rama abandoning pregnant Sita in the forest and the suggestion of a second fire test (in book 7).
43. Lutgendorf, *Life of a Text*, 396–397; for narrative context, see Lutgendorf, "Book Five: Sundar Kand," 179–180.
44. Lutgendorf, "Secret Life of Ramcandra of Ayodhya," in Richman, *Many Ramayanas*, 217.
45. Lutgendorf, *Life of a Text*, 9; on Kaithi, see de Bruijn, *Ruby in the Dust*, 77.
46. Lutgendorf, *Life of a Text*, 254.

47. E.g., there are Sanskrit plays based on the Ramayana, such as by Bhavabhuti (*Rama's Last Act*, eighth century); also note references to a Nepali performance of a Ramayana in the fourteenth century (Formigatti, "Towards a Cultural History of Nepal," 60).

48. Truschke, "Silencing Sita."

49. O'Hanlon, "Speaking from Siva's Temple," 266.

50. Wright, "History in the Abstract," 1044n9.

51. O'Hanlon and Minkowski, "What Makes People Who They Are?"

52. Wright, "History in the Abstract," 1055–1062, citing the *Brahmanatvavada*.

53. O'Halnon, "Letters Home," 217–218.

54. Adapted from translation in Wright, "History in the Abstract," 1048; Sanskrit printed in Gode, "Some New Evidence Regarding Devabhatta Mahasabde," 133–134.

55. Busch, *Poetry of Kings*, 148–151 (dhrupads); Gandhi, "Prince and the *Muvahhid*," 81–82 (*Yogavasishtha*).

56. The *Kavindrachandrodaya* (Sanskrit) and *Kavindrachandrika* (Hindi). Gode, *Studies in Indian Literary History*, 2:364–379; Truschke, "Contested History."

57. Pollock, "Death of Sanskrit," 407–408; Bernier, *Travels*, 2:41 ("Athens of India").

58. Minkowski, "Nilakantha's Mahabharata."

59. Pollock, "Languages of Science," 34.

60. Truschke, "Defining the Other," 645–655.

61. Pollock, "Death of Sanskrit," 409.

62. Athavale, "New Light"; Pollock, "Sanskrit Literary Culture," 97–98.

63. Quoted in Pollock, "Death of Sanskrit," 409 (Pollock's translation).

64. Bronkhorst, "Bhattoji Diksita on Sphota," 15.

65. E.g., see the account of stressing out a turkey by taking it around Manhattan (Patricia Marx, "Pets Allowed," *New Yorker*, October 13, 2014, https://www.newyorker.com/magazine/2014/10/20/pets-allowed).

66. Jahangir, *Jahangirnama*, 280 (Thackston's translation).

67. The painting is held today in the Smithsonian's Freer Gallery (F1945.9a).

68. Moosvi, "Mughal Encounter with Vedanta," 20.

69. Jahangir, *Jahangirnama*, 209 (Thackston's translation).

70. Asher, "Appropriating the Past," 4–8. Allahabad is where three rivers are believed to converge: Ganges, Yamuna, and (the invisible) Saraswati. On other places on which Jahangir had his Timurid lineage carved, see Lefevre, *Consolidating Empire*, 106–107.

71. Findly, *Nur Jahan*, 220.

72. Jahangir, *Jahangirnama*, 260 (Thackston's translation).

73. Loomba, "Of Gifts, Ambassadors, and Copy-cats," 41–46. Roe was probably the source of the painting of King James referenced earlier in this paragraph (Chida-Razvi, "Perception of Reception," 281–282).

74. Foster, *Embassy of Sir Thomas Roe*, 2:322–323, and Terry quoted in 2:322–323n3.

75. Chida-Razvi, "Perception of Reception," 275–276 (Roe on gifts).

76. Quoted in translation in Subrahmanyam, "Taking Stock of the Franks," 69; Luard and Hosten, *Travels of Fray Sebastien Manrique*, 2:219 (I adapt from both translations).

77. Schrader, *Rembrandt and the Inspiration of India*; also note other European artists, such as Willem Schellinks (d. 1678) and Johann Melchior Dinglinger (d. 1731) who created art featuring the Mughals (Koch, *Complete Taj Mahal*, 14–15).

78. Findly, *Nur Jahan*, 252–257; Sharma, *Mughal Arcadia*, 81–82.

79. Jahangir, *Jahangirnama*, 332 (Thackston's translation).

80. Moosvi, "World of Labour," 251.

81. Kaw, "Famines in Kashmir," 59–60.

82. Kinra, *Writing Self*, 138 (Kinra's translation lightly adapted).

83. Quoted in Kinra, *Writing Self*, 137, and Sharma, *Mughal Arcadia*, 107.

84. Kinra, *Writing Self*, 127 (ten million); Koch, *Complete Taj Mahal*, 100 (five million).

85. Lefevre, *Consolidating Empire*, 106 (Timur Ruby and Jahangir); the Timur Ruby is actually a red spinel.

86. Bokhari, "'Light' of the Timuria."

87. Asher, *Architecture of Mughal India*, 225–226.

88. Koch, *Complete Taj Mahal*, 18.

89. I draw in this paragraph and the next from Koch, *Complete Taj Mahal*.

90. An oft-repeated apocryphal story is that Shah Jahan cut off the hands of the Taj Mahal's builders so that they could never again construct such a wonder. This false story is not unique to the Taj and pops up as a recurrent motif concerning famous buildings across Asia and Europe (Koch, *Complete Taj Mahal*, 250).

91. Koch, *Complete Taj Mahal*, 92.

92. Translated in Koch, *Complete Taj Mahal*, 224–228.

93. Fisher, *Short History of the Mughal Empire*, 168.

94. Quoted in Koch, *Complete Taj Mahal*, 83 (Koch's translation).

95. Kinra, *Writing Self*, 54–59. Today, visitors are greeted by expansive lawns throughout the Taj Mahal complex, a hangover of British colonial tastes.

96. Quoted in Kinra, *Writing Self*, 55 (Kinra's translation).

97. The final resting places of the first six Mughal kings are as follows: Babur in Kabul, Humayun in Delhi, Akbar in Agra, Jahangir in Lahore, Shah Jahan in Agra, and Aurangzeb Alamgir in Khuldabad, Maharashtra.

98. Koch methodically catalogs Agra as it appeared in the seventeenth century versus now (*Complete Taj Mahal*, chap. 1).

99. On Hindu nationalist "conspiratorial claims" that the Taj Mahal is a Shiva temple, see Kumar, "Manipulated Facts," 33–36, and Tillotson, *Taj Mahal*, 112–115.

100. Tillotson, *Taj Mahal*, 114.

101. Jason Burke, "Taj Mahal Threatened by Polluted Air and Water," *Guardian*, December 2, 2010, https://www.theguardian.com/world/2010/dec/02/taj-mahal-threatened-pollution.

15. AURANGZEB'S EMPIRE AND TWO SHUDRA LINEAGES

1. Rao and Shulman, *Classical Telugu Poetry*, 243 (Rao and Shulman's translation).

2. Habib, "Postal Communications in Mughal India," 239.

3. Fisher, *Short History of the Mughal Empire*, 1; Richards, *Mughal Empire*, 1.

4. Habib, "Population," 171.

5. Specialists familiar with Aurangzeb Alamgir will notice that I leave out many details of Aurangzeb as an individual. I do this pursuant to my goal of avoiding Great Man history (and, frankly, if there is a criticism to be made of this chapter on that score, it is that I do not avoid that approach enough). Some non-specialists may be familiar with mythologies of Aurangzeb, which are exceedingly common today and driven by Hindu nationalist ideology. I briefly mention misleading views of Aurangzeb later in the book, when they arose in history (chapter 18), but otherwise I stick to the facts. I offer more detail on Hindu nationalism and its extreme Islamophobia at several points (especially chapters 21, 23, and 24).

6. Quoted in Mikkelson, "Aurangzeb and Dara Shukuh's Struggle," 246 (Mikkelson's translation).

7. Quoted in Eaton, *India in the Persianate Age*, 301; the expression also exists in the variants *ya takht ya tabut* (Manucci, *Storia do Mogor*, 1:242) and *takht ast ya takhta* (Khafi Khan, *Muntakhab al-Lubab*, 2:596).

8. Choudhury, "Eventful Politics of Difference," 279–281.

9. All Mughal sources agree on the beheading, but only some mention that Aurangzeb first accused Dara Shukoh of apostasy.

10. Faruqui, *Princes of the Mughal Empire*, 252.

11. Jain, "Piety, Laity and Royalty," 86–87.

12. Bilgrami, "Shaykh 'Abd al-Wahhab," 101–102; Husain, *Structure of Politics under Aurangzeb*, 31.

13. For recent scholarly overviews of Aurangzeb, see Eaton, *India in the Persianate Age*, chap. 7; Truschke, *Aurangzeb*.

14. Truschke, *Aurangzeb*, 72–74; e.g., see the discussion of people stealing wood during Holi in Lokhandwala, *Mirat-i-Ahmadi*, 233.

15. Rezavi, *Fathpur Sikri Revisited*, 40 (prostitutes); Wink, *Akbar*, 58 (alcohol and gambling, citing Qandahari).

16. Rezavi, "Organization of Education," 393–394.

17. Saqi Mustad Khan, *Maasir-i-'Alamgiri*, 13–14 (Sarkar's translation lightly adapted). On this history, see Kulke, "Mughal Munsi at Work."

18. Bhimsen, *Tarikh-i-Dilkasha*, 215.

19. Guenther, "Hanafi *Fiqh* in Mughal India"; Khalfaoui, "al-Fatawa l-'Alamgiriyya."

20. Asher, *Architecture of Mughal India*, 257–260.

21. Brown, "Did Aurangzeb Ban Music?," 88–89; Wade, *Imaging Sound*, 187 (musicians).

22. Brown, "Did Aurangzeb Ban Music?," 94.

23. Richards, *Mughal Administration in Golconda*, 51.

24. Sarkar, *History of Aurangzib*, 4:366.

25. Truschke, *Aurangzeb*, 70.

26. Gommans, *Mughal Warfare*, 193.

27. Bhimsen, *Tarikh-i-Dilkusha*, 223 (Sarkar's translation).

28. Bhimsen, *Tarikh-i-Dilkusha*, 231; Manucci, *Storia do Mogor*, 2:415.

29. Careri in Sen, *Indian Travels*, 216; Bilimoria, *Ruka'at-i-Alamgiri*, 26–27.

30. Quoted in translation in in Ali, *Mughal Nobility under Aurangzeb*, 92.

31. Truschke, "Hindu," 256–260.

32. Quoted in Flynn, "English Translation of the Adab-i-'Alamgiri," 200 (Flynn's translation); see also Shahnavaz Khan, *Maasir al-Umara*, 1:807; Brown, "Did Aurangzeb Ban Music?," 82–85.

33. Bilimoria, *Ruka'at-i-Alamgiri*, 74.

34. Truschke, *Aurangzeb*, 57–58.

35. Quotation from *Mirat al-Muluk*, an early eighteenth-century Sufi-authored work in Askari, "Mirat-ul-Muluk," 34.

36. Hallissey, *Rajput Rebellion*.

37. Ali, *Mughal Nobility under Aurangzeb*, 31–32.

38. Chandraman's ca. 1690s *Nargisistan* and Amar Singh's 1705 *Amar Prakash*.

39. Pillai, "Remembering and Removing Aurangzeb," 357.

40. Eaton, "Temple Desecration and Indo-Muslim States," 71 (Eaton's translation). The same order prohibited further temple building in Benares, which some have misunderstood as applying to the entire empire. It is unclear to me whether this was enforced in Benares.

41. Truschke, *Aurangzeb*, 78–83; Goswamy and Grewal, *Mughals and the Jogis*.

42. Quoted in Ernst, "Admiring the Work of the Ancients," 109.

43. Eaton, "Temple Desecration and Indo-Muslim States," 74–75.

44. Pauwels, "Tale of Two Temples," 288–290.

45. E.g., Saqi Mustad Khan's *Maasir-i-'Alamgiri*.

46. Quoted in Talbot, "Poetic Record," 472 (Talbot's translation lightly adapted).

47. In Aurangzeb's empire, Rajput and Maratha state officials and Brahmin religious leaders were exempt from the jizya; Jains, Sikhs, and others were required to pay.

48. Ali, *Mughal India*, 207; Hallissey, *Rajput Rebellion*, 87–88.

49. Letter printed in Sarkar, *History of Aurangzib*, 3:286–290.

50. On Mughal *sulh-i kull*, se Kinra, "Revisiting the History and Historiography of Mughal Pluralism."

51. Chandra, *Mughal Religious Policies*, 182.

52. Sheikh, "Aurangzeb as Seen from Gujarat," 570–571. For a brief overview of the Satnamis in the context of discussing Hinduism, see Doniger, *Hindus*, 633.

53. Fisher, *Short History of the Mughal Empire*, 195.

54. Shackle and Mandair, *Teachings of the Sikh Gurus*, 141 (Shackle and Mandair's translation).
55. Farman quoted in Pinch, *Warrior Ascetics*, 72.
56. Sheikh, "Aurangzeb as Seen from Gujarat," 569.
57. Sarkar, *Anecdotes of Aurangzib*, 99 (adapted from Sarkar's translation).
58. Gordon, *Marathas*, 41–44; Guha, "Bad Language and Good Language," 56–57.
59. Benke, "Sudracarasiromani of Krsna Sesa," 239.
60. Laine, "*dharma* of Islam," 302.
61. Gordon, *Marathas*, 67–68.
62. Thevenot in Sen, *Indian Travels*, 41.
63. Gordon, *Marathas*, 71–75.
64. Jasper, "Commemorating Shivaji," 50.
65. Jasper, "Commemorating Shivaji," 50.
66. Vajpeyi, "History of Caste," 304.
67. Bendrey, *Coronation of Shivaji*.
68. For a rare, mythological exception, see Sathaye, *Crossing the Lines of Caste* on Vishvamitra.
69. Bendrey, *Coronation of Shivaji*, 51.
70. Vajpeyi, "Excavating Identity," 242–243.
71. Sarkar, *House of Shivaji*, 143.
72. Chandra, "Social Background," 215–216.
73. On this and other modern remembrances of Shivaji, see Jasper, "Commemorating Shivaji," and Laine, *Shivaji*.
74. Cf. Dirks, *Hollow Crown*, which distinguishes kingship and purity concerns regarding caste.
75. Vajpeyi, "Excavating Identity."
76. Vajpeyi, "Excavating Identity," 244 (on early modern Brahmins benefiting financially from Shudras through ritual performances more generally, see Benke, "Sudracarasiromani of Krsna Sesa," 257).
77. Bendrey, *Coronation of Shivaji*, 42–46.
78. Vajpeyi, "Excavating Identity," 247, 247n9.
79. Burchett, *Genealogy of Devotion*, 30–31; Fisher, *Hindu Pluralism*, 36.
80. Laine in Paramananda, *Epic of Shivaji*, 24–25; Sardesai, *New History of the Marathas*, 1:224–225; Salomon, "Sivarajarajyabhisekakalpataru," 70–89.
81. Bendrey, *Coronation of Shivaji*, 53–54.
82. Salomon, "Sivarajarajyabhisekakalpataru," 70–71.
83. Guha, "Bad Language and Good Language," 60–62; Truschke, "Defining the Other," 660–661.
84. The text is better known as *Shivabharata*.
85. Gordon, *Marathas*, 66.
86. Paramananda, *Epic of Shivaji*, 262.
87. Paramananda, *Suryavamsha* 18.21 (my translation).
88. Karashima, *Concise History of South India*, 227–228. Ekoji ended Nayaka rule in Thanjavur in the 1670s, and the Jinji Nayakas were dominated by Bijapur and Golconda earlier.
89. Rao, Shulman, and Subrahmanyam, *Symbols of Substance*, 75 (Rao, Shulman, and Subrahmanyam's translation).
90. Rao, Shulman, and Subrahmanyam, *Symbols of Substance*, 75 (Rao, Shulman, and Subrahmanyam's translation).
91. Eaton, *India in the Persianate Age*, 178; Rao, Shulman, and Subrahmanyam, *Symbols of Substance*, 67–70.
92. Rao, Shulman, and Subrahmanyam, *Symbols of Substance*, 87.
93. Rao, Shulman, and Subrahmanyam, *Symbols of Substance*, 90 (Catholic), and Bayly, "Islam in Southern India," 54 (Sufi dargahs).
94. Fisher, *Hindu Pluralism*, 179.
95. Hudson, "Siva, Minaksi, Vishnu," 111.
96. Bronner and Shulman, "Cloud Turned Goose," 8 (Bronner and Shulman's translation).

97. Translation adapted from Sanderson, "Saiva Age," 289n690 (see also quotations in 289n689).

98. Wagoner, *Tidings of the King*, 82 (see also Wagoner's comments in 186n23).

99. Benke, "Sudracarasiromani of Krsna Sesa," 241–249 (see pp. 11–16 for a list of texts).

100. Benke, "Sudracarasiromani of Krsna Sesa," 256.

101. Rao and Shulman, *Classical Telugu Poetry*, 257; Subrahmanyam, "Hearing Voices," 84.

102. Rao and Shulman, *Classical Telugu Poetry*, 260.

103. Rao and Shulman, *Classical Telugu Poetry*, 264–265 (Rao and Shulman's translation).

104. Rao and Shulman, *Classical Telugu Poetry*, 267 (Rao and Shulman's translation).

105. Still, courtesans, known as *devadasis*, occupied a morally ambiguous place in Nayaka society (Soneji, *Unfinished Gestures*, 3).

106. Rao and Shulman, *Classical Telugu Poetry*, 273; Subrahmanyam, "Hearing Voices," 89.

107. Rao and Shulman, *Classical Telugu Poetry*, 275 (Rao and Shulman's translation).

108. Rao and Shulman, *Classical Telugu Poetry*, 277 (Rao and Shulman's translation).

109. Busch, "Classical Past," 658–659 (Busch's translation).

110. Guha, *Beyond Caste*, 25.

111. Katz, "South Asian Judaisms," 149–150.

16. REGIONAL FLOURISHING, 1720–1780

1. Quoted in Cherian, *Merchants of Virtue*, 144 (Cherian's translation).

2. Cherian, *Merchants of Virtue*, 144–146.

3. Kadam, "Institution of Marriage," 347.

4. Chandra, *Parties and Politics*.

5. Lakshmipati, *Nripatinitigarbhitavritta*, 31–32; see Truschke, *Language of History*, Appendix A.8 for a translation.

6. Alam, *Crisis of Empire*, xix–xx.

7. Irvine and Sarkar, *Later Mughals*, 257–263; Kaicker, *King and the People*, 256–290.

8. Chandra, *Parties and Politics*, 247–256; Fisher, *Short History of the Mughal Empire*, 216–217.

9. Kaicker, *King and the People*, 44.

10. Held at the Victoria and Albert Museum, IM.20-1919 (https://collections.vam.ac.uk/item/O81782/portrait-of-nadir-shah-painting/).

11. Sarkar, *Nadir Shah*, 67.

12. Ananda Ranga Pillai, *Private Diary*, 1:95.

13. Ananda Ranga Pillai, *Private Diary*, 1:94 (Price and Rangachari's translation).

14. E.g., Alam, *Crisis of Empire*, introduction; Bhargava, *Decline*; Chandra, *Parties and Politics*, introduction; Faruqui, *Princes of the Mughal Empire*, conclusion.

15. Mir, *Zikr-i Mir*, 70 (Naim's translation).

16. Keshavmurthy, *Persian Authorship*; Kovacs, "Challenges of and Strategies for Translating Indo-Persian Poetry."

17. Dudney, *India in the Persian World of Letters*, chap. 2.

18. Dudney, *India in the Persian World of Letters*, 35–37.

19. Dadlani and Sharma, "Beyond the Taj Mahal," 1065–1067.

20. Dallal, "Origins and Objectives of Islamic Revivalist Thought."

21. Eaton, *India in the Persianate Age*, 321–322.

22. Wilson, *India Conquered*, 59; on Janjira's rulers, see Jasdanwalla, "Invincible Fort."

23. Guha, "Maratha Empire."

24. Bayly, "Pre-history of 'Communalism,'" 181.

25. Chakravarti, "Wifehood," 6–7.

26. Kadam, "Institution of Marriage," 342.

27. Subrahmanyam, "Warfare and State Finance," 220–223.

28. Chitnis, *Nawabs of Savanur*, 84–85 and 174–176.

29. Ghosh, "Two Kings."

30. Faruqui, "Empire's End," 17–18; much of this paragraph draws on Faruqui's article.

31. Faruqui, "Empire's End," 28–32.

32. Several individuals are described in Kia, *Persianate Selves*, xv–xxii.

33. Johnson-Roerh, "Centering the *Charbagh*," 32 and 34–37. I draw on this article throughout this paragraph; note Johnson-Roerh's arguments, which I find compelling, against "Vedic design" in Jaipur.

34. Sachdev and Tillotson, *Building Jaipur*, 52.

35. Michell, "Jaipur," 78.

36. Johnson-Roerh, "Centering the *Charbagh*," 31–32.

37. Asher, "Mapping Hindu-Muslim Identities," 138–139.

38. Quoted in Gode, "Two Contemporary Tributes," 292, v. 197.

39. The *Kashikhanda* section of the *Skandapurana* was composed in the mid-second millennium CE, post-Ghurids (Dalmia, *Nationalization of Hindu Traditions*, 51); the *Kashirahasya* is among the latest puranas (Eck, "Survey of Sanskrit Sources," 85).

40. Asher, "Making Sense of Temples," 16–17.

41. Mishra, *Banaras in Transition*, chap. 3 (violence, marriage); Bayly, *Rulers*, 18 (caste base).

42. Mishra, *Banaras in Transition*, 74–78.

43. Desai, *Banaras Reconstructed*, 74–77.

44. Desai, *Banaras Reconstructed*, 129.

45. Shantanu Guha Ray, "In Varanasi, a Lifetime Spent in a World of Death," *New York Times*, March 16, 2014, https://archive.nytimes.com/india.blogs.nytimes.com/2014/03/16/in-varanasi-a-lifetime-spent-in-a-world-of-death/.

46. Dalmia, *Nationalization of Hindu Traditions*, 96.

47. Dalmia, *Nationalization of Hindu Traditions*, 95–96.

48. Respectively, Alam, *Crisis of Empire*, xlii, and Altekar quoted in Eck, *Banaras*, 90.

49. Desai, *Banaras Reconstructed*, chap. 3; Hatcher, *Hinduism before Reform*, 113 (named as Rani Bhabani).

50. Bose, "Royal Matronage," 46–47; Desai, *Banaras Reconstructed*, 83.

51. Desai, *Banaras Reconstructed*, 110–112.

52. Alam, "Trade," 50; Mishra, *Banaras in Transition*, 108.

53. Mishra, *Banaras in Transition*, 97–100.

54. On armed ascetic groups more broadly in early modern India, see Pinch, *Warrior Ascetics*.

55. Mishra, *Banaras in Transition*, 10–12, 49; I draw on Mishra's book throughout this paragraph.

56. Dalmia, *Nationalization of Hindu Traditions*, 64.

57. Bayly, *Rulers*, 152.

58. Gough, "Situating Parsva's Biography"; "self-consciously" quote in Dalmia, *Nationalization of Hindu Traditions*, 60.

59. Lee, "Alleyways of Banaras," 213–215.

60. Khairuddin, *Bulwuntnamah*, 77–84.

61. Dalmia, *Nationalization of Hindu Traditions*, 69 (Persian and Braj); Orsini, "Between *Qasbas* and Cities," 73–74 (Persian).

62. Lorenzen, "Who Invented Hinduism?," 646–654; Truschke, "Hindu," 249–260.

63. Cherian, *Merchants of Virtue*; I draw on Cherian's book in the following several paragraphs.

64. Cherian, *Merchants of Virtue*, 19.

65. E.g., the Osval community of the region encompasses Jains and Vaishnavas (Dundas, *Jains*, 148–149).

66. Cherian, *Merchants of Virtue*, 103–104.

67. Cherian, *Merchants of Virtue*, 110.

68. Cherian, *Merchants of Virtue*, 88–89 and 117–123.

69. Cherian, *Merchants of Virtue*, 50 (1775 example) and 56 (water example).

70. Cherian, *Merchants of Virtue*, 201n70.

71. Cherian, *Merchants of Virtue*, 76–77.

72. Ananda Ranga Pillai, *Private Diary*, 1:293–295 (Price and Rangachari's translation, lightly amended).

73. Washbrook, "Envisioning the Social Order."

74. Bangha, "Rekhta," 25–26.

75. Some scholars propose that Urdu dates back to the advent of Indo-Persian in the early second millennium CE, but the claims are unsubstantiated (Bangha, "Rekhta," 23–24). Other scholars put Urdu's birth in the nineteenth century, often affiliating it with writing in the Perso-Arabic script, but this is anachronistic. The association between Urdu and Perso-Arabic letters came later, in the nineteenth century; it was first articulated by colonial thinkers and later embraced by South Asians (Orsini, "Introduction," 3–4). Both ideas—about Urdu's undue longevity and its advent only in the colonial period—stem from the same bad set of assumptions that there is a primordial link between language, script, and religion (i.e., Urdu, Perso-Arabic script, and Islam, quite often opposed to Hindi, Devanagari script, and Hinduism). This set of bad assumptions has a history of its own, dating to the nineteenth and twentieth centuries. Still, bad modern ideas do not help us understand premodern complexities. Regarding nomenclatures, a poet named Mushafi defined Rekhta as *zaban-i urdu*, possibly using "urdu" to mean Delhi around 1780 (Faruqi, "Long History of Urdu," 806). However, "Urdu" did not replace "Rekhta" as the common name for the language until the nineteenth century.

76. Hashmi, *Kulliyat-i Vali*, 172 (my translation). Dhavan and Pauwels, "Controversies Surrounding the Reception"; Pauwels, "Literary Moments of Exchange."

77. Dhavan and Pauwels, "Controversies Surrounding the Reception," 628.

78. Quoted in Alam, *Crisis of Empire*, xxxv (adapted from Alam's translation).

79. Pauwels, "Literary Moments of Exchange"; Bangha, "Rekhta," 71–80.

80. Pauwels, "Literary Moments of Exchange," 82 (Pauwels's translation).

81. Bangha, "Rekhta," 62.

82. Bangha, "Rekhta," 63 (Bangha's translation); Orsini, "Barahmasas," 154–159 (on the *Bikat Kahani* more generally).

83. Shackle, "Introduction," xxvii.

84. Shackle, introduction to *Shah Abdul Latif Risalo*, vii–viii.

85. Burchett, *Genealogy of Devotion*, 78–80, and Ernst, "Situating Sufism and Yoga," 23–24 (Nath yogi and Sufi shared practices); Schimmel, *Pain and Grace*, 220 (Shah Latif and Nath yogis).

86. Dean Accardi quoted in Burchett, *Genealogy of Devotion*, 80.

87. Shackle, *Shah Abdul Latif Risalo*, 425–429 (Shackle's translation; for the full poem, see pp. 424–469).

17. COMPANY BAHADUR

1. Quoted in *Shahrashob*, 133 (see also translation in Alam, *Crisis of Empire*, xxii).

2. Robertson, *Essential Writings of Raja Rammohan Ray*, 267–270; on the episode, see Robertson, "English Writings of Raja Rammohan Ray," 27–31.

3. Stern, *Company-State*.

4. Quoted in Guha, "Maratha Empire" (Guha's translation).

5. Barrow, *East India Company*, 139.

6. Wilson, *India Conquered*, 28–30.

7. On Calcutta's founding, see Hasan, "Indigenous Cooperation."

8. Bayly, *Indian Society*, 68 (Calcutta, I round down from Bayly's estimate); Ahuja, "Labour Unsettled," 390 (Madras; cf. Bayly's more robust estimate); Commander, "Malthus," 681 (Bombay).

9. Chakrabarti, "Neither of Meate nor Drinke," 3 (quote); Travers, "Death and the Nabob," 87 and 109–110 (Bengal death rate for Britishers).

10. E.g., Gravestone of Richard Becher, quoted in Derozario, *Complete Monumental Register*, 30.

11. Hasan, "Indigenous Cooperation," 72–74.

12. Chatterjee, *Merchants*, 102–106; Chaudhury, *Trade*, 153.

13. Jasanoff, *Edge of Empire*, 28; Mukherjee, "What Made the East India Company So Successful?"

14. Wilson, *India Conquered*, 106.

15. Roy, "Military Synthesis," 685 (sepoy and European numbers); Wilson, *India Conquered*, 110 (one-quarter died or seriously injured).

16. Travers, *Empires of Complaints*.

17. Kanda, "Competition or Collaboration?," 249 (salt); Markovitz, "Political Economy of Opium Smuggling," 90–91 (opium).

18. Ghulam Hussain Khan, *Seir Mutaqherin*, 3:32.

19. Ghulam Hussain Khan, *Seir Mutaqherin*, 3:162.

20. Ghulam Hussain Khan, *Seir Mutaqherin*, 3:26.

21. Wilson, *India Conquered*, 114–115.

22. Quoted in Kaye, *Administration of the East India Company*, 242.

23. Wilson, *India Conquered*, 121.

24. Raman, *Document Raj*, 176–177; Wilson, *India Conquered*, 223–224 (makes this comparison).

25. Travers, "Death and the Nabob," 97–103.

26. Ghulam Hussain Khan, *Seir Mutaqherin*, 3:161.

27. Shore, *Notes on Indian Affairs*, 10.

28. Jasanoff, *Edge of Empire*, 49 (Calcutta); Washbrook, "South India," 485–486 (Madras).

29. Hawes, *Poor Relations*, 4.

30. Bayly, *Empire and Information*, 91–93.

31. Ghosh, *Sex and the Family*, 103–105.

32. There were four Anglo-Mysore wars (1767–1769, 1780–1784, 1790–1792, and 1799) and three Anglo-Maratha conflicts (1775–1782, 1803–1805, and 1817–1818).

33. Irschick, *Dialogue and History*, 207n4.

34. Sivasundaram, *Islanded*, 4.

35. It seems to me that many scholars have confused Indian history and British history. To be sure, the two were intertwined for 200 years, which complicates matters but excuses neither sloppiness nor carelessness. The fact of the matter is that if one writes a story that is primarily about British institutions, British people, debates in Britain, English-medium sources written by British men, and British decisions, then one is generally writing British history. I have no objection to that project, except insofar as British history is sometimes mislabeled as Indian history and thereby obscures the agency and stories of Indians. Additionally, some scholars go further and, following bad Orientalist assumptions, depict India as merely a land to be conquered and whose people only enacted historical changes until the British showed up. I reject such views as inaccurate and unethical. In a sense, my point is banal, namely that Indians—along with their decisions, sources, ideas, texts, communities, and struggles—are definitionally the fulcrum of Indian history. And yet, given the state of scholarship, centering Indian agency is a stance I feel compelled to state explicitly here (see also the Historiography essay). Some readers may feel adrift without the standard lineup of British male names for this period, but I propose that such unmooring can prompt critical and productive thinking.

36. Yang, *Limited Raj*.

37. Wilson, *India Conquered*, 158–161.

38. Khazeni, *City and the Wilderness*, 76–78.

39. Brittlebank, *Tipu Sultan's Search for Legitimacy*, 42–43 (Sufis) and 127–129 (temples); Davis, "Muslim Princess," 148 (Vishnu temple dispute); Simmons, *Devotional Sovereignty*, chap. 2 (both).

40. Brittlebank, *Tiger*, 8–9.

41. Quoted in Brittlebank, "Accessing the Unseen Realm," 164.

42. Stronge, *Tipu's Tigers*.

43. Marsh, *India in the French Imagination*, 32–40 (Versailles embassy).

44. Travers, "Death and the Nabob," 110. British East India Company troops included continental Europeans, who were about 15 percent of Madras Presidency troops in 1766 and 20 percent in 1800 (Jasanoff, *Edge of Empire*, 48–49).

45. Peers, "South Asia," 46.

46. Kolff, *Naukar, Rajput and Sepoy*, 27.

47. Teltscher, "Shampooing Surgeon," 411–413.

48. Alavi, *Sepoys and the Company*, 44–55.

49. Mukherjee, *Year of Blood*, 112.

50. Alavi, *Sepoys and the Company*, 279.

51. Chakrabarti, "Neither of Meate nor Drinke," 32.

52. Bayly, *Empire and Information*, 157.

53. Chakrabarti, "Neither of Meate nor Drinke," 23–26 (joint training) and 18 (aloe and mercury).

54. This and the following few sentences draw from Bayly, *Empire and Information*, 60–64.

55. Bayly, *Empire and Information*, 133.

56. Quoted in Viswanath, *Pariah Problem*, 5; I draw from this book's introduction in this paragraph.

57. Discussed in contributions by Eaton, Fisher, Guha, and Sreenivasan to Chatterjee and Eaton, *Slavery and South Asian History*.

58. Sharp, *Selections from Educational Records*, 109.

59. Figueira, *Translating the Orient*, 8–9 (*Shakuntala*); Marchignoli, "Canonizing an Indian Text?," 254 (Bhagavadgita). More generally, see Mufti, "Orientalism."

60. Figueira, *Translating the Orient*, 23.

61. Figueira, *Translating the Orient*, 12.

62. Cohn, *Colonialism*, 26–30 and chap. 3; Travers, *Empires of Complaints*, chap. 3 (esp. on the Mughal context).

63. Bhattacharyya, *Empire and Ecology*, 86.

64. Asif, *Loss of Hindustan*.

65. Satia, *Time's Monster*, 74 (on the impact of Mill's work).

66. Chatterjee, *Nation and Its Fragments*, 77–86.

67. Many have written on this (e.g., Pandey, *Construction of Communalism*; van der Veer, *Religious Nationalism*).

68. White, *Little London to Little Bengal*, 61.

69. On Gilchrist, see Lelyveld, "Fate of Hindustani."

70. Orsini, "Introduction," 3.

71. Mantena, *Origins of Modern Historiography*, 95–121 (as Mantena notes, there were five brothers, but Mackenzie worked closely with three of them).

72. Khera, *Place of Many Moods*, chap. 4; Talbot, *Last Hindu Emperor*, chap. 6.

73. Thompson, *Women's Travel Writings in India*, 1:2–3.

74. Kindersley in Thompson, *Women's Travel Writings in India*, 1:108.

75. Graham in Thompson, *Women's Travel Writings in India*, 1:137–308.

76. Guha-Thakurta, *Monuments*, 95.

77. Trautmann, "Inventing the History of South India," 39–40.

78. Durba Ghosh offers a fuller definition: "'Bhadralok' was used to identify upper-caste, typically Hindu, landholding elites who were educated, often in English, and were trained for 'respectable,' or white-collar, jobs in the colonial administration" (*Gentlemanly Terrorists*, 1).

79. Hatcher, *Bourgeois Hinduism*, 25–26; Kopf, *Brahmo Samaj*, chap. 1.

80. Truschke, "Hindu," 262.

81. On how Brahmo Samaj thinkers negotiated Vaishnava movements, see Barua, *Brahmo Samaj*.

82. Kopf, *Brahmo Samaj*, 99–100.

83. Hatcher, *Bourgeois Hinduism*, 23–24.

84. Robertson, "English Writings of Raja Rammohan Ray," 32.

85. Robertson, *Essential Writings of Raja Rammohan Ray*, 31–32.

86. Roberts, *Scenes and Characteristics of Hindostan*, 3:179.

87. Roberts, *Scenes and Characteristics of Hindostan*, 3:180.

88. Fisher, *Short History of the Mughal Empire*, 224.

89. Naim, "Syed Ahmad and His Two Books," 694n70 (*khalq khuda ki / mulk padshah ka / hukm kampani bahadur ka*).

18. SEPOY REBELLION AND DAWN OF THE BRITISH RAJ

1. Quoted in Broughton, "Letters from a Competition Wallah," 9–10 (*sub lal hogea hai*); translation and transliteration given in article.

2. Chaturvedi, *Hindutva and Violence*, 181 (maps); Wagner, *Great Fear*, 76–77 (blood, uniforms). I am not certain that this saying was actually printed in 1857, although the English press was reporting that it had been by the mid-1860s. Like so much about the Sepoy Rebellion, an air of uncertainty and rumor remains.

3. Cook, *Annexation and the Unhappy Valley*, chap. 1.

4. Markovits, "Political Economy of Opium Smuggling," 108–109.

5. Doniger, *On Hinduism*, 560.

6. Fisher, *Politics of the British Annexation*, 22.

7. Atwal, *Royals and Rebels*, 43; Grewal, *Sikhs of the Punjab*, 100.

8. Dhavan, *When Sparrows Became Hawks*, 72–73.

9. Grewal, *Sikhs of the Punjab*, 100.

10. Atwal, *Royals and Rebels*, 55 (marriages); Grewal, *Sikhs of the Punjab*, 108–109 (patronage).

11. Kapuria, "Music and the Maharaja," 666.

12. Sohan Lal, *Umdat-ut-Tawarikh*, 3:505.

13. Dhavan, *When Sparrows Became Hawks*, 142.

14. Grewal, *Sikhs of the Punjab*, 101–103.

15. Atwal, *Royals and Rebels*, chap. 4.

16. Quoted in Grewal, *Sikhs of the Punjab*, 124.

17. *Papers Relating to the Punjab*, 26 (both letters); also quoted in Atwal, *Royals and Rebels*, 193–194.

18. *Papers Relating to the Punjab*, 53.

19. Ballantyne, *Between Colonialism and Diaspora*, chap. 3; Singh, *Sikhism*, 139–140.

20. Tarshis, "Koh-i-Noor Diamond," 140.

21. On the contemporary British reception of loot from India, see Cohn, *Colonialism*, 102–105.

22. Barnett, "Awadh."

23. Quoted in Mukherjee, *Awadh in Revolt*, 32.

24. Barnett, "Awadh."

25. Cole, *Roots of North Indian Shi'ism*, 96–98.

26. Sharma, "Famine," 167.

27. Williams, "Hindustani Music," chaps. 3–4.

28. Varady, "Rail and Road Transport," 30–47.

29. Stark, *Empire of Books*, 42 (press); Wilson, *India Conquered*, 216 (steamboat).

30. Lucas, *Dacoitee in Excelsis*, iii.

31. Wajid Ali Shah, *Reply to the Charges*, 54.

32. Shcheglova, "Lithography."

33. Stark, *Empire of Books*, 49 (Tulsidas) and 51 (Quran).

34. Stark, *Empire of Books*, 31, quoting Avril Powell; see also Bayly, *Empire and Information*, 191–192, and Jones, *Religious Controversy*.

35. Bayly, *Empire and Information*, 133.

36. Frykenberg, "Modern Education in South India," 46.

37. E.g., Bombay Education Society (1815), Calcutta School Book Society (1817), and Madras School Book Society (1820) (Ramaswamy, *Terrestrial Lessons*, 72–73, 163–164, 267).

38. Suntharalingam, *Politics and Nationalist Awakening*, 37.

39. Sender, "Kashmiri Brahmins," 175 (dining); Bayly, *Empire and Information*, 231 (aryavarta).

40. Sender, "Kashmiri Brahmins," 176.

41. Suntharalingam, *Politics and Nationalist Awakening*, 35–36 (such cases were repeated in subsequent decades, 306–307).

42. Judge, "Reform in Fragments," 1127.

43. Ballantyne, *Between Colonialism and Diaspora*, 93–94; Singh, *Sikhism*, 140.

44. Singh, *Maharaja Duleep Singh Correspondence*, no. 428.

45. E.g., see essays in Pati, *Great Rebellion*, and Bates et al., *Mutiny at the Margins*, vols. 1–6.

46. *Hindoo Patriot*, quoted in Bates and Carter, *Mutiny at the Margins*, 7:70. Historians have spilled much ink debating what to call the Sepoy Rebellion, and much of that ink would probably have been put to better use analyzing the pertinent historical events (or, better yet, less-discussed historical events in nineteenth-century South Asia). All the same, my admittedly mild defense of "Sepoy Rebellion" as opposed to other descriptors is as follows. I reject as ahistorical the suggestion that this was "India's First War of Independence." The British called it a "mutiny" at the time, and some British historians still do so. I decline to use that term since it is British-centric and carries a negative judgment, which can impede historical analysis. I am somewhat agnostic on "revolt" versus "uprising" versus "rebellion," and I use all three here. I favor "rebellion" because it sounds neutral while demarcating armed resistance. Some have argued for replacing "sepoy" with either "Indian" or the year 1857, in part because Indians beyond sepoys participated in this armed pushback against the Company. That argument is sound, but "Indian Rebellion" introduces a new problem in that it appears to wrongly project onto the entirety of the subcontinent what was geographically limited to parts of British India. There is also the issue that there were many Indian rebellions against the British, not just one. In summary, I find "Sepoy Rebellion" the most neutral, specific, and historically accurate of the commonly understood, succinct descriptors.

47. Sitaram and Bahadur Shah Zafar quoted in Mukherjee, *Year of Blood*, 29–30n2; Sitaram's text was either heavily edited or outrightly authored by a Britisher (Wagner, "Marginal Mutiny," 762).

48. James W. Frey, "The Sepoy Speaks: Discerning the Significance of the Vellore Mutiny," in Bates and Rand, *Mutiny at the Margins*, 4:7.

49. Quoted in Bates and Carter, *Mutiny at the Margins*, 7:8.

50. The Company had four major armies in (respectively) Bombay, Madras, and Bengal presidencies as well as the Punjab Irregular Force, totaling more than 220,000 sepoys in 1857 (Bates and Rand, *Mutiny at the Margins*, 4:xvii and 4:xxviin7). Bengal boasted 120,000 sepoy troops as of 1857 (Roy, *Army in British India*, 8; cf. to nearly 140,000 in Habib, "Coming of 1857," 6); only 8,000 remained in service by September 1858 (Habib, "Coming of 1857," 8). Note that some sepoys went home instead of joining the revolt (Stokes, *Peasant Armed*, 54–55).

51. Mukherjee, *Year of Blood*, 103–135; Wagner, *Great Fear*, chap. 4.

52. Wagner, *Great Fear*, chap. 1; for some additional sepoy grievances, see Peers, "South Asia," 47–48.

53. Habib "Coming of 1857," 7 (Brahmins); Wagner, *Great Fear*, 33.

54. Mukherjee, *Year of Blood*, 128–129.

55. Mukherjee, *Awadh in Revolt*, 135.

56. Quoted in Mukherjee, *Year of Blood*, 41.

57. Mukherjee, *Year of Blood*, 42; Roy, *Politics of a Popular Uprising*, 30. On later imaginations of Rani Lakshmibai of Jhansi, see Deshpande, "Making of an Indian Nationalist Archive."

58. Chapatis were noticed and feared by the British as early as February 1857 (Bates and Carter, *Mutiny at the Margins*, 7:31–32, citing the *Delhi Gazette*), although some interpreted them as a talisman to eliminate cholera (Wagner, *Great Fear*, 64–65).

59. Bayly, *Empire and Information*, 323.

60. Printed in Bates and Carter, *Mutiny at the Margins*, 7:61–65.

61. E.g., quoted by Crispin Bates and Marina Carter, "Holy Warriors: Religion as Military Modus Operandi," in Bates and Rand, *Mutiny at the Margins*, 4:48 (*deen ka jai*), and quoted by Nupur Chaudhuri and Rajat Kanta Ray, "'We' and 'They' in an Altered Ecumene: The Mutiny from the Mutineers' Mouths," in Bates, *Mutiny at the Margins*, 5:41–42 (*deen*).

62. Quoted in Jafri, "Issue of Religion in 1857," 84 (adapted from Jafri's translation).

63. Quoted in Mukherjee, *Year of Blood*, 68.

64. Bates and Carter, *Mutiny at the Margins*, 7:58 (Nana Sahib).

65. Mukherjee, *Year of Blood*, 54.

66. Islam, "Backlash in Delhi"; Stokes, *Peasant Armed*, 94.

67. Quoted in Islam, "Backlash in Delhi," 202.

68. Islam, "Backlash in Delhi," 204 (beheadings); Narang and Abel, "Ghalib and the Rebellion," 47 (gallows).

69. Madhurima Sen, "Contested Sites: The Prison, Penal Laws and the 1857 Revolt," in Pati, *Great Rebellion*, 90–91.

70. Islam, "Backlash in Delhi," 199.

71. Quoted in Hasan, *Moral Reckoning*, 190.

72. Peers, "South Asia," 48–49.

73. Cited by Chhanda Chatterjee, "Contextualising Truth: Deconstructing the Poet Khazan Singh's Account of the War of Delhi, 1857," in Bates, *Mutiny at the Margins*, 1:143.

74. Wilson, *India Conquered*, 249–251. In generally on jihad, see Jalal, *Partisans of Allah.*

75. Nayar, *Penguin 1857 Reader*, 214.

76. Quoted in Yadav, *Sovereign*, 365.

77. Bayly, *Empire and Information*, 324.

78. Dadlani and Sharma, "Beyond the Taj Mahal," 1076.

79. *East India (Proclamations)*, 2–3 (capitalization, spelling, and punctuation as in original).

80. Fisher, *Politics of the British Annexation*, 24.

81. Taylor, *Empress*, 1–2.

19. KNOWING INDIA AND INDIANS, 1860–1900

1. *kos kos par badle pani, char kos par bani* (my translation).

2. Raj, *Relocating Modern Science*, 196–199.

3. Majeed, *Colonialism and Knowledge*, 1.

4. Gottschalk, *Religion, Science, and Empire*, 184–186.

5. Cohn, *Colonialism*, 8.

6. Kashmir was not included until the 1891 census (Natarajan, *Census of India*, 9). After partition and independence in 1947, the British transferred the census to India and Pakistan, respectively, and Bangladesh began its own census after breaking off from Pakistan in 1971. Of the three nations, Bangladesh has come closest to continuing the British schedule, completing its 2021 census in 2022 due to COVID-19 pandemic delays (as of the time of writing in summer 2024, Pakistan does not have a regular census schedule, and India has not conducted a census since 2011).

7. Cohn, *Colonialism*, 16 ("conquest of knowledge").

8. Gottschalk, *Religion, Science, and Empire*, 183 ("epistemic regime").

9. Beverley, *Report on the Census of Bengal 1872*, chap. 4.

10. Gottschalk, *Religion, Science, and Empire*, 222.

11. Beverley, *Report on the Census of Bengal 1872*, 54–55; see also Cornish, *Report on the Census of the Madras Presidency 1871*, 39.

12. Cohn, *Colonialism*, 8.

13. Gottschalk, *Religion, Science, and Empire*, 209.

14. Cornish, *Report on the Census of the Madras Presidency 1871*, 42 (the "Jeypore hill tribes" discussed here should not be confused with the northern Indian city of Jaipur); also see comments in Beverley, *Report on the Census of Bengal 1872*, 54.

15. Printed in *Report on the Census of Assam for 1881*, 16.

16. The British conducted a Religious Census in 1851, and the experiment met with opposition and criticism; it was not repeated. Religion was added to the British census as an optional category in 2001. Religion has never been included on the American census.

17. Quoted in Cohn, *Anthropologist among the Historians*, 227.

18. Gottschalk, *Religion, Science, and Empire*, 204.

19. Sharma, "If There Is a Paradise on Earth," 250–251.

20. Quoted in Cohn, *Anthropologist among the Historians*, 245.

21. Gottschalk, *Religion, Science, and Empire*, 213.

22. Nanjundayya, *Ethnographical Survey of Mysore.*

23. Wilson, *India Conquered*, 278.

24. Wilson, *India Conquered*, 321.

25. Quoted in Lopez, *Buddhism and Science*, 130 (Lopez's translation).

26. Patel, *Naoroji*, 233–234 (book circulated widely).

27. Arvind Chhabra, "Punjab's Drug Menace: 'I Wanted My Son to Die,'" BBC News, November 23, 2018, https://www.bbc.com/news/world-asia-india-46218646.

28. Naoroji, *Poverty and Un-British Rule in India*, 215.

29. Natarajan, *Census of India*, i. Some scholars describe early modern India as "literacy aware," but the fact remains that India overall had low literacy and general schooling rates as compared to other parts of Asia (Bayly, *Empire and Information*, 39).

30. Suntharalingam, *Politics and Nationalist Awakening*, 113–114.

31. Kumar, *Science and the Raj*, 145–146.

32. Quoted in Suntharalingam, *Politics and Nationalist Awakening*, 157.

33. Cohn, *Colonialism*, 119–121.

34. Cohn, *Colonialism*, 125–126.

35. Peers, "South Asia," 54; see also Metcalf, *Ideologies*, 196.

36. Quoted in Suntharalingam, *Politics and Nationalist Awakening*, 152.

37. Metcalf, *Ideologies of the Raj*, 205–213.

38. Chatterjee, *Nation and Its Fragments*, 20–21.

39. April 1883 Poona publication, cited in Seal, *Emergence of Indian Nationalism*, 259 (misattributed to Bengali *Amrit Bazar Patrika* in Wilson, *India Conquered*, 333).

40. Quoted in Suntharalingam, *Politics and Nationalist Awakening*, 207.

41. Anagol-McGinn, "Age of Consent Act," 102–103.

42. Hindu Lady, "Infant Marriage and Enforced Widowhood."

43. Metcalf, *Ideologies of the Raj*, 106–107; Anagol-McGinn, "Age of Consent Act," 114.

44. Anagol-McGinn, "Age of Consent Act," 112; Muller, "Story of an Indian Child-Wife." Cf. to Muller's negative comments on infant marriages in other writings (e.g., Muller, *Life and Letters*, 2:210–212).

45. Quoted in Anagol-McGinn, "Age of Consent Act," 112.

46. Suntharalingam, *Politics and Nationalist Awakening*, 317 (newspapers); Chandrachud, *Independent, Colonial Judiciary*, chap. 2 (Ranade's support); Kosambi, "Women," 40 (Ranade's child marriage). Ranade was a Chitpavan Brahmin, like Tilak.

47. Lahore *Tribune*, March 30, 1889, quoted in Jones, *Socio-Religious Reform Movements*, 1.

48. Morgenstein Fuerst, *Indian Muslim Minorities*, chap. 2; Metcalf, *Ideologies of the Raj*, 140–141.

49. Khan Bahadur, *Review on Dr. Hunter's Indian Musalmans*, 6.

50. Morgenstein Fuerst, *Indian Muslim Minorities*, 87–88; this paragraph draws on Morgenstein Fuerst's book.

51. Lavan, *Ahmadiyah Movement*, 92–93.

52. Jones, *Socio-Religious Reform Movements*, 117.

53. Metcalf, *Ideologies of the Raj*, 82–84; Pollock, "Deep Orientalism"; van der Veer, *Imperial Encounters*, chap 6.

54. "Convention of 1884," 2.

55. Dalmia, *Nationalization of Hindu Traditions*, 35n17 (arya dharma).

56. T. V. Vaswani quoted in Bayly, "Hindu Modernisers," 97.

57. Jones, *Socio-Religious Reform Movements*, 96.

58. Dalmia, *Nationalization of Hindu Traditions*. Many European Orientalist backed the emphasis on Vaishnava ideas and texts (Dalmia, "Only Real Religion," 195–197).

59. Dalmia, *Nationalization of Hindu Traditions*, 384.

60. Dalmia, *Nationalization of Hindu Traditions*, 363–364 and 384.

61. Cort, "Jain Identity and the Public Sphere," 116–117.

62. Jones, *Socio-Religious Reform Movements*, 100–101.

63. Jaffrelot, *Religion, Caste, and Politics*, 145–150 (mimicking); Jones, "Communalism in the Punjab," 47–52 (timing and targets).

64. Jones, *Socio-Religious Reform Movements*, 113–114.

65. Rawat, *Reconsidering Untouchability*, 143–144.

66. Christophe Jaffrelot, "'Reconversion' Paradoxes," *Indian Express*, January 7, 2015, republished by Carnegie Endowment for International Peace, https://carnegieendowment.org/2015/01/07/reconversion-paradoxes-pub-57664.

67. Jha, *Myth of the Holy Cow*, chap. 1.

68. Gundimeda and Ashwin, "Cow Protection in India," 159.

69. Pandey, *Construction of Communalism*, 94; Rawat, *Reconsidering Untouchability*, 11.

70. Rawat, *Reconsidering Untouchability*, chap. 1.

71. Pandey, *Construction of Communalism*, 262 (Pandey's translation lightly adapted).

72. "Violent Cow Protection in India: Vigilante Groups Attack Minorities," Human Rights Watch, February 18, 2019, https://www.hrw.org/report/2019/02/19/violent-cow-protection-india/vigilante-groups-attack-minorities.

73. Quoted in Gundimeda and Ashwin, "Cow Protection in India," 158.

74. Powell, "History Textbooks," 124–125.

75. "Timeline: Ayodhya Holy Site Crisis," BBC News, December 6, 2012, https://www.bbc.com/news/world-south-asia-11436552.

76. Prior, "British Administration of Hinduism," 98.

77. Bayly, *Saints, Goddesses and Kings*, 313–314.

78. Stephens, *Governing Islam*, 132.

79. Quoted in Etter, "Antiquarian Knowledge," 87.

80. Quoted in Guha-Thakurta, *Monuments*, 30.

81. Guha-Thakurta, *Monuments*, chap 3.

82. Guha-Thakurta, *Monuments*, 40.

83. Gottschalk, *Religion, Science, and Empire*, 281–184.

84. Gottschalk, *Religion, Science, and Empire*, 275; Metcalf, *Ideologies of the Raj*, 152–153.

85. Metcalf, *Ideologies of the Raj*, 153–154.

86. Guha-Thakurta, *Monuments*, 79–80.

87. Chaudhuri, "Birth of Museum," 5 (1864); Singh, "Material Fantasy," 52 (1913).

88. Singh, "Material Fantasy," 52.

89. *Conference of Orientalists*, 117 (weddings, note from Vogel); Singh, "Material Fantasy," 52 (Pongol).

90. Guha-Thakurta, *Monuments*, 74–75.

91. Cunningham, *Archaeological Survey of India Report for the Year 1872–73*, 106–107.

92. Singh, *Discovery of Ancient India*, 97–98.

93. Cunningham, *Archaeological Survey of India Report for the Year 1872–73*, 108.

20. INDIANS ON THE MOVE, 1880–1920

1. *Stri Dharma Niti*, quoted in Kosambi, *Pandita Ramabai*, 46 (Kosambi's translation).

2. Prasad, *Tracks of Change*, 2.

3. Tumbe, *India Moving*, 69–70.

4. Prasad, *Tracks of Change*, 74.

5. Prasad, *Tracks of Change*, 38–40.

6. Hindu stories say that the invincible Saraswati River also converges at Allahabad.

7. Maclean, *Pilgrimage and Power*, 134–137 (I draw on this book throughout this paragraph).

8. Tumbe, "Towards Financial Inclusion," 414.

9. Tumbe, *India Moving*, 49–50.

10. Jahan, "Sultana's Dream: Purdah Reversed," in Hossain, *Sultana's Dream*, 1.

11. Hossain, *Sultana's Dream*, 8–9 and 14.

12. Jahan "Chronology," in Hossain, *Sultana's Dream*, xi.

13. Wagner, *Thuggee*, 121.

14. Nijhar, *Law and Imperialism*, 124.

15. Nijhar, *Law and Imperialism*, chap. 7.

16. Major, "State and Criminal Tribes," 657.

17. Pearson, *Indian Ocean*, 243.

18. Between 1834 and 1937, more than 90 percent of all Indian emigrants went to Ceylon, Burma, and the Malay Peninsula (Amrith, "South Indian Migration," 122, citing Kingsley Davis).

19. Cohn, *Colonialism*, 149; Pearson, *Indian Ocean*, 200. Cohn gives the Suez Canal's opening date as 1867, which is when the first ship passed through.

20. Pearson, *Indian Ocean*, 193 (volume); Markovits, "Indian Merchant Networks," 885 (quarter of a million).

21. Markovits, "South Asian Business," 71.

22. Balachandran, "South Asian Seafarers," 188; Broeze, "Muscles of Empire," 44–45.

23. Broeze, "Muscles of Empire," 50.

24. Tinker, *New System of Slavery*, chap. 1.

25. Machado, *Ocean of Trade*, 230–239.

26. Quoted in Tinker, *New System of Slavery*, 46.

27. Lal, "Indian Indenture," 83–84. "Coolie" can be a slur in modern times, although reclaimed by some descendants of indentured laborers (Bahadur, "Preface: The C-Word," in *Coolie Woman*); it can also refer to a porter in India.

28. See numbers in Lal, "Indian Indenture," 79; Shepherd, *Maharani's Misery*, 4.

29. Amrith, "South Indian Migration," 142 (on Southeast Asia; this system is sometimes called *kangani*, which is akin to indenture); Rawat, *Reconsidering Untouchability*, 76 (Chamar family migration).

30. Bahadur, *Coolie Woman*, 137–138.

31. Bahadur, *Coolie Woman*, 31.

32. Bahadur, *Coolie Woman*, 17–18.

33. Tinker, *New System of Slavery*, 124–130 (kidnapping); Bahadur, *Coolie Woman*, 48 (contradictory stories).

34. Shepherd, *Maharani's Misery*.

35. Bahadur, *Coolie Woman*, chap. 7.

36. Vahed, "Evil Thing," 667.

37. Tinker, *New System of Slavery*, chap. 9.

38. Bahadur, *Coolie Woman*, 168–172.

39. Bahadur, *Coolie Woman*, 169.

40. Cohn, *Colonialism*, 110.

41. Roy, "Combat Motivation," 46.

42. Quoted in Bose, *Hundred Horizons*, 126.

43. Arnold, "Death and the Modern Empire"; Tumbe, *Age of Pandemics*, chap. 4.

44. Englesberg, "Bellingham 'Anti-Hindu' Riot."

45. "Hindu" persisted as a racial category for decades in the United States, appearing on American censuses between 1920 and 1940 to categorize all South Asians and recurring as late as the 1980s in New Jersey (Truschke, "Hindu," 265 on census; Bahadur, "Unmaking Asian Exceptionalism" on the racialized sense of "Hindu" in the Dotbuster attacks of 1987).

46. Leonard, *Making Ethnic Choices*, chaps. 3–4.

47. Leonard, *Making Ethnic Choices*, 126.

48. Mukherjee, *Century of Trust*, 13 (toured America), 22 (date), 40–41 (on replacing American and European staff in the 1920s).

49. Anandibai gives her age as eighteen in "Letter of Anandibai Joshee to Alfred Jones," June 28, 1883, Legacy Center Archives, Drexel University College of Medicine, https://www.saada.org/item/20120711-721.

50. Chakravarti, *Rewriting History*, 211–212; on Anandibai as a child bride, see Anagol, "Rebellious Wives," 463n89.

51. "Letter from Anandibai Joshee to Alfred Jones," June 28, 1883, Legacy Center Archives, Drexel University College of Medicine, https://www.saada.org/item/20120711-721.

52. Chakravarti, *Rewriting History*, 211.

53. Quoted in Chakravarti, *Rewriting History*, 213.

54. Quoted in Kosambi, *Pandita Ramabai*, 130.

55. Chakravarti, *Rewriting History*, 215.

56. Chakravarti, *Rewriting History*, 215 and 242n45.

57. Quoted in Rachel L. Bodley's introduction to Ramabai, *High-Caste Hindu Woman*, vi.

58. This paragraph draws on Chakravarti, *Rewriting History*, 303–310; Kosambi, *Pandita Ramabai*, chap. 1.

59. Chakravarti, *Rewriting History*, 307.

60. Quoted in Chakravarti, *Rewriting History*, 310.

61. Quoted in Kosambi, *Pandita Ramabai*, 29.

62. Kosambi, *Pandita Ramabai*, 122.

63. Kosambi, *Pandita Ramabai*, 133–134.

64. Kosambi, *Pandita Ramabai*, 128.

65. Jones, *Socio-Religious Reform Movements*, 42; Sharma, *Restatement of Religion*, xii.

66. Sharma, *Restatement of Religion*, 150.

67. Poster reproduced in Kaplish "Vivekananda's Journey."

68. Vivekananda, *Speeches and Writings*, 5.

69. Quoted in Jones, *Socio-Religious Reform Movements*, 45.

70. Jones, *Socio-Religious Reform Movements*, 43–44.

71. Quoted in Chowdhury-Sengupta, "Reconstructing Hinduism," 28.

72. Quoted in Sharma, *Restatement of Religion*, 272.

73. Sharma, *Restatement of Religion*, xii.

74. Chowdhury-Sengupta, "Reconstructing Hinduism," 22.

75. Not traveling abroad remains a self-imposed restriction by nearly all Jain monks today.

76. Quoted in Harvard University, "Parliament of Religions." On Dharmapala's views on Buddhism as an aryan religion, see Lopez, *Buddhism and Science*, 92–102.

77. Some have doubted in recent years whether Vivekananda began with "Sisters and Brothers of America." The line was printed with the speech quite quickly (e.g., Houghton, *Neely's History of the Parliament of Religions*, 64, published in 1894); it was also remembered by attendees (e.g., Roxie Blodgett quoted in Bramen, "Christian Maidens and Heathen Monks," 201).

78. Printed in Houghton, *Neely's History of the Parliament of Religions*, 64–65.

79. Quoted in Bayly, "Hindu Modernisers," 103.

80. Chakravarti, *Rewriting History*, 333–336.

81. Baumfield, "Science and Sanskrit," 205–206.

82. Quoted in Gambhirananda, *History of the Ramakrishna Math*, 136.

83. Chakravarti, *Rewriting History*, 312.

84. Kosambi, *Pandita Ramabai*, 208.

85. Reverenda is the English "reverend" plus the long -a Sanskrit feminine ending, making it parallel to "pandita" (Kosambi, *Pandita Ramabai*, 209).

86. Quoted in Kosambi, *Pandita Ramabai*, 86 (Kosambi's translation).

87. Gould, "Social and Religious Reform."

88. Jangam, *Dalits and the Making of Modern India*, 22–26.

89. O'Hanlon, *Caste*, chap. 5.

90. Salunke, "Reclaiming Savitribai Phule," 58–60.

91. Omvedt, "Teacher and a Leader," 28–29.

92. Tumbe, *Age of Pandemics*, 86.

93. Quoted in Sardar and Paul, "Pioneering Engaged Writing," 66–67 (Sardar and Paul's translation).

94. Prasad, *Tracks of Change*, 63–67 (railways); Basu, "Turbans in the Trenches," 17–19 (sepoys).

95. Viswanath, *Pariah Problem*.

96. Ayyathurai, "Foundations of Anti-Caste Consciousness," 23–25.

97. Paul, "Dalit Conversion Memories," 189; Kannan, "Caste," 846 (on the reluctance to end slavery in Travancore).

98. Quoted in Sardar, "Love Letters," 44–45 (Sardar's translation).

99. Rawat, *Reconsidering Untouchability*, 124.

100. Jangam, *Dalits and the Making of Modern India*, 114.

101. Rawat, *Reconsidering Untouchability*, 133 (Chamar sabhas); Jangam, *Dalits and the Making of Modern India*, 144–145 (Adi-Hindu Conference).

102. Scholars rejected the Aryan Invasion Theory (AIT) decades ago. It mainly arises in modern times in Hindu nationalist discourse, where they deploy it as a strawman argument. A theory that posits aryan migrations (i.e., Indo-European speaker migrations) is current scholarly consensus. As compared to the predecessor AIT, current thinking regarding early aryan migrations is more precise regarding dates and does not stipulate widespread violence. As discussed in chapter 2, that Indo-European speakers migrated to the subcontinent in the second millennium BCE is backed by overwhelming linguistic evidence, as well as convergent genetic evidence and similarities between ancient beliefs systems.

103. Jaywant, "Reshaping the Figure of the Shudra."

104. Thapar, "Some Appropriations," 18.

105. O'Hanlon, *Caste*, 141–142.

106. Quoted in O'Hanlon, *Caste*, 142.

107. Geetha and Rajadurai, "Dalits and Non-Brahmin Consciousness," 2092 (using the spelling Ayothidas).

108. Geetha and Rajadurai, *Towards a Non-Brahmin Millennium*, 46.

109. Chakrabarti, *Bacteriology*, 1–2; Kumar, *Science and the Raj*, 92–93.

110. Pratik Chakrabarti quoted in Joel Gunter and Vikas Pandey, "Waldemar Haffkine: The Vaccine Pioneer the World Forgot." BBC News, December 10, 2020, sec. India, https://www.bbc.com/news/world-asia-india-55050012.

111. Jehan Begum, *Hayat-i-Shahjehani*, 71–72.

21. ADVOCATING FOR INDEPENDENCE, NATIONALISM, AND EQUAL RIGHTS

1. Quoted in translation in Jangam, *Dalits and the Making of Modern India*, 174.

2. Rawat, *Reconsidering Untouchability*, 159–161.

3. Suntharalingam, *Politics and Nationalist Awakening*, 231.

4. Talbot and Kamran, *Colonial Lahore*, 110.

5. Quoted in Suntharalingam, *Politics and Nationalist Awakening*, 248.

6. Pirzada, *Foundations of Pakistan*, 1:xix.

7. Quoted in Pirzada, *Foundations of Pakistan*, 1:xxiv.

8. At different points, the group also went by the names "Mohammedan Educational Congress" and "Anglo-Oriental Educational Conference."

9. Sarkar, *Swadeshi Movement*, 312.

10. Deepanjan Ghosh, "Durga Puja 2021: When Pandals Depict Political Themes," *Outlook India*, October 13, 2021, https://www.outlookindia.com/national/india-news-durga-puja-2021-when-pandals-depict-political-themes-news-397565.

11. Mukherjee, *Century of Trust*; Raianu, *Tata* (chap. 1 on the opium and cotton origins).

12. Resolution 1 adopted at Dacca, quoted in Pirzada, *Foundations of Pakistan*, 1:6.

13. Noorani, "Vande Mataram," 1039.

14. Sarkar, *Hindu Nationalism*, 39–40.

15. Aurobindo, *Complete Works*, 5:465–466 (Aurobindo's translation).

16. Orsini, *Hindi Public Sphere*, chap. 5; Pandey, *Construction of Communalism*, chaps. 6–7. By this point, "Hindustan" generally meant India.

17. Bapu, *Hindu Mahasabha*, 126; on Malaviya's promotion of similar ideas in the 1890s, see Mufti, *Enlightenment in the Colony*, 146.

18. Ramaswamy, *Passions of the Tongue*, 233–242 (on Periyar and the Dravidian movement).

19. Quoted in Bapat, *Reminiscences and Anecdotes*, 3.

20. Noorani, *Indian Political Trials*, 116.

21. Pinney, "Tiger's Nature," 407.

22. Noorani, *Indian Political Trials*, chap. 4.

23. Tilak, *Bhagavadgita-Rahasya* 1:75 (on karma including killing) and 1:548 (on killing "evil-doers"); Davis, *Bhagavad Gita*, 130–131.

24. Ghosh, *Gentlemanly Terrorists*.

25. Ghosh, *Gentlemanly Terrorists*, 28–29; Wilson, *India Conquered*, 404–405.

26. Ghosh, *Gentlemanly Terrorists*, 30.

27. Wagner, "Calculated to Strike Terror," 186.

28. Quoted in Wagner, "Calculated to Strike Terror," 194.

29. Quoted in Wagner, "Calculated to Strike Terror," 194.

30. I rely on Rajmohan Gandhi (*Mohandas*) and David Arnold (*Gandhi*) for details about Gandhi's life.

31. Mongia, *Indian Migration and Empire*, chap. 3 (pp. 99–101 on female participation).

32. Gandhi, *Hind Swaraj*, 48.

33. Gandhi, *Hind Swaraj*, 27–28.

34. Independent India's flag is based on Congress's flag, but Gandhi's charkha has been replaced by Ashoka's wheel of justice.

35. Amin, "Gandhi as Mahatma," 289–290.

36. Amin, "Gandhi as Mahatma," 290–291 (avatar); Kapila, "Gandhi before Mahatma," 431 (not God).

37. Gandhi, *Collected Works*, 20:283.

38. Sharafi, *Law and Identity*, 253.

39. Gandhi, *Mohandas*, 282.

40. Ghosh, *Gentlemanly Terrorists*, 93.

41. Ghosh, *Gentlemanly Terrorists*, 119.

42. Hardiman, "Gandhi's Global Legacy," 240–243 (influence on the U.S. Civil Rights Movement).

43. Gandhi, *Mohandas*, 334.

44. Gottschalk, *Religion, Science, and Empire*, 215.

45. Arnold, *Gandhi*, 153 (Churchill's exact comment was more verbose than what I have given here).

46. Geetha and Rajadurai, *Towards a Non-Brahmin Millennium*, 64, describing a column in the Tamil weekly *Tamizhan*.

47. Jangam, *Dalits and the Making of Modern India*, 175.

48. Quoted in translation in Jangam, *Dalits and the Making of Modern India*, 174.

49. Dirks, *Castes of Mind*, 259; Venkatachalapathy, "Periyar."

50. Rawat, *Reconsidering Untouchability*, 166.

51. Gandhi, *Collected Works*, 23:44.

52. Gandhi, *Collected Works*, 23:44.

53. Quoted in Sarkar, "Gandhi and Social Relations," 180.

54. Gandhi, *Collected Works*, 23:44; Sarkar, "Gandhi and Social Relations," 182 ("upper-caste penance").

55. Metcalf and Metcalf, *Concise History of Modern India*, 174 ("harshly coercive," speaking of Gandhi's fasts generally); Roy, "Doctor and the Saint," 125 ("barefaced blackmail").

56. Quoted in Jaffrelot, *Ambedkar and Untouchability*, 66.

57. Quoted in Jaffrelot, *Ambedkar and Untouchability*, 66.

58. Rawat, *Reconsidering Untouchability*, 169.

59. Brown, "Introduction," 7.

60. Pirzada, *Foundations of Pakistan*, 1:lxviii, quoting *Star of India*.

61. Jaffrelot, *Modi's India*, 12 ("ideology") and 14 ("to ensure their [Hindu] domination").

62. Chaturvedi, *Hindutva and Violence*, 155 and 157–158 (quotes from Savarkar).

63. Sen, "Hindu Conservative Negotiates Modernity," 178.

64. Bakhle, *Savarkar*; Chaturvedi, *Hindutva and Violence*; Jaffrelot, *Hindu Nationalism*.

65. Chaturvedi, *Hindutva and Violence*, 142; Savarkar, *Hindutva*, 1.

66. Bakhle, "Country First?"; Jaffrelot, *Hindu Nationalism*, 86.

67. E.g., see Bakhle, *Savarkar*, 23 on the "affective power of his [Savarkar's] poetry," especially "the rage of his anti-Muslim diatribes."

68. Savarkar's *Hindutva* quoted in Jaffrelot, *Hindu Nationalism*, 95–96.

69. Savarkar, *Six Glorious Epochs*; Chaturvedi, *Hindutva and Violence*.

70. Quoted in Bakhle, *Savarkar*, 4.

71. Chaturvedi, *Hindutva and Violence*, 164–165.

72. Chaturvedi, *Hindutva and Violence*, 82–83.

73. Savarkar, *Hindutva*.

74. Chaturvedi, *Hindutva and Violence*, 374 ("super-savage cruelty" and "arch-devils") and 377–379 (rape).

75. Nehru described the RSS as "in the nature of a private army" (quoted in Nussbaum, *Clash Within*, 167); the group has been open about its Hindu nationalist ideals from the start and remains so today.

76. Casolari, *Shadow of the Swastika*, 34.

77. Casolari, "Hindutva's Foreign Tie-up."

78. Bakhle, *Savarkar*, 5.

79. Casolari, *Shadow of the Swastika*, 84n80.

80. Chaturvedi, *Hindutva and Violence*, 24.

81. Quoted in Chaturvedi, *Hindutva and Violence*, 334.

82. Cited in Egorova, *Jews and India*, 42.

83. Jaffrelot, *Hindu Nationalism*, 14.

84. Quoted in Chaturvedi, *Hindutva and Violence*, 334.

85. Jaffrelot, *Hindu Nationalism*, 16.

86. Gandhi, "Hindutva and the Shared Scripts of the Global Right"; Pinherio-Machado and Vargas-Maia, *Radical Right in the Global South*.

87. Jaffrelot, *Hindu Nationalism*, 17–19.

88. Sharma, "Political Mobilization" (on Hindutva disinformation generally; see p. 147 on the Sangh Parivar's "propaganda machine").

89. Jaffrelot, *Ambedkar and Untouchability*, 19.

90. Jaffrelot, *Ambedkar and Untouchability*, 26–27.

91. Roy, "Doctor and the Saint," 95–96.

92. Jaffrelot, *Ambedkar and Untouchability*, 27.

93. Sarkar, "Gandhi and Social Relations," 182.

94. Rao, *Caste Question*, 15.

95. Ambedkar, *Annihilation of Caste*, 244–246 and 295. In 1937, Ambedkar emended "silenced" to read "frozen instantly it is told" and changed the last line to "But all the slaves are not equal in status" (Ambedkar, *Annihilation of Caste*, 295nn132–133).

96. Ambedkar, *Annihilation of Caste*, 285.

97. Zelliot, "Understanding Dr. B. R. Ambedkar," 807 (context); quoted in Rao, *Caste Question*, 118 (i.e., Ambedkar's Yeola statement).

98. Ambedkar, *Writings and Speeches*, 9:296.

99. Ambedkar, *Writings and Speeches*, 9:249.

100. Jaffrelot, *Ambedkar and Untouchability*, 134–136; Rao, *Caste Question*, 118–119.

101. Ambedkar, *Buddha and His Dhamma*.

102. Ambedkar, *Annihilation of Caste*, 316–317.

22. DIVIDING INDIA IN 1947

1. Manto, *Black Margins*, 220 (Memon's translation).

2. "Two Indian Nations Emerge on World Scene," *New York Times*, August 15, 1947, https://www.nytimes.com/1947/08/15/archives/india-and-pakistan-become-nations-clashes-continue-ceremonies-at.html.

3. On historiographical trends in interpreting and explaining partition, see Gilmartin, "Historiography of India's Partition."

4. Pirzada, *Foundations of Pakistan*, 2:159.

5. Pirzada, *Foundations of Pakistan*, 2:160 and 2:154, respectively.

6. Kamran, "Choudhary Rahmat Ali," 95.

7. Khan, *Great Partition*, 43.

8. Jalal, *Sole Spokesman*, 2.

9. Jalal, *Sole Spokesman*, 171–172.

10. Pirzada, *Foundations of Pakistan*, 2:341.

11. Quoted in Gandhi, *Collected Works*, 77:303n2.

12. Azad, "Presidential Address," 66–67.

13. Khan, *Great Partition*, 34–36.

14. Quoted in Jones, "Pakistan That Is Going to be Sunnistan," 350.

15. I remain agnostic about the argument, associated with Ayesha Jalal, that Jinnah intended Pakistan as a bargaining chip. I find it more productive here to stick to events, rather than parsing intentions.

16. Bose, *Hundred Horizons*, 125.

17. Nehru, *Selected Works* (first series), 10:197.

18. Jalal, *Sole Spokesman*, 72.

19. Gandhi, *Collected Works*, 83:197 (italics in original).

20. Khan, *Raj at War*, 193.

21. Nehru, *Discovery of India*, 9.

22. Khan, *Raj at War*, 193.

23. Dyson and Maharatna, "Excess Mortality" (two million). Many have cited, or repeated without citing, Amartya Sen's estimate of three million dead; Dyson and Maharatna review the evidence on why two million is a more accurate estimate. Aberigh-Mackay, *Twenty-one Days in India*, 129.

24. Khan, *Great Partition*, 17.

25. Gordon, *Brothers against the Raj*, 484.

26. Sundaram, "Indian National Army."

27. There were many rumors about Bose's death being manufactured or, alternatively, faked at the time, and many conspiracy theories persist today.

28. Bird and Sherwin, *American Prometheus*, 99–100; Hijiya, "*Gita* of J. Robert Oppenheimer," 130 and 151.

29. Sinha, "Orienting America."

30. Davis, *Bhagavad Gita*, 172–173 and 224n19; Hijiya, "*Gita* of J. Robert Oppenheimer," 123–124n3. This quote is sometimes given as "destroyer of worlds," based on a televised interview that Oppenheimer gave in 1965; I give it here in its earlier attested version.

31. Jalal, *Sole Spokesman*, 129–132.

32. Moon, *Wavell*, 142 (entry for June 16, 1945).

33. Jalal, *Sole Spokesman*, 171–172; Metcalf and Metcalf, *Concise History of Modern India*, 213.

34. This paragraph draws on Khan, *Great Partition*, chap. 2.

35. Khan, *Great Partition*, 27.

36. Quoted in Khan, *Great Partition*, 55.

37. Das, *Communal Riots in Bengal*, 167–170.

38. *Dawn* and *Eastern Times*, quoted in Khan, *Great Partition*, 64.

39. Chatterji, *Bengal Divided*, 232.

40. Chatterji, *Bengal Divided*, 232–240.

41. Chatterji, *Bengal Divided*, 233.

42. Das, *Sardar Patel's Correspondence*, 3:182.

43. Markovits, "Calcutta Riots."

44. Khan, *Great Partition*, 83–84.

45. Khan, *Great Partition*, 1–3; excerpts were carried in international papers, such as the *New York Times* (June 4, 1947, https://timesmachine.nytimes.com/timesmachine/1947/06/04/issue.html).

46. Chughtai, *My Friend*, 3 (Naqvi's translation).

47. Khan, *Great Partition*, 125.

48. E.g., see the map from June 1947 in Satia, *Time's Monster*, 216.

49. Mansergh, *Transfer of Power*, 12:230.

50. Justices Muhammad Munir, Din Muhammad, Mehr Chand Mahajan, and Teja Singh constituted the Punjab Boundary Commission. Justices Abu Saleh Akram, S. A. Rahman, C. C. Biswas, and Bijan Kumar Mukherjea constituted the Bengal Boundary Commission. All four League representatives were Muslim, and the Congress men included three Hindus and one Sikh.

51. There are mild discrepancies in how many days scholars report that each boundary commission met, seemingly explained by whether one counts Sundays, which the Bengal Boundary Commission took off (Ghosh, "Protracted Process of Boundary Formation," 38).

52. Fitzpatrick, "Space of the Courtroom," 189.

53. Chatterji, *Partition's Legacies*, 93–94.

54. Chester, *Borders and Conflict*, 55 (Radcliffe's dates); Khan, *Great Partition*, 105 (3,800 miles).

55. Chatterji "Fashioning of a Frontier" 224 (not attending); Chester, *Borders and Conflict*, 117–118 (plane trip).

56. Chester, *Borders and Conflict*, 29.

57. Chester, *Borders and Conflict*, 62–63.

58. Chester, *Borders and Conflict*, 107–108; Khan, *Great Partition*, 125.

59. Talbot, *Pakistan*, 95.

60. Butalia, *Other Side of Silence*, 85.

61. Butalia, *Other Side of Silence*, 86; Radcliffe destroyed most of his own documents and papers, which adds to the challenge of trying to recover his reasoning (Chester, *Borders and Conflict*, 41).

62. Nehru, *Selected Works* (second series), 3:135.

63. Afzal, *Selected Speeches*, 428–429.

64. Afzal, *Selected Speeches*, 428–430 (Jinnah); Nehru, *Selected Works* (second series), 3:135–136.

65. Quoted in Chester, *Borders and Conflict*, 101. Pakistan later shifted its independence celebrations to August 14.

66. Mansergh, *Transfer of Power*, 12:692.

67. Quoted in Aslan, *Tablet and Pen*, 439 (V. G. Kiernan's translation).

68. Jalal, *Pity of Partition*.

69. Mufti, *Enlightenment in the Colony*, 203; all three stories are printed in Manto, *Black Margins*, 200–220.

70. Manto, *Stars from Another Sky*, 74–75 (Hasan's translation).

71. Chughtai, *My Friend*, 3–4 (Naqvi's translation).

72. Butalia, *Other Side of Silence*, 73.

73. Quoted in Nair, *Changing Homelands*, 215.

74. Copland, "Further Shores of Partition."

75. Bourke-White, *Halfway to Freedom*, chap. 1.

76. Khan, *Great Partition*, 156.

77. Khan, *Great Partition*, 163–164.

78. Quoted in Khan, *Great Partition*, 145.

79. Butalia, *Other Side of Silence*, 3.

80. Khan, *Great Partition*, 134.

81. Butalia, *Other Side of Silence*, chap 5.

82. Butalia, *Other Side of Silence*, 160–164.

83. Khan, *Great Partition*, 118–119.

84. Roy, "Paper Rights"; Zamindar, *Long Partition*, chaps. 5–6. These passports were discontinued in the 1960s.

85. Chester, *Borders and Conflict*, 170–171.

86. Wilson, *India Conquered*, 482.

87. Vallabhbhai Patel quoted in Sherman, "Integration of the Princely State of Hyderabad," 491–492.

88. Witmer, "1947–1948 India-Hyderabad Conflict," 2–3.

89. Sunderlal Committee, "Sunderlal Committee Report" (in the report, his name is also spelled Sunder Lal and Sundarlal).

90. Zutshi, *Languages of Belonging*, 49.

91. Haines, *Rivers Divided*, chap. 3.

92. Rai, *Hindu Rulers*, 9.

93. Rai, *Hindu Rulers*, chap. 5.

94. Wilson, *India Conquered*, 431.

95. Hussain, *Kashmir in the Aftermath of Partition*, chap. 4.

96. On Godse's RSS affiliation, see Jha, "Apostle of Hate"; Arnold, *Gandhi*, 34 ("Maharashtrian Brahmin").

97. See citations in chapter 21.

98. Pinney, "Tiger's Nature," 413.

99. Gandhi, *Mohandas*, 642.

100. Chaturvedi, *Hindutva and Violence*, 5.

101. Bakhle, *Savarkar*, 150.

102. Quoted in Gandhi, *Mohandas*, 682.

103. Quoted in Trivedi, "Literary and Visual Portrayals," 199.

104. Zamindar, *Long Partition*, 86–88.

105. Khan, *Great Partition*, 181.

106. Godse, *May It Please Your Honour*, 42.

107. Godse, *May It Please Your Honour*, 77.

108. Gandhi, *Mohandas*, 686.

109. This is owing to the established links of Godse with both the RSS and Savarkar (Jha, "Apostle of Hate").

110. Quoted in Nussbaum, *Clash Within*, 167.

111. "V.D. Savarkar Is Dead at 83; An Indian Nationalist Leader," *New York Times*, February 27, 1966, p. 85, https://www.nytimes.com/1966/02/27/archives/vd-savarkar-is-dead-at-83-an-indian-nationalist-leader.html.

112. Nussbaum, *Clash Within*, 168–169.

113. E.g., Butalia, *Other Side of Silence*; "1947 Partition Archive," https://www.1947partitionarchive.org/ (begun in 2008).

114. Quoted in Butalia, *Other Side of Silence*, 357.

23. NEW NATION-STATES, 1947–1990

1. Nawaz, *Heart Divided*, 272 (Mumtaz Shah Nawaz died in 1948, and the novel was published posthumously).

2. Crews, *Afghan Modern*, chap 5.

3. Wickramasinghe, *Sri Lanka*, 157–161.

4. Quoted in DeVotta, *Blowback*, 76.

5. I draw on Wickramasinghe, *Sri Lanka*, throughout this paragraph.

6. *Exhibition of Indian Art*, v.

7. *Exhibition of Indian Art*, v.

8. Guha-Thakurta, *Monuments*, 201 (chap. 6 on the exhibit generally).

9. Sherman, *Nehru's India*, 65 (Christianity is not represented in the sixteen stamps).

10. Nehru, *Jawaharlal Nehru's Speeches*, 3:35.

11. The Constituent Assembly began with fifteen female members (six of whom resigned before the constitution was enacted) and added two more (Chetan, *Founding Mothers of the Indian Republic*, 12n2).

12. The word count of India's constitution has gone up since its initial ratification, owing to additions and amendments.

13. De, *People's Constitution*, 2; Khosla, *India's Founding Moment*, 8.

14. January 26 had been celebrated by the Congress Party as "Independence Day," pursuant to that goal, since the 1929 Purna Swaraj resolution (see chapter 22).

15. *Constitution of India*, preamble.

16. E.g., the Indian Constitution was a potent symbol during protests against the BJP's Citizenship Amendment Act that rocked India between December 2019 and March 2020.

17. De, *People's Constitution*, 7–8.

18. Bandyopadhyay, *Decolonization in South Asia*, 94–100; for a history of postcolonial emergency laws, see Ghosh, *Gentlemanly Terrorists*, 252–256.

19. *Constitution of India*, preamble.

20. Quoted in Mukherjee, *Great Speeches*, 218–219.

21. Quoted in Hasan, *Legacy of a Divided Nation*, 135.

22. Quoted in Nair, *Changing Homelands*, 81.

23. Talbot, *Pakistan*, 24.

24. Talbot, *Pakistan*, 26.

25. Quoted in Malik, *State and Civil Society*, 63.

26. Pork and liquor are prohibited by most readings of Muslim teachings.

27. Quoted in Jalal, *State of Martial Rule*, 279.

28. Jalal, *State of Martial Rule*, 281.

29. *Constituent Assembly of Pakistan Debates*, 5(1): 3.

30. Jalal, *State of Martial Rule*, 281–282.

31. *Report of the Court of Inquiry*, 214–218.

32. Isambard Wilkinson, "Pakistan Brewery Produces Muslim World's First 20-Year Whisky," *Telegraph*, February 26, 2007, https://www.telegraph.co.uk/news/worldnews/1543915/Pakistan-brewery-produces-Muslim-worlds-first-20-year-whisky.html, quoting a member of the brewery's owning family.

33. Quoted in Khan, *Constitutional and Political History*, 57.

34. Quoted in Khan, *Constitutional and Political History*, 57.

35. Qadir, "Parliamentary Hereticization," 139; Nair, *Hurt Sentiments*, 233–234.

36. Shani, "Women and the Vote," 244–245.

37. Chester, *Borders and Conflict*, 57.

38. Talbot, *Pakistan*, 97–98.

39. Talbot, *Pakistan*, 171.

40. Khilnani, *Idea of India*, 64–88.

41. Balakrishnan, *Economic Growth in India*, 55–61; Hatekar and Dongre, "Structural Breaks in India's Growth," 1433.

42. Quoted in Amrith, *Unruly Waters*, 198 (p. 195 on second tallest).

43. Quoted in Anumeha Yadav, "The Anger of Adivasis Turns to Poetry of Anguish and Hope in a Young Woman's Hands," Scroll.in, June 5, 2016, http://scroll.in/article/808591/the-anger-of-adivasis-turns-to-poetry-of-anguish-and-hope-in-a-young-womans-hands.

44. Dreze and Sen, *India*, 132.

45. Dreze and Sen, *India*, 133.

46. For a discussion of the green revolution in Asia and its impacts given additional factors, see Asian Development Bank, *Rural Asia*.

47. Roy, "Indian Economy after Independence" (India); Talbot, *Pakistan*, 42 (Pakistan).

48. Balakrishnan, *Economic Growth in India*, 217 (point 1); Dreze and Sen, *India*, chap. 7 (point 2).

49. Dreze and Sen, *India*, 12 (India); Talbot, *Pakistan*, 23 (Pakistan).

50. Numbers are based on Pakistan's 2017 census and India's 2011 census; Pakistan conducted a 2023 census, but the results were not yet available at the time of writing.

51. World Bank, "Literacy Rate," World Bank Open Data, accessed April 18, 2024, https://genderdata.worldbank.org/indicators/se-adt/ (Sri Lankan literacy rates).

52. Dreze and Sen, *India*, 85.

53. Dreze and Sen, *India*, 90–92.

54. World Bank, "Labor Force, Female," World Bank Open Data, accessed August 17, 2023, https://data.worldbank.org/indicator/SL.TLF.TOTL.FE.ZS.

55. Sherman, *Nehru's India*, 26–28.

56. Roy, "Indian Economy after Independence."

57. Mukherjee, *Jawaharlal Nehru*, 100–104.

58. Biswas, "Indus Water Treaty," 203.

59. Michel, *Indus Rivers*, 256.

60. Cf. Haines, *Rivers Divided*, chap. 5 that argues for cooperation as a discursive strategy, as much as a reality, in representations of the Indus Treaty.

61. Talbot, *Pakistan*, 185.

62. Indira Gandhi's surname is by marriage to her husband, Feroze Gandhi; she is not related to Mohandas Gandhi.

63. Bass, *Blood Telegram*, 95.

64. "Moth-eaten" is from Jinnah (Jalal, *Sole Spokesman*, 121).

65. Bass, *Blood Telegram*, 95.

66. Bass, *Blood Telegram*, 72.

67. Gandhi, "Letter from Indian Prime Minister," writing to U.S. president Nixon.

68. Bass's *Blood Telegram* documents this evidence.

69. Hindus were 13.5 percent of the Bangladesh population in the 1974 census as compared to 18.5 percent (of East Pakistan) as of the 1961 census.

70. Bose, *Secular States*, 124.

71. Fisher, *Environmental History*, 198.

72. This nuclear test is commonly called "Smiling Buddha," although the phrase may postdate the test and reflects the official government line that India's pursuit of nuclear technology was peaceful (Sarkar, *Ploughshares and Swords*, 178 and 253n67).

73. Jaffrelot and Anil, *India's First Dictatorship*, 6–8.

74. Bass, *Blood Telegram*, 38.

75. For the next several paragraphs, I draw on Jaffrelot and Anil, *India's First Dictatorship*, and Prakash, *Emergency Chronicles*.

76. Amnesty International, "Report 1975–76," 127–132; Amnesty International, "Report 1977," 179–186; Jaffrelot and Anil, *India's First Dictatorship*, 40–41; Prakash, *Emergency Chronicles*, 186–187.

77. Jaffrelot and Anil, *India's First Dictatorship*, 165.

78. Prakash, *Emergency Chronicles*, 267–268.

79. Jaffrelot and Anil, *India's First Dictatorship*, 152–153.

80. Lewis M. Simons and Washington Post Foreign Services, "Compulsory Sterilization Provokes Fear, Contempt," *Washington Post*, July 4, 1977, https://www.washingtonpost.com/archive/politics/1977/07/04/compulsory-sterilization-provokes-fear-contempt/c2e28747-b5f1-4551-9bfe-98b552d8603f/.

81. Jaffrelot and Anil, *India's First Dictatorship*, 155.

82. Jaya Prakash Narayan, quoted in William Borders, "Opposition Accuses Mrs. Gandhi of 'Murdering' India's Democracy," *New York Times*, January 24, 1977, https://www.nytimes.com/1977/01/24/archives/opposition-accuses-mrs-gandhi-of-murdering-indias-democracy.html.

83. Jaffrelot and Anil, *India's First Dictatorship*, 454–455.

84. Shani, *Sikh Nationalism*, 51–53; Nair, *Changing Homelands*, 167.

85. Quoted in Bhatt, *Secession and Security*, 101–102.

86. Human Rights Watch, "India."

87. Wickramasinghe, *Sri Lanka*, 296.

88. Wickramasinghe, *Sri Lanka*, 303–306 (on India's attempted intervention).

89. Mapping Militant Organizations, "Liberation Tigers."

90. Hachhethu and Gellner, "Nepal," 144; Human Rights Watch, "We Don't Want to Be Refugees Again."

91. Quoted in Richter, "Political Dynamics of Islamic Resurgence," 555.

92. Jahangir and Jilani, *Hudood Ordinances*, 21.

93. Talbot, *Pakistan*, 273.

94. Chadbourne, "Never Wear Your Shoes after Midnight," 217–227.

95. Ashfaq, "Voices from Prison."

96. Staff Reporter, "Women Remember Iconic 1983 Demo, Vow to Fight Oppression," *Dawn*, February 13, 2019, https://www.dawn.com/news/1463551.

97. Nair, *Hurt Sentiments*, 235–236.

98. RSS and BJP membership overlaps substantially; that said, the two groups have diverged at times, especially in the 1980s (Jaffrelot and Andersen, "Hindu Nationalism," 472).

99. BJP, "Towards a New Polity," 397.

100. See chapter 22; Godse, *May It Please Your Honour*, 77.

101. BJP, "Vote BJP," 146–147.

102. Mandal Commission, *Report of the Backward Classes Commission*, 1:56.

103. Mandal Commission, *Report of the Backward Classes Commission*, 1:64.

104. Mandal Commission, *Report of the Backward Classes Commission*, 1:62.

105. Phoolan Devi's life was later popularized by Mala Sen's biography *India's Bandit Queen* (1991), which was subsequently made into a film (1994).

106. Rawat and Satyanarayana, "Dalit Studies," 4.

107. Chakravarti, *Gendering Caste*, 1–5.

108. Tharu and Niranjana, "Problems for a Contemporary Theory of Gender," 93.

24. EVERYDAY LIFE IN CONTEMPORARY SOUTH ASIA

1. Quoted in Ghosh, "Bones of Our Mother," 444.

2. Amrith, *Unruly Waters*, 6.

3. Dreze and Sen, *India*, 189 (one-billionth); Hannah Ellis-Petersen, "India Overtakes China to Become World's Most Populous Country," *Guardian*, April 24, 2023, https://www.theguardian.com/world/2023/apr/24/india-overtakes-china-to-become-worlds-most-populous-country (most populous).

4. Shakeel Ahmad, "Unleashing the Potential of a Young Pakistan," United Nations Human Development Programme, July 24, 2018, https://hdr.undp.org/content/unleashing-potential-young-pakistan (Pakistan); Laura Silver, Christine Huang, and Laura Clancy, "Key Facts as India Surpasses China as the World's Most Populous Country," Pew Research Center, February 9, 2023, https://www.pewresearch.org/short-reads/2023/02/09/key-facts-as-india-surpasses-china-as-the-worlds-most-populous-country/ (India); "World Population Dashboard: Bangladesh," United Nations Population Fund, accessed March 15, 2024, https://www.unfpa.org/data/world-population/BD.

5. Dreze and Sen, *India*, vi.

6. See UNICEF malnutrition data, available at https://data.unicef.org/topic/nutrition/malnutrition/.

7. This is based on United Nations World Urbanization Prospects data from 2018, highlights available at https://population.un.org/wup/Publications/Files/WUP2018-Highlights.pdf.

8. van Schendel, *History of Bangladesh*, 276 (Dhaka); Fisher, *Environmental History*, 249 (Bangladesh generally).

9. Projected by United Nations World Urbanization Prospects data.

10. Ambade, "Air Pollution during Diwali."

11. Neha Tandon Sharma, "Almost Twice as Tall as Big Ben," Luxury Launches, November 20, 2022, https://luxurylaunches.com/celebrities/antilia-the-most-expensive-home-in-the-world.php.

12. Saglio-Yatzimirsky, *Dharavi*, 1.

13. Martin-Brehm Christensen et al., "Survival of the Richest: How We Must Tax the Super-Rich Now to Fight Inequality," Oxfam International, 2023, https://oxfamilibrary.openrepository.com/bitstream/10546/621477/7/bp-survival-of-the-richest-160123-en.pdf.

14. Maurice Landes, Alex Melton, and Seanicaa Edwards, "From Where the Buffalo Roam: India's Beef Exports," USDA, Economic Research Service, June 2016, https://www.ers.usda.gov/publications/pub-details/?pubid=37673 (on beef).

15. Ari Hoffman and Jeanne Batalova, "Indian Immigrants in the United States," Migration Policy Institute, December 7, 2022, https://www.migrationpolicy.org/article/indian-immigrants-united-states.

16. World Trade Organization, "World Trade Statistical Review 2023," accessed February 10, 2024, https://www.wto.org/english/res_e/publications_e/wtsr_2023_e.htm, p. 80.

17. van Schendel, *History of Bangladesh*, 282–283.

18. Labowitz and Baumann-Pauly, "Business as Usual Is Not an Option," 9.

19. Siddiqui, "Scandalising the Supply Chain."

20. Labowitz and Baumann-Pauly, "Beyond the Tip of the Iceberg"; on paths forward, see Saxena, *Labor*.

21. Kai McNamee, "10 Years after the Deadliest Garment Factory Accident," NPR, *All Things Considered*, April 26, 2023, https://www.npr.org/2023/04/26/1172289981/10-years-after-the-deadliest-garment-factory-accident.

22. Ruwanpura, *Garments without Guilt?*

23. World Bank, "People Practicing Open Defecation (% of Population)," World Bank Open Data, accessed April 18, 2024, https://data.worldbank.org/indicator/SH.STA.ODFC.ZS.

24. Fisher, *Environmental History*, 230.

25. Gatade, "Silencing Caste, Sanitising Oppression."

26. Nagar, "Unfair Selection."

27. E.g., India Today Web Desk, "Just Learnt What Kalu Meant: Darren Sammy Furious at Racial Barb Directed during IPL," *India Today*, June 6, 2020, https://www.indiatoday.in/sports/cricket/story/darren-sammy-says-he-thisara-perera-were-called-kalu-playing-in-ipl-1686277-2020-06-06. On the history of cricket in India, see Ramachandra Guha, *A Corner of a Foreign Field: The Indian History of a British Sport* (Delhi: Pan Macmillan, 2002).

28. Ghosh, "Bones of Our Mother," 444.

29. Bhukya, *Roots of the Periphery*, 179.

30. Jha, "Code of Silence."

31. Elias, *Wings of Diesel*; Jamal J. Elias, "On Wings of Diesel: The Decorated Trucks of Pakistan," *Amherst Magazine*, Spring 2005, https://www.amherst.edu/news/magazine/issue-archive/2005_spring/wings (quote).

32. Sherman, *Nehru's India*, 197.

33. Peterson and Soneji, "Introduction," 4–8.

34. Morcom, *Illicit Worlds of Indian Dance* (on devadasis and tawaifs); Soneji, *Unfinished Gestures* (on devadasis).

35. Soneji, "Critical Steps."

36. Web Desk, "13 Musicians and Artists Killed in Pakistan since 2008," *News International*, June 23, 2016, https://www.thenews.com.pk/latest/130121-13-musicians-artists-killed-Pakistan-since-2008.

37. Muneeza Naqvi, "Indian Artist M.F. Husain Dies at 95," *Washington Post*, June 9, 2011, https://www.washingtonpost.com/local/obituaries/indian-artist-mf-husain-dies-at-95/2011/06/09/AGrU2hNH_story.html.

38. Sherman, *Nehru's India*, 199.

39. Gilmartin and Metcalf, "Art on Trial," 56. I used the award dates as given on the Government of India's website.

40. William Grimes, "Maqbool Fida Husain, India's Most Famous Painter, Dies at 95," *New York Times*, June 9, 2011, https://www.nytimes.com/2011/06/10/arts/design/maqbool-fida-husain-indias-most-famous-painter-dies-at-95.html; Somini Sengupta, "An Artist in Exile Tests India's Democratic Ideals," *New York Times*, November 8, 2008, https://www.nytimes.com/2008/11/09/world/asia/09india.html. On the international context of these attacks, see Anderson, "Neo-Hindutva."

41. E.g., see essays in Dudrah and Desai, *Bollywood Reader*.

42. Debasish Roy Chowdhury, "How Bollywood Rolled Over to Hindu Supremacists," *Time*, January 26, 2023, https://time.com/6250414/bollywood-hindu-supremacists/.

43. Chowdhury, "How Bollywood Rolled Over to Hindu Supremacists"; see also Samanth Subramanian, "When the Hindu Right Came for Bollywood," *New Yorker*, October 10, 2022, https://www.newyorker.com/magazine/2022/10/17/when-the-hindu-right-came-for-bollywood.

44. Simon Abrams, "The Man Behind India's Controversial Global Blockbuster 'RRR,'" *New Yorker*, February 16, 2023, https://www.newyorker.com/culture/the-new-yorker-interview/the-man-behind-indias-controversial-global-blockbuster-rrr-s-s-rajamouli.

45. Chowdhury, "How Bollywood Rolled Over to Hindu Supremacists."

46. See Freedom House democracy rankings, especially https://freedomhouse.org/country/india.

47. V-Dem Institute, "Democracy Report 2022: Autocratization Changing Nature?," https://v-dem.net/media/publications/dr_2022.pdf.

48. Ananya Vajpeyi, "Secular India or Hindu Nation: A Short History," *Contending Modernities*, April 19, 2024, https://contendingmodernities.nd.edu/global-currents/secular-india-hindu-nation/.

49. E.g., see India reports by Amnesty International, Human Rights Watch, and the United States Commission on International Religious Freedom (USCIRF).

50. Alex Travelli and Suhasini Raj, "Modi Calls Muslims 'Infiltrators' Who Would Take India's Wealth," *New York Times*, April 26, 2024, https://www.nytimes.com/2024/04/22/world/asia/modi-speech-muslims.html.

51. "Timeline: Ayodhya Holy Site Crisis," BBC News, December 6, 2012, https://www.bbc.com/news/world-south-asia-11436552.

52. Jaffrelot, *Modi's India*, 16–17 (the Bajrang Dal is the VHP's youth movement).

53. Disinformation continues to circulate about the Babri Masjid site, including allegations of a temple being located beneath the ruins of the mosque. Sometimes, proponents of this theory cite an archaeological excavation of the site, led by the Archaeological Survey of India in 2003. However, the excavation is unreliable, owing to its many flaws, irregularities, and outdated methods. On this, see Menon and Varma, "Was There a Temple."

54. See map in Hasan, *Legacy of a Divided Nation*, 257.

55. Press Trust of India, "26 Years on: Ayodhya Residents Recall the Horrors of 1992 Tragedy," *Hindustan Times*, December 5, 2018, https://www.hindustantimes.com/india-news/26-years-on-ayodhya-residents-recall-the-horrors-of-1992-tragedy/story-2lb84or3KmxKCRyw7vEteO.html.

56. "Timeline: Ayodhya Holy Site Crisis."

57. Metcalf, *Ideologies of the Raj*, 155.

58. Jaffrelot, *Modi's India*, 34–38 (Modi's RSS membership).

59. Jaffrelot, *Modi's India*, 39–41.

60. Jaffrelot, "2002 Pogrom in Gujarat," 176.

61. BBC Two, "India: The Modi Question" (documentary), February 2023, episode 1, https://www.bbc.co.uk/programmes/p0dkb144.

62. Jaffrelot, *Modi's India*, 451; James Mann, "Why Narendra Modi Was Banned from the U.S.," *Wall Street Journal*, May 2, 2014, https://www.wsj.com/articles/why-narendra-modi-was-banned-from-the-u-s-1399062010 ("severe violations of religious freedom").

63. BBC Two, "India: The Modi Question" (documentary), February 2023.

64. Jaffrelot, *Modi's India*, 33 ("right conduit") and 59 ("strongman").

65. Jaffrelot, *Modi's India*, 150.

66. Echeverri-Gent, Sinha, and Wyatt, "Economic Distress amidst Political Success."

67. This paragraph draws on human rights reports published between 2014 and 2020 (about events through 2019) by Human Rights Watch, Amnesty International, and the United States Commission on International Religious Freedom.

68. Amnesty International, "India: Hate Crimes against Muslims and Rising Islamophobia Must Be Condemned," June 28, 2017, https://www.amnesty.org/en/latest/press-release/2017/06/india-hate-crimes-against-muslims-and-rising-islamophobia-must-be-condemned/.

69. United Nations, "UN Experts Call on India to Protect Journalist Rana Ayyub from Online Hate Campaign," May 24, 2018, https://www.ohchr.org/en/press-releases/2018/05/un-experts-call-india-protect-journalist-rana-ayyub-online-hate-campaign.

70. "Violent Cow Protection in India: Vigilante Groups Attack Minorities," Human Rights Watch, February 18, 2019, https://www.hrw.org/report/2019/02/19/violent-cow-protection-india/vigilante-groups-attack-minorities.

71. Jaffrelot, *Modi's India*, chap. 7.

72. Christophe Jaffrelot, "Bajrang Dal and Making of the Deeper State," *Indian Express*, August 2, 2023, https://indianexpress.com/article/opinion/columns/karnataka-election-result-poll-campaign-congress-bjp-8645595/ ("deeper state").

73. On India's freedom of the press, see annual rankings by Reporters Without Borders (Reporters sans Frontieres).

74. Dexter Filkins, "Blood and Soil in Narendra Modi's India." *New Yorker*, December 2, 2019, https://www.newyorker.com/magazine/2019/12/09/blood-and-soil-in-narendra-modis-india.

75. M Siddiq (D) Thr Lrs v. Mahant Suresh Das & Ors., decided November 9, 2019.

76. Truschke, "Ayodhya Verdict."

77. Patel, *Our Hindu Rashtra*, chap. 4 ("garbled mantras").

78. Jaffrelot, *Modi's India*, 276–289.

79. Mujib Mashal and Hari Kumar, "Modi Opens a Giant Temple in a Triumph for India's Hindu Nationalists," *New York Times*, January 22, 2024, https://www.nytimes.com/2024/01/22/world/asia/modi-india-ram-temple.html.

80. Ranking by Reporters sans Frontieres, "India," 2023, https://rsf.org/en/country/india.

81. Reporters sans Frontieres, "India," 2024, https://rsf.org/en/country/india.

82. Khilnani, *Idea of India*, xii.

83. Patel, *Our Hindu Rashtra*, vii.

84. Translated by Shabana Mir in "Fahmida Riaz on Fundamentalism on Both Sides," April 11, 2014, https://koonjblog.wordpress.com/2014/04/11/india-awash-in-fundamentalism-hail-fellow-well-met/.

85. Amnesty International, "India 2023," 2024, https://www.amnesty.org/en/location/asia-and-the-pacific/south-asia/india/report-india/.

86. *Constitution of India*, preamble.

87. Amrith, *Unruly Waters*, 303.

88. Amrith, *Unruly Waters*, 3; World Bank, "How Is India Addressing Its Water Needs?," World Bank Brief, February 14, 2023, https://www.worldbank.org/en/country/india/brief/world-water-day-2022-how-india-is-addressing-its-water-needs.

89. Agarwal, Chopra, and Sharma, *State of India's Environment 1982*, 23.

90. Agarwal, Chopra, and Sharma, *State of India's Environment 1982*, 20.

91. Agarwal, Chopra, and Sharma, *State of India's Environment 1982*, 26.

92. Amrith, *Unruly Waters*, 269.

93. The Indian government did not voluntarily release this information; Vivek Mishra, "Sewage Overload: Why the Ganga Remains Polluted Despite Cleanliness Drives," *Down to Earth*, April 16, 2023, https://www.downtoearth.org.in/news/environment/sewage-overload-why-the-ganga-remains-polluted-despite-cleanliness-drives-88651.

94. Amrith, *Unruly Waters*, 312.

95. Iqbal, "Bengal Delta."

96. Fisher, *Environmental History of India*, 220–221.

97. Dasgupta et al., *Urban Flooding of Greater Dhaka*.

98. Amrith, *Unruly Waters*, 309 (1970 and 2007 numbers); Iqbal, "Governing Mass Migration to Dhaka," 28 (1991 number).

99. Pequeno et al., "Climate Impact."

100. Im, Pal, and Eltahir, "Deadly Heat Waves."

101. Fisher, *Environmental History*, 224.

102. Quoted in Sadhika Tiwari, "Me the Change: Meet Dayamani Barla, Tribal Activist and a Climate Warrior," *The Quint*, March 19, 2022, https://www.thequint.com/climate-change/meet-climate-change-warrior-dayamani-barla-a-tribal-activist-from-jharkhand.

AFTERWORD

1. Quoted in Shoma Chaudhury, "The Master in his Absurd Exile," February 2, 2008, https://shomachaudhury.com/the-master-in-his-absurd-exile/.

2. United Nations, "International Migrant Stock 2020," https://www.un.org/development/desa/pd/content/international-migrant-stock (I round up slightly, given that I write in 2024 and the data dates to 2020).

3. Rajan, "Migration in South Asia," figure 1.2 (Saudi Arabia) and pp. 3–4 (majority); UN Migration, *World Migration Report 2022*, https://publications.iom.int/books/world-migration-report-2022, p. 75.

4. South Asian Americans Leading Together, "Demographic Information," https://saalt.org/south-asians-in-the-us/demographic-information/, accessed February 12, 2024 (United States); Minority Rights Group, "South Asians in the United Kingdom" (2022), https://minorityrights.org/communities/south-asians/ (United Kingdom).

5. Rajan, "Migration in South Asia," 6–7.

6. Nisha Anand, "Over 87,000 Indians Gave Up Their Citizenship So Far in 2023, Says MEA," *Hindustan Times*, July 23, 2023, https://www.hindustantimes.com/india-news/how-many-indian-giving-up-indian-citizenship-2023-data-multiple-citizenship-indian-laws-lok-sabha-news-101690116422019.html.

7. Chakravorty, Kapur, and Singh, *Other One Percent*, 27 (chaps. 1–2 more broadly).

8. Also see Sumitra Badrinathan, Devesh Kapur, Jonathan Kay, and Milan Vaishnav, "Social Realities of Indian Americans: Results from the 2020 Indian American Attitudes Survey," Carnegie Endowment for International Peace, June 9, 2021, https://carnegieendowment.org/2021/06/09/social-realities-of-indian-americans-results-from-2020-indian-american-attitudes-survey-pub-84667.

9. Mishra, *Desis Divided*, 226n18.

10. Mishra, *Desis Divided*, 31 and 226n18.

11. Badrinathan et al., "Social Realities of Indian Americans."

12. Truschke, "Hindu Right in the United States"; not all members of the student groups are aware of their extremist origins and ties.

13. Truschke, "Hindu Right in the United States."

14. Casolari, "Hindutva's Foreign Tie-up"; Casolari, *Shadow of the Swastika*.

15. Falcone, "Garba with Attitude."

16. Kurien, "Hinduism in the United States," 148–149 (as Kurien notes, a north-south divide remains).

17. On the 2020 Delhi Riots, see Delhi Minorities Commission, "Report of the DMC Fact-Finding Committee on North-East Delhi Riots of February 2020," Government of NCT of Delhi, 2020.

18. Freedom House democracy rankings, https://freedomhouse.org/country/india.

19. See reports and investigations by Amnesty International, Human Rights Watch, and USCIRF.

20. On Hindutva as fascism, see sources ranging from Jawaharlal Nehru (discussed in Jaffrelot, *Modi's India*, 18) to Patnaik, "Fascism of Our Times."

HISTORIOGRAPHY

1. Nora, "Between Memory and History," 9.

2. Thapar, *Our History*, chaps. 3–4; Truschke, "Hindutva's Dangerous Rewriting of History."

3. On Hindutva attacks on scholars in North America over the last several decades, see South Asia Scholar Activist Collective, "Timeline of Specific Incidents of Hindutva Harassment."

4. I am grateful to Harbans Mukhia for this insight, especially in his January 24, 2021, remarks on the subject "How Muslim Was the Medieval Indian State?" (virtual event).

5. For some historians, "positivism" is a dirty word (hence my avoidance of it here). Vocabulary aside, I find it astonishing, in good and bad ways, that some historians consider themselves to be almost post-truth. Part of me envies historians of other regions who do not face anti-intellectual harassment from far-right movements and so are free to question the centrality of facts to the historian's craft. Another part of me is appalled that some historians have become so enamored with their own theories that they are willing to sell short that we write about real people and real lives. We owe our subjects—prior generations of people—our best efforts to get their stories right and present them accurately and truthfully.

6. Benjamin, *Illuminations*, 256.

7. I borrow "Brahminical archive" from Taylor, *Fall of the Indigo Jackal*.

8. On early European imaginations of "timeless India," see Asif, *Loss of Hindustan*, 19–21, and Satia, *Time's Monster*.

9. See Eaton, "(Re)imag(in)ing Other^{2}ness" for a postmortem.

10. Margaret Atwood, "Who Tells the Story: Narrative Point of View," Master Class, accessed August 21, 2023, https://www.masterclass.com/classes/margaret-atwood-teaches-creative-writing/chapters/who-tells-the-story-narrative-point-of-view.

11. Cf. to the argument that engagement with Western theory alongside Indian sources can be productive (e.g., Kaviraj, "What Is Western").

12. Others have made this objection as well (e.g., Atwal, *Royals and Rebels*, 7, specifically about scholarship on the Sikh Empire).

13. Salman Rushdie, *The Satanic Verses: A Novel* (New York: Picador, 2000), 353.

14. Cf. Asher and Talbot, *India before Europe*; Jha, *Ancient India*; Thapar, *Early India*.

15. Cf. Keay, *India*, chap. 7 (in emphasis and tone).

16. Parker, *Making of Roman India*, 85.

17. Williams, *Art of Gupta India*, 3, published in 1982.

18. Cf. Khilnani, *Idea of India*.

19. Keune, *Shared Devotion*, 21.

20. Gangl, "Essential Tension."

21. Ernst, *Eternal Garden*, 22–23; Truschke, "Hindu."

22. English "monsoon" comes from the Arabic "mausim," via Portuguese "moncao" (Amrith, *Unruly Waters*, 22).

POSTSCRIPT AND ACKNOWLEDGMENTS

1. *Kural*, 60 (Sundaram's translation).

2. Meena Alexander, *Fault Lines: A Memoir* (New York: Feminist Press at the City University of New York, 1993), 193.

3. Abul Fazl, *History of Akbar*, 1:59 (Thackston's translation).

Bibliography

PRIMARY SOURCES

Abdur Rahman. *Samdesarasaka of Abdul Rahman*. Translated by C. M. Mayrhofer. Delhi: Motilal Banarsidass, 1998.

Aberigh-Mackay, George. *Twenty-One Days in India, or the Tour of Sir Ali Baba, K.C.B.* 3rd ed. London: W. H. Allen, 1881.

Abul Fazl ibn Mubarak. *Ain-i Akbari*. Edited by H. Blochmann. 2 vols. Calcutta: Asiatic Society of Bengal, 1867–1877.

———. *The History of Akbar*. Translated by Wheeler M. Thackston. 8 vols. Cambridge, MA: Harvard University Press, 2015–2022.

Afzal, M. Rafique, ed. *Selected Speeches and Statements of the Quaid-i-Azam Mohammad Ali Jinnah, 1911–34 and 1947–48*. Lahore: Research Society of Pakistan, University of the Punjab, 1980.

Ahmad, Naim, ed. *Shahrashob: Ma'muqaddimah o Havashi*. Delhi: Maktabah-yi jamah, 1968.

Ambedkar, B. R. *Annihilation of Caste: The Annotated Critical Edition*. Edited by S. Anand. London: Verso, 2014.

———. *The Buddha and His Dhamma: A Critical Edition*. Edited by Aakash Singh Rathore and Ajay Verma. New Delhi: Oxford University Press, 2011.

———. *Dr. Babasaheb Ambedkar: Writings and Speeches*. 17 vols. Bombay: Education Department, Government of Maharashtra, 1979.

Amir Khusraw. *Khazainul Futuh*, published as *The Campaigns of 'Ala'u'd-Din Khilji: Being the Khaza'inul Futuh (Treasures of Victory)*. Translated by Muhammad Habib. Madras: Diocesan Press, 1931.

Ananda Ranga Pillai. *The Private Diary of Ananda Ranga Pillai, Dubash to Joseph Francois Dupleix, Knight of the Order of St. Michael, and Governor of Pondichery*. Vol. 1. Translated and edited by J. Frederick Price and K. Rangachari. Madras: Government Press, 1904.

Arthashastra. Published as *King, Governance, and Law in Ancient India: Kautilya's Arthasastra*. Edited and translated by Patrick Olivelle. New York: Oxford University Press, 2013.

Asad Beg Qazvini. *Waqai Asad Beg Qazvini*. Edited by Chander Shekhar. Delhi: National Mission for Manuscripts, 2017.

Aslan, Reza, ed. *Tablet and Pen: Literary Landscapes from the Modern Middle East*. New York: W. W. Norton, 2011.

Aurobindo. *The Complete Works of Sri Aurobindo*. Vol. 5, *Translations*. Pondicherry: Sri Aurobindo Ashram Press, 1999.

Azad, Maulana. "Presidential Address of Abul Kalam Azad—Ramgarh, December 1940." In *India's Partition: Process, Strategy and Mobilization*, edited by Mushirul Hasan, 59–68. Delhi: Oxford University Press, 1993.

Babur. *The Baburnama: Memoirs of Babur, Prince and Emperor*. Translated by Wheeler M. Thackston. Washington, DC: Freer Gallery of Art and Arthur M. Sackler Gallery, Smithsonian Institution, 1996.

Badauni. *Muntakhab al-Tavarikh*. Edited by W. N. Lees and Munshi Ahmad Ali. Vol. 2. Calcutta: College Press, 1865.

Bailey, Greg, ed. and trans. *Love Lyrics by Amaru, Bhartrihari, and Bilhana*. New York: New York University Press, 2005.

Bana. *The Harsa-Carita of Bana*. Translated by E. B. Cowell and F. W. Thomas. London: Royal Asiatic Society, 1897.

Banarasidas. *Ardhakathanaka: Half a Tale*. Translated by Mukund Lath. New Delhi: Rupa, 2005.

Bapat, S. V., ed. *The Reminiscences and Anecdotes of Lokamanya Tilak*. Poona: Jagadhitechu Press, 1924.

Baqir, Muhammad. *Advice on the Art of Governance: An Indo-Islamic Mirror for Princes: Mau'izah-i Jahangiri of Muhammad Baqir Najm-i Sani*. Translated by Sajida Sultana Alvi. Albany: State University of New York Press, 1989.

Barani. *Tarikh-i Firuzshahi*. Edited by Saiyid Ahmad Khan and W. Nassau Lees. Calcutta: Asiatic Society of Bengal, 1860.

Bates, Crispin, and Marina Carter, eds. *Mutiny at the Margins: New Perspectives on the Indian Uprising of 1857*. Vol. 7. New Delhi: Sage, 2017.

Bernier, Francis. *Travels in the Mogul Empire*. Translated by Irving Brock. Vol. 2. London: William Pickering, 1826.

Beverley, H. *Report on the Census of Bengal 1872*. Calcutta: Bengal Secretariat Press, 1872.

The Bhagavad-Gita: Krishna's Counsel in Time of War. Translated by Barbara Stoler Miller. New York: Bantam Books, 2004.

The Bhagavadgita in the Mahabharata: Text and Translation. Translated by J.A.B. van Buitenen. Chicago: University of Chicago Press, 1994.

Bhartrhari. *Subhashitatrishati, with the Commentary of Ramachandrabudhendra*. Edited by Narayana Rama Acharya and Damodara Dharmananda Kosambi. Varanasi: Chaukhambha Sanskrit Sansthan, 1987.

Bhatavadekar, Krishna Shastri, and Udhav Shastree Ainapure, eds. *Subhashitaratnakara*. Bombay: Gopal Narayen, 1903.

Bhimsen. *Tarikh-i-Dilkasha: Memoirs of Bhimsen Relating to Aurangzib's Deccan Campaigns*. Translated by Jadunath Sarkar. Edited by V. G. Khobrekar. Bombay: Department of Archives, Maharashtra, 1972.

Bilhana. *Vikramankadevacharita*. Edited by Georg Buhler. Bombay: Government Central Book Depot, 1875.

Bilimoria, Jamshid H., trans. *Ruka'at-i-Alamgiri or Letters of Aurungzebe: With Historical and Explanatory Notes*. Calcutta: Cherag Printing Press, 1908.

Biruni. *Alberuni's India: An Account of the Religion, Philosophy, Literature, Geography, Chronology, Astronomy, Customs, Laws and Astrology of India about A.D. 1030*. Translated by Edward C. Sachau. 2 vols. Delhi: S. Chand, 1965.

———. *Kitab al-Biruni fi tahqiq ma li-al-hind min maqula maqbula fi al-'aql aw mardula*. Edited by Edward C. Sachau. London: Trubner, 1887.

BJP. "Towards a New Polity: Election Manifesto, Lok Sabha Election—1984." 1984.

———. "Vote BJP: Election Manifesto 1998." 1998.

Bolts, William. *Considerations on India Affairs: Particularly Respecting the Present State of Bengal and Its Dependencies*. 2nd ed. London: J. Almon, 1772.

Bourke-White, Margaret. *Halfway to Freedom: A Report on the New India in the Words and Photographs of Margaret Bourke-White*. New York: Simon and Schuster, 1949.

Brodbeck, Simon, trans. *Krishna's Lineage: The Harivamsha of Vyasa's Mahabharata*. New York: Oxford University Press, 2019.

Broughton, H. "Letters from a Competition Wallah: Letter XII." *Macmillan's Magazine*, May 1864, 1–17.

Casson, Lionel. *The Periplus Maris Erythraei: Text with Introduction, Translation, and Commentary*. Princeton, NJ: Princeton University Press, 1989.

Chughtai, Ismat. *My Friend, My Enemy: Essays, Reminiscences, Portraits*. Translated by Tahira Naqvi. New Delhi: Kali for Women, 2001.

The Conference of Orientalists Including Museums and Archaeology Conference Held at Simla, July 1911. Simla: Government Central Branch Press, 1911.

Constituent Assembly of Pakistan Debates: Monday, 7th March, 1949. Vol. 5(1). Karachi: Government of Pakistan, 1949.

Constitution of India. Delhi: Government of India Press, 1949.

"The Convention of 1884." *Supplement to the Theosophist* 4, no. 5 (1885): 1–3.

Cornish, W. R. *Report on the Census of the Madras Presidency 1871, with Appendix Containing the Results of the Census Arranged in Standard Forms Prescribed by the Government of India*. Madras: Government Gazette Press, 1874.

Corpus Inscriptionum Indicarum. Vol. 3 (revised), *Inscriptions of the Early Gupta*

Kings. Edited by Devadatta Ramakrishna Bhandarkar, Bahadurchand Chhabra, Govind Swamirao Gai, and John Faithfull Fleet. New Delhi: Archaeological Survey of India, 1981.

Corpus Inscriptionum Indicarum. Vol. 5, *Inscriptions of the Vakatakas*. Edited by Vasudev Vishnu Mirashi. Oootacamund: Government Epigraphist for India, 1963.

Cunningham, Alexander. *Archaeological Survey of India Report for the Year 1872–73*. Vol. 5. Calcutta: Office of the Superintendent of Government Printing, 1875.

Das, Durga, ed. *Sardar Patel's Correspondence 1945–50*. Vol. 3. Ahmedabad: Navajivan Publishing House, 1972.

Derozario, M. *The Complete Monumental Register: Containing All the Epitaphs, Inscriptions, etc. in the Different Churches and Burial-Grounds, in and about Calcutta*. Calcutta: P. Ferris, 1815.

de Silva, Chandra R., ed. *Portuguese Encounters with Sri Lanka and the Maldives: Translated Texts from the Age of Discoveries*. New York: Routledge, 2016.

Devavimala. *Hirasaubhagya*. Edited by Mahamahopadhyaya Pandit Sivadatta and Kashinath Pandurang Parab. Bombay: Tukaram Javaji, 1900.

Dharmasvamin. *Biography of Dharmasvamin: (Chag lo tsa-ba Chos-rje-dpal): A Tibetan Monk Pilgrim*. Translated by George Roerich. Patna: K. P. Jayaswal Research Institute, 1959.

Doniger, Wendy, trans. *The Rig Veda: An Anthology: One Hundred and Eight Hymns*. London: Penguin, 2005.

East India (Proclamations): Ordered by the House of Commons, to Be Printed, 13 November 1908. London: Majesty's Stationery Office, 1908.

Edgerton, Franklin, ed. *The Panchatantra Reconstructed: An Attempt to Establish the Lost Original Sanskrit Text of the Most Famous of Indian Story-Collections on the Basis of the Principal Extant Versions*. 2 vols. New Haven, CT: American Oriental Society, 1924.

The Electronic Text Corpus of Sumerian Literature. University of Oxford, last updated 2016. https://etcsl.orinst.ox.ac.uk/.

Epigraphia Indica of the Archaeological Survey of India. Calcutta/Delhi: Asiatic Society, 1892–.

Exhibition of Indian Art Held at the Government House November 6–December 31, 1948 Catalogue. New Delhi: Department of Archaeology, 1948.

Ferdowsi. *Shahnameh*, published as *Sunset of Empire: Stories from the Shahnameh of Ferdowsi*. Vol. 3. Translated by Dick Davis. Washington, DC: Mage, 2004.

Firishta, Muhammad Qasim. *History of the Rise of the Mahomedan Power in India, till the Year A.D. 1612*. Translated by John Briggs. Vol. 2. London: Longman, Rees, Orme, Brown, and Green, 1829.

Fitzgerald, James L., trans. *The Mahabharata, Volume 7: Book 11: The Book of the Women; Book, 12: The Book of Peace, Part 1*. Chicago: University of Chicago Press, 2004.

Foster, William, ed. *The Embassy of Sir Thomas Roe to the Court of the Great Mogul, 1615–1619*. Vol. 2. London: Hakluyt Society, 1899.

Gambhirananda, Swami. *History of the Ramakrishna Math and Mission*. Calcutta: Advaita Ashrama, 1957.

Gandhi, Indira. "Letter from Indian Prime Minister Gandhi to President Nixon, May 13, 1971." In *Foreign Relations of the United States, 1969–1976*, vol. 9, edited by Louis J. Smith, document 46. Washington, DC: United States Government Printing Office, 1971. https://history.state.gov/historicaldocuments/frus1969-76v11/d46.

Gandhi, Mohandas. *The Collected Works of Mahatma Gandhi*. 98 vols. New Delhi: Government of India, 1999.

———. *Hind Swaraj and Other Writings*. Edited by Anthony J. Parel. Cambridge: Cambridge University Press, 1997.

Gangadevi. *Madhuravijaya*. Edited by S. Thiruvenkatachari. Annamalainagar: Annamalai University, 1957.

Geiger, Wilhelm, and Mabel Haynes Bode, trans. The *Mahavamsa, or The Great Chronicle of Ceylon*. London: Pali Text Society, 1912.

Geiger, Wilhelm, and C. Mabel Rickmers, trans. *Culavamsa: Being the More Recent Part of the Mahavamsa*. 2 vols. London: Pali Text Society, 1929–1930.

Gethin, Rupert, trans. *Sayings of the Buddha: A Selection of Suttas from the Pali Nikayas.* Oxford: Oxford University Press, 2008.

Ghulam Hussain Khan, Seid. *The Seir Mutaqherin, or Review of Modern Times, Being an History of India, from the Year 1118, to Year 1194, of the Hedjrah.* Calcutta: Cambray, 1902–1903.

Godse, Nathuram. *May It Please Your Honour.* 3rd ed. Delhi: Surya Prakashan, 1987.

Hafiz. *Divan-i Hafiz.* Edited by Parviz Natil Khanlari. Tehran: Intisharat-i Khvarazmi, 1983.

Hala. *Poems on Life and Love in Ancient India: Hala's* Sattasai. Translated by Peter Khoroche and Herman Tieken. Albany, NY: Excelsior Editions, 2009.

Hallisey, Charles, trans. *Therigatha: Poems of the First Buddhist Women.* Cambridge, MA: Harvard University Press, 2015.

Hart, George L., and Hank Heifetz, trans. *The Four Hundred Songs of War and Wisdom: An Anthology of Poems from Classical Tamil, The Purananuru.* New York: Columbia University Press, 1999.

Hashmi, Nurul Hasan, ed. *Kulliyat-i Vali.* Lucknow: Uttar Pradesh Urdu Academy, 2008.

Herodotus. *The Histories.* Translated by Tom Holland. London: Penguin, 2013.

A Hindu Lady. "Infant Marriage and Enforced Widowhood." *Times of India*, June 26, 1885. retyped and available at https://scalar.lehigh.edu/kiplings/infant-marriage-and-enforced-widowhood-rukhmabai-june-1885.

Hossain, Rokeya Sakhawat. *Sultana's Dream: A Feminist Utopia, and Selections from The Secluded Ones.* Edited and translated by Roushan Jahan. New York: Feminist Press at the City University of New York, 1988.

Houghton, Walter R., ed. *Neely's History of the Parliament of Religions and Religious Congresses at the World's Columbian Exposition.* 4th ed. Chicago: F. Tennyson Neely, 1894.

Hultzsch, E. *Inscriptions of Asoka.* New ed. with 55 plates. Vol. 1. Oxford: Clarendon Press, 1925.

Hyecho. *Hye Ch'o Diary: A Memoir of the Pilgrimage to the Five Regions of India.* Translated and edited by Han-Sung Yang, Yun-Hua Jan, Shotaro Iida, and Laurence W. Preston. Berkeley: Asian Humanities Press, 1984.

Ibn al-Athir, 'Izz al-Din. *The Chronicle of Ibn al-Athir for the Crusading Period from al-Kamil Fi'l-Ta'rikh.* Translated by D. S. Richards. Vol. 3. Aldershot, UK: Ashgate, 2008.

Ibn Battuta. *The Rehla of Ibn Battuta (India, Maldive Islands and Ceylon).* Translated by Mahdi Husain. Baroda: Oriental Institute, 1976.

———. *The Travels of Ibn Battuta, A.D. 1325–1354.* Edited and translated by H.A.R. Gibb and C. F. Beckingham. 4 vols. London: Routledge, 2016.

Ibrahim Adil Shah II. *Kitab-i-Nauras.* Translated by Nazir Ahmad. New Delhi: Bharatiya Kala Kendra, 1956.

Isami. *Futuhus-Salatin.* Edited by A. S. Usha. Madras: University of Madras, 1948.

Jaffrelot, Christophe, ed. *Hindu Nationalism: A Reader.* Princeton, NJ: Princeton University Press, 2007.

Jahangir. *The Jahangirnama: Memoirs of Jahangir, Emperor of India.* Translated by Wheeler H. Thackston. Washington, DC: Freer Gallery of Art and Arthur M. Sackler Gallery, Smithsonian Institution, 1999.

Jayanaka. *Prithvirajavijaya.* Edited by Gaurishankar Hirachand Ojha and Chandradhar Sharma Guleri. Ajmer: Vedic Yantralaya, 1941.

Jehan Begum, Nawab Sultan. *Hayat-i-Shahjehani: Life of Her Highness the Late Nawab Shahjehan Begum of Bhopal, C.I., G.C.S.I.* Translated by B. Ghosal. Bombay: Times Press, 1926.

Jonaraja. *Rajatarangini*, published as *Kingship in Kasmir (AD 1148–1459): From the Pen of Jonaraja, Court Pandit to Sultan Zayn al-'Abidin.* Edited and translated by Walter Slaje. Halle, Germany: Universitatsverlag Halle-Wittenberg, 2014.

Kabir. *The Bijak of Kabir.* Translated by Linda Hess and Shukdeo Singh. Oxford: Oxford University Press, 2002.

———. *Kabir Granthavali (Doha).* Edited by Charlotte Vaudeville. Pondichery: Institut Francais D'Indologie, 1957.

Kakka. *Nabhinandanajinoddhara.* Edited and translated (into Gujarati) by Bhagvandas Harakhchand. Limdi: Shri Hemachandra-charya Jain Granthamala, 1929.

Kalhana. *Kalhana's Rajatarangini: A Chronicle of the Kings of Kasmir*. Edited by M. A. Stein. Reprinted, Delhi: Motilal Banarsidass, 1989.

Kalidasa. *The Recognition of Shakuntala*. Translated by Somadeva Vasudeva. New York: New York University Press, 2006.

Kanaganayakam, Chelva, ed. *Lutesong and Lament: Tamil Writing from Sri Lanka*. Ontario: TSAR Publications, 2001.

Kaul, Srikanth, ed. *Rajatarangini of Shrivara and Shuka*. Hoshiarpur: Vishveshvar-anand Institute, 1966.

Kaye, John William. *The Administration of the East India Company: A History of Indian Progress*. London: Richard Bentley, 1853.

Khafi Khan. *Muntakhab al-Lubab*. Edited by Maulavi Kabir al-Din Ahmed. Vol 2. Calcutta: College Press, 1874.

Khairuddin. *The Bulwuntnamah Translated from the Tuhfa-i-Taza of Fakir Khair-ud-Din Khan*. Translated by Frederick Curwen. Allahabad: North-Western Provinces Government Press, 1875.

Khan Bahadur, Syed Ahmad. *Review on Dr. Hunter's Indian Musalmans: Are They Bound in Conscience to Rebel against the Queen?* Benares: Medical Hall Press, 1872.

Klijn, A.F.J. *The Acts of Thomas: Introduction, Text, and Commentary*. 2nd rev. ed. Leiden: Brill, 2003.

Kramer, Samuel Noah. *Enmerkar and the Lord of Aratta: A Sumerian Epic Tale of Iraq and Iran*. Philadelphia: University of Pennsylvania, 1952.

Krishnadasa. *Parasiprakasha*. Edited by Vibhuti Bhushan Bhattacharya. Varanasi: Varanaseya Sanskrit Vishvavidyalaya, 1965.

The Kural of Tiruvalluvar. Translated by P. S. Sundaram. London: Penguin, 1990.

Lakshmipati. *Nripatinitigarbhitavritta*. Edited by Jatindra Bimal Chaudhuri. Calcutta: Pracyavani, 1959.

Lawrence, Bruce B., trans. *Morals for the Heart: Conversations of Shaykh Nizam Ad-Din Awliya Recorded by Amir Hasan Sijzi*. New York: Paulist Press, 1992.

Legge, James, trans. *A Record of Buddhistic Kingdoms: Being an Account by the Chinese Monk Fa-Hien of His Travels in India and Ceylon (A.D. 399–414)*. Oxford: Clarendon Press, 1886.

Lilavati. Translated by Colebrooke, with notes by Haran Chandra Banerji. Allahabad: Kitab Mahal, 1967.

Lokhandwala, M. F., trans. *Mirat-i-Ahmadi: A Persian History of Gujarat (English Translation), Translated from the Persian Original of Ali Muhammad Khan*. Baroda: Oriental Institute, 1965.

The Longman Anthology of World Literature. Edited by David Damrosch et al. 6 vols. New York: Longman, 2004.

Losensky, Paul E., and Sunil Sharma, trans. *In the Bazaar of Love: The Selected Poetry of Amir Khusrau*. New Delhi: Penguin, 2011.

Luard, C. Eckford, and H. Hosten, trans. *Travels of Fray Sebastien Manrique, 1629–1643: A Translation of the Itinerario de Las Missiones Orientales*. 2 vols. Oxford: Hakluyt Society, 1927.

Lucas, Samuel. *Dacoitee in Excelsis, or, The Spoliation of Oude, by the East India Company, Faithfully Recounted with Notes and Documentary Illustrations*. London: J. R. Taylor, 1857.

Lutgendorf, Philip. "Book Five: Sundar Kand." *Indian Literature* 45, no. 3 (2001): 149–181.

The Mahabharata. Translated by J.A.B. van Buitenen. 3 vols. Chicago: University of Chicago Press, 1973–1978.

Mahabharata, published as *The Mahabharata, for the First Time Critically Edited*. Edited by Vishnu S. Sukthankar, S. K. Belvalkar, P. L. Vaidya, et al. 19 vols. Poona: Bhandarkar Oriental Research Institute, 1933–1966.

Mahalingam, T. V. *A Topographical List of Inscriptions in the Tamil Nadu and Kerala States*. Vol. 7, *Thanjavur District*. New Delhi: Indian Council of Historical Research, 1992.

Mallinson, James, trans. *Messenger Poems by Kalidasa, Dhoyi, and Rupagosvamin*. New York: New York University Press, 2006.

Mandal Commission. *Report of the Backward Classes Commission*. 2 vols. Delhi: Government of India, 1980.

Mansergh, Nicholas, ed. *The Transfer of Power 1942–7*. 12 vols. London: Her Majesty's Stationery Office, 1970–1983.

Manto, Saadat Hasan. *Black Margins: Sa'adat Hasan Manto Stories*. Edited and translated by Muhammad Umar Memon. New Delhi: Katha, 2003.

Manto, Saadat Hasan. *Stars from Another Sky: The Bombay Film World in the 1940s*. Translated by Khalid Hasan. New Delhi: Penguin Books, 1998.

Manu. *Manu's Code of Law: A Critical Edition and Translation of the* Manava-Dharmasastra. Translated by Patrick Olivelle. New York: Oxford University Press, 2005.

Manucci, Niccolao. *Storia do Mogor or, Mogul India, 1653–1708*. Translated by William Irvine. 4 vols. London: John Murray, 1907–1908.

McLeod, W. H., ed. and trans. *The B40 Janam-Sakhi: An English Translation with Introduction and Annotations of the India Office Library Gurmukhi Manuscript Panj. B40, a Janam-Sakhi of Guru Nanak compiled in A.D. 1733 by Daya Ram Abrol*. Amritsar: Guru Nanak Dev University, 1980.

Merutunga. *Prabandhachintamani*. Edited by Jinavijaya Muni. Shantiniketan: Adhisthata Singhi Jaina Jnanapitha, 1933.

Mir. *Zikr-i Mir: The Autobiography of the Eighteenth Century Mughal Poet, Mir Muhammad Taqi 'Mir' (1723–1810)*. Translated by C. M. Naim. New Delhi: Oxford University Press, 1999.

Moon, Penderel, ed. *Wavell: The Viceroy's Journal*. London: Oxford University Press, 1973.

Mukherjee, Rudranghsu, ed. *The Great Speeches of Modern India*. Noida: Random House India, 2011.

Muller, F. Max. "The Story of an Indian Child-Wife." *The Contemporary Review* 60 (1891): 183–187.

Muller, Georgina Adelaide, ed. *The Life and Letters of the Right Honourable Friedrich Max Muller*. 2 vols. London: Longmans, Green, 1902.

Nanjundayya, H. V. *The Ethnographical Survey of Mysore*. Bangalore: Government Press, 1906.

Naoroji, Dadabhai. *Poverty and Un-British Rule in India*. London: Swan Sonnenschein, 1901.

Narayan, R. K. *The Ramayana: A Shortened Modern Prose Version of the Indian Epic (Suggested by the Tamil Version of Kamban)*. New York: Penguin, 2006.

Natarajan, D. *Census of India 1971: Census Centenary Monograph no. 9 (Extracts from the All India Census Reports on Literacy)*. Delhi: Ministry of Home Affairs, 1972.

Nawaz, Mumtaz Shah. *The Heart Divided*. Lahore: ASR Publications, 1990.

Nayar, Pramod K., ed. *The Penguin 1857 Reader*. New Delhi: Penguin, 2007.

Nehru, Jawaharlal. *The Discovery of India*. Delhi: Oxford University Press, 1985.

———. *Jawaharlal Nehru's Speeches*. Vol. 3, *March 1953–August 1957*. Delhi: Ministry of Information and Broadcasting, Government of India, 1958.

———. *Selected Works*. Edited by S. Gopal. Vol. 10. First Series. New Delhi: Orient Longman, 1977.

———. *Selected Works*. Edited by S. Gopal. Vol. 3. Second Series. New Delhi: Jawaharlal Nehru Memorial Fund, 1985.

Nikitin, Athanasius. "The Travels of Athanasius Nikitin of Twer: Voyage to India." In *India in the Fifteenth Century*, edited by R. H. Major, 3–32. London: Hakluyt Society, 1857.

Olivelle, Patrick, ed. and trans. *The Early Upanisads: Annotated Text and Translation*. New York: Oxford University Press, 1998.

———, trans. *Pancatantra: The Book of India's Folk Wisdom*. Oxford: Oxford University Press, 1999.

Padmasagara. *Jagadgurukavya*. Edited by Hargovinddas and Becardas. Benares: Harakhchand Bhurabhai, 1910.

Papers Relating to the Punjab 1847–1849. Vol. 12, *Accounts and Papers*. London: Harrison and Son, 1849.

Paramananda, Kavindra. *The Epic of Shivaji*. Translated by James W. Laine and S. S. Bahulkar. Hyderabad: Orient Longman, 2001.

———. *Suryavamsha*, published as *Shrishivabharata*. Edited by Sadashiva Mahadeva Divekar. Poona: Ganesh Printing Press, 1927.

Paranavitana, S. *Sigiri Graffiti: Being Sinhalese Verses of the Eight, Ninth and Tenth Centuries*. Vol. 2. London: Published for the Government of Ceylon by Geoffrey Cumerlege, Oxford University Press, 1956.

Parthasarathy, R., ed. and trans. *The Cilappatikaram of Ilanko Atikal: An Epic of South*

India. New York: Columbia University Press, 1993.

Pirzada, Syed Sharifuddin, ed. *Foundations of Pakistan: All-India Muslim League Documents*. 2 vols. Karachi: National Publishing House Limited, 1969–1970.

Pliny the Elder. *Natural History*. Translated by H. Rackham. Vol. 3. Cambridge, MA: Harvard University Press, 1940.

———. *Natural History*. Vol. 6. Translated by W.H.S. Jones. Cambridge, MA: Harvard University Press, 1961.

Pollock, Sheldon, ed. and trans. *A Rasa Reader: Classical Indian Aesthetics*. New York: Columbia University Press, 2016.

Prasad, Pushpa. *Sanskrit Inscriptions of Delhi Sultanate, 1191–1526*. Delhi: Oxford University Press, 1990.

Ramabai Sarasvati, Pundita. *The High-Caste Hindu Woman*. Philadelphia: Jas B. Rodgers, 1888.

Ramanujan, A. K., trans. *Speaking of Siva*. Harmondsworth, UK: Penguin, 1973.

The Ramayana of Valmiki: An Epic of Ancient India. Edited and translated by Robert P. Goldman et al. 7 vols. Princeton, NJ: Princeton University Press, 1984–2017.

Rao, Velcheru Narayana, and David Shulman, trans. and eds. *Classical Telugu Poetry: An Anthology*. Berkeley: University of California Press, 2002.

[Razmnama] Mahabharata: The Oldest and Longest Sanskrit Epic. Translated by Mir Ghayasuddin Ali Qazvini Known as Naqib Khan (d. 1023 AH). Edited by Sayyid Muhammad Reza Jalali Naini and N. S. Shukla. 4 vols. Tehran: Kitabkhanah i Tahuri, 1979–1981.

Report of the Court of Inquiry Constituted under Punjab Act II of 1954 to Enquire into the Punjab Disturbances of 1953. Lahore: Superintendent, Government Printing, 1954.

Report on the Census of Assam for 1881. Calcutta: Office of Superintendent of Government Printing, 1883.

Rhys Davids, T. W., and Hermann Oldenberg, trans. *Vinaya Texts*. Vol. 1. Oxford: Clarendon Press, 1881.

The Rigveda: The Earliest Religious Poetry of India. Edited by Stephanie W. Jamison and Joel P. Brereton. 3 vols. New York: Oxford University Press, 2014.

Roberts, Emma. *Scenes and Characteristics of Hindostan with Sketches of Anglo-Indian Society*. Vol. 3. London: Allen, 1835.

Robertson, Bruce Carlisle, ed. *The Essential Writings of Raja Rammohan Ray*. Delhi: Oxford University Press, 1999.

Sadi. *The Gulistan (Rose Garden) of Sa'di: Bilingual English and Persian Edition with Vocabulary*. Translated by W. M. Thackston. Bethesda, MD: Ibex, 2008.

Saqi Mustad Khan. *Maasir-i Alamgiri: A History of the Emperor Aurangzib-'Alamgir (Reign 1658–1707 A.D.)*. Translated by Jadunath Sarkar. Calcutta: Royal Asiatic Society of Bengal, 1947.

Sarvananda. *The Jagaducharita of Sarvananda: A Historical Romance from Gujarat*. Edited by Georg Buhler. Vienna: Akademie der Wissenschaften, 1892.

The Satapatha-Brahmana According to the Text of the Madhyandina School. Translated by Julius Eggeling. Vol. 2. Oxford: Clarendon Press, 1885.

Savarkar, Vinayak Damodar. *Hindutva: Who Is a Hindu?* Bombay: Veer Savarkar Prakashan, 1969.

Selby, Martha Ann, trans. *Tamil Love Poetry: The Five Hundred Short Poems of the* Ainkurunuru, *an Early Third Century Anthology*. New York: Columbia University Press, 2011.

Sen, Surendranath, ed. *Indian Travels of Thevenot and Careri: Being the Third Part of the Travels of M. de Thevenot into the Levant and the Third Part of a Voyage Round the World by Dr. John Francis Gemelli Careri*. New Delhi: National Archives of India, 1949.

Shackle, Christopher, trans. *Shah Abdul Latif Risalo*. Cambridge, MA: Harvard University Press, 2018.

Shackle, Christopher, and Arvind-Pal Singh Mandair, eds. and trans. *Teachings of the Sikh Gurus: Selections from the Sikh Scriptures*. London: Routledge, 2005.

Shahnavaz Khan. *Maasir al-Umara*, published as *The Maathir-ul-Umara, Being Biographies of the Muhammadan and Hindu Officers of the Timurid Sovereigns of India from 1500 to about 1780 A.D. by*

Nawwab Samsam-ud-Daula Shah Nawaz Khan and His Son 'Abdul Hayy. Translated by H. Beveridge and Baini Prashad. Vol. 1. Patna: Janaki Prakashan, 1979.

Sharp, H. *Selections from Educational Records: Part I, 1781–1839.* Calcutta: Superintendent, Government Printing, 1920.

Shilpaprakasha: Medieval Orissan Sanskrit Text on Temple Architecture. Edited by Ramacandra Mahapatra Kaula Bhattaraka. Delhi: Indira Gandhi National Centre for the Arts, 2005.

Shore, Frederick John. *Notes on Indian Affairs.* Vol. 1. London: John W. Parker, 1837.

Singh, Ganda, ed. *Maharaja Duleep Singh Correspondence.* Vol. 3. Patiala: Punjabi University, 1977.

Singh, Nikky-Guninder Kaur, trans. *Verses of the Sikh Gurus: The Name of My Beloved.* New Delhi: Penguin Books, 1995.

Smith, John D., trans. *Mahabharata.* London: Penguin, 2009.

Sohan Lal. *Umdat-ut-Tawarikh: Chronicle of the Reign of Maharaja Ranjit Singh, 1831–1839 A.D.* Translated by V. S. Suri. Vol. 3. Delhi: S. Chand, 1961.

South-Indian Inscriptions. Madras: Archaeological Survey of India, 1890–.

Sunderlal Committee. "The Sunderlal Committee Report on the Massacres in Hyderabad." New Delhi, 1948.

Tavernier, Jean Baptiste. *Travels in India, by Jean Baptiste Tavernier, Baron of Aubonne, Translated from the Original French Edition of 1676 with a Biographical Sketch of the Author, Notes, Appendices, etc.* Translated by V. Ball. Vol. 2. London: Macmillan, 1889.

Thackston, Wheeler M., trans. "Kamaluddin Abdul-Razzaq Samarqandi: Mission to Calicut and Vijayanagar." In *A Century of Princes: Sources on Timurid History and Art*, edited by Wheeler M. Thackston, 299–321. Cambridge, MA: Aga Khan Program for Islamic Architecture, 1989.

———, trans. *Three Memoirs of Homayun.* Costa Mesa, CA: Mazda, 2009.

Tharu, Susie, and K. Lalita, eds. *Women Writing in India: 600 B.C. to the Present.* New York: Feminist Press at the City University of New York, 1991.

Thompson, Carl, ed. *Women's Travel Writings in India 1777–1854.* Vol. 1. London: Routledge, 2020.

Tilak, B. G. *Sri Bhagavadgita-Rahasya or Karma-Yogasastra (English Translation).* Translated by B. S. Sukthankar. Vol. 1. Poona: Tilak Bros., 1935.

Titley, Norah M., trans. *The Ni'matnama Manuscript of the Sultans of Mandu: The Sultan's Book of Delights.* London: Routledge, 2005.

Travancore Archaeological Series. Vol. 2. Trivandrum: Trivandrum Department of Archaeology, Government of Travancore, 1910.

University of Mysore. *Annual Report of the Mysore Archaeological Department for the Year 1929.* Bangalore: Government Press, 1931.

The Valmiki Ramayana: Critical Edition. Edited by G. H. Bhatt et al. 7 vols. Baroda: Oriental Institute: 1960–75.

van Kooij, Karel Rijk, trans. *Worship of the Goddess According to the Kalikapurana: Part 1, A Translation with an Introduction and Notes of Chapters 54–69.* Leiden: Brill, 1972.

Varahamihira's Brihatsamhita. Edited by V. Panditabhushana, Subrahmanya Sastri, and Vidwan M. Ramakrishna Bhat. Bangalore: V. B. Soobbiah & Sons, 1946.

Vatsyayana. *Kamasutra.* Edited and translated by Wendy Doniger and Sudhir Kakar. Oxford: Oxford University Press, 2003.

Vidyapati. *Kirttilata.* Edited by Shashinath Jha. Bihar: Madhubani, 1997.

Vivekananda, Swami. *Speeches and Writings.* 3rd ed., revised and enlarged. Madras: G. A. Natesan, 1899.

Vividhatirthakalpa of Jinaprabhasuri and Vidyatilaka. Edited by Jinavijaya. Shantiniketan: Adhisthata Singhi Jaina Jnanapitha, 1934.

Wajid Ali Shah. *Reply to the Charges against the King of Oude.* Calcutta: Englishman Press, 1856.

Yadav, K. C., ed. *The Sovereign, Subject, and Colonial Justice: Revisiting the Trial of Bahadur Shah, 1858.* New York: Routledge, 2023.

Yajnavalkya. *A Treatise on Dharma.* Edited and translated by Patrick Olivelle. Cambridge, MA: Harvard University Press, 2019.

Xuanzang. *A Biography of the Tripitaka Master of the Great Ci'en Monastery of the Great Tang Dynasty: Translated from the Chinese* of Sramana Huili and Shi Yancong. Translated by Li Rongxi. Berkeley: Numata Center for Buddhist Translation and Research, 1995.

———. *Buddhist Records of the Western World.* Translated by Samuel Beal. 2 vols. London: Trubner, 1906.

SECONDARY SOURCES

Abeydeera, Ananda. "The Geographical Perceptions of India and Ceylon in the *Periplus Maris Erythraei* and in Ptolemy's *Geography*." *Terrae Incognitae* 30, no. 1 (1998): 1–25.

Abraham, Meera. *Two Medieval Merchant Guilds of South India.* New Delhi: Manohar, 1988.

Abu-Lughod, Janet L. *Before European Hegemony: The World System A.D. 1250–1350.* New York: Oxford University Press, 1989.

Acri, Andrea. "Tantrism 'Seen from the East.'" In *Spirits and Ships: Cultural Transfers in Early Monsoon Asia*, edited by Andrea Acri, Roger Blench, and Alexandra Landmann, 71–144. Singapore: ISEAS, 2017.

Acri, Andrea, Roger Blench, and Alexandra Landmann. "Introduction: Re-Connecting Histories Across the Indo-Pacific." In *Spirits and Ships: Cultural Transfers in Early Monsoon Asia*, edited by Andrea Acri, Roger Blench, and Alexandra Landmann, 1–37. Singapore: ISEAS, 2017.

Adamjee, Qamar, and Audrey Truschke. "Reimagining the 'Idol Temple of Hindustan': Textual and Visual Translation of Sanskrit Texts in Mughal India." In *Pearls on a String: Artists, Patrons, and Poets at the Great Islamic Courts*, edited by Amy S. Landau, 141–165. Baltimore: Walters Art Museum, in association with University of Washington Press, 2015.

Agarwal, Anil, Ravi Chopra, and Kalpana Sharma. *The State of India's Environment 1982: A Citizens' Report.* New Delhi: Centre for Science and Environment, 1982.

Ahuja, Ravi. "Labour Unsettled: Mobility and Protest in the Madras Region, 1750–1800." *Indian Economic and Social History Review* 35, no. 4 (1998): 381–404.

Akhtar, Jawaid. "Mercantile and Financial Operations of Virji Vora, the Great 17th Century Merchant of Surat." *Proceedings of the Indian History Congress* 57 (1996): 316–322.

Aktor, Mikael. "Social Classes: *Varna*." In *Hindu Law: A New History of Dharmasastra*, edited by Patrick Olivelle and Donald R. Davis, 60–77. Oxford: Oxford University Press, 2018.

Alam, Muzaffar. *The Crisis of Empire in Mughal North India: Awadh and the Punjab, 1707–1748.* 2nd ed. New Delhi: Oxford University Press, 2013.

———. "The Culture and Politics of Persian in Precolonial Hindustan." In *Literary Cultures in History: Reconstructions from South Asia*, edited by Sheldon Pollock, 131–198. Berkeley: University of California Press, 2003.

———. *The Languages of Political Islam: India 1200–1800.* Chicago: University of Chicago Press, 2004.

Alam, Muzaffar, and Sanjay Subrahmanyam. *Indo-Persian Travels in the Age of Discoveries, 1400–1800.* Cambridge: Cambridge University Press, 2007.

———. "Iran and the Doors to the Deccan, ca. 1400–1650: Some Aspects." In *Iran and the Deccan: Persianate Art, Culture, and Talent in Circulation, 1400–1700*, edited by Keelan Overton, 77–103. Bloomington: Indiana University Press, 2020.

———. "Love, Passion and Reason in Faizi's Nal-Daman." In *Love in South Asia: A Cultural History*, edited by Francesca Orsini, 109–141. Cambridge: Cambridge University Press, 2006.

———. *Writing the Mughal World: Studies on Culture and Politics.* New York: Columbia University Press, 2012.

Alam, Parvez. "Trade, Textile and Other Industrial Activities: A Study of Banaras Region in Medieval India." *Journal of Indian Studies* 3, no. 1 (2017): 49–56.

Alavi, Seema. *The Sepoys and the Company: Tradition and Transition in Northern India, 1770–1830.* Delhi: Oxford University Press, 1995.

Ali, Daud. "Between Market and Court: The Careers of Two Courtier-Merchants in the

Twelfth-Century Deccan." *Journal of the Economic and Social History of the Orient* 53, no. 1/2 (2010): 185–211.

———. *Courtly Culture and Political Life in Early Medieval India*. New Delhi: Cambridge University Press, 2006.

———. "The Death of a Friend: Companionship, Loyalty and Affiliation in Chola South India." *Studies in History* 33, no. 1 (2017): 36–60.

———. "Royal Eulogy as World History: Rethinking Copper-Plate Inscriptions in Cola India." In *Querying the Medieval: Texts and the History of Practices in South Asia*, edited by Ronald Inden, Jonathan Walters, and Daud Ali, 165–229. Oxford: Oxford University Press, 2000.

———. "War, Servitude, and the Imperial Household: A Study of Palace Women in the Chola Empire." In *Slavery and South Asian History*, edited by Indrani Chatterjee and Richard M. Eaton, 44–62. Bloomington: Indiana University Press, 2006.

Ali, M. Athar. *Mughal India: Studies in Polity, Ideas, Society, and Culture*. New Delhi: Oxford University Press, 2006.

———. *The Mughal Nobility under Aurangzeb*. Bombay: Published for the Department of History, Aligarh Muslim University by Asia Publishing House, 1966.

Amar, Abhishek S. "Buddhist Responses to Brahmana Challenges in Medieval India: Bodhgaya and Gaya." *Journal of the Royal Asiatic Society* 22, no. 1 (2012): 155–185.

———. "Reassessing the Muslim Attacks and the Decline of Buddhist Monasteries in the Thirteenth Century Magadha." In *Encountering Buddhism and Islam in Premodern Central and South Asia*, edited by Blain Auer and Ingo Strauch, 48–74. Berlin: De Gruyter, 2019.

Ambade, Balram. "The Air Pollution during Diwali Festival by the Burning of Fireworks in Jamshedpur City, India." *Urban Climate* 26 (2018): 149–160.

Amin, Shahid. "Gandhi as Mahatma: Gorakhpur District, Eastern UP, 1921–2." In *Selected Subaltern Studies*, edited by Ranajit Guha and Gayatri Chakravorty Spivak, 288–348. New York: Oxford University Press, 1988.

Amnesty International. "The Amnesty International Report 1 June 1975–31 May 1976." London: Amnesty International Publications, 1976.

———. "The Amnesty International Report 1977." London: Amnesty International Publications, 1977.

Amrith, Sunil. "Rebellious Wives and Dysfunctional Marriages: Indian Women's Discourses and Participation in the Debates over Restitution of Conjugal Rights and the Child Marriage Controversy in the 1880s and 1890s." In *Women and Social Reform in Modern India: A Reader*, edited by Sumit Sarkar and Tanika Sarkar, 1:420–465. Ranikhet, India: Permanent Black, 2007.

———. "South Indian Migration, c. 1800–1950." In *Globalising Migration History: The Eurasian Experience (16th–21st Centuries)*, edited by Jan Lucassen and Leo Lucassen, 122–148. Leiden: Brill, 2014.

———. *Unruly Waters: How Rains, Rivers, Coasts, and Seas Have Shaped Asia's History*. New York: Basic Books, 2018.

Anagol-McGinn, Padma. "The Age of Consent Act (1891) Reconsidered: Women's Perspectives and Participation in the Child-Marriage Controversy in India." *South Asia Research* 12, no. 2 (1992): 100–118.

Anderson, Carol S. "Four Noble Truths." In *Oxford Research Encyclopedia of Religion*. Published online, 2016. https://doi.org/10.1093/acrefore/9780199340378.013.180.

Anderson, Edward. "'Neo-Hindutva': The Asia House M. F. Husain Campaign and the Mainstreaming of Hindu Nationalist Rhetoric in Britain." *Contemporary South Asia* 23, no. 1 (2015): 45–66.

Anderson, Gregory D. S. "Introduction to the Munda Languages." In *The Munda Languages*, edited by Gregory D. S. Anderson, 1–10. London: Routledge, 2008.

Appleton, Naomi. *Jataka Stories in Theravada Buddhism: Narrating the Bodhisatta Path*. Farnham, UK: Ashgate, 2010.

Arnold, David. "Death and the Modern Empire: The 1918–19 Influenza Epidemic in India." *Transactions of the Royal Historical Society* 29 (2019): 181–200.

———. *Gandhi*. London: Routledge, 2001.

Arrizabalaga, Jon. "Garcia de Orta in the Context of the Sephardic Diaspora." In *Medicine, Trade and Empire: Garcia de*

Orta's Colloquies on the Simples and Drugs of India *(1563) in Context*, edited by Palmira Fontes da Costa, 11–32. London: Routledge, 2016.

Asani, Ali S. "At the Crossroads of Indic and Iranian Civilizations: Sindhi Literary Culture." In *Literary Cultures in History: Reconstructions from South Asia*, edited by Sheldon Pollock, 612–646. Berkeley: University of California Press, 2003.

Asher, Catherine B. "Appropriating the Past: Jahangir's Pillars." *Islamic Culture* 71, no. 4 (1977): 1–15.

———. *Architecture of Mughal India*. Cambridge: Cambridge University Press, 1992.

———. "The Architecture of Raja Man Singh: A Study of Sub-Imperial Patronage." In *The Powers of Art: Patronage in Indian Culture*, edited by Barbara Stoler Miller, 183–201. Delhi: Oxford University Press, 1992.

———. *Delhi's Qutb Complex: The Minar, Mosque and Mehrauli*. Mumbai: Marg, 2017.

———. "Kacchavaha Pride and Prestige: The Temple Patronage of Raja Mana Simha." In *Govindadeva: A Dialogue in Stone*, edited by Margaret H. Case, 215–238. New Delhi: Indira Gandhi National Centre for the Arts, 1996.

———. "Making Sense of Temples and Tirthas: Rajput Construction under Mughal Rule." *The Medieval History Journal* 23, no. 1 (2020): 9–49.

———. "Mapping Hindu-Muslim Identities through the Architecture of Shahjahanabad and Jaipur." In *Beyond Turk and Hindu: Rethinking Religious Identities in Islamicate South Asia*, edited by David Gilmartin and Bruce B. Lawrence, 121–148. Gainesville: University Press of Florida, 2000.

Asher, Catherine B., and Cynthia Talbot. *India before Europe*. 2nd ed. Cambridge: Cambridge University Press, 2023.

Asher, Frederick M. *Bodh Gaya*. New Delhi: Oxford University Press, 2008.

———. "Early Indian Art Reconsidered." In *Between the Empires: Society in India 300 BCE to 400 CE*, edited by Patrick Olivelle, 50–66. New York: Oxford University Press, 2006.

———. "India Abroad: Evidence for Ancient Indian Maritime Activity." In *The Indian Ocean Trade in Antiquity: Political, Cultural, and Economic Impacts*, edited by Matthew Adam Cobb, 157–167. Abingdon, UK: Routledge, 2019.

———. "India, Magadha, Nalanda: Ecology and a Premodern World System." In *Records, Recoveries, Remnants and Inter-Asian Interconnections: Decoding Cultural Heritage*, edited by Anjana Sharma, 51–69. Singapore: ISEAS, 2018.

———. *Nalanda: Situating the Great Monastery*. Mumbai: Marg, 2015.

———. *Sarnath: A Critical History of the Place where Buddhism Began*. Los Angeles: Getty Research Institute, 2020.

Ashfaq, Abira. "Voices from Prison and a Call for Repeal: The Hudood Laws of Pakistan." *New Politics* 10, no. 4 (2006): https://newpol.org/issue_post/voices-prison-and-call-repeal-hudood-laws-pakistan/.

Asian Development Bank. *Rural Asia: Beyond the Green Revolution*. N.p.: Asian Development Bank, 2000.

Asif, Manan Ahmed. *A Book of Conquest: The* Chachnama *and Muslim Origins in South Asia*. Cambridge, MA: Harvard University Press, 2016.

———. *The Loss of Hindustan: The Invention of India*. Cambridge, MA: Harvard University Press, 2020.

Askari, Syed Hasan. "Mirat-ul-Muluk: A Contemporary Work Containing Reflections on Later Mughal Administration." In *Indica: The Indian Historical Research Institute Silver Jubilee Commemoration Volume*, 27–37. Bombay: St. Xavier's College, 1953.

Asouti, Eleni, and Dorian Q. Fuller. *Trees and Woodlands of South India: Archaeological Perspectives*. Walnut Creek, CA: Left Coast Press, 2007.

Athavale, R. B. "New Light on the Life of Panditaraja Jagannatha." *Annals of the Bhandarkar Oriental Research Institute* 48/49 (1968): 415–420.

Atwal, Priya. *Royals and Rebels: The Rise and Fall of the Sikh Empire*. Oxford: Oxford University Press, 2020.

Auer, Blain. "Chishti Muʿin Al-Din." In *Encyclopaedia of Islam Three*, edited by Kate Fleet, Gudrun Kramer, Denis Matringe, John Nawas, and Devin J.

Stewart. Published online, 2015. http://dx.doi.org/10.1163/1573-3912_ei3_COM_25501.

Ayyathurai, Gajendran. "Foundations of Anti-Caste Consciousness: Pandit Iyothee Thass, Tamil Buddhism, and the Marginalized in South India." PhD diss., Columbia University, 2011.

Bahadur, Gaiutra. *Coolie Woman: The Odyssey of Indenture*. Chicago: University of Chicago Press, 2014.

———. "Unmaking Asian Exceptionalism." *Boston Review*, April 4, 2023. https://www.bostonreview.net/articles/unmaking-asian-exceptionalism-bahadur/.

Bahura, Gopal Narayan. "Sri Govinda Gatha: Service Rendered to Govinda by the Rulers of Amera and Jayapura." In *Govindadeva: A Dialogue in Stone*, edited by Margaret H. Case, 195–213. New Delhi: Indira Gandhi National Centre for the Arts, 1996.

Bailey, Gregory. "*Sthavirabuddhayah* in the Markandeyasamasyaparvan of the Mahabharata. Problems in Locating Critiques of Buddhism in the Mahabharata." In *Devadattiyam: Johannes Bronkhorst Felicitation Volume*, edited by Francois Voegeli, Vincent Eltschinger, Danielle Feller, Maria Piera Candotti, Bogdan Diaconescu, and Malhar Kulkarni, 685–701. Berlin: Peter Lang, 2012.

Bakhle, Janaki. "Country First? Vinayak Damodar Savarkar (1883–1966) and the Writing of *Essentials of Hindutva*." *Public Culture* 22, no. 1 (2010): 149–186.

———. *Savarkar and the Making of Hindutva*. Princeton, NJ: Princeton University Press, 2024.

Bakker, Hans. "Royal Patronage and Religious Tolerance: The Formative Period of Gupta—Vakataka Culture." *Journal of the Royal Asiatic Society* 20, no. 4 (2010): 461–475.

———. "A Theatre of Broken Dreams 2.0: Vidisa in the Days of Gupta Hegemony." In *The Routledge Handbook of the State in Premodern India*, edited by Hermann Kulke and Bhairabi Prasad Sahu, 191–207. London: Routledge, 2022.

Balabanlilar, Lisa. *The Emperor Jahangir: Power and Kingship in Mughal India*. London: I. B. Tauris, 2020.

Balachandran, G. "South Asian Seafarers and Their Worlds: c. 1870–1930s." In *Seascapes, Maritime Histories, Littoral Cultures, and Transoceanic Exchanges*, edited by Jerry H. Bentley, Renate Bridenthal, and Karen Wigen, 186–202. Honolulu: University of Hawaiʻi Press, 2007.

Balakrishnan, Pulapre. *Economic Growth in India: History and Prospect*. Delhi: Oxford University Press, 2010.

Balbir, Nalini. "A Propos des Hymnes Jaina Multilingues (Sanskrit, Prakrit, Persan)." In *Indica et Tibetica: Festschrift fur Michael Hahn*, edited by Konrad Klaus and Jens-Uwe Hartmann, 39–61. Vienna: Arbeitskreis fur Tibetische und Buddhistische Studien, 2007.

Ballantyne, Tony. *Between Colonialism and Diaspora: Sikh Cultural Formations in an Imperial World*. Durham, NC: Duke University Press, 2006.

Bandyopadhyay, Sekhar. *Decolonization in South Asia: Meanings of Freedom in Post-Independence West Bengal, 1947–52*. New York: Routledge, 2009.

Bangha, Imre. "Early Hindi Epic Poetry in Gwalior: Beginnings and Continuities in the Ramayan of Vishnudas." In *After Timur Left: Culture and Circulation in Fifteenth-Century North India*, edited by Francesca Orsini and Samira Sheikh, 365–402. New Delhi: Oxford University Press, 2014.

———. "Rekhta: Poetry in Mixed Language—The Emergence of Khari Boli Literature in North India." In *Before the Divide: Hindi and Urdu Literary Culture*, edited by Francesca Orsini, 21–83. New Delhi: Orient Blackswan, 2010.

Bano, Shadab. "The Acquisition and Trade of Elite Slaves in the Thirteenth Century." *Proceedings of the Indian History Congress* 59 (1998): 229–236.

Bapu, Prabhu. *Hindu Mahasabha in Colonial North India, 1915–1930: Constructing Nation and History*. London: Routledge, 2013.

Barnes, Ruth. "Introduction." In *Textiles in Indian Ocean Societies*, edited by Ruth Barnes, 1–9. London: Routledge, 2005.

Barnett, Richard B. "Awadh." In *Encyclopaedia of Islam Three*, edited by Kate Fleet, Gudrun Kramer, Denis Matringe, John

Nawas, and Devin J. Stewart. Published online, 2008. http://dx.doi.org/10.1163/1573-3912_ei3_COM_26360.

Barrow, Ian. *The East India Company, 1600–1858: A Short History with Documents.* Indianapolis, IN: Hackett, 2017.

Barua, Ankur. *The Brahmo Samaj and Its Vaisnava Milieus: Intersections of Hindu Knowledge and Love in Nineteenth Century Bengal.* Leiden: Brill, 2021.

Basham, A. L. *History and Doctrines of the Ajivikas, a Vanished Indian Religion.* Delhi: Motilal Banarsidass, 1981.

Bass, Gary J. *The Blood Telegram: Nixon, Kissinger, and a Forgotten Genocide.* New York: Knopf, 2013.

Basu, Shrabani. "Turbans in the Trenches: Indian Sepoys and Sowars on the Western Front during the Great War." In *Indian Soldiers in the First World War: Re-Visiting a Global Conflict*, edited by Ashutosh Kumar and Claude Markovits, 11–40. London: Routledge, 2021.

Bates, Crispin, Andrea Major, Marina Carter, and Gavin Rand, eds. *Mutiny at the Margins: New Perspectives on the Indian Uprising of 1857.* 6 vols. New Delhi: Sage, 2013–2016.

Baumfield, Vivienne. "Science and Sanskrit: Vivekananda's Views on Education." In *Swami Vivekananda and the Modernization of Hinduism*, edited by William Radice, 194–212. Delhi: Oxford University Press, 1998.

Baums, Stephan. "Inventing the *Pothi*: The Adoption and Spread of a New Manuscript Format in Indian Buddhism." In *Body and Cosmos: Studies in Early Indian Medical and Astral Sciences in Honor of Kenneth G. Zysk*, edited by Toke Lindegaard Knudsen, Jacob Schmidt-Madsen, and Sara Speyer, 343–362. Leiden: Brill, 2020.

Bayly, C. A. *Empire and Information: Intelligence Gathering and Social Communication in India, 1780–1870.* Cambridge: Cambridge University Press, 1996.

———. *Indian Society and the Making of the British Empire.* Cambridge: Cambridge University Press, 1988.

———. "The Pre-History of 'Communalism'? Religious Conflict in India, 1700–1860." *Modern Asian Studies* 19, no. 2 (1985): 177–203.

———. *Rulers, Townsmen, and Bazaars: North Indian Society in the Age of British Expansion, 1770–1870.* 3rd ed. Delhi: Oxford University Press, 2012.

Bayly, Susan. "Hindu Modernisers and the 'Public' Arena: Indigenous Critiques of Caste in Colonial India." In *Swami Vivekananda and the Modernization of Hinduism*, edited by William Radice, 93–137. Delhi: Oxford University Press, 1998.

———. "Islam in Southern India: 'Purist' or 'Syncretic'?" In *Two Colonial Empires: Comparative Essays on the History of India and Indonesia in the Nineteenth Century*, edited by C. A. Bayly and D.H.A. Kolff, 35–73. Dordrecht: Martinus Nijhoff Publishers, 1986.

———. *Saints, Goddesses and Kings: Muslims and Christians in South Indian Society, 1700–1900.* Cambridge: Cambridge University Press, 1989.

Beach, Milo Cleveland. *Mughal and Rajput Painting.* Cambridge: Cambridge University Press, 1992.

Behl, Aditya. *Love's Subtle Magic: An Indian Islamic Literary Tradition, 1379–1545.* Edited by Wendy Doniger. New York: Oxford University Press, 2013.

Bellwood, Peter. *First Farmers: The Origins of Agricultural Societies.* 2nd ed. Hoboken, NJ: Wiley-Blackwell, 2023.

Bendrey, V. S. *Coronation of Shivaji the Great, or the Procedure of the Religious Ceremony Performed by Gagabhatta for the Consecration of Shivaji as a Hindu King.* Bombay: P.P.H. Bookstall, 1960

Benjamin, Walter. *Illuminations: Essays and Reflections.* Edited by Hannah Arendt. Translated by Henry Zohn. New York: Schocken Books, 1969.

Benke, Theodore. "The Sudracarasiromani of Krsna Sesa: A 16th Century Manual of Dharma for Sudras." PhD diss., University of Pennsylvania, 2010.

Berkwitz, Stephen C. *Buddhist Poetry and Colonialism: Alagiyavanna and the Portuguese in Sri Lanka.* New York: Oxford University Press, 2013.

Bernier, Ronald M. *Himalayan Architecture.* Madison, NJ: Fairleigh Dickinson University Press, 1997.

Bharadwaj, Surajbhan. "Migration, Mobility and Memories: Meos in the Processes of Peasantisation and Islamisation in Medieval Period." *Indian Historical Review* 39, no. 2 (2012): 217–250.

Bhargava, Meena, ed. *The Decline of the Mughal Empire*. New Delhi: Oxford University Press, 2014.

Bhatt, Ahsan I. *Secession and Security: Explaining State Strategy against Separatists*. Ithaca, NY: Cornell University Press, 2017.

Bhattacharya, Ramkrishna. "Carvaka Fragments: A New Collection." *Journal of Indian Philosophy* 30, no. 6 (2002): 597–640.

Bhattacharyya, Debjani. *Empire and Ecology in the Bengal Delta: The Making of Calcutta*. Cambridge: Cambridge University Press, 2018.

Bhukya, Bhangya. *The Roots of the Periphery: A History of the Gonds of Deccan India*. New Delhi: Oxford University Press, 2017.

Bilgrami, Rafat. "Shaykh 'Abd al-Wahhab and His Family under 'Alamgir." *Journal of the Pakistan Historical Society* 31, no. 2 (1983): 100–114.

Bird, Kai, and Martin J. Sherwin. *American Prometheus: The Triumph and Tragedy of J. Robert Oppenheimer*. New York: Vintage Books, 2006.

Bisschop, Peter C., and Elizabeth A. Cecil. "Primary Sources and Asian Pasts: Beyond the Boundaries of the 'Gupta Period.'" In *Primary Sources and Asian Pasts*, edited by Peter C. Bisschop and Elizabeth A. Cecil, 1–17. Berlin: De Gruyter, 2021.

Biswas, Asit K. "Indus Water Treaty: The Negotiating Process." *Water International* 17, no. 4 (1992): 201–209.

Blackburn, Anne M. *Locations of Buddhism: Colonialism and Modernity in Sri Lanka*. Chicago: University of Chicago Press, 2010.

Blackburn, Stuart. "The Brahmin and the Mongoose: The Narrative Context of a Well-Travelled Tale." *Bulletin of the School of Oriental and African Studies* 59, no. 3 (1996): 494–507.

Blair, Sheila, and Jonathan Bloom. "From Iran to the Deccan: Architectural Transmission and the Madrasa of Mahmud Gavan at Bidar." In *Iran and the Deccan: Persianate Art, Culture, and Talent in Circulation, 1400–1700*, edited by Keelan Overton, 175–202. Bloomington: Indiana University Press, 2020.

Blankinship, Kevin. "Tales of Two Jackals." *Aeon*, March 11, 2022. https://aeon.co/essays/kalila-and-dimnas-ethically-murky-ancient-parables-on-power.

Boehrer, Bruce Thomas. *Parrot Culture: Our 2,500-Year-Long Fascination with the World's Most Talkative Bird*. Philadelphia: University of Pennsylvania Press, 2004.

Boivin, Nicole. "Proto-Globalisation and Biotic Exchange in the Old World." In *Human Dispersal and Species Movement: From Prehistory to the Present*, edited by Nicole Boivin, Remy Crassard, and Michael Petraglia, 349–408. Cambridge: Cambridge University Press, 2017.

Bokhari, Afshan. "The 'Light' of the Timuria: Jahan Ara Begum's Patronage, Piety, and Poetry in 17th-Century Mughal India." *Marg* 60, no. 1 (2008): 52–61.

Bollee, Willem. *A Cultural Encyclopaedia of the Kathasaritsagara in Keywords: Complementary to Norman Penzer's General Index on Charles Tawney's Translation*. Halle, Germany: Universitatsverlag Halle-Wittenberg, 2015.

Bose, Melia Belli. "Royal Matronage and a Visual Vocabulary of Indian Queenship: Ahilyabai Holkar's Memorial Commissions." In *Women, Gender and Art in Asia, c. 1500–1900*, edited by Melia Belli Bose, 41–62. New York: Routledge, 2016.

Bose, Sugata. *A Hundred Horizons: The Indian Ocean in the Age of Global Empire*. Cambridge, MA: Harvard University Press, 2006.

Bose, Sumantra. *Secular States, Religious Politics: India, Turkey, and the Future of Secularism*. Cambridge: Cambridge University Press, 2018.

Bowles, Adam. *Dharma, Disorder, and the Political in Ancient India: The Apaddharmaparvan of the Mahabharata*. Leiden: Brill, 2007.

Bragg, Melvyn. "The Hittites." *In Our Time*, December 23, 2022. https://www.bbc.co.uk/sounds/play/m0012q5n.

Bramen, Carrie Tirado. "Christian Maidens and Heathen Monks: Oratorical Seduction at the 1893 World's Parliament of Religions."

In *The Puritan Origins of American Sex: Religion, Sexuality, and National Identity in American Literature*, edited by Tracy Fessenden, Nicholas F. Radel, and Magdalena J. Zaborowska, 191–212. London: Routledge, 2001.

Brereton, Joel P. "'*Tat Tvam Asi*' in Context." *Zeitschrift Der Deutschen Morgenlandischen Gesellschaft* 136, no. 1 (1986): 98–109.

Brittlebank, Kate. "Accessing the Unseen Realm: The Historical and Textual Contexts of Tipu Sultan's Dream Register." *Journal of the Royal Asiatic Society* 21, no. 2 (2011): 159–175.

———. *Tiger: The Life of Tipu Sultan*. New Delhi: Juggernaut, 2016.

———. *Tipu Sultan's Search for Legitimacy: Islam and Kingship in a Hindu Domain*. Delhi: Oxford University Press, 1997.

Brockington, John. *The Sanskrit Epics*. Leiden: Brill, 1998.

Broeze, F.J.A. "The Muscles of Empire—Indian Seamen and the Raj 1919–1939." *Indian Economic and Social History Review* 18, no. 1 (1981): 43–67.

Bronkhorst, Johannes. "Bhattoji Diksita on Sphota." *Journal of Indian Philosophy* 33, no. 1 (2005): 3–41.

———. *Greater Magadha: Studies in the Culture of Early India*. Leiden: Brill, 2007.

———. *How the Brahmins Won: From Alexander to the Guptas*. Leiden: Brill, 2016.

———. "Plagues and Brahmins: Did a Combination of Epidemics and Ideology Empty India's Cities?" In *Body and Cosmos: Studies in Early Indian Medical and Astral Sciences in Honor of Kenneth G. Zysk*, edited by Toke Lindegaard Knudsen, Jacob Schmidt-Madsen, and Sara Speyer, 184–208. Leiden: Brill, 2021.

———. "Sacrifice in the *Mahabharata* and beyond or Did the Author(s) of the *Mahabharata* Understand Vedic Sacrifice Better than We Do?" In *Mythic Landscapes and Argumentative Trails in Sanskrit Epic Literature: Proceedings of the Sixth Dubrovnik International Conference on the Sanskrit Epics and Puranas*, edited by Ivan Andrijanic and Sven Sellmer, 23–38. Zagreb: Croation Academy of Sciences and Arts, 2022.

———. "The Spread of Sanskrit in Southeast Asia." In *Early Interactions between South and Southeast Asia: Reflections on Cross-Cultural Exchange*, edited by Pierre-Yves Manguin, A. Mani, and Geoff Wade, 263–275. New Delhi: Manohar, 2011.

Bronner, Yigal. *Extreme Poetry: The South Asian Movement of Simultaneous Narration*. New York: Columbia University Press, 2010.

Bronner, Yigal, and David Shulman. "'A Cloud Turned Goose': Sanskrit in the Vernacular Millennium." *Indian Economic and Social History Review* 43, no. 1 (2006): 1–30.

Brose, Benjamin. *Xuanzang: China's Legendary Pilgrim and Translator*. Boulder, CO: Shambhala, 2021.

Brough, John. *The Early Brahmanical System of Gotra and Pravara: A Translation of the Gotra-Pravara-Manjari of Purusottama-Pandita*. Cambridge: Cambridge University Press, 1953.

Brown, Judith M. "Introduction." In *The Cambridge Companion to Gandhi*, edited by Judith M. Brown and Anthony Parel, 1–8. New York: Cambridge University Press, 2011.

Brown, Katherine Butler. "Did Aurangzeb Ban Music? Questions for the Historiography of His Reign." *Modern Asian Studies* 41, no. 1 (2007): 77–120.

Brown, Michael, and Claire Rasmussen. "Bestiality and the Queering of the Human Animal." *Environment and Planning D: Society and Space* 28, no. 1 (2010): 158–177.

Burchett, Patton E. *A Genealogy of Devotion:* Bhakti, *Tantra, Yoga, and Sufism in North India*. New York: Columbia University Press, 2019.

Busch, Allison. "The Classical Past in the Mughal Present: The Brajbhasha *Riti* Tradition." In *Innovations and Turning Points: Toward a History of Kavya Literature*, edited by Yigal Bronner, David Shulman, and Gary A. Tubb, 648–690. New Delhi: Oxford University Press, 2014.

———. "Hidden in Plain View: Brajbhasha Poets at the Mughal Court." *Modern Asian Studies* 44, no. 2 (2010): 267–309.

———. *Poetry of Kings: The Classical Hindi Literature of Mughal India*. New York: Oxford University Press, 2011.

———. “Riti and Register: Lexical Variation in Courtly Braj Bhasha Texts.” In *Before the Divide: Hindi and Urdu Literary Culture*, edited by Francesca Orsini, 84–120. New Delhi: Orient Blackswan, 2010.

Butalia, Urvashi. *The Other Side of Silence: Voices from the Partition of India*. New Delhi: Penguin, 1998.

Cagle, Hugh. “Cultures of Inquiry, Myths of Empire: Natural History in Colonial Goa.” In *Medicine, Trade and Empire: Garcia de Orta's* Colloquies on the Simples and Drugs of India *(1563) in Context*, edited by Palmira Fontes da Costa, 107–128. London: Routledge, 2016.

Carratelli, G. Pugliese, and G. Garbini. *A Bilingual Graeco-Aramaic Edict by Asoka: The First Greek Inscription Discovered in Afghanistan*. Rome: Istituto Italiano Per il Medio ed Estremo Oriente, 1964.

Casolari, Marzia. “Hindutva's Foreign Tie-up in the 1930s: Archival Evidence.” *Economic and Political Weekly* 35, no. 4 (2000): 218–228.

———. *In the Shadow of the Swastika: The Relationships between Indian Radical Nationalism, Italian Fascism and Nazism*. London: Routledge, 2020.

Casson, Lionel. “Ancient Naval Technology and the Route to India.” In *Rome and India: The Ancient Sea Trade*, edited by Vimala Begley and Richard Daniel De Puma, 8–11. Madison: University of Wisconsin Press, 1991.

Chadbourne, Julie Dror. “Never Wear Your Shoes after Midnight: Legal Trends under the Pakistan Zina Ordinance.” *Wisconsin International Law Journal* 17 (1999): 179–280.

Chakrabarti, Dilip K. *India: An Archaeological History, Palaeolithic Beginnings to Early Historic Foundations*. 2nd ed. Oxford: Oxford University Press, 2009.

———, ed. *Indus Civilization Sites in India: New Discoveries*. Mumbai: Marg Publications on behalf of the National Centre for the Performing Arts, 2004.

———. *The Oxford Companion to Indian Archaeology: The Archaeological Foundations of Ancient India, Stone Age to AD 13th Century*. New Delhi: Oxford University Press, 2006.

———. “Rajagriha: An Early Historic Site in East India.” *World Archaeology* 7, no. 3 (1976): 261–268.

Chakrabarti, Dilip K., and Nayanjot Lahiri. “The Iron Age in India: The Beginning and Consequences.” *Puratattva* 24 (1994): 12–32.

Chakrabarti, Pratik. *Bacteriology in British India: Laboratory Medicine and the Tropics*. Rochester, NY: University of Rochester Press, 2012.

———. “‘Neither of Meate nor Drinke, but What the Doctor Alloweth’: Medicine amidst War and Commerce in Eighteenth-Century Madras.” *Bulletin of the History of Medicine* 80, no. 1 (2006): 1–38.

Chakrabarty, Dipesh. *Provincializing Europe: Postcolonial Thought and Historical Difference*. Princeton, NJ: Princeton University Press, 2008.

Chakravarti, Ananya. *The Empire of Apostles: Religion,* Accommodatio, *and the Imagination of Empire in Early Modern Brazil and India*. New Delhi: Oxford University Press, 2018.

———. “Mapping ‘Gabriel’: Space, Identity and Slavery in the Late Sixteenth-Century Indian Ocean.” *Past & Present* 243, no. 1 (2019): 5–34.

Chakravarti, Ranabir. “Monarchs, Merchants and a Matha in Northern Konkan (c. AD 900–1053).” In *Trade in Early India*, edited by Ranabir Chakravarti, 257–281. New Delhi: Oxford University Press, 2001.

———. *Trade and Traders in Early Indian Society*. 3rd ed. London: Routledge, 2020.

Chakravarti, Uma. *Gendering Caste through a Feminist Lens*. Rev. ed. Los Angeles: Sage, 2018.

———. *Rewriting History: The Life and Times of Pandita Ramabai*. New Delhi: Zubaan, 2013.

———. *The Social Dimensions of Early Buddhism*. Delhi: Munshiram Manoharlal, 1996.

———. “Wifehood, Widowhood and Adultery: Female Sexuality, Surveillance and the State in 18th Century Maharashtra.” *Contributions to Indian Sociology* 29, no. 1–2 (1995): 3–21.

Chakravorty, Sanjoy, Devesh Kapur, and Nirvikar Singh. *The Other One Percent:*

Indians in America. New York: Oxford University Press, 2017.

Champakalakshmi, R. *Trade, Ideology and Urbanization: South India 300 BC to AD 1300*. Delhi: Oxford University Press, 1996.

Chandra, Satish. *Medieval India: From Sultanat to the Mughals*. Part 1: Delhi Sultanate (1206–1526). Rev. ed. New Delhi: Har-Anand Publications, 2004.

———. *Mughal Religious Policies: The Rajputs & the Deccan*. New Delhi: Vikas, 1993.

———. *Parties and Politics at the Mughal Court, 1707–1740*. 2nd ed. New Delhi: People's Publishing House, 1972.

———. "Social Background to the Rise of the Maratha Movement during the 17th Century in India." *Indian Economic and Social History Review* 10, no. 3 (1973): 209–217.

Chandrachud, Abhinav. *An Independent, Colonial Judiciary: A History of the Bombay High Court during the British Raj, 1862–1947*. New Delhi: Oxford University Press, 2015.

Charney, Michael W. "Where Jambudipa and Islamdom Converged: Religious Change and the Emergence of Buddhist Communalism in Early Modern Arakan (Fifteenth to Nineteenth Centuries)." PhD diss., University of Michigan, 1999.

Chase, Bradley Allen. "Meat Provisioning and the Integration of the Indus Civilization: A Perspective from Gujarat (India)." PhD diss., University of Wisconsin–Madison, 2007.

Chatterjee, Indrani. "*Adivasis*, Tribes and Other Neologisms for Erasing Precolonial Pasts: An Example from Northeast India." *Indian Economic and Social History Review* 53, no. 1 (2016): 9–40.

Chatterjee, Indrani, and Richard M. Eaton, eds. *Slavery and South Asian History*. Bloomington: Indiana University Press, 2006.

Chatterjee, Kumkum. *Merchants, Politics and Society in Early Modern India: Bihar, 1733–1820*. Leiden: Brill, 1996.

Chatterjee, Nandini. *Negotiating Mughal Law: A Family of Landlords across Three Indian Empires*. Cambridge: Cambridge University Press, 2020.

Chatterjee, Partha. *The Nation and Its Fragments: Colonial and Postcolonial Histories*. Princeton, NJ: Princeton University Press, 1993.

Chatterji, Joya. *Bengal Divided: Hindu Communalism and Partition, 1932–1947*. Cambridge: Cambridge University Press, 1994.

———. "The Fashioning of a Frontier: The Radcliffe Line and Bengal's Border Landscape, 1947–52." *Modern Asian Studies* 33, no. 1 (1999): 185–242.

———. *Partition's Legacies*. Albany: State University of New York Press, 2021.

Chattopadhyaya, Brajadulal. *Studying Early India: Archaeology, Texts, and Historical Issues*. Delhi: Permanent Black, 2003.

Chaturvedi, Vinayak. *Hindutva and Violence: V.D. Savarkar and the Politics of History*. Albany: State University of New York Press, 2022.

Chaudhuri, Sibdas. "Birth of Museum in Modern India and the Asiatic Society." *The Calcutta Review* 3, no. 1–2 (1971): 1–11.

Chaudhury, Sushil. *Trade, Politics and Society: The Indian Milieu in the Early Modern Era*. London: Routledge, 2017.

Cherian, Divya. *Merchants of Virtue: Hindus, Muslims, and Untouchables in Eighteenth-Century South Asia*. Oakland: University of California Press, 2023.

Chester, Lucy P. *Borders and Conflict in South Asia: The Radcliffe Boundary Commission and the Partition of Punjab*. Manchester, UK: Manchester University Press, 2009.

Chetan, Achyut. *Founding Mothers of the Indian Republic: Gender Politics of the Framing of the Constitution*. Cambridge: Cambridge University Press, 2022.

Chew, Sing C. *The Southeast Asia Connection: Trade and Polities in the Eurasian World Economy, 500 BC–AD 500*. New York: Berghahn Books, 2018.

Chida-Razvi, Mehreen M. "The Perception of Reception: The Importance of Sir Thomas Roe at the Mughal Court of Jahangir." *Journal of World History* 25, no. 2/3 (2014): 263–284.

Chitnis, K. N. *The Nawabs of Savanur*. New Delhi: Atlantic Publishers and Distributors, 2000.

Choudhury, Rishad. "An Eventful Politics of Difference and Its Afterlife: Chittagong Frontier, Bengal, c. 1657–1757." *Indian Economic and Social History Review* 52, no. 3 (2015): 271–296.

Chowdhury, Zirwat. "An Imperial Mughal Tent and Mobile Sovereignty in Eighteenth-Century Jodhpur." *Art History* 38, no. 4 (2015): 668–681.

Chowdhury-Sengupta, Indira. "Reconstructing Hinduism on a World Platform: The World's First Parliament of Religions, Chicago 1892." In *Swami Vivekananda and the Modernization of Hinduism*, edited by William Radice, 17–35. Delhi: Oxford University Press, 1998.

Clooney, Francis X., and Tony K. Stewart. "Vaisnava." In *The Hindu World*, edited by Sushil Mittal and Gene R. Thursby, 162–184. London: Routledge, 2004.

Clothey, Fred W. *The Many Faces of Murukan: The History and Meaning of a South Indian God*. The Hague: Mouton, 1978.

Cobb, Matthew A. "Black Pepper Consumption in the Roman Empire." *Journal of the Economic and Social History of the Orient* 61, no. 4 (2018): 519–559.

———. "Mediterranean Goods in an Indian Context: The Use of Transcultural Theory for the Study of the Ancient Indian Ocean World." In *Globalization and Transculturality from Antiquity to the Pre-Modern World*, edited by Serena Autiero and Matthew Adam Cobb, 165–182. London: Routledge, 2022.

———. *Rome and the Indian Ocean Trade from Augustus to the Early Third Century CE*. Leiden: Brill, 2018.

Cohn, Bernard S. *An Anthropologist among the Historians and Other Essays*. Delhi: Oxford University Press, 1987.

———. *Colonialism and Its Forms of Knowledge: The British in India*. Princeton, NJ: Princeton University Press, 1996.

Cole, J.R.I. *Roots of North Indian Shi'ism in Iran and Iraq: Religion and State in Awadh, 1722–1859*. Berkeley: University of California Press, 1988.

Cole, W. Owen. "Sikh Interactions with Other Religions." In *The Oxford Handbook of Sikh Studies*, edited by Pashaura Singh and Louis E. Fenech, 250–261. Oxford: Oxford University Press, 2014.

Collins, Charles Dillard. *The Iconography and Ritual of Siva at Elephanta*. Albany: State University of New York Press, 1988.

Commander, Simon. "Malthus and the Theory of 'Unequal Powers': Population and Food Production in India, 1800–1947." *Modern Asian Studies* 20, no. 4 (1986): 661–701.

Commissariat, Khan Bahadur M. S. "Imperial Mughal Farmans in Gujarat: Being Farmans Mainly Issued in Favour of Shantidas Jawahari of Ahmadabad by the Mughal Emperors." *Journal of the University of Bombay* 9, no. 1 (1940): 1–56.

Coningham, Robin. "Beyond and before the Imperial Frontiers: Early Historic Sri Lanka and the Origins of Indian Ocean Trade." *Man and Environment* 27, no. 1 (2002): 99–108.

Coningham, Robin, and Ruth Young. *The Archaeology of South Asia: From the Indus to Asoka, c. 6500 BCE–200 CE*. Cambridge: Cambridge University Press, 2015.

Cook, Matthew A. *Annexation and the Unhappy Valley: The Historical Anthropology of Sindh's Colonization*. Leiden: Brill, 2016.

Copland, Ian. "The Further Shores of Partition: Ethnic Cleansing in Rajasthan 1947." *Past & Present* 160, no. 1 (1998): 203–239.

Cort, John E. *Framing the Jina: Narratives of Icons and Idols in Jain History*. New York: Oxford University Press, 2010.

———. "Jain Identity and the Public Sphere in Nineteenth-Century India." In *Religious Interactions in Modern India*, edited by Martin Fuchs and Vasudha Dalmia, 99–137. New Delhi: Oxford University Press, 2019.

Courtright, Paul B. *Ganesa: Lord of Obstacles, Lord of Beginnings*. New York: Oxford University Press, 1989.

Cox, Whitney. *Politics, Kingship, and Poetry in Medieval South India: Moonset on Sunrise Mountain*. Cambridge: Cambridge University Press, 2016.

Crews, Robert D. *Afghan Modern: The History of a Global Nation*. Cambridge, MA: Belknap Press of Harvard University Press, 2015.

Czekalska, Renata, and Agnieszka Kuczkiewicz-Fras. "From Africans in India to African Indians." *Politeja* 13, no. 42 (2016): 189–212.

da Costa, Palmira Fontes. "Introduction." In *Medicine, Trade and Empire: Garcia de*

Orta's Colloquies on the Simples and Drugs of India *(1563) in Context*, edited by Palmira Fontes da Costa, 1–9. London: Routledge, 2016.

Dadlani, Chanchal, and Yuthika Sharma. "Beyond the Taj Mahal: Late Mughal Visual Culture." In *A Companion to Islamic Art and Architecture*, edited by Finbarr Barry Flood and Gulru Necipoglu, 2:1055–1081. Hoboken, NJ: Wiley-Blackwell, 2017.

Dale, Stephen F. *The Garden of the Eight Paradises: Babur and the Culture of Empire in Central Asia, Afghanistan and India (1483–1530)*. Leiden: Brill, 2004.

———. "A Safavid Poet in the Heart of Darkness: The Indian Poems of Ashraf Mazandarani." *Iranian Studies* 36, no. 2 (2003): 197–212.

———. "Trade, Conversion and the Growth of the Islamic Community of Kerala, South India." *Studia Islamica*, no. 71 (1990): 155–175.

Dallal, Ahmad. "The Origins and Objectives of Islamic Revivalist Thought, 1750–1850." *Journal of the American Oriental Society* 113, no. 3 (1993): 341–359.

Dallapiccola, Anna L., John M. Fritz, George Michell, and S. Rajasekhara. *The Ramachandra Temple at Vijayanagara*. New Delhi: Manohar, American Institute of Indian Studies, 1992.

Dalmia, Vasudha. *The Nationalization of Hindu Traditions: Bharatendu Harischandra and Nineteenth-Century Banaras*. Ranikhet, India: Permanent Black, 2010.

———. "'The Only Real Religion of the Hindus': Vaisnava Self-Representation in the Late Nineteenth Century." In *Representing Hinduism: The Construction of Religious Traditions and National Identity*, edited by Vasudha Dalmia and Heinrich von Stietencron, 176–210. New Delhi: Sage, 1995.

Das, Suranjan. *Communal Riots in Bengal, 1905–1947*. Delhi: Oxford University Press, 1991.

Dasgupta, Susmita, Asif Mohammed Zaman, Subhendu Roy, Mainul Huq, Sarwar Jahan, and Ainun Nishat. *Urban Flooding of Greater Dhaka in a Changing Climate: Building Local Resilience to Disaster Risk*. Washington, DC: World Bank, 2015.

Davis, Donald R. "Introduction." In *Hindu Law: A New History of Dharmasastra*, edited by Patrick Olivelle and Donald R. Davis, 1–11. Oxford: Oxford University Press, 2018.

———. "Seeing through the Law: A Debate on Caste in Medieval *Dharmasastra*." *Contributions to Indian Sociology* 56, no. 1 (2022): 17–40.

———. "Slaves and Slavery in the *Smrtican-drika*." *Indian Economic and Social History Review* 57, no. 3 (2020): 299–326.

Davis, Richard H. *The Bhagavad Gita: A Biography*. Princeton, NJ: Princeton University Press, 2015.

———. "Chola Bronzes in Procession." In *The Sensuous and the Sacred: Chola Bronzes from South India*, edited by Vidya Dehejia, 46–63. Seattle: University of Washington Press, 2002.

———. *Global India circa 100 CE: South Asia in Early World History*. Ann Arbor, MI: Association for Asian Studies, 2009.

———. *Lives of Indian Images*. Princeton, NJ: Princeton University Press, 1997.

———. "A Muslim Princess in the Temples of Visnu." *International Journal of Hindu Studies* 8, no. 1–3 (2004): 137–156.

———. "The Origin of Linga Worship." In *Religions of India in Practice*, edited by Donald S. Lopez, 637–648. Princeton, NJ: Princeton University Press, 1995.

———. *Ritual in an Oscillating Universe: Worshipping Siva in Medieval India*. Princeton, NJ: Princeton University Press, 1991.

———. "The Story of the Disappearing Jains: Retelling the Saiva-Jain Encounter in Medieval South India." In *Open Boundaries: Jain Communities and Culture in Indian History*, edited by John E. Cort, 213–224. Albany: State University of New York Press, 1998.

De, Rohit. *A People's Constitution: The Everyday Life of Law in the Indian Republic*. Princeton, NJ: Princeton University Press, 2018.

de Bruijn, Thomas. *Ruby in the Dust: Poetry and History in Padmavat by the South Asian Sufi Poet Muhammad Jayasi*. Leiden: Leiden University Press, 2012.

de Clercq, Eva. "Apabhramsha as a Literary Medium in Fifteenth-Century North

India." In *After Timur Left: Culture and Circulation in Fifteenth-Century North India*, edited by Francesca Orsini and Samira Sheikh, 339–364. New Delhi: Oxford University Press, 2014.

Deeg, Max. "Chinese Buddhist Travelers: Faxian, Xuanzang, and Yijing." In *Oxford Research Encyclopedia of Asian History*. Published online, 2019. https://doi.org/10.1093/acrefore/9780190277727.013.217.

———. "Describing the Own Other: Chinese Buddhist Travelogues between Literary Tropes and Educational Narratives." In *Primary Sources and Asian Pasts*, edited by Peter C. Bisschop and Elizabeth A. Cecil, 129–151. Berlin: De Gruyter, 2021.

———. "Has Xuanzang Really Been in Mathura? Interpretatio Sinica or Interpretatio Occidentalia—How to Critically Read the Records of the Chinese Pilgrim." In *Essays on East Asian Religion and Culture: Festschrift in Honour of Nishiwaki Tsuneki on the Occasion of His 65th Birthday*, edited by Christian Wittern and Shi Lishan, 35–73. Kyoto: Editorial Committee for the Festschrift in Honour of Nishiwaki Tsuneki, 2007.

———. "Many Biographies—Multiple Individualities: The Identities of the Chinese Buddhist Monk Xuanzang." In *Religious Individualisation: Historical Dimensions and Comparative Perspectives*, edited by Martin Fusch, Antje Linkenbach, Martin Mulsow, Bernd-Christian Otto, Rahul Bjorn Parson, and Jorg Rupke, 1:913–937. Berlin: De Gruyter, 2019.

Dehejia, Vidya. *The Body Adorned: Dissolving Boundaries between Sacred and Profane in India's Art*. New York: Columbia University Press, 2009.

———. "Chola Bronzes: How, When, and Why." In *The Sensuous and the Sacred: Chola Bronzes from South India*, edited by Vidya Dehejia, 10–26. Seattle: University of Washington Press, 2002.

———. *Discourse in Early Buddhist Art: Visual Narratives of India*. Delhi: Munshiram Manoharlal, 1997.

———. "Reading Love Imagery on the Indian Temple." In *Love in Asian Art and Culture*, edited by Karen Sagstetter, 97–113. Washington, DC: Arthur M. Sackler Gallery, Smithsonian Institution, 1998.

———. *The Thief Who Stole My Heart: The Material Life of Sacred Bronzes from Chola India, 855–1280*. Princeton, NJ: Princeton University Press, 2021.

De Puma, Richard Daniel. "The Roman Bronzes from Kolhapur." In *Rome and India: The Ancient Sea Trade*, edited by Vimala Begley and Richard Daniel De Puma, 82–112. Madison: University of Wisconsin Press, 1991.

De Romanis, Federico. *The Indo-Roman Pepper Trade and the Muziris Papyrus*. Oxford: Oxford University Press, 2020.

Desai, Devangana. *The Religious Imagery of Khajuraho*. Mumbai: Franco-Indian Research, 1996.

Desai, Madhuri. *Banaras Reconstructed: Architecture and Sacred Space in a Hindu Holy City*. Seattle: University of Washington Press, 2017.

de Saxce, Ariane. "Local Networks and Long-Distance Trade: The Role of the Exchanges between Sri Lanka and India during the Mediterranean Trade." In *Imperial Rome, Indian Ocean Regions and Muziris: New Perspectives on Maritime Trade*, edited by K. S. Mathew, 53–73. London: Routledge, 2017.

Deshpande, Madhav M. "Changing Perspectives in the Sanskrit Grammatical Tradition and the Changing Political Configurations in Ancient India." In *Between the Empires: Society in India 300 BCE to 400 CE*, edited by Patrick Olivelle, 215–225. New York: Oxford University Press, 2006.

———. "From Orality to Writing: Transmission and Interpretation of Panini's Astadhyayi." In *Travaux de Symposium International: Le Livre, La Roumanie, l'Europe: Troisieme Edition, 20 a 24 Septembre 2010*, vol. 3, 57–100. Bucharest: Bibliotheque de Bucarest, 2011.

———. "Interpreting the Asokan Epithet *devanampiya*." In *Asoka in History and Historical Memory*, edited by Patrick Olivelle, 19–43. Delhi: Motilal Banarsidass Publishers, 2009.

———. *Sanskrit and Prakrit: Sociolinguistic Issues*. Delhi: Motilal Banarsidass Publishers, 1993.

———. "Vedic Aryans, Non-Vedic Aryans, and Non-Aryans: Judging the Linguistic Evidence of the Veda." In *The Indo-Aryans of Ancient South Asia: Language, Material Culture and Ethnicity*, edited by George Erdosy, 67–84. Berlin: De Gruyter, 1995.

Deshpande, Prachi. "The Making of an Indian Nationalist Archive: Lakshmibai, Jhansi, and 1857." *Journal of Asian Studies* 67, no. 3 (2008): 855–879.

DeVotta, Neil. *Blowback: Linguistic Nationalism, Institutional Decay, and Ethnic Conflict in Sri Lanka*. Stanford, CA: Stanford University Press, 2004.

Dewaraja, Lorna. "Cheng Ho's Visits to Sri Lanka and the Galle Trilingual Inscription in the National Museum in Colombo." *Journal of the Royal Asiatic Society of Sri Lanka* 52 (2006): 59–74.

Dhand, Arti. "Paradigms of the Good in the *Mahabharata*: Suka and Sulabha in Quagmires of Ethics." In *Gender and Narrative in the* Mahabharata, edited by Simon Brodbeck and Brian Black, 258–278. London: Routledge, 2007.

Dhavan, Purnima. *When Sparrows Became Hawks: The Making of the Sikh Warrior Tradition, 1699–1799*. New York: Oxford University Press, 2011.

Dhavan, Purnima, and Heidi Pauwels. "Controversies Surrounding the Reception of Vali 'Dakhani' (1665?–1707?) In Early Tazkirahs of Urdu Poets." *Journal of the Royal Asiatic Society* 25, no. 4 (2015): 625–646.

Digby, Simon. "After Timur Left: North India in the Fifteenth Century." In *After Timur Left: Culture and Circulation in Fifteenth-Century North India*, edited by Francesca Orsini and Samira Sheikh, 47–59. New Delhi: Oxford University Press, 2014.

———. "Before Timur Came: Provincialization of the Delhi Sultanate through the Fourteenth Century." *Journal of the Economic and Social History of the Orient* 47, no. 3 (2004): 298–356.

———. "The Sufi Shaykh and the Sultan: A Conflict of Claims to Authority in Medieval India." *Iran* 28 (1990): 71–81.

Dirks, Nicholas B. *Castes of Mind: Colonialism and the Making of Modern India*. Princeton, NJ: Princeton University Press, 2001.

———. *The Hollow Crown: Ethnohistory of an Indian Kingdom*. Cambridge: Cambridge University Press, 1987.

Disney, A. R. *A History of Portugal and the Portuguese Empire: From Beginnings to 1807*. Cambridge: Cambridge University Press, 2009.

Doniger, Wendy. *The Hindus: An Alternative History*. New York: Penguin, 2009.

——— (under Doniger O'Flaherty). "The Myths Depicted at Elephanta," in *Elephanta: The Cave of Shiva*, edited by Carmel Berkson, Wendy Doniger O'Flaherty, and George Michell, 27–39. Princeton, NJ: Princeton University Press, 1983.

———. *On Hinduism*. New York: Oxford University Press, 2014.

———. *Siva: The Erotic Ascetic*. New York: Oxford University Press, 1973.

———. *Winged Stallions and Wicked Mares: Horses in Indian Myth and History*. Charlottesville: University of Virginia Press, 2021.

Dreze, Jean, and Amartya Sen. *India: Development and Participation*. 2nd ed. Oxford: Oxford University Press, 2002.

Dudney, Arthur. *India in the Persian World of Letters: Khan-i Arzu among the Eighteenth-Century Philologists*. New York: Oxford University Press, 2022.

Dudrah, Rajinder, and Jigna Desai, eds. *Bollywood Reader*. Berkshire: Open University Press, 2008.

Dundas, Paul. "Floods, Taxes, and a Stone Cow: A Jain Apocalyptic Account of the Gupta Period." *South Asian Studies* 30, no. 2 (2014): 230–244.

———. *History, Scripture and Controversy in a Medieval Jain Sect*. London: Routledge, 2007.

———. "Jain Perceptions of Islam in the Early Modern Period." *Indo-Iranian Journal* 42, no. 1 (1999): 35–46.

———. *The Jains*. 2nd ed. London: Routledge, 2002.

Durrani, F. A., Ihsan Ali, and G. Erdosy. "Further Excavations at Rehman Dheri." *Ancient Pakistan* 7 (1991): 61–151.

———. "Introduction: Excavations in the Gomal Valley (Rehman Dheri Report No. 2)." *Ancient Pakistan* 10 (1994): 1–13.

———. "New Perspectives on Indus Urbanism from Rehman Dheri." *East and West* 45, no. 1/4 (1995): 81–96.

Dyson, Tim, and Arup Maharatna. "Excess Mortality during the Bengal Famine: A

Re-Evaluation." *Indian Economic and Social History Review* 28, no. 3 (1991): 281–297.
Eaton, Richard M. "Gisu-Daraz." In *Encyclopaedia Iranica*, 2012. http://www.iranicaonline.org/articles/gisu-daraz.
———. *India in the Persianate Age, 1000–1765.* Oakland: University of California Press, 2019.
———. "Introduction." In *Slavery and South Asian History*, edited by Indrani Chatterjee and Richard M. Eaton, 1–16. Bloomington: Indiana University Press, 2006.
———. "The Persian Cosmopolis (900–1900) and the Sanskrit Cosmopolis (400–1400)." In *The Persianate World: Rethinking a Shared Sphere*, edited by Abbas Amanat and Assef Ashraf, 63–83. Leiden: Brill, 2019.
———. "(Re)Imag(in)Ing Other²ness: A Postmortem for the Postmodern in India." *Journal of World History* 11, no. 1 (2000): 57–78.
———. "The Rise and Fall of Military Slavery in the Deccan, 1450–1650." In *Slavery and South Asian History*, edited by Indrani Chatterjee and Richard M. Eaton, 115–135. Bloomington: Indiana University Press, 2006.
———. *The Rise of Islam and the Bengal Frontier, 1204–1760.* Berkeley: University of California Press, 1993.
———. "The Rise of Written Vernaculars: The Deccan, 1450–1650." In *After Timur Left: Culture and Circulation in Fifteenth-Century North India*, edited by Francesca Orsini and Samira Sheikh, 111–129. New Delhi: Oxford University Press, 2014.
———. *A Social History of the Deccan, 1300–1761: Eight Indian Lives.* Cambridge: Cambridge University Press, 2005.
———. "Temple Desecration and Indo-Muslim States." *Frontline*, January 5, 2001, 70–77.
———. "Temple Desecration in Pre-Modern India." *Frontline*, December 22, 2000, 62–70.
Eaton, Richard M., and Phillip B. Wagoner. *Power, Memory, Architecture: Contested Sites on India's Deccan Plateau, 1300–1600.* New Delhi: Oxford University Press, 2014.
Echeverri-Gent, John, Aseema Sinha, and Andrew Wyatt. "Economic Distress amidst Political Success: India's Economic Policy under Modi, 2014–2019." *India Review* 20, no. 4 (2021): 402–435.
Eck, Diana L. *Banaras, City of Light.* Princeton, NJ: Princeton University Press, 1982.
———. *Darsan: Seeing the Divine Image in India.* 3rd ed. New York: Columbia University Press, 1998.
———. *India: A Sacred Geography.* New York: Harmony Books, 2012.
———. "A Survey of Sanskrit Sources for the Study of Varanasi." *Purana* 22, no. 1 (1980): 81–101.
Egorova, Yulia. *Jews and India: Perceptions and Image.* London: Routledge, 2006.
Elias, Jamal J. *On Wings of Diesel: Trucks, Identity and Culture in Pakistan.* Oxford: Oneworld, 2011.
Elverskog, Johan. *Buddhism and Islam on the Silk Road.* Philadelphia: University of Pennsylvania Press, 2010.
Englesberg, Paul. "The Bellingham 'Anti-Hindu' Riot." In *Our Stories: An Introduction to South Asian America*, 28–35. Philadelphia: South Asian American Digital Archive, 2021.
Erndl, Kathleen M. "Sakta." In *The Hindu World*, edited by Sushil Mittal and Gene R. Thursby, 140–161. London: Routledge, 2004.
Ernst, Carl W. "Admiring the Work of the Ancients: The Ellora Temples as Viewed by Indo-Muslim Authors." In *Beyond Turk and Hindu: Rethinking Religious Identities in Islamicate South Asia*, edited by David Gilmartin and Bruce B. Lawrence, 98–120. Gainesville: University Press of Florida, 2000.
———. *Eternal Garden: Mysticism, History, and Politics at a South Asian Sufi Center.* Albany: State University of New York Press, 1992.
———. "The Islamization of Yoga in the 'Amrtakunda' Translations." *Journal of the Royal Asiatic Society* 13, no. 2 (2003): 199–226.
———. "Muslim Studies of Hinduism? A Reconsideration of Arabic and Persian Translations from Indian Languages." *Iranian Studies* 36, no. 2 (2003): 173–195.
———. "Situating Sufism and Yoga." *Journal of the Royal Asiatic Society* 15, no. 1 (2005): 15–43.

Ernst, Carl W., and Bruce B. Lawrence. *Sufi Martyrs of Love: The Chishti Order in South Asia and Beyond*. New York: Palgrave Macmillan, 2002.

Etter, Anne-Julie. "Antiquarian Knowledge and Preservation of Indian Monuments at the Beginning of the Nineteenth Century." In *Knowledge Production, Pedagogy, and Institutions in Colonial India*, edited by Daud Ali and Indra Sengupta, 75–95. New York: Palgrave Macmillan, 2011.

Falcone, Jessica Marie. "'Garba with Attitude': Creative Nostalgia in Competitive Collegiate Gujarati American Folk Dancing." *Journal of Asian American Studies* 16, no. 1 (2013): 57–89.

Falk, Harry. *Asokan Sites and Artefacts: A Source-Book with Bibliography*. Mainz: Verlag Philipp von Zabern, 2006.

———. "Indian Gold Crossing the Indian Ocean through the Millennia." In *Across the Ocean: Nine Essays on Indo-Mediterranean Trade*, edited by Federico De Romanis and Marco Maiuro, 97–113. Leiden: Brill, 2015.

———. "Owners' Graffiti on Pottery from Tissamaharama." *Zeitschrift fur Archaologie Aussereuropaischer Kulturen* 6 (2014): 45–94.

———. "Remarks on the Minor Rock Edict of Asoka at Ratanpurwa." *Jnana-Pravaha Research Journal* 16 (2013): 29–48.

Fallon, Oliver. "Introduction." In *Bhatti's Poem: The Death of Ravana by Bhatti*, xix–xxxvii. New York: New York University Press, 2009.

Farge, Arlette. *The Allure of the Archives*. Translated by Thomas Scott-Railton. New Haven, CT: Yale University Press, 2013.

Farmer, Steve. "Claims Concerning the Longest Indus 'Inscription.'" Steve Farmer's Personal Website, February 24, 2023. https://safarmer.com/indus-longest inscription/.

Farmer, Steve, Richard Sproat, and Michael Witzel. "The Collapse of the Indus-Script Thesis: The Myth of a Literate Harappan Civilization." *Electronic Journal of Vedic Studies* 11, no. 2 (2004): 19–57.

Faruqi, Shamsur Rahman. "A Long History of Urdu Literary Culture, Part 1: Naming and Placing a Literary Culture." In *Literary Cultures in History: Reconstructions from South Asia*, edited by Sheldon Pollock, 805–863. Berkeley: University of California Press, 2003.

Faruqui, Munis D. "At Empire's End: The Nizam, Hyderabad and Eighteenth-Century India." *Modern Asian Studies* 43, no. 1 (2009): 5–43.

———. *The Princes of the Mughal Empire, 1504–1719*. New York: Cambridge University Press, 2012.

Felbur, Rafal. "Kumarajiva: 'Great Man' and Cultural Event." In *A Companion to World Literature*, edited by Ken Seigneurie, 1–13. New York: John Wiley & Sons, 2019.

Fenech, Louis E. "Martyrdom and the Sikh Tradition." *Journal of the American Oriental Society* 117, no. 4 (1997): 623–642.

Fenech, Louis E., and W. H. McLeod. *Historical Dictionary of Sikhism*. 3rd ed. Lanham, MD: Rowman & Littlefield, 2014.

Ferstl, Christian. "Bana's Literary Representation of a South Indian Saivite." In *Tantric Communities in Context*, edited by Nina Mirnig, Marion Rastelli, and Vincent Eltschinger, 171–201. Vienna: Austrian Academy of Sciences Press, 2019.

Figueira, Dorothy Matilda. *Translating the Orient: The Reception of* Sakuntala *in Nineteenth-Century Europe*. Albany: State University of New York Press, 1991.

Findly, Ellison Banks. *Nur Jahan: Empress of Mughal India*. New York: Oxford University Press, 1993.

Fischel, Roy S. *Local States in an Imperial World: Identity, Society and Politics in the Early Modern Deccan*. Edinburgh: Edinburgh University Press, 2020.

Fisher, Elaine M. *Hindu Pluralism: Religion and the Public Sphere in Early Modern South India*. Oakland: University of California Press, 2017.

Fisher, Michael H. *An Environmental History of India: From Earliest Times to the Twenty-First Century*. Cambridge: Cambridge University Press, 2018.

———. "Islam in Mughal India." In *Oxford Research Encyclopedia of Religion*. Published online, 2018. https://doi.org/10.1093/acrefore/9780199340378.013.648.

———, ed. *The Politics of the British Annexation of India, 1757–1857*. Delhi: Oxford University Press, 1993.

———. *A Short History of the Mughal Empire.* London: I. B. Tauris, 2016.

Fitzgerald, James L. "The Great Epic of India as Religious Rhetoric: A Fresh Look at the 'Mahabharata.'" *Journal of the American Academy of Religion* 51, no. 4 (1983): 611–630.

———. "India's Fifth Veda: The *Mahabharata*'s Presentation of Itself." *Journal of South Asian Literature* 20, no. 1 (1985): 125–140.

———. "Mahabharata." In *The Hindu World*, edited by Sushil Mittal and Gene R. Thursby, 52–74. London: Routledge, 2004.

Fitzpatrick, Hannah. "The Space of the Courtroom and the Role of Geographical Evidence in the Punjab Boundary Commission Hearings, July 1947." *South Asia: Journal of South Asian Studies* 42, no. 1 (2019): 188–207.

Flatt, Emma J. *The Courts of the Deccan Sultanates: Living Well in the Persian Cosmopolis.* Cambridge: Cambridge University Press, 2019.

Flood, Finbarr B. *Objects of Translation: Material Culture and Medieval "Hindu-Muslim" Encounter.* Princeton, NJ: Princeton University Press, 2009.

———. "Pillars, Palimpsests, and Princely Practices: Translating the Past in Sultanate Delhi." *Res: Anthropology and Aesthetics* 43 (2003): 95–116.

Flood, Gavin. *An Introduction to Hinduism.* Cambridge: Cambridge University Press, 1996.

Floyd, Jessica. "Engaging Imperfect Texts: The Ballad Tradition and the Investigation of Chanteys." *Restoration: Studies in English Literary Culture, 1660–1700* 44, no. 2 (2020): 111–138.

Flynn, Vincent John Adams. "An English Translation of the Adab-i-'Alamgiri: The Period before the War of Succession being the Letters of Prince Muhammad Aurangzib Bahadur to Muhammad Shihabu'd-din Shah Jahan Sahib-i-Qiran-i-Sani Emperor of Hindustan." PhD diss., Australian National University, 1974.

Fogelin, Lars. "Ritual and Presentation in Early Buddhist Religious Architecture." *Asian Perspectives* 42, no. 1 (2003): 129–154.

Ford, L. A., A. M. Pollard, R.A.E. Coningham, and B. Stern. "A Geochemical Investigation of the Origin of Rouletted and Other Related South Asian Fine Wares." *Antiquity* 79, no. 306 (2005): 909–920.

Formigatti, Camillo A. "Towards a Cultural History of Nepal, 14th–17th Century: A Nepalese Renaissance?" In *Studies in Honour of Luciano Petech: A Commemoration Volume 1914–2014*, edited by Elena De Rossi Filibeck, Giorgio Milanetti, Michela Clemente, Federica Venturi, and Oscar Nalesini, 51–66. Pisa: Fabrizio Serra Editore, 2016.

Framarin, Christopher G. "Environmental Ethics and the *Mahabharata*: The Case of the Burning of the Khandava Forest." *Sophia* 52, no. 1 (2013): 185–204.

Francis, Peter. *Asia's Maritime Bead Trade: 300 B.C. to the Present.* Honolulu: University of Hawai'i Press, 2002.

———. "Beads and Selected Small Finds from the 1989–92 Excavations." In *The Ancient Port of Arikamedu: New Excavations and Researches, 1989–1992*, edited by Vimala Begley, Peter Francis, Noboru Karashima, K. V. Raman, Steven E. Sidebotham, and Elizabeth Lyding Will, 2:447–604. Paris: Ecole Francaise d'Extreme-Orient, 2004.

Franco, Eli. *The Spitzer Manuscript: The Oldest Philosophical Manuscript in Sanskrit.* 2 vols. Vienna: Verlag der Osterreichischen Akademie der Wissenschaften, 2004.

Frankopan, Peter. *The Silk Roads: A New History of the World.* New York: Knopf, 2016.

Frykenberg, Robert Eric. *Christianity in India: From Beginnings to the Present.* Oxford: Oxford University Press, 2008.

———. "Modern Education in South India, 1784–1854: Its Roots and Its Role as a Vehicle of Integration under Company Raj." *American Historical Review* 91, no. 1 (1986): 37–65.

Fuller, Dorian Q. "Agricultural Origins and Frontiers in South Asia: A Working Synthesis." *Journal of World Prehistory* 20, no. 1 (2006): 1–86.

Gabbay, Alyssa. "In Reality a Man: Sultan Iltutmish, His Daughter, Raziya, and Gender Ambiguity in Thirteenth Century Northern India." *Journal of Persianate Studies* 4, no. 1 (2011): 45–63.

———. "The Language of Tolerance: Amir Khusraw and the Development of

Indo-Persian Culture." PhD diss., University of Chicago, 2007.

Galewicz, Cezary. *A Commentator in Service of the Empire: Sayana and the Royal Project of Commenting on the Whole of the Veda*. Vienna: Sammlung de Nobili, 2009.

Gandhi, Rajmohan. *Mohandas: A True Story of a Man, His People and an Empire*. Noida: Penguin, 2006.

Gandhi, Supriya. *The Emperor Who Never Was: Dara Shukoh in Mughal India*. Cambridge, MA: Belknap Press of Harvard University Press, 2020.

———. "Hindutva and the Shared Scripts of the Global Right." *The Immanent Frame*, October 12, 2022. https://tif.ssrc.org/2022/10/12/hindutva-and-the-shared-scripts-of-the-global-right/.

———. "The Prince and the *Muvahhid*: Dara Shikoh and Mughal Engagements with Vedanta." In *Religious Interactions in Mughal India*, edited by Vasudha Dalmia and Munis D. Faruqui, 65–101. Delhi: Oxford University Press, 2014.

Gangl, Georg. "The Essential Tension: Historical Knowledge between Past and Present." *History and Theory* 60, no. 3 (2021): 513–533.

Gatade, Subhash. "Silencing Caste, Sanitising Oppression: Understanding Swachh Bharat Abhiyan." *Economic and Political Weekly* 50, no. 44 (2015): 29–35.

Geetha, V., and S. V. Rajadurai. "Dalits and Non-Brahmin Consciousness in Colonial Tamil Nadu." *Economic and Political Weekly* 28, no. 39 (1993): 2091–2098.

———. *Towards a Non-Brahmin Millennium: From Iyothee Thass to Periyar*. Calcutta: Samya, 1998.

Gerety, Finnian M. M. "Between Sound and Silence in Early Yoga: Meditation on 'Om' at Death." *History of Religions* 60, no. 3 (2021): 209–244.

———. "This Whole World Is OM: Song, Soteriology, and the Emergence of the Sacred Syllable." PhD diss., Harvard University, 2015.

Ghosh, Devleena. "The Bones of Our Mother: Adivasi Dispossession in an Indian State." In *The Routledge Companion to Global Indigenous History*, edited by Ann McGrath and Lynette Russell, 443–463. London: Routledge, 2021.

Ghosh, Durba. *Gentlemanly Terrorists: Political Violence and the Colonial State in India, 1919–1947*. Cambridge: Cambridge University Press, 2017.

———. *Sex and the Family in Colonial India: The Making of Empire*. Cambridge: Cambridge University Press, 2006.

Ghosh, Samyak. "'Two Kings' in the Tungkhungia Court? Love and Courtly Culture in Early Eighteenth-Century Hindustan." *Comparative Studies of South Asia, Africa and the Middle East* 42, no. 2 (2020): 348–355.

Ghosh, Subhasri. "The Protracted Process of Boundary Formation: The Making of the *Nadia-Kushtia* Border, 1947–1971." In *The 1947 Partition in The East: Trends and Trajectories*, edited by Subhasri Ghosh, 36–68. London: Routledge, 2022.

Gillespie, Thomas W., Monica L. Smith, Scott Barron, Kanika Kalra, and Corey Rovzar. "Predictive Modelling for Archaeological Sites: Ashokan Edicts from the Indian Subcontinent." *Current Science* 110, no. 10 (2016): 1916–1921.

Gilmartin, David. "The Historiography of India's Partition: Between Civilization and Modernity." *Journal of Asian Studies* 74, no. 1 (2015): 23–41.

Gilmartin, David, and Barbara D. Metcalf. "Art on Trial: Civilisation and Religion in the Persona and Painting of M. F. Husain." In *Barefoot across the Nation: Maqbool Fida Husain and the Idea of India*, edited by Sumathi Ramaswamy, 54–74. New York: Routledge, 2011.

Gode, P. K. "Some New Evidence Regarding Devabhatta Mahasabde, the Father of Ratnakarabhatta, the Guru of Sevai Jaising of Amber (A.D. 1699–1743)." *Poona Orientalist* 8, no. 3/4 (1933–34): 129–138.

———. *Studies in Indian Cultural History*. Vol. 1. Hoshiarpur: Vishveshvaranand Vedic Research Institute, 1961.

———. *Studies in Indian Literary History*. Vol. 2. Bombay: Singhi Jain Shastra Shikshapith, 1954.

———. "Two Contemporary Tributes to Minister Vidyadhara, the Bengali Architect of Jaipur at the Court of Sevai Jaising of Amber (A.D. 1699–1743)." In *Dr. C. Kunhan Raja Presentation Volume*, 285–294. Madras: Adyar Library, 1946.

Goitein, S. D., and Mordechai Akiya Friedman. *India Traders of the Middle Ages: Documents from the Cairo Geniza ("India Book")*. Leiden: Brill, 2008.

Goldman, Robert P., and Sally J. Sutherland Goldman. "Ramayana." In *The Hindu World*, edited by Sushil Mittal and Gene R. Thursby, 75–96. London: Routledge, 2004.

Gommans, Jos. *Mughal Warfare: Indian Frontiers and Highroads to Empire, 1500–1700*. New York: Routledge, 2002.

———. "Warhorse and Gunpowder in India c. 1000–1850." In *War in The Early Modern World, 1450–1815*, edited by Jeremy Black, 105–127. London: Routledge, 1999.

Gopal, Surendra. *Jains in India: Historical Essays*. London: Routledge, 2019.

Gordon, Leonard A. *Brothers against the Raj: A Biography of Indian Nationalists Sarat and Subhas Chandra Bose*. New York: Columbia University Press, 1990.

Gordon, Stewart. *The Marathas, 1600–1818*. Cambridge: Cambridge University Press, 1993.

———. *When Asia Was the World*. Cambridge, MA: Da Capo Press, 2008.

Goswamy, B. N., and J. S. Grewal. *The Mughals and the Jogis of Jakhbar: Some Madad-i-Ma'ash and Other Documents*. Simla: Indian Institute of Advanced Study, 1967.

Gottschalk, Peter. *Religion, Science, and Empire: Classifying Hinduism and Islam in British India*. New York: Oxford University Press, 2013.

Gough, Ellen. *Making a Mantra: Tantric Ritual and Renunciation on the Jain Path to Liberation*. Chicago: University of Chicago Press, 2021.

———. "Situating Parsva's Biography in Varanasi." *Religions* 11, no. 3 (2020): 1–25.

Gould, William. "Social and Religious Reform in 19th-Century India." In *Oxford Research Encyclopedia of Asian History*. Published online, 2020. https://doi.org/10.1093/acrefore/9780190277727.013.382.

Granoff, Phyllis. "Mountains of Eternity: Raidhu and the Colossal Jinas of Gwalior." *Rivista Di Studi Sudasiatici* 1 (2006): 31–50.

Green, Adam S. "Killing the Priest-King: Addressing Egalitarianism in the Indus Civilization." *Journal of Archaeological Research* 29, no. 2 (2021): 153–202.

Green, Nile. "Introduction: The Frontiers of the Persianate World (ca. 800–1900)." In *The Persianate World: The Frontiers of a Eurasian Lingua Franca*, edited by Nile Green, 1–71. Oakland: University of California Press, 2019.

Green, Peter. *Alexander of Macedon 356–323 B.C.: A Historical Biography*. Berkeley: University of California Press, 2013.

Grewal, J. S. *The Sikhs of the Punjab*. Rev. ed. Cambridge: Cambridge University Press, 1990.

Guenther, Alan M. "Hanafi *Fiqh* in Mughal India: The *Fatawa-i 'Alamgiri*." In *India's Islamic Traditions, 711–1750*, edited by Richard M. Eaton, 209–230. New Delhi: Oxford University Press, 2003.

Guha, Sumit. "Bad Language and Good Language: Lexical Awareness in the Cultural Politics of Peninsular India, ca. 1300–1800." In *Forms of Knowledge in Early Modern Asia: Explorations in the Intellectual History of India and Tibet, 1500–1800*, edited by Sheldon Pollock, 49–68. Durham, NC: Duke University Press, 2011.

———. *Beyond Caste: Identity and Power in South Asia, Past and Present*. Leiden: Brill, 2013.

———. "The Maratha Empire." In *Oxford Research Encyclopedia of Asian History*. Published online, 2019. https://doi.org/10.1093/acrefore/9780190277727.013.356.

Guha-Thakurta, Tapati. *Monuments, Objects, Histories: Institutions of Art in Colonial and Postcolonial India*. New York: Columbia University Press, 2004.

Gundimeda, Sambaiah, and V. S. Ashwin. "Cow Protection in India: From Secularising to Legitimating Debates." *South Asia Research* 38, no. 2 (2018): 156–176.

Gupta, P. L., and T. R. Hardaker. *Punchmarked Coinage of the Indian Subcontinent: Magadha-Mauryan Series*. Mumbai: IIRNS, 2014.

Gurukkal, Rajan. "Forms of Production and Forces of Change in Ancient Tamil Society." *Studies in History* 5, no. 2 (1989): 159–175.

Gutas, Dimitri. *Greek Thought, Arabic Culture: The Graeco-Arabic Translation Movement in Baghdad and Early 'Abbasid Society (2nd–4th/8th–10th centuries)*. London: Routledge, 1998.

Guy, John. *Tree and Serpent: Early Buddhist Art in India*. New York: Metropolitan Museum of Art, 2023.

Habib, Irfan. "The Coming of 1857." *Social Scientist* 26, no. 1/4 (1998): 6–15.

———. "Linguistic Materials from Eighth-Century Sind: An Exploration of the *Chachnama*." In *Recording the Progress of Indian History: Symposia Papers of the Indian History Congress 1992–2010*, edited by S.Z.H. Jafri, 79–89. Delhi: Primus Books, 2012.

———. "Population." In *The Cambridge Economic History of India*. Vol. 1, *c. 1200–c. 1750*, edited by Tapan Raychaudhuri and Irfan Habib, 163–171. Cambridge: Cambridge University Press, 1982.

———. "Postal Communications in Mughal India." *Proceedings of the Indian History Congress* 46 (1985): 236–252.

———. "Review of Manan Ahmad Asif, *A Book of Conquest: The Chachnama and Muslim Origins in South Asia*." *Studies in People's History* 4, no. 1 (2017): 105–109.

Hachhethu, Krishna, and David N. Gellner. "Nepal: Trajectories of Democracy and Restructuring of the State." In *Routledge Handbook of South Asian Politics: India, Pakistan, Bangladesh, Sri Lanka, and Nepal*, edited by Paul R. Brass, 131–146. London: Routledge, 2010.

Haeri, Shahla. *The Unforgettable Queens of Islam: Succession, Authority, Gender*. Cambridge: Cambridge University Press, 2020.

Haidar, Navina Najat. "The *Kitab-i Nauras*: Key to Bijapur's Golden Age." In *Sultans of the South: Arts of India's Deccan Courts, 1323–1687*, edited by Navina Najat Haidar and Marika Sardar, 26–43. New York: Metropolitan Museum of Art, 2011.

Haines, Daniel. *Rivers Divided: Indus Basin Waters in the Making of India and Pakistan*. New York: Oxford University Press, 2016.

Hall, Edith. "Iphigenia in Oxyrhynchus and India: Greek Tragedy for Everyone." In *Parachoregema: Meletemata Gia to Archaio Theatro Pros Timen Tou Kathegete Gregore M. Sephake*, edited by S. Tsitsirides, 393–417. Heraklion: Crete University Press, 2010.

Hallisey, Charles. "Works and Persons in Sinhala Literary Culture." In *Literary Cultures in History: Reconstructions from South Asia*, edited by Sheldon Pollock, 689–746. Berkeley: University of California Press, 2003.

Hallissey, Robert C. *The Rajput Rebellion against Aurangzeb: A Study of the Mughal Empire in Seventeenth-Century India*. Columbia: University of Missouri Press, 1977.

Hamza, Shireen. "A Hakim's Tale: A Physician's Reflections from Medieval India." *Asian Medicine* 15, no. 1 (2020): 63–82.

Hardiman, David. "Gandhi's Global Legacy." In *The Cambridge Companion to Gandhi*, edited by Judith M. Brown and Anthony Parel, 239–257. New York: Cambridge University Press, 2011.

Harding, Robert. "Rajgir and Its Hinterland." PhD diss., Pembroke College, University of Cambridge, 2003.

Hardy, Peter. "Abul Fazl's Portrait of the Perfect Padshah: A Political Philosophy for Mughal India—or a Personal Puff for a Pal?" In *Islam in India: Studies and Commentaries*, edited by Christian W. Troll, 2:114–137. New Delhi: Vikas, 1985.

———. *Historians of Medieval India: Studies in Indo-Muslim Historical Writing*. London: Luzac, 1960.

Harrison, Paul. "Some Reflections on the Personality of the Buddha." *Otani Gakuho* 74, no. 4 (1995): 1–29.

Hart, George L. *The Poems of Ancient Tamil: Their Milieu and Their Sanskrit Counterparts*. Berkeley: University of California Press, 1975.

Harvard University. "Parliament of Religions, 1893." *The Pluralism Project*, 2020. https://pluralism.org/parliament-of-religions-1893.

Harvey, Peter. "*Dukkha*, Non-Self, and the Teaching on the Four 'Noble Truths.'" In *A Companion to Buddhist Philosophy*, edited by Steven M. Emmanuel, 26–45. Malden, MA: John Wiley & Sons, 2013.

Hasan, Farhat. "Indigenous Cooperation and the Birth of a Colonial City: Calcutta, c. 1698–1750." *Modern Asian Studies* 26, no. 1 (1992): 65–82.

Hasan, Mushirul. *Legacy of a Divided Nation: India's Muslims since Independence*. London: Routledge, 2018.

———. *A Moral Reckoning: Muslim Intellectuals in Nineteenth-Century Delhi*. New Delhi: Oxford University Press, 2007.

Hatcher, Brian A. *Bourgeois Hinduism, or the Faith of the Modern Vedantists: Rare Discourses from Early Colonial Bengal.* Oxford: Oxford University Press, 2008.

———. *Hinduism before Reform.* Cambridge, MA: Harvard University Press, 2020.

Hatekar, Neeraj, and Ambrish Dongre. "Structural Breaks in India's Growth: Revisiting the Debate with a Longer Perspective." *Economic and Political Weekly* 40, no. 14 (2005): 1432–1435.

Hawes, C. J. *Poor Relations: The Making of a Eurasian Community in British India, 1773–1833.* London: Routledge, 2013.

Hawley, John Stratton. "Naming Hinduism." *Wilson Quarterly* 15, no. 3 (1991): 20–34.

———. *Three Bhakti Voices: Mirabai, Surdas, and Kabir in Their Times and Ours.* New Delhi: Oxford University Press, 2005.

Hawley, John Stratton, and Mark Juergensmeyer. *Songs of the Saints of India.* New Delhi: Oxford University Press, 2004.

Hawley, Nell Shapiro, and Sohini Sarah Pillai. "An Introduction to the Literature of the Mahabharata." In *Many Mahabharatas*, edited by Nell Shapiro Hawley and Sohini Sarah Pillai, 1–34. Albany: State University of New York Press, 2021.

Hegarty, James. *Religion, Narrative and Public Imagination in South Asia: Past and Place in the Sanskrit Mahabharata.* London: Routledge, 2012.

Hens, Sander. "Beyond Power and Praise: Nayacandra Suri's Tragic-Historical Epic Hammira-mahakavya as a Subversive Response to Hero Glorification in Early Tomar Gwalior." *South Asian History and Culture* 11, no. 2 (2020): 40–59.

Hess, Linda. "Rejecting Sita: Indian Responses to the Ideal Man's Cruel Treatment of His Ideal Wife." *Journal of the American Academy of Religion* 67, no. 1 (1999): 1–32.

Hijiya, James A. "The *Gita* of J. Robert Oppenheimer." *Proceedings of the American Philosophical Society* 144, no. 2 (2000): 123–167.

Hinnells, John R. "Parsi Communities i. Early History." In *Encyclopaedia Iranica*, 2008. https://iranicaonline.org/articles/parsi-communities-i-early-history.

Hiroyuki, Mashita. "A Historiographical Study of the So-called *Ahwal-i Asad Big*." *Zinbun* 36, no. 1 (2001/2002): 51–103.

Hooykaas, C. *The Old-Javanese Ramayana: An Exemplary Kakawin as to Form and Content.* Amsterdam: N.V. Noord-Hollandsche Uitgevers Maatschappij, 1958.

Houghteling, Sylvia. *The Art of Cloth in Mughal India.* Princeton, NJ: Princeton University Press, 2022.

Hudson, Dennis. "Siva, Minaksi, Vishnu—Reflections on a Popular Myth in Madurai." *Indian Economic and Social History Review* 14, no. 1 (1977): 107–118.

Hudson, Emily T. *Disorienting Dharma: Ethics and the Aesthetics of Suffering in the Mahabharata.* New York: Oxford University Press, 2013.

Human Rights Watch. "India: No Justice for 1984 Anti-Sikh Bloodshed." October 29, 2014. https://www.hrw.org/news/2014/10/29/india-no-justice-1984-anti-sikh-bloodshed.

———. "'We Don't Want to Be Refugees Again': A Human Rights Watch Briefing Paper for the Fourteenth Ministerial Joint Committee of Bhutan and Nepal, May 19, 2003." May 2003. https://www.hrw.org/legacy/backgrounder/wrd/refugees/.

Husain, S. M. Azizuddin. *Structure of Politics under Aurangzeb, 1658–1707.* New Delhi: Kanishka, 2002.

Hussain, Shahla. *Kashmir in the Aftermath of Partition.* Cambridge: Cambridge University Press, 2021.

Hutton, Deborah. *Art of the Court of Bijapur.* Bloomington: Indiana University Press, 2006.

Hutton, Deborah, and Rebecca Tucker. "A Dutch Artist in Bijapur." In *The Visual World of Muslim India: The Art, Culture and Society of the Deccan in the Early Modern Era*, edited by Laura E. Parodi, 205–232. London: I. B. Tauris, 2014.

Im, Eun-Soon, Jeremy S. Pal, and Elfatih A. B. Eltahir. "Deadly Heat Waves Projected in the Densely Populated Agricultural Regions of South Asia." *Science Advances* 3, no. 8 (2017): 1–7.

Iqbal, Iftekhar. "Bengal Delta." In *Oxford Research Encyclopedia of Asian History.* Published online, 2020. https://doi.org/10.1093/acrefore/9780190277727.013.19.

———. "Governing Mass Migration to Dhaka: Revisiting Climate Factors." *Economic and*

Political Weekly 54, no. 36 (September 7, 2019): 26–31.

Irschick, Eugene F. *Dialogue and History: Constructing South India, 1795–1895*. Berkeley: University of California Press, 1994.

Irvine, William, and Jadunath Sarkar. *Later Mughals*. Vol. 2, *1719–1739*. Calcutta: M. C. Sarkar & Sons, 1922.

Isayeva, Natalia. *Shankara and Indian Philosophy*. Albany: State University of New York Press, 1993.

Islam, Arshad. "The Backlash in Delhi: British Treatment of the Mughal Royal Family Following the Indian 'Sepoy Mutiny' of 1857." *Journal of Muslim Minority Affairs* 31, no. 2 (2011): 197–215.

Jackson, Peter. *The Delhi Sultanate: A Political and Military History*. Cambridge: Cambridge University Press, 1999.

———. "Turkish Slaves on Islam's Indian Frontier." In *Slavery and South Asian History*, edited by Indrani Chatterjee and Richard M. Eaton, 63–82. Bloomington: Indiana University Press, 2006.

Jaffrelot, Christophe. *Dr Ambedkar and Untouchability: Analysing and Fighting Caste*. London: Hurst, 2005.

———. *Modi's India: Hindu Nationalism and the Rise of Ethnic Democracy*. Translated by Cynthia Schoch. Princeton, NJ: Princeton University Press, 2021.

———. *Religion, Caste, and Politics in India*. New York: Columbia University Press, 2011.

———. "The 2002 Pogrom in Gujarat: The Post-9/11 Face of Hindu Nationalist Anti-Muslim Violence." In *Religion and Violence in South Asia: Theory and Practice*, edited by John R. Hinnells and Richard King, 164–182. London: Routledge, 2007.

Jaffrelot, Christophe, and Edward Anderson. "Hindu Nationalism and the 'Saffronisation of the Public Sphere': An Interview with Christophe Jaffrelot." *Contemporary South Asia* 26, no. 4 (2018): 468–482.

Jaffrelot, Christophe, and Pratinav Anil. *India's First Dictatorship: The Emergency, 1975–1977*. New York: Columbia University Press, 2020.

Jafri, S.Z.H. "The Issue of Religion in 1857: Three Documents." *Studies in People's History* 4, no. 1 (2017): 77–90.

Jahangir, Asma, and Hina Jilani. *The Hudood Ordinances, a Divine Sanction? A Research Study of the Hudood Ordinances and Their Effect on the Disadvantaged Sections of Pakistan Society*. Lahore: Sang-e-Meel, 2003.

Jain, Shalin. "Jain Elites and the Mughal State under Shahjahan." *Indian Historical Review* 42, no. 2 (2015): 210–225.

———. "Piety, Laity and Royalty: Jains under the Mughals in the First Half of the Seventeenth Century." *Indian Historical Review* 40, no. 1 (2013): 67–92.

Jalal, Ayesha. *Partisans of Allah: Jihad in South Asia*. Cambridge, MA: Harvard University Press, 2008.

———. *The Pity of Partition: Manto's Life, Times, and Work across the India-Pakistan Divide*. Princeton, NJ: Princeton University Press, 2013.

———. *The Sole Spokesman: Jinnah, the Muslim League, and the Demand for Pakistan*. New York: Cambridge University Press, 1994.

———. *The State of Martial Rule: The Origins of Pakistan's Political Economy of Defence*. Cambridge: Cambridge University Press, 1990.

Jalali, S. Farrukh Ali, and S. M. Razaullah Ansari. "Persian Translation of Varahamihira's Brhatsamhita." *Studies in History of Medicine and Science* 9, no. 3–4 (1985): 161–169.

Jamison, Stephanie W. "Marriage and the Householder: *Vivaha, grhastha*." In *Hindu Law: A New History of Dharmasastra*, edited by Patrick Olivelle and Donald R. Davis, 125–136. Oxford: Oxford University Press, 2018.

———. *The Ravenous Hyenas and the Wounded Sun: Myth and Ritual in Ancient India*. Ithaca, NY: Cornell University Press, 1991.

———. *Sacrificed Wife / Sacrificer's Wife: Women, Ritual, and Hospitality in Ancient India*. New York: Oxford University Press, 1996.

———. "The Secret Lives of Texts." *Journal of the American Oriental Society* 131, no. 1 (2011): 1–7.

———. "Women 'between the Empires' and 'between the Lines.'" In *Between the Empires: Society in India 300 BCE to 400 CE*, edited by Patrick Olivelle, 191–214. New York: Oxford University Press, 2006.

Jangam, Chinnaiah. *Dalits and the Making of Modern India*. New Delhi: Oxford University Press, 2017.

Jarrige, Jean-Francois, Catherine Jarrige, Gonzague Quivron, Luc Wengler, and David Sarmiento Castillo. *Mehrgarh: Neolithic Period—Seasons 1997–2000—Pakistan*. Paris: Mission Archeologique de l'Indus, 2013.

Jasanoff, Maya. *Edge of Empire: Lives, Culture, and Conquest in the East, 1750–1850*. New York: Knopf, 2005.

Jasdanwalla, Faaeza. "The Invincible Fort of the Nawabs of Janjira." *Journal of African Diaspora Archaeology and Heritage* 4, no. 1 (2015): 72–91.

Jasper, Daniel Alan. "Commemorating Shivaji: Regional and Religious Identity in Maharashtra, India." PhD diss., New School for Social Research, 2002.

Jaywant, Ketaki. "Reshaping the Figure of the Shudra: Tukaram Padwal's *Jatibhed Viveksar* (Reflections on the Institution of Caste)." *Modern Asian Studies* 57 (2023): 380–408.

Jha, Arun Kumar. "Chemical Industries in Ancient India (From the Mauryan Era to the Gupta Age)." *Proceedings of the Indian History Congress* 64 (2003): 122–131.

Jha, D. N. *Ancient India in Historical Outline: Revised and Enlarged Edition*. Delhi: Manohar, 2009.

———. *The Myth of the Holy Cow*. London: Verso, 2002.

Jha, Dhirendra K. "The Apostle of Hate: Historical Records Expose the Lie That Nathuram Godse Left the RSS." *The Caravan*, January 1, 2020. https://caravanmagazine.in/reportage/historical-record-expose-lie-godse-left-rss.

———. "Code of Silence: Why the Demand for the Sarna Code Rattles the RSS." *The Caravan*, December 28, 2022. https://caravanmagazine.in/politics/rss-sarna-code-jharkhand-adivasi.

Jha, Pankaj. *A Political History of Literature: Vidyapati and the Fifteenth Century*. Delhi: Oxford University Press, 2019.

Joffee, Jennifer Beth. "Art, Architecture and Politics in Mewar, 1628–1710." PhD diss., University of Minnesota, 2005.

Johansen, Peter G. "Issues and Problems of Ashmound Research in the Neolithic South Deccan: Contemporary Perspectives." In *Beyond Stones and More Stones*, edited by Ravi Korisettar, 2:170–207. Bengaluru: Mythic Society, 2018.

———. "Landscape, Monumental Architecture, and Ritual: A Reconsideration of the South Indian Ashmounds." *Journal of Anthropological Archaeology* 23, no. 3 (2004): 309–330.

Johnson-Roehr, Susan N. "Centering the *Charbagh*: The Mughal Garden as Design Module for the Jaipur City Plan." *Journal of the Society of Architectural Historians* 72, no. 1 (2013): 28–47.

Jones, Justin. "'The Pakistan That Is Going to Be Sunnistan': Indian Shi'a Responses to the Pakistan Movement." In *Muslims against the Muslim League: Critiques of the Idea of Pakistan*, edited by Ali Usman Qasmi and Megan Eaton Robb, 350–380. Cambridge: Cambridge University Press, 2017.

Jones, Kenneth W. "Communalism in the Punjab: The Arya Samaj Contribution." *Journal of Asian Studies* 28, no. 1 (1968): 39–54.

———, ed. *Religious Controversy in British India: Dialogues in South Asian Languages*. Albany: State University of New York Press, 1992.

———. *Socio-Religious Reform Movements in British India*. Cambridge: Cambridge University Press, 1989.

Joseph, Tony. *Early Indians: The Story of Our Ancestors and Where We Came From*. New Delhi: Juggernaut, 2018.

Joshi, P. M. "Asad Beg's Mission to Bijapur, 1603–1604." In *Mahamahopadhyaya Prof. D. V. Potdar Sixty-First Birthday Commemoration Volume: Studies in Historical and Indological Research Presented to M. M. Prof. Datto Vaman Potdar by His Friends and Old Pupils in Honour of His 61st Birthday*, edited by Surendra Nath Sen, 184–196. Poona: D. K. Sathe, 1950.

Judge, Rajbir Singh. "Reform in Fragments: Sovereignty, Colonialism, and the Sikh Tradition." *Modern Asian Studies* 56, no. 4 (2022): 1125–1152.

Kachru, Sonam. "Ashoka's Moral Empire." *Aeon*, July 2, 2020. https://aeon.co/essays/ashokas-ethical-infrastructure-is-carved-into-indias-rocks.

Kadam, V. S. "The Institution of Marriage and Position of Women in Eighteenth Century Maharashtra." *Indian Economic and Social History Review* 25, no. 3 (1988): 341–370.

Kaicker, Abhishek. *The King and the People: Sovereignty and Popular Politics in Mughal Delhi*. New York: Oxford University Press, 2020.

Kamran, Tahir. "Choudhary Rahmat Ali and His Political Imagination: Pak Plan and the Continent of Dinia." In *Muslims against the Muslim League: Critiques of the Idea of Pakistan*, edited by Ali Usman Qasmi and Megan Eaton Robb, 82–108. Cambridge: Cambridge University Press, 2017.

Kanda, Sayako. "Competition or Collaboration? Importers of Salt, the East India Company, and the Salt Market in Eastern India, c. 1780–1836." In *Memory, Identity and the Colonial Encounter in India: Essays in Honour of Peter Robb*, edited by Ezra Rashkow, Sanjukta Ghosh, and Upal Chakrabarti, 249–275. London: Routledge, 2018.

Kanjilal, Sucheta. "From Excluded to Exceptional: Caste in Contemporary Mahabharatas." In *Many Mahabharatas*, edited by Nell Shapiro Hawley and Sohini Sarah Pillai, 343–360. Albany: State University of New York Press, 2021.

Kannan, Divya. "Caste, Space, and Schooling in Nineteenth Century South India." *Children's Geographies* 20, no. 6 (2022): 845–860.

Kapadia, Aparna. *In Praise of Kings: Rajputs, Sultans and Poets in Fifteenth-Century Gujarat*. Cambridge: Cambridge University Press, 2018.

Kapila, Shruti. "Gandhi before Mahatma: The Foundations of Political Truth." *Public Culture* 23, no. 2 (2011): 431–448.

Kaplish, Lalita. "Vivekananda's Journey." Wellcome Collection, January 18, 2018. https://wellcomecollection.org/articles/Wk9TyyQAACUAPB3_.

Kapuria, Radha. "Of Music and the Maharaja: Gender, Affect, and Power in Ranjit Singh's Lahore." *Modern Asian Studies* 54, no. 2 (2020): 654–690.

Karashima, Noboru. "Allur and Isanamangalam: Two South Indian Villages of the Cola Times." *Indian Economic and Social History Review* 3, no. 2 (1966): 150–162.

———, ed. *A Concise History of South India: Issues and Interpretations*. New Delhi: Oxford University Press, 2014.

Karttunen, Klaus. *Yonas and Yavanas in Indian Literature*. Helsinki: Finnish Oriental Society, 2015.

Katz, Nathan. "South Asian Judaisms: Practicing Tradition Today." In *South Asian Religions: Tradition and Today*, edited by Karen Pechilis and Selva J. Raj, 143–158. London: Routledge, 2013.

Kaul, Jayalal. *Lal Ded*. New Delhi: Sahitya Akademi, 1973.

Kaushik, Garima. *Women and Monastic Buddhism in Early South Asia: Rediscovering the Invisible Believers*. London: Routledge, 2016.

Kaviraj, Sudipta. "What Is Western about Western Thought?" *Sophia* 62, no. 3 (2023): 485–514.

Kaw, Mushtaq A. "Famines in Kashmir, 1586–1819: The Policy of the Mughal and Afghan Rulers." *Indian Economic and Social History Review* 33, no. 1 (1996): 59–68.

Keay, John. *India: A History*. New York: Atlantic Monthly Press, 2000.

Kellens, J. "Avesta i. Survey of the History and Contents of the Book." *Encyclopaedia Iranica*, 2011. http://www.iranicaonline.org/articles/avesta-holy-book.

Kelly, Gwendolyn. "Craft Specialization, Technology and Social Change: A Study of Material Culture in Iron Age and Early Historic South India (c. 1200 BCE–400 CE). PhD diss., University of Wisconsin–Madison, 2013.

———. "The Megalithic Bleached Carnelian Beads of the Deccan: Chronology and Use as a Medium of Exchange." In *Deccan: Culture, Heritage and Literature*, edited by Mohammad Nazrul Bari and H. M. Maheshwaraiah, 105–139. New Delhi: Manak, 2017.

Kelting, M. Whitney. "Jain Traditions: Practicing Tradition Today." In *South Asian Religions: Tradition and Today*, edited by Karen Pechilis and Selva J. Raj, 73–98. London: Routledge, 2013.

Kenoyer, J. M., and R. H. Meadow. "Excavations at Harappa, 1986–2010: New Insights on the Indus Civilization and Harappan Burial Traditions." In *A Companion to*

South Asia in the Past, edited by Gwen Robbins Schug and Subhash R. Walimbe, 145–168. Chichester, UK: Wiley, 2016.

Kenoyer, J. Mark, T. Douglas Price, and James H. Burton. "A New Approach to Tracking Connections between the Indus Valley and Mesopotamia: Initial Results of Strontium Isotope Analyses from Harappa and Ur." *Journal of Archaeological Science* 40, no. 5 (2013): 2286–2297.

Kenoyer, Jonathan Mark. *Ancient Cities of the Indus Valley Civilization*. Oxford: Oxford University Press, 1998.

———. "The Archaeology of Indus Urbanism: Comparing Mohenjo Daro, Harappa and Dholavira." 2021. https://youtube.com/watch?v=CWeuu2ltl5E.

———. "Households and Neighborhoods of the Indus Tradition: An Overview." In *New Perspectives on Household Archaeology*, edited by Bradley J. Parker and Catherine P. Foster, 373–406. Winona Lake, PA: Eisenbrauns, 2012.

———. "Iconography of the Indus Unicorn: Origins and Legacy." In *Connections and Complexity: New Approaches to the Archaeology of South Asia*, edited by Shinu Anna Abraham, Praveena Gullapalli, Teresa P. Raczek, and Uzma Z. Rizvi. 107–125. Walnut Creek, CA: Left Coast Press, 2013.

———. "The Integration and Diversity in the Indus Tradition (2600–1900 BCE): Comparing Cities, Towns and Villages." *Heritage: Journal of Multidisciplinary Studies in Archaeology* 9 (2021–2022): 1–29.

———. "Origin and Development of the Indus Script: Insights from Harappa and Other Sites." In *Studies on Indus Script*, edited by K. Lashari, 217–270. Karachi: National Fund for Mohenjodaro, 2020.

———. "Uncovering the Keys to the Lost Indus Cities." *Scientific American* 289, no. 1 (2003): 66–75.

Keshavmurthy, Prashant. *Persian Authorship and Canonicity in Late Mughal Delhi: Building an Ark*. New York: Routledge, 2016.

Keune, Jon. *Shared Devotion, Shared Food: Equality and the Bhakti-Caste Question in Western India*. New York: Oxford University Press, 2021.

Khalfaoui, Mouez. "Al-Fatawa l-'Alamgiriyya." In *Encyclopaedia of Islam Three*, edited by Kate Fleet, Gudrun Kramer, Denis Matringe, John Nawas, and Devin J. Stewart. Published online, 2012. http://dx.doi.org/10.1163/1573-3912_ei3_COM_27028.

Khan, Hamid. *Constitutional and Political History of Pakistan*. 3rd ed. Karachi: Oxford University Press, 2017.

Khan, Iqtidar Alam. "Coming of Gunpowder to the Islamic World and North India: Spotlight on the Role of the Mongols." *Journal of Asian History* 30, no. 1 (1996): 27–45.

Khan, Kunwar Refaqat Ali. *The Kachhwahas under Akbar and Jahangir*. New Delhi: Kitab Publishing House, 1976.

Khan, Mohammad Ishaq. "The Rishi Movement as a Social Force in Medieval Kashmir." In *The Making of Indo-Persian Culture: Indian and French Studies*, edited by Muzaffar Alam, Francoise "Nalini" Delvoye, and Marc Gaborieau, 129–147. Delhi: Manohar, 2000.

Khan, Yasmin. *The Great Partition: The Making of India and Pakistan, New Edition*. New Haven, CT: Yale University Press, 2017.

———. *The Raj at War: A People's History of India's Second World War*. London: Bodley Head, 2015.

Khazeni, Arash. *The City and the Wilderness: Indo-Persian Encounters in Southeast Asia*. Oakland: University of California Press, 2020.

———. *Sky Blue Stone: The Turquoise Trade in World History*. Berkeley: University of California Press, 2014.

Khera, Dipti. *The Place of Many Moods: Udaipur's Painted Lands and India's Eighteenth Century*. Princeton, NJ: Princeton University Press, 2020.

Khilnani, Sunil. *The Idea of India*. New Delhi: Penguin, 2012.

———. "Panini: Catching the Ocean in a Cow's Hoofprint." Incarnations: India in 50 Lives, January 21, 2016. Accessed October 30, 2023. https://www.bbc.co.uk/programmes/b05tlvb2.

Khosla, Madhav. *India's Founding Moment: The Constitution of a Most Surprising Democracy*. Cambridge, MA: Harvard University Press, 2020.

Kia, Mana. *Persianate Selves: Memories of Place and Origin before Nationalism*. Stanford, CA: Stanford University Press, 2020.

Kim, Jinah. *Receptacle of the Sacred: Illustrated Manuscripts and the Buddhist Book Cult in South Asia*. Berkeley: University of California Press, 2013.

Kinra, Rajeev. "Revisiting the History and Historiography of Mughal Pluralism." *ReOrient* 5, no. 2 (2020): 137–182.

———. *Writing Self, Writing Empire: Chandar Bhan Brahman and the Cultural World of the Indo-Persian State Secretary*. Oakland: University of California Press, 2015.

Klein, Martin A. "Looking for Slavery in Colonial Archives: French West Africa." In *African Voices on Slavery and the Slave Trade*, edited by Alice Bellagamba, Sandra E. Greene, and Martin A. Klein, 2:114–131. Cambridge: Cambridge University Press, 2016.

Knutson, Jesse Ross. *Into the Twilight of Sanskrit Court Poetry: The Sena Salon of Bengal and Beyond*. Berkeley: University of California Press, 2014.

Koch, Ebba. *The Complete Taj Mahal and the Riverfront Gardens of Agra*. London: Thames & Hudson, 2006.

———. "Solomonic Angels in a Mughal Sky: The Wall Paintings of the Kala Burj at the Lahore Fort Revisited and Their Reception in Later South Asian and Qajar Art." In *Spirits in Transcultural Skies: Auspicious and Protective Spirits in Artefacts and Architecture Between East and West*, edited by Niels Gutschow and Katharina Weiler, 151–171. Cham, Switzerland: Springer, 2015.

Kolff, Dirk H. A. *Naukar, Rajput and Sepoy: The Ethnohistory of the Military Labour Market in Hindustan, 1450–1850*. Cambridge: Cambridge University Press, 1990.

Kopf, David. *The Brahmo Samaj and the Shaping of the Modern Indian Mind*. Princeton, NJ: Princeton University Press, 1979.

Kosambi, Meera. *Pandita Ramabai: Life and Landmark Writings*. London: Routledge, 2016.

———. "Women, Emancipation and Equality: Pandita Ramabai's Contribution to Women's Cause." *Economic and Political Weekly* 23, no. 44 (October 29, 1988): 38–49.

Kosmin, Paul J. *The Land of the Elephant Kings: Space, Territory, and Ideology in the Seleucid Empire*. Cambridge, MA: Harvard University Press, 2014.

Kovacs, Hajnalka. "Challenges of and Strategies for Translating Indo-Persian Poetry and Prose: The Case of Bedil (1644–1720)." In *The Routledge Handbook of Persian Literary Translation*, edited by Pouneh Shabani-Jadidi, Patricia J. Higgins, and Michelle Quay, 110–130. London: Routledge, 2022.

Krishnamurti, Bhadriraju. *The Dravidian Languages*. Cambridge: Cambridge University Press, 2003.

Kulke, Hermann. "The Naval Expeditions of the Cholas in the Context of Asian History." In *Nagapattinam to Suvarnadwipa: Reflections on the Chola Naval Expeditions to Southeast Asia*, edited by Hermann Kulke, K. Kesavapany, and Vijay Sakhuja, 1–19. Singapore: Institute of Southeast Asian Studies, 2009.

Kulke, Tilmann. "A Mughal Munsi at Work: Conflicts and Emotions in Musta'idd Han's *Ma'asir-i Alamgiri*. A Narratological Investigation." PhD diss., European University Institute, 2016.

Kumar, Deepak. *Science and the Raj: A Study of British India*. 2nd ed. New Delhi: Oxford University Press, 2006.

Kumar, Sangeet. "Manipulated Facts and Spreadable Fantasies: Battles over History in the Indian Digital Sphere." In *Disinformation in the Global South*, edited by Herman Wasserman and Dani Madrid-Morales, 26–40. Hoboken, NJ: John Wiley & Sons, 2022.

Kumar, Sunil. *The Emergence of the Delhi Sultanate, 1192–1286*. Ranikhet, India: Permanent Black, 2007.

Kurien, Prema. "Hinduism in the United States." In *Hinduism in the Modern World*, edited by Brian A. Hatcher, 143–157. New York: Routledge, 2016.

Labowitz, Sarah, and Dorothee Baumann-Pauly. "Beyond the Tip of the Iceberg: Bangladesh's Forgotten Apparel Workers." New York: Center for Business and Human Rights, New York University, December 2015. https://people.stern.nyu.edu

/twadhwa/bangladesh/downloads/beyond_the_tip_of_the_iceberg_report.pdf.

———. "Business as Usual Is Not an Option: Supply Chains and Sourcing after Rana Plaza." New York: Center for Business and Human Rights, New York University, April 2014. https://www.stern.nyu.edu/sites/default/files/assets/documents/con_047408.pdf.

Lahiri, Nayanjot. "Archaeology and Some Aspects of the Social History of Early India." In *A Social History of Early India*, edited by Brajadulal Chattopadhyaya, 3–17. New Delhi: Pearson Education, 2009.

———. *Ashoka in Ancient India*. Cambridge, MA: Harvard University Press, 2015.

———, ed. *The Decline and Fall of the Indus Civilization*. Delhi: Permanent Black, 2000.

Laine, James W. "The *dharma* of Islam and the *din* of Hinduism: Hindus and Muslims in the Age of Sivaji." *International Journal of Hindu Studies* 3, no. 3 (1999): 299–318.

———. *Shivaji: Hindu King in Islamic India*. New York: Oxford University Press, 2003.

Lal, Brij V. "Indian Indenture: Experiment and Experience." In *Routledge Handbook of the South Asian Diaspora*, edited by Joya Chatterji and David Washbrook, 79–95. London: Routledge, 2013.

Lal, Makhan. "Iron Tools, Forest Clearance, and Urbanization in the Gangetic Plains." In *India's Environmental History: From Ancient Times to the Colonial Period, A Reader*, edited by Mahesh Rangarajan and K. Sivaramakrishnan, 1:65–79. Ranikhet, India: Permanent Black, 2012.

Lal, Ruby. *Domesticity and Power in the Early Mughal World*. Cambridge: Cambridge University Press, 2005.

Lavan, Spencer. *The Ahmadiyah Movement: A History and Perspective*. Delhi: Manohar, 1974.

Lee, Christopher. "'The Alleyways of Banaras' and 'The Ka'aba of Hindustan': Varanasi through Banarsi Muslim Poetry." In *Banaras: Urban Forms and Cultural Histories*, edited by Michael S. Dodson, 213–233. New Delhi: Routledge, 2012.

Lee, Risha. "Constructing Community: Tamil Merchant Temples in India and China, 850–1281." PhD diss., Columbia University, 2012.

Leemans, W. F. *Foreign Trade in the Old Babylonian Period*. Leiden: Brill, 1960.

Lefevre, Corinne. *Consolidating Empire: Power and Elites in Jahangir's India 1605–1627*. Translated by Renuka George and Corinne Lefevre. Ranikhet, India: Permanent Black, 2022.

———. "The Court of 'Abd-ur-Rahim Khan-i Khanan as a Bridge between Iranian and Indian Cultural Traditions." In *Culture and Circulation: Literature in Motion in Early Modern India*, edited by Thomas de Bruin and Allison Busch, 75–106. Leiden: Brill, 2014.

———. "Din-i Ilahi." In *Encyclopaedia of Islam Three*, edited by Kate Fleet, Gudrun Kramer, Denis Matringe, John Nawas, and Devin J. Stewart, 81–83. Published online, 2015. http://dx.doi.org/10.1163/1573-3912_ei3_COM_26038.

Lelyveld, David. "The Fate of Hindustani: Colonial Knowledge and the Project of a National Language." In *Orientalism and the Postcolonial Predicament: Perspectives on South Asia*, edited by Carol A. Breckenridge and Peter van der Veer, 189–214. Philadelphia: University of Pennsylvania Press, 1993.

Leonard, Karen Isaksen. *Making Ethnic Choices: California's Punjabi Mexican Americans*. Philadelphia: Temple University Press, 1992.

Lien, Le Thi. "Hindu Deities in Southern Vietnam: Images on Small Archaeological Artefacts." In *Early Interactions between South and Southeast Asia: Reflections on Cross-Cultural Exchange*, edited by Pierre-Yves Manguin, A. Mani, and Geoff Wade, 407–431. Singapore: ISEAS, 2011.

Lienhard, Siegfried. *A History of Classical Poetry: Sanskrit-Pali-Prakrit*. Wiesbaden: Otto Harrassowitz, 1984.

Loomba, Ania. "Of Gifts, Ambassadors, and Copy-Cats: Diplomacy, Exchange, and Difference in Early Modern India." In *Emissaries in Early Modern Literature and Culture: Mediation, Transmission, Traffic, 1550–1700*, edited by Brinda Charry and Gitanjali Shahani, 41–75. Farnham, UK: Ashgate, 2009.

Lopez, Donald S. *Buddhism and Science: A Guide for the Perplexed*. Chicago: University of Chicago Press, 2008.

———. *Hyecho's Journey: The World of Buddhism*. Chicago: University of Chicago Press, 2017.

———. *The Lotus Sutra: A Biography*. Princeton, NJ: Princeton University Press, 2016.

Lorenzen, David N. "Historians and the Gupta Empire." In *Reappraising Gupta History for S.R. Goyal*, edited by B. Ch. Chhabra, P. K. Agrawala, Ashvini Agrawal, and Shankar Goyal, 47–60. New Delhi: Aditya Prakashan, 1992.

———. *The Kapalikas and Kalamukhas: Two Lost Saivite Sects*. New Delhi: Motilal Banarsidass, 1991.

———. "A Parody of the Kapalikas in the *Mattavilasa*." In *Tantra in Practice*, edited by David Gordon White, 81–96. Princeton, NJ: Princeton University Press, 2000.

———. *Praises to a Formless God: Nirguni Texts from North India*. Albany: State University of New York Press, 1996.

———. "Who Invented Hinduism?" *Comparative Studies in Society and History* 41, no. 4 (1999): 630–659.

Lothspeich, Pamela. "Draupadi, Yajnaseni, Pancali, Krsna: Representations of an Epic Heroine in Three Novels." In *Many Mahabharatas*, edited by Nell Shapiro Hawley and Sohini Sarah Pillai, 325–342. Albany: State University of New York Press, 2021.

Lubin, Timothy. "Asoka's Disparagement of Domestic Ritual and Its Validation by the Brahmins." *Journal of Indian Philosophy* 41, no. 1 (2013): 29–41.

———. "Writing and the Recognition of Customary Law in Premodern India and Java." *Journal of the American Oriental Society* 135, no. 2 (2015): 225–259.

Lutgendorf, Philip. *The Life of a Text: Performing the* Ramcaritmanas *of Tulsidas*. Berkeley: University of California Press, 1991.

MacCulloch, Diarmaid. "Is There Still Value in 'Great Man' History?" *History Today* 69, no. 9 (September 9, 2019): 8.

Machado, Pedro. *Ocean of Trade: South Asian Merchants, Africa and the Indian Ocean, c. 1750–1850*. Cambridge: Cambridge University Press, 2014.

Maclagan, E. D. "The Jesuit Missions to the Emperor Akbar." *Journal of the Asiatic Society of Bengal* 65 (1896): 38–113.

Maclean, Derryl N. *Religion and Society in Arab Sind*. Leiden: Brill, 1989.

Maclean, Kama. *Pilgrimage and Power: The Kumbh Mela in Allahabad, 1765–1954*. New York: Oxford University Press, 2008.

Magee, Peter, Cameron Petrie, Robert Knox, Farid Khan, and Ken Thomas. "The Achaemenid Empire in South Asia and Recent Excavations in Akra in Northwest Pakistan." *American Journal of Archaeology* 109, no. 4 (2005): 711–741.

Mahadevan, Thennilapuram P. "On the Southern Recension of the *Mahabharata*, Brahman Migrations, and Brahmi Paleography." *Electronic Journal of Vedic Studies* 15, no. 2 (2008): 1–143.

Mahalakshmi, Rakesh. "Chola (Cola) Empire." In *The Encyclopedia of Empire*, edited by John M. MacKenzie, 1–7. New York: John Wiley & Sons, 2016. http://onlinelibrary.wiley.com/book/10.1002/9781118455074.

Majeed, Javed. *Colonialism and Knowledge in Grierson's* Linguistic Survey of India. London: Routledge, 2019.

Major, Andrew J. "State and Criminal Tribes in Colonial Punjab: Surveillance, Control and Reclamation of the 'Dangerous Classes.'" *Modern Asian Studies* 33, no. 3 (1999): 657–688.

Malekandathil, Pius. "The Sassanids and the Maritime Trade of India during the Early Medieval Period." *Proceedings of the Indian History Congress* 63 (2002): 156–173.

Malik, Iftikhar H. *State and Civil Society in Pakistan: Politics of Authority, Ideology, and Ethnicity*. Basingstoke, UK: Macmillan, 1997.

Mallinson, James, and Mark Singleton, "Introduction." In *Roots of Yoga*, edited by James Mallinson and Mark Singleton, ix–xxxviii. London: Penguin Books, 2017.

Manatunga, Anura. "Sri Lanka and Southeast Asia during the Period of the Polonnaruva Kingdom." In *Nagapattinam to Suvarnadwipa: Reflections on the Chola Naval Expeditions to Southeast Asia*, edited by Hermann Kulke, K. Kesavapany, and Vijay Sakhuja, 193–207. Singapore: Institute of Southeast Asian Studies, 2009.

Mann, Gurinder Singh. *The Making of Sikh Scripture*. Oxford: Oxford University Press, 2001.

Mann, Richard D. *The Rise of Mahasena: The Transformation of Skanda-Karttikeya in North India from the Kusana to Gupta Empires*. Leiden: Brill, 2012.

Mantena, Rama Sundari. *The Origins of Modern Historiography in India: Antiquarianism and Philology, 1780–1880*. New York: Palgrave Macmillan, 2012.

Manz, Beatrice F. "Timur Lang." In *The Encyclopaedia of Islam*. New ed., 10:510–513. Leiden: Brill, 2000.

Mapping Militant Organizations. "Liberation Tigers of Tamil Elam." Stanford, CA: Stanford University, last modified June 2018. https://cisac.fsi.stanford.edu/mappingmilitants/profiles/liberation-tigers-tamil-elam.

Marchignoli, Saverio. "Canonizing an Indian Text? A.W. Schlegel, W. von Humboldt, Hegel, and the *Bhagavadgita*." In *Sanskrit and "Orientalism": Indology and Comparative Linguistics in Germany, 1750–1958*, edited by Douglas T. McGetchin, Peter K. J. Park, and D. R. Sardesai, 245–270. New Delhi: Manohar, 2004.

Markovits, Claude. "The Calcutta Riots of 1946." In *Mass Violence and Resistance*. Paris: Sciences Po, 2007. https://www.sciencespo.fr/mass-violence-war-massacre-resistance/fr/document/calcutta-riots-1946.html.

———. "Indian Merchant Networks outside India in the Nineteenth and Twentieth Centuries: A Preliminary Survey." *Modern Asian Studies* 33, no. 4 (1999): 883–911.

———. "The Political Economy of Opium Smuggling in Early Nineteenth Century India: Leakage or Resistance?" *Modern Asian Studies* 43, no. 1 (2009): 89–111.

———. "South Asian Business in the Empire and Beyond c. 1800–1950." In *Routledge Handbook of the South Asian Diaspora*, edited by Joya Chatterji and David Washbrook, 69–78. London: Routledge, 2013.

Marsh, Kate. *India in the French Imagination: Peripheral Voices, 1754–1815*. London: Pickering & Chatto, 2009.

Marshall, John. *Taxila: An Illustrated Account of Archaeological Excavations Carried out at Taxila under the Orders of the Government of India between the Years 1913 and 1934*. Vol. 1. Cambridge: Cambridge University Press, 1951.

Mathpal, Yasodhar. *Prehistoric Rock Paintings of Bhimbetka, Central India*. New Delhi: Abhinav Publications, 1984.

Mazzarella, William. "Cultural Politics of Branding: Promoting 'KamaSutra' in India." In *Consumer Culture, Modernity and Identity*, edited by Nita Mathur, 204–238. London: Routledge, 2014.

McClish, Mark. *The History of the Arthasastra: Sovereignty and Sacred Law in Ancient India*. Cambridge: Cambridge University Press, 2019.

McCrea, Lawrence. "The Hierarchical Organization of Language in Mimamsa Interpretive Theory." *Journal of Indian Philosophy* 28, no. 5/6 (2000): 429–459.

McHugh, James. *Sandalwood and Carrion: Smell in Indian Religion and Culture*. Oxford: Oxford University Press, 2012.

———. *An Unholy Brew: Alcohol in Indian History and Religions*. New York: Oxford University Press, 2021.

McIntosh, Jane. *The Ancient Indus Valley: New Perspectives*. Santa Barbara, CA: Bloomsbury, 2008.

McKeown, Arthur Philip. *Guardian of a Dying Flame: Sariputra (c. 1335–1426) and the End of Late Indian Buddhism*. Cambridge, MA: Department of South Asian Studies, Harvard University, 2018.

McLaughlin, Raoul. *Rome and the Distant East: Trade Routes to the Ancient Lands of Arabia, India and China*. London: Continuum, 2010.

Mehta, Makrand. *Indian Merchants and Entrepreneurs in Historical Perspective: With Special Reference to Shroffs of Gujarat, 17th to 19th Centuries*. Delhi: Academic Foundation, 1991.

Meisami, Julie Scott. "Ghaznavid Panegyrics: Some Political Implications." *Iran* 28 (1990): 31–44.

Menon, Jaya, and Supriya Varma. "Was There a Temple under the Babri Masjid? Reading the Archaeological 'Evidence.'" *Economic and Political Weekly* 54, no. 50 (December 11–17, 2010): 61–72.

Menon, Meena, and Uzramma. *A Frayed History: The Journey of Cotton in India*. New Delhi: Oxford University Press, 2017.

Metcalf, Barbara D. "Ibn Battuta as a Qadi in the Maldives." In *Islam in South Asia in Practice*, edited by Barbara D. Metcalf, 271–278. Princeton, NJ: Princeton University Press, 2009.

Metcalf, Barbara D., and Thomas R. Metcalf. *A Concise History of Modern India*. 3rd ed. Cambridge: Cambridge University Press, 2012.

Metcalf, Thomas R. *Ideologies of the Raj*. Cambridge: Cambridge University Press, 1995.

Metropolitan Museum of Art. *Art of the First Cities: The Third Millennium B.C. from the Mediterranean to the Indus*, edited by Joan Aruz and Ronald Wallenfels. New York: Metropolitan Museum of Art, 2003.

Michel, Aloys Arthur. *The Indus Rivers: A Study of the Effects of Partition*. New Haven, CT: Yale University Press, 1967.

Michell, George. "Jaipur: Form and Origins." In *Stadt und Ritual: Beitrage eines internationalen Symposions zur Stadtbaugeschichte Sud- u. Ostasiens*, edited by Niels Gutschow and Thomas Sieverts, 78–81. Darmstadt: Technische Hochschule, 1977.

Mikkelson, Jane. "The Way of Tradition and the Path of Innovation: Aurangzeb and Dara Shukuh's Struggle for the Mughal Throne." In *The Empires of the Near East and India: Source Studies of the Safavid, Ottoman, and Mughal Literate Communities*, edited by Hani Khafipour, 240–260. New York: Columbia University Press, 2019.

Miller, Barbara Stoler. "Jayadeva: The Wandering Poet." In *Gitagovinda of Jayadeva: Love Song of the Dark Lord*, edited and translated by Barbara Stoler Miller, 3–37. Delhi: Motilal Banarsidass, 1984.

Minkowski, Christopher. "Learned Brahmins and the Mughal Court: *The Jyotisas*." In *Religious Interactions in Mughal India*, edited by Vasudha Dalmia and Munis D. Faruqui, 102–134. New Delhi: Oxford University Press, 2014.

———. "Nilakantha's Mahabharata." *India Seminar* 608 (2010).

Mir, Rayees Ahmad, Mohammad Abass Ahanger, and R. M. Agarwal. "Marigold: From Mandap to Medicine and from Ornamentation to Remediation." *American Journal of Plant Sciences* 10, no. 2 (2019): 309–338.

Mishra, Kamala Prasad. *Banaras in Transition, 1738–1795: A Socioeconomic Study*. New Delhi: Munshiram Manoharlal, 1975.

Mishra, Om Prakash, and S. Pradhan. "Sati Memorials and Cenotaphs of Madhya Pradesh—A Study." *Proceedings of the Indian History Congress* 62 (2001): 1013–1019.

Mishra, Sangay K. *Desis Divided: The Political Lives of South Asian Americans*. Minneapolis: University of Minnesota Press, 2016.

Moin, A. Azfar. *The Millennial Sovereign: Sacred Kingship and Sainthood in Islam*. New York: Columbia University Press, 2012.

Mondini, Sara. "Architectural Heritage and Modern Rituals: The Ahmad Shah Bahmani Mausoleum between Old Political Concerns and New Religious Perceptions." In *Objects of Worship in South Asian Religions: Forms, Practices and Meanings*, edited by Knut A. Jacobsen, Mikael Aktor, and Kristina Myrvold, 129–142. London: Routledge, 2014.

Mongia, Radhika. *Indian Migration and Empire: A Colonial Genealogy of the Modern State*. Durham, NC: Duke University Press, 2018.

Monius, Anne. "'*And We Shall Compose a Poem to Establish These Truths*': The Power of Narrative Art in South Asian Literary Cultures." In *Narrative, Philosophy and Life*, edited by Allen Speight, 151–165. Dordrecht: Springer, 2015.

Moore, Jennifer. "When Not Just Any Wine Will Do . . . ? The Proliferation of Coan-Type Wine and Amphoras in the Greco-Roman World." *Marburger Beitrage zur Antiken Handels-, Wirtschafts- und Sozialgeschichte* 28 (2010): 89–122.

Moorjani, Priya, Kumarasamy Thangaraj, Nick Patterson, Mark Lipson, Po-Ru Loh, Periyasamy Govindaraj, Bonnie Berger, David Reich, and Lalji Singh. "Genetic Evidence for Recent Population Mixture in India." *American Journal of Human Genetics* 93, no. 3 (2013): 422–438.

Moosvi, Shireen. "The Mughal Encounter with Vedanta: Recovering the Biography of 'Jadrup.'" *Social Scientist* 30, no. 7/8 (2002): 13–23.

———. "The Silver Influx, Money Supply, Prices and Revenue-Extraction in Mughal

India." *Journal of the Economic and Social History of the Orient* 30, no. 1 (1987): 47–94.

———. "The World of Labour in Mughal India (c. 1500–1750)." *International Review of Social History* 56, no. S19 (2011): 245–261.

Morcom, Anna. *Illicit Worlds of Indian Dance: Cultures of Exclusion*. New York: Oxford University Press, 2013.

Morgenstein Fuerst, Ilyse R. *Indian Muslim Minorities and the 1857 Rebellion: Religion, Rebels, and Jihad*. London: I. B. Tauris, 2017.

Mubayi, Yaaminey. "'Malik Ambar ki Pipeline': Reconstructing the Past through Community Memories." *The Medieval History Journal* 23, no. 2 (2020): 370–398.

Mufti, Aamir R. *Enlightenment in the Colony: The Jewish Question and the Crisis of Postcolonial Culture*. Princeton, NJ: Princeton University Press, 2007.

———. "Orientalism and the Institution of World Literatures." *Critical Inquiry* 36, no. 3 (2010): 458–493.

Mughal, Mohammad Rafique. "The Early Harappan Period in the Greater Indus Valley and Northern Baluchistan (c. 3000–2400 B.C.)." PhD diss., University of Pennsylvania, 1970.

Mujtabai, Fathullah. *Aspects of Hindu Muslim Cultural Relations*. New Delhi: National Book Bureau, 1978.

Mukherjee, Rudrangshu. *Awadh in Revolt, 1857–1858: A Study of Popular Resistance*. Delhi: Oxford University Press, 1984.

———. *A Century of Trust: The Story of Tata Steel*. New Delhi: Penguin Books, 2008.

———. *Jawaharlal Nehru*. New Delhi: Oxford University Press, 2019.

———. "What Made the East India Company So Successful?" *The India Forum*, October 10, 2019. https://www.theindiaforum.in/article/what-made-east-india-company-so-successful.

———. *The Year of Blood: Essays on the Revolt of 1857*. London: Routledge, 2018.

Murphy, Anne. "The Utility of 'South Asia.'" *South Asian Review* 38, no. 3 (2017): 91–98.

Nagar, Itisha. "The Unfair Selection: A Study on Skin-Color Bias in Arranged Indian Marriages." *SAGE Open* 8, no. 2 (2018): 1–8.

Nagaraj, D. R. "Critical Tensions in the History of Kannada Literary Culture." In *Literary Cultures in History: Reconstructions from South Asia*, edited by Sheldon Pollock, 323–382. Berkeley: University of California Press, 2003.

Naik, Chhotubhai Ranchhodji. *'Abdu'r-Rahim Khan-i-Khanan and His Literary Circle*. Ahmedabad: Gujarat University, 1966.

Naim, C. M. "Syed Ahmad and His Two Books Called 'Asar-al-Sanadid.'" *Modern Asian Studies* 45, no. 3 (2011): 669–708.

Nair, Neeti. *Changing Homelands: Hindu Politics and the Partition of India*. Cambridge, MA: Harvard University Press, 2011.

———. *Hurt Sentiments: Secularism and Belonging in South Asia*. Cambridge, MA: Harvard University Press, 2023.

Nair, Shankar. *Translating Wisdom: Hindu-Muslim Intellectual Interactions in Early Modern South Asia*. Oakland: University of California Press, 2020.

Nandy, Ashis. "The Idea of South Asia: A Personal Note on Post-Bandung Blues." *Inter-Asia Cultural Studies* 6, no. 4 (2005): 541–545.

Narang, G. C., and Leslie Abel. "Ghalib and the Rebellion of 1857." *Mahfil* 5, no. 4 (1968–1969): 45–57.

Narasimhan, Vagheesh M. et al. "The Formation of Human Populations in South and Central Asia." *Science* 365, no. 6457 (2019).

Nath, Pratyay. *Climate of Conquest: War, Environment, and Empire in Mughal North India*. New Delhi: Oxford University Press, 2019.

Nattier, Jan. *Once upon a Future Time: Studies in a Buddhist Prophecy of Decline*. Berkeley, CA: Asian Humanities Press, 1991.

Newman, John. "Islam in the Kalacakra Tantra." *Journal of the International Association of Buddhist Studies* 21, no. 2 (1998): 311–371.

Nijhar, Preeti. *Law and Imperialism: Criminality and Constitution in Colonial India and Victorian England*. London: Pickering & Chatto, 2009.

Noorani, A. G. *Indian Political Trials 1775–1947*. New Delhi: Oxford University Press, 2005.

———. "Vande Mataram: A Historical Lesson." *Economic and Political Weekly* 8, no. 23 (1973): 1039–1043.

Nora, Pierre. "Between Memory and History: Les Lieux de Memoire." *Representations*, no. 26 (1989): 7–24.

Norman, K. R. "Introduction" to *The Elders' Verses II: Therigatha*, xix–xci. Lancaster: Pali Text Society, 2007.

———. *Pali Literature: Including the Canonical Literature in Prakrit and Sanskrit of All the Hinayana Schools of Buddhism*. Wiesbaden: Otto Harrassowitz, 1983.

Novetzke, Christian Lee. *The Quotidian Revolution: Vernacularization, Religion, and the Premodern Public Sphere in India*. New York: Columbia University Press, 2016.

Nussbaum, Martha C. *The Clash Within: Democracy, Religious Violence, and India's Future*. Cambridge, MA: Belknap Press of Harvard University Press, 2007.

Obrock, Luther. "*Mahabharata*: Brahmins, Kings, and the South Asian Social World." In *A Companion to World Literature*, edited by Ken Seigneurie, 1–11. New York: John Wiley & Sons, 2019.

———. "Muslim *Mahakavyas*: Sanskrit and Translation in the Sultanates." In *Text and Tradition in Early Modern North India*, edited by Tyler Williams, Anshu Malhotra, and John Stratton Hawley, 58–76. Delhi: Oxford University Press, 2018.

———. "Uddhara's World: Geographies of Piety and Trade in Sultanate South Asia." *Journal of the Royal Asiatic Society* 32, no. 1 (2022): 59–81.

O'Hanlon, Rosalind. *Caste, Conflict, and Ideology: Mahatma Jotirao Phule and Low Caste Protest in Nineteenth-Century Western India*. Cambridge: Cambridge University Press, 1985.

———. "Contested Conjunctures: Brahman Communities and 'Early Modernity' in India." *American Historical Review* 118, no. 3 (2013): 765–787.

———. "Kingdom, Household and Body: History, Gender and Imperial Service under Akbar." *Modern Asian Studies* 41, no. 5 (2007): 889–923.

———. "Letters Home: Banaras Pandits and the Maratha Regions in Early Modern India." *Modern Asian Studies* 44, no. 2 (2010): 201–240.

———. "Speaking from Siva's Temple: Banaras Scholar Households and the Brahman 'Ecumene' of Mughal India." *South Asian History and Culture* 2, no. 2 (2011): 253–277.

O'Hanlon, Rosalind, and Christopher Minkowski. "What Makes People Who They Are? Pandit Networks and the Problem of Livelihoods in Early Modern Western India." *Indian Economic and Social History Review* 45, no. 3 (2008): 381–416.

Olivelle, Patrick. *Ashoka: Portrait of a Philosopher King*. New Haven, CT: Yale University Press, 2023.

———. "Asoka's Inscriptions as Text and Ideology." In *Reimagining Asoka: Memory and History*, edited by Patrick Olivelle, Janice Leoshko, and Himanshu Prabha Ray, 157–183. New Delhi: Oxford University Press, 2012.

———. *The Asrama System: The History and Hermeneutics of a Religious Institution*. New York: Oxford University Press, 1993.

———. "Introduction." In *A Dharma Reader: Classical Indian Law*, edited by Patrick Olivelle, 1–47. New York: Columbia University Press, 2017.

———. "The Semantic History of Dharma: The Middle and Late Vedic Periods." *Journal of Indian Philosophy* 32, no. 5/6 (2004): 491–511.

Ollett, Andrew. "Attempted Iconoclasm: Mahmud of Ghazna, King Yoga, and the Poet Dhanapala." *Comparative Studies of South Asia, Africa and the Middle East* 42, no. 2 (2022): 309–324.

———. "Ghosts from the Past: India's Undead Languages." *Indian Economic and Social History Review* 51, no. 4 (2014): 405–456.

———. *Language of the Snakes: Prakrit, Sanskrit, and the Language Order of Premodern India*. Oakland: University of California Press, 2017.

———. "Making It Nice: Kavya in the Second Century." *Journal of Indian Philosophy* 47, no. 2 (2019): 269–287.

Olson, Christopher R., Devin C. Owen, Andrey E. Ryabinin, and Claudio V. Mello. "Drinking Songs: Alcohol Effects on Learned Song of Zebra Finches." *PLoS ONE* 9, no. 12 (2014).

Omvedt, Gail. "A Teacher and a Leader." In *A Forgotten Liberator: The Life and Struggle of Savitribai Phule*, edited by Braj Ranjan

Mani and Pamela Sardar, 28–31. New Delhi: Mountain Peak, 2008.

Orr, Leslie C. *Donors, Devotees, and Daughters of God: Temple Women in Medieval Tamilnadu*. New York: Oxford University Press, 2000.

———. "Jain and Hindu 'Religious Women' in Early Medieval Tamilnadu." In *Open Boundaries: Jain Communities and Culture in Indian History*, edited by John E. Cort, 187–212. Albany: State University of New York Press, 1998.

Orsini, Francesca. "Barahmasas in Hindi and Urdu." In *Before the Divide: Hindi and Urdu Literary Culture*, edited by Francesca Orsini, 142–177. New Delhi: Orient Blackswan, 2010.

———. "Between *Qasbas* and Cities: Language Shifts and Literary Continuities in North India in the Long Eighteenth Century." *Comparative Studies of South Asia, Africa and the Middle East* 39, no. 1 (2019): 68–81.

———. *The Hindi Public Sphere 1920–1940: Language and Literature in the Age of Nationalism*. New Delhi: Oxford University Press, 2002.

———. "Introduction." In *Before the Divide: Hindi and Urdu Literary Culture*, edited by Francesca Orsini, 1–20. New Delhi: Orient Blackswan, 2010.

Orsini, Francesca, and Samira Sheikh. "Introduction." In *After Timur Left: Culture and Circulation in Fifteenth-Century North India*, edited by Francesca Orsini and Samira Sheikh, 1–44. New Delhi: Oxford University Press, 2014.

Orthmann, Eva. "Circular Motions: Private Pleasure and Public Prognostication in the Nativities of the Mughal Emperor Akbar." In *Horoscopes and Public Spheres: Essays on the History of Astrology*, edited by Gunther Oestmann, H. Darrel Rutkin, and Kocku von Stuckrad, 101–114. Berlin: De Gruyter, 2005.

Overton, Keelan. "Book Culture, Royal Libraries, and Persianate Painting in Bijapur, circa 1580–1630." *Muqarnas* 33 (2016): 91–154.

———. "Farrukh Husayn." In *Encyclopaedia of Islam Three*, edited by Kate Fleet, Gudrun Kramer, Denis Matringe, John Nawas, and Devin J. Stewart. Published online, 2017. http://dx.doi.org/10.1163/1573-3912_ei3_COM_27826.

———. "Introduction to Iranian Mobilities and Persianate Mediations in the Deccan." In *Iran and the Deccan: Persianate Art, Culture, and Talent in Circulation, 1400–1700*, edited by Keelan Overton, 3–76. Bloomington: Indiana University Press, 2020.

———. "Vida de Jacques de Coutre: A Flemish Account of Bijapuri Visual Culture in the Shadow of Mughal Felicity." In *The Visual World of Muslim India: The Art, Culture and Society of the Deccan in the Early Modern Era*, edited by Laura E. Parodi, 233–264. London: I. B. Tauris, 2014.

Paddayya, K. "The Problem of Ashmounds of Southern Deccan in the Light of Recent Research." In *Recent Studies in Indian Archaeology*, edited by K. Paddayya, 81–111. New Delhi: Munshiram Manoharlal, 2002.

Padoux, Andre. *The Hindu Tantric World: An Overview*. Chicago: University of Chicago Press, 2017.

Pandey, Gyanendra. *The Construction of Communalism in Colonial North India*. Delhi: Oxford University Press, 1990.

Parasher-Sen, Aloka. "Naming and Social Exclusion: The Outcast and the Outsider." In *Between the Empires: Society in India 300 BCE to 400 CE*, edited by Patrick Olivelle, 415–455. New York: Oxford University Press, 2006.

———. "Of Tribes, Hunters, and Barbarians: Forest Dwellers in the Mauryan Period." In *India's Environmental History: From Ancient Times to the Colonial Period, A Reader*, edited by Mahesh Rangarajan and K. Sivaramakrishnan, 1:127–151. Ranikhet, India: Permanent Black, 2012.

Parker, Grant. "Ex Oriente Luxuria: Indian Commodities and Roman Experience." *Journal of the Economic and Social History of the Orient* 45, no. 1 (2002): 40–95.

———. *The Making of Roman India*. Cambridge: Cambridge University Press, 2008.

Parpola, Asko. *Deciphering the Indus Script*. Cambridge: Cambridge University Press, 1994.

Parpola, Simo, Asko Parpola, and Robert H. Brunswig. "The Meluhha Village: Evidence of Acculturation of Harappan

Traders in Late Third Millennium Mesopotamia?" *Journal of the Economic and Social History of the Orient* 20, no. 2 (1977): 129–165.

Patel, Aakar. *Our Hindu Rashtra: What It Is. How We Got Here.* Chennai: Westland, 2020.

Patel, Alka. "Expanding the Ghurid Architectural Corpus East of the Indus: The Jagesvara Temple at Sadadi, Rajasthan." *Archives of Asian Art* 59, no. 1 (2009): 33–56.

———. "The Historiography of Reuse in South Asia." *Archives of Asian Art* 59, no. 1 (2009): 1–5.

———. "The Mosque in South Asia: Beginnings." In *Piety and Politics in the Early Indian Mosque*, edited by Finbarr Barry Flood, 3–26. New Delhi: Oxford University Press, 2008.

Patel, Dinyar. *Naoroji: Pioneer of Indian Nationalism.* Cambridge, MA: Harvard University Press, 2020.

Pati, Biswamoy, ed. *The Great Rebellion of 1857 in India: Exploring Transgressions, Contests and Diversities.* London: Routledge, 2010.

Patnaik, Prabhat. "The Fascism of Our Times." *Social Scientist* 21, no. 3/4 (1993): 69–77.

Patton, Laurie L. *Bringing the Gods to Mind: Mantra and Ritual in Early Indian Sacrifice.* Berkeley: University of California Press, 2005.

Paul, Vinil Baby. "Dalit Conversion Memories in Colonial Kerala and Decolonisation of Knowledge." *South Asia Research* 41, no. 2 (2021): 187–202.

Pauwels, Heidi. "Literary Moments of Exchange in the 18th Century: The New Urdu Vogue Meets Krishna Bhakti." In *Indo-Muslim Cultures in Transition*, edited by Alka Patel and Karen Leonard, 61–85. Leiden: Brill, 2012.

———. "A Tale of Two Temples: Mathura's Kesavadeva and Orccha's Caturbhuja-deva." *South Asian History and Culture* 2, no. 2 (2011): 278–299.

Pearson, Michael. *The Indian Ocean.* London: Routledge, 2003.

———. "Locating Garcia de Orta in the Port City of Goa and the Indian Ocean World." In *Medicine, Trade and Empire: Garcia de Orta's* Colloquies on the Simples and Drugs of India *(1563) in Context*, edited by Palmira Fontes da Costa, 33–48. London: Routledge, 2016.

Peers, Douglas. "South Asia." In *War in the Modern World since 1815*, edited by Jeremy Black, 41–74. New York: Routledge, 2003.

Pequeno, Diego N. L., Ixchel M. Hernandez-Ochoa, Matthew Reynolds, Kai Sonder, Anabel Molero Milan, Richard D. Robertson, Marta S. Lopes, Wei Xiong, Martin Kropff, and Senthold Asseng. "Climate Impact and Adaptation to Heat and Drought Stress of Regional and Global Wheat Production." *Environmental Research Letters* 16, no. 5 (2021): 1–17.

Pescatello, Ann M. "The African Presence in Portuguese India." *Journal of Asian History* 11, no. 1 (1977): 26–48.

Peterson, Indira Viswanathan. *Poems to Siva: The Hymns of the Tamil Saints.* Delhi: Motilal Banarsidass, 1991.

Peterson, Indira Viswanathan, and Davesh Soneji. "Introduction." In *Performing Pasts: Reinventing the Arts in Modern South India*, edited by Indira Viswanathan Peterson and Davesh Soneji, 1–40. New Delhi: Oxford University Press, 2008.

Phillips, Robert Lowell. "Garden of Endless Blossoms: Urdu *Ramayans* of the 19th and Early 20th Century." PhD diss., University of Wisconsin–Madison, 2010.

Phukan, Shantanu. "Through a Persian Prism: Hindu and Padmavat in the Mughal Imagination." PhD diss., University of Chicago, 2000.

Pillai, Sohini Sarah. "The Mahabharata as Krsnacarita: Draupadi's Prayer in Two Regional Retellings." *Journal of Hindu Studies* 14, no. 3 (2021): 259–278.

———. "Remembering and Removing Aurangzeb: The Manuscript History of Sabalsingh Chauhan's *Mahabharat.*" *Comparative Studies of South Asia, Africa and the Middle East* 42, no. 2 (2022): 356–361.

Pinch, William R. *Warrior Ascetics and Indian Empires.* New Delhi: Cambridge University Press, 2006.

Pinheiro-Machado, Rosana, and Tatiana Vargas-Maia, eds. *The Rise of the Radical Right in the Global South.* London: Routledge, 2023.

Pinney, Christopher. "The Tiger's Nature, but Not the Tiger: Bal Gangadhar Tilak as

Mohandas Karamchand Gandhi's Counter-Guru." *Public Culture* 23, no. 2 (2011): 395–416.

Plofker, Kim. *Mathematics in India*. Princeton, NJ: Princeton University Press, 2009.

Pollock, Sheldon. "The Death of Sanskrit." *Comparative Studies in Society and History* 43, no. 2 (2001): 392–426.

———. "Deep Orientalism? Notes on Sanskrit and Power Beyond the Raj." In *Orientalism and the Postcolonial Predicament: Perspectives on South Asia*, edited by Carol A. Breckenridge and Peter van der Veer, 76–133. Philadelphia: University of Pennsylvania Press, 1993.

———. "The Divine King in the Indian Epic." *Journal of the American Oriental Society* 104, no. 3 (1984): 505–528.

———. *The Ends of Man at the End of Premodernity*. Amsterdam: Royal Netherlands Academy of Arts and Sciences, 2005.

———. "Introduction." In *Forms of Knowledge in Early Modern Asia: Explorations in the Intellectual History of India and Tibet, 1500–1800*, edited by Sheldon Pollock, 1–16. Durham, NC: Duke University Press, 2011.

———. "Introduction." In *Literary Cultures in History: Reconstructions from South Asia*, edited by Sheldon Pollock, 1–36. Berkeley: University of California Press, 2003.

———. *The Language of the Gods in the World of Men: Sanskrit, Culture, and Power in Premodern India*. Berkeley: University of California Press, 2006.

———. "The Languages of Science in Early Modern India." In *Forms of Knowledge in Early Modern Asia: Explorations in the Intellectual History of India and Tibet, 1500–1800*, edited by Sheldon Pollock, 19–48. Durham, NC: Duke University Press, 2011.

———. "Literary Culture and Manuscript Culture in Precolonial India." In *Literary Cultures and the Material Book*, edited by Simon Eliot, Andrew Nash, and Ian Willison, 77–94. London: British Library, 2007.

———. "Mimamsa and the Problem of History in Traditional India." *Journal of the American Oriental Society* 109, no. 4 (1989): 603–610.

———. "Ramayana and Political Imagination in India." *Journal of Asian Studies* 52, no. 2 (1993): 261–297.

———. "Sanskrit Literary Culture from the Inside Out." In *Literary Cultures in History: Reconstructions from South Asia*, edited by Sheldon Pollock, 39–130. Berkeley: University of California Press, 2003.

Possehl, Gregory L. *The Indus Civilization: A Contemporary Perspective*. Lanham, MD: AltaMira Press, 2002.

———. "Shu-ilishu's Cylinder Seal." *Expedition* 48, no. 1 (2006): 42–43.

———. "The Transformation of the Indus Civilization." *Journal of World Prehistory* 11, no. 4 (1997): 425–472.

Powell, Avril A. "History Textbooks and the Transmission of the Pre-colonial Past in North-western India in the 1860s and 1870s." In *Invoking the Past: The Uses of History in South Asia*, edited by Daud Ali, 91–133. New Delhi: Oxford University Press, 1999.

Prakash, Gyan. *Emergency Chronicles: Indira Gandhi and Democracy's Turning Point*. Princeton, NJ: Princeton University Press, 2019.

Prakash, Om. *The Dutch East India Company and the Economy of Bengal, 1630–1720*. Princeton, NJ: Princeton University Press, 1985.

Prasad, Ritika. *Tracks of Change: Railways and Everyday Life in Colonial India*. New Delhi: Cambridge University Press, 2015.

Prebish, Charles S. "Cooking the Buddhist Books: The Implications of the New Dating of the Buddha for the History of Early Indian Buddhism." *Journal of Buddhist Ethics* 15 (2008): 1–21.

Prior, Katherine. "The British Administration of Hinduism in North India, 1780–1900." PhD diss., University of Cambridge, 1990.

Qadir, Ali. "Parliamentary Hereticization of the Ahmadiyya in Pakistan: The Modern World Implicated in Islamic Crises." In *Religion in Times of Crisis*, edited by Gladys Ganiel, Heidemarie Winkel, and Christophe Monnot, 135–152. Leiden: Brill, 2014.

Quintanilla, Sonya Rhie. "Closer to Heaven than the Gods: Jain Monks in the Art of Pre-Kushan Mathura." *Marg* 52, no. 3 (2001): 57–68.

Rabe, Michael D. *The Great Penance at Mamallapuram: Deciphering a Visual Text*. Chennai: Institute of Asian Studies, 2001.

———. "Secret Yantras and Erotic Display for Hindu Temples." In *Tantra in Practice*, edited by David Gordon White, 434–446. Princeton, NJ: Princeton University Press, 2000.

Rai, Mridu. *Hindu Rulers, Muslim Subjects: Islam, Rights, and the History of Kashmir*. Princeton, NJ: Princeton University Press, 2004.

Raianu, Mircea. *Tata: The Global Corporation That Built Indian Capitalism*. Cambridge, MA: Harvard University Press, 2021.

Raj, Kapil. *Relocating Modern Science: Circulation and the Construction of Knowledge in South Asia and Europe, 1650–1900*. Basingstoke, UK: Palgrave Macmillan, 2007.

Rajan, K. "Emergence of Early Historic Trade in Peninsular India." In *Early Interactions between South and Southeast Asia: Reflections on Cross-Cultural Exchange*, edited by Pierre-Yves Manguin, A. Mani, and Geoff Wade, 177–196. Singapore: ISEAS, 2011.

———. "Kodumanal Excavations—A Report." In *Gauravam: Recent Researches in Indology: Prof. B. K. Gururaja Rao Felicitation Volume*, edited by K. V. Ramesh, V. Shivanand, M. D. Sampath, and L. N. Swamy, 72–85. New Delhi: Harman, 1996.

———. "Situating the Beginning of Early Historic Times in Tamil Nadu: Some Issues and Reflections." *Social Scientist* 36, no. 1/2 (2008): 40–78.

Rajan, S. Irudaya. "Migration in South Asia: Old and New Mobilities." In *Migration in South Asia: IMISCOE Regional Reader*, edited by S. Irudaya Rajan, 3–15. Cham, Switzerland: Springer, 2023.

Rajendran, C. P., Kusala Rajendran, S. Srinivasalu, Vanessa Andrade, P. Aravazhi, and Jaishri Sanwal. "Geoarchaeological Evidence of a Chola-Period Tsunami from an Ancient Port at Kaveripattinam on the Southeastern Coast of India." *Geoarchaeology* 26, no. 6 (2011): 867–887.

Raman, Bhavani. *Document Raj: Writing and Scribes in Early Colonial South India*. Chicago: University of Chicago Press, 2012.

Ramanujan, A. K. *The Collected Essays of A. K. Ramanujan*. Edited by Vinay Dharwadker. New Delhi: Oxford University Press, 1999.

Ramaswamy, Sumathi. *Passions of the Tongue: Language Devotion in Tamil India, 1891–1970*. Berkeley: University of California Press, 1997.

———. "Remains of the Race: Archaeology, Nationalism, and the Yearning for Civilisation in the Indus Valley." *Indian Economic and Social History Review* 38, no. 2 (2001): 105–145.

———. *Terrestrial Lessons: The Conquest of the World as Globe*. Chicago: University of Chicago Press, 2017.

Rambachan, Anantanand. *The Advaita Worldview: God, World, and Humanity*. Albany: State University of New York Press, 2006.

Rao, Anupama. *The Caste Question: Dalits and the Politics of Modern India*. Berkeley: University of California Press, 2009.

Rao, S. R. "Shipping and Maritime Trade of the Indus People." *Expedition* 7, no. 3 (1965): 30–37.

Rao, Velcheru Narayana. "Multiple Literary Cultures in Telugu: Court, Temple, and Public." In *Literary Cultures in History: Reconstructions from South Asia*, edited by Sheldon Pollock, 383–436. Berkeley: University of California Press, 2003.

Rao, Velcheru Narayana, David Shulman, and Sanjay Subrahmanyam. "A New Imperial Idiom in the Sixteenth Century: Krishnadevaraya and His Political Theory of Vijayanagara." In *Forms of Knowledge in Early Modern Asia: Explorations in the Intellectual History of India and Tibet, 1500–1800*, edited by Sheldon Pollock, 69–111. Durham, NC: Duke University Press, 2011.

———. *Symbols of Substance: Court and State in Nayaka Period Tamilnadu*. Delhi: Oxford University Press, 1992.

Rawat, Ramnarayan S. *Reconsidering Untouchability: Chamars and Dalit History in North India*. Bloomington: Indiana University Press, 2011.

Rawat, Ramnarayan S., and K. Satyanarayana. "Dalit Studies: New Perspectives on Indian History and Society." In *Dalit*

Studies, edited by Ramnarayan S. Rawat and K. Satyanarayana, 1–30. Durham, NC: Duke University Press, 2016.

Ray, Himanshu Prabha. *The Archaeology of Seafaring in Ancient South Asia*. Cambridge: Cambridge University Press, 2003.

———. "The Axial Age in Asia: The Archaeology of Buddhism (500 B.C.–A.D. 500)." In *Archaeology of Asia*, edited by Miriam T. Stark, 303–323. Malden, MA: Blackwell, 2006.

———. "Colonial Archaeology in South Asia: Epigraphic Research." In *Oxford Research Encyclopedia of Anthropology*. Published online, 2022. https://doi.org/10.1093/acrefore/9780190854584.013.322.

———. *Colonial Archaeology in South Asia: The Legacy of Sir Mortimer Wheeler*. New Delhi: Oxford University Press, 2008.

———. "Ethnographies of Sailing: From the Red Sea to the Bay of Bengal in Antiquity." In *The Indian Ocean Trade in Antiquity: Political, Cultural, and Economic Impacts*, edited by Matthew Adam Cobb, 73–94. Abingdon, UK: Routledge, 2019.

Ray, Sugata. *Climate Change and the Art of Devotion: Geoaesthetics in the Land of Krishna, 1550–1850*. Seattle: University of Washington Press, 2019.

Raymond, Catherine. "Religious and Scholarly Exchanges between the Singhalese Sangha and the Arakanese and Burmese Theravadin Communities: Historical Documentation and Physical Evidence." In *Commerce and Culture in the Bay of Bengal, 1500–1800*, edited by Om Prakash and Denys Lombard, 87–105. New Delhi: Manohar, 1999.

Reich, David. *Who We Are and How We Got Here: Ancient DNA and the New Science of the Human Past*. Oxford: Oxford University Press, 2018.

Reich, David, Kumarasamy Thangaraj, Nick Patterson, Alkes L. Price, and Lalji Singh. "Reconstructing Indian Population History." *Nature* 461, no. 7263 (2009): 489–494.

Reich, Tamar C. "Sacrificial Violence and Textual Battles: Inner Textual Interpretation in the Sanskrit Mahabharata." *History of Religions* 41, no. 2 (2001): 142–169.

Rezavi, Syed Ali Nadeem. "Antiquarian Interests in Medieval India: The Relocation of Ashokan Pillars by Firuzshah Tughluq." *Proceedings of the Indian History Congress* 70 (2009–2010): 994–1010.

———. *Fathpur Sikri Revisited*. New Delhi: Oxford University Press, 2013.

———. "The Organization of Education in Mughal India." *Proceedings of the Indian History Congress* 68 (2007): 389–397.

Rice, Yael. "Workshop as Network: A Case Study from Mughal South Asia." *Artl@s Bulletin* 6, no. 3 (2017): 50–65.

Richards, John F. "Early Modern India and World History." *Journal of World History* 8, no. 2 (1997): 197–209.

———. *Mughal Administration in Golconda*. Oxford: Clarendon Press, 1975.

———. *The Mughal Empire*. Cambridge: Cambridge University Press, 1995.

Richman, Paula, ed. *Many Ramayanas: The Diversity of a Narrative Tradition in South Asia*. Berkeley: University of California Press, 1991.

———, ed. *Ramayana Stories in Modern South India: An Anthology*. Bloomington: Indiana University Press, 2008.

Richter, William L. "The Political Dynamics of Islamic Resurgence in Pakistan." *Asian Survey* 19, no. 6 (1979): 547–557.

Robbins Schug, Gwen, K. Elaine Blevins, Brett Cox, Kelsey Gray, and V. Mushrif-Tripathy. "Infection, Disease, and Biosocial Processes at the End of the Indus Civilization." *PLoS ONE* 8, no. 12 (2013).

Roberts, Michael. *Caste Conflict and Elite Formation: The Rise of a Karava Elite in Sri Lanka, 1500–1931*. Cambridge: Cambridge University Press, 1982.

Robertson, Bruce Carlisle. "The English Writings of Raja Rammohan Ray." In *An Illustrated History of Indian Literature in English*, edited by Arvind Krishna Mehrotra, 27–40. Delhi: Permanent Black, 2003.

Robinson, Rowena. "The Cross: Contestation and Transformation of a Religious Symbol in Southern Goa." *Economic and Political Weekly* 29, no. 3 (1994): 94–98.

Roy, Arundhati. "The Doctor and the Saint." In *Annihilation of Caste: The Annotated Critical Edition*, edited by S. Anand, 15–179. London: Verso, 2014.

Roy, Haimanti. "Paper Rights: The Emergence of Documentary Identities in Post-Colonial India, 1950–67." *South Asia: Journal of South Asian Studies* 39, no. 2 (2016): 329–349.

Roy, Kaushik. *The Army in British India: From Colonial Warfare to Total War 1857–1947*. London: Bloomsbury, 2013.

———. "Combat Motivation of the Sepoys and Sowars during the First World War." In *Indian Soldiers in the First World War: Re-Visiting a Global Conflict*, edited by Ashutosh Kumar and Claude Markovits, 41–62. London: Routledge, 2021.

———. "Military Synthesis in South Asia: Armies, Warfare, and Indian Society, c. 1740–1849." *Journal of Military History* 69, no. 3 (2005): 651–690.

Roy, Tapti. *The Politics of a Popular Uprising: Bundelkhand in 1857*. Delhi: Oxford University Press, 1994.

Roy, Tirthankar. "The Indian Economy after Independence." In *Oxford Research Encyclopedia of Economics and Finance*. Published online, 2020. https://doi.org/10.1093/acrefore/9780190625979.013.563.

Ruwanpura, Kanchana N. *Garments without Guilt? Global Labour Justice and Ethical Codes in Sri Lankan Apparels*. New Delhi: Cambridge University Press, 2022.

Sachdev, Vibhuti, and Giles Tillotson. *Building Jaipur: The Making of an Indian City*. London: Reaktion Books, 2002.

Saglio-Yatzimirsky, Marie-Caroline. *Dharavi: From Mega-Slum to Urban Paradigm*. London: Routledge, 2013.

Sakhuja, Vijay, and Sangeeta Sakhuja. "Rajendra Chola I's Naval Expedition to Southeast Asia: A Nautical Perspective." In *Nagapattinam to Suvarnadwipa: Reflections on the Chola Naval Expeditions to Southeast Asia*, edited by Hermann Kulke, K. Kesavapany, and Vijay Sakhuja, 76–90. Singapore: Institute of Southeast Asian Studies, 2009.

Salomon, Richard. *Ancient Buddhist Scrolls from Gandhara: The British Library Kharosthi Fragments*. Seattle: University of Washington Press, 1999.

———. *Indian Epigraphy: A Guide to the Study of Inscriptions in Sanskrit, Prakrit, and the Other Indo-Aryan Languages*. New York: Oxford University Press, 1998.

———. "On the Origin of the Early Indian Scripts." *Journal of the American Oriental Society* 115, no. 2 (1995): 271–279.

———. "The Sivarajarajyabhisekakalpataru: A Sanskrit Text on Sivaji." *Journal of the Oriental Institute, M. S. University of Baroda* 28 (1979): 70–89.

Salunke, Nilekha. "Reclaiming Savitribai Phule: Life and Times of a Forgotten Liberator." In *The Routledge Handbook of the Other Backward Classes in India: Thought, Movements and Development*, edited by Simhadri Somanaboina and Akhileshwari Ramagoud, 54–69. London: Routledge, 2022.

Salvadore, Matteo. "Between the Red Sea Slave Trade and the Goa Inquisition: The Odyssey of Gabriel, a Sixteenth-Century Ethiopian Jew." *Journal of World History* 31, no. 2 (2020): 327–360.

Sanderson, Alexis. "How Public Was Saivism?" In *Tantric Communities in Context*, edited by Nina Mirnig, Marion Rastelli, and Vincent Eltschinger, 1–46. Vienna: Austrian Academy of Sciences Press, 2019.

———. "The Saiva Age: The Rise and Dominance of Saivism during the Early Medieval Period." In *Genesis and Development of Tantrism*, edited by Shingo Einoo, 41–349. Tokyo: Institute of Oriental Culture, University of Tokyo, 2009.

Saraiva, Antonio Jose. *The Marrano Factory: The Portuguese Inquisition and Its New Christians 1536–1765*. Translated by H. P. Salomon and I.S.D. Sassoon. Leiden: Brill, 2001.

Sardar, Sunil. "Love Letters Unlike Any Other: Savitri's Three Letters to Jotiba." In *A Forgotten Liberator: The Life and Struggle of Savitribai Phule*, edited by Braj Ranjan Mani and Pamela Sardar, 39–47. New Delhi: Mountain Peak, 2008.

Sardar, Sunil, and Victor Paul. "Pioneering Engaged Writing: Savitribai Phule's Poetry." In *A Forgotten Liberator: The Life and Struggle of Savitribai Phule*, edited by Braj Ranjan Mani and Pamela Sardar, 65–69. New Delhi: Mountain Peak, 2008.

Sardesai, Govind Sakharam. *New History of the Marathas*. Vol. 1, *Shivaji and His Line (1600–1707)*. Bombay: Phoenix Publications, 1957.

Sarkar, H. B. "Chinese Texts on Chia-Na-t'iao/Kanthi: Its Identification as a Trans-Continental Port of India." *Indologica Taurinensia* 21–22 (1995–1996): 271–284.

Sarkar, Jadunath. *Anecdotes of Aurangzib and Historical Essays*. Calcutta: M. C. Sarkar & Sons, 1917.

———. *History of Aurangzib Based on Original Sources*. 5 vols. Calcutta: M. C. Sarkar & Sons, 1912–1924.

———. *A History of Jaipur, c. 1503–1938*. Edited by Raghubir Sinh. Hyderabad: Orient Longman, 1984.

———. *House of Shivaji: Studies and Documents on Maratha History, Royal Period*. New Delhi: Orient Longman, 1978.

———. *Nadir Shah in India*. Calcutta: Naya Prokash, 1973.

Sarkar, Jayita. *Ploughshares and Swords: India's Nuclear Program in the Global Cold War*. Ithaca, NY: Cornell University Press, 2022.

Sarkar, Sumit. *The Swadeshi Movement in Bengal, 1903–1908*. New Delhi: People's Publishing House, 1973.

Sarkar, Tanika. "Gandhi and Social Relations." In *The Cambridge Companion to Gandhi*, edited by Judith M. Brown and Anthony Parel, 173–195. New York: Cambridge University Press, 2011.

———. *Hindu Nationalism in India*. New York: Oxford University Press, 2022.

Sarma, Sreeramula Rajeswara. "A Jain Assayer at the Sultan's Mint: Thakkura Pheru and His *Dravyapariksa*." In *Jaina Studies: Proceedings of the DOT 2010 Panel in Marburg, Germany*, edited by Jayandra Soni, 7–32. New Delhi: Aditya Prakashan, 2012.

———. "Translation of Scientific Texts into Sanskrit under Sawai Jai Singh." *Sri Venkateswara University Oriental Journal* 41 (1998): 67–87.

Sastri, Hirananda. *Ancient Vijnaptipatras*. Baroda: Baroda State Press, 1942.

Sastri, K. A. Nilakanta. *The Colas*. 2nd ed. Madras: University of Madras, 1955.

Sathaye, Adheesh A. *Crossing the Lines of Caste: Visvamitra and the Construction of Brahmin Power in Hindu Mythology*. New York: Oxford University Press, 2015.

Satia, Priya. *Time's Monster: How History Makes History*. Cambridge, MA: Belknap Press of Harvard University Press, 2020.

Saxena, Sanchita Banerjee, ed. *Labor, Global Supply Chains, and the Garment Industry in South Asia: Bangladesh after Rana Plaza*. London: Routledge, 2020.

Schimmel, Annemarie. *Pain and Grace: A Study of Two Mystical Writers of Eighteenth-Century Muslim India*. Leiden: Brill, 1976.

Schopen, Gregory. *Bones, Stones, and Buddhist Monks: Collected Papers on the Archaeology, Epigraphy, and Texts of Monastic Buddhism in India*. Honolulu: University of Hawai'i Press, 1997.

Schrader, Stephanie, ed. *Rembrandt and the Inspiration of India*. Los Angeles: Getty Museum, 2018.

Scott, James C. *Against the Grain: A Deep History of the Earliest States*. New Haven, CT: Yale University Press, 2017.

Seal, Anil. *The Emergence of Indian Nationalism: Competition and Collaboration in the Later Nineteenth Century*. Cambridge: Cambridge University Press, 1968.

Sears, Tamara I. "Ibn Battuta's Buddhists: Monuments, Memory, and the Materiality of Travel." In *Encountering Buddhism and Islam in Premodern Central and South Asia*, edited by Blain Auer and Ingo Strauch, 97–127. Berlin: De Gruyter, 2019.

———. *Worldly Gurus and Spiritual Kings: Architecture and Asceticism in Medieval India*. New Haven, CT: Yale University Press, 2014.

Sen, Amiya P. "A Hindu Conservative Negotiates Modernity: Chandranath Basu (1844–1910) and Reflections on the Self and Culture in Colonial Bengal." In *HerStory: Historical Scholarship between South Asia and Europe. Festschrift in Honour of Gita Dharampal-Frick*, edited by Rafael Klober and Manju Ludwig, 175–188. Heidelberg: Heidelberg University Library, 2018.

Sen, Tansen. "The Military Campaigns of Rajendra Chola and the Chola-Srivijaya-China Triangle." In *Nagapattinam to Suvarnadwipa: Reflections on the Chola Naval Expeditions to Southeast Asia*, edited by Hermann Kulke, K. Kesavapany, and Vijay Sakhuja, 61–75. Singapore: Institute of Southeast Asian Studies, 2009.

Sender, Henriette M. "The Kashmiri Brahmins (Pandits) up to 1930: Cultural Change in the Cities of North India." PhD diss., University of Wisconsin–Madison, 1981.

Seyller, John. *Workshop and Patron in Mughal India: The Freer Ramayana and Other Illustrated Manuscripts of 'Abd al-Rahim.* Zurich: Artibus Asiae, 1999.

Shackle, Christopher. "Introduction." In *Bullhe Shah Sufi Lyrics*, edited and translated by Christopher Shackle, vii–xxx. Cambridge, MA: Harvard University Press, 2015.

Shackle, Christopher, and Zawahir Moir. *Ismaili Hymns from South Asia: An Introduction to the Ginans.* London: Routledge, 2000.

Shaffer, Jim G. "The Later Prehistoric Periods." In *The Archaeology of Afghanistan from Earliest Times to the Timurid Period*, edited by F. R. Allchin and Norman Hammond, 71–186. London: Academic Press, 1978.

Shani, Giorgio. *Sikh Nationalism and Identity in a Global Age.* London: Routledge, 2008.

Shani, Ornit. "Women and the Vote: Registration, Representation and Participation in the Run-Up to India's First Elections, 1951–52." *South Asia: Journal of South Asian Studies* 44, no. 2 (2021): 228–246.

Sharafi, Mitra. *Law and Identity in Colonial South Asia: Parsi Legal Culture, 1772–1947.* New York: Cambridge University Press, 2014.

Sharma, Amogh Dhar. "Political Mobilization in an Era of 'Post-Truth Politics': Disinformation and the Hindu Right in India (1980s–2010s)." In *The Rise of the Radical Right in the Global South*, edited by Rosana Pinheiro-Machado and Tatiana Vargas-Maia, 141–157. London: Routledge, 2023.

Sharma, Jyotirmaya. *A Restatement of Religion: Swami Vivekananda and the Making of Hindu Nationalism.* New Haven, CT: Yale University Press, 2013.

Sharma, Sanjay. "Famine, Relief and Rhetoric of Welfare in Colonial North India." In *An Economic History of Famine Resilience*, edited by Jessica Dijkman and Bas van Leeuwen, 162–181. London: Routledge, 2020.

Sharma, Sunil. *Amir Khusraw: The Poet of Sufis and Sultans.* Oxford: Oneworld, 2005.

———. "Forging a Canon of Dakhni Literature: Translations and Retellings from Persian." In *Iran and the Deccan: Persianate Art, Culture, and Talent in Circulation, 1400–1700*, edited by Keelan Overton, 401–420. Bloomington: Indiana University Press, 2020.

———. "'If There Is a Paradise on Earth, It Is Here': Urban Ethnography in Indo-Persian Poetic and Historical Texts." In *Forms of Knowledge in Early Modern Asia: Explorations in the Intellectual History of India and Tibet, 1500–1800*, edited by Sheldon Pollock, 240–256. Durham, NC: Duke University Press, 2011.

———. *Mughal Arcadia: Persian Literature in an Indian Court.* Cambridge, MA: Harvard University Press, 2017.

———. "The Nizamshahi Persianate Garden in Zuhuri's *Saqinama*." In *Garden and Landscape Practices in Pre-Colonial India: Histories from the Deccan*, edited by Daud Ali and Emma J. Flatt, 159–171. New Delhi: Routledge, 2012.

Shaw, Sarah. "Introduction." In *The Jatakas: Birth Stories of the Bodhisatta*, xix–lxvii. New Delhi: Penguin Books, 2006.

Shcheglova, Olimpiada P. "Lithography ii. In India." In *Encyclopaedia Iranica*, 2009. https://www.iranicaonline.org/articles/lithography-ii-in-india.

Sheikh, Samira. "Aurangzeb as Seen from Gujarat: Shi'i and Millenarian Challenges to Mughal Sovereignty." *Journal of the Royal Asiatic Society* 28, no. 3 (2018): 557–581.

Shepherd, Verene A. *Maharani's Misery: Narratives of a Passage from India to the Caribbean.* Kingston: University of the West Indies Press, 2002.

Sherman, Taylor C. "The Integration of the Princely State of Hyderabad and the Making of the Postcolonial State in India, 1948–56." *Indian Economic and Social History Review* 44, no. 4 (2007): 489–516.

———. *Nehru's India: A History in Seven Myths.* Princeton, NJ: Princeton University Press, 2022.

Sherwani, Haroon Khan. *The Bahmanis of the Deccan: An Objective Study.* Hyderabad: Saood Manzil, 1953.

Shinde, Vasant et al. "An Ancient Harappan Genome Lacks Ancestry from Steppe Pastoralists or Iranian Farmers." *Cell* 179 (2019): 729–735.

Shokoohy, Mehrdad. "Sasanian Royal Emblems and Their Reemergence in the

Fourteenth-Century Deccan." *Muqarnas* 11 (1994): 65–78.

Shulman, David. *Tamil: A Biography*. Cambridge, MA: Belknap Press of Harvard University Press, 2016.

Siddiqui, Dina M. "Scandalising the Supply Chain: Looking Back at 40 Years of Bangladesh's Garment Industry." *Himal Southasian*, January 2022. https://www.himalmag.com/scandalising-the-supply-chain-bangladesh-2022/.

Sidebotham, Steven E. *Berenike and the Ancient Maritime Spice Route*. Berkeley: University of California Press, 2011.

Simmons, Caleb. *Devotional Sovereignty: Kingship and Religion in India*. New York: Oxford University Press, 2020.

Singh, Gurdip. "Environmental Changes in Southern Asia during the Holocene." In *Current Perspectives in Palynological Research*, edited by Sunirmal Chanda, 277–296. New Delhi: Today & Tomorrow, 1991.

Singh, Kavita. "Material Fantasy: The Museum in Colonial India." In *Art and Visual Culture in India, 1857–2007*, edited by Gayatri Sinha, 40–57. Mumbai: Marg, 2009.

Singh, Nikky-Guninder Kaur. "Sikh Art." In *The Oxford Handbook of Sikh Studies*, edited by Pashaura Singh and Louis E. Fenech, 419–429. Oxford: Oxford University Press, 2014.

———. *Sikhism: An Introduction*. London: I. B. Tauris, 2011.

Singh, Pashaura. "The Guru Granth Sahib." In *The Oxford Handbook of Sikh Studies*, edited by Pashaura Singh and Louis E. Fenech, 125–135. Oxford: Oxford University Press, 2014.

Singh, Simran Jeet. "The Life of the Puratan Janamsakhi: Tracing the Earliest Memories of Guru Nanak." PhD diss., Columbia University, 2016.

Singh, Upinder. *The Discovery of Ancient India: Early Archaeologists and the Beginnings of Archaeology*. Delhi: Permanent Black, 2004.

———. *A History of Ancient and Early Medieval India: From the Stone Age to the 12th Century*. New Delhi: Pearson Education, 2008.

———. *Political Violence in Ancient India*. Cambridge, MA: Harvard University Press, 2017.

Sinha, Mishka. "Orienting America: Sanskrit and Modern Scholarship in the United States, 1836–1894." In *Debating Orientalism*, edited by Ziad Elmarsafy, Anna Bernard, and David Attwell, 73–93. London: Palgrave Macmillan, 2013.

Sinopoli, Carla M. "Human Representation in the South Indian Iron Age: Examples from Kadebakele, South India." *Man in India* 91, no. 2 (2011): 375–385.

Sircar, D. C. *Asokan Studies*. Calcutta: Indian Museum, 1979.

Sivasundaram, Sujit. *Islanded: Britain, Sri Lanka, and the Bounds of an Indian Ocean Colony*. Chicago: University of Chicago Press, 2013.

Skelton, Robert. "Farrukh Beg in the Deccan: An Update." In *Sultans of the South: Arts of India's Deccan Courts, 1323–1687*, edited by Navina Najat Haidar and Marika Sardar, 12–25. New York: Metropolitan Museum of Art, 2011.

Slaje, Walter. "Buddhism and Islam in Kashmir as Represented by Rajatarangini Authors." In *Encountering Buddhism and Islam in Premodern Central and South Asia*, edited by Blain Auer and Ingo Strauch, 128–160. Berlin: De Gruyter, 2019.

Sohoni, Pushkar. *The Architecture of a Deccan Sultanate: Courtly Practice and Royal Authority in Late Medieval India*. London: I. B. Tauris, 2018.

Soneji, Davesh. "Critical Steps: Thinking through Bharatanatyam in the Twenty-First Century." In *Bharatanatyam: A Reader*, edited by Davesh Soneji, xi–li. New Delhi: Oxford University Press, 2010.

———. *Unfinished Gestures:* Devadasis, *Memory, and Modernity in South India*. Chicago: University of Chicago Press, 2012.

South Asia Scholar Activist Collective. "Timeline of Specific Incidents of Hindutva Harassment of Academics in North America." *Journal of the American Academy of Religion* 90, no. 4 (2022): 788–794.

Southworth, Franklin C. *Linguistic Archaeology of South Asia*. London: Routledge Curzon, 2005.

Speziale, Fabrizio. "Introduction." In *Hospitals in Iran and India, 1500–1950s*, edited by Fabrizio Speziale, 1–26. Leiden: Brill, 2012.

Srinivasan, Doris. "Unhinging Siva from the Indus Civilization." *Journal of the Royal Asiatic Society of Great Britain and Ireland*, no. 1 (1984): 77–89.

Srinivasan, Sharada. "Shiva as 'Cosmic Dancer': On Pallava Origins for the Nataraja Bronze." *World Archaeology* 36, no. 3 (2004): 432–450.

Staal, Frits. *Discovering the Vedas: Origins, Mantras, Rituals, Insights*. New Delhi: Penguin, 2008.

Stark, Ulrike. *An Empire of Books: The Naval Kishore Press and the Diffusion of the Printed Word in Colonial India*. Ranikhet, India: Permanent Black, 2007.

Staubwasser, M., F. Sirocko, P. M. Grootes, and M. Segl. "Climate Change at the 4.2 ka BP Termination of the Indus Valley Civilization and Holocene South Asian Monsoon Variability." *Geophysical Research Letters* 30, no. 8 (2003).

Stein, Burton. "South India: Some General Considerations of the Region and Its Early History." In *The Cambridge Economic History of India*. Vol. 1, *c. 1200–c. 1750*, edited by Tapan Raychaudhuri and Irfan Habib, 14–42. Cambridge: Cambridge University Press, 1982.

Stein, M. A. "A Sanskrit Deed of Sale Concerning a Kasmirian Mahabharata Manuscript." *Journal of the Royal Asiatic Society of Great Britain and Ireland* (April 1900): 187–194.

Stephens, Julia. *Governing Islam: Law, Empire, and Secularism in South Asia*. Cambridge: Cambridge University Press, 2018.

Stern, Philip J. *The Company-State: Corporate Sovereignty and the Early Modern Foundations of the British Empire in India*. Oxford: Oxford University Press, 2011.

Stokes, Eric. *The Peasant Armed: The Indian Revolt of 1857*. Edited by C. A. Bayly. Oxford: Clarendon Press, 1986.

Strauch, Ingo, ed. "The Character of the Indian Kharosthi Script and the 'Sanskrit Revolution': A Writing System between Identity and Assimilation." In *The Idea of Writing: Writing across Borders*, edited by Alex de Voogt and Joachim Friedrich Quack, 131–168. Leiden: Brill, 2012.

———. *Foreign Sailors on Socotra: The Inscriptions and Drawings from the Cave Hoq*. Bremen: Hempen Verlag, 2012.

Stronge, Susan. *Tipu's Tigers*. London: Victoria and Albert Museum, 2009.

Subbarayalu, Y. "Anjuvannam: A Maritime Trade Guild of Medieval Times." In *Nagapattinam to Suvarnadwipa: Reflections on the Chola Naval Expeditions to Southeast Asia*, edited by Hermann Kulke, K. Kesavapany, and Vijay Sakhuja, 158–167. Singapore: Institute of Southeast Asian Studies, 2009.

———. *South India under the Cholas*. New Delhi: Oxford University Press, 2012.

Subrahmanyam, Sanjay. *The Career and Legend of Vasco Da Gama*. Cambridge: Cambridge University Press, 1997.

———. "Hearing Voices: Vignettes of Early Modernity in South Asia, 1400–1750." *Daedalus* 127, no. 3 (1998): 75–104.

———. "Of Imarat and Tijarat: Asian Merchants and State Power in the Western Indian Ocean, 1400 to 1750." *Comparative Studies in Society and History* 37, no. 4 (1995): 750–780.

———. "Taking Stock of the Franks: South Asian Views of Europeans and Europe, 1500–1800." *Indian Economic and Social History Review* 42, no. 1 (2005): 69–100.

———. "Warfare and State Finance in Wodeyar Mysore, 1724–25: A Missionary Perspective." *Indian Economic and Social History Review* 26, no. 2 (1989): 203–233.

———. "Written on Water: Designs and Dynamics in the Portuguese *Estado da India*." In *Empires: Perspectives from Archaeology and History*, edited by Susan E. Alcock, Terence N. D'Altroy, Kathleen D. Morrison, and Carla M. Sinopoli, 42–69. Cambridge: Cambridge University Press, 2001.

Sundaram, Chandar S. "The Indian National Army: Towards a Balanced and Critical Appraisal." *Economic and Political Weekly* 50, no. 30 (July 25, 2015): 21–24.

Suntharalingam, R. *Politics and Nationalist Awakening in South India, 1852–1891*. Jaipur: Rawat Publications, 1958.

Sussman, George D. "Was the Black Death in India and China?" *Bulletin of the History of Medicine* 85, no. 3 (2011): 319–355.

Talbot, Cynthia. "Inscribing the Other, Inscribing the Self: Hindu-Muslim Identities in Pre-Colonial India."

Comparative Studies in Society and History 37, no. 4 (1995): 692–722.
———. "Justifying Defeat: A Rajput Perspective on the Age of Akbar." *Journal of the Economic and Social History of the Orient* 55, no. 2/3 (2012): 329–368.
———. *The Last Hindu Emperor: Prithviraj Chauhan and the Indian Past, 1200–2000*. Cambridge: Cambridge University Press, 2016.
———. "The Mewar Court's Construction of History." In *Kingdom of the Sun: Indian Court and Village Art from the Princely State of Mewar*, edited by Joanna Williams, 13–33. San Francisco: Asian Art Museum, 2007.
———. "A Poetic Record of the Rajput Rebellion, c. 1680." *Journal of the Royal Asiatic Society* 28, no. 3 (2018): 461–483.
Talbot, Ian. *Pakistan: A Modern History*. London: Hurst, 1998.
Talbot, Ian, and Tahir Kamran. *Colonial Lahore: A History of the City and Beyond*. Oxford: Oxford University Press, 2016.
Tanner, Harold M. *China: A History*. Indianapolis, IN: Hackett, 2009.
Tarshis, Dena K. "The Koh-i-Noor Diamond and Its Glass Replica at the Crystal Palace Exhibition." *Journal of Glass Studies* 42 (2000): 133–143.
Taylor, McComas. *The Fall of the Indigo Jackal: The Discourse of Division and Purnabhadra's* Pancatantra. Albany: State University of New York Press, 2007.
———. "The *Panchatantra*: World Literature before 'World Literature.'" In *A Companion to World Literature*, edited by Ken Seigneurie, 1–13. New York: John Wiley & Sons, 2019.
Taylor, Miles. *Empress: Queen Victoria and India*. New Haven, CT: Yale University Press, 2018.
Teltscher, Kate. "The Shampooing Surgeon and the Persian Prince: Two Indians in Early Nineteenth-Century Britain." *Interventions* 2, no. 3 (2000): 409–423.
Thakur, Vijay Kumar. "Forced Labour in the Gupta Period." *Proceedings of the Indian History Congress* 38 (1977): 145–151.
Thapar, Romila. "Ashoka—A Retrospective." *Economic and Political Weekly* 44, no. 45 (2009): 31–37.
———. *Asoka and the Decline of the Mauryas*. 3rd ed. New Delhi: Oxford University Press, 2012.
———. "Asokan India and the Gupta Age." In *A Cultural History of India*, edited by A. L. Basham, 38–50. New Delhi: Oxford University Press, 1975.
———. *Early India: From the Origins to AD 1300*. London: Allen Lane, 2002.
———. *From Lineage to State: Social Formations in the Mid-First Millennium B.C. in the Ganga Valley*. New Delhi: Oxford University Press, 1984.
———. *Our History, Their History, Whose History?* Calcutta: Seagull Books, 2023.
———. *The Past before Us: Historical Traditions of Early North India*. Cambridge, MA: Harvard University Press, 2013.
———. "Perceiving the Forest: Early India." In *India's Environmental History: From Ancient Times to the Colonial Period, A Reader*, edited by Mahesh Rangarajan and K. Sivaramakrishnan, 1:105–126. Ranikhet, India: Permanent Black, 2012.
———. *Somanatha: The Many Voices of a History*. London: Verso, 2005.
———. "Some Appropriations of the Theory of Aryan Race Relating to the Beginnings of Indian History." In *Invoking the Past: The Uses of History in South Asia*, edited by Daud Ali, 15–35. New Delhi: Oxford University Press, 1999.
Thapar, Romila, Michael Witzel, Jaya Menon, Kai Friese, and Razib Khan. *Which of Us Are Aryans? Rethinking the Concept of Our Origins*. New Delhi: Aleph, 2019.
Tharu, Susie, and Tejaswini Niranjana. "Problems for a Contemporary Theory of Gender." *Social Scientist* 22, no. 3/4 (1994): 93–117.
Thornton, Christopher P. "Mesopotamia, Meluhha, and Those in Between." In *The Sumerian World*, edited by Harriet Crawford, 600–619. London: Routledge, 2012.
Tieken, Herman. *The Asoka Inscriptions: Analysing a Corpus*. New Delhi: Primus, 2023.
———. *Kavya in South India: Old Tamil Cankam Poetry*. Groningen, Netherlands: Egbert Forsten, 2001.
Tillemans, Tom. "Dharmakirti." In *The Stanford Encyclopedia of Philosophy*, edited by

Edward N. Zalta, Spring 2021. https://plato.stanford.edu/archives/spr2021/entries/dharmakiirti/.
Tillotson, Giles. *Taj Mahal*. Cambridge, MA: Harvard University Press, 2008.
Tinker, Hugh. *A New System of Slavery: The Export of Indian Labour Overseas, 1830–1920*. London: Oxford University Press, 1974.
Trautmann, Thomas R. "Elephants and the Mauryas." In *India's Environmental History: From Ancient Times to the Colonial Period, A Reader*, edited by Mahesh Rangarajan and K. Sivaramakrishnan, 1:152–181. Ranikhet, India: Permanent Black, 2012.
———. "Inventing the History of South India." In *Invoking the Past: The Uses of History in South Asia*, edited by Daud Ali, 36–54. New Delhi: Oxford University Press, 1999.
Travers, Robert. "Death and the Nabob: Imperialism and Commemoration in Eighteenth-Century India." *Past & Present* 196, no. 1 (2007): 83–124.
———. *Empires of Complaints: Mughal Law and the Making of British India, 1765–1793*. Cambridge: Cambridge University Press, 2022.
Tremblay, Jennifer Carrie. "The Mauryan Horizon: An Archaeological Analysis of Early Buddhism and the Mauryan Empire at Lumbini, Nepal." PhD diss., Durham University, 2014.
Trivedi, Harish. "Literary and Visual Portrayals of Gandhi." In *The Cambridge Companion to Gandhi*, edited by Judith M. Brown and Anthony Parel, 199–218. New York: Cambridge University Press, 2011.
Truschke, Audrey. *Aurangzeb: The Life and Legacy of India's Most Controversial King*. Stanford, CA: Stanford University Press, 2017.
———. "The Ayodhya Verdict Is a Cornerstone of the Hindu Rashtra." *The Caravan*, December 5, 2019. https://caravanmagazine.in/religion/ayodhya-babri-masjid-ram-mandir-supreme-court-audrey-truschke.
———. "Contested History: Brahmanical Memories of Relations with the Mughals." *Journal of the Economic and Social History of the Orient* 58, no. 4 (2015): 419–452.
———. *Culture of Encounters: Sanskrit at the Mughal Court*. New York: Columbia University Press, 2016.
———. "Defining the Other: An Intellectual History of Sanskrit Lexicons and Grammars of Persian." *Journal of Indian Philosophy* 40, no. 6 (2012): 635–668.
———. "Hindu: A History." *Comparative Studies in Society and History* 65, no. 2 (2023): 246–271.
———. "The Hindu Right in the United States." In *Oxford Research Encyclopedia of American History*. Published online, 2022. https://doi.org/10.1093/acrefore/9780199329175.013.1070.
———. "Hindutva's Dangerous Rewriting of History." *South Asia Multidisciplinary Academic Journal*, no. 24/25 (2020).
———. *The Language of History: Sanskrit Narratives of Indo-Muslim Rule*. New York: Columbia University Press, 2021.
———. "A Padshah like Manu: Political Advice for Akbar in the Persian *Mahabharata*." *Philological Encounters* 5, no. 2 (2020): 1–22.
———. "The Power of the Islamic Sword in Narrating the Death of Indian Buddhism." *History of Religions* 57, no. 4 (2018): 406–435.
———. "Silencing Sita: Why the Ramayana's Many Voices Provoke Outrage." *The Caravan*, May 31, 2018. https://caravanmagazine.in/perspectives/sita-ramayana-many-voices-outrage.
Tryjanowski, Piotr, Mateusz Hetman, Paweł Czechowski, Grzegorz Grzywaczewski, Petr Sklenicka, Klaudia Ziemblinska, and Tim H. Sparks. "Birds Drinking Alcohol: Species and Relationship with People. A Review of Information from Scientific Literature and Social Media." *Animals* 10, no. 2 (2020): 270.
Tubb, Gary A. "*Santarasa* in the *Mahabharata*." *Journal of South Asian Literature* 20, no. 1 (1985): 141–168.
Tull, Herman W. "Karma." In *The Hindu World*, edited by Sushil Mittal and Gene R. Thursby, 309–331. London: Routledge, 2004.
Tumbe, Chinmay. *The Age of Pandemics (1817–1920): How They Shaped India and the World*. Noida: HarperCollins, 2020.

———. *India Moving: A History of Migration.* Gurgaon: Viking, 2018.

———. "Towards Financial Inclusion: The Post Office of India as a Financial Institution, 1880–2010." *Indian Economic and Social History Review* 52, no. 4 (2015): 409–437.

Turner, Paula J. *Roman Coins from India.* London: Royal Numismatic Society, 1989.

Urban, Hugh B. *The Power of Tantra: Religion, Sexuality and the Politics of South Asian Studies.* London: I. B. Tauris, 2010.

Vahed, Goolam. "'An Evil Thing': Gandhi and Indian Indentured Labour in South Africa, 1893–1914." *South Asia: Journal of South Asian Studies* 42, no. 4 (2019): 654–674.

Vajpeyi, Ananya. "Excavating Identity through Tradition: Who Was Shivaji?" In *Traditions in Motion: Religion and Society in History*, edited by Satish Saberwal and Supriya Varma, 240–271. New Delhi: Oxford University Press, 2005.

———. "A History of Caste in South Asia: From Pre-colonial Polity to Biopolitical State." In *Shared Histories of Modernity: China, India and the Ottoman Empire*, edited by Huri Islamoglu and Peter C. Perdue, 299–320. London: Routledge, 2009.

Vallavanthara, Antony. *India in 1500 A.D.: The Narratives of Joseph the Indian.* Mannanam: Research Institute for Studies in History, 1984.

van Bladel, Kevin. "Eighth-Century Indian Astronomy in the Two Cities of Peace." In *Islamic Cultures, Islamic Contexts: Essays in Honor of Professor Patricia Crone*, edited by Behnam Sadeghi, Asad Q. Ahmed, Adam Silverstein, and Robert Hoyland, 257–294. Leiden: Brill, 2015.

Van der Veen, Marijke, and Jacob Morales. "The Roman and Islamic Spice Trade: New Archaeological Evidence." *Journal of Ethnopharmacology* 167 (2015): 54–63.

van der Veer, Peter. *Imperial Encounters: Religion and Modernity in India and Britain.* Princeton, NJ: Princeton University Press, 2001.

———. *Religious Nationalism: Hindus and Muslims in India.* Berkeley: University of California Press, 1994.

van Schendel, Willem. *A History of Bangladesh.* 2nd ed. Cambridge: Cambridge University Press, 2020.

Varadarajan, Lotika. "Konkan Ports and Medieval Trade." *Indica* 22, no. 1 (1985): 9–16.

Varady, Robert Gabriel. "Rail and Road Transport in Nineteenth Century Awadh: Competition in a North Indian Province." PhD diss., University of Arizona, 1981.

Venkatachalapathy, A. R. "Periyar E. V. Ramasamy." In *Oxford Research Encyclopedia of Asian History.* Published online, 2020. https://doi.org/10.1093/acrefore/9780190277727.013.340.

Verma, Anjali. *Women and Society in Early Medieval India: Re-Interpreting Epigraphs.* New York: Routledge, 2019.

Verma, Som Prakash. *Mughal Painters and Their Work: A Biographical Survey and Comprehensive Catalogue.* Delhi: Oxford University Press, 1994.

Vidale, Massimo. "Growing in a Foreign World: For a History of the 'Meluhha Villages' in Mesopotamia in the 3rd Millennium BC." In *Proceedings of the Fourth Symposium of the Melammu Project Held in Ravenna, Italy, October 13–17, 2001*, edited by A. Panaino and A. Piras, 261–280. Milan: Universita di Bologna & IsIao, 2004.

Viswanath, Rupa. *The Pariah Problem: Caste, Religion, and the Social in Modern India.* New York: Columbia University Press, 2014.

Vose, Steven M. "The Making of a Medieval Jain Monk: Language, Power, and Authority in the Works of Jinaprabhasuri (c. 1261–1333)." PhD diss., University of Pennsylvania, 2013.

Wade, Bonnie C. *Imaging Sound: An Ethnomusicological Study of Music, Art, and Culture in Mughal India.* Chicago: University of Chicago Press, 1998.

Wagner, Kim A. "'Calculated to Strike Terror': The Amritsar Massacre and the Spectacle of Colonial Violence." *Past & Present* 233, no. 1 (2016): 185–225.

———. *The Great Fear of 1857: Rumours, Conspiracies and the Making of the Indian Uprising.* Oxford: Peter Lang, 2010.

———. "The Marginal Mutiny: The New Historiography of the Indian Uprising of 1857." *History Compass* 9, no. 10 (2011): 760–766.

———. *Thuggee: Banditry and the British in Early Nineteenth-Century India.* London: Palgrave Macmillan, 2007.

Wagoner, Phillip B. "Fortuitous Convergences and Essential Ambiguities: Transcultural Political Elites in the Medieval Deccan." *International Journal of Hindu Studies* 3, no. 3 (1999): 241–264.

———. "Harihara, Bukka, and the Sultan: The Delhi Sultanate in the Political Imagination of Vijayanagara." In *Beyond Turk and Hindu: Rethinking Religious Identities in Islamicate South Asia*, edited by David Gilmartin and Bruce B. Lawrence, 300–326. Gainesville: University Press of Florida, 2000.

———. "'Sultan among Hindu Kings': Dress, Titles, and the Islamicization of Hindu Culture at Vijayanagara." *Journal of Asian Studies* 55, no. 4 (1996): 851–880.

———. *Tidings of the King: A Translation and Ethnohistorical Analysis of the* Rayavacakamu. Honolulu: University of Hawai'i Press, 1993.

Wahab, Shaista, and Barry Youngerman. *A Brief History of Afghanistan*. 2nd ed. New York: Infobase Publishing, 2010.

Wang, Yongjin, Hai Cheng, R. Lawrence Edwards, Yaoqi He, Xinggong Kong, Zhisheng An, Jiangying Wu, Megan J. Kelly, Carolyn A. Dykoski, and Xiangdong Li. "The Holocene Asian Monsoon: Links to Solar Changes and North Atlantic Climate." *Science* 308, no. 5723 (2005): 854–857.

Washbrook, David. "Envisioning the Social Order in a Southern Port City: The Tamil Diary of Ananda Ranga Pillai." *South Asian History and Culture* 6, no. 1 (2015): 172–185.

———. "South India 1770–1840: The Colonial Transition." *Modern Asian Studies* 38, no. 3 (2004): 479–516.

Weerakkody, D.P.M. *Taprobane: Ancient Sri Lanka as known to Greeks and Romans*. Turnhout, Belgium: Brepols, 1997.

Weinstein, Laura R. "The Indian Figurine from Pompeii as an Emblem of East-West Trade in the Early Roman Imperial Era." In *Globalization and Transculturality from Antiquity to the Pre-Modern World*, edited by Serena Autiero and Matthew A. Cobb, 183–204. London: Routledge, 2022.

Welch, Anthony, Hussein Keshani, and Alexandra Bain. "Epigraphs, Scripture, and Architecture in the Early Delhi Sultanate." *Muqarnas* 19 (2002): 12–43.

Wen, Xin. *The King's Road: Diplomacy and the Remaking of the Silk Road*. Princeton, NJ: Princeton University Press, 2023.

White, Daniel E. *From Little London to Little Bengal: Religion, Print, and Modernity in Early British India, 1793–1835*. Baltimore: Johns Hopkins University Press, 2013.

White, David Gordon. *Kiss of the Yogini: "Tantric Sex" in Its South Asian Contexts*. Chicago: University of Chicago Press, 2006.

———. "Tantra in Practice: Mapping a Tradition." In *Tantra in Practice*, edited by David Gordon White, 3–38. Princeton, NJ: Princeton University Press, 2000.

———. *The Yoga Sutra of Patanjali: A Biography*. Princeton, NJ: Princeton University Press, 2014.

Wickramasinghe, Nira. *Sri Lanka in the Modern Age: A History*. New Delhi: Oxford University Press, 2014.

Williams, Joanna. *The Art of Gupta India: Empire and Province*. Princeton, NJ: Princeton University Press, 1982.

Williams, Richard David. "Hindustani Music between Awadh and Bengal c. 1758–1905." PhD diss., King's College London, 2014.

Willis, Michael. *The Archaeology of Hindu Ritual: Temples and the Establishment of the Gods*. Cambridge: Cambridge University Press, 2009.

———. "Later Gupta History: Inscriptions, Coins and Historical Ideology." *Journal of the Royal Asiatic Society* 15, no. 2 (2005): 131–150.

Wilson, Jon. *India Conquered: Britain's Raj and the Chaos of Empire*. London: Simon & Schuster, 2016.

Wink, Andre. *Akbar*. Oxford: Oneworld, 2009.

Wirkud, Harshada. "Discussing the Importance of the Ass Curse Steles Issued by Muslim Rulers in the Corpus of Gadhegals." *Bulletin of the Deccan College Post-Graduate and Research Institute* 77 (2017): 131–138.

———. "Gadhegals from Goa, India." *Heritage: Journal of Multidisciplinary Studies in Archaeology* 5 (2017): 201–211.

Witmer, Michael David. "The 1947–1948 India-Hyderabad Conflict: Realpolitik and the Formation of the Modern Indian State." PhD diss., Temple University, 1996.

Witzel, Michael. "The Brahmins of Kashmir." Provisional paper published on Michael

Witzel's faculty website (September 1991): 1–56.

———. "Early Sanskritization: Origins and Development of the Kuru State." *Electronic Journal of Vedic Studies* 1, no. 4 (1995): 1–26.

———. "The Realm of the Kuru: Origins and Development of the First State in India." *Electronic Journal of Vedic Studies* 28, no. 1 (2023): 1–165.

———. "Rgvedic History: Poets, Chieftains and Polities." In *The Indo-Aryans of Ancient South Asia: Language, Material Culture and Ethnicity*, edited by George Erdosy, 307–352. Berlin: De Gruyter, 1995.

———. "The Vedas and the Epics: Some Comparative Notes on Persons, Lineages, Geography, and Grammar." In *Epics, Khilas, and Puranas: Continuities and Ruptures, Proceedings of the Third Dubrovnik International Conference on the Sanskrit Epics and Puranas, September 2002*, edited by Petteri Koskikallio, 21–80. Zagreb: Croatian Academy of Sciences and Arts, 2005.

———. "Vedas and Upanisads." In *The Blackwell Companion to Hinduism*, edited by Gavin Flood, 68–101. Malden, MA: Blackwell, 2003.

Witzel, Michael, and Steve Farmer. "Horseplay in Harappa: The Indus Valley Decipherment Hoax." *Frontline*, October 13, 2000, 4–16.

Wright, Rita P. *The Ancient Indus: Urbanism, Economy, and Society*. Cambridge: Cambridge University Press, 2010.

Wright, Samuel. "History in the Abstract: 'Brahman-ness' and the Discipline of Nyaya in Seventeenth-Century Varanasi." *Journal of Indian Philosophy* 44, no. 5 (2016): 1041–1069.

Wujastyk, Dominik. "From Balkh to Baghdad: Indian Science and the Birth of the Islamic Golden Age in the Eighth Century." *Indian Journal of History of Science* 51, no. 4 (2016): 679–690.

———. "Indian Manuscripts." In *Manuscript Cultures: Mapping the Field*, edited by Jorg Quenzer, Dmitry Bondarev, and Jan-Ulrich Sobisch, 159–181. Berlin: De Gruyter, 2014.

Yang, Anand A. *The Limited Raj: Agrarian Relations in Colonial India, Saran District, 1793–1920*. Berkeley: University of California Press, 1989.

Yucesoy, Hayrettin. "Translation as Self-Consciousness: Ancient Sciences, Antediluvian Wisdom, and the 'Abbasid Translation Movement." *Journal of World History* 20, no. 4 (2009): 523–557.

Zaman, Taymiya R. "The Mughal Conquest of Chittor: Study of Akbar's Letter of Victory." In *The Empires of the Near East and India: Source Studies of the Safavid, Ottoman, and Mughal Literate Communities*, edited by Hani Khafipour, 287–300. New York: Columbia University Press, 2019.

Zamindar, Vazira Fazila-Yacoobali. *The Long Partition and the Making of Modern South Asia: Refugees, Boundaries, Histories*. New York: Columbia University Press, 2010.

Zeder, Melinda A. "The Origins of Agriculture in the Near East." *Current Anthropology* 52, Supplement 4 (2011): S221–S235.

Zelliot, Eleanor. "Understanding Dr. B. R. Ambedkar." *Religion Compass* 2, no. 5 (2008): 804–818.

Zupanov, Ines G. "Garcia de Orta's *Coloquios*: Context and Afterlife of a Dialogue." In *Medicine, Trade and Empire: Garcia de Orta's* Colloquies on the Simples and Drugs of India *(1563) in Context*, edited by Palmira Fontes da Costa, 49–65. London: Routledge, 2016.

Zutshi, Chitralekha. *Languages of Belonging: Islam, Regional Identity, and the Making of Kashmir*. New York: Oxford University Press, 2004.

Zvelebil, Kamil. *The Smile of Murugan on Tamil Literature of South India*. Leiden: Brill, 1973.

Index

Note: Page numbers in *italics* indicate figures.